SYMBOLIC ANALYSIS
CROSS-CULTURALLY

SYMBOLIC ANALYSIS CROSS-CULTURALLY

The Rorschach Test

GEORGE A. DE VOS AND L. BRYCE BOYER

Contributions by Orin Borders, Ruth M. Boyer, Richard Day, Horace Miner, Eiji Murakami, and Mayumi Taniguchi

UNIVERSITY OF CALIFORNIA PRESS
BERKELEY   LOS ANGELES   LONDON

University of California Press
Berkeley and Los Angeles, California

University of California Press, Ltd.
London, England

Copyright © 1989 by The Regents of the University of California

Library of Congress Cataloging-in-Publication Data

De Vos, George A.
  Symbolic analysis cross-culturally.

  Includes bibliographies.
  Partial contents: The Japanese—Algerian Arabs—
Native Americans.
  1. Ethnopsychology.   2. Symbolism (Psychology)
3. Rorschach test.   I. Boyer, L. Bryce.   II. Borders,
Orin.   III. Title.
GN508.D43   1988   155.8   87-30087
ISBN 0-520-06086-5 (alk. paper)

Printed in the United States of America

1 2 3 4 5 6 7 8 9

*This volume is dedicated to the late Donald MacKinnon and
to colleagues and the staff of IPAR, the Institute of
Personality Assessment and Research at University of California,
Berkeley, where first, under the
direction of Donald MacKinnon, then Harrison Gough,
and most recently Ken Craik,
creative research assessing "personality" has been encouraged
and ventured.*

Contents

Tables

Preface

The following chapters are based on two essential premises. First, there is the presumption of universals in human capacities in thought processes. Any psychodynamic approach to human nature is based on the assumption that people everywhere are fundamentally the same psychobiologically and are subject to developmental vicissitudes regardless of the culture into which they are born. Being human means that everyone starts with the same mental apparatus and that progression in the development of thought assumes forms of social communication and interaction that channelize basic drives and organize biological capacities through the child-rearing processes that are common to one's culture.

However, cultures differ greatly in the normative experiences of their infants and children through the continuing socialization into adulthood. These culturally normative experiences profoundly influence perception, thought, and the modes of automatic control exercised over the expression of drive derivatives or impulses and affective reactions to outer stimuli. Differential individual capacities as well as differential socialization experiences and the drives they channelize will be found represented symbolically in different behavioral expressions, including language.

The second unifying theme in these chapters is our demonstration that the Rorschach test, a projective technique, can be used cross-culturally to examine modalities of thought and affective control through an analysis of verbal responses to the stimuli afforded by a series of inkblots. Indeed, we hold that a cross-cultural comparison of psychological tests is not only possible but essential for further research in social psychiatry, psychological anthropology, as well as developmental psychology.

Part One

Introduction

Chapter One

Humans as Symbolic Animals: A Psychocultural Perspective

George A. De Vos and L. Bryce Boyer

Symbolism in Anthropology

Human beings have become culture-bearing animals because they have acquired the capacity to control symbolic thought adaptively. Within the wide variations of culture developed in the evolution of humanity, there have come into being an awesome diversity of concepts and beliefs through which humans seek to communicate their experience of the outer world as well as their inner psychological states.

To encompass the complexities of experience, each individual resorts to symbolic means of representation in communication. These symbols are not invented sui generis but become available progressively as the infant, then child, and finally adult partakes of the culturally transmissible collective representations of the particular group. At the same time the individual is also drawing upon the available inner experiences of his or her own bodily processes as psychophysiological functioning matures. Each gradually learns to give communicable representations of inner states of pain, anxiety, and pleasure to the self as well as to others. The collective culturally available representations are necessary for social continuity. They are not only available in the ephemera of verbal or gestural interchange but are embedded in forms of art, enacted in religious rituals, and embodied in myths and cosmologies, that is to say, human "expressive culture."

Almost all human behavior can be considered for its symbolic value. As a social animal each human is constantly in communication with others for both instrumental and expressive purposes. It is, indeed, the development of symbolic thought that characterizes "The Human Animal," as Weston La Barre titled his 1954 work.

Anthropology, in recent years (i.e., Geertz 1973, 1983; Lévi-Strauss 1955, 1966, 1967; Turner 1967, 1978), has witnessed a number of divergent approaches to symbolism. Many in these new traditions, however, continue to avoid the fact that in symbolizing humans utilize associative pathways governed by the same psychodynamic principles that guide the development of thought and causal reasoning through psychosexual stages starting from early infancy. The precausal residues of these earlier developmental phases are embedded in every form of institutionalized communication—in ritual, myth, and custom. The interpretations offered in the newer schools calling themselves "symbolic anthropology" or "interpretive anthropology" are often characterized by a studious avoidance of the usual psychoanalytic insights emphasizing the role of unconscious precausal processes operative in all societies, both idiosyncratically within the individual as well as in the collective symbols found in expressive culture.

Such avoidance is very evident in so called structuralists influenced by the British social anthropological tradition founded by Radcliffe-Brown. This approach is most cogently represented in the writings of Mary Douglas (1966, 1970), critically reviewed by De Vos (1975). Although not avowedly antagonistic to psychoanalysis per se, other structuralists, following the work of Lévi-Strauss in analyzing myth or ritual, scarcely heed Freudian mental mechanisms, no matter how evident their appearance is in the verbatim material. Thus Kuper and Stone (1982) held that the Irma dream, "the dream specimen of psychoanalysis" (Erikson 1954), could be better understood using the approach of Lévi-Strauss than it had been by Freud himself. Their position has been rebutted sharply by Thoden van Velsen (1988).

We contend that there is an inherent duality in all symbolic behavior. It is not that a structural-functionalist approach offers no insight into human behavior; it is, rather, that such an approach ignores the necessity to make continual judgments as to the relative determinative effect of role expectations versus psychological processes when examining any act or thought in its cultural context. In similar fashion, so-called cognitive anthropologists draw heavily upon linguistic analysis but ignore evident psychodynamic symbolic sequences in the texts they examine. For them, human symbolism can be understood essentially as a grammar. For some, thought is implicitly reducible to language, which is then understandable in terms of a series of structures. Syntactic relationships become, for them, the essence of human association.

This structuralist approach to linguistics is personified by Chomsky (1957, 1968), who is concerned with the universality of "deep structures." He is not interested basically in the contribution of interactional patterns to the laying in of cognitive schemata that characterize culturally induced distinctions developed by social learning. It is these distinctions that come to differentiate the thought patterns embedded in the language of given cultures. But as social scientists we must include consideration of the divergences that occur in thought and communication within cultures, as well as the universals that are manifest throughout humanity in the development of thought regardless of social nexus.

It should be obvious that the laws of association guiding the flow of thought have their beginning primarily in an emotional matrix (Arieti 1948, Freud 1915, Kasanin 1944, Ogden 1986). Affective considerations continue to manifest their influence despite the subsequent development of formal logic and instrumental problem solving, which also come to characterize human thought regardless of differences in cultural context.

Some structural approaches are totally opposed to a psychodynamic view that assumes that any directional flow in thought continues to be governed by affectivity as well as by more rational cognitive rules. The continuing presence of inchoate, disturbing, or even disruptive so-called primary-process thinking in all symbolic processes is ignored. Such affectively driven concatenated thought cannot be avoided, rather, it must be of major concern to social scientists in understanding even the most focused, seemingly rational problem-solving behavior.

Early anthropologists such as Frazer (1894, 1910, 1913) and
Lévy-Bruhl (1910, 1928) attempted to understand these "laws
of association" in unraveling the mysteries of myth and ritual,
magical and religious beliefs. Frazer's understanding of *similarity*
and *contiguity* is not far different from these psychological concepts as used either in contemporary studies of conditioning or in
"dreamwork" as understood in psychoanalysis (Altman 1969;
Freud 1900). For example, Frazer's understanding of how contiguity and similarity explain sympathetic magic is not unlike
Freud's approach to understanding dream symbols: namely, like-
appearing objects can represent one another in disguise, should
there be "danger" in direct representation. Long cylindrical objects symbolize the phallus and potency whether in paleolithic
caves or in the dreams of modern men (La Barre 1984). Encompassing objects represent the fertility and generativity of the
female and carry across in representation from direct images to
symbolic forms in cave art to that of all later eras.

The laws of contiguity are found to be basic to studies of conditioning both in animals and man, in the type of conditioning
that precedes conscious control over the voluntary musculature.
Contiguity in occurrence of events shapes the human experience
of causality. Contiguity of occurrence relates inner thought to
outer consequence in us all. It is basic to our sense of animate
power. So too, discriminations of similarity and difference eventually are developed into capacities for analysis and synthesis.
Nevertheless, any sense of discrimination begins as affectively
guided associations of objects one with another.

Aside from understanding these very basic laws of association
so well studied in behaviorist psychology, one has to go further
and understand the pathways of association in terms of our affect-
laden early experiences, which give content as well as direction to
the affective flow of early associations. These experiences are
processed by a developing ego structure utilizing what are termed
mental mechanisms, coping mechanisms, or "defense" mechanisms.

Symbol, by its very nature, is a mode of guided communication
and cannot be considered independently from the process of communication itself. Man's thought is inherently interactive. Earlier
work in the understanding of causality in developmental psychol-

ogy, represented by Piaget (1928, 1929, 1930, 1974) and Vigotsky (1934, 1939*a*, 1939*b*), dealt both with the physiological, maturational development of language and symbol into causal patterns and the innately interactive processes involved in social learning which culturally transmit patterns of thought from one generation to the next (see also Rapaport 1950, 1951). However, for purposes of understanding cognition purely and ideally without the interference of affect, cognitive psychologists often studiously fail to consider what processes contribute to the continuance of precausality in given individual or cultural situations.

Anthropologists, in contrast to psychologists, are interested not only in the psychology of causality per se or the universal psychological principles underlying symbolism but also more specifically in the deciphering of culturally unique behavior as it reflects human experience within particular settings. In this sense, symbolism must be understood socially as well as personally in terms of what Durkheim (1947) and his followers have called "collective representations." But in their efforts to understand such cultural patterns of symbolic thought, anthropologists cannot avoid some disciplined understanding of psychodynamic principles that are elicited in the detailed clinical work of psychoanalysts, who in examining crises in human experience follow the pathways of primary as well as secondary-process thinking revealed in individual case studies.

The principles of association that psychoanalytic anthropologists such as La Barre (1954, 1980, 1984) and Devereux (1951, 1961, 1967, 1978, 1980) have often treated are thus quite unlike the principles of association used in structuralist anthropological approaches influenced by linguistics. This distinction occurs despite some apparent similarities between the use of a concept of ego structure and the concept of deep structure in either Chomsky or Lévi-Strauss. These approaches all suggest that patterns are innate in the human mind (see also Ogden 1986, chap. 2). However, psychoanalysis is clinical as well as interactional and therefore concerned with differential and idiosyncratic childhood experiences.

While there are universal occurrences that inescapably mark the human condition as developmental crises in the so-called oral, anal, phallic, and genital stages of psychosexual development,

there are also experiential differences among individuals that are
quickly apparent. Psychoanalysis is not simply a structuralist
approach to invariant stages. It is deeply concerned with the vicissitudes that govern the social interaction of the human being from
childbirth on. Indeed, modern culturally oriented psychoanalysis,
which is symbolized very often by the figure of Erikson (1950,
1964), takes an avowedly interactional approach to psychosexual
development. Moreover, recent psychoanalytic theory in respect
to ego psychology and object relations has gone far toward a
more interpersonal approach to behavior in attempting to understand not only psychological structure but the interactional patterns special to various groups that develop their own modes of
symbolizing.

Earlier on, in some of the anthropological approaches of the
so-called neo-Freudian period characterized by Fromm (1941,
1944, 1950, 1951), Horney (1937, 1939, 1945, 1950), and Kardiner
(1939, 1945), there was an attempted withdrawal from concern
with energy or drive aspects in psychoanalytic theory and instead
an insistent emphasis on an interactional approach. Recently
there has been better recognition that neither concern negates the
other; it is rather a question of emphasis. There has been a re-
assertion, within the mainstream of psychoanalysis itself, of the
necessity to consider not only the energizing affects of drives in
the understanding of psychosexual development in any cultural
setting, but also drives as an aid to understanding the energizing
of associative symbolism within specific cultures.

Some difference in emphasis is still apparent within recent clinical psychoanalysis in the theoretical division between Kernberg
(1975) and others who follow the approach as to object relations,
synthesizing the views of (Bowlby 1958, 1969, 1988; Fairbairn
1952; Jacobson 1964; Klein 1921, 1931, 1932; Mahler et al. 1975,
and Winnicott 1953), on the one hand and on the other hand the
individualistic approach of Kohut (1971), which is considered
by some to play down drives and the unconscious in attempting
to emphasize the interactional aspects of consciousness and self-
hood. It would seem, then, that within contemporary espousers
of psychoanalytic theory, one continues to find, generally speaking, two schools, one of which is more rationalistic and plays

down a theory of needs and drives and the other which remains more clinically focused on the continuity of unconscious structures in human behavior.

There is implicit in this division of approaches another tendency, noticeable in the works of many social scientists, that is, an inclination to be uncomfortable with the idea of the irrational and a preference therefore to emphasize the rational, utilitarian trend in all human intentionality.

There is very little relationship between the psychoanalytic approach in anthropology and the newer interests of some anthropologists in sociobiology. Sociobiologists cannot deal well with the determinant effects of learned symbolic communication. In their view, so much of human behavior is genetically organized rather than learned that the human capacity to symbolize is of little importance as the principal determinant of flexibility in human culture.

The capacity to symbolize is inherent as an *adaptive* trait of human beings. Indeed, the sociobiologists on the one hand and the more rationalistic structuralists such as Lévi-Strauss (1967) on the other hand, take the extreme positions possible between biological determinism and some form of rationalistic volunteerism in understanding social behavior. Psychoanalytic theory does not discard concern with the rational capacity of human consciousness as determinative of behavior, although there is a tendency in some proponents of psychoanalytic thought to reduce the understanding of the "emic" experiential self or self-consciousness to the "etic" structural concept of the ego.

It is helpful to distinguish between these two concepts. *Ego* is an "etic" concept, that is, a concept used by the outside observer to distinguish a variety of mental mechanisms that comprise the selective perception, integration, and execution of behavior in individuals. These mechanisms for the most part operate automatically without self-consciousness. The *self* is an experiential concept that designates the subjective experience of the individual or, when applied by anthropologists to cultural analysis, is an "emic" approach that takes into consideration the inner view of individuals in a culture as opposed to a structural analysis based solely on the a priori application of a theory of the dynamics of either psychological or social structures determining human behavior.

It would be our view that either structuralist approach is reductionist and that, indeed, the optimistic statement made by Freud about progress in therapy indicated that where "id" was, one could hope to find conscious direction and control at work henceforth. This hope for greater "self" determination resulting from therapy is no concept of the individual as hopelessly subject only to the irrational in the course of history, whether personal or collective. An increasing capacity for some conscious control is to be sought leading to a greater self-determination of one's behavior. Human beings do not remain subject only to the irrational impulses with which human life commences, nor do they have no conscious influence over the larger social forces that determine their history.

We (Boyer 1979; De Vos 1986) have considered three dimensions that characterize psychoanalytically oriented symbolic approaches to anthropology. First, psychoanalytic anthropology, in dealing with *symbols*, has recourse to an understanding of ego-defensive maneuvers such as projection and repression. But this is not to negate the fact that human communication is overdetermined and multileveled and takes place through patterned collective representations such as those delineated in other forms of structural analysis.

Second, in understanding *causality* in human thought psychoanalysis commences with a concern with so-called primaryprocess thinking. This is not to dismiss the necessity to understand the cognitive principles underlying causal thought, but to insist that affective experiences such as the internal experience of power or helplessness continue to be represented in human logic, and that rationality continually remains subject to forms of affective interference. Irrationality as well as rationality can be studied systematically.

Third, comprehending the operation of ego defense mechanisms or *coping mechanisms* and the vicissitudes that influence their transmutation into mature forms of adaptive thought is central to the understanding of moral development or internalization as integral to becoming a social animal in any specific cultural context.

The Development of the Capacity to Symbolize

There is a vast literature on human creativity from a psycho-analytic standpoint (Bergler 1950; Bonaparte 1933; Deri 1984; Eissler 1963; Giovacchini 1971; Greenacre 1957; Kris 1952; Rank 1932; Rickman 1940; Sachs 1942). From the earliest days of psychoanalysis, attention has been directed toward learning about the development in the child of a capacity to create and communicate through symbols. Thus in 1909 Freud wrote that Little Hans equated the horse with his internal picture of his father as a fearful rival. Subsequently, Whiting (1960) noted that Ferenczi's (1913) Little Arpad had also used the horse, but for him the horse was a maternal symbol. While Jones (1916) claimed that only what is repressed is, or must be, symbolized, Melanie Klein (1921, 1932) challenged this inflexible view and suggested that children's play can be sublimated activity that is a symbolic expression of both anxieties and positive wishes. Klein (1931) also raised the problem of inhibition in symbol formation. She concluded that an autistic child of four she had examined failed to endow the world about him with symbolic meaning. She reasoned, therefore, that the whole development of the ego is arrested if some form of symbolization does not occur.

Over the past fifty years, studies of symbols and their use, prin-cipally by the British, have included a redirection of interest to-ward their appearance in early childhood. British ideas concern-ing the development of object relations have complemented those of others who have more or less rigidly followed what has been considered a more standard structural theory (Arlow and Brenner 1964; Anna Freud 1936; Hartmann, Kris, and Loewen-stein 1946; Jacobson 1964; Mahler, Pine, and Bergman 1975; Rapaport 1950, 1951).

Winnicott (1962) perhaps best represents contemporary British object relations theorists who have modified the initial views of Klein. Comparisons of the positions taken by these theorists, as well as the interactions among their positions, are to be found in the writings of Kernberg (1980), Ogden (1983, 1986), and Winni-cott (1962). Winnicott had the advantage of much direct contact with Klein without coming under her tutelage by way of a personal or didactic analysis. Therefore, he retained a critical objectivity that allowed him to emphasize her most valuable contributions to theory without having to accept those hypotheses more generally considered erroneous or untestable by other observers.

Practicing pediatrics for years before becoming a psychoanalyst himself, Winnicott became an astute and empathic observer, who in his communication with small children came to understand their symbolic logic (Winnicott 1971*a*, 1971*b*). Later, as an analyst, he did not limit himself to the treatment of children but specialized also in the psychoanalytic treatment of severely disturbed patients, such as those termed *borderline* or even frankly schizophrenic. In his therapeutic approach, he encouraged rather than discouraged regression to their infantile states in his consultation room. While recognizing the similar thought processes in early childhood and in disturbed adults, he considered he learned more about early thinking from his regressed patients.

Winnicott's first major contribution to the study of symbolism (1953) was his concept of "transitional objects" (Grolnick, Barkin, and Meunsterberger 1978), considered a landmark in the theory of object relationships. He defined the transitional object as the first "not-me object" produced by the child. It exists in an illusory fashion, bonding child to mother, and globally symbolizing child and mother as well as the sensory stimulation of the oral zone and satisfaction of oral stimuli, all in "quiet union." A related concept, "transitional phenomena" and "transitional objects," both designate "the intermediate area of experience, between the thumb and the teddy bear, between oral eroticism and true object relationship, between primary creativity and projection of what has already been introjected, between primary unawareness of indebtedness and the acknowledgment of indebtedness" (Winnicott 1953:230).

In Winnicott's (1965) view, the adequate mother provides a "holding environment" that facilitates the unfolding of her baby's innate psychological growth capacities. The degree to which she can provide that environment depends on her capacity to have empathy with her baby's needs and her own identification with the child, as reflected in attitude and behavior. Initially, she more or less provides a milieu within which the infant's wants are anticipated relatively free of frustrations or a knowledge of want. At first she forms only a background and is an indistinguishable part of the baby's psychological existence. As the mother begins to interfere with the infant's spontaneous gestures, a developing sense of self includes experiences of traumatic disruption (Ogden 1983: 231).

Following the introduction of the concept of the transitional object, Winnicott gradually developed a concept of "potential space," perhaps his most important and elusive idea. It is this term that he used to refer to an intermediate area of experiencing that lies between fantasy and reality in the development of human consciousness (Ogden 1986, chap. 8). Winnicott admonished us to allow the paradoxes

. . . to be accepted, tolerated and respected, . . . and not be resolved (1971*a*:xii). Potential space . . . is the hypothetical area that exists (but cannot exist) between the baby and the object (mother or part of mother) during the phase of the repudiation of the object as not-me, that is, at the end of being merged with the object (1971*a*:107). Playing, creativity, transitional phenomena, psychotherapy and cultural experience, all have a place in which they occur (1971*a*:99). That place, potential space, is not *inside* by any sense of the word . . . nor is it *outside*, that is to say that it is not part of the repudiated world, the not-me, that which the individual has decided to recognize (with whatever difficulty and even pain) as truly external, which is outside magical control (1971*a*:41). Potential space is an intermediate area of experiencing that lies between (a) the inner world, "inner psychic reality" (1971*a*:106), and (b) "actual or external reality" (1971*a*:41).

It lies "between the subjective object and the object objectively perceived, between me-extensions and not-me" (Ogden 1986:100). It is, then within this psychological "potential space" that frustrations stimulate the infant to begin to use its innate capacity to create first mental representations of mother and self, objectivity and subjectivity, and symbols for both. Rapaport (1951:689–730) presented as a model for the development of thinking, affect, psychic structure, and memory, the restlessness of the hungry infant who hallucinates initially some vague representation of the breast that temporarily satisfies until hunger tension becomes too strong. In Winnicott's view, the first creativity occurs within potential space in the form of initially indefinite but subsequently ever clearer symbols that will be chosen on the basis of their having qualities in common with that which they symbolize.

The Logic of the Unconscious

Two different types of logic are involved in human thought as it unfolds from this early incomplete separation of self and object: that generally employed by the conscious mind, known for its "Aristotelian" logic, and that characteristic of the unconscious mind, called by various names such as "paleologic," "autistic," "prelogical," or "primary process" thinking. Primary-process thinking is typical both of the immature mind and of individuals during periods of psychological regression and altered ego states including sleep, trance and, perhaps, to a lesser degree, reverie and periods of creativity. It involves a high mobility of drive cathexes (that is, the investment of affect into attachments to a person or persons), the absence of a concept of time, and the use of two mental mechanisms known as displacement and condensation (Brenner 1955; Freud 1915). Displacement involves the transference of a cathexis or affective investment from one idea or object to another; condensation entails the representation of several ideas or images by a single word or image, or even a part of one.

During the maturation of the ego, drive cathexes become bound and stable, conceptualized as committed investments of "meaning" in things and beings outside oneself (Hartmann 1939; Hartmann, Kris, and Loewenstein 1946), but earlier, their mobility had enhanced the tendency to immediate gratification or discharge of cathexis, dominant in infancy and childhood, in the dream state, and during some periods of regression. The pent-up cathexis is perceived as anxiety or tension in some affectual form. In the event that drive cathexes must be shifted from their original objects or methods of gratification, drive discharge can be accomplished, at least in part, through symbolic representation. The lonely or hungry baby or small child seeks to suck its thumb, which has come to symbolize its mother or her nipple. Previous pleasurable play with feces is now forbidden, but the toddler may enjoy making mud pies, and unconscious elements of the initial source of satisfaction may be retained even later by the most highly creative and mature ceramist.

Although some schools of psychology hold that mental contents are themselves inherited so that people are born with inherent symbolic representations (Jung 1916*a*, 1916*b*, 1928), most students of the mind believe such a hypothesis to be untestable and hold more conservatively that the *capacity* to achieve symbolic representation is innate. The literature on the psychology of the infant and young child is replete with graphic examples of their early use of symbols (see especially Milner 1952, 1957, 1969; Segal 1957; Winnicott 1953, 1971*a*, 1977*b*).

As discussed above in reference to the so-called laws of association, the use of a different idea or image as an object of displacement or condensation depends on its having some quality or qualities in common with the initial idea or image. As examples, there may be a similarity of form, texture, color, odor, taste, of the nature of motion or potential motion. These dimensions, related to sensory modalities, in effect are operative in the "determinants" governing the response patterns to Rorschach stimuli, as will be apparent in the following chapters.

The symbols that will be created by the infant and small child will be simple, based on the relative absence of complexity of its wishes, the demands made on it, and its physical and emotional environment—its world. Such symbols will very likely be universal in their earliest forms. Indeed, they have appeared as such in the clinical practice of the psychoanalytic author, who has treated people of all colors and from many cultures in his practice. Simple and sophisticated people alike use the same basic symbols in their dreams, reveries, and parapraxes.

Early in his study of dreams and neurotic symptoms, Freud (1900) found symbolic representations that were relatively constant from patient to patient and were unknown to the patients themselves; subsequently analysts throughout the world have validated his observations. Thus "hills" and "two sisters" in a dream always stood for thoughts about breasts; it is interesting in this regard that Apache Indians of New Mexico call three mountains that look like breasts the Three Sisters and believe supernatural, nurturing power emanates from tunnels within them

(Boyer 1979). Freud also found that a "journey" or the phenomenon of "absence" stood for death, "money" stood for feces, and so on. Such equations are regularly made unconsciously by the audiences of joke tellers, regardless of their cultural background.

The list of what may be represented by a symbol by the infant is quite short, inasmuch as his interests and environment are sharply limited. It comprises the body and its parts, initially skin, breasts, buttocks, anus, urinary and alimentary tracts, the experiences of motoric control and kinesthetic sensibility (De Vos 1988), and perhaps a bit later the sexual organs; members of the immediate family; certain bodily functions and experiences, including sexual intercourse, excretory activities, eating, weeping, rage, and sexual excitement; birth, death, and a few others. It must be remembered that, given the timelessness of the unconscious, the initial symbolic representations created by the infant and toddler will remain forever in his unconscious mind and retain their original meanings, regardless of whatever subsequent meanings may be attached to them by condensation, whether dictated by the needs of the growing individual or by societal teaching. What is of particular importance from the standpoint of this book is that regardless of how many subsequent additional meanings are attached to symbols, at some level of unconsciousness they also retain their primitive, simple meanings.

The unconscious affect as well as conscious emotion which will be attached to a symbol will depend upon the experiences of the individual and the complexities of his personality structure. Thus for one person, the hill or sister will have a positive valence, reflecting remembered warmth and gratitude and the feeling of being loved while being cared for by his mother figure. For another, perhaps less tenderly nurtured, the breast symbol will have come to represent also displaced or projected rage, and perhaps he will see it as representative of a "bad mother" wanting to devour him. Surely such symbolic meanings are rife in the folklore of many groups, as, for example, the Eskimo (Birket-Smith 1953; Boas 1904; Garber 1940; Hippler and Wood 1977).

Scientists have long sought to understand the logic involved in the thinking of the regressed or otherwise autistic person. Perhaps the most illuminating insight has been provided by von

Domarus (1925, 1944). Focusing specifically on communication through symbols, he formulated a principle which, in slightly modified form, is as follows: "Whereas the normal person accepts identity only nominatively upon the basis of identical subjects, the paleologician accepts identity based on identical predicates" (Arieti, 1948:326). At times the communications of the psychotic become exceedingly complex due to the nature of the similarities which determine the communicating symbols. Such complex communications would only be used by a person who had undergone learning and then regressed. Thus, a patient of von Domarus (Arieti 1948:327) thought that Jesus, cigar boxes, and females were identical. The common predicate found in this delusion that led to its comprehension was the state of being "encircled." According to the patient, the head of a saint or of Jesus is encircled by a halo, the box of cigars by the tax band, and a woman by the sexual glance of the man. Usually the meanings of symbols are more easily detected. As an example, a psychotic patient of Segal's (1957:391) was once asked by his doctor why it was that since his illness he had stopped playing the violin. He responded angrily: "Why! Do you expect me to masturbate in public?"

Duality in Symbolic Analysis

To encompass the increasing complexities of social experience, the infant becoming a socialized child reaches out beyond the body and primary attachments. Through an increasing capacity for verbal as well as gestural communication, the increasingly social child resorts to symbolic means of representation that include experiences of the social and natural world about. These symbols are not invented from within but become available as the infant, then child, and finally adult progressively partakes of the collective representations of his or her group.

Some schools of anthropology, discomforted by the illusive and irrational as well as by the concept of unconscious process, would forgo any form of psychological analysis that would force its members to consider how the earlier infantile and childhood period representations remain embedded in and influence social communication. As has been noted earlier, this exclusory attitude has characterized the position of the structural-functional approach of British social anthropology. A theoretical separation from psychology was deemed necessary by Radcliffe-Brown (1922) if one hoped to be systematic in developing knowledge of social structure as an independent science of man. For him and his followers the motivations of the individual are unimportant in understanding systems of social behavior.

Malinowski (1926, 1927, 1929, 1935, 1955) dared what were considered theoretical inconsistences by insisting that the motivational strategies of the individual color the manner in which cultural patterns are expressed somewhat imperfectly by societal constituents (see also Spiro 1982). American cultural anthropologists such as Hallowell (1940, 1955), Kluckhohn, Murray, and Schneider (1959), Kroeber (1923, 1952), Kroeber and Kluckhohn (1952), Linton (1945, 1955, 1956), Mead (1949*a*, 1949*b*), and Spindler (1978) were more sympathetic to what developed as a "culture and personality approach." Those sympathetic to this approach see the collective symbols of humans not solely as representations of outer social realities or institutional structures, but, in addition, as commonly held symbols that in many instances are deeply expressive of inner affective states that cannot be directly related to social structure per se. This alternative functionalist approach to symbolic analysis has been related consistently, but somewhat critically, to psychoanalytic psychology. Indeed, it has been influential in overcoming a tendency to ethnocentric interpretations in clinical practice, as if these symbols appeared exclusively within a given class of Western society.

Psychoanalytic psychology, as applied to the analysis of cultural behavior, has made us deeply aware of the possible vicissitudes occurring in the normal processes of the development of thought. The inchoate forms of thought, termed *primary processes*, which are characteristic of infantile maturational stages, are transmuted through social living within family and community into *secondary processes* shared by the group as a whole. Nevertheless, as we have been indicating, adult thought content, whatever the society studied, still includes vestiges of the more primitive forms of logic in its seemingly scientific principles as well as in the magically and religiously based beliefs and concepts peculiar to the particular society and its history.

The "socialization" of thought consists of transforming into communicable forms associative processes with their primary, yet autistically incommunicable, attempts at symbolism. The early spontaneous affectively guided associations, aptly described by Piaget (1930) as "ego-centric" and "syncretic," gradually, through social interaction, become consciously guided communication more often characterized by objectivity, reciprocity, and mutuality. In short, thought becomes permeable to cultural experience and to external regularities of social logic, whatever its imperfections in any particular society.

Some scholars attempt to understand man as a symbolizing animal solely in terms of his development of *verbal* communication as either an inner language or a mode of external communication. The artist or dancer would never make such a mistake. Those working in the plastic or graphic arts as well as in dance seek consciously to control and to represent outwardly in visual form inner perceptions of which the person is deeply aware but which may have no ready verbal referent. One may speculate that inner experiences are perhaps communicated symbolically to the conscious mind before they are expressed in outer communication. The reverse, however, is also possible. By active participation in performance one may acquire an inner experience. These inner experiences, or inner affective states, usually occur in other modalities than solely verbal ones. Kinesthesis, visual imagery, smell, or taste are prior forms of experience. But since sensory experiences, albeit conscious, are less subject to abstraction in communication, they remain more inchoate, more "primitive," or more subject to primary-process associations and less subject to ego controls. Visual images prevail in dreams, although other sensory modalities also are represented, and use of verbal condensations is not uncommon.

With the development and evolution of consciousness, the capacity to symbolize comes progressively under the direction of objectively organized ego functions. Consciousness begets more unconsciousness as coping or defense mechanisms exclude the disorganized, inconsistent, and dangerous stimuli, past and present, that would threaten a more ordered and socially acceptable self.

The most obvious aspect of this development in control is found in "language." The origin of language is enshrouded in that dim prehistoric time when outwardly expressed signs of affective

or kinetic states such as facial postures somehow became more
deliberately controlled and ordered in discriminant verbal symbols. Language, even in its simplest form, is symbolic. Therefore,
these verbal symbols, operative socially, are used first of all to
indicate something which is not visually present in the situation.
As defined by Webster (1983), "A symbol is a sign by which one
knows or infers a thing. It is that which suggests something else by
reason of relationship, association, or convention. It can be a visible sign of something invisible, such as an idea, a quality."

In its more technical use in psychoanalysis, a symbol is often an
object, act, or thought representing an unconscious desire or
even a conflict constellation. As Durkheim (1947) uses the term,
a "representation" to be analyzed symbolically in a sociological
framework is defined as "an act or instance of representing,
through a likeness, picture, model, image or other reproduction." Durkheim included dramatic reproductions or performances.

The word *symbol* as used in this volume is broadly defined to
include unconscious representations considered in a sociological
as well as a psychological frame of reference. As collective representations are described by Durkheim, their functions or intentions are not necessarily self-conscious to participants. Those engaged in the telling of a myth or taking part in a ritual are usually
unaware that by so doing they are representing their social solidarity. Nor may they be concerned with the educative functions
of folklore, or the alleviation or expression of psychological tensions. Nevertheless, there is a great deal of unconscious understanding of what is being presented and communicated by both
teller and audience (Arlow 1961; Bascom 1954; Boyer 1979;
Dundes 1965).

What is termed "symbolic analysis" by either the sociologically
or psychologically oriented social scientist is usually *not* the analysis of graphic or verbal symbols used consciously. Rather, attention is usually focused on what is *inadvertently* expressed as a "by-
product" either in religious beliefs and rituals, dreams, or even
ordinary conversation or, as we shall consider in the following
chapters, in such projective tests as the Rorschach. The social
scientist intends to analyze symbolic expressions as they are related to underlying social or psychological processes, and as these

expressions are conceptually understood etically by the scientific analyst within his own frame of reference. These symbolic expressions are not necessarily self-consciously understood by the bearers of the culture examined. To make this distinction between inadvertent and conscious use of symbols clear, let us very briefly consider some of the functions of a symbol in both its cognitive and its affective-expressive aspects.

Psychological Functions of Symbolic Communication

One important function of any symbol, used consciously or not, is to communicate something that has no immediate concrete referent. Symbols involve various forms of control and directionality. For example:

1. Symbols are used for *precise conceptual economy* in communication when concepts are of a complex nature. If a set of abstract symbols is mutually understood, communication is more rapid and economical. This is the disciplined, objective use of symbols found in its most complex development in such fields as mathematics.

2. Symbols are used less precisely to convey *concepts* that are felt to be *too complex for comprehension*, but when some communication is necessary. Humans are still prone to symbolize, even when they feel that something is conceptually beyond their power to comprehend fully. Individuals often feel themselves to be in some relation to certain invisible realities. It is then necessary to represent what is ill understood or what cannot be directly comprehended by verbal terms, graphic design, or expressive gesture. The concept of "god" and religious terms and rituals in their cognitive aspects have such symbolic function. Representations of this nature were the basis of the approach developed by Durkheim in his analysis of cultural behavior. The cabalists of the Middle Ages developed a very complex system of "incomprehensible" symbols as a means of "comprehending" reality. Zen Buddhism seeks truth or enlightenment reached only through a sudden comprehension. Obscure symbolic conundrums with manifest incongruity are used to stimulate the seeker into sudden realization.

3. Symbols can be used to convey *complex emotional states.* What is to be communicated may be not only a complex cognition but also an associated complex feeling. Usually both cognitive and affective elements are present in symbols, but in certain instances the emphasis is more on one than on the other. When one becomes conscious of oneself, one may become conscious of the complexity of one's emotional nature as well and attempt to communicate this complexity to others.

Such communication, to be effective, demands means other than direct cognitive communication, since the goal is often to arouse like states in others. Art, drama, and literature, especially in such forms as lyric poetry, depend upon artistic ability in symbolic expressive media to produce in audiences certain emotional states which allow them to comprehend at least affectively, if not cognitively, the intent of the artist. The French Symbolist poets, exemplified by Verlaine, despaired of communicating general truths or the "inner cosmos" except by means of indirect, vaguely apprehended, affect-laden symbolic statements. Religious rituals, similarly, function to create in their participants certain states of affect related to what has deep meaning for the group as a whole, as well as for its individual members. Great drama, as well as simple folktales, depend on an undercurrent of symbolic meanings to produce emotional impact as well as to convey cognitive significance.

Both sociological and psychological interpretations of such cultural expressions are possible. It is often the artful, mostly unconscious use of primary process associations with psychosexual developmental referents *common to members of a particular group* that cause these artistic creations to be treasured and preserved. Conversely, in a Durkheimian sense they also bear meanings of great value to the social life of the group, whether consciously or unconsciously understood.

4. Finally, symbols in a broadly psychoanalytic sense are *projections of inner states.* In this form of symbolic expression the very manner in which an individual perceives an object, answers a question, recounts an event, or tells a spontaneous story is of symbolic significance to the trained observer of behavior, as is well exemplified in the chapters of this book. This is the form of symbolism with which we have been particularly concerned in the

use of projective tests cross-culturally. The material elicited has both manifest and latent meanings. In the psychoanalytic sense it performs one very important function of a symbol, namely to express indirectly what cannot be directly expressed due to the presence of negative sanctions.

Note well, however, that the term *repression* refers both to the exercise of social-political sanctions which may lead to distorted or hidden forms of dissidence and protest as well as to the intrapsychic defenses against unconscious pressures within the individual that seek some form of outer expression. Symbolizing is indeed sometimes used consciously by politically helpless dissident groups within a culture whose values or behavior are opposed by the dominant group or by the majority; but it is also possible to find examples of what are both intrapsychically and socially repressed feelings expressing underlying "dangerous" attitudes. They may be expressed socially, but most often unconsciously, only in so-called rituals of rebellion (Bateson 1936; Gluckman 1954), wherein social roles are temporarily reversed as a form of ceremonial play. In other cultural contexts, they may become manifest only in altered states of consciousness such as trance (Bourguignon 1966), which allows for experiences of power not directly appreciable in the normal conscious state.

The socially conforming individual often expresses affect symbolically so as not to arouse the censorship of his or her own ego, which acts as an internalized representative of socially held values. For the individual, as for the group, some feelings or thoughts challenging the status quo are unconscionable in direct naked form, yet are of such importance that they seek some form of expression. They may be disguised from direct view by being put in a form which is seemingly nonsymbolic or supposedly consciously acceptable and symbolic of something else shared by those in communication.

Dramas such as *Hamlet*, therefore, inescapably have multiple meanings. First, there is the overt problem faced by Hamlet and its solution, which fulfills the necessary requisites of noble tragic drama according to Aristotelian aesthetics. Second, as analyzed by Ernest Jones (1948), there is the basic Oedipal theme, more or less unconsciously shared by members of the audience witnessing the play. Shakespeare's masterful use of condensation is attested to by the fact that there are numerous psychoanalytic studies of *Hamlet*, many of which uncover meanings other than those detected by Jones (e.g., Clatton-Brock 1922; Eissler 1963; Glaz 1961, 1962; Mairet 1969; Moloney and Rockelein 1949; Reik 1952).

While it is a far cry from the analysis of a single set of Rorschach responses to the analysis of *Hamlet*, both are related to inherent expressive symbolizing functions of man's intellect. No matter in what culture, humans cannot help symbolizing more than is their conscious intention. They can never escape their own primary affective associations in their attempts at controlled thought, regardless of what energy they expend to remain objective. Each night humans must, albeit sometimes reluctantly, return to the past and to the primitive when returning to sleep and rest. In so doing the human mind reverts to less disciplined patterns. Somatic and affective referents guide the residues of associations through regressive modes requiring less controlled psychic energy for direction.

So, too, even in the waking state the individual cannot always escape the influence of strong emotions. Hard-won objective controls may give way under the sway of uncontrollable feelings that color total perception. Less overtly, some of these patterns of emotion, especially those involved in primary relationships, are constantly coloring the world for any particular individual. All perception is influenced by past experience in an affective as well as cognitive sense. The degree of strength exercised by affective considerations differs radically with circumstance, but also with the individual and with the group considered. Using standardized stimuli is one means to attempt assessing such differences. In this volume we have attempted to present studies using methods of quantification as well as those depending directly on qualitative forms of analysis. Although the capacity to demonstrate systematic occurrences by quantification is reassuring and ultimately necessary for scientific progress, a case approach is also scientific in its purpose of increasing our knowledge and directing our attention toward possible generalizations to be further tested. Interpretation of symbolism cannot escape the disciplined insight of the trained observer in either approach.

References

Abraham, Karl
  1913   *Dreams and Myths*. New York: Nervous and Mental Disease
         Publications.
Altman, Leon L.
  1969   *The Dream in Psychoanalysis*. New York: International Uni-
         versities Press.
Arieti, Silvano
  1948   Special Logic of Schizophrenia and Other Types of Autistic
         Thought. *Psychiatry* 11:325–338.
Arlow, Jacob A.
  1961   Ego Psychology and the Study of Mythology. *Journal of the
         American Psychoanalytic Association* 9:371–393.
Arlow, Jacob A., and Charles Brenner
  1964   *Psychoanalytic Concepts and the Structural Theory*. New
         York: International Universities Press.
Bascom, William
  1954   Four Functions of Folklore. *Journal of American Folklore*
         66:333–349.
Bateson, Gregory
  1936   *Naven*. Cambridge: Cambridge University Press.
Bergler, Edmund
  1950   *The Writer and Psychoanalysis*. New York: Doubleday.
Birket-Smith, Kaj
  1953   *The Chugach Eskimo*. Copenhagen: Nationalmuseetts Publi-
         kationsford.
Boas, Franz
  1904   The Folklore of the Eskimo. *Journal of American Folklore*
         17:1–13.
Bonaparte, Marie
  1933   *The Life and Works of Edgar Allan Poe: A Psychoanalytic
         Interpretation*. London: Imago Publishing Company.
Bourguignon, Erika
  1966   World Distribution and Patterns of Possession States,
         Raymond Prince, ed. *Trance and Possession States*, pp. 3–340.
         Montreal: Bucks Memorial Society.
Bowlby, John
  1958   The Nature of the Child's Tie to Its Mother. *International
         Journal of Psychoanalysis* 39:350–373.
  1969   *Attachment and Loss*. Vol. 1, *Attachment*. New York: Basic
         Books.

1988   Developmental Psychiatry Comes of Age, *American Journal of Psychiatry* 145:1–10.

Boyer, L. Bryce
1979   *Childhood and Folklore: A Psychoanalytic Study of Apache Personality.* New York: Library of Psychological Anthropology.

Brenner, Charles
1955   *An Elementary Textbook of Psychoanalysis.* Revised and expanded edition. Garden City, N.Y.: Anchor Press, 1974.

Chomsky, Noam
1957   *Syntactic Structures.* The Hague: Mouton.
1968   *Language and Mind.* New York: Harcourt Brace Jovanovich.

Clatton-Brock, A.
1922   *Shakespeare's Hamlet.* London: Methuen.

Deri, Susan K.
1984   *Symbolization and Creativity.* New York: International Universities Press.

Devereux, George
1951   *Reality and Dream: Psychotherapy of a Plains Indian.* New York: International Universities Press.
1961   *Mohave Ethnopsychiatry and Suicide: the Psychiatric Knowledge and the Psychic Disturbances of an Indian Tribe.* Smithsonian Institution, Bureau of American Ethology, Bulletin 175.
1967   *From Anxiety to Method in the Behavioral Sciences.* Paris: Mouton.
1978   *Ethnopsychoanalysis.* Berkeley, Los Angeles, London: University of California Press.
1980   *Basic Problems of Ethnopsychiatry.* Chicago: University of Chicago Press.

De Vos, George A.
1975   The Dangers of Pure Theory in Social Anthropology. *Ethos* 3:77–91.
1986   Insight and Symbol: Dimensions of Analysis in Psychoanalytic Anthropology. *Journal of Psychoanalytic Anthropology* 9(3):199–233.
1988   Empathy to Alienation: Problems in Human Belonging. *Personality in the Construction of Society.* David Jordan and Marc Swartz, eds. University: University of Alabama Press.

Douglas, Mary
1966   *Purity and Danger: An Analysis of Concepts of Pollution and Taboo.* New York: Praeger.
1970   *Natural Symbols: Explorations in Cosmology.* London: Cresset Press.

Dundes, Alan, ed.
1965   *The Study of Folklore*. Englewood Cliffs, N.J.: Prentice-Hall.
Durkheim, Emile
1947   *The Elementary Forms of the Religious Life*. J. W. Swain, trans. Glencoe, Ill.: Free Press.
Eissler, Kurt
1963   *Goethe: A Psychoanalytic Study, 1775–1786*. 2 vol. Detroit: Wayne State University Press.
Erikson, Erik H.
1950   *Childhood and Society*. New York: Norton.
1954   The Dream Specimen of Psychoanalysis. *Journal of the American Psychoanalytic Association* 50:131–170.
1964   *Insight and Responsibility*. New York: Norton.
Fairbairn, W. R. O.
1952   *An Object Relations Theory of Personality*. New York: Basic Books.
Ferenczi, Sándor
1913   A Little Chanticleer. *Sex and Psychoanalysis*, pp. 240–252. New York: Basic Books [1959].
Frazer, James G.
1894   *The Golden Bough*. 2 vol. New York: Macmillan.
1910   *Totemism and Exogamy*. 4 vol. London: Macmillan.
1913   *Psyche's Task*. London: Macmillan.
Freud, Anna
1936   *The Ego and the Mechanisms of Defense*. New York: International Universities Press, 1946.
Freud, Sigmund
1900   *The Interpretation of Dreams*. Standard edition, 1953, Vols. 4 and 5. London: Hogarth Press.
1909   *Analysis of a Phobia in a Five-year-old Boy*. Standard edition, 1955, 10:5–147. London: Hogarth Press.
1915   *The Unconscious*. Standard edition, 1957, 14:159–215. London: Hogarth Press.
Fromm, Erich
1941   *Escape from Freedom*. New York: Rinehart.
1944   Individual and Social Origins of Neurosis. *American Sociological Review* 9:380–384.
1950   *Psychoanalysis and Religion*. New Haven: Yale University Press.
1951   *The Forgotten Language*. New York: Rinehart.
Garber, Clark M.
1940   *Stories and Legends of the Bering Strait Eskimos*. Boston:

Christopher.

Geertz, Clifford
1973   *The Interpretation of Culture*. New York: Basic Books.
1983   *Local Knowledge: Further Essays in Interpretation*. New York: Basic Books.

Giovacchini, Peter L.
1971   Creativity and Character. *Journal of the American Psychoanalytic Association* 19:524–542.

Glaz, A. André
1961   Hamlet, or the Tragedy of Shakespeare. *American Imago* 18:129–158.
1962   Iago, or Moral Sadism. *American Imago* 19:323–348.

Gluckman, Max
1954   *Rituals of Rebellion*. Manchester: Manchester University Press.

Greenacre, Phyllis
1957   The Childhood of the Artist: Libidinal Phase Development and Giftedness. *Psychoanalytic Study of the Child* 12:47–72. New York: International University Press.

Grolnick, Simon A., Leonard Barkin, and Werner Muensterberger
1978   *Between Reality and Fantasy: Transitional Objects and Phenomena*. New York: Jason Aronson.

Hallowell, A. Irving
1940   Aggression in Saulteaux Society. *Psychiatry* 3:395–407.
1955   *Culture and Experience*. Philadelphia: University of Pennsylvania Press.

Hartmann, Heinz
1939   *Ego Psychology and the Problem of Adaptation*. New York: International Universities Press, 1958.

Hartmann, Heinz, Ernst Kris, and Rudolph M. Loewenstein
1946   Comments on the Formation of Psychic Structure. *Psychoanalytic Study of the Child* 2:11–38. New York: International Universities Press.

Hippler, Arthur E., and John Wood
1977   *The Eskimos: A Selected Annotated Bibliography*. Fairbanks: University of Alaska, I.S.E.G.R.

Horney, Karen
1937   *The Neurotic Personality of Our Time*. New York: Norton.
1939   *New Ways in Psychoanalysis*. New York: Norton.
1945   *Our Inner Conflicts: A Constructive Theory of Neurosis*. New York: Norton.
1946   *Are You Considering Psychoanalysis?* New York: Norton.

1950   *Neurosis and Human Growth: The Struggle Toward Self-Realization*. New York: Norton.
Jacobson, Edith
1964   *Psychotic Conflict and Reality*. New York: International Universities Press.
Jones, Ernest
1916   The Theory of Symbolism. *Papers on Psychoanalysis*, pp. 87–144. 5th edition. Baltimore: Williams and Wilkins, 1949.
1948   The Death of Hamlet's Father. *Essays on Applied Psychoanalysis*. 1:323–328. London: Hogarth Press.
Jung, Carl G.
1916a   *Psychology of the Unconscious*. London: Kegan Paul.
1916b   *Collected Papers on Analytical Psychology*. London: Balliere, Tindall and Cox.
1928   *Contributions to Analytical Psychology*. London: Kegan Paul, Trench and Trubner.
Kardiner, Abram
1939   *The Individual and His Society*. New York: Columbia University Press.
1945   *The Psychological Frontiers of Society*. New York: Columbia University Press.
Kasanin, Jacob S., ed.
1944   *Language and Thought in Schizophrenia: Collected Papers*. Berkeley: University of California Press.
Kernberg, Otto F.
1975   *Borderline Conditions and Pathological Narcissism*. New York: Jason Aronson.
1980   *Internal World and External Reality*. New York: Jason Aronson.
Klein, Melanie
1921   The Development of a Child: Sexual Enlightenment and Permissiveness in Their Influence on the Intellectual Development of the Child. *International Journal of Psycho-Analysis* 4:419–474.
1931   A Contribution to the Theory of Intellectual Inhibition. *International Journal of Psychoanalysis* 13:206–218.
1932   *The Psycho-Analysis of Children*. London: Hogarth Press [1950].
Kluckhohn, Clyde, Henry A. Murray, and David Schneider, eds.
1959   *Personality in Nature, Society, and Culture*. New York: Alfred A. Knopf.
Kohut, Heinz
1971   *The Analysis of the Self: A Systematic Approach to the*

Psychoanalytic Treatment of the Narcissistic Disorders. New York: International Universities Press.

Kris, Ernst
1952   *Psychoanalytic Explorations in Art*. New York: International Universities Press.

Kroeber, Alfred
1923   *Anthropology*. New York: Harcourt, Brace, 1948.
1952   *The Nature of Culture*. Chicago: University of Chicago Press.

Kroeber, Alfred, and Clyde Kluckhohn
1952   Culture: A Critical Review of Concepts and Definitions. *Papers of the Peabody Museum* 47:1.

Kuper, Adam, and Alan A. Stone
1982   The Dream of Irma's Injection: A Structural Analysis. *American Journal of Psychiatry* 139:1225–1234.

La Barre, Weston
1954   *The Human Animal*. Chicago: University of Chicago Press.
1980   *Culture in Context*. Durham: Duke University Press.
1984   *Muelos: A Stone Age Superstition about Sexuality*. New York: Columbia University Press.

Lévi-Strauss, Claude
1955   The Structural Study of Myth. *Journal of American Folklore* 68:428–444.
1966   *Le Totemisme Aujourd'hui*. Paris: Presses Universitaires de France.
1967   *Structural Anthropology*. New York: Doubleday.

Lévy-Bruhl, Lucien
1910   *Primitive Mentality*. Boston: Beacon Press, 1923.

Linton, Ralph
1945   *The Cultural Background of Personality*. New York: D. Appleton-Century.
1955   *The Tree of Culture*. New York: Alfred A. Knopf.
1956   *Culture and Mental Disorders*. Springfield, Ill.: C. C. Thomas.

Mahler, Margaret S., Fred Pine, and Anni Bergman
1975   *The Psychological Birth of the Human Infant*. New York: Basic Books.

Mairet, Philippe
1969   Hamlet as a Study in Individual Psychology. *Journal of Individual Psychology* 25:71–78.

Malinowski, Brownislaw
1926   *Crime and Custom in Savage Society*. London: Kegan Paul, Trench, and Trubner.
1927   *Sex and Repression in Savage Society*. New York: Meridian

[1955].

1929   *The Sexual Lives of Savages*. London: Routledge and Kegan Paul [1953].

1935   *Coral Gardens and Their Magic*. New York: American Book Company.

1955   *Magic, Science, and Religion and Other Essays*. Garden City: Doubleday–Anchor Books.

Mead, Margaret

1949*a*   *Male and Female: A Study of the Sexes in a Changing World*. New York: Mentor Books, 1955.

1949*b*   The Mountain Arapesh V. The Record of Unabelin with Rorschach Analysis. Anthropological Papers of the American Museum of Natural History.

Milner, Marion

1952   Aspects of Symbolism in Comprehension of the Not-Self. *International Journal of Psychoanalysis* 33:181–195.

1957   *On Not Being Able to Paint*. New York: International Universities Press.

1969   *The Hands of the Living God: An Account of a Psychoanalytic Treatment*. New York: International Universities Press.

Moloney, James Clarke, and Laurence A. Rockelein

1949   A New Interpretation of Hamlet. *International Journal of Psycho-Analysis* 30:92–107.

Ogden, Thomas H.

1983   *Projective Identification and Psychotherapeutic Technique*. New York: Aronson.

1986   *The Matrix of the Mind: Object Relations in the Psychoanalytic Dialogue*. Northdale, N.J.: Aronson.

Piaget, Jean

1928   *Judgment and Reasoning in the Child*. New York: Harcourt, Brace.

1929   *The Child's Conception of the World*. New York: Harcourt, Brace.

1930   *The Child's Conception of Causality*. London: Kegan Paul.

1974   *Understanding Causality*. New York: W. W. Norton.

Radcliffe-Brown, Alfred R.

1922   *The Andaman Islanders*. Glencoe, Ill.: Free Press [1948].

Rank, Otto

1932   *Art and Artist: Creative Urge and Personality Development*. New York: Alfred A. Knopf.

Rapaport, David

1950   *Emotions and Memory*. New York: International Universities

Press.

Rapaport, David, ed.
   1951   *Organization and Pathology of Thought: Selected Papers.* New
          York: Columbia University Press.
Reik, Theodor
   1952   In My Mind's Eye. *Horatio Complex,* 7:15–31. New York:
          Grune and Stratton.
Rickman, John
   1940   On the Nature of Ugliness and the Creative Impulse. *Interna-
          tional Journal of Psycho-Analysis* 21:294–313.
Sachs, Hans
   1942   *The Creative Unconscious.* Cambridge: Sci-Art Publishers.
Segal, Hanna
   1957   Notes on Symbol Formation. *The Works of Hanna Segal: A
          Kleinian Approach to Clinical Practice,* pp. 49–65. New York:
          Aronson, 1981.   .
Spindler, George
   1978   *The Making of Psychological Anthropology.* Berkeley, Los
          Angeles, London: University of California Press.
Spiro, Melford E.
   1982   *Oedipus in the Trobriands.* Chicago: University of Chicago
          Press.
Thoden Van Velsen, H. U. E.
   1988   Irma's Rape: The Hermeneutics of Structuralism and
          Psychoanalysis Compared. L. Bryce Boyer and Simon A. Grol-
          nick, eds. *The Psychoanalytic Study of Society,* 12:102–140. Hills-
          dale, N.J.: Analytic Press.
Turner, Victor
   1967   *The Forest of Symbol: Aspects of Ndembu Ritual.* Ithaca,
          N.Y.: Cornell University Press.
   1978   *Image and Pilgrimage in Christian Culture: Anthropological
          Perspectives.* New York: Columbia University Press.
Vigotsky, L.
   1934   *Thought and Language.* Cambridge, Mass.: MIT Press.
   1939a Thought in Schizophrenia. *Archives of Neurology and
          Psychiatry* 31:1063–1077.
   1939b Thought in Speech. *Psychiatry* 2:29–54.
Von Domarus, E.
   1925   The Specific Laws of Logic and Schizophrenia. Jacob Kasinen,
          ed. *Language and Thought in Schizophrenia:* pp. 104–114. Ber-
          keley: University of California Press.

Whiting, John W. M.
1960 Totem and Taboo—A Re-evaluation. Jules H. Masserman, ed. *Science and Psychoanalysis*. Vol. 3; *Psychoanalysis and Human Values*, pp. 150–155. New York: Grune and Stratton.
Winnicott, D. W.
1953 Transitional Objects And Transitional Phenomena. *Collected Papers: Through Paediatrics to Psychoanalysis*, pp. 229–242. New York: Basic Books.
1962 A Personal View of the Kleinian Contribution. *The Maturational Processes and the Facilitating Environment*, pp. 171–178. New York: International Universities Press.
1965 *The Maturational Processes and the Facilitating Environment: Studies in the Theory of Emotional Development*. New York: International Universities Press.
1971a *Playing and Reality*. London: Tavistock Publications.
1971b *Therapeutic Consultations in Child Psychiatry*. London: Hogarth Press.

Chapter Two

Transcultural Studies: Normative and Clinical

George A. De Vos

As cultures become more complex and geographic and social mobility increases, previously unnoticed rigidities within individuals become manifest as hindrances to new patterns of social adaptation. The increase in intercultural communication changes the perspective of the theory and application of social thought. Knowledge both of human biology and of the determinative effects of society upon its members has aimed, albeit imperfectly, to transcend the boundaries of any particular cultural heritage. In science, inevitably, concepts of treatment, whether medical or psychiatric, must come to transcend local definitions. Concern with *social* as well as *biological* features of personal disturbances becomes a necessary part of modern psychiatry in a multiethnic world.

The Relationship of Cross-Cultural Psychology to Transcultural Psychiatry

Psychiatry is being influenced progressively by the social sciences that are involved in the study of social maladaptation, and thus it is increasingly concerned with the possibilities of amelioration through better forms of intervention in both the natural and social environment. Especially when viewed from a cross-cultural or "transcultural" perspective, the study of internal, intrapsychic maladjustment cannot artificially be kept separate from problems

34

of social maladaptation arising out of forms of social stress, from such social ills as maldistribution of economic resources or, as we shall touch on in some of the following chapters, from the psychological as well as social effects of discrimination directed toward particular groups. Several of the chapters in this volume deal with Native Americans, Algerian Arabs, and Japanese Americans, some of whose members have been influenced stressfully by their minority status.

Social psychiatry has been searching transculturally for universals in the specific forms of psychological as well as physiological disturbance (cf. various WHO reports; De Vos 1976, 1980). There can be some consensus now that there are universals that manifest themselves in mental disorder, whether they appear in Africa, Asia, Europe, or the Americas. We assume, given biological universals, that the psychiatric symptoms that appear in situations of stress are universal to human nature, due to structural variations in both physiology and in personality organization common to the human species. Psychological functioning is governed by a finite number of mental processes, known as coping mechanisms or defense mechanisms, which are involved in the development of affective and intellectual controls. Although influenced differentially by the practices of childhood socialization found in particular cultures, psychological functioning depends upon certain underlying physiological, hereditary structures common to all *Homo sapiens*. Universals, therefore, are to be found cross-culturally in forms of intrapsychic maladjustment that appear as behavioral maladaptations, however they are defined or understood in local contexts.

The lines of inquiry now taken in social psychiatry call upon more difficult, complementary forms of systematic exploration in collaboration with the other social sciences, especially anthropology. The stresses which affect adaptation in different groups vary greatly, since there are cultural differences in the types of situations that give rise to inner feelings of stress in the individual. Therefore transcultural psychiatry as a specialized discipline becomes involved, not only in seeking out universal patterns related to physiology, but also in systematic attempts to understand how particular patterns of adaptation are related to given forms of social stress.

Freud's early writings (1900, 1905) were among the first to direct psychiatric attention to causes of psychiatric breakdown found related to situations of social stress as well as directly attributable to difficulties in socialization. Subsequently, there has been an increasing awareness that psychological "dis-eases" or maladjustments frequently are heightened by social circumstances. Indeed, many psychiatrists are deeply aware of new types of stress that are not manifest in simple isolated communities, where people live throughout their lives in relatively unchanging conditions. It is this common condition of an internal sense of rapidly changing social life that is producing new challenges for ameliorative intervention, and for cross-cultural studies of normative as well as deviant psychological functioning.

This is not to gainsay that modern social conditions may alleviate some forms of difficulty inherent in living in tightly knit traditional communities. Alex Inkeles and David Smith (1976) have well demonstrated that modernization of itself is not detrimental to mental health. In testing levels of mental health in urban migrants in six different cultures, they found that the scores obtained favored those moving into the city over those remaining in the rural setting. In each case studied, however, those migrating were not moving into a minority role, as is true for those who become part of a racial minority as immigrants.

Some continuities in childhood socialization patterns are resistive to other forms of social change (Caudill 1976). These continuities may facilitate adaptation, as in the case of the modernizing Japanese in Japan and the United States, as I discuss in chapter 4. In the case of the Arabs and Apaches, as discussed in later chapters, social change may create new difficulties in adaptation.

In attempting psychological studies of either normative or deviant behavior cross-culturally, there are difficulties to overcome. In order to objectify transcultural studies, social scientists must be able to free themselves from ethnocentric and personal biases (Boyer 1964). Their very perceptions and concepts are all too often organized around the social realities and values of the cultures within which they were developed. Thus far, those cultures have been predominantly Western. Sometimes published studies reveal how the social scientist authors have failed to avoid clinical or disciplinary, even political, dogmatism in pursuing their empirical research from a Western perspective.

Prejudgments related to overriding personal as well as social values are always present to some degree. The very perceptions and concepts around which the still separate social sciences are organized tend to be heavily influenced by the ethnocentrically perceived social realities of the Western culture in which they were developed. In many instances social scientists discount the psychological determinants of history. They fail to observe how a positivistic reductionism causes them to pass over consideration of culturally influenced child-rearing patterns that influence intrapsychic development and consequent social behavior (De Vos, Marsella, and Hsu 1984: Introduction). The intrapsychic problems of humans are sometimes discounted as socially or historically irrelevant. Such social scientists explain psychological maladjustments solely on the basis of maladaptive processes arising in the larger structural patterns that organize society, and ignore the socializing effects of family continuity.

Conversely, there are the biological determinists, according to whom explanations for human behavior, both normal and pathological, can be reduced to the physiological or the sociobiological. Hereditary patterns are considered to govern social life even in complex modern societies.

Both the psychiatrists and the anthropologists of the nineteenth and much of the early twentieth century could not accept any evidence to contradict their view that all behavior was organically determined, whether the "organicity" was to be found in neurophysiology or social structure. Although Freud was one of the pioneers in demolishing the position taken by the organicist psychiatrists, the so-called neo-Freudian group of analysts, including, among others, Horney, Kardiner, Fromm, Sullivan, and Thompson, considered his libido theory unduly restrictive and organic.

A number of anthropologists in the United States rebelled against the racialistic conservatism of turn-of-the-century social and biological theory. Most influential in this movement was Franz Boas (Stocking 1982). Among his graduate students were some, such as Klineberg, Sapir, Benedict, and Mead, who became very influential in stressing the role of cultural influences on childhood socialization. There developed a great deal of mutual interaction between psychoanalysis and what became the field of culture and personality in anthropology (see Boyer 1982; Marcuse 1955, 1957).

In this volume we hold explicitly to a dualistic theoretical position which also acknowledges the irreducibility of human behavior influenced by consciousness (De Vos, Marsella, and Hsu 1984). Although all human behavior is influenced by *both* social and psychological structures, it cannot be totally understood in terms of either. Some form of explicit dualism in structural explanations is necessary to resolve some of the issues raised in behavioral or cognitive studies cross-culturally. As we have already indicated, this duality is especially necessary in developing any satisfactory symbolic analysis. Relevant to transcultural psychiatry is the question of how one can read expressive behavior that refers to social tensions as well as to personal malaise.

Ultimately, from the perspective of man's common heritage, one has to maintain a *nonrelativistic* assumption of common inherited potential which is normatively *not* realized in a different fashion in different cultures. That is, we can look at problems of psychophysiological maturation and development in terms of ever-present but potentially unnecessary forms of intrapsychic rigidity which interfere with the full potential realization of human cognitive or emotional growth. We have ideals of what human nature can become that seldom see full realization.

It is necessary, therefore, to reject, on the one hand, the quite prevalent relativistic anthropological position that qualifies *all* judgments about human behavior as value laden or culture bound. From a scientific standpoint, on the other hand, it is also necessary to reject as insufficient to full understanding of any behavior, sociological contentions that seek to ignore underlying common psychological functioning.

If we believe in a universal psychological potential, we cannot be relativistic when we observe certain rigidities that incapacitate members of certain cultures as they seek to adapt to a modern world and communicate adaptively within it. Some emotional and physical states of disorder or "emotional" problems cause human misery, regardless of the culture in which they occur. Therefore a transcultural ameliorative science of psychiatry is not only a possibility but a necessity, and it cannot simply give way to a total relativism that says that no judgments can be made about the possible inadequate mental functioning of people in other cultures.

Although we oppose such a total relativism, we do not deny that, given a supportive environment, an individual with a particular form of rigidity or a particular form of illogical thought processes can remain socially adaptive as long as he remains in his own protective cultural milieu. That is to say, there is some possible justification for a relativistic position if it is concerned *only* with the question of social adaptation. The degree to which certain relatively maladjustive personality systems are in harmony with the requirements of a given social milieu can differ widely. We shall illustrate this position later, especially when we attempt to analyze the records of Algerian Arabs in chapters 8 and 9.

Adaptation vs. Adjustment

A necessary distinction to be made in psychiatry as well as in the social sciences dealing with human behavior is the differentiation between social maladaptation on the one hand, and intrapsychic maladjustment on the other. The concepts of adaptation and adjustment as generally used are so blurred in most writings that the semantically poor communication that exists between the sociologically oriented social sciences and the more psychologically oriented disciplines causes difficulty in separating the levels of analysis and the salient determinants which refer to either social structure or to psychological structures.

For the most part in the literature of psychology as well as that of anthropology and sociology, concepts of "adjustment" and "adaptation" are loosely used in a roughly equivalent manner. They refer simultaneously both to the internal structures which are subsume under the concept of personality or, in many instances, to mutually adaptive processes of communication and interaction that can occur in social role relationships. More generally, these terms are used indiscriminately as concepts referring to human responses to the environment. The converse concepts, maladjustment and maladaptation, can refer to some deficiency or *structural* incapacity for response in an individual, or they can refer simply to some form of social role response that is inadequate for realizing the purposes of the individual. Hence there is a continuing confusion which calls for some explicit distinction.

We have consistently used the term "adjustment" in our work in this volume and in other contexts as a term referring to *psychological structure*, to suggest that human adjustment has to be seen in respect to some optimal potential within humanity generally. Adjustment as we use it here assumes an ideal progression of maturation that is potential in all human beings, the realization of which may be culturally fostered or deformed. Moreover, the realization of a fuller maturation may be considerably influenced by physiological factors.

"Adaptation" is a social term and is judged by social criteria considering the relative adequacy of behavioral interaction with others. It refers to behavior regardless of the underlying structure of personality.

It has been said, for example, that a "well-adjusted" person in a "bad environment" would be socially maladaptive. Social behavior is not simple to assess psychologically. Testing of the Nazi Eichmann was considered to have revealed a personality functioning within the normal range as judged from the adjustive mechanisms measured in psychological tests. This type of finding does not necessarily bring the validity of testing into question, but should make us cautious about any direct inferences between social behavior within a given set of social conditions, and personality structure. Too often, forms of socially pathological behavior are called forth as expedient—and hence "adaptive"—to socially pathological conditions. Such behavior reflects less about psychological structure and more about generally distorted social values. Reactions to conditions of social pathology without a loss of humanistic values derivative of "good" psychological adjustment can either facilitate one's survival or lead to death depending on particular exigencies or opportunities.

However, it should not be entirely surprising that an adequate psychological adjustment does not preclude a distorted set of social values that were learned throughout childhood and later reinforced in the context of given social conditions. Moral sensibility and psychological adjustment are *not* necessarily congruent, no matter how we would wish them to be. A "well-adjusted" individual may well adapt to a society that systematically dehumanizes a segment of its population. In situations of severe status discrimination against women, for example, one can find psychologically mature individuals of both sexes adapting without protest. Or, conversely, adjustively disturbed individuals can help lead a drive for social justice.

We are likely, therefore, to confuse adaptation and adjustment through our desire to inflexibly equate good psychological adjustment with good social adaptation. Indeed, alongside the "well-adjusted" Eichmanns were many who were so deformed maturationally that they could well adapt to the situations of human brutality that came to characterize Nazi Germany. One cannot presume one way or another ahead of time about the relationship of adaptation and adjustment in given individuals simply on the basis of their public behavior.

We do often assume, again from a value standpoint, that while it may be possible for an internally well-adjusted person to survive in a bad environment, such an individual will attempt to strive for ameliorative social change. Again, we may assume that a person who is maladjusted will not be well equipped to bring about a desired betterment of conditions. Unfortunately, however, adjustment must be defined in terms of maturational potential rather than in terms of moral imperatives to action. In sum, it is most helpful theoretically to maintain a clear distinction between an internal structuring of personality relating to the concept of "adjustment," and social behavioral responses which can be seen as adaptive or maladaptive for the individual in a particular social nexus.

Levels of Analysis

To complicate such a dualist-functional theory further, one must point out that a structural-functional analysis in anthropology or social psychiatry is incomplete when limited to but one level. What is involved in psychocultural research is a necessity to examine and explain human behavior on a series of interrelated levels. In the analysis of human behavior one must relate one level of social functioning to an understanding of social structure, and conversely on another level we must observe psychological functioning that is governed to some extent by an underlying psychological structure of a fairly fixed nature.

To illustrate, a sociologist or anthropologist can study a pattern of "possession" behavior as a function of social *structure*. But a psychological anthropologist or social psychiatrist is also concerned with how "possesson" behavior in given individuals is or is not related to adjustive personality patterns in those individuals (see also Crapanzano 1977). He or she must attempt to understand the complex interrelationships of social organization, possession behavior, *and* personality. In considering possession phenomena or other forms of curious social behavior, one must use a dual level of analysis with a structural-functional distinction in order to adjudge how salient the personality structure of an individual is in the performance of an expected social role. One must interrelate adjustment to psychological *structure* on the one hand, and adaptation to social functioning on the other. Each level of behavior has its "structural" referents, and these structures, be they of role patterns in a society *or* rigid limits within a given personality structure, influence behavioral functioning.

In understanding a possession state, the concept of psychological structure itself can be subdivided and examined on another level of analysis. There is a necessity to explore the relationship between adjustive psychological functioning using a possession state and the underlying psychological structuring. The possession state of a particular individual may result from a preponderance of psychogenic components or may be caused by organic features due to neurophysiological deficiencies resulting from constitutional defects. Organic features may also be due to trauma or to temporary drug toxicities.

Whatever contributes to given acts, the human psychic structure has a limited number of variables or problems that can cause malfunction. These processes can be conductive to malfunction through environmental stress without any great physiological deficit within the organism. Or malfunctioning can be due to particular lesions or physiological trauma or toxic effects on the body.

It has been a traditional problem in psychiatry to distinguish between structure and function in respect to organic problems versus adjustment problems. In transcultural psychiatry, however, a new dichotomy appears. A distinction must now be made as to whether or not relatively debilitating or painful adjustments or maladjustments can at the same time be socially adaptive or maladaptive within different cultural contexts.

Psychiatrists or psychologists, when viewing "mental health," are concerned specifically with psychological adjustive mechanisms with which they have become familiar in Western culture, and to this extent they tend to slip into ethnocentric value judgments which govern the diagnosis and treatment of what they perceive to be psychiatric illness. Anthropologists, in turn, are focused more on patterns of social adaptation, that is, whether the individual remains in, or how he or she was brought into or excluded from, social participation. Caudill (1959) has suggested that the comprehension of the working relationship between anthropology and psychology requires, for the psychiatrist as well as others, some understanding of culture as a key concept, just as it is necessary for anthropologists to understand personality structure or personality functioning as related to motivated human behavior. We must avoid tendencies to reductionism in either direction in studying the interrelationship of these systems.

For some psychiatrists, treating individuals outside Western culture, there is the somewhat disturbing consideration that in functional nonorganic disorders, knowledge of the cause of malfunctioning, by itself, may not help treatment. There needs to be, if therapy is administered through a system of verbal communication, a sharing of belief and symbol. Therapist and patient must share belief in the efficacy of the treatment experience. To this degree, psychotherapy is irreducibly symbolic communication.

What is already apparent to some psychiatrists in extending or reinterpreting the "cause" of mental illness is the necessity to clarify or differentiate between those concepts or definitions of behavior pervading a given culture and those concepts that are imposed externally upon the meaning of behavior from a Western psychiatric framework. If no attention is paid to indigenous perceptions of "mental illness" or to the meaning of its particular forms within a culture, there can be no therapeutic process. Western-trained psychologists or psychiatrists studying what are recognizably disturbed patients in radically different cultures tend to rely too heavily on their own background in their diagnoses, perhaps using traditional descriptive psychiatric or psychoanalytic formulations which, in a sense, alienate them from symbolic communication with members of the culture in which they are functioning (Prince 1964).

The anthropologist very often notes what might be considered clinically bizarre behavior, but he also notes how it is highly integrated and socially adaptive within its cultural setting. The Arab patterns we shall examine in chapters 8 and 9 are a case in point. Cultural usage or the cultural definitions given to the behavior seem to alter the "meaning" of the symptom for the individual so that he or she in fact remains socially integrated within the group. In our culture what we now define readily as "neuroticism" was in a previous age defined as sainthood or "scrupulosity" in adhering to religious directives.

Certain forms of internal maladjustment in other cultural contexts may be seen as requiring not treatment but a special vocation, such as that of the shaman. A deviant way of life may be proposed for the sufferer, who can thus employ a specialized, socially adaptive pattern that may relieve internal pressures resulting from the experience of inner stress. The Apache shaman considered in chapter 12 is one such instance; the particular symptoms of "illness" are channelized in such a manner that the behavior becomes more controllable, and hence, useful socially. The personality structure may not change, but a socially positive climate fosters adaptation rather than alienation. We have not as yet explored in any systematic way, for example, how some shamans learn to use "ecstasy" rather than remain passive subjects to seizures. When several shamans are studied, it becomes apparent that their personality patterns vary considerably. Often psychiatric symptoms are mimicked by others who "borrow" such symptoms as signs of possession for religious purposes.

The Distinction Between Culturally Normative Functioning and Clinical Symptoms

The relationship between adaptation and adjustment is, indeed, complex when we are trying to understand how the behavior of someone such as a shaman is a result of fulfilling a social role while also being driven by inner promptings. It is even more complex when we seek to examine the similar behavior of other individuals in other contexts. To help clarify this difficulty in the context of special religious behavior, Theodore Schwartz (1976) has introduced the innovative concept "pathomimetic behavior."

Pathomimetic behavior can appear as socially adaptive when, for purposes of strengthening a collective belief in possession by a deity, an individual mimics, unconsciously or consciously, forms of behavior which are usually indicative of internal maladjustment or organic pathology. A shaman may indicate that he is "possessed" by a deity by exhibiting "seizure" phenomena of a type observed to occur in epileptics. In native medicine, epileptic seizure, a frightening form of behavior to behold, is usually explained as the intrusion of an alien force, often a deity or demon, into the body. Therefore, any person who manifests a seizure is "possessed." In a true epileptic, the behavior is maladjustive in a structural sense. In the shaman, whatever his state of consciousness or self-hypnosis, seizure behavior becomes socially adaptive as a socially usable symbol of "possession," a special condition of communication with the supernatural. In pathomimetic phenomena, the possessed individual has somehow learned to manifest convulsions as a sign that a spirit has entered his body so that direct communication with the supernatural becomes possible.

Is there any way to make a scientifically objective judgment of adjustive behavior by ascertaining something about personality structure cross-culturally? We hold that there is, and psychological testing procedures can aid in this endeavor. Unfortunately, some previous attempts to delineate adjustment or maladjustment as distinct from adaptive behavior have not been free of ethnocentric judgments; but past failures in any field of scientific endeavor should not deter future efforts.

Some attempts at cross-cultural testing have been based on improper assumptions, and tests have been improperly used. Again these failures do not mean that better attempts should not be made. Despite criticism to the contrary, we hold that one can make some objective judgments of psychological structures comparatively, and that estimating the relative prevalence of any given psychological adjustment pattern in different populations is just as possible as the comparison of the incidence of physical difficulties. Both individual and group differences in adjustive functioning are obtainable cross-culturally.

We must concede, however, that generally speaking, adequate training in the use of testing procedures, not only in other countries but in the United States, which has been the center for most training in clinical psychology, has not been forthcoming to the degree necessary to provide more than sporadic examples of what might be accomplished if more money, effort, and talent were devoted to cross-cultural work in personality psychology.

In the course of our work in applying psychological tests such as the Rorschach and the Thematic Apperception Test (TAT) cross-culturally, it has become apparent that it is necessary to make some distinctions between the relative presence of psychiatrically recognizable states of social and personal maladjustment and the relative presence within any given culture of "coping" or "defense" mechanisms and patterns of cognitive functioning operative as aspects of personality. The problem is a very complex one. Here we can only attempt to briefly touch upon some of the main dimensions.

1. *There is a cross-culturally based universality in the appearance of organically based mental illness which is to be distinguished from functional disorders.* In every culture, therefore, physiologically based impairments of cognition or emotional expression must be distinguished from nonorganic "defenses" in personality patterns. Peculiarities in aberrant thought content, interesting as they may be, tell us little about the possible organic causes of psychiatric pathology.

2. *There are cultural differences in the universally recognizable capacities of human beings to go through a process of maturation.* All human beings have the potential to think rationally or "causally" in problem solving, but there are cultural differences in how such a potential maturation is facilitated or impeded. There are also differences in the areas of culture (technological, political, social) in the degree to which rational problem solving is permitted or emphasized.

3. *A propensity to "regress" to precausal cognitive patterns under emotional duress or stress is also a universal in human beings regardless of culture.* Given cultures differ in the degree of readiness with which their members will manifest regression of

this nature. Cultures also differ in the degree to which they "educate" their members toward rational causal thinking, or the degree to which they induce in many of their members severe traumatic experiences, which result in defensive personality rigidifications impeding both cognitive and emotional maturation. That is to say, in comparing cultures and assessing levels of maturation of members, one must distinguish between cultural limitations impeding growth and actual traumatic impairments which result in defensive and maladjustive ego maneuvers.

4. *A psychological universal in human beings is what might be broadly termed the capacity for altered states of consciousness which may or may not betoken the presence of psychopathology.* A distinction must be made between the capacity to utilize some form of dissociation (for example, a possession state or trance) and the uncontrolled appearance of a dissociated state as part of a hysterical neurosis of a temporary or chronic nature. For example, certain features of personality structure in Balinese individuals going into trance in religious drama as reported by Bateson and Mead (1942) may or may not resemble those of someone developing a "dual personality" in the United States at the turn of the twentieth century, or those in a more recent outbreak of hysterical possession phenomena in a girls' school in Malaysia (Tan 1972). Regardless, in each instance the mechanism of repression is brought into play; but the social and personal contexts are greatly different. In Bali the condition is induced within a religious ritual. In the United States the debility may be part of an individual neurosis, whereas in the last instance cited it is part of a collectively reinforced outbreak of hysterical acting out on the part of immature adolescent girls.

5. *So-called "magical thinking" is universal.* Malinowski (1948) cautioned us from falling into the error of Lévy-Bruhl (1926), who tended to dichotomize too absolutely between so-called rational man and so-called primitive man (see also Jacoby 1967). The biological and social factors that govern the development of maturational capacities regardless of culture are the same. As Malinowski pointed out, a Trobriand Islander learns to use "scientific" methods when they are culturally available, as in planting crops. But when rational problem-solving behavior is insufficient, one resorts in the Trobriands, or in the modern city,

to magical practices or religious supplication, especially when one is uncertain or anxious about the outcome of highly desired endeavors. A "modern" man or woman in a social, technological, or personal crisis may consult astrology or offer prayers to a personal god, who is anthropomorphically endowed with a sense of pity which may cause him to intervene, superseding the usual laws of nature on behalf of his supplicant. In modern settings, praying is usually not regarded as evidence of using primitive thought or being mentally ill. The people in a Texas town who call in Indian rainmakers to dance during a drought display the same level of helplessness and consequent anxiety with capricious nature as did the Indians who lived before them on the same land with the same problems.

Granted the universality of the human capacity to think illogically or "superstitiously" as well as logically or objectively, one can nevertheless find differences in cultures in the degree to which the individual is "educated" or socialized toward the use of objectivity and logic in solving problems and the degree to which he or she is discouraged from giving way to the press of emotionalized thought associations. One must distinguish, for example, between cultural explanations taken from a precausal view of nature or the world which result from a lack of available knowledge and such explanations resulting from a maladjustive or immature personality pattern with defensive needs (see Boyer 1983).

6. *Behavior is not personality.* One must also distinguish between a culturally permitted emotional display of temper in interpersonal crises related to relative status positions, and forms of structured incapacities that may indeed be fairly common to a culture due to its methods of socialization of emotional controls. In some situations display of affect is permitted in given status positions. Individuals with the same personality but located in lower-status positions (for example, in gender status situations) may be forced by severe sanctions to control displays of anger. Hence there are patterns in which controls are reinforced externally in some status situations, whereas they are permitted in others.

This fact of social life leads to considerable difficulty in making direct assumptions about the relationship of adjustive patterns to visible behavior. In the use of the Rorschach test in Japan there were almost no differences in structural aspects of personality to be noted between the men and women tested (Muramatsu et al. 1960). Yet Japanese men and women behave very differently from one another, and their conscious thought and social perceptions as measured on other instruments such as the Thematic Apperception Test may be quite different (De Vos 1973). Normatively, for most members of a population, behavior is actualized in accordance with self-consistent role expectations, and is not simply an expression of underlying personality propensities.

7. *Intellectual and emotional maturation are not congruent.* There are obvious difficulties in social or psychological theory related to a "conceptual" capacity to express adequately the complex and continuous interrelationships existing between structural intellectual maturation and the maturation of emotional components of the individual. Problems resulting from relative ego weakness cause difficulties in managing previously unresolved conflicts and influence strongly the course of maturation of intellectual processes in all stages of cognitive development. However, this interrelationship between the cognitive and emotional fields depends on differences in defensive structures. Individuals prone to obsessive-compulsive types of defenses encounter less interference with progression in the development of ideation or control of the outer world through the maturation of thought than do individuals using massive forms of repression usually found with hysterical types of personality. Different cognitive orientations are manifest normatively in members of Japanese society compared either with Algerian Arabs or with Native Americans, as is well demonstrated in this volume.

8. *Deviant beliefs common to individuals of a given culture are not necessarily signs of adjustive pathology.* Questions of "psychopathology," therefore, do not relate as much to the cultural content of beliefs as to the type of personality structure that is found in individuals sharing in given beliefs. This was patently illustrated among the Arabs of Algeria, where what might be considered paranoid patterns of ideation were widespread. One could not, therefore, presuppose that every individual sharing these beliefs socially was so doing on the basis of his personality characteristics. Some individuals sharing current beliefs may have more

mature personality characteristics than others regardless of the paucity of scientific knowledge available within that culture. While treating Apaches with psychoanalytic psychotherapy, Boyer once helped a man rid himself of culturally instituted fears of commonly accepted bogies. Once free of them, he was a cultural deviant. He laughingly said he had to pretend to continue to be afraid of canines, ghosts, and owls to be "normal."

9. *By and large, better adjusted individuals will be more capable of flexibility in the face of new experiences and capable of responding adaptively with problem-solving behavior when confronted with new instrumental needs.* Conversely, an individual with some form of rigidification in personality is less capable of adapting in situations of change.

As we shall illustrate in this volume, Miner not only obtained samples from various informants in Algeria but also carefully noted to what degree certain beliefs in widespread magical practices, or attitudes about the chaperonage of women, were found in specific individuals. Inflexibility or intensity of belief could be matched with the Rorschach protocols of a number of individuals. In our work together, we were able to find that there was indeed systematic correspondence between personality rigidity and the strength of particular magical beliefs and projective attitudes on the part of given individuals (see chap. 8).

In another cultural context, Japan, where we made a within-group comparison of delinquent and nondelinquent Japanese, we were able to establish systematic differences between experimental and control groups (see chap. 6). However, we have also cautioned that one cannot take the statistical differences so established and use them to make an individual diagnosis of proneness to delinquency. One must distinguish between establishing significant differences in group norms and judging any individual record by itself as sufficiently indicative to permit a clinical diagnosis. Fathers of delinquents have a mean high score for rigidity, but a high score in an individual record does not therefore place that record in the category of delinquent fathers.

10. *Variability is considerable in all contemporary cultural environmentals, but regularities occur which distinguish groups from one another.* To make scientific progress in culture and personality research, one cannot simply try to formulate the personality

system common to a given group. Especially in times of change, one must go further and attempt to demonstrate how given members of the group do not equally share in either common beliefs or common modalities of thought. Nor do all members of any groups share completely or even partially in the psychological or structural characteristics of personality that may be normative or common for the group. For example, we found that paranoid thinking was common for a number of individuals in Miner's samples of Algerians, to a degree that group norms could readily distinguish these individuals from samples of American Indians or Japanese. There was at the same time considerable variation among those included in the sample. However, as we shall demonstrate, in the case of the Algerian Arabs one was able to identify most records as characteristically "Algerian." There was sufficient propensity in these records to employ arbitrary forms of thought, putting together percepts that had no logical juxtaposition. There were in a number of these records types of suspiciousness and defensiveness expressed in symbolic content which gave ample evidence of the use of projection as a prominent mechanism of defense.

The Feasibility and Validity of Testing Cross-Culturally

In considering material examined cross-culturally, the first question asked is whether or not the material obtained is valid. Can we, indeed, give the Rorschach test to people of another culture and obtain material from which to make valid comparative inferences about thought processes? One can readily find in a number of critiques of psychological anthropology, opinions that such comparative work is impossible. However, one must also look for the actual experience of those who make such judgments. In most instances they are individuals who themselves have had no familiarity with projective tests or any actual testing experience in any setting within or outside of their own culture. Their judgments are on a completely presumptive basis.

As this book attests, we have found test materials from several different cultural settings to be useful in understanding the individuals tested. Individuals within groups can be well differentiated from one another. However, we have used considerable caution before making diagnostic, clinical interpretations of features found normative for a group. There is a difference between psychological propensities and the appearance of what becomes clinically evident as psychopathology.

I must note that I do not believe in a type of analysis that depends simply on a quantitative analysis of percentages followed by a reified, mechanical interpretation of equations which implies perforce a particular personality pattern. One must maintain a configurational approach and a flexibility in understanding the very great perceptual differences of members of different cultures. The danger to validity in using the Rorschach test cross-culturally is not that, once sufficient rapport with subjects is established, one obtains invalid material, but that individuals trained only in clinical practice may make overly rigid interpretations. Anthropologists, on the other hand, without some test experience have no qualifications for making flexible interpretations of data. They are often limited to a mechanical, textbook application of what they find in clinical volumes.

In the particular case of the Algerian material, I have concluded that there is evidence suggesting maladjustment in a percentage of the population which exceeds that found in other cultures tested. These tendencies, for example, are notably lacking in Native Americans by and large, although in the case of the shaman in chapter 12, we also found in a particular record some suggestions of paranoid ideation at work. The Apache shaman record is *not* characteristic of the group, whereas, relatively speaking, such material is found to be more prevalent in Algerian protocols. It must be noted that in my work I have generally been cautious about assessments of comparative overall social adaptation of the cultural groups concerned. Such assessments involve value judgments to some degree.

Nevertheless, it is possible to make some judgment of relative intragroup and intergroup adaptations. One cannot argue against the fact that the Japanese by most criteria would be seen as more adaptive economically in modern society than either the Algerian Arabs or the Native American groups considered. There are historical, economic, and other social determinants of this adaptation, but I would nevertheless argue that the Japanese overall, in normative personality variables, have the type of cognitive development and capacity for emotional control that gives them advantage in social situations of change. Many Native Americans and Arabs manifest forms of rigidification that make for difficulties in adapting to new situations, if not in maintaining themselves within their traditional cultural patternings.

In each group examined there are within-group individual differences in adaptation as shown in test results. We examined three Apache brothers (chapter 11), who were tested three times over a period of twenty years. The brother who became an artist certainly has maintained himself better than his two sibs. In chapter 9 we illustrate a number of different adaptations noted by Miner among the Arabs of his sample. We found no simple direct correspondence between the Rorschach results and general social adaptability, but there was indeed notable correspondence between beliefs and Rorschach scores in a number of the cases. In Canadian Athabascan records completed with June Helm, but not discussed in this volume (Helm, De Vos, and Carterette 1960), we found considerable differences between Athabascan records obtained from two villages. From a Slavey group we gained an overall impression of a capacity for normal adaptation. However, a number of members of a Dogrib community manifested in their Rorschach responses more severe forms of psychological constriction and debilitation. The Athabascan Apache records we report on in chapter 10 also manifested progressive constriction, but the Dogrib material was far in excess of that obtained from the Apache or from other Native American samples we have seen. The Native American records I have examined are quite generally characterized most by simple intellectual constriction without pathological ideation. These records generally are somewhat different from the type of rigidification found in some Japanese with their strong intellectual striving, or the type of defensive rigidification with forced logic which is more generally true for Algerian Arabs.

In general, then, I would consider it possible, given a sufficiently large number of records and observational data from a group, to judge within-group differences in social adaptation in societies other than our own. The Rorschach test may have only very limited capacity to predict adaptive breakdown or social incapacitation. First, working blindly on the Algerian Arab data without access to behavioral content, as we did at first at the University of Michigan, I found it easier to predict protocols that I judged to be superior to the group norms than to differentiate relative social incapacity among those with more disturbed records. In other words, an above-the-norm Rorschach is more readily predictive of relatively good social adaptation than a relatively poor Rorschach is predictive of manifestly poor adaptation.

Using ordinary clinical criteria in working with Japanese protocols, I found it not too difficult to make assessments of the different types of neurotic behavior to be expected of given individuals who came to the attention of psychiatrists at Nagoya National University, where I worked in the university's psychiatric clinic for two years. In general, among the normative population in Japan, we found relatively few signs of severe paranoid symptomatology in the 724 records obtained in the two cities and the three villages studied. In this normative population we found only one record of obsessive sexual content. One can see that in such a social context, any appearance of florid sexual content would mark the respondent as highly deviant from the group. Therefore, when sexual responses appear, they are quickly marked with peculiar significance in the context of a Japanese Rorschach. The absence of sexual responses in the Japanese records was indicative of the general type of control over symbolic expression that is characteristically Japanese in the test situation.

Several years back while working in Paris as a consultant with an Israeli psychologist, Margalit Cohen, who was conducting her doctoral research on the acculturation of Moroccan Jews to Paris, I noted in her protocols the appearance of several records with rich obsessional sexual material, of such proportion that the individuals were not able to respond adequately with other associations. Such protocols were found particularly among individuals she knew to be not acculturating well to social life in Paris, but who had been living there for some years in an encapsulated situation. Obviously, by maintaining themselves in isolation, these individuals could handle their internal difficulties in such a way as to avoid direct contact with professionals in the psychiatric community.

To summarize, in my experiences of within-group comparisons

of social adaptation, I have found that the Rorschach results can differentiate among individuals in normative populations taken from a number of cultures. However, the norms from which one works are different, depending upon a culture's normative percepts and patternings. There is a tendency, whatever the normative patterning, for some responses to be common in one group but aberrant in another setting. This normative patterning suggests some form of acceptable social adaptation in a given group. There can, therefore, be no direct correspondence between internal adjustments of specific groups and the American standards for psychopathology suggestive of observable clinical breakdown.

Mental Mechanisms Cross-Culturally

It has become my conviction that a normative population of any culture can be approached with testing procedures allowing for some forms of personality assessment. One aim of such procedures would be to determine the relative utilization of universally present coping mechanisms related to progressive maturational levels. The relative use of defensive coping mechanisms, as in repression or projection, in members of a given culture group can be elicited if the tester uses some already existing tests such as the Rorschach and adapts them to the special problems of gaining rapport and improving communication.

What, then, is the relationship between evidence of the ready use of projection/repression and psychopathology in the predictive sense? It stands to reason that tests cannot be rigidly applied by seeking quantitative results predicting psychopathology directly in cross-cultural work. Certain test results obtained from individuals who manifest disturbed behavior in an American or European psychiatric setting may be indicative of social malfunctioning. However, similar protocols in many individuals in other cultural settings may not be accompanied by any manifest maladaptation. The question again arises whether such test results are valid only when measured against manifest breakdown, or whether they remain suitable for general personality assessment without focus on psychopathology. I would hold that the tests are in one way or another universals of *maturation* in psychological (not biological) functioning. Manifest immaturities in thought

processes or primitiveness in emotional control, however, do not
bear a one-to-one relationship to either socially or psychiatrically
recognizable symptoms.

I have witnessed results obtained with the Rorschach on Americans outside psychiatric clinics which indicate the wider presence
in the American normative population of some very primitive
modalities of thought. For example, the presence of "prelogical,
magical" thinking, emotional rigidifications, and the like are
found in a large number of individuals who have never manifested obvious psychiatric symptomatology. Test signs indicating
a propensity to use immature coping mechanisms are not limited
to individuals whose obvious disturbances have brought them to
the attention of a psychiatric or psychological facility in the
United States. The tests do indicate, in clinically obvious cases
at least, that signs of primitive emotional functioning, or primary-
process thinking, will be significantly overrepresented in a psychiatric population. These tests work especially well to distinguish between the various psychotic structural problems in the
personality organization of individuals whose disturbed behavior
has caused them to refer themselves or be referred by others to a
psychiatric facility. The point is, however, that tests of personality do not usually control or measure the stresses of the social
environment that partially determine whether or not certain personality rigidifications or immaturities will result in the acute or
chronic appearance of an obvious symptom in the usual psychiatric sense. Notice that in defense of my scoring system in the following chapters, I have emphasized the use of positive percepts as
differentiators. It is curious to note that I have found no other
scoring system which suggests "positive" symbolism as diagnostic
in the Rorschach. There tends to be a "clinical" bias among those
using the test diagnostically. Testers tend to look for pathology,
especially in symbolic content. They may overlook the possibility
that integrative features can also be quantified and hence help
to differentiate systematically. I have made such distinctions in
analyzing Japanese protocols (see chap. 4).

One can conclude as a result of psychological assessment of a
nonclinical group that a particular individual may be what is
termed a "schizoid" personality. Such a judgment may be based
on test results indicating that the individual may cope by with-

drawing from social communication, coupled with evidence of some form or other of primary-processes thinking. Whether or not the particular individual will at some time become manifestly psychotic and be diagnosed psychiatrically as a schizophrenic is not within the power of the testing procedure to determine, since the important environmental factors involved may not be readily available to the tester. Such an individual may continue to function tolerably well in simple, undemanding social situations which do not require the use of complex reasoning processes that are relatively free of emotional interference or incapacitating preoccupations.

On tests individuals may reveal a proneness to employ an arbitrary type of thinking termed "paranoid," as did some of the Algerian Arabs (see chaps. 8 and 9). The degree to which such propensities become manifest or recognizable would depend on the sensitivity of the individuals' social group, as well as the necessity of the individual concerned to make reasoned decisions under stress. What Miner and I concluded, in the case of the Algerians in our sample, was that a propensity for paranoid like thought processes was indeed present in some persons. Such thinking was not too easily recognizable as socially disruptive. What would be taken in Europe or the United States as a sign of psychosis, such as sitting mute or unwashed in the street for several days, in Algeria would be more likely to result in the individual's being classified as a "holy man." Should a man immodestly remove his clothes, however, he would be immediately recognized as "crazy." Algerians who shared in socially current beliefs about the conspiracies and plots of Jews and French to undermine their health and potency would not be considered "queer" by fellow Algerians. For thinking to be recognized as "queer" it must go beyond that allowable by the society. Paranoid Americans who join a special Christian religious group or the John Birch Society to protect their nation against a "Communist conspiracy" are usually not judged to be "paranoid" with the same rapidity as those citizens whose delusional thinking leads them to believe they are famous persons or that they are being persecuted by radio waves from Mars.

There are in all cultures some crisis situations in which collective behavior calls into existence more primitive levels of ego functioning. Not every Algerian who shared the beliefs about a Jewish-French conspiracy and later took up arms against French colonialism was paranoid. Not every American who approved of the relocation of Japanese Americans during World War II because they were dangerous was paranoid, nor was every Japanese who participated in the postearthquake mass hysteria in 1923, in which over 6,000 Koreans were killed in the Tokyo area (Lee and De Vos 1981).

Psychological tests such as the Rorschach are confined to suggesting the relative proneness to regression in given individuals. Individuals can be in a state of remission until meeting a situation with which they cannot cope. I have already cited the study by Samuel J. Beck at Michael Reese Hospital in Chicago in the early 1950s when individuals were tested during their manifest schizophrenic episodes. Five years later, when retested, many of these individuals had made more or less satisfactory social adaptations. In one instance, for example, the individual confided to me that he had learned not to reveal his hallucinatory experiences to others because such revelations "disturbed" people. Overall, the Rorschach retest results were noticeably stable, showing little change in personality patterning despite the fact that most of the respondents had made at least marginal social adaptations. In the judgment of its users at Michael Reese, the Rorschach test was valid in revealing persistent schizophrenic personality structures in the sample of subjects. It was incapable, however, of commenting on whether or not the social environment would be supportive enough to allow for some level of social adaptation by the former patients, given the limitations of schizophrenic weakness in the ego.

Potential maladjustment due to personality immaturity becomes evident when the individual reveals that he or she is incapable of some forms of coping. The potentially maladjusted individuals become rigidified in such a way that they cannot alter their behavior to adapt to reality stresses. They have not matured to the point of being able to exercise alternative capacities except under optimal conditions. Under stress they resort to less adequate, more primitive psychological levels of functioning. It is more taxing, and hence very costly in mental and emotional energy, to maintain functioning at a higher level; they are less "structured" to do so. Tney more readily "regress" under duress to the use of less adequate and more primitive levels of coping. It is this tendency to regress to earlier forms of maturational capacity that characterizes maladjusted individuals. On a social level, one must also look at what is socially available as patterns of either knowledge or behavior to aid the individual in coping with particular situations. Given their social roles, expectations can support or impede. Social role expectations may pull the individual toward one form or another of behavior acceptable or unacceptable. If, for example, a woman in a given society is forbidden direct expression of overt aggressive behavior, she may feel constrained and may therefore adopt some masochistic forms of behavior to handle the affect engendered by highly emotional situations. Masochism can therefore become a socially reinforced behavior in certain social circumstances. On a personality level the individual may be capable of alternative forms of action, but because of strict social definitions of self, she is incapable of exercising potentials beyond those allowable socially.

Reluctance in the Use of the Concept "Psychopathology"

While I am firmly of the opinion that cross-cultural evaluations can be made in terms of maturation, I agree to some extent with the point made by some of the cultural relativists who criticize the too-ready use of the concept of psychopathology to label various forms of incomplete maturation which appear in every culture. Optimal maturation is relatively rare; it is an ideal state seldom realized in any society. It is not the scientific task of comparative psychological anthropology to judge "pathology" per se or to suggest that if one finds witchcraft, for example, in a particular society this group should be compelled to initiate some kind of social amelioration program of personal therapy. The task, rather, is to objectively describe personality functioning as well as possible and to recognize how social adaptation occurs. In most instances what one perceives in comparing patterns operative in one society with those in another are alternative forms of less than optimal realizations of social harmony or development of personal capacity. Value judgments come in readily when one attempts to assess the relative virtue of one imperfect pattern compared with another. It is indeed difficult to judge what is relatively satisfying or unsatisfying as a mode of life in another society.

Social Adaptation and Social Stress

When we compare the American normative material with the Japanese, some questions arise with regard to the type of neurotic rigidification which may be adaptive or nonadaptive in the two instances. In the United States individuals tend to be socialized toward the greatest possible development of "individualistic" life patterns, stressing hard work and long-range goals leading to success. American culture demands much of its members in the way of competition, at least in its middle-class segment. They are subject to a great deal of tension and strain as a result. In such a culture, there is some social advantage for workers in many occupations to have some obsessive-compulsive personality propensities. An individual with such propensities may be able to function quite successfully in a number of occupational roles where obsessive-compulsive traits are socially adaptive. The strains an individual feels may come out more in the incapacity to relate closely to others and may cause feelings of painful isolation. In the Japanese culture similar goals of hard work, striving, and covert competition are stressed but the value of family and social harmony is generally more important than social independence and individualism. Japanese society also produces its share of individuals who may be considered obsessive-compulsive from a psychiatric standpoint and also produces individuals who feel a great deal of stress over social demands. Work in a psychiatric clinic in Japan revealed to me the presence of individuals with the same structural personality problems as would appear in an American clinic, and in some instances, the person might chance seeking resolution through psychotherapy. It should be noted that in some instances the psychotherapy that "works" is the therapy that is comprehended by the clients (Reynolds 1980; Ticho 1971). In Japanese Morita therapy the therapeutic encounter conduces the individual to conform to his society rather than helping him with an individualistic resolution, such as allowing him to leave his present work or family. The individual in Japan is very often, through either formal or informal counseling, helped to subdue idiosyncratic propensities and feelings. The opposite is true in the United States.

Methodological Approaches to Use of the Rorschach Cross-Culturally

We have selected the various chapters of this volume to illustrate a number of methodological approaches and a number of problems. All the following chapters illustrate problems of social adaptation. However, in each instance there is no direct, simple relationship between the Rorschach findings and adaptation. Nevertheless, the Rorschach can help *ex post facto* to explain some forms of behavior and show the pattern taken by individuals in adapting to their social environment.

Two of these chapters are quite directly clinical, asking direct questions of the relationship of the Rorschach symbolism to psychopathology. In chapter 3, we compare the affective symbolism of normal, neurotic, and schizophrenic Americans as a base for comparing two generations of Japanese Americans in chapter 4. In chapter 7, we illustrate from Japan two types of psychodiagnostic conditions that can be inferred from particular test results. Chapters 5 and 6 relate to comparisons of delinquents and nondelinquents in respect to content symbolism. They demonstrate systematic differences between Japanese delinquent and nondelinquent groups in the handling of Rorschach cards.

Chapter 10 reports longitudinal research among Apache and demonstrates how the Rorschach can be useful in understanding nonlearning; this material is highly suggestive of the maladaptation of adjustive patterns in respect to formal learning in the schools. Chapter 11 is a more qualitative assessment of three brothers from this longitudinal study, showing how the Rorschach reflects a different occupational career in one brother compared with his less adaptive sibs. Chapter 12 is a detailed study over a two-year period of a woman who became a shaman.

The methods of approach differ in each of the chapters. Some of them are basically quantitative in approach, while some are qualitative. We have tried to supply overall quantifications for the various categories and subcategories of content symbolism (see chap. 3). Patterns of constriction related to excessive use of *neutral* content are found in chapter 5, in which Japanese delinquents are seen as more guarded and constricted than normals in their expression of symbolic material, and in chapter 10, in which Apache youth are seen as increasingly constricted as they move into adulthood.

The statistically different use of *positive* symbolism is depicted in the comparison of Japanese Americans and in American clinical samples in chapter 3. The relatively good adaption of individuals with positive symbolism is delineated in the case of individual Arabs in chapter 9, and in the comparison of the three Apache brothers in chapter 11.

Discussion of both the clincial and normative meaning of *dependency* symbolism is found in chapter 6, contrasting delinquents and nondelinquents and their families in Japan; and in chapter 7 we find an unusual appearance of dependency symbolism in a record considered clinically, taken from a Japanese village headman with an ulcer. The significance appearance of *body preoccupation* and sadomasochistic material is recorded quantitatively in chapter 9 in reporting on acculturated Arabs and Japanese Americans. The significance of particular types of *hostile* symbolism is found both quantitatively and qualitatively in the Arab records of chapters 8 and 9.

What is offered in these various chapters are a number of alternative methods of approaching Rorschach symbolism cross culturally with specific problems in mind. Too often attempts are made to use a Rorschach comparative study in too diffuse and global a fashion. More is to be gained by using the Rorschach or other projective techniques to examine specific problems in which symbolic analysis or personality structure plays a particular part in a given cultural or social context. We found the test useful clinically in analyses of thought processes and in helping us understand very different forms of cognitive response to social situations as well as the modulation of affectivity in different cultural contexts. If more individuals were to use the tests along with other forms of systematic tests or interviews, we could examine more realistically the effects of differential socialization cross-culturally. It is our common heritage to mature in sequences of development. It is our common destiny to face vicissitudes in childhood and adulthood that make us all fall short in one or another way of our actual full potential in our specific lives as humans.

References

Bateson, Gregory, and Margaret Mead
  1942   *Balinese Character: A Photographic Analysis.* New York: New York Academy of Sciences.
Boyer, L. Bryce
  1964   Psychoanalytic Insights in Working with Ethnic Minorities. *Social Casework* 45:519–526.
  1982   Historical Development of Psychoanalytic Psychotherapy of the Schizophrenic: The Followers of Freud. L. Bryce Boyer and Peter L. Giovacchini, eds. *Psychoanalytic Treatment of Schizophrenic, Borderline, and Characterological Disorders*, pp. 111–117. 2d edition, revised and enlarged. New York: Aronson.
  1983   Approaching Cross-Cultural Psychotherapy. *Journal of Psychoanalytic Anthropology* 6:237–245.
Caudill, William
  1959   The Relationship of Anthropology to Psychiatry in the Study of Culture and Personality. *Japanese Journal of Psychoanalysis* 6:468–482.
  1976   Social Change and Cultural Continuity in Modern Japan. George A. De Vos, ed. *Responses to Change: Society, Culture, and Personality*, pp. 18–44. New York: D. Van Nostrand.
Crapanzano, Vincent
  1977   Introduction. Vincent Crapanzano and Vivian Garrison, eds. *Studies in Spirit Possession*, pp. 1–40. New York: John Wiley.
De Vos, George A., ed.
  1973   *Socialization for Achievement: Essays on the Cultural Psychology of the Japanese.* Berkeley, Los Angeles, London: University of California Press.
  1976   The Interrelationship of Social and Psychological Structures in Transcultural Psychiatry. William P. Lebra, ed. *Culture-Bound Syndromes, Ethnopsychiatry, and Alternate Therapies*, pp. 278–298. Honolulu: University of Hawaii Press.
  1980   Book review of "Schizophrenia: An International Follow-up Study." *Social Science and Medicine*: 50:262–263.

De Vos, George A., A. Marsella, and F. Hsu
  1984   Approaches to the Self from a Psychocultural Perspective: Introduction. George A. De Vos, A. Marsella, and F. Hsu, eds. *Culture and Self*, pp. 1–55. London: Metheun.
Freud, Sigmund
  1900   *The Interpretation of Dreams*. Standard edition, 1953, Vols. 4 and 5. London: Hogarth Press.
  1905   *Three Essays on the Theory of Sexuality*. Standard edition, 1953, 7:123–245. London: Hogarth Press.
Helm, June, George A. De Vos, and Teresa Carterette
  1960   Variations in Personality and Ego Identification Within a Slave Indian Kin-Community. National Museum of Canada Bulletin 190, *Contributions to Anthropology*, Part 2.
Inkeles, Alex, and David Smith
  1976   Personal Adjustment and Modernization. George A. De Vos, ed. *Responses to Change: Society, Culture, and Personality*, pp. 214–233. New York: D. Van Nostrand.
Jacoby, Jacob
  1967   The Construct of Abnormality: Some Cross-Cultural Considerations. *Journal of Experimental Research in Personality* 2:1–15.
Lee, Changsoo, and George A. De Vos
  1981   *Koreans in Japan: Ethnic Conflict and Accommodation*. Berkeley, Los Angeles, London: University of California Press.
Lévy-Bruhl, Lucien
  1926   *How Natives Think*. London: Allen and Unwin.
Malinowski, Bronislaw
  1948   *Magic, Science, and Religion*. Glencoe, Ill.: Free Press.
Marcuse, Herbert
  1955   *Eros and Civilization: A Philosophical Inquiry into Freud*. Boston: Beacon Press.
  1957   Kritik des Neo-Freudianischen Revisionismus. *Psyche* (Heidelberg) 11:801–820.
Muramatsu, T., ed.
  1960   *Nipponjin—Bunka to Pāsonaritī no Jisshō-Teki Kenkyū* (The Japanese: An Empirical Study in Culture and Personality). Tokyo: Reimei Shobo.
Prince, Raymond
  1964   Indigenous Yoruba Psychiatry. Ari Kiev, ed. *Magic, Faith, and Healing*, pp. 84–120. New York: Free Press.
Reynolds, David
  1980   *The Quiet Therapies*. Honolulu: University of Hawaii Press.

Schwartz, Theodore
  1976   The Cargo Cult: A Melanesian Type Response to Change. George A. De Vos, ed. *Responses to Change: Society, Culture, and Personality*, pp. 157–206. New York: D. Van Nostrand.
Stocking, George
  1982   *Race, Culture, and Evolution: Essays in the History of Anthropology*. Chicago: University of Chicago Press.
Tan, Eng-Seong
  1972   Prospects of Psychiatric Research in a Multiracial Developing Community—West Malaysia. William Lebra, ed. *Transcultural Research in Mental Health*, pp. 262–280. Honolulu: University Press of Hawaii.
Ticho, Gertrude R.
  1971   Cultural Aspects of Transference and Counter-Transference. *Bulletin of the Menninger Foundation* 35:313–334.

Chapter Three

Quantitative Analysis of Rorschach Symbolism

George A. De Vos

Symbolic Analysis Using the Rorschach in Cross-Cultural Research

It is curious that one of the least exploited aspects of the Rorschach test is its potential value for standard analysis of the content of responses as related to affective symbolism in various cultures.[1] This neglect is basically a reflection of the relative lack of systematic attention to content found generally in Rorschach work.[2]

There are a number of reasons for this lack of quantification in the area of content analysis. First and foremost is that Herman Rorschach himself (1921) set the direction of interest in the use of his test toward understanding the *structure* of personality and its relation to perception. In establishing the validity of his test he was concerned most with the relatively inflexible modes of perception found in characteristic personality traits, especially those signifying pathological aberrations. He devoted most of his attention, therefore, to establishing norms with respect to the *formal* nature of the blots, i.e., use of form, color, shading, and other determinants of the "structure" of a response, specifically the modes of perception that were selective as to location, size, and complexity of the responses given. The *symbolic* stimulus value of the unstructured blots received no systematic attention by those adopting and adapting Rorschach's method of scoring, although interpretations of the content have become an essential part of individual clinical analysis.

This lack of quantification of content in terms of its affective or symbolic referents has created a serious problem for those attempting to use the test with varying cultural groups. Sometimes the most meaningful differences are found in the use of affect-laden content rather than in the formal determinants traditionally scored.

The Importance of Context in Quantification and Interpretation

Roy Schafer (1954) recognized that the *content* of Rorschach responses as traditionally scored is static and categorical rather than dynamic; that is, the quantitative scoring of animals, art, anatomy, and so on is formal and not related by inference to any psychological process. What is necessary is to consider some "thematic" categories in organizing and scoring the content.

In reflecting human thought processes, Rorschach responses are on a continuum from autistic perceptions to those more governed by outer reality. Being psychoanalytically oriented, Schafer was more concerned with relating the thematic psychodynamic value of content analysis to other test material than with quantifying the relative number of responses within given categories. He himself did not have in mind, however, how to set up a system of quantification of the thematic data as a means of comparing groups. While Schafer (pp. 131 ff.) listed a number of oral, anal, and dependent themes, he argued well against the objection that a thematic approach to content analysis necessarily ascribes invariant meaning to specific images (p. 124). He took into account possible different interpretations of similar responses related to differences in age, sex, cultural background, and pathological syndromes.

He illustrated that the "ovaries" seen by a twenty-year-old woman have different implications than those seen by a fifty-year-old. What may imply concern with female reproduction differs with age. One must be concerned with responses that suggest a denial of hostility or, on a deeper level, are counterphobic. Schafer also considered that responses differ in thematic implications in given social settings, for example, between rural and urban individuals. One has to examine the cultural context. Permissiveness to see given content differs within given social groups. Particular responses of an "oral" nature embedded in one record may have different implications than those found in another record.

None of these cautionary considerations, however, obviates the capacity to score the responses in different categories or subcategories. A secondary interpretation of the use of content categories can be made depending on cultural differences. I would agree with Schafer that any thematic analysis of imagery need not and should not assume invariant meanings except on a general level of interpretation. The scoring system I have developed attempts to score on this general level rather than accounting for the nuances that may be attributed to specific subcategories in cultural settings. Therefore, while agreeing with Schafer's caution that any one-to-one correlation between the interpretation of given responses without attention to context should be avoided, I would argue that this consideration of context does not mean that we must neglect quantification, any more than the scoring of a "W," or holistic response to the entire blot area, should be neglected, because the use of given whole responses can have different implications in different records.

Responses by themselves are seldom diagnostic, but must be seen in the context of the total response protocol of given individuals. Schafer (p. 130) illustrated that oral aggressive imagery may be conspicuously present in records of alcoholics, depressives, and schizophrenics, and may even be present in records of certain well-functioning normals. What is important for us, however, is our understanding of the orally aggressive implications of a given response in a given complex personality, rather than our seeking to make a direct clinical inference to a diagnostic category from single responses.

The Quantification of Affective Inferences

It was immediately apparent to me in working with Japanese materials that the symbolic material of the Rorschach protocols would be significantly compelling in considering cultural differences between Japanese and Americans. The symbolic content was as pertinent to the understanding of personality variables as was the material traditionally quantified in clinical work. How could I compare differences?

In order to overcome this problem in my initial comparative research with Japanese-Americans (De Vos 1954, 1955), I developed a systematic, quantifiable notational system which permited a statistically reliable scoring of each Rorschach response for its "affective inference" in addition to the customary scoring then in use (De Vos 1952). As delineated in Appendix A, I devised overall indices of responses connoting hostility, anxiety, body preoccupation, dependency, and positive content, as well as content seemingly neutral in affective tone. Each of these indices was comprised of specific scorable subcategories. Since the initial publication, as a result of use by others as well as myself (Singer n.d.; Speisman and Singer 1961; Streitfeld 1954; Thaler et al. 1957; Weiner et al. 1957; Wynne and Singer 1966), I have been assisted by others in revising my manual describing the subcategories, and further refining the criteria used for scoring (see appendix A). The system as outlined has been developed to aid in the quantification of the Rorschach for research purposes, as well as to provide a teaching guide for use in clinical Rorschach work.

This system of scoring the underlying affective symbolism is organized around three major affective categories common to most understandings of the emotions, namely *positive* valences toward objects; *hostile*, destructive, or antagonistic feelings; and dread, fear, or *anxiety* of a diffused or focused nature.

Additionally for separate consideration I have brought together as one category various expressions of helplessness and *dependent* need, subservience to authority, and symbols of security. The responses in this category reflect "object cathexis" or attachment in which dependency is salient, in contrast to those under the *positive* category, in which pleasure is uppermost. Approximately half the responses of many records are best considered a reaction to the form of the blots themselves rather than a direct reflection of inner states. Here the content is banal and basically *neutral* in tone. Some additional responses, not easily categorizable, I have relegated to a special *miscellaneous* category.

The system herein outlined proposes a supplementary way of

scoring all responses on the Rorschach for their affective connotations just as they are generally scored for location, form, and other determinants, and specific content. All responses given in the free association to the blots are examined for their affective tone and their symbolic representation of underlying feelings. Just as is true for determining location, form, and so on, the affective connotation of responses can be made more precise by judicious, nonsuggestive questions during the inquiry period. Even though direct explanatory evidence of affective tone is lacking in the records of more laconic individuals, certain responses, highly suggestive of underlying affective pressure, can be scored according to established psychoanalytic interpretations of the meaning of given symbolism.

None of the inferences from a response can be considered final, given the human capacity for psychological complexity; hence interpretation has to be flexibly related to the particular individual record and the particular social and cultural context in which the response is given. The scoring criteria are hypotheses that must be continually reexamined in context. Nevertheless, as the following chapters testify, I have found the scoring system to offer cross-cultural evidence of the validity of assuming associative universals to be at work in thought and affect.

In working with other Rorschach specialists for a sufficient period to acquaint them with the scoring criteria, I have found that the system offers a reliable guide allowing for a quantifiable, organized approach to content symbolism. To aid in the precision of scoring and interpretation, the criterion statements have been made explicit and the rationale of the categories has been made directly pertinent to the psychoanalytic theory of libidinal progression and object cathexis, i.e., the relative strength of oral, anal, and genital preoccupations, and how humans are in a complex manner invested with feelings of a positive or negative valence. The inferences made are not simply a referral to affective tone (see next section of this chapter).

Although I have made some modification of subcategories since my first publication (De Vos 1952), the major categories have proved their worth, as have most of the initial subcategories. In modifying the system in the direction of a half-dozen more subcategories, I have kept in mind the dangers of a too free proliferation, which would result from trying to handle individualistically toned responses. New subcategories have been added only if they seemed to add some elemental affective constituent not already specifically delineated. Further precision would vitiate our purpose of quantifying significant differences between groups.

Relation of the Scoring System to Psychoanalytic Theory

This system of scoring the underlying affective symbolism is highly dependent on psychoanalytic theory for its rationale. It is not devoted solely to a recording of the affective tone of Rorschach responses, but is concerned also with the nature of content symbolism as indicating the relative strength of libidinal vectors attached to the various stages of psychosexual development. It is equally concerned with the cultural structuring of object cathexis into special content as implied in Rorschach responses from different groups. These differences, however, are not included in the basic manual.

The various factors involved in analyzing content symbolism according to the present system are as follows:

a. The overall positive or negative affective tone of specific content. Is there a relative balance in the production of positive, negative, or neutral percepts?

b. The nature of the cathexis involved in affective drives. Is cathexis basically of other persons or of self? Does the content suggest positively or destructively toned narcissism? To what extent is the narcissism of a primitive or secondary, socialized variety? Is object cathexis essentially constructive or destructive in nature?

c. The psychosexual developmental level of the responses. What does the content suggest about continuing concern with given libidinal development stages? Are there suggestions of fixation on or regression to earlier stages of development? Content often suggests in some manner the relative amount of energy or interest directed toward pregenital oral-tactual, anal-control, phallic-genital development stages as well as sublimations in libidinal expression.

d. The degree and nature of the socialization of the ego as a mediator between outer pressures and inner needs. What is the nature of the socialization and sublimation of libidinal interests? Are libidinal concerns expressed in a more or less direct manner in the content? Are ego defenses used to handle impulses, or are they used to guard against affective stimulation from the outside? Is repression, denial, projection, or displacement overused? Is affective responsiveness active or passive on balance? Is it diffuse or focused?

e. The attitudinal stance or "set" taken toward given external objects. Is the effective relationship to objects structured in active or passive terms? Are outside objects related to in terms of dependent needs or in terms of active interests?

These five analytic factors are used to classify responses within the scoring system. Some of the complexity derives from the many combinations of these factors possible in responses and from differences in their relative pertinence to the particular responses. Most responses showing any kind of affective determination are located between the polarities of content, suggesting: (a) positive, (b) outer-object oriented, (c) mature, (d) sublimated, or (e) active or (f) passive receptive characteristics; and content suggesting: (a') destructive, (b') narcissistic, (c') primitive or aggressive, (d') non-socialized or (e') defensive characteristics.

There are six major categories organized to include subcategories which are more or less sensitive to these analytic factors.

The Hostile, Anxious, and Positive categories are primarily organized around affective tone (a and a'). Within these categories as well as the others, relative degrees of maturation or primitiveness are apparent (c, c'). In the Hostile and Anxious categories there is an active or passive stance (e, f) taken toward destructiveness or fear of destructiveness.

Body Preoccupation responses reflect most directly the nature of body cathexis (b'), and the relative failure of satisfactory externalization of both impulses and affective responsiveness (d'). Many of these responses are narcissistic in tone (b').

The Dependent category reflects an attitudinal stance toward outside objects of a passive or receptive nature (f), a seeking for strength and protection outside. No matter how primitive the level on which this seeking takes place, there is attachment to the social world.

Responses in the Positive category reflect positively toned attachments to objects and persons in the social world (a).

Variations in level of psychosexual development is found throughout these major categories. By means of the various subcategories one can specifically note the various nuances in the expression of oral, tactual, anal, and phallic as well as genital or sublimated vectors in libidinal expression.

In the course of the following chapters we shall draw attention to specific categories or subcategories as they demonstrate personality features of a particular individual or group, or help to systematically differentiate the various groups we have studied with our method.

Problems of Reliability and Validity

In my original article (De Vos 1952), I published a reliability study using four experienced users of the Rorschach as judges who were briefly instructed in the scoring system and there I reported having high reliability in "Bodily Preoccupations" of .99; in "Anxious" content, .88; Hostility, .77; and "Unpleasant overall" (a combination of the Hostile, Anxious, and Body preoccupation categories) of .88. Dependent content was .68. The "Positive" category was .91; and Neutral, .85. (see table 3.1).

TABLE 3.1

Product Moment Correlation on Each Affective Index of Each
of Four Judges with Examiner D in Rorschach Records

Judge	Host.	Anx.	Bod.	Unpl.	Dep.	Pos.	Neut.	Means r of Judge
C	.83	.81	1.00	.85	.33	.91	.82	.78
R	.81	.92	.98	.88	.84	.95	.86	.89
S	.85	.92	.99	.91	.87	.84	.91	.90
T	.60	.89	1.00	.88	.71	.93	.82	.83
Mean r of categories	.77	.88	.99	.88	.68	.91	.85	

What I found in this study of scoring reliability was that in two instances, a particular scorer had a problem with a given category. One had difficulty scoring hostility (.60), and one had trouble with dependency responses (.33). With further coaching both overcame these difficulties. What it pointed up, however, is something all clinicians have experienced either in their own learning or in teaching others, namely that one's personal propensities must be overcome in dealing objectively with psychodynamic materials. Countertransference is always operative in either undue sensitivity or relative blindness to given thematic implications. Even experienced clinicians may at first have problems with particular content. This problem recurred when I later instructed others in scoring thematic material. By and large, such difficulties can be surmounted by working over a period of time with several individuals comparing their use of the scoring system on the same test protocols.

Initially, one is puzzled by some very complex responses that are open to a variety of interpretations. This type of complexity cannot be avoided. What I have asked users to do is to score only the most salient features of the response. (In complex responses, no more than three scores are considered.) Some of the subtleties of given responses that may be picked up by some individuals are not picked up by others. For some there is a danger of overscoring. However, with use and some initial checking with others, the overall effect is that reliability becomes sufficiently high to ensure that the over sixty subcategories are adequately comparable between groups when scored by different individuals.

Some Remarks on Clinical Validity

It may be helpful here to recapitulate some of the tests of significance used with the clinical categories of normal, neurotic, and schizophrenics as first scored at Michael Reese Hospital with this method (see tables 3.2 and 3.3). Three methods were initially used with subsamples of 60 normals, 30 neurotics, and 30 schizophrenics from the Michael Reese files to ascertain how adequately the summary indices functioned in differentiating clinical groups. Subsequent to the initial publication I further tested another subsample with equal results.

TABLE 3.2

Comparison of the Means, Standard Deviations, and Critical
Ratios of Affective Indices Among Normal, Neurotic, and
Schizophrenic Groups

Major Categories		Normal Means S.D.		Neurotic Means S.D.		Schiz. Means S.D.		Critical Ratio P Level
				Means and S.D.				* = .05
								† = .01
								‡ = .001
Hostility	M	9.2	6.5	15.4	12.1	10.9	8.3	Nor. vs. Neu. = 1.04
	F	9.5	7.5	8.1	5.6	5.6	6.9	Nor. vs. Sch. = .62
	T	**9.4**	**7.1**	**11.6**	**8.3**	**8.3**	**7.7**	Neu. vs. Sch. = 1.35
Anxiety	M	14.9	8.2	22.7	12.3	24.3	14.5	Nor. vs. Neu. = 3.68‡
	F	12.7	7.0	22.5	11.2	22.6	13.6	Nor. vs. Sch. = 3.55‡
	T	**13.8**	**7.6**	**22.6**	**11.8**	**12.7**	**14.1**	Neu. vs. Sch. = .32
Bodily Preoccup.	M	5.4	6.7	10.3	9.7	15.9	14.5	Nor. vs. Neu. = 2.16*
	F	2.8	3.1	8.3	15.9	22.7	31.8	Nor. vs. Sch. = 3.68‡
	T	**4.1**	**4.9**	**9.3**	**12.8**	**19.3**	**23.1**	Neu. vs. Sch. − 2.08*
Total Unpleasant Affect	M	31.17	12.9	47.8	16.3	51.5	17.2	Nor. vs. Neu. = 4.30‡
	F	24.83	11.1	37.5	10.2	51.8	22.8	Nor. vs. Sch. = 6.12‡
	T	**27.5**	**12.0**	**42.7**	**13.2**	**51.7**	**20.0**	Neu. vs. Sch. = 2.07*
Dependency	M	4.6	4.8	7.6	6.6	7.5	5.8	Nor. vs. Neu. = 1.67
	F	4.6	4.3	6.5	8.0	4.6	7.5	Nor. vs. Sch. = 1.07
	T	**4.6**	**4.6**	**7.0**	**7.4**	**6.0**	**6.8**	Neu. vs. Sch. = .53
Positive Affect	M	16.1	11.1	11.3	9.0	7.3	6.0	Nor. vs. Neu. = 2.30*
	F	18.2	10.7	12.5	10.6	6.5	5.6	Nor. vs. Sch. = 5.80‡
	T	**17.1**	**10.9**	**11.9**	**9.8**	**6.9**	**5.8**	Neu. vs. Sch. = 2.39*
Neutral	M	48.5	14.7	37.6	21.0	33.8	19.3	Nor. vs. Neu. = .96
	F	50.1	16.4	52.9	16.0	35.4	18.8	Nor. vs. Sch. = 3.64‡
	T	**49.3**	**15.6**	**45.3**	**19.2**	**34.6**	**19.1**	Neu. vs. Sch. = 2.10*

Significance Tests on Each of the Affective Indices

Critical ratios were obtained of the differences in mean percentages of normal, neurotics, and schizophrenics on each of the
major categories. Then I used chi square tests to bring out more
directly the differentiating value of the various indices by comparing the numbers of individuals in the neurotic and schizophrenic
groups who scored one or two standard deviations above the

TABLE 3.3

Number of Cases in Each Affective Index by Standard
Deviations from the Normal Group Mean in 60 Normal,
30 Neurotic, and 30 Schizophrenic Records

						Chi Square		P level
								* = .05
						n.t. (not testable)		† = .01
								‡ = .001

Index	Normal		Neurotic		Schizophr.		Nor. vs. Neu.	Nor. vs. Sch.	Neu. vs. Sch.
Normals	N	%	N	%	N	%			
A High *hostile* content									
Mean σ 1σ=17	9	15	6	20	7	23	-	-	-
9.4 ± 7.1 2σ=24	2	3	4	13	1	3	-	-	-
B High *anxious* content									
Mean σ 1σ=22	13	23	13	43	15	50	4.67*	7.22*	-
13.8 ± 8.0 2σ=30	0		8	27	6	20	n.t.	n.t.	-
C High *bodily* content									
Mean σ 1σ=10	6	10	6	20	17	57	n.t.	22.65‡	8.52†
4.1 ± 4.9 2σ=14	3	5	5	17	15	50	n.t.	25.29‡	7.50†
D High *total unpleasant* content									
Mean σ 1σ=40	8	13	19	63	22	73	23.51‡	25.60‡	-
27.9 ± 12.0 2σ=50	3	5	9	30	16	53	n.t.	21.70‡	-
E High *dependent* content									
Mean σ 1σ=10	8	13	8	27	6	20	-	-	-
4.6 ± 4.6 2σ=14	1	1.6	3	10	4	13	n.t.	n.t.	n.t.
F1 Low *positive* content									
Mean σ 1σ=6	11	18	12	40	16	53	4.86*	11.66‡	-
17.1 ± 10.9 2σ=0	2	3	4	10	9	30	n.t.	14.06‡	-
F2 High *positive* content									
Mean 17	28	47	8	27	1	3	-	16.22‡	n.t.
1σ=28	9	15	3	10	0	-	n.t.	n.t.	n.t.
2σ=39	4	7	0	-	0	-	n.t.	n.t.	n.t.
G1 Low *neutral* content									
Mean σ 1σ=34	12	20	9	30	16	53	-	10.47‡	3.36 (P=.07)
49.3 ± 15.6 2σ=18	0	-	3	10	5	17	n.t.	n.t.	n.t.
G2 High *neutral* content									
1σ=65	11	18	5	17	2	7	-	-	n.t.
2σ=80	2	3	3	10	0	-	n.t.	n.t.	n.t.

mean of the normal control group. Theoretically these should include 16% and 2.3% of the normal and schizophrenic groups, respectively. If any index is to discriminate well it should include far more individuals with high or low scores in the neurotic or schizophrenic groups, so that one could consider the appearance of certain high or low scores as indicative of probable maladjustment. The critical value of scores two standard deviations from the mean would be the most valuable, since the theoretical possibility of such an individual being in the normal range is only two chances in a hundred.

Comparing Differentiating Value of Affective Indices by Means of Critical Checks

In comparing the differentiating value of the thematic affective indices, we used a critical check for each score exceeding two standard deviations away from the normal mean. The number of records in the normal, neurotic, and schizophrenic groups receiving no check were compared with the number receiving one or two checks by means of chi square.

Fisher Maladjustment Scores Correlated with the Index of Total Unpleasant Affect

My principal method of validation was to compute a correlation between the index of total unpleasant affect and the configurational Maladjustment Score developed by Fisher (1950). I demonstrated a high relationship between unpleasant affect and maladjustment. Fisher's criteria held up as a good differentiator not only on his own samples of normal, neurotics, and schizophrenics, but also when tested subsequently on the Michael Reese sample. Fisher's score was composed of weighted points for given various imbalances for infirmities or pathological signs usually noted in a clinical evaluation of a record. His system of scoring several criteria with weighted points permits one to obtain a single overall number in rating a record.

Because a few items that were scored for affective content also obtained points in Fisher's system, I ran two correlations, one on the total maladjustment score and the second on the total maladjustment score minus items appearing in both scoring systems. The later correlation of maladjustment with unpleasant affect was .69. As this early validation study indicated, my classification system of inferences concerning negatively valenced affective symbolism and other Rorschach indices was valid quantitatively in cases placed within normal, neurotic, and maladjusted groups as previously judged by other psychiatric criteria.

In comparing the Beck samples with the original material forwarded by Fisher, we found a mean of 33.1 for our normal group on Fisher's scale compared with 36.9 for his own normal group; we obtained 59.4 on our neurotic group compared with Fisher's 59.7; we obtained a mean of 85.2 for our schizophrenic group compared with 85.5 reported for his schizophrenics—a remarkably close correspondence between the two sets of scoring samples.

A Comparison of Affective Categories

As tables 3.2 and 3.3 indicate, certain of the thematic indices show significant differences between clinical groups while others do not. Schizophrenics are best differentiated from normals by:

1. *A Lack of Positive Content.* A score of about 20% on the Index of Positive Affect excluded all schizophrenics in the Michael Reese study. Only one schizophrenic scored as high as 17%, which was the mean for the normal group. This result strongly suggests that a high Positive score would contradict schizophrenia in any record. In subsequent work in many of our cross-cultural samples we have found this result to hold up. In some of the cultural samples in which we obtained strong indications of Unpleasant material, as in many Japanese, we found Unpleasant material to be counterpoised by a considerable number of Positive responses. Since these scores were obtained from individuals who were tested in nonclinical settings, we came to rely on the Index of Positive Affect as counterindicative of clinical manifestations of maladjustment. I now hold that a high Positive content score on the Rorschach suggests a considerable amount of positive social-object cathexis, and hence a positive desire to maintain continuing affective relationships with the social world. A very low score, on the contrary, suggests a possible lack of such object cathexis or lack of positive interests or outlets to counteract underlying unresolved regressive problems. Low scores beyond two standard deviations which reach to 0% are definitely rare in normal groups and are found more often in schizophrenics than in neurotics, as was true in our initial research.

Tables 3.2 and 3.3 demonstrate that normals may be differentiated from maladjusted groups by a high Positive content, pro-portionately roughly twice as many normals were at the normal mean (28 of 60), whereas 8 out of 30 neurotics and only 1 out of 30 schizophrenics reached 17%. At one standard deviation above the normal mean, the difference between normal and neurotic was somewhat less, 15% of the normal reached this level and 10% of the neurotic group gave 28% positive responses. At two standard deviations above the mean (39%) we still found 4 of the 60 normal records, but no neurotic or schizophrenics.

2. *Low or High Neutral Content.* A relatively lower amount of Neutral content is found in schizophrenic records, although the evidence is not firm. Schizophrenics tend to have a low neutral score to a statistically significant degree. Over 50% of schizophre-nics have such low scores of Neutral Rorschach responses. This is true for only 30% of the neurotics and 20% of the normals at one standard deviation below the normal mean. I believe that these results support the idea that schizophrenics cannot generally handle affectivity in a controlled manner. They, both consciously and unconsciously, experience affective pressures which influence their perceptual apparatus to an undue extent.

Excessively high scores in Neutral content, however, suggest constriction used to block out the expression of affective feelings, even to the point of preventing the occurrence of any sort of ob-vious unconscious symbolic expression. Such blocking, as will be reported in some of the following chapters, is found especially in groups tending toward high levels of ideational constriction, such as is found to characterize many Native Americans. The exact relationship of this sort of constriction to symbolic production generally is not yet well understood, but American schizophre-nics seem prone to symbolize more of their responses than do either normals or neurotics. However, I did not find that hospital-ized Japanese psychotics did so; curiously enough, many of those tested tended to have very flat records. In Japan, it was the neurotic records that tended to be the most flamboyant in the use of affective material.

By and large, the better adjusted as well as adaptive an indi-vidual appears to be, the more free he seems to be to express a certain amount of affective content of both a positive and nega-tive variety. The defensive structure of individuals in whose records little or no negative content appears needs further syste-

matic exploration. However, every cross-cultural sample I have
personally viewed has a relative number of individuals practicing
extreme forms of affective constriction.

3. *Bodily Preoccupation and Sexual Content*. Anatomical and
sexual material constituting more than 14% of the responses was
found in 50% of the schizophrenics, in contrast to 17% of the
neurotics and 5% of the normal group. With the exception of
some unusual professional groups such as artists, an excessive
amount of such material suggests withdrawal of affect from the
external world and the presence of pathological narcissism.
Perseveration on anatomical material may be interpreted differently in some cases, especially when the material is of the pelvic
and backbone type, as seen in some neurotic records. By and
large the inordinate use of anatomy cross-culturally was highly
suggestive of pathology, whatever the group studied. It has been
suggested a priori by some that hunters and gatherers, since they
hunt and butcher animals, would see more anatomical shapes. No
such results are forthcoming. Many other easy suppositions about
how interests or occupations would conduce toward given types
of Rorschach responses similarly have been found to be negated.

4. *Low Anxious Responses*. Anxious responses are significantly less prevalent in normal groups. One finds 23% of the normals
compared with 43% of the neurotics and 50% of the schizophrenics at one standard deviation above the mean. At two standard
deviations, one still finds more than one fourth of the neurotics
and 24% of the schizophrenics, but no normal records reached
30% "high anxiety" in content. Note that there is little difference
between neurotics and schizophrenics in the production of anxiety material.

5. *Low Total Unpleasant Scores*. Normals definitely have a
lower amount of total Unpleasant content. Records with a score
of 50% Unpleasant content include only 5% of the normals but
30% of the neurotics and 53% of the schizophrenics. A scoring in
which 50% of the responses have an unpleasant content suggests
that there is a sufficient degree of disturbance in the emotional
life of the person to consider him critically maladjusted, with
considerable affective energy tied up in internal conflict. There
is a tendency for normal and neurotic men to score higher on
Unpleasant content than normal and neurotic women.

6. *Dependent Content as a Differentiator*. The normal and

neurotic group did not produce as many individuals with high Dependent content as did the schizophrenic group, but the differences were not significant. Both in the United States and in other cultures I consider Dependent content can be ego-centric in some individuals, but at the same time it is suggestive of an attachment to social life, albeit of a passive nature. This need may not be seen as evidence of maladjustment, and can even be culturally adaptive as in the case of the Japanese. Nevertheless, an unusual emphasis on Dependent content in a record can be of clinical significance. In chapter 7 I shall report one case in which dependent responses were confirming of psychosomatic difficulty.

7. *Hostile Content as a Differentiator.* Interestingly enough, an overall Index of Hostility was not a critical score differentiating maladjusted individuals from normals, nor has the overall score of Hostility been critical in other subsequent uses of this system. There are, however, interesting clinical differences in the subcategories of hostility which are disguised by the overall hostile score.

Hostile content on the Rorschach is very often of an active nature and thereby may indicate a more active stance in the personality. It is therefore somewhat counterindicative of any social retreat. In some records it is the form taken by Hostile content which seems significant, not the overall score, as I comment further in chapter 6, comparing the families of delinquents and nondelinquents in Japan. The meaning of hostile responses in the Rorschach has not received much consensus in the literature generally. What is demonstrated quantitatively in our studies is that Hostile content does not add up to overall high scores in most records regardless of the groups studied. Nevertheless, some specific subcategories such as (Hsm) hostile sadomasochism become highly significant differentiators in given sub groups.

Comparison of F+ as a Significant Differentiator

A critical separation of clinical groups was checked for each score exceeding two standard deviations from the normal mean by particular category, excluding high positive affect. It was found that the affective scorings considered together are as valid in differentiating between a normal and a maladjusted individual as is F+% (the percentage of responses considered to have "good form," or a plausible percept for the area of blot used). The overall percentage of responses with adequate fit between blot form and the response given is a good measure of reality testing.

The correspondence between these measures was brought out by comparing the proportionate number of normals, neurotics, and schizophrenics showing *two* critically high affective inferences with the proportionate number receiving an F+ scoring of less than 60% over their whole record, or conversely, being so rigidly concerned with form accuracy that they received a score of more than 96%. Only 12% of the normals had an aberrant F+%, whereas 23% of the neurotics and 46% of the schizophrenics had aberrant scores. Two or more critical affective indices include only 5% of the normals compared with 40% of the neurotics and 60% of the schizophrenics. This evidence argues strongly for the use of these indices as clinical differentiators. However, the results are statistical; it is apparent that they are not infallible differentiators. The Rorschach itself is not infallible but indicative of a variety of possible aberrancies. Just like any other individual Rorschach variable, one has to judge what these indices of affect suggest in the context of the total record.

These cases were characterized on the basis of psychiatric evaluations which were also open to a certain percentage of error. Then, too, it is expected that a certain percentage of seriously maladjusted individuals will find their way into any sampling of a supposedly normal population. All things considered, the major categories of affective Indices seem to be as useful as indicators as any Rorschach variables tested quantitatively.

The various *subcategories* based on psychoanalytic literature held up in overall quantification with clinical groups. In subsequent chapters, we will demonstrate how certain subcategories as well as the major indices are useful in differentiating among members of cultural groups. We turn from a study here of clinical purpose to a study of cross-cultural comparison.

Notes

1. This chapter is modified from George A. De Vos, "A Quantitative Approach to Affective Symbolism in Rorschach Responses," *Journal of Projective Techniques*, 1952, 16:133–150.

2. In briefly reviewing various symbolic approaches to the Rorschach, I have found the writing of Roy Schafer (1954) to be the most congenial to the assumptions which have guided my own efforts to develop a quantitative system for the comparison of data cross-culturally.

References

Beck, Samuel J., Roy R. Grinker, and William Stephenson
 1954 *The Six Schizophrenias: Reaction Patterns in Children and Adults.* New York: American Orthopsychiatric Association.
Boyer, L. Bryce, George A. De Vos, Orin Borders, and Alice Borders
 1978 The Burnt Child Reaction Among the Yukon Eskimos. *Journal of Psychological Anthropology* 1(1):7–56.
Boyer, L. Bryce, Ruth M. Boyer, and George A. De Vos
 1982 An Apache Woman's Account of Her Recent Acquisition of the Shamanistic Status. *Journal of Psychoanalytic Anthropology* 5(3):299–331.
 1983 On the Acquisition of the Shamanistic Status: A Clinical and Rorschach Study of a Specific Case. G. Devereux and Hans Peter Duerr, eds. *Die Wilde Seele: Kritische Aufsatze Zur Ethnopsychiatrie*, pp. 102–140. Frankfurt: Syndikat. English transl., Wildman Press, New York.
Boyer, L. Bryce, Christine M. Miller, and George A. De Vos
 1984 A Comparison of Rorschach Protocols Obtained from Two Groups of Laplanders from Northern Finland. *Journal of Psychoanalytic Anthropology* 7(4):379–396.
Boyer, L. Bryce, George A. De Vos, and Ruth M. Boyer
 1985 Crisis and Continuity in the Personality of an Apache Shaman. *Psychoanalytical Study of Society*, Vol. 11. Hillsdale, N.Y., London: Analytic Press.
Day, Richard, L. Bryce Boyer, and George A. De Vos
 1975 Two Styles of Ego Development: A Cross-Cultural Longitudinal Comparison of Apache and Anglo School Children. *Ethos* 3(3).
De Vos, George A.
 1952 A Quantitative Approach to Affective Symbolism in Rorschach Responses. *Journal of Projective Techniques* 16(2):133–150.
 1954 A Comparison of the Personality Differences in Two Generations of Japanese Americans by Means of the Rorschach Test. *Nagoya Journal of Medical Science* 17(3):153–265.
 1955 A Quantitative Rorschach Assessment of Maladjustment and Rigidity in Acculturating Japanese Americans. *Genetic Psychology Monographs* 52:51–87.

1961 Symbolic Analysis in the Cross-Cultural Study of Personality. Bert Kaplan, ed. *Studying Personality Cross-Culturally*, pp. 599–634. Evanston, Ill.: Row-Peterson.

De Vos, George A., and Orin Borders
  1979 A Rorschach Comparison of Delinquent and Nondelinquent Japanese Family Members. *Journal of Psychological Anthropology* 2(4):425–442.

De Vos, George A., and L. Bryce Boyer
  1987 *Studying Personality Cross-Culturally*. Evanston, Ill.: Row, Peterson.

De Vos, George A., and Horace Miner
  1959 Oasis and Casbah: A Study in Acculturative Stress. Marvin K. Opler, ed. *Culture and Mental Health*, pp. 333–359. New York: Macmillan.

Fisher, Seymour
  1950 Patterns of Personality Rigidity and Some of Their Determinants. *Psychological Monographs: General and Applied* 64(1):1–64.

Helm, June, George A. De Vos, and Teresa Carterette
  1960 Variations in Personality and Ego Identification Within a Slave Indian Kin-Community. National Museum of Canada Bulletin 190, *Contributions to Anthropology*, Part 2.

Rabkin, Leslie Y.
  1986 Longitudinal Continuities in the Personality of a Kibbutznik. *Journal of Psychoanalytic Anthropology* 9(3):319–338.

Rorschach, Hermann
  1921 *Psychodiagnostics*. Reprinted by Grune and Stratton, New York [1949].

Schafer, Roy
  1954 Psychoanalytic Interpretation in Rorschach Testing: Theory and Application. New York: Grune and Stratton.

Singer, Margaret Thaler
  1962 Personality Measurement in the Aging. James Birran, ed. *Human Aging: Biological, Social and Psychological*. Birran, ed. Washington, D.C.: Government Printing Office.

Speisman, Joseph, and Margaret Thaler Singer
  1961 Rorschach Content: Correlates in Five Groups with Organic Pathology. *Journal of Projective Techniques* 25:356–359.

Streitfelt, H. S.
  1954 Specificity of Peptic Ulcer to Intense Oral Conflicts. *Psychosomatic Medicine* 16:315–326.

Thaler, Margaret, Herbert Weiner, and Morton Reiser
1957 Exploration of the Doctor-Patient Relationship Through Projective Techniques. *Psychosomatic Medicine* 19:228–239.
Wagatsuma, Hiroshi, and George A. De Vos
1985 *Heritage of Endurance: Family Patterns and Delinquency Formation in Urban Japan.* Berkeley, Los Angeles, London: University of California Press.
Weiner, Herbert, Margaret Thaler (Singer), and Morton Reiser
1957 Etiology of the Peptic Ulcer. Part I: Relation of Specific Psychological Characteristics to Gastric Secretion (Serum Pepsinogen). *Psychosomatic Medicine*, Vol. 19.
Weiner, Herbert, Margaret Thaler (Singer), Morton Reiser, and L. Minsky
1957 Etiology of Duodenal Ulcer. *Psychosomatic Medicine* 19(1):1–10.
Wynne, Lyman, and Margaret Thaler-Singer
1966 Principles of Scoring Communication Defects and Deviances in Parents of Schizophrenics. *Psychiatry* 29:260–298.

Part II

The Japanese

George A. De Vos

This section of our volume presents some major excerpts from my specific research work with the Rorschach test that has been directed toward the understanding of Japanese culture and personality. My undergraduate experience was in sociology. After three and a half years in the army in World War II (1943–1946), during which I spent much of my time learning the Japanese language, I returned to the University of Chicago and entered graduate school in anthropology. Under the direction of W. Lloyd Warner, the social anthropologist, I was enrolled in an interdisciplinary program organized by the Committee on Human Development. I had become intrigued both by Ruth Benedict's essay on the Japanese, *The Chrysanthemum and The Sword* (1946), and what was at the time the very general interest in anthropology in "culture and personality," which sought to combine psychodynamic psychology with the understanding of cultural behavior. I had been most impressed by the work of Abram Kardiner and Ralph Linton (1939), and then of Cora Du Bois (1944), in her attempt to combine fieldwork observation and the use of the Rorschach test with preliterate peoples as analyzed by Emil Oberholzer in Du Bois' *The People of Alor.*

I was drawn to studying the Rorschach test, and over a period of two years received initial intensive instruction from psychologists Al Hunsicker and Hedda Bolgar. In early 1947 I heard that two fellow graduate students, William Caudill, in anthropology, and Setsuko Nishi, in sociology, were planning a study of the more than 17,000 Japanese Americans who were resettling in the

Chicago area after leaving their wartime internment camps. I joined Caudill and Nishi's effort, determined to use the Rorschach test in complementary fashion to the Thematic Apperception Test which was being used by Caudill (1952). I was eventually able to overlap with Caudill's sample most of my sample of 140 Issei immigrants and Nisei, American-born subjects, drawn from the Chicago population (Caudill and De Vos 1956). In addition, I made a special study of Kibei, or American-born children of Issei immigrants who had been sent back to Japan during their formative school years to enter Japanese schools. Nishi, for her part, did intensive interviewing with members of the newly forming community.

Realizing that further psychological training in testing would be necessary for a proper understanding of psychodiagnosis, I applied for a clinical internship with David Shakow, then director of psychology at the Illinois Psychiatric Institute, and eventually received my doctorate in psychology at the University of Chicago.

Charlotte Babcock of the Chicago Institute for Psychoanalysis joined our efforts and began intensive psychoanalysis with a number of Nisei. Just at this time Samuel J. Beck, with the assistance of Herman Molish and William Thetford, was engaged in a study of schizophrenia at Michael Reese Hospital in Chicago. Beck (Beck et al. 1954) had collected a normative sample of 157 nonclinical Rorschachs as well as extensive samples of Psychoneurotic and Schizophrenic subjects and welcomed my use of samples taken from his data.

From 1948 to 1950 I was engaged in visiting Japanese American homes and also working with my selected Beck control samples of 60 normals, 50 neurotic, and 50 schizophrenic records at Michael Reese. I was extremely dissatisfied with what was being published on the Rorschach test cross-culturally, since the very rich psychodynamic possibilities of the content of the responses received, at best, only anecdotal reporting. As a means of systematically comparing the symbolic material both clinically and normatively (see chap. 3), I developed the scoring system herein reported.

The orienting concern of our collaborative research with Japanese Americans was the possible traumatic social and personal effects of their wartime relocation experience. They had been forcefully removed from their homes in California and sent to camps because they were thought to be untrustworthy and dangerous to the national security as a result of the wave of collective hysteria that had engulfed the American government and a large section of the American white population after the Japanese attack on Pearl Harbor.

We were prepared to find a great deal of social and personal malaise, and were therefore surprised to find how quickly the Japanese American community was reconstituting itself, surmounting difficulties without manifesting much visible evidence of either social disorganization or personal maladaptation. In the sample of 50 Issei I did find evidence, however (see chap. 4) in some protocols, especially of older women, of considerable personal maladjustment. These specific patterns were, no doubt, of long standing, but the general effects of social discrimination on the groups as a whole were also suggested by some of the content (see chaps. 4 and 9).

Among the American-born, I completed a sample of 60 Nisei, who had spent their entire childhood in the United States, and a special sample of 30 "Kibei," American born who by my criterion had spent at least five years in Japan in school, having been sent there by their parents to learn the Japanese language and culture. They had thus been in a Japanese peer group for a considerable period of their formative years. These records, too, revealed some special psychological problems (see chap. 4).

Although my background in sociology and social anthropology had equipped me with considerable initial skepticism about testing cross-culturally, by 1949 I had become deeply impressed with the consistencies that were appearing in the Rorschach protocols. There were distinctly different perceptual patterns between the immigrant generation and their children. In contrast with the Issei, the Nisei norms approximated in many respects the statistical norms of the American groups. The Kibei sample varied widely, but when averaged tended to fall remarkably close to midway between the Issei and Nisei records.

In 1951 Professor Tsuneo Muramatsu, head of psychiatry at Nagoya National University, visited the Institute for Psychoanalysis in Chicago at a time when our research team was formally presenting our findings. He became enthusiastic about doing a large-scale project on normative personality in Japan and was able to obtain funding from the Rockefeller Foundation and the Foundation's Fund For Research in Psychiatry. In 1953, I received a Fulbright research grant for two years and introduced the Rorschach, the Thematic Apperception Test, and the "Insight Test" of Helen Sargent (1953) to the Japanese psychologists working on the project, as well as the F scale of the Authoritarian Personality study of Adorno, Frenkl-Brunswik, and Sanford (Adorno et al. 1950). With an interdisciplinary staff of over 30 researchers, we developed several social opinion scales and selected a representative farm village, a fishing village, and a mountain village, and also conducted doing block sampling of census tracts in the cities of Okayama and Nagoya. In all, approximately 2,400 individuals were interviewed. Of the 724 given the Rorschach, over 600 were also given both the Problem Situation Test and the TAT. In chapter 4, I briefly mention some of the comparative findings as they related to work with Japanese Americans. What was remarkable to me was that the statistical norms obtained in Japan on the Rorschach were very similar to those obtained from the much smaller sample of Issei gathered five years earlier in Chicago.

Chapter 5 reports on a special sample of delinquent youth and their normal controls we studied during my time at the Nagoya Department of Psychiatry. Chapters 6 and 7 report on interview and testing materials obtained during an intensive study of fifty Japanese families from Arakawa Ward, Tokyo. These latter materials were gathered as part of a large-scale study of delinquency in Japan which I directed for eight years (1960–68), sponsored by the National Institute of Mental Health, at the Institute for Human Development at the University of California, Berkeley. This family study (De Vos 1973, 1980; De Vos and Wagatsuma 1973; Wagatsuma and De Vos 1985) was unique in that it is probably the only one in the field of delinquency research in which the personality patterns of parents and children in both an experimental and control group have been systematically compared by means of projective test instruments.

Finally, chapter 7 of this section gives us a very brief glimpse into the usability of the Rorschach cross-culturally in clinical diagnostic work. I report from the 1954 Japanese ethnographic materials (De Vos 1961) on a village man with an ulcer, and from the delinquency research sample of 1960–1965 (Wagatsuma and De Vos 1984), on a delinquent youth guilty of rape, who produced a schizophrenic Rorschach protocol.

References

Adorno, T. W., Else Frenkel-Brunswik, D. Levinson, and N. Sanford
1950 *The Authoritarian Personality.* New York: Harper and Brothers.

Beck, Samuel Jacob
1954 *The Six Schizophrenias: Reaction Patterns in Children and Adults.* New York: American Orthopsychiatric Association, Monograph 6.

Benedict, Ruth
1946 *The Chrysanthemum and the Sword.* Boston: Houghton-Mifflin.

Caudill, William
1952 *Japanese American Personality and Acculturation.* Genetic Psychological Monograph, 45:2–102.

Caudill, William, and George De Vos
1956 Achievement, Culture, and Personality: The Case of the Japanese Americans. *American Anthropologist* 58:6:1102–1126.

De Vos, George A.
1961 Symbolic Analysis in Cross-Cultural Study of Personality. B. Kaplan, ed. *Studying Personality Cross-Culturally*, pp. 599–634. Evanston: Row, Peterson.
1973 *Socialization for Achievement: Essays on the Cultural Psychology of the Japanese.* Berkeley, Los Angeles, London: University of California Press.
1980 Delinquency and Minority Status: A Psychoculture Perspective. G. Newman, ed. *Crime and Deviancy: A Comparative Perspective*, pp. 130–180. Beverly Hills: Sage Publications.

De Vos, George A., and Hiroshi Wagatsuma
1972 Family Life and Delinquency: Some Perspectives from Japanese Research. William P. Lebra, ed. *Transcultural Research in Mental Health*, pp. 59–87. Honolulu: University of Hawaii Press.

Du Bois, Cora
1944 *The People of Alor.* Minneapolis: University of Minnesota Press.

Kardiner, Abram, and Ralph Linton
  1939   *The Individual and His Society: The Psychodynamics of Primitive Social Organization.* New York: Columbia University Press.
Sargent, Helen D.
  1953   *The Insight Test: A Verbal Projective Test for Personality Study.* New York: Grune and Stratton.
Wagatsuma, Hiroshi, and George A. De Vos
  1984   *Heritage of Endurance: Family and Delinquency in Urban Japan.* Berkeley, Los Angeles, London: University of California Press.

Chapter Four

Personality Continuities and Cultural Change in Japanese Americans

George A. De Vos

Socialized to Succeed

Before World War II, an overwhelming majority of Japanese Americans lived on the West Coast or in Hawaii. In the 1940 census only 360 Japanese Americans were listed in the census of the Chicago area. Following the wartime relocation from the West Coast, the estimates of newly arrived Japanese-Americans ranged from 16,000 to 19,000. Some figure above 17,000 is considered most nearly correct for the 1947 base year of our Chicago study. A larger number of individuals had settled there temporarily, but by this time some considerable number had returned to California. As discussed in my original monograph (De Vos 1954:162 ff.), we were able to obtain a representative sample of individuals of all ages from this population with very few refusals of cooperation.

By the late 1940s a number of books and articles had appeared about "Japanese personality," many of the interpretations written in negative tones due to the feelings aroused by war and conflict (ibid.: 157 ff.). What I found most intriguing in the background literature were earlier reports of various forms of intelligence and school achievement testing of the American-born Nisei children in the California schools, well summarized by Edward K. Strong (1934) and Reginald Bell (1933). When Nisei youth were systematically compared with those of the majority white population of the state, it was found that the Japanese Nisei had succeeded remarkably well in the American school environment compared with other ethnic minorities (De Vos 1954: 165 ff.).

In postwar Chicago, Charlotte Babcock (1962) was finding a number of psychological tensions which reflected evident cultural continuities in the childhood experience of the Nisei (De Vos 1954:169 ff.). For example, the Nisei remained especially sensitive to the pressure of their parents, who not only wished them to conform socially but expected them to excel in American society for the sake of the prestige and well-being of the family as it was judged within the Japanese community. These expectations were held at the price of individually considered potential. Great emphasis was placed on what was owed parents, and guilt was aroused through reminding children of the parental sacrifices made on their behalf. Gratification was experienced through conforming socially, especially if conforming led one to be socially successful and productive.

Anxiety about any inclination not to conform was concealed under the great pressure of an inner demand to maintain acceptance from the parent. There was often a conflict between self-realization and self-sacrifice which resulted in serious psychological stress. Any frustration or anxiety resulting from conflicts about conformity was handled largely by suppression, withdrawal, and limiting the external expression of all emotions.

It seems ironic today to me to hear many complaints by Sansei (the "third generation") about their Nisei parents. Being so thoroughly American in their own thinking, despite their strong Japanese identity, many Sansei cannot understand why their parents did not protest more vehemently against the injustice done to them by the wartime relocation. They consider their parental generation to have been too passive and nonconfrontational. By way of asserting their own "Japanese" identity they use characteristic contemporary "American" methods of self-assertion. They have little sensitivity to the stronger repressive forces that were applied to an earlier generation of Japanese, nor do they comprehend the very "Japanese" nature of their law-abiding, conformist, but persistent and enduring parents (Wagatsuma and De Vos 1984) who, nevertheless, ultimately gained social recognition and respect within a highly bigoted society.

The law-abiding nature of the Nisei generation has been borne out by statistics on delinquency and crime in California. For example, in statistics from the Department of Corrections I found that the delinquency rate for the Nisei in the state as a whole was one-eightieth that of the majority white population. The major offenses of Japanese generally were related either to gambling or to traffic delicts.

Babcock (1962) found that Nisei often experienced feelings of inadequacy as a means of handling guilt toward their parents and other siblings; our subsequent work in Japan revealed this process very clearly. These feelings are the surface manifestations of deep reactive hostility to the severe expectations placed on the growing individual. This almost totally unconscious hostility is often experienced masochistically, since individually toned self-assertion is seldom tolerated after early childhood. Guilt can be experienced consciously and also unconsciously through psychosomatic phenomena. Shame seems to predominate over guilt on a manifest level because the formation of the superego has been notably influenced by the early disciplinary use of the group as the prohibiting agent.

Whereas Japanese society puts a great deal of emphasis at an early age on the shame (Benedict 1946) and ostracism which the child's bad behavior will bring to the family, the American middle class puts more emphasis on how a child has disgraced himself or herself. While this personal disgrace may secondarily bring shame on the family, such disgrace is much less the focus of attention than it is for the Japanese child, who must bear the guilt (De Vos 1960) for the negative effects incurred by all the family members as a result of his or her wayward or inadequate behavior.

Despite the status of the father in Japanese society, in the experience of some of the conflicted patients seen in therapy by Babcock there was a tendency for the mother to belittle the father. In my own work with normative samples in Japan, I found such overt depreciation of the head of the family to be a relatively rare occurrence in comparison with American families. Nevertheless, when it did occur in a Japanese family it was significantly related to the appearance of delinquency in a child (Wagatsuma and De Vos 1984).

Although the Nisei showed forms of tension that differed from those evident in Japan, highly similar interpersonal family pat-

terns appeared in the sample of Thematic Apperception Test
material of Caudill (1952) and in the normative TATs obtained
by the Nagoya group (Muramatsu et al. 1960). In the various
reports by Wagatsuma and myself on TAT materials from two
Japanese villages, we commented on patterns of somatization
(De Vos and Wagatsuma 1959), guilt (De Vos 1960), wive's attitudes of respect toward husbands (De Vos and Wagatsuma 1961),
and the need to repay parental sacrifice and mentorship (De Vos
1975).

In our Chicago research on acculturative change as expressed
in the fantasy material on interpersonal relations, we found, in
general, a continual emphasis in both the immigrant Issei and the
Nisei on educational and vocational striving. In their perception
of social roles the Nisei were driven to gain acceptance within the
American middle-class environment; nevertheless their behavior
was based on certain inculcated Japanese values passed on to
them by the Issei parents (Caudill and De Vos 1956). These inculcated values were in many respects conducive to quick adaptive
acculturation, but in some respects they were also conducive to
producing internal tensions, as I shall presently discuss.

The intrapsychic tensions were such that they did not jeopar-
dize the Nisei's overt social acceptance, although they did interfere somewhat with the formation of intimate relations with
"Caucasians." Emphasis on social conformity made the Nisei
highly acceptable to majority whites, whereas the older values of
personal submergence to family obligation and strong control
over ready emotional expressiveness constituted a considerable
source of internal conflict for them as they continued to inhabit a
minority status within American society.

Perceptual Organization of Japanese Americans

The results and the interpretation of a comparison of the location
and determinants used in standard Rorschach scoring are reported in detail in the original monograph (De Vos 1954). What I
shall excerpt here is a brief summary of my general findings followed by a more detailed recapitulation of the results obtained by
my systematic comparison of the symbolic content in respect to its
affective connotations.

Mental Approach: Quality Ambition in
Perceptual Organization

I used three samples of Japanese-American adults: 50 immigrant Issei ("first generation"), 60 American-born Nisei ("second generation"), and a special group of 30 Nisei termed by themselves, "Kibei" ("return Americans") who as children had been sent to Japan and returned to the United States after at least five years of education in Japanese schools. In all three groups, the entire mental approach to the blots is different from that found in the American samples. The Japanese American perceptual organization is much more concerned with achieving some overall complex integration of the card, with a relative neglect of easier separate details, and with less emphasis on small unusual details. This approach, organizing the blots into complex concepts or configurations, indicates a striving in the intellectual sphere greater than that found in Beck's normative sample of Americans (table 4.1). The later normative statistics obtained in Japan substantiated these findings as a characteristically "Japanese" pattern.

The Beck American normative group, in comparison with whom the Japanese tendency toward striving seems so marked, may reflect a certain environmental selectivity related to the occupations available in the Chicago area mail-order business, with its various levels of management and labor, which was used

TABLE 4.1

Means and Standard Deviations of the Various Groups
on Items Measuring Mental Approach

Groups	Means (and Standard Deviations)					Groups	Confidence Levels of Significant Differences of Means				
	W	R	W (%)	D (%)	Dd (%)		W	R	W (%)	D (%)	Dd (%)
Issei	6.2	18.8	35.6	58.8	5.7	Is - Ki	-	-	-	-	-
	(4.0)	(11.0)	(18.9)	(25.4)	(9.8)	Is - Ni	-	0.001	-	-	-
Kibei	5.5	18.2	36.2	58.9	5.2	Ki - Ni	0.01	0.05	-	-	-
	(2.6)	(11.4)	(20.3)	(27.6)	(5.7)						
Nisei	7.4	26.0	34.8	59.3	6.6	Is - No	-	0.001	0.001	0.001	-
	(3.7)	(16.4)	(19.4)	(18.7)	(6.9)	Ki - No	-	0.001	0.001	0.01	-
Normal	5.0	30.9	18.6	73.5	8.7	Ni - No	0.001	0.05	0.001	0.001	-
	(3.5)	(12.8)	(13.6)	(11.4)	(7.1)						
Neur.	5.3	32.7	19.3	72.1	9.2	No - Ne	-	-	-	-	-
	(3.2)	(29.8)	(10.7)	(10.7)	(7.2)	No - Sc	0.01	-	-	-	0.01
Schiz.	3.6	31.2	16.5	72.0	12.3	Ne - Sc	0.01	-	-	-	-
	(2.3)	(19.0)	(20.3)	(18.4)	(12.1)						

to gather protocols. In Beck's group as a whole there was a tendency to show a certain sluggishness of intellectual drive. The difference between this Normal group and the Nisei may relate to the fact that the Normal group was composed of lower as well as middle-class persons (unskilled and skilled laborers, in addition to an executive group). Certain intellectual traits in the Nisei records such as ambition and drive, if attributed to a middle-class orientation, would tend to put the Nisei in a favorable light vis-à-vis Beck's Normal sample, just as in the schools in California the Nisei obtained better grades than did other children coming from diverse social-class backgrounds. The Japanese American records have yet to be compared with those of a group with specifically middle-class American background.

The fact that a large number of individuals in the Japanese American groups showed imbalances between their liberated creative capacities measured by Movement responses (M) and their intellectual strivings measured by Whole responses (W) in a (W:M) ratio suggests that the strong drive to succeed outstripped in some cases the actual capacities available to the individual (table 4.2). In the Issei the associative blocking was prevalent,

TABLE 4.2

Distribution of Cases in Regard to W : M Ratio

Groups	3W : 1M (W>6)			W>M			W= or >M			Groups	Confidence Levels of Sig. Diff. by X^2 W : M Ratio
	M	F	T	M	F	T	M	F	T		
Issei	10	5	15	11	18	29	4	2	6	Is - Ki	-
										Is - Ni	-
Kibei	6	1	7	7	12	19	2	2	4	Ki - Ni	-
Nisei	8	7	15	18	16	34	4	7	11	Is - No	0.001
										Ki - No	-
Normal	1	6	7	17	14	31	12	10	22	Ni - Ne	0.05
Neur.	3	2	5	9	13	22	3	0	3	No - No	-
										No - Sc	-
Schiz.	1	2	3	8	9	17	6	4	10	Ne - Sc	-

W = whole responses; M = movement responses. In lower headings, M = male; F = female; T = totals.

TABLE 4.3

Distribution of Cases, Means, and Standard Deviations of Variables
Measuring Associative Blocking

Groups	Rejections 0			1			2			R (number) 0-19			20-40			41-			Groups	Confidence Levels of Sig. Diff. by X^2 Rej.	R.
	M	F	T	M	F	T	M	F	T	M	F	T	M	F	T	M	F	T			
Issei	13	16	*29*	2	4	*6*	10	5	*15*	17	17	*34*	6	7	*13*	2	1	*3*	Is - Ki	-	-
																			Is - Ni	0.05	0.01
Kibei	6	9	*15*	2	3	*5*	7	3	*10*	11	9	*20*	3	4	*7*	1	2	*3*	Ki - Ni	0.01	n.t
Nisei	23	27	*50*	3	0	*3*	4	3	*7*	15	11	*26*	12	15	*27*	3	4	*7*	Is - No	0.001	0.001
																			Ki - No	0.001	0.001
Normal	23	28	*56*	2	2	*4*	0	0	*0*	4	5	*9*	18	20	*38*	8	5	*13*	Ni - No	-	0.001
Neur.	13	12	*25*	0	1	*1*	2	2	*4*	3	4	*7*	9	8	*17*	3	3	*6*	No - Ne	n.t.	-
																			No - Sc	n.t.	0.06
Schiz.	11	11	*22*	1	2	*3*	3	2	*5*	5	5	*10*	5	7	*12*	5	3	*8*	Ne - Sc	-	-

Groups	Means (and Standard Deviations) R (mean) M	F	T	T / IR M	F	T	Groups	Confidence Levels of Sig. Diff. (C.R.) R	T / IT
Issei	19.3	18.3	*18.8*	61.4*	39.8	*50.6*	Is - Ki	-	0.001
	(14.3)	(7.7)	*(11.0)*	(41.3)	(21.6)	*(34.7)*	Is - Ni	0.01	0.001
Kibei	17.5	18.8	*18.2*	41.0	34.3	*37.7*	Ki - Ni	0.5	-
	(16.6)	(16.2)	*(16.4)*	(39.2)	(24.4)	*(33.3)*			
Nisei	23.8	28.2	*26.0*	30.7	21.0	*25.8*	Is - No	0.001	0.001
	(13.6)	(18.8)	*(16.4)*	(23.6)	(17.6)	*(21.4)*	Ki - No	0.001	-
Normal	32.2	30.6	*30.9*	31.0	33.3	*32.4*	Ni - No	0.06	0.05
	(12.5)	(12.9)	*(12.7)*	(16.5)	(18.8)	*(15.2)*			
Neur.	30.5	28.2	*29.3*	38.3	33.0	*35.7*	No - Ne	-	-
	(29.1)	(23.1)	*(26.1)*	(13.1)	(12.2)	*(17.5)*	No - Sc	-	-
Schiz.	30.5	25.8	*28.2*	48.3	28.3	*38.3*	Ne - Sc	-	-
	(24.3)	(20.1)	*(22.2)*	(41.6)	(23.6)	*(32.6)*			

* Issei M vs. Issei F = 0.02.
R = responses.

often accompanied by verbalization of a sense of defeat when the individual could not give an overall integrative response to a complex card because it was "too difficult." When on a test of limits the examiner attempted to have individuals respond to some details, in numerous instances they would not do so, feeling that they had already failed in a task of integration. They would state again the most used words, "Ammari muzukashii" ("It's just too difficult"), with a shake of the head.

TABLE 4.4

Means and Standard Deviations
of F+ % (Good Form, as Measure of Ego Control)

Groups	Means (and Standard Deviations) F+ %			Groups	Confidence Levels of Sig. Diff. of Mean F+ %
	M	F	T		
Issei	72.3 (23.9)	63.9 (19.1)	*68.1 (21.2)*	Is - Ki	-
				Is - Ni	0.001
Kibei	71.8 (14.0)	71.5 (20.4)	*71.1 (17.5)*	Ki - Ni	0.05
Nisei	79.8 (18.5)	80.6 (13.5)	*80.2 (16.2)*	Is - No	0.001
				Ki - No	0.01
Normal	80.3 (9.1)	81.0 (10.4)	*80.7 (9.8)*	Ni - No	-
Neur.	63.8 (16.4)	76.8 (13.9)	*70.4 (16.1)*	No - Ne	0.01
				No - Sc	0.001
Schiz.	63.8 (19.9)	57.5 (24.9)	*60.7 (22.4)*	Ne - Sc	0.05

The generally high regard for accuracy in finding "good" responses (see table 4.4) that fit the general form of the inkblots failed some of the Japanese Americans at times. This failure seemed to be related to their intense sense of striving. There was then some tendency to produce "confabulatory" wholes, forcing a whole response from a large detail. Some produced vague abstract responses, others, poorly conceived anatomical responses in which the parts were ill defined at best. These various forms of (W) all served to confirm a high organizational drive and a strain to accomplish. The use of such an integrative approach in spite of personal limitations was related in many cases to relatively high rigidity scores (see chap. 6), personal constriction, and other inner malfunctions.

The prevalence of such excessive intellectual rigidity in a number of the Issei and Kibei groups was found to a lesser extent in the Nisei. Where rigidity appeared, it usually led to excessive associative blocking, suggesting a lack of liberation of intellectual potential. In some cases, however, it was related to an intense preoccupation with bodily functions, and inferentially with a considerably narrowed range of interest in objects outside the self. On the other hand, the American Normal group shows more tendency to exhibit caution and momentary blocking in associative functioning than did the Nisei group.

TABLE 4.5

Distribution of Cases According to Total Number of
Space Responses Per Record (Oppositional Trends)

Groups	Space Responses												Groups	Confidence Levels of Sig. Diff. by X^2	
	0			1-2			3-4			5+				$S = 0$	$S = 3+*$
	M	F	T	M	F	T	M	F	T	M	F	T			
Issei	17	11	*28*	7	13	*20*	1	1	*2*	0	0	*0*	Is - Ki	-	-
													Is - Ni	-	0.001
Kibei	8	9	*17*	4	5	*9*	3	1	*4*	0	0	*0*	Ki - Ni	-	0.05
Nisei	12	13	*25*	13	3	*16*	4	9	*13*	1	5	*6*	Is - No	0.01	0.01
													Ki - No	0.01	-
Normal†	8	10	*18*	14	15	*29*	5	3	*8*	3	2	*5*	Ni - No	-	-
Neur.	3	7	*10*	6	6	*12*	3	0	*3*	3	2	*5*	No - Ne	-	-
													No - Sc	-	-
Schiz.	3	4	*7*	7	9	*16*	5	0	*5*	0	2	*2*	Ne - Sc	-	-

* Nisei M vs. Nisei F = 0.05.

† A later breakdown of the American normal sample into occupational subgroups revealed a greater tendency in the American executive subgroup toward such imbalances than in other subgroups.

Rather than the severe and permanent blocking found in the Issei, the American Normal controls who blocked recovered and gave responses, whereas in many cases the Issei and Kibei totally rejected the stimulus material, producing more card rejections than were found in the American controls (see table 4.3).

Observing the relative use of the *white spaces* on the cards, (WS, DS) suggesting oppositional trends, I found that they were most prevalent in the Nisei women (see table 4.5). The psychotherapy material of extended treatment cases of three of the Nisei women seen by Charlotte Babcock (1962) supported the oppositional meaning of the space responses in Nisei women. A strong theme running through all three cases was more or less conscious opposition to the mother, which was demonstrated in various subtle ways. In none of these cases was continuing difficulty with authority or supervisory figures expressed through any direct opposition. Instead, opposition was manifested more indirectly in the way that assigned tasks were done. Rebelliousness was more prevalent against older women than against male

authorities. In all three cases, some break with the family occurred eventually, with each young woman determined to make
her own way despite considerable internal turmoil and strong
guilt feelings over neglecting an internalized obligation to her
family.

Space responses were less common in the Nisei men and were
quite sparse in the Issei and Kibei groups. The Issei and Kibei
handled the test situation compliantly, conforming as best they
could to the wishes of the "authority" as represented by a scholar
doing research testing. Excessive blocking in some cases, however, can be related to a rigid negativism that permits no overt
external expression, but instead constricts an individual to a
position of total inactivity. That such self-paralysis could be a
mark of pervasive unconscious negativism was borne out in
the psychotherapy of one Nisei male among the cases seen by
Babcock.

If one sees rigidity and blocking as related to unconscious negativism, as seems true in some Rorschachs taken from delinquent
subjects, the inference is that such negativism is unacceptable to
the ego in contrast to the more conscious type of negativism suggested by (WS, DS) responses. The space response, an attitude
very close to consciousness, suggests that there is awareness of
the behavioral manifestations of resistance or contrariness.

Vicissitudes in the Use of Emotional Controls

The more acculturated Nisei were notably freer than the immigrant Issei in the overall use of the blot determinants: form (F),
movement (M), color (FC, CF, C), texture (FT, TF, T), shading
(FY, YF, Y), achromatic color, (FC', C'F), and vista (FV). The
Nisei scores, in more respects, tended to resemble the representative sample of American Normals. However, as I shall note,
despite their shift from the generally rigid defensive patterning
more characteristic for the Issei, the Nisei still manifested certain
features characteristic for the Japanese American records generally. The differences between the generations, since they invariably were in the direction of American norms, suggested an
acculturation in prevailing patterns of emotional control (De Vos
1954:221 ff.).

TABLE 4.6

Means and Standard Deviations of F% (Beck)*
(Constrictive Control)

Groups	Means (and Standard Deviations) F% (Beck)			Groups	Confidence Levels of Sig. Diff. of Mean F% (Beck)
	M	F	T		
Issei	64.3 (18.2)	71.3 (12.8)	*67.8 (16.1)*	Is - Ki	-
				Is - Ni	0.001
Kibei	60.2 (19.1)	69.5 (22.1)	*64.8 (21.1)*	Ki - Ni	-
Nisei	60.1 (19.5)	55.8 (15.5)	*57.9 (17.5)*	Is - No	-
				Ki - No	-
Normal	71.0 (14.8)	71.5 (13.6)	*71.3 (14.3)*	Ni - No	0.001
Neur.	71.2 (13.5)	78.2 (12.6)	*74.7 (13.1)*	No - Ne	-
				No - Sc	-
Schiz.	71.5 (14.1)	73.2 (15.7)	*72.3 (14.9)*	Ne - Sc	-

* Beck's F%, or "Lambda Index," includes FM, animal movement, and m, inanimate movement, which are not considered separately in Beck's scoring system.

The more culturally marginal Kibei, in their interviews, seemed to have a confused identity, upset by the formative years they had spent in Japan. On the Rorschach they presented a very mixed picture that averaged out intermediate to the Issei and Nisei.

Differences by sex revealed a consistent pattern in which the Nisei women showed the greatest distance from the Issei norms on all determinants. The Issei women were consistently the group least like the American Normal sample. The Japanese American women differed much more radically from their parents than did the men.

The Beck Normal sample and the Japanese American groups both differed in certain characteristics from the optimal norms used as standards in Rorschach analysis. The Beck Normals showed a relatively high degree of overall emotional constriction, with a mean percentage of pure form responses without enlivenment (F%) that was well above the level generally considered indicative of constriction (see table 4.6).

However, the Issei and, to a lesser extent, the Kibei, in manifesting a certain degree of overall constriction, did so with a relative distribution of determinants radically different from that found in the American Normals. The Nisei men showed their

TABLE 4.7

Distribution of Cases, Means, and Standard Deviations in
Movement Responses

Distribution of Cases

Groups	M												M- (poor form)						M in Dd (in small details)					
	0			1			2-4			5-			0			1			0-1			2-		
	M	F	T	M	F	T	M	F	T	M	F	T	M	F	T	M	F	T	M	F	T	M	F	T
Issei	6	11	17	7	8	15	9	5	14	3	1	4	25	23	48	0	2	2	25	23	48	0	2	2
Kibei	4	5	9	4	2	6	5	5	10	2	3	5	11	12	23	4	3	7	12	14	26	3	1	4
Nisei	7	1	8	4	2	6	12	19	31	7	8	15	25	22	47	5	8	13	27	27	54	3	3	6
Norm.	5	4	9	4	3	7	10	17	27	11	6	17	24	23	47	6	7	13	27	27	54	3	3	6
Neur.	6	6	12	2	3	5	3	5	8	4	1	5	11	13	24	4	2	6	12	15	27	3	0	3
Schiz.	5	7	12	1	2	3	7	4	11	2	2	4	6	10	16	9	5	14	12	14	26	3	1	4

Groups	Means (and Standard Deviations) of M			Groups	Confidence Levels of Sig. Diff. Chi Square		
	M	F	Total		M	M-	M in Dd
Issei	2.0 (1.9)	1.2 (1.6)	1.6 (1.8)	Is - Ki	-	-	-
				Is - Ni	0.001	0.05	-
Kibei	2.1 (2.5)	2.5 (2.9)	2.3 (2.7)	Ki - Ni	0.05	-	-
Nisei	3.1 (3.1)	4.0 (3.2)	3.9 (3.1)	Is - No	0.001	0.05	-
				Ki - No	0.10	-	-
Normal	3.9 (3.7)	3.0 (2.6)	3.4 (3.0)	Ni - No	-	-	-
Neur.	3.7 (5.2)	1.4 (1.5)	2.6 (4.0)	No - Ne	0.05	-	-
				No - Sc	0.05	0.05	-
Schiz.	2.5 (3.1)	2.9 (5.1)	2.7 (4.2)	Ne - Sc	-	0.05	-

a: Nisei M vs. Nisei F = 0.05.
b: Nisei M vs. Normal M = 0.10.

greatest constriction in their lower number of movement responses (table 4.7). The Kibei men also tended to use fewer movement than color responses. The Issei women were lowest in seeing human movement.

The American Normals, closer to expectations of maturity in the use of movement responses came nowhere near the norms of mature outer control usually considered desirable as measured by their color responses (De Vos 1954:202). The Normals as well as the Neurotics showed less than optimal use of the color variable, but with little card rejection or diminution of responses to colored cards (tables 4.8 and 4.9). Some Issei and Kibei, and, to a much lesser extent, Nisei showed difficulties in mature affective responsiveness by fewer responses or by actual rejection of some of the colored cards.

TABLE 4.8

Proportionate Distribution of Color Responses
According to Form Quality

Groups	Total color responses	Mean % of total color responses				Total Percentages
		FC	CF	FC-, CF-	C, Cn	
Issei	137	18	37	24	21	100
Kibei	81	35	34	16	15	100
Nisei	228	29	34	19	18	100
Norm.	197	32	28	21	19	100
Neur.	83	29	28	29	14	100
Schiz.	97	14	19	34	33	100

TABLE 4.9

Distribution of Card Rejections in the Various Groups

Groups	Cards										Rejection						Grand Total
											Black Cards			Colored Cards			
	I	II	III	IV	V	VI	VII	VIII	IX	X	M	F	T	M	F	T	
Issei	0	3	6	6	2	5	9	0	14	6	17	5	22	15	14	29	51
Kibei	0	1	4	6	2	4	8	2	8	6	12	8	20	16	5	21	41
Nisei	1	3	0	1	1	3	0	2	4	4	4	2	6	9	4	13	19
Total	1	7	10	13	5	12	17	4	26	16	33	15	48	40	23	63	111
Norm.	0	0	0	0	0	1	0	0	3	0	1	0	1	1	2	3	4
Neur.	0	2	1	2	1	2	2	0	3	1	3	4	7	3	4	7	14
Schiz.	0	1	2	3	2	4	3	0	1	3	7	5	12	3	4	7	19
Total	0	3	3	5	3	7	5	0	7	4	11	9	20	7	10	17	37

Only 24 of 60 Normals approximated a maturely adjustive affective balance, and of these, two-thirds were markedly constricted. The Japanese American groups showed an even more notable lack of mature affective balance in their records. A number of Issei records tended to show either a severe constriction, being totally without color, or a single, egocentric color response. In a few of the more open Japanese-American records there was a predominance of poorly controlled color responses (see tables 4.10 and 4.11).

While the Nisei showed almost the same proportion of individuals with predominant egocentric affect as did the Issei (table 4.10), as a group they were relatively freer of constrictive trends

TABLE 4.10

Distribution of Cases in Relative Prevalence
of FC Responses as Measure of Affective Maturity

Groups	FC Responses 0			1			2			Groups	Confidence Levels of Sig. Diff. by X^{2*}
	M	F	T	M	F	T	M	F	T		
Issei	16	15	*31*	7	8	*15*	2	2	*4*	Is - Ki	-
										Is - Ni	-
Kibei	7	8	*15*	6	2	*8*	2	6	*8*	Ki - Ni	-
Nisei	17	10	*27*	5	14	*19*	8	9	*17*	Is - No	0.01
										Ki - No	-
Norm.	11	10	*21*	12	11	*23*	7	9	*16*	Ni - No	-
Neur.	6	9	*15*	4	4	*8*	5	2	*7*	No - Ne	-
										No - Sc	-
Schiz.	10	11	*21*	4	3	*7*	1	1	*2*	Ne - Sc	0.05

* Nisei M vs. Nisei F = 0.05.

TABLE 4.11

Distribution of Cases According to Form Dominance in Color -
Determined Responses and According to Relative Constriction*

	FC > FC-, CF, C			FC < FC-, CF, C		Confidence Levels of Sig. Diff. by X^2, FC-, Dominant: FC, CF, C Dominant	
	FC = 2	FC = 1	C = 0	FC-, CF, C = 1	FC-, CF, C = 2		
	Relatively Open Records	Constricted Records			Relatively Open Records		
Issei	1	6	7	12	24	Is - Ki	0.05
						Is - Ni	-
Kibei	6	5	3	3	13	Ki - Ni	-
Nisei	8	5	6	8	33	Is - No	0.001
						Ki - No	-
Norm.	8	16	7	4	25	Ni - No	0.05
Neur.	5	3	7	3	12	No - Ne	-
						No - Sc	0.001
Schiz.	0	2	4	7	17	Ne - Sc	0.05

* These results point up not only the value but also the necessity of working with ideal concepts in the field of maturity and adjustment as well as modalities. Such concepts are pertinent to many tests dealing with personality. One of the difficulties encountered in standardizing tests of personality is the implicit assumption that conformity to a population norm is a basis for assessing personality adjustment *per se*.

than were either the Issei or the American Normal sample. These results suggest that in the process of acculturation the Nisei tended to maintain the underlying egocentric propensities found in many Issei, even though, relatively speaking, they did not use constriction as a major mode of control. They show a relatively greater basic potential for affective lability than do the sample of American Normals. Inferentially, this potential for quick responsiveness was inhibited by ego controls that countered affective display. The relatively large number of shading responses (TY) in many of the records were an evident balance controlling labile propensities (see tables 4.12, 4.13, and 4.14).

In the Issei and Kibei, a large proportion of cases scored high on Fisher's Rigidity Scale (Fisher 1950). The less rigid Nisei had more recourse to some form of passive inactivity, as suggested by their higher balance of shading responses measured against color responses (TY > C). They also showed more recourse to introversive controls as represented by the number of records in which movement responses predominant over color responses (M > sum C) (see table 4.15).

Of all the groups considered, American and Japanese, the Nisei showed the greatest use of shading. Without the defensive rigidity so prevalent among Issei and Kibei, it can be inferred that

TABLE 4.12

Distribution of Cases According to Relative Presence of Texture and Shading Responses

T-Y Responses

Groups	0			1-4			5			Groups	Confidence Levels of Sig. Diff. by X^2*
	M	F	T	M	F	T	M	F	T		
Issei	7	7	*14*	14	18	*32*	4	0	*4*	Is - Ki	-
										Is - Ni	0.001
Kibei	4	7	*11*	9	7	*16*	2	1	*3*	Ki - Ni	0.001
Nisei	2	1	*3*	24	18	*42*	4	11	*15**	Is - No	-
										Ki - No	-
Norm.	8	10	*18*	17	16	*33*	5	4	9	Ni - No	0.001
Neur.	3	2	5	17	11	*28*	5	2	7	No - Ne	-
										No - Sc	0.10
Schiz.	8	8	*16*	6	5	*11*	1	2	3	Ne - Sc	0.01

* Nisei M vs. Nisei F = 0.05.

TABLE 4.13

Distribution of Cases of Possible Defenses Against Egocentric Affect

Groups		Egocentric without Constriction					Groups	Confidence Levels of Sig. Diff. by X^2			
		Total No.*	Rigidity >40	TY>C	M>C	Others		Rig. 40	TY >C	M>C	Other
Issei	36	12	24	11	5	4	7	Is - Ki	-	-	-	-
								Is - Ni	0.05	0.05	-	-
Kibei	16	3	13	7	4	2	1	Ki - Ni	n.t.	-	-	-
Nisei	41	8	33	6	16	11	9	Is - No	0.01	-	-	-
								Ki - No	n.t.	-	-	-
Norm.	29	4	25	3	5	5	13	Ni - No	-	0.04	-	-
Neur.	15	3	12	2	6	3	2	No - Ne	-	-	-	-
								No - Sc	n.t.	-	-	-
Schiz.	24	7	17	6	2	4	5	Ne - Sc	-	-	-	-

* Each record can show more than one type of defense.

TABLE 4.14

Distribution of Cases on Ratio of Shading to Color Responses

TY:C Ratio of Shading to Color

Groups	TY>C			TY<C			C = TY = 0			Groups	Confidence Levels of Sig. Diff. of X^2
	M	F	T	M	F	T	M	F	T		
Issei	12	10	*22*	13	14	*27*	0	1	*1*	Is - Ki	-
										Is - Ni	-
Kibei	7	4	*11*	7	11	*18*	0	1	*1*	Ki - Ni	-
Nisei	16	16	*32*	14	14	*28*	0	0	*0*	Is - No	-
										Ki - No	-
Norm.	11	10	*21*	15	19	*34*	4	1	*5*	Ni - No	0.10
Neur.	5	9	*14*	9	5	*14*	1	1	*2*	No - Ne	-
										No - Sc	-
Schiz.	3	3	*6*	10	11	*21*	2	1	*3*	Ne - Sc	0.05

they experienced a greater tendency to feel anxiety directly. While the prevalence of shading responses in the Nisei suggests inactivity as a characteristic defense, the well-controlled nature of the responses in which shading was used as a determinant also suggests more tact and circumspection than was found in the

TABLE 4.15

Distribution of Introversive and Extratensive Balances
in Japanese American and American Groups

		M/ΣC Ratio						
Groups	M/ΣC=0	Introversive M>ΣC (M=1-4)	(M=5+)	Ambi-equal M=ΣC	Extratensive M<ΣC C=(.5-4.5)	(5+)	Groups	Confidence Levels of Sig. Diff. of X^2 (M>C, M<C)
Issei	1	12	3	5	17	12	Is - Ki	-
							Is - Ni	-
Kibei	3	7	4	1	11	4	Ki - Ni	-
Nisei	2	16	11	2	11	15	Is - No	0.05
							Ki - No	-
Norm.	3	17	13	5	12	10	Ni - No	-
Neur.	4	6	4	1	12	3	No - Ne	-
							No - Sc	-
Schiz	2	8	4	1	8	7	Ne - Sc	*

ΣC = the sum of all the color responses.

American Normal group. It is interesting that the statistical differences in shading found between Normals and Nisei were due specifically to the those records of Nisei whose emotional balance tended in an egocentric direction. These were the records of emotionally open individuals who used inactivity or, in a positive sense, circumspection to hold back what might have become displays of less controlled affect. There was no difference in the use of shading between Normals and Nisei in the other records.

The results with the vista determinant (FV) were difficult to interpret (see discussion in De Vos 1954:213). This determinant was significantly infrequent in all Japanese American groups excepting some Nisei women who, as with many other variables, showed the greatest overall similarity to the American Normal group.

The differential results for the Issei, Kibei, and Nisei in regard to the use of Movement (M) as a determinant confirm the general impressions suggested by the other results. The Issei, most markedly Issei women, showed severe blocking or, it may be inferred, suppression of impulses and stifling of the more creative aspects of personality (see table 4.7). The differences between the generations were most marked in the women in regard to this variable. The Kibei women, the most highly varied in respect to (M), had a mean intermediate to the Issei and Nisei women. Among the Nisei men there were enough individuals with serious constriction so that their bimodal distribution gave them an average not significantly higher than that of the Issei men. On the other hand, their mean production of movement responses was not low enough to differentiate them significantly from the American Normal men.

The Nisei women, in contrast to the men, showed a more frequent use of movement responses, matching that found in the American Normal group. The Nisei, especially the women, showed a tendency to express their tensions, attitudes, and even autistic concerns more freely in the movement symbolism than did the Issei. These tendencies were part of a general picture of greater freedom of expression in Nisei than in Issei.

In the Nisei there were generally active attitudes expressed in an abundance of movement responses that extended to or depicted the use of musculature (table 4.16). Such responses by the Nisei showed a generally more active orientation than was found in the American Normals. The active-passive balance in the responses of the Normal group was intermediate to that found in Issei as compared with Nisei. While the Issei movement responses were somewhat more passive in their postures than were the Normals group, the differences did not reach significance. The differences between Nisei and Issei however, were highly significant, suggesting that the Nisei were assuming a more "active" attitudinal stance than the older Issei.

The Introversive-extratensive orientation is of major interest in Rorschach interpretation as an indication of overall personality tendencies to be turned inward toward the self or to be outward-oriented, concerned with the outer social world. The records of the Issei were extratensive to a degree not found in the other groups (see table 4.15). While the results suggest a greater prevalence of an outward orientation in Japanese Americans generally, they were not conclusively so as measured by statistical comparisons. Individuals with introversive trends were in evidence both among the Issei and Nisei. However, the total lack of movement

TABLE 4.16

Distribution of Active and Passive Movement Responses
in Japanese American and American Groups*

Groups	Active Responses									Passive Responses								
	0			1-2			3+			0			1-2			3+		
	M	F	T	M	F	T	M	F	T	M	F	T	M	F	T	M	F	T
Issei	7	10	*17*	11	9	*20*	7	6	*13*	5	7	*12*	6	13	*19*	14	5	*19*
Kibei	3	7	*10*	6	5	*11*	6	3	*9*	5	4	*9*	7	5	*12*	3	6	*9*
Nisei	4	2	*6*	10	6	*16*	16	22	*38*	8	2	*10*	10	11	*21*	12	17	*29*
Norm.	3	8	*11*	9	11	*20*	18	11	*29*	8	2	*10*	5	13	*18*	17	15	*32*
Neur.	4	7	*11*	6	7	*13*	5	1	*6*	3	5	*8*	4	8	*12*	8	2	*10*
Schiz.	7	6	*13*	5	7	*12*	3	2	*5*	2	6	*8*	5	6	*11*	8	3	*11*

	Ratio of Active to Passive Responses												Confidence Levels of Sig.	
Groups	3a:1p			a>p			a<p			a+p=0			Groups	Diff. by X^2 (a>p, a<p)
	M	F	T	M	F	T	M	F	T	M	F	T		
Issei	0	1	*1*	9	10	*19*	13	9	*22*	3	5	*8*	Is - Ki	-
													Is - Ni	0.001
Kibei	3	0	*3*	6	6	*12*	4	6	*10*	2	3	*5*	Ki - Ni	-
Nisei	7	9	*16*	14	11	*25*	6	10	*16*	3	0	*3*	Is - No	-
													Ki - No	-
Norm.	4	5	*9*	15	11	*26*	9	14	*23*	2	0	*2*	Ni - No	-
Neur.	0	0	*0*	4	4	*8*	9	6	*15*	2	5	*7*	No - Ne	0.01
													No - Sc	0.03
Schiz.	0	1	*1*	3	6	*9*	10	5	*15*	2	3	*5*	Ne - Sc	-

* This table includes the distribution of individuals according to the number of active and passive responses in each record. It then demonstrates the distribution of records according to whether the ratio between responses is predominantly active or passive.

The American groups were rescored so that any response showing any animation was judged arbitrarily either predominantly active or passive in nature. The general criteria for active or passive orientation were:

Active: Use of extensor muscles - including figures seen as walking, pulling, lifting, running, climbing, fighting, and struggling, as well as explosions, birds flying, and the like.

Passive: Figures seen as looking, observing, bent over, bowing, lying down, kissing, facing each other. This same criteria was also applied to animals and inanimate objects - hanging, crushed, dead, drooping, falling.

responses in many of the Issei (table 4.16) indicated that constriction of inner life was even more characteristic of them than was constriction of affective responsiveness.

The use of the more immature animal movement responses (FM) showed no proportionate difference between the generations (table 4.17). The inanimate movement responses (Fm, mF) were much more in evidence in the Nisei than in the Issei or Kibei (table 4.18). These results are in line with the results demonstrating lesser constriction in the Nisei group.

The Japanese

TABLE 4.17

Distribution of Cases in Japanese American Groups on
Ratio of Human Movement to Animal Movement*

M/FM

Groups	M>FM			M≤FM			M/FM=0		
	M	F	T	M	F	T	M	F	T
Issei	13	12	25	9	7	16	3	6	9
Kibei	8	9	17	5	3	8	2	3	5
Nisei	19	23	42	7	7	14	4	0	4

* No significant differences between groups.

It is my contention that the use of M is related directly to the use of such variables as Y and T in the Nisei, thus showing a handling of problems in a more differentiated manner rather than by total constriction of personality. The repressive defenses in individuals using M are more apt to be used in localized areas than in the blanket fashion used by highly constricted individuals.

TABLE 4.18

Distribution of Animal Movement and Inanimate Movement
Responses in Japanese American Groups

Groups	FM												Fm, m												Groups	Confidence Levels of Sig. Diff. by X^2	
	0			1-2			3-4			5+			0			1			2			3				FM (0:1+)	Fm, m (0:1+)
	M	F	T	M	F	T	M	F	T	M	F	T	M	F	T	M	F	T	M	F	T	M	F	T			
Issei	5	14	19	13	8	21	5	2	7	2	1	3	18	21	39	4	3	7	2	0	2	1	1	2	Is - Ki	-	-
Kibei	7	6	13	4	7	11	3	1	4	2	1	3	10	13	23	5	2	7	0	0	0	0	0	0	Is - Ni	-	0.01
Nisei	9	4	13	8	10	18	6	15	21	7	1	8	16	16	32	6	7	13	5	3	8	3	4	7	Ki - Ni	0.06	0.05

The attitudes expressed in the movement responses further confirm the results mentioned previously in regard to intellectual aspects of personality. As reported above there is evidence of a strong tendency in both Issei and Nisei toward a striving for achievement that often outstrips the amount of constructive imaginative potential available to implement this striving. In the Issei the relative constriction in M as well as the resigned, passive nature of some responses (Mp) is seemingly predictive of a lack of realization of many of their strivings. In contrast, the active attitudes in Nisei movement responses (Ma) give added weight to the evidence of their desire to externalize their strivings into actual accomplishment.

Continuity and Change in Content Symbolism

As we shall demonstrate, the content symbolism revealed two major findings in respect to the acculturation of Japanese Americans. First, it helped us understand the balance in personality which allows for an adaptive social responsiveness despite intrapsychic tensions, and second, it suggested the personal cost paid by some who were facing the social tensions of their minority status in American society, a cost that became more evident when we later compared their records with the normative samples of Japanese in Japan.

Hostile Symbolism

A Comparison of Groups on the Index of Hostile Affect. The mean indices of Hostile content do not show significant differences between the groups (table 4.19). There is, however, a trend toward differences according to sex. Men in the Issei and Kibei groups, and even more so, men in the American Neurotic and Schizophrenic groups, score higher on Hostile affect than do women. The later normative Japanese sample gathered in 1954 and scored by Murakami (Muramatsu et al. 1960:223, 226, 230) showed a somewhat lower level of hostility in two of the villages, but the overall percentages were strikingly similar to our American and Japanese normative samples (see table 4.20).

Group Differences in the Number of Individuals Using Subcategories of Hostile Affect. Neither the "oral aggressive" (Hor) nor the "distorted" percepts with parts missing (Hhad) responses showed any noteworthy differences between American and Japanese groups (table 4.19). The direct hostility (HH) responses were significantly prevalent in the Issei compared with either the Nisei or American Normal groups (see app. A).

The sadomasochistic (Hsm) responses were significantly more prevalent in all the Japanese groups, with a chi-square between the American Normal and each of the Japanese Americans groups significant beyond the 1% confidence level. This was the

TABLE 4.19

Hostile Affect

(a) Means (and Standard Deviations) of Index of Hostile Affect

Groups	N	Means* (and Standard Deviations)		
		M	F	T
Issei	50	12.2 (9.9)	8.2 (8.1)	10.2 (9.3)
Kibei	30	13.1 (9.2)	9.7 (11.9)	11.4 (10.7)
Nisei	60	10.7 (10.7)	11.5 (8.3)	11.1 (9.6)
Normal	60	9.2 (6.5)	9.5 (7.5)	9.4 (7.1)
Neur.	30	15.1 (12.1)	9.5 (5.6)	11.6 (6.9)
Schiz.	30	10.4 (8.3)	8.1 (6.9)	8.3 (7.7)

* No significant differences of means between groups.

(b) Distribution of Cases Showing Responses in Various Subcategories of Hostile Affect

Groups	Hor			Hdpr			HH			Hh			Hha			HHat			Hsm			Hhad		
	M	F	T	M	F	T	M	F	T	M	F	T	M	F	T	M	F	T	M	F	T	M	F	T
Issei	6	4	10	8	3	11	3	2	5	5	5	10	8	8	16	4	0	4	9	7	16	1	2	3
Kibei	1	2	3	2	3	5	3	2	5	3	2	5	3	2	5	4	0	4	5	6	11	2	1	3
Nisei	7	7	14	9	13	22	7	9	16	4	12	16	5	10	15	5	5	10	12	6	18	2	4	6
Norm.	4	9	13	8	14	22	7	8	15	7	12	19	16	10	26	10	1	11	2	4	6	3	2	5
Neur.	4	6	10	6	6	12	6	4	10	5	3	8	12	6	18	5	2	7	4	1	5	2	3	5
Schiz.	5	2	7	4	1	5	3	0	3	7	6	13	9	3	12	6	1	7	3	2	5	1	2	3

Confidence Levels of Significant Differences by X^2 †

	Hor	Hdpr	HH	Hh	Hha	HHat	Hsm	Hhad
Is - Ki	-	-	-	-	-	-	-	-
Is - Ni	-	-	0.05	-	-	-	-	-
Ki - Ni	-	0.05	-	-	-	-	-	-
Is - No	-	-	0.05	-	-	-	0.01	-
Ki - No	-	-	-	-	0.001	-	0.01	-
Ni - No	-	-	-	-	0.05	-	0.01	-
No - Ne	-	-	-	-	-	-	-	-
No - Sc	-	-	-	-	-	-	-	-
Ne - Sc	-	-	-	-	-	-	-	-

† Issei F - Nisei F (Hor=0.05).
  Issei F - Normal F (Hdpr=0.05).
  Nisei M - Nisei F (Hh=0.05).
  Nisei M - Normal M (Hha=0.01).
  Normal M - Normal F (Hhat=0.01).

TABLE 4.20

Japanese Rural and Urban Rorschach Records
Scored for Major Affective Categories*

Means (and Standard Deviations)

	Rural			Urban	
Location	Saku (Fishing)	Nagura (Mtn.)	Niike (Farm)	Nagoya	Okayama
N	88	71	60	381	124
Hostile	7.40 (7.22)	10.13 (8.51)	7.61 (7.50)	9.75 (7.74)	9.90 (7.58)
Anxious	22.52 (14.10)	22.90 (17.65)	26.85 (20.67)	23.04 (15.62)	21.07 (12.66)
Bod. Preocc.	6.00 (8.43)	5.88 (8.43)	5.18 (5.54)	7.01 (8.48)	5.59 (6.21)
Tot. Unpleas.	37.08 (17.73)	38.07 (18.54)	37.27 (22.57)	38.29 (15.85)	35.15 (13.99)
Dependent	6.14 (5.51)	6.04 (5.34)	5.99 (5.81)	6.17 (5.14)	5.87 (4.60)
Positive	11.11 (9.14)	11.21 (9.16)	10.99 (8.24)	17.04 (11.67)	17.81 (11.17)
Miscellan.	2.71 (1.72)	2.62 (1.74)	2.81 (2.16)	2.68 (2.03)	2.65 (2.30)
Neutral	48.01 (17.73)	41.98 (17.70)	46.73 (19.32)	39.32 (15.45)	41.60 (15.73)

* Adapted from Muramatsu et al. 1960: 226, 230.

most clear-cut trend of any subcategory in the Hostile category. The individual responses given by the Japanese Americans in this category seem to have had predominantly anatomical connotations, e.g., crushed lungs, dissections, and wounds. The prevalence of such responses seems related to my observation of a general prevalence of sadomasochistic orientation turned toward the body.

The hostile anxious (IIha) responses were used by a lesser number of Nisei men than women. In the American Normal group the trend was for more men than women to show such responses. My impression from inspecting the individual records was that sadomasochistic (Hsm) or anatomical responses (Bb, Bf, etc.), given by more Issei and Nisei men than women, may be alternatives to the hostile anxious responses found to be more prevalent in the American Normal men. Hha responses are often very indirect symbols suggestive of what is termed "castration anxiety," appearing in such forms as pincers, tweezers, and the claw of a crab, whereas the Hsm responses show actual "crushing" or violation of tissue by tearing, ripping, cutting open, and so on.

Most of the other differences noted in the use of the subcategories were due to differential distribution of responses between the sexes. Larger samples of records would be necessary to estab-

lish in a definitive fashion the significance of the various sex differences noted as trends in "hostile" material. The results, nevertheless, are highly suggestive of the fact that such differences
exist. The hostile anxious tension (Hhat) responses, such as explosions or jet planes, appeared almost exclusively in men, with
the exception of the Nisei group, where they appeared in an equal
number of women. More Nisei and American Normal women
used indirect hostile (Hh) responses, although the trend reached
significance only in the Nisei women.

Hostile depreciatory (Hdpr) responses ("clowns," "silly old
men," etc.) were more prevalent in both Nisei and American
Normal women than in the men, although not to a significant
extent. In the Issei the opposite was the case, with women giving
very few such responses. Only 3 out of 25 Issei women showed
depreciatory responses in comparison to nearly half the Nisei and
the Normal women. This finding suggests a loosening of patterns
of social respect and a greater tendency toward derogation in
social relationships in American women, and a greater tension
about attitudes of social respect.

Comparison of Groups on the Index of
Anxious Affect

Although the means of each of the Japanese American groups
were higher than that of the American Normal group on anxious
affect, the Kibei was the only group in which the difference became significant (see table 4.21). The Neurotic and Schizophrenic
groups both showed means that were significantly higher than
that of the American Normal group. The Issei women showed a
considerably lower anxiety mean than the Issei men (this difference was due to their tendency to give more anatomical material
than of anxiety responses; see below), but due to the large standard deviations, differences between the means were not significant.

The overall levels of anxiety in the Nagoya normative samples
(table 4.20 above) appeared to be significantly higher than in the
American and Japanese American normative groups. Some of
this difference was due to their proneness toward card rejection.

The Japanese and American groups I tested did not show sig-

TABLE 4.21

Anxious Affect

(a) Means and Standard Deviations of Index of Anxious Affect

Groups	Means (and Standard Deviations)			Groups	Confidence Levels of Sig. Diff. of Means
	M	F	T		
Issei	21.1 (17.4)	14.4 (14.2)	*17.7*	*(16.3)*	Is - Ki	-
					Is - Ni	-
Kibei	25.5 (15.3)	20.8 (19.3)	*23.1*	*(17.6)*	Ki - Ni	-
Nisei	16.4 (10.3)	17.5 (10.8)	*17.0*	*(10.6)*	Is - No	0.07
					Ki - No	0.001
Norm.	14.9 (8.2)	12.7 (7.0)	*13.8*	*(7.6)*	Ni - No	0.07
Neur.	22.7 (12.3)	22.5 (11.2)	*22.6*	*(11.6)*	No - Ne	0.001
					No - Sc	0.001
Schiz.	24.3 (14.5)	22.6 (13.6)	*23.7*	*(14.1)*	Ne - Sc	-

(b) Distribution of Cases Showing Responses in Various Subcategories of Anxious Affect

Groups	Adis	Ath	Aa	Afc	Aev	Arej	Agl	Abal	Acon	Adeh	Asex	Afant
Issei 50	0	3	25	5	10	23	1	2	2	14	0	3
Kibei 30	3	8	22	2	2	15	1	1	0	3	2	1
Nisei 60	6	24	46	7	5	11	6	5	4	2	1	9
Norm. 60	4	22	56	8	14	4	3	0	1	6	2	3
Neur. 30	9	11	28	5	9	7	2	5	2	2	2	8
Schiz. 30	5	7	22	3	11	7	2	2	0	8	2	9

Confidence Levels of Significant Differences by X^2

	Adis	Ath	Aa	Afc	Aev	Arej	Agl	Abal	Acon	Adeh	Asex	Afant
Is - Ki	-	n.t.*	0.05	-	-	-	-	-	-	0.05	-	-
Is - Ni	-	0.001	0.01	-	-	0.001	-	-	-	0.001	-	-
Ki - Ni	-	-	-	-	-	0.001	-	-	-	-	-	n.t.
Is - No	-	0.001	0.001	-	-	0.001	-	-	-	0.05	-	-
Ki - No	-	-	n.t.	-	0.05	0.001	-	-	-	-	-	-
Ni - No	-	-	0.01	-	0.05	0.05	-	-	-	-	-	-
No - Ne	n.t.	-	-	-	-	n.t.	-	n.t.	-	-	-	n.t.
No - Sc	-	-	n.t.	-	-	n.t.	-	-	-	n.t.	-	n.t.
Ne - Sc	-	-	-	-	-	-	-	-	-	-	-	-

* n.t. = not testable.

nificant differences in six of my subcategories (Adis, Aobs, Agl, Abal, Acnph, and Asex; see table 4.21). Rejection (Arej) was significantly prevalent as a mode of expressing anxiety in all three Japanese groups in comparison with the American Normals. The Issei and Kibei showed significantly more rejection than the Nisei. The Issei showed significantly less direct anxiety through perceiving threatening figures (Athr) than did the Nisei. The Kibei were intermediate, with more similarity to the Nisei than the Issei in this regard. Neither American-born group, the Nisei or Kibei, differed significantly from the American Normals.

The results with the indirect anxiety responses (Aa), (which I later separated into several subcategories, see appendix A) showed the Issei with proportionately fewer individuals giving such responses than either the Kibei and Nisei, who in turn had fewer individuals show these responses than the American Normal group. There was a trend for the American Normal men to use evasive responses (Aev), a trend that led to a difference at the 5% level between the Normals, the Kibei and Nisei.

The Issei showed a significant trend toward dehumanizing the human form (Adeh) in comparison with the Nisei and Kibei as well as the American Normal group. The Nisei, in turn, showed a trend approaching significance for the use of responses with forced combinations of animal, human, or inanimate objects (Afant).

In sum, there was an overall pattern of difference between Issei and American Normals in respect to symbolic expressions of anxiety. Anxiety was handled by the Issei much more through overall blocking than through indirect symbolic expression. They showed significantly more individuals with total rejection of cards and the binding up of affect in anatomical responses (see below). The higher statistical means for anxiety responses in the Kibei and Issei group were due principally to the inclusion of card rejection as an indication of anxiety. This higher anxiety score was found also in the normative results in Japan.

The Nisei group showed an overall similarity to the American Normal group in the distribution of anxiety responses with one exception. As shown in the following section, Anatomy tends to predominate in the Nisei in contrast to the type of responses included in the other indirect anxiety categories found more often in the American Normal group. In this respect the Nisei still remain similar to the Issei.

Comparison of Groups on the Index of Body Preoccupation

Body preoccupation responses were the most notable differentiators between the Japanese American groups and the American Normal group (table 4.22). The Nisei had a total mean percentage of bodily oriented responses as high as that of the Neurotic group, and the Issei had an even higher mean which almost approximated that of the American Schizophrenic group. The Kibei mean was intermediate between those of the Issei and Nisei. (The social implications of these results are discussed more fully in chap. 8.)

In the American Normal and Nisei groups the characteristic pattern was for men to have significantly higher percentages of bodily oriented responses than the women. This trend was also found in Kibei and in the Neurotic samples, but not to a significant degree. In both the Issei and Schizophrenic groups the trend was reversed, the women producing more anatomy responses, but again the difference was not significant.

In the Japanese American groups differences between the generations on body preoccupation responses appeared in the women tested. Differences between the Issei and Nisei men were not significant. These findings reinforced other trends in which the records of women were farther removed from the patterns evident in the Issei, whereas again the Issei and Nisei men showed less difference from one another.

In comparing the maladjusted and normative Americans, we found greater differences among the groups in the women than in the men. This was due to the fact that Normal and Neurotic men revealed a higher body preoccupation score, and the Schizophrenic men a lower score than did the women in their groups.

In the later results obtained in Japan in 1953–1954, the normative samples revealed an overall level of body preoccupation which was lower than that of the Japanese-American samples. Sadomasochistic material, such as the "crushed" anatomical responses I found in the Japanese-American content, did not

TABLE 4.22

Body Preoccupation

(a) Means and Standard Deviations of Index of Body Preoccupation

Groups	Means (and Standard Deviations)			Groups	Confidence Levels of Sig. Diff. of Mean
	M	F	T		
Issei	14.8 (24.1)	23.8 (31.2)	*19.3 (27.6)*	Is - Ki	-
				Is - Ni	0.05
Kibei	10.5 (8.6)	16.3 (24.6)	*13.4 (16.6)*	Ki - Ni	-
Nisei	12.7*(15.8)	6.6 (6.6)	*9.6 (10.7)*	Is - No	0.001
				Ki - No	0.01
Norm.	5.4† (9.7)	2.8 (3.1)	*4.1 (4.9)*	Ni - No	0.01
Neur.	10.3 (9.7)	8.3 (15.9)	*9.3 (12.8)*	No - Ne	0.05
				No - Sc	0.001
Schiz.	15.9 (14.5)	22.7 (31.8)	*19.3 (23.2)*	Ne - Sc	0.05

(b) Distribution of Cases Showing Responses in Various Subcategories of Body Preoccupation

Subcategories

Groups	Bb M	F	T	Bf M	F	T	Bs M	F	T	Bso M	F	T	Ban M	F	T	Bdi M	F	T	Bch M	F	T
Issei	13	7	*20*	8	7	*15*	0	3	*3*	2	5	*7*	2	7	*9*	2	1	*3*	0	7	*7*
Kibei	10	6	*16*	6	4	*10*	1	1	*2*	2	0	*2*	1	0	*1*	0	1	*1*	0	0	*0*
Nisei	17	16	*33*	19	10	*29*	1	1	*2*	1	1	*2*	3	1	*4*	2	1	*3*	0	0	*0*
Norm.	15	12	*27*	8	5	*13*	1	1	*2*	1	0	*1*	3	0	*3*	0	1	*1*	0	0	*0*
Neur.	11	19	*20*	7	4	*11*	1	0	*1*	2	0	*2*	1	0	*1*	0	0	*0*	0	0	*0*
Schiz.	9	5	*14*	8	4	*12*	3	1	*4*	4	4	*8*	4	3	*7*	2	3	*5*	2	1	*3*

Confidence Levels of Significant Differences by X^2‡

Is - Ki	-	-	-	-	n.t.	-	n.t.
Is - Ni	-	0.05	-	n.t.	-	-	n.t.
Ki - Ni	-	-	-	-	-	-	-
Is - No	-	-	-	n.t.	0.05	-	n.t.
Ki - No	-	-	-	-	-	-	-
Ni - No	-	0.001	-	-	-	-	-
No - Ne	0.06	0.05	-	-	-	-	-
No - Sc	-	0.05	n.t.	n.t.	n.t.	n.t.	-
Ne - Sc	-	-	-	n.t.	n.t.	n.t.	-

* Nisei M - Nisei F = 0.05.

† Normal M - Normal F = 0.05.

‡ Nisei M - Nisei F (Bf = 0.05).
  Issei M - Issei F (Ban = n.t.).
  Issei M - Issei F (Bch = n.t.).

appear in proportionate numbers. However, some similar anatomical responses were found in Japan specifically in the age group of men who saw service in World War II.

The Nisei, Kibei, and American Normal groups showed a similar distribution of individuals giving responses within the various subcategories. The higher means in the Kibei and Nisei were attributable to general increases rather than to any difference in emphasis on particular subcategories; an exception was flesh anatomy (Bf) responses, which were much more common in the Japanese American groups in general, most notably in the men.

While the responses of the Issei men were similar to those of the Nisei, Kibei, and American Normal groups, the Issei women showed a tendency toward types of anatomical responses found characteristically only in American Schizophrenics. The twenty-five Issei women in five cases produced sex organ (Bso) responses, in seven cases anal (Ban) responses, and in seven, childbirth (Bch) responses. Many of these responses were of a patently autistic nature, with very little consideration given to the formal qualities of the blots. Most often such responses were accompanied in the same records by a great deal of other anatomical material; in four subjects over 40 percent of the total number of responses given to the cards was anatomical. These results were strongly suggestive of a high rate of maladjustment in Issei women. Many never learned English, and lived a very circumscribed life within the home.

Total Unpleasant Affect

The differences noted between the groups in reference to hostile, anxious, and body preoccupation content are more strongly emphasized when these three categories are combined into a total Index of Unpleasant Affect (table 4.23). This index gives us an overall evaluation of the relative adjustment level of a record on the basis of the relative percentage of negative content. It can be assumed that when a relatively high percentage of the total responses of a record has connotations of hostility, anxiety, and/or body preoccupation, there is a sufficient degree of disturbance in the emotional life of the individual to consider him or her critically maladjusted, with considerable emotional or intellectual energy tied up in internal disturbance. The presence of a few

TABLE 4.23

Means and Standard Deviations of Index of Unpleasant Affect

Groups	Means (and Standard Deviations)			Groups	Confidence Levels of Sig. Diff. of Mean
	M	F	T		
Issei	46.5 (22.8)	45.9 (24.7)	46.2 (23.4)	Is - Ki	-
				Is - Ni	0.05
Kibei	49.8 (23.4)	47.8 (21.8)	48.8 (22.8)	Ki - Ni	0.05
Nisei	40.2 (21.3)	33.4 (14.6)	36.3 (17.9)	Is - No	0.001
				Ki - No	0.001
Norm.	31.2* (12.9)	24.8 (11.1)	27.5 (12.0)	Ni - No	0.001
Neur.	47.8† (16.3)	37.5 (10.2)	42.7 (13.2)	No - Ne	0.001
				No - Sc	0.001
Schiz.	51.6 (17.2)	51.8 (22.8)	51.7 (20.0)	Ne - Sc	0.05

* Normal M - Normal F = 0.05.
† Neurotic M - Neurotic F = 0.05.

negatively toned, even dramatically negative responses is to be found among normative records in individuals who may have unresolved problems but continue to function adaptively. A more telling differentiator between groups and individuals considered clinically is the accumulation in single records of a high proportion of negatively toned symbolic responses.

The means of the Issei and Kibei on total unpleasant affect were significantly higher than the means of the American Normal groups at the 0.1 percent level of probability. The means of the Nisei groups placed them intermediate between the American Normal and Neurotic groups. The Nisei averaged significantly higher than the Normals, to the degree that they did not differ significantly from the Neurotic American group. The Issei and Kibei groups had means intermediate to those of the Neurotic and Schizophrenic American groups.

Comparing sex differences, there was a significant tendency for the men in both the American Normal and Neurotic groups to give more unpleasant content than the women. This trend also appeared in the Nisei men, but the results were not significant due to a higher standard deviation for this group compared to the other groups. In the Issei and Kibei groups men and women showed total unpleasant scores similar to one another.

These results, based solely on a quantitative index of negatively toned symbolic material are highly correlated with results obtained by using a Maladjustment Scale developed by Fisher. As discussed in the previous chapter, his scale is based on a rather complex method of weighting certain deviations in the use of location, determinants, and content scored according to Beck's system. When corrected for interdependent items the 300 records used in my study showed a correlation of 0.62 between the Index of Unpleasant Affect and Fisher's Maladjustment Scale. These results placed the Issei and Kibei closer to the Neurotic and Schizophrenic groups than to either the Normal Americans or the Nisei. The Nisei showed means on both measures intermediate to those of the Normal and Neurotic Americans.

Such results suggest that, regardless of their positive social adaptation, intrapsychic tensions or disturbances were quite prevalent in Japanese Americans. The relationship between these disturbances and cultural variables is complex. Suffice it to repeat here that a theme of this volume is that adaptation and adjustment may not be congruent. An individual considered well adapted in terms of contemporary social expectations may pay an intrapsychic price.

One cultural setting may provide an adaptive *modus vivendi* for modes of behavior that cause difficulties when they are brought into another cultural setting. Japanese immigrants and their children have given no evidence of any lack of adaptive capacity. Very few have revealed any difficulties that required professional attention. However, inflexible neurotic adjustments or even underlying psychotic processes can be masked socially by general cultural acceptance of rigidified patterns of behavior. Automatic conforming behavior may have masked the high internal disturbance suggested in several of the Issei women, most of whom came to the United States as "picture brides" sent from their villages to be married to bachelor emigrants who had accumulated sufficient funds.

During extended conversations with Issei men whom I visited in their residences, in two instances I encountered patterns of benign paranoia. These two men were living alone as bachelors who had never married. As inquiry about themselves progressed, they gradually revealed grandiose systems of thought. One claimed to be an inventor who had had his major inventions stolen from him, the other had taken on the task of writing a book on "mondology" which he was preparing to send to the U.S. State Department as a means of assuring world peace.

The Issei women, almost all of whom I interviewed in Japanese, were laconic but polite and cooperative. Their behavior was formal and circumspect. The aberrant material of their records was given with a blandness of affect. As far as I could observe, they were living sheltered lives within the bosoms of their families, a situation that did not demand of them any contact with outside society.

The Japanese records in Japan showed higher overall unpleasant scores than did the American normative sample (cf. tables 4.20 and 4.23), principally due to their higher anxiety scores, which were partially a result of frequent card rejections. The amount of anatomical material was less, and the aberrant body preoccupation responses of the type noted in Issei women did not appear in any of the subsamples of the Nagoya research.

A Comparison of Groups on the Index of Dependent Affect

The Nisei groups were significantly higher in dependency responses than either the American Normal or the Issei groups (table 4.24). The American Normal, Neurotic, and Schizophrenic groups were not significantly different from each other, although there was a slight tendency for the maladjusted groups to average a bit higher.

Dependent responses with a childish quality (Dch, such as "kitties," "puppies," "a little doll") were found in two-thirds of the Nisei women. Kibei and Issei women were also somewhat more prone than the men to give such responses but such a trend was absent in the Normal American group. The production of such responses may be related to the role identity of Japanese women, who as mothers are inclined to see the world vicariously through their children's eyes. Childlike attention to young animals, toys, and so on is consistent with their career definitions as mothers. These "Dch" responses also appeared in good numbers among the women tested in the Japanese normative samples.

Dependent oral responses (Dor, such as licking or sucking)

TABLE 4.24

Dependent Affect

(a) Means and Standard Deviations of Index of Dependent Affect

Groups	Means (and Standard Deviations)			Groups	Confidence Levels of Sig. Diff. of Means
	M	F	T		
Issei	3.3 (5.0)	4.6 (6.3)	*3.9* *(5.8)*	Is - Ki	-
				Is - Ni	0.01
Kibei	3.5 (6.5)	5.5 (5.4)	*4.5* *(6.0)*	Ki - Ni	0.05
Nisei	6.5 (7.2)	7.1 (5.4)	*6.8* *(6.3)*	Is - No	-
				Ki - No	-
Norm.	4.6 (4.8)	4.6 (4.3)	*4.6* *(4.6)*	Ni - No	0.05
Neur.	7.6 (6.6)	6.5 (8.0)	*7.0* *(7.4)*	No - Ne	-
				No - Sc	-
Schiz.	7.5 (5.8)	4.6 (7.5)	*6.0* *(6.8)*	Ne - Sc	-

(b) Distribution of Cases Showing Responses in Various Subcategories of Dependent Affect

Subcategories

Groups	Df M F T	Dor M F T	Dd M F T	Dsec M F T	Dch M F T	Dlo M F T	Drel M F T
Issei	1 3 *4*	8 1 *9*	3 1 *4*	1 2 *3*	3 8 *11*	1 2 *3*	1 3 *4*
Kibei	0 2 *2*	1 2 *3*	2 0 *2*	0 0 *0*	1 7 *8*	0 1 *1*	1 3 *4*
Nisei	6 1 *7*	7 3 *10*	2 4 *6*	4 3 *7*	11 20 *31*	3 3 *6*	1 4 *5*
Norm.	3 0 *3*	3 1 *4*	1 4 *5*	7 8 *15*	10 10 *20*	5 3 *8*	6 6 *12*
Neur.	3 0 *3*	2 2 *4*	3 1 *4*	2 2 *4*	10 7 *17*	2 1 *3*	3 1 *4*
Schiz.	4 1 *5*	6 2 *8*	2 1 *3*	4 1 *5*	6 4 *10*	0 1 *1*	3 3 *6*

Confidence Levels of Significant Differences by X^{2*}

	Df	Dor	Dd	Dsec	Dch	Dlo	Drel
Is Vs Ki	-	-	-	-	-	-	-
Is Vs Ni	-	-	-	-	0.01	-	-
Ki Vs Ni	-	-	-	-	0.05	-	-
Is Vs No	-	-	-	0.05	-	-	-
Ki Vs No	-	-	-	0.05	-	-	-
Ni Vs No	-	-	-	0.06	0.05	-	-
No Vs Ne	-	-	-	-	0.05	-	-
No Vs Sc	n.t.	n.t.	-	-	-	-	-
Ne Vs Sc	-	-	-	-	-	-	-

* Nisei M - Nisei F (Dcl=0.05).

tended to be primarily a male response, especially high in the Issei, Nisei, and Schizophrenic male groups.

Although generally rare and hence not usually subject to differential testing, responses identifying fetuses or small infants (Df) were given by a number of Japanese men, especially among the Nisei. This response in my judgment was a symbolic parallel to the appearance of childbirth responses among Issei women. These remarkable responses found in our smaller sample of Japanese American records were not found later in the normative testing done in Japan. The oral dependent responses made their appearance more in men than in women.

The American Normals both men and women, tended to give more responses categorized as related to security needs (Dsec). Some of these responses were of a wish-fulfillment variety and were in that sense positively toned. There was also a noticeable trend, which did not reach significance for the American groups, to give more religious responses (Drel). In chapter 6 below I discuss in detail some of the differences in dependent symbolism in our later research in Tokyo which marked the family members of nondelinquent children compared with those having a delinquent child.

A Comparison of Groups on the Index of Positive Affect

As reported above, the means of the American Normal, Neurotic, and Schizophrenic groups, in regard to seeing positively toned objects or scenes, were significantly different from one another beyond the 2 percent level of significance. The Issei and Kibei had means essentially similar to the American Normal group (see table 4.25). The overall Nisei mean was significantly higher than the other groups mainly because the Nisei women scored higher than any other group tested. The trend differentiating the two generations of Japanese women but not the men was again in evidence. The range of differences within each group was wide, but the Issei men showed the greatest variation in their symbols of positive affect.

As table 4.25 demonstrates, all groups showed a remarkably similar proportion of individuals producing Positive responses

TABLE 4.25

Positive Affect

(a) Means and Standard Deviations of Index of Positive Affect

Groups	Means (and Standard Deviations)			Groups	Confidence Levels of Sig. Diff. of Means
	M	F	T		
Issei	17.6 (13.3)	14.1*(14.8)	*15.6 (14.1)*	Is - Ki	-
				Is - Ni	0.05
Kibei	17.3 (10.6)	15.6 (13.9)	*16.5 (12.4)*	Ki - Ni	0.05
Nisei	18.3†(10.4)	25.9 (13.6)	*22.1 (12.7)*	Is - No	-
				Ki - No	-
Norm.	16.1 (11.1)	18.2 (10.7)	*17.2 (10.9)*	Ni - No	0.05
Neur.	11.3 (9.0)	12.5 (10.6)	*11.9 (9.8)*	No - Ne	0.05
				No - Sc	0.001
Schiz.	7.3 (6.0)	6.5 (5.6)	*6.9 (5.8)*	Ne - Sc	0.05

(b) Distribution of Cases Showing Responses in Various Subcategories of Positive Affect

Subcategories

Groups	Por			Ps			Pch:Dch			Pch			Psec			Pnat			Porn		
	M	F	T	M	F	T	M	F	T	M	F	T	M	F	T	M	F	T	M	F	T
Issei	5	2	*7*	16	8	*24*	2	3	*5*	1	1	*2*	8	5	*13*	10	15	*25*	12	8	*20*
Kibei	2	0	*2*	7	9	*16*	2	1	*3*	2	0	*2*	9	6	*15*	8	5	*13*	4	4	*8*
Nisei	7	12	*19*	25	23	*48*	6	14	*20*	6	5	*11*	16	18	*34*	14	23	*37*	13	12	*25*
Norm.	8	8	*16*	25	25	*50*	7	3	*10*	2	3	*5*	12	16	*28*	21	19	*40*	14	15	*29*
Neur.	7	6	*13*	9	10	*19*	1	2	*3*	0	0	*0*	6	4	*10*	9	6	*15*	5	6	*11*
Schiz.	6	4	*10*	6	5	*11*	3	0	*3*	0	0	*0*	6	3	*9*	5	7	*12*	5	6	*11*

Confidence Levels of Significant Differences by X^2

	Por	Ps	Pch:Dch	Pch	Psec	Pnat	Porn
Is - Ki	-	-	-	-	0.01	-	-
Is - Ni	0.05	0.01	0.001	0.05	0.001	-	-
Ki - Ni	0.01	0.01	0.05	-	-	-	-
Is - No	-	0.001	-	-	0.05	-	-
Ki - No	0.05	0.01	-	-	-	-	0.05
Ni - No	-	-	0.05	-	-	-	-
No - Ne	-	0.05	-	-	-	0.05	-
No - Sc	-	0.001	-	-	-	0.05	-
Ne - Sc	-	0.05	-	-	-	-	-

* Issei F - Nisei F = 0.01.

† Nisei M - Nisei F = 0.05.

within each of these respective subcategories. However, the number of individuals within the Issei and Kibei, as well as in the American Neurotic and Schizophrenic groups, that gave responses in the subcategories of positive affect was smaller in proportion to group size when compared with the Nisei and American Normals.

The fact that a relatively lower number of Issei and Kibei individuals appeared in the distribution in each positive subcategory was not, however, inconsistent with the previously mentioned fact that they had a higher mean score of positive content. Two factors will explain the apparent inconsistency: (1) the overall response total was lower for the Issei and Kibei. It took fewer positive responses per record to give the individual a higher percentage of positive responses; (2) when they did give positive responses, there was a slight tendency to give less variety in them than was found in the American Normal and Nisei groups.

The only trend appearing between the sexes was for both more Issei and Nisei women to give more positively toned nature responses (Pnat). The Nisei women produced more childishly toned positive responses (Pch), parallel to their production of childishly toned dependent responses. The Issei women, on the other hand, gave significantly fewer positive sensual responses (Ps) than did the men. These trends may be related to culturally defined male and female roles. The man is considered somewhat more free to express sensuality directly than the married woman.

In general, one can state that the number of individuals represented in each of the subcategories of the positive responses was remarkably similar between the Nisei and American Normal groups. There were proportionately fewer individuals in each of the categories in the Issei and Kibei, but the relative emphasis among all the subcategories seemed to be the same for all the groups considered.

It is interesting to note that the urban sample in Japan, taken in the cities of Nagoya and Okayama had a percentage of positive responses comparable to the American normative population (table 4.20). The village samples, however, had a positive average some 5 points lower than the urban Japanese. This difference suggests a more freely open range of positive interests in urban as contrasted with rural Japanese living in more traditional village settings in 1954.

Neutral Responses

Neutral responses are so categorized because the affective push is judged to be minimal in 40% to 50% of the responses elicited. Many such responses are of animals.

While, strictly speaking, no response is completely without possible affective connotations, a large number of responses are seemingly much more directly related to shape and other formal characteristics of the blots and do not appear to have affective implications. Too large a proportion of such "neutral" responses—for example, an index above 80%—suggests affective constriction, as does a high level of pure form responses, F%. Affectivity in such records shows no easy flow in any direction, so that one can presume the presence of severe personal strictures at work, blocking the imagination. On the other hand, a low level of neutral responses in a record can at times suggest such affective lability that there may be minimal use of ego controls over either healthy or pathologically structured impulses and affective reactions. Such lability may be reflected in an outbreak of pathology, in continuous obsessional preoccupations with certain impulses trying to break through, or in a general imbalance and instability in relating to the environment, whether it is expressed behaviorally or experienced in constant inner agitation.

Neutral responses comprise roughly 50% of the total responses in most of the Normative American records (table 4.26). The Schizophrenic group differed significantly from both the Normal

TABLE 4.26

Means and Standard Deviations of Index of Neutral Affect

Groups	Means (and Standard Deviations)			Groups	Confidence Levels of Sig. Diff. of Means
	M	F	T		
Issei	44.5 (25.3)	45.9 (24.5)	*45.2 (24.9)*	Is - Ki	0.05
				Is - Ni	-
Kibei	36.7 (19.2)	33.5 (20.6)	*35.1 (20.0)*	Ki - Ni	-
Nisei	40.3 (14.7)	38.1 (18.0)	*39.3 (16.4)*	Is - No	-
				Ki - No	0.001
Norm.	48.5 (14.7)	50.1 (16.4)	*49.3 (15.6)*	Ni - No	0.001
Neur.	37.6 (21.0)	52.9 (16.0)	*45.3 (19.2)*	No - Ne	-
				No - Sc	0.001
Schiz.	33.8 (19.3)	35.4 (18.8)	*34.6 (19.1)*	Ne - Sc	0.05

and Neurotic groups in producing a lower percentage of Neutral responses. The mean of the Issei group was roughly comparable to that of the American Normal group, whereas the means of both Nisei and Kibei were significantly lower than that of the American Normal group. The Kibei mean was even significantly lower than that of the Issei.

The records reveal that there were a number of individuals in each of the Japanese American groups below 2 Standard Deviations of the American Normal group mean, whereas no American Normals had such a low percentage of neutral content. The numbers were not large enough to test by chi square, but with more cases they would probably prove to be significant. The standard deviations in the Issei were the highest, emphasizing the very great variability of this group in the production of neutral affect. Some records are very constricted, others have almost no Neutral content.

In Japan the general level of Neutral content was somewhat lower than for the American Normative group. This overall difference is probably due both to the proportionately higher anxiety scores, due to a proneness to reject specific cards, and to the quality rather than quantity ambition producing complex responses that were more likely to have affective connotations.

Conclusions and Brief Discussion

The most general findings concerning the Japanese-American groups were:

1. The Issei (immigrant) group showed an overall pattern stressing Body Preoccupation with Sadomasochistic symbolism. Blocking and constriction rather than symbolic expression of anxiety or dependency were characteristic for many of this group. Positive affect, however, was as proportionately prevalent in the Issei as in the American Normal group. The overall amount of Unpleasant affect suggested a great deal of maladjustment in the Issei, especially in the women, whose Body Preoccupation responses were in many cases as autistic as those found in Schizophrenic records. The later normative sampling in Japan itself revealed no such elevation of anatomy in any of the normative women's records. However, the means for the age group of men

who were likely to have participated as soldiers in World War II showed some elevation of Body Preoccupation responses, some with sadomasochistic content.

2. The Kibei group, the group consisting of American-born Japanese Americans who had been sent to Japan for at least five years during childhood, showed results intermediate to the Issei and Nisei, though they showed more intrapersonal difficulty in the overall expression of Unpleasant Affect. They were freer than the Issei and more like the Nisei in the expression of anxiety through content material.

3. The Nisei records demonstrated a definite similarity to the American Normal sample in most symbolic material. While they resembled the Japanese older generation in respect to sadoma-sochism and body preoccupation, they were more like the American group in every other measure. The Nisei women differed more from the Issei women than the Nisei men did from the Issei men. The Nisei were generally more expressive of affect than the Normal sample in both positive and negative directions.

The outstanding overall differences between the groups of Japanese Americans and the American Normal groups were: (1) the large amount of body preoccupation appearing in the Japanese Americans; (2) the significantly larger number of sadomasochistic responses found in all the Japanese American groups. Such somatization as part of a defensive syndrome was often brought out in psychotherapy material in the initial Chicago interdisciplinary study. Expressed culturally, it often appeared as an emphasis on bodily endurance. There was anger directed toward one's body for being weak or inadequate should there be failure to accomplish goals. One's body was supposed to withstand strain without comment as part of *Yamato damashi*, the indomitable Japanese spirit. Projection of the cause of failure as due to outside forces or situational factors was not permitted as readily as in American society. The body, rather than outside influences, tended to be the "scapegoat." It is noteworthy that responses such as "crushed lungs" and "dissections" were frequent among these responses. Fear of diseases such as tuberculosis was at that time extreme in the Japanese community. The disease in one family member made that family a bad marriage risk. In one of the Nisei therapy cases under analysis, this disease definitely had the meaning of punishment which was related to the manner in which the person handled her guilt feelings.

The large incidence of anatomy responses in the records supported my impression from observation of behavior that hypochondriasis was prevalent in both Issei and Nisei groups. The possible relation of these body preoccupation responses to minority status within American society is discussed further in chapter 8 below in the context of a comparison with other groups showing stress characteristics that are possibly related to similar minority status conflicts.

The inner disturbances suggested by responses with anatomical content were most pronounced in the Issei women. The Nisei women, on the contrary, showed proportionally the least use of anatomy responses of any Japanese American group. The men showed no significant differences between generations. The fact that anal, sexual, fetal, as well as childbirth responses usually appeared in the most disturbed records of the Issei women but were absent in the Issei men renders questionable an explanation of these results in terms of "lack of cultural repression" of such material. The Issei women were the only group that showed a definite tendency toward specific types of anatomical material found characteristically only in the American Schizophrenics. Most noteworthy were the responses dealing directly with childbirth.

Nisei men also showed a trend toward fetal and embryo responses. Oral dependent responses were notably present in both the Issei and Nisei men. Speculatively, the appearance of fetal and oral dependent responses in the men would suggest that the concern in the mother over childbearing and early dependency was somehow conveyed to the male child in a telling fashion so that it played a continuing role in the regressive fantasy structure of the individual.

The anatomical responses in the Issei women were of a markedly autistic nature and contributed to the low average form level found in the records of some of the women. These findings may be overdetermined and may be related not only to the age of the Issei women (many of them were in the involutional period) but to the general nature of their affective relationships, and their social role in the family. As the "okusan" or wife (literally, person who stays in the back), her traditional role was to withdraw herself. Issei women did not develop interests outside circumscribed and routinized family duties. The fact that the later testing in Japan did not substantiate these results with anatomy leads us to question the possible selectivity of those sent to the United States before 1924 as "picture brides." It could well be that certain young women were selected to be sent overseas because they were considered more difficult to marry off in their native villages for psychological reasons.

Motivational factors of a libidinal nature must also be included as a probable strong influence accentuating the withdrawal of affect into hypochondriacal concerns. Personality patterning is relatively fixed and has to be seen in relation to the entire developmental life span of the individual. Elsewhere in this volume I discuss relative consistencies of test and retest records. By and large, Rorschach protocols do not simply reflect immediate circumstances. As was indicated in my analysis of the structural aspects of personality of the Issei women (De Vos 1954), there was a repression of inner impulses as well as of expressive outlets in many of these individuals, so that a secondary narcissistic withdrawal is not an unlikely direction to take. It is to be noted that this trend was found in each of the Japanese American groups, but not to the degree represented in the records of the Issei women.

An outstanding instance in which the Nisei resembled the American Normal sample in contrast to the Issei and, to a lesser extent, the Kibei is the manner of expressing anxiety through symbolic content. The Issei gave so few responses specifically in this category, other than card rejection, that it may be concluded that they handled anxiety less directly through symbolic expression and much more through mental blocking, evasion, or, inferentially, through resort to anatomical responses. The averages of the Kibei and Issei in respect to anxiety responses were higher than those of the Nisei or American Normal groups only due to the inclusion of card rejection as an anxiety response. These results seem to be related to those obtained with the shading responses. In both cases the Nisei showed their anxiety more on a symbolic level, closer to the surface and less bound up in inflexible patterns, than did the Issei.

A difference appeared between Issei and Nisei in the dependent category in the greater tendency for the Nisei to give responses of a childish dependent nature. The possible meaning of this difference is not clear. It may be that feelings of childhood dependency related to similar cultural experiences in early childhood remained strong in both groups, but were expressed more through content in the less rigid Nisei. The Nisei women gave significantly more of these responses than the men, in a "little girl" attitude suggestive of the Oedipal stage of psychosexual development. As mentioned above, the men, especially the Nisei, showed symbolism of a more infantile sort of dependency going back to the primary relationship to the mother.

Direct hostile responses were relatively lacking in the Issei group when compared with the American Normal and Nisei groups. The Hostile Depreciatory response was found more often in American Normal and Nisei women than in the Issei women. The findings suggest that difficulty in human relationships may have been expressed by blocking and by somatically bound affect in the Issei women. They did not show the negatively toned conscious attitudes or the autistically contrived human responses that were found in a few of the Nisei men and women. It must be noted that the Issei men did give depreciatory responses to human percepts as much as did the Nisei men, although their overall blocking with the human form was also considerable.

The Index of Unpleasant Affect demonstrated results highly similar to those gained by applying Fisher's Maladjustment Scale to the records. The Issei and Kibei means were intermediate to those of the American Neurotic and Schizophrenic samples and the Nisei showed a mean intermediate to that of the American Normal and Neurotic groups. These results again emphasize the prevalence of patterns of personality integration, especially in the Issei and Kibei and to the lesser extent in the Nisei, which suggest maladjustment according to American clinical standards.

The fact that these two independent measures (Fisher's Maladjustment Scale and the Index of Unpleasant Affect) produced strikingly similar results emphasizes the presence of intrapsychic disturbance in the Japanese Americans as a group. The Nisei's better adjustment than that of the more culturally marginal Kibei is indicative of the greater strain placed on the Kibei, who were sent to Japan during their school years, often to be rejected or made objects of scorn by their age-mates. The fact that the Nisei records are closer to the American Normal records is confirmatory evidence of their general acculturation to American modes of symbolic expression.

An answer to the question of how the Japanese Americans continued to function well in spite of signs of intrapsychic difficulty is partially suggested by the fact that the Japanese American records are not only more expressive of negative affect than the American Normals but, in contrast to the maladjusted American groups, compare very favorably with an American Normal group in the expression of positive affect.

A low Neutral score, indicative of affective lability although more prevalent in each of the Japanese American groups, was less often combined with a low positive score than in the American Neurotic and Schizophrenic groups. Those who failed to have Positive responses with a low Neutral score in the Japanese Americans most often showed anatomical perseveration. These high anatomical records accounted for the somewhat bimodal distribution of positive scores in the Issei and Kibei.

If Positive responses are some measure of the amount of affectivity turned outward in positive object cathexes or investment beyond the self of various sorts, then the Japanese Americans as a group showed a considerable number of individuals with such cathexes. These results and those obtained in comparing the active-passive orientation of the Movement responses were two areas in which the Issei and Kibei groups had some direct contrasts to the maladjusted American groups, whom they resembled in some of the other variables tested.

Both the positive responses and the movement responses pointed to more vigor in the intellectual and emotional life in the Japanese Americans. Active movement responses may be considered as reflecting an active attitudinal stance toward social life, and the Positive affective responses, a considerable degree of object cathexis. Both these qualities seem to be lacking in many more of the American maladjusted records than in those of Japanese Americans of all groups.

References

Babcock, Charlotte E.
   1962 Reflections on Dependency Phenomena as Seen in Nisei in the United States. R. J. Smith and R. K. Beardsley, eds. *Japanese Culture: Its Developments and Characteristics*, pp. 172–185. Chicago: Aldine Press.
Caudill, William
   1952 Japanese American Acculturation and Personality. *Genetic Psychology Monographs* 45:3–102.
De Vos, George A.
   1954 A Comparison of the Personality Differences in Two Generations of Japanese Americans by Means of the Rorschach Test. *Nagoya Journal of Medical Science* 17(3):153–265 (reprinted no. 34, 1966).
   1955 A Quantitative Rorschach Assessment of Maladjustment and Rigidity in Acculturating Japanese Americans. *Genetic Psychology Monographs* 52:51–87.
   1960 The Relation of Guilt Toward Parents to Achievement and Arranged Marriage Among the Japanese. *Psychiatry* 23:287–301.
   1975 Apprenticeship and Paternalism: Psychocultural Continuities Underlying Japanese Social Organization. Ezra Vogel, ed. *Modern Japanese Organization and Decision Making*, pp. 210–227. Berkeley, Los Angeles, London: University of California Press.
De Vos, George A., and Hiroshi Wagatsuma
   1959 Psychocultural Significance of Concern over Death and Illness Among Rural Japanese. *International Journal of Social Psychiatry* 5:6–19.
   1961 Value Attitudes Toward Role Behavior of Women in Two Japanese Villages. *American Anthropologist* 63:1204–30.
Muramatsu, T., ed.
   1960 *Nipponjin—Bunka to Pāsonaritī no Jisshō-Teki Kenkyū* (The Japanese—An Empirical Study in Culture and Personality). Tokyo: Reimei Shobō.
Wagatsuma, Hiroshi, and George A. De Vos
   1984 *Heritage of Endurance: Family Patterns and Delinquency Formation in Urban Japan*. Berkeley, Los Angeles, London: University of California Press.

Chapter Five

"Mother" and "Father" Cards: A Comparison of Delinquent and Nondelinquent Youth

Mayumi Taniguchi, George A. De Vos, and
Eiji Murakami

Japanese culture has traditionally emphasized very strongly defined parental roles (De Vos 1973: chap. 2). The father, ideally conceived, is a dignified authority figure who has very little to do with the actual discipline of his children. As head of the family he commands unquestioned respect. The ideal mother inculcates in her children a feeling of reverence and awe for the father, no matter what his shortcomings are in actuality. She is the source of warmth and comfort, completely devoted to the care of her husband and children as her chief reason for existence. She is expected to be cheerfully compliant no matter what hardships she must face in accomplishing this task. She disciplines by indirection in the name of the father's authority and according to the purposes and traditions of the family lineage that she joined as a bride.

In 1955, Mayumi Taniguchi had the opportunity to give the Rorschach test in Nagoya, Japan, to a large number of delinquent and nondelinquent Japanese adolescents. She was interested in finding whether the Rorschach could possibly shed light on differences in attitudes toward parents between these two groups. It was hypothesized that a delinquent group would reveal striking differences in attitudes from a nondelinquent group. De Vos was interested in how a symbolic analysis of responses to the cards would reflect conscious and unconscious attitudes toward parents.

Analysis and interpretation of the stimulus value of the Rorschach cards had led certain authors (Bochner and Halpern 1942; Meers and Singer 1950; Phillips and Smith 1953; Rosen 1951) to conclude that subjects are particularly prone to perceive parental figures in specific Rorschach cards. Card IV is often considered by clinicians to be the "father" or authority card, and Card VII the "mother" card. In order to ascertain the stimulus values of the various Rorschach cards in reference to both parents in a delinquent and a nondelinquent group, a special test of limits requesting choice of cards as related to parental figures was given by Taniguchi following a standard administration of the Rorschach test. In essence the procedures used replicated those reported in a previous study by Meers and Singer (1950).

Design and Procedure

A total of 100 subjects were tested from November 1955 through May 1956. These included a group of 50 delinquents (mean age 18.3: divided equally by sex). The delinquent group was interviewed in a juvenile classification office, where they had been sent after committing some offense. The nondelinquent or normal group chosen were college students (mean age 19.4) at Nagoya National University who were fulfilling their roles as proper children by pursuing higher education. Obtaining higher education is a strongly respected value throughout the various strata of Japanese society. A dutiful son or daughter according to Japanese values repays deeply felt obligations (*on-gaeshi*) to parents by excellence in school. The college population in Japan is by no means predominantly urban middle class in background. National universities select students for merit on the basis of highly competitive examinations (De Vos 1973). The college group also was divided equally by sex. In both groups only those with both parents alive were considered in the study.

There was no opportunity to control the groups used in respect to intelligence. One must bear in mind, however, that the college students of a Japanese national university would be a selected group intellectually in comparison with the delinquent group.[1] However, there is nothing to suggest a priori that the specific delinquent group used would have a mean IQ below the Japanese national standard. Other prison samples have tested out on a normative level.

After the proper administraton of the Rorschach test the ten cards were placed before the subjects, who were asked to designate one card as the one that most reminded them of their father and another that most reminded them of their mother. They were given as much time as needed for the selection. The subjects were then asked to give the reason why they selected these cards as father card and mother card. They then were required to rank all the cards from most liked to most disliked. Chi-square and a test of different proportions were used to test the degree to which observed frequency of choices deviated from chance expectancy. Yates correction for continuity was necessary in certain instances because of the small numbers in each cell. The nature of the affective symbolism in the content of responses on the cards was compared with the affective implications of the remaining cards.

Results

In selecting a father card the nondelinquent Japanese group in almost half the cases (24 out of 50) chose Black and White Card IV (P greater than .001). A smaller number (10) opted for Card I (see table 5.1). No one chose Cards VII or X. These results differed in some respects from those reported by Meers and Singer (1950), testing Americans. Comparably, in their study, Card IV was the most common choice; but in contrast, Card II was selected as a secondary father card with Card I third. Meers and Singer noted that Card II, with a red and white interior design, was occasionally selected by Americans for its "massive quality" as a father card, but in the Japanese study it was chosen much more rarely. Color was probably an important consideration. Red color is related to female gender role in Japan.

Radically different results were obtained for the Japanese delinquent group (see table 5.1). Their choice of father cards was much more scattered, with Card III (two bowing figures with peripheral splotches of red) receiving the majority of votes (13

TABLE 5.1

Choice of Father and Mother Cards in Japanese
Nondelinquent and Delinquent Youth

Card	Father Card						Mother Card						Card Chosen as Father Card More than Mother Card	Card Chosen as Mother Card More than Father Card
	Nondelinquents			Delinquent			Nondelinquents			Delinquent				
	M	F	T	M	F	T	M*	F	T	M†	F†	T		
N	25	25	*50*	25	25	*50*	25	25	*50*	25	25	*50*		
I	7	3	*10*	2	3	*5*	1	_	*1*	_	_	_	Nor.>.01	
II	2	3	*5*	2	2	*4*	1*	1	*2*	2†	4†	*6*	Del.>.01	
III	1	3	*4*	8	5	*13‡*	4*	3	*7*	3†	4†	*7*	Nor.>.01	
IV	13**	11**	*24**	4	4	*8*	_	1	*1*	_	1	*1*	Nor.>.01	
V	1	1	*2*	3	3	*6*	2	2	*4*	4	1	*5*		
VI	1	2	*3*	2	1	*3*	1	1	*2*	_	_	_		
VII	_	_	_	2	2	*4*	3	8	*11††*	3	1	*4*		Nor.>.01
VIII	_	1	*1*	_	3	*3*	5*	1	*6*	7†	3†	*10*		Del.>.01
IX	_	1	*1*	1	_	*1*	4*	3	*7*	2†	5†	*7*		
X	_	_	_	1	2	*3*	4*	5	*9*	4†	6†	*10*		Nor.>.01

* Choice of colored cards as mother card significant at the .05 level.
† Choice of colored cards as mother card significant at the .01 level.
‡ Choice of card III as father card significant at the .05 level.
** Choice of card IV as father card significant at the .001 level.
†† Choice of card VII as mother card significant at the .05 level.

cases; P greater than .05). Card IV was a second choice only, occurring in 8 out of 50 instances.

The results of the Japanese normal group in essence agreed with those reported by Meers and Singer for American normals. In the choice of a mother card by the Japanese nondelinquent group, Card VII (black and white, but soft and "feminine" in appearance) was selected most frequently (11 cases of 50, 8 of them girls), barely reaching significance at the .05 level. Out of the 39 remaining options, 22 were of colored cards (VIII to X), with Card X the most popular (9 cases). It seems obvious that the bright, gay colors were an important consideration in the selection of a mother card. Traditionally, use of color was stringently defined by sex and age in Japan. Red is a color worn only by women, usually those under thirty.

Among delinquents the choice of a mother card seems even more determined by color than by form. The feminine form of Card VII was selected as a mother card by only 4 of 50 individuals, which would be expected on a chance basis, whereas 27 (13 out of 25 boys and 14 out of 25 girls) picked a colored blot as

TABLE 5.2

Reasons Given for Choice of Father or Mother Cards
by Nondelinquent and Delinquent Japanese Youth on Cards Most Frequently Chosen

			Nondelinquent			Delinquent
Father Card	I	1	masculine, sturdy	III	1	like father's mind
		2	self-confident, secure		1	suffering the torment of
		2	generous			daily life
		3	imposing		1	giving advice to children
		1	fearful		10	from the form (shape)
		_1_	from the form and color		—	
		10			13	
	IV	7	masculine, sturdy, etc.	IV	1	fierce
		8	dignified		2	big, strong
		6	balanced, secure, self		1	looks like it
			confident		4	from the form
		1	masterful, dominating			
		_2_	fearful		—	
		24			8	
Mother Card	VII	8	tenderness, warmness	VIII	1	beautiful
		1	taking care of children		2	tenderness
		2	from the shape		1	simple
					2	strong character
					_4_	from the shape and color
		—			10	
		11				
	X	5	tenderness, warmness	X	3	tenderness
		1	buoyant, cheerful		3	bright, cheerful
		1	complicated		4	shape, color
		_2_	from the color, shape		—	
		9			10	

the mother card. Cards VIII and X were most frequently selected, with 10 choices each. In the study, Card X was a second option as a mother card in the American normal group. Card IV received only one vote out of 50 in the delinquent group as a mother card. In the normal group Card VII received no choices as a father card, whereas in the delinquent group there were 4 such selections out of the 50.

The stated reason given for card choice varied (see table 5.2). In the normal group the explanations for choosing Card IV as a father card often involved such adjectives as "sturdy," "self-confident," "masculine," and "dignified." More negatively toned adjectives such as "fearful," "masterful," or "dominating" appeared only three times. A similar distribution of descriptive adjectives appeared for (achromatic) Card I. These results, again, are similar to American explanations reported by Meers and Singer. Only once was a simple statement "from the form and color" used by a Japanese normal as a reason for selecting either Card I or Card IV. In the delinquent group, however, form was appealed to as the explanation for the choice of Card III (the bowing figures) as father card (in 10 of 13 cases). More positively toned descriptive adjectives were almost entirely lacking in this group.

In regard to the reasons given for the choice of a mother card, there were few differences for the choice of black and white Card VII or Card X in either the normal of delinquent groups. The main adjectives used for both cards were such positively toned descriptions as "warm," "tender," and "bright and cheerful." In general, the descriptions given fit closely to what a mother should be in Japan.

Comparison of Card Choice to
Spontaneous Affective Content

Scoring the content according to our system of affective inferences (see above) reveals certain differences between the normal sample and the delinquent group (table 5.3). Significantly more anxious responses were given by the normal group to the cards chosen as the father card than to the remainder of the blots. In a number of cases responses involving direct or indirect feelings were forthcoming, such as "gorilla," "baboon," "two Deva kings" (called *Nio*—fierce-looking guardians of Buddha), and "demons." Anxious responses were *less* common in the delinquent group to the cards selected as representing the father. In general, the delinquents tended to give more neutral or evasive responses to these cards. The amount of anxiety symbolism in their responses to the remaining blots, however, was greater than that found on those chosen as the father card.

One can infer from these results that, in normal Japanese, descriptions of cards given in the test of limits are more closely related to conscious attitudes of what a father should be like than is the actual content symbolism associated spontaneously to the cards.

TABLE 5.3

Affective Symbolism on Cards Chosen as Father Card and Mother Card

| | Nondelinquents | | | Delinquents | | | Significant Difference in Percentage of Affective Content Between Cards Chosen and All Other Cards | |
	Father	Mother	Other Cards	Father	Mother	Other Cards	Father	Mother
Hostility	7.4	9.7	13.9	3.7	4.9	6.6		
Anxiety	27.3*	8.0	13.5	11.6*	8.2	16.8	.001 (Nor.)	.05 (Del.)
Bodily Preoccupation	5.0	3.6	4.9	6.8	4.9	3.1		
Total								.05 (Nor.)
Unpleasant	39.7†	21.3	32.3	22.0†	18.0	26.5		.05 (Del.)
Dependent	5.9	16.7‡	4.5	5.3	1.7‡	3.9		.001 (Nor.)
Pleasant	10.9	34.0**	22.2	14.7	23.0**	12.3		
Miscellaneous	1.0	4.6	1.0	-	1.0	0.4		
Neutral	42.5	23.4††	40.0	57.9	56.3††	56.9		

Significant differences between normals and delinquents as to mean percentage of affect on cards chosen as mother or father cards are as follows:

*P>.01
†P>.05
‡P>.001
**P>.05
††P>.001

In the delinquent group obvious characterological defenses against anxiety are used in the choice of cards. Moreover, the father is less likely to be consciously perceived in a positive light.

The affective content on the mother cards chosen by the normal group revealed a significantly higher number of positive and *dependent* affective responses, often characterized by a somewhat childish tone, such as "rabbits making rice cakes" (*mochi*), "the kingdom of Heaven," "fairyland," "square dance by Lilliputians," and "floral design." In the delinquent group, however, very little dependent affect was shown in the content of the chosen cards (see chap. 6). Although somewhat more positive affect was present on the blots chosen as the mother card for the delinquent group than on the other cards, the overall amount of positive affect in the records was significantly lower than that found in the nondelinquent group. Instead, the delinquent group was significantly higher on neutral responses throughout. But again, the mother card, while described in positive terms, did not evoke as much positive or dependent affect in the content symbolism given spontaneously to the cards as it did in the normal group.

One may infer that, generally, delinquents give flatter, more evasive records and avoid producing affectively laden responses (see chap. 6). Avoidance of deep relationships has often been described in reference to criminal and psychopathic groups (Cleckey 1941; Lindner 1944).

Relative Choice of Cards Ranked According to "Like" and "Dislike"

In ranking the blots according to likes and dislikes, those chosen as the mother card were ranked first by 18 of 25 normal girls and 10 of 25 delinquent girls (table 5.4). For the boys a converse trend held. Only 5 normal boys ranked the mother card first, as compared with 11 of 25 delinquents. There was much variation in ranking in respect to the father card, which was most often second choice in both the nondelinquent and delinquent groups. There was a tendency, however, for normal boys to choose the

TABLE 5.4

Ranking of Father and Mother Cards with All Other Cards in
Nondelinquent and Delinquent Japanese Youth

Rank[*] of Card Chosen as:	Father Card						Mother Card					
	Nondelinquents			Delinquents			Nondelinquents			Delinquents		
	M	F	T	M	F	T	M	F	T	M	F	T
1	7	_	7	2	3	5	5	18‡	23‡	11†	10†	21‡
2	6	13**	19**	8	9	17**	6	2	8	3	3	6
3	2	2	4	2	4	6	4	2	6	5	3	8
4	3	2	5	4	1	5	4	1	5	1	4	5
5	1	2	3	3	2	5	2	_	2	2	1	3
6	2	1	3	1	_	1	3	1	4	1	1	2
7	2	_	2	_	1	1	_	1	1	1	1	2
8	2	2	4	3	1	4	1	_	1	1	_	1
9	_	2	2	2	3	5	_	_	_	_	_	_
10	_	1	1	_	1	1	_	_	_	_	2	2
Total	25	25	50	25	25	50	25	25	50	25	25	50

* Each individual rank ordered all the cards. The relative position of the cards previously chosen as "father" and "mother" cards were noted for each individual regardless of what specific cards were chosen.
† P>.05 for frequency of ranking mother card first choice.
‡ P>.01 for frequency of ranking mother card first choice.
** P>.01 for frequency of ranking father card second choice.

father card first (7 cases). In both nondelinquent and delinquent groups the mother card ranked higher than the father card (in 35 of 50 cases). However, there was a significant trend for the normal boys (in 13 cases) to rank the father ahead of the mother as compared with the normal girls, only 2 of whom did so. The reverse was true for the delinquent group, where boys ranked the father first in 6 cases, and girls in 9.

It is obvious that first asking for a designation of cards as reminiscent of either father or mother influenced the subsequent ranking of the ten cards as to likes and dislikes. It has been the usual experience with American groups that Card IV is rarely chosen in a test as a "most liked" card. Its appearance as a preferred card among certain normal Japanese boys seemed to be related to conscious attitudes about what one's feelings toward a father should be.

Negative choices for ranking a card low were related strongly to conscious attitudes toward a parent. This relationship became evident in subsequent interviews with the delinquent group. For example, one delinquent who ranked the father card first and the mother card tenth said, "My father is kind to me and loves me, but my mother is selfish and cruel. I have not heard from her for awhile. My neighbors sympathize with me because of my mother's coldness." Another delinquent who ranked the mother card third and the father card tenth stated that he hated his father "because he always got angry at trifles."

Conclusions and Discussion

The above results comparing normal and delinquent Japanese youth on the basis of their selection of specific Rorschach cards as related to the mother or father suggest several conclusions.

1. A cross-cultural applicability of the Rorschach test is validated. As in the studies with normal Americans, the choice of Card IV as a father card corroborates the clinical impressions of this blot as representing dominance and authority, with possible underlying threatening implications for many subjects.

2. The tendency to select Card VII as a mother card was evident, at least in nondelinquent Japanese girls, but color, especially when interpreted as gay and pleasant in nature, seemed

to act as a more immediate stimulus to choice than did the soft, feminine configurations of the achromatic Card VII.

3. The conscious reasons presented by normals for choice of Card IV as a father card emphasized the more positive attributes of masculine dominance, whereas more threatening affective symbolism was found in the content given spontaneously. These results suggest that normal Japanese youth, boys especially, are apt to see the father and his authority in a positive light and to seek to emphasize the positive virtues of an adult authority figure, although the underlying threat implied in the relationship to the father seemed to remain unresolved in many instances.

4. There was less divergence between conscious attitudes and spontaneous responses to the cards chosen as reminiscent of mother in both normal and delinquent groups. However, the delinquent group produced less positive and dependent affective content.

5. There was a trend for the ranking of father and mother cards to be related to sex. In normal Japanese girls, the mother card was overwhelmingly ranked as most liked, in some contrast to the boys, who in some cases choose the father over the mother cards.

6. Card choice in the delinquent group was further complicated by the inferential presence of certain character defences related to delinquent behavior. Authority threat was avoided, rather than translated into positive terms, as it was in many of the nondelinquent group. Affective symbolism, of either a positive or negative variety, was restricted in the protocols. Even less affective content was found on the cards selected as the father card than in the others. The relatively few choices of Card IV by the delinquent group compared with the nondelinquent group suggests an avoidance of that blot and its implied threat by an evasive selection of another, more neutral card.

The results obtained are consonant with descriptions of characterological avoidance of strong affective relationships found in delinquent character reactions. This trend is especially noted in reference to the choice of a father card.

The results in general are consonant with impressions gained by observation that suggest that the conforming, socially adapting person in Japan tends to emphasize consciously the positive or dependent features of relationships to the parents. This tendency holds regardless of whatever unconscious unresolved feelings, particularly toward the father, may be present. The relationship to the mother tends in both groups tested to be more spontaneous and warm, with less discrepancy between conscious and unconscious attitudes. The conclusions of this study were further strengthened by the results of later tests reported in the following chapter.

Notes

1. The Japanese schools use well-standardized versions of both the Binet and Wechsler intelligence scales. In an informal comparison of the Japanese translation of the "Wechsler" intelligence scale with the American version, the author De Vos felt that the Japanese test was somewhat more exacting in the precision demanded in answers to vocabulary items. The most noteworthy difference that could be directly compared was in respect to the Japanese standards on the Block Design subtest. The Japanese norm of "10" on the identical subtest used in the American version of "Wechsler I" is comparable to our level of "12." In other words, the Japanese norm of 100 would be achieved only by Americans gaining a score of 120. This disparity is of significance in considering differences between the highest attainments of Japanese children in mathematics and science when compared with American children (cf. Stevenson, Azuma, and Hakuta 1986).

References

Bochner, R., and F. Halpern
   1942   *The Clinical Application of the Rorschach Test.* New York: Grune and Stratton.
Cleckley, H.
   1941   *The Mask of Sanity.* St. Louis: C. V. Mosby.
De Vos, G. A.
   1952   A Quantitative Approach to Affective Symbolism in Rorschach Responses. *Journal of Projective Techniques* 16:133–150.
   1954   A Comparison of the Personality Difference in Two Generations of Japanese Americans by Means of the Rorschach Test. *Nagoya Journal of Medical Science* 17:133–261.
Lindner, R.
   1944   *Rebel Without a Cause.* New York: Grune and Stratton.

1946 Content Analysis in Rorschach Work. *Rorschach Research Exchange* 10:121–129.

Meers, B., and S. L. Singer
1950 A Note on the "Father" and "Mother" Cards in Rorschach Inkblots. *Journal of Consulting Psychology* 14:482–484.

Mitchell, Mildred B.
1952 Preferences for Rorschach Cards. *Journal of Projective Techniques* 16:203–211.

Phillips, L., and J. Smith
1953 *Rorschach Interpretation: Advanced Technique.* New York: Grune and Stratton.

Rosen, E.
1951 Symbolic Meanings in Rorschach Cards: A Statistical Study. *Journal of Clinical Psychology* 7:239–244.

Chapter Six

A Comparison of Delinquent and Nondelinquent Families

George A. De Vos and Orin Borders

The Rorschach test was used as part of a large-scale research project on juvenile delinquency in Japan conducted during the 1960s (see Wagatsuma and De Vos 1985). Our major research effort was done with an experimental sample of thirty-one families, each with a delinquent son who was 13 to 15 years old. These families were compared with the families of nineteen nondelinquent age-mate controls taken from the same junior high schools. The samples were controlled stringently for parents' education, family occupation, and other features of class background. Each father and mother as well as each subject and control was interviewed and tested with the Rorschach and TAT during two or more interview sessions lasting a minimum of six hours per person.

The families were all obtained from Arakawa ward, Tokyo, an area of prevailingly lower-status petty artisans and merchants living on the northeast fringes of metropolitan Tokyo. Our contact with the parents was facilitated through members of the local school system, the police, and clinical psychologists working in various child welfare agencies. The present sample took over four years to collect, interview, and test.

This study reveals again that it is difficult to use the Rorschach test to do individual diagnostic comparisons related specifically to problems of delinquency. Nevertheless, as our results demonstrate, it is possible to find significant group differences both in

149

children who commit delinquent offenses and in members of their families as compared with normal children and their families.

The Rorschach records were compared thoroughly on the standard scoring categories. In addition, Fisher's Rigidity and Maladjustment scales were used (see chap. 4), as well as the De Vos system of scoring content symbolism (see chap. 3 and app. A). Results with the present sample confirmed previous results reporting the overall usefulness of the Rorschach technique in clinical diagnosis in Japan. The present research findings also highlight the potential importance of testing and interviewing family members as well as subjects themselves in any clinical study.

A Comparison of Rorschach Test Results

Overall results with the Rorschach test in Arakawa were similar to the normative testing previously mentioned in chapter 4. As discussed there, the Rorschach results in Japan reported by Murakami (1959, 1960) revealed an overall pattern similar to that obtained from American *Issei* immigrants in my initial study in Chicago with Japanese immigrant *Issei* and American-born *Nisei* (De Vos 1952, 1954, 1955). Whereas the overall level of personality rigidity was considerably higher for Japanese than for American subjects, the sense of social reality was very strong, (principally measured by "good form" responses or F+). The Japanese generally revealed on the Rorschach a higher regard for good form (F+) in the percepts than did American subjects. While there was a high degree of overlap in what are termed "popular" (P) or frequently seen percepts between the two populations, Japanese were less apt to utilize some particular details (D) that were popular for Americans. By contrast, they produced a popular response in the form of a flower given to the center of Card VIII, which rarely appeared in American reports (Murakami 1959).

Characteristically, the Japanese gave far fewer responses (R) than did American subjects. The average number of responses for the Japanese were approximately seventeen compared with twenty-eight to thirty-two responses for American populations (De Vos 1954; Murakami 1959). The Japanese generally strove to give a single well-integrated response to each card (W organized with Z), showing a strong intellectual organizational drive. Americans were more apt to give a simple response to some detail of the card when they did not perceive a total, complex integrated whole. The Japanese, in contrast, were more likely to reject a card (rej) when they were unable to give what they believed to be a satisfactory response. Clinical application of the Rorschach in Japan reveals that it can be used with the same diagnostic credibility as in the United States (chap. 7).

In the present study we used the Rorschach in examining individual family members as an aid to understanding the personality dynamics underlying expressed attitudes and observed behavior. We were also interested to learn whether there were any particular diagnostic features that would be indicative of personality differences distinguishing between delinquent and nondelinquent subjects and their parents. We can report that we did indeed find significant statistical differences between groups, but we do not feel that any of these differences permitted an individual diagnosis related to social deviancy.

We did find higher overall rigidity as a personality characteristic in the parents of delinquents. But a high parental rigidity score of itself, or any of the other differences by themselves, are *not* diagnostic of potential delinquency in a child. For example, there were on the average significantly fewer human movement responses (H) to the Rorschach in both parents and subjects among the delinquent sample. While this finding was highly significant statistically for the group, we could not thereby determine that the absence of movement responses (M) in a Rorschach protocol was indicative of delinquency vs. nondelinquency in a particular parent or subject. Nevertheless, the overall results are worth reporting because they are in line with various assumptions about how particular personality patterns may contribute to the appearance of delinquent or criminal behavior in particular individuals.

The Rorschach Rigidity and Maladjustment Scales (Fisher 1950) reported on in other chapters of this volume were used to test differences in the Japanese family units as to certain qualitative features of a record. There are twelve items which comprise the rigidity scale, and the maladjustment scale has twenty-four separate items. Some of the items overlap from one scale to the other. Both scales measure aberrancies in responses concerned with location, formal determinants, color, shading, response totals, form quality, and various content features such as percentage of animal responses (A). Overall, the rigidity scale attempts to measure the level of stereotypy, or lack of flexibility in personality.

The Maladjustment scale, in contrast, is a composite measure of those Rorschach variables which have traditionally and empirically been demonstrated to relate to psychopathology in the more restricted clinical sense. While there is some correlation and overlap between the two systems, a high score on the rigidity scale does not always indicate a serious maladjustment, and vice versa.

Fisher characterized his rigidity scale as a moderately good measure of what might be called a general rigidity trend in a personality. Variables contributing to a high rigidity score include the percentage of pure form (F%); low response total (R); high percentage of animal responses (A%); too high F+% (above 95); no card turning; low number of color (FC, CF, C), shading (T, Y), or human movement responses (H); high use of whole responses (W); unusual details (Dd); stereotypy in response content; and slow initial response time.

The maladjustment scale of Fisher is highly complex, composed of many variables. In general, they first include what are termed perceptual "approach" variables (the ratio of responses to the whole of the card (W%), or to large details (D%), or rarely seen details (Dd%). The scale includes several variables suggestive of intrapsychic "looseness" or fluidity not found in the rigidity scale (as an example, poor form level [low F+%]). Variables contributing to high maladjustment scores also include an excessive use of whole responses or unusual details; a low number of color and human movement responses, poor form quality, card rejection, poorly controlled shading responses, sex or anatomy content, inappropriate animal content; sex confusion, contamination, and confabulation.

Rigidity and Maladjustment Results from Our Sample

Individual T-test and chi-square comparisons of significant differences were performed on the various subsamples, as well as on the totals of the delinquent and nondelinquent family members considered together. Table 6.1 presents the mean scores of significance on the rigidity and maladjustment scales. In this and other tables the T-test was used for the parametric variables, whereas the chi-square was reserved for the nominal variables.

In considering the maladjustment scores, we found that where sons, fathers, and mothers in a group were all considered together, the nondelinquent controls received lower maladjustment scores than did their counterparts. However, only in the instance of the mothers, where there was a difference of 13 points, was there a statistically significant difference; the mothers of nondelinquents scored notably lower than any of the other subgroups, in contrast to the relatively high score found in the mothers of delinquents. Overall, there was a very high variability in maladjustment scores, which contributed to the lack of statistical significance in the total samples when they were compared. The principal difference in the subcategories included in the maladjustment scale was due to the relative lack of movement responses in all the delinquent subsamples. The general lack of enrichment in the delinquent records suggested that constriction and rigidity contributed more to any maladjustment noted than did signs of "looseness" or poor reality contact. The records as a whole in both groups gave us relatively little indication of autistic or pathological thinking or an inadequate sense of social reality. These findings become clearer when we examine the results of the rigidity scale.

As table 6.1 demonstrates, when the scores of sons, mothers, and fathers in a group were averaged together, the delinquent group showed a significantly higher average rigidity than the nondelinquent group. Because of the small size of the sample, however, only the mothers of delinquents, when compared separately, showed a statistical difference from the mothers of nondelinquents at the 5% level. An examination of the subcategories of the rigidity scale suggests that the difference between delinquent and nondelinquent groups rested primarily on a much greater use of form without the enrichment of the major determinants (color, movement, or shading) among the delinquent groups. What was again particularly noteworthy was the general lack of human movement responses in the delinquent sample.

TABLE 6.1

Differences in Total Fisher's Rigidity and Maladjustment
Scores and Various Specific Subscores

	Nondelinquents				Delinquents			
	Fa	Mo	Sons	Tot	Fa	Mo	Sons	Tot
Total Rigidity Score	37.17	29.78	32.83	33.26	46.17*	44.17‡	39.20	43.18‡
F% (pure form)	53.89	51.89	56.22	54.00	63.70*	66.07†	64.93	64.90‡
F indefinite (Fv)	.50	.78	.94	.74	.27	.73	.70	.57
Z (organizational responses)	5.61†	7.00†	6.83†	6.48†	3.20	3.57	4.40	3.72
No card turning	.50	.67	.50	.56*	.47	.43	.43	.40
Total Maladjustment Score	42.00	34.94	38.11	38.35	48.33	47.87†	44.03	46.74†
Total populars (P)	5.22	5.11	4.67	5.00*	4.70	4.70	4.23	4.54
No popular on Card V	.67	.83	.67	.72	.87	.86	.93†	.89†
No popular on Card VIII	.56	.67	.61	.61	.83†	.80	.63	.76
Animal percentage (A%)	55.28	46.17*	55.78	52.41	56.83	55.03	57.63	56.50
Humans (H)	2.17†	2.50‡	2.61†	2.43‡	1.00	1.30	1.50	1.27
Human detail (Hd)	.28	.41	.72	.47†	.13	.20	.37	.23
"Humanoid" responses	.39	1.00†	1.11	.83	.60	.46	1.17	.74
Aesthetic responses	1.17†	.78	.67	.87†	.23	.77	.23	.41
Anatomy	.72	.94	.17	.61	.86	.67	1.07†	.87
Sex, anality	.28	.22*	.00	.17*	.13	.03	.00	.06

*(p<.10)
†(p<.05)
‡(p<.01)

The delinquent sample also showed, on the average, a lack of form-dominated color and good form responses. These differences reached significance only when the total groups were considered together.

Another notable difference between the two groups was in the number of responses that contained superior organization (the Z-score). Such responses are usually indicative of a highly internalized push to organize the world cognitively in a comprehensible fashion. Our results revealed far fewer such responses among the delinquent sample and provided significant evidence that highly motivated, conflict-free cognitive functioning was considerably less prominent in delinquent families than in nondelinquent families. We speculated that this was not only an intrapsychic reality of the individuals in such families, but also an important aspect of the family atmosphere and environment.

But what did this difference in cognitive organization and lack of movement, color, and shading responses in the members of families of delinquents imply? It is our opinion that this evidence suggested a general tendency toward greater use of denial and repression on the part of individuals in delinquent families when compared with nondelinquent families. Movement, color, and shading responses are significant on the Rorschach in that they indicate various levels of ego-syntonic emotional responsiveness and involvement with the interpersonal world. The capacity to give a goodly number and balance of such responses is suggestive of fairly well-developed abilities to integrate the various facets of emotional experience into comfortable social behavior. Together with other Rorschach indicators (a high form level score), a good balance of such responses also suggests a more mature level in the use of coping mechanisms. The gross lowering or absence of all such responses in some delinquent families suggested a discomfort with spontaneous emotional expression generally, and a propensity to cope with emotionally significant social events by the rigid application of less mature defense mechanisms. Speaking more phenomenologically, it appears more difficult for individuals in delinquent families to both acknowledge to themselves or to others the full spectrum of their feelings and to respond spontaneously to feelings in a socially nondisruptive way. At the same time, they are prone to what is termed "acting-out" behavior, unmodulated by prior thought. From this, we might infer that members of delinquent families will often try to cope with their inner life and feelings toward others by either ignoring or denying many of their emotions.

The sons, fathers, and mothers of nondelinquents all gave more responses containing human percepts. Such responses are generally connected with the capacity for empathy and the ability to identity with the experiences of others. From this point of view, the low frequency of such responses among all the delinquent subgroups suggested less well-developed empathic attitudes and concern for the feelings of others among the individuals in delinquent families when compared with nondelinquent families.

When we compare the movement, color, and shading responses of the two groups as they related to what is termed in Rorschach parlance as "inner and outer control," our results in general conform to the observation that delinquency-prone individuals are more "motoric," that is, behave more "externally" than "ideationally," whereas nondelinquent individuals more often show a tendency to resolve or react to stimuli by internal processes involving thinking through of experience rather than giving overt behavioral responses.

Measures of Inner and Outer Control

The most notable differences between the groups was in what is considered in Rorschach assessment as the areas of "inner control" and "outer control." As we shall presently discuss, the use of kinesthetic or movement responses to the Rorschach is assumed to reveal a capacity for an "inner life," hence inner control, and the ability to problem-solve in thought rather than resorting to externally observable behavioral responses to resolve inner promptings.

Color responses measure "outer control," the ability to modulate in a controlled way one's reactivity to external stimuli. The results obtained with the delinquent samples suggested an excessive utilization of constrictive defenses. Such overall constriction prevents both more modulated responses to one's own inner impulses and ego-modulated reactions to emotional arousal by outside stimuli. Hence, one assumes there might be the periodic appearance of uncontrolled behavior which could bring the individual into social difficulty.

Deviant behavior in many instances is consequent to a lack of inner control, outer control, or some combination thereof. For example, it can result from strong impulses to express a sense of hostility or resentment. Some delinquents "need" to flout authority. Again, delinquency can symbolize the person's need for affection. Deviant behavior may also result from immoderate or uncontrolled reactions to outer provocations. In contrast, a nondelinquent person can "keep his cool" despite provocation, exercising a wariness about possible social disapproval. Some individuals can be termed "hostile" or given to aggressive behavior arising from within; others are uncontrolled in their reactions and thereby become alienated and are treated as immature or deviant by those who are in contact with them. Of course, the behavior of most deviant individuals results from a composite of inner promptings combined with environmental events which "justify their actions." In brief, a typical delinquent has resentful attitudes that he acts upon and can justify, pointing out that he is rejected or treated badly by authorities or adults generally. Some, certain that they will be deprived or "picked on," steal first, in symbolic retribution.

"Inner Control": Human Movement Percepts

As already noted, the most highly significant differentiation between our samples appeared in the overall use of human percepts and their animation (see table 6.2). The capacity for kinesthetic interpretation of the Rorschach blots, whether in the form of human, animal, or inanimate motion, was given more freely by the

TABLE 6.2

Significant Differences in Movement Responses

	Nondelinquents				Delinquents			
	Fa	Mo	Sons	Tot	Fa	Mo	Sons	Tot
Total human movement	2.33†	2.78‡	3.78‡	2.96‡	1.27	1.47	1.87	1.53
M with minus form (M-)	.28‡	.06	.72	.35*	.00	.10	.17	.09
M on Card III	.78	1.00	.83	.87	.70	.53‡	.57*	.60‡
Active M	1.17†	1.22	2.17‡	1.52‡	.53	.80	.80	.71
Passive M	.72	1.22†	1.06	1.00†	.57	.50	.73	.60
Animal movement (FM)	3.83*	4.78*	3.83	4.15‡	2.57	3.03	3.40	3.00
Active animal movement (FM_a)	2.06*	2.61*	2.78	2.48	1.17	1.47	2.10	1.57
Total inanimate movement (Fm)	.67	1.78‡	1.17	1.20†	.53	.80	.83	.72
Total active movement (M_a)	3.33†	4.67†	5.00*	4.33‡	1.93	2.60	3.47	2.67
Total passive movement (M_p)	2.39†	3.00†	2.39	2.59‡	1.40	1.50	1.67	1.52

*(p<.10)
†(p<.05)
‡(p<.01)

nondelinquent than by the delinquent group. The overall suggestion is, therefore, that there is greater constriction of inner life in
the delinquent sample and, therefore, a lack of maturation of
conscious concern with humans and their motivations.

Our finding is consonant with one of the major assumptions of
Rorschach diagnosis concerning ego constriction versus ideational freedom. It is therefore a significant substantiation of the
meaning of this variable in Rorschach interpretations. These are
clinical conclusions that agree with other studies indicating that
individuals institutionalized for delinquent behavior generally
tend to be more "motor"-oriented in coping with the environment; in other words, they are not likely to resolve problems in
their minds before going into action. By contrast, other individuals are better able to interpose forms of ideational control
that can modulate the direct expression of attitudes or impulses.
In a stress situation, such a person can experience emotional
arousal internally without making a visible outer response.
According to clinical inference, the capacity to see human movement on the Rorschach is related to forms of self-control over
behavior which can prevent an individual from getting into social
difficulty. He or she can consciously or unconsciously inhibit the
commission of an act that would prompt social disapprobation.

Some of the fathers in the nondelinquent sample, by and large
petty merchants and artisans, occasionally produced movement
responses of "poor form" quality, that is movement was given for
figures conforming very poorly to the form of the blot (M−). This
suggests a tendency toward maladjustive looseness in thought
processes. That is to say, in some cases the percepts given did
not correspond well to the shape of the blot area. Such responses
are a minor indication that some of these economically marginal
men of Arakawa ward, Tokyo (Wagatsuma and De Vos 1984:
chap. 6), showed certain marginal psychological qualities that
may have been related to their occupational difficulties in a
competitive society. They revealed in their human movement perceptions a form of maladjustment that might have been socially
maladaptive. But these inner problems did not relate to behavioral deviancy in the direction of delinquency. Statistically
the nondelinquent fathers did not, as a variable group, differ
widely in their mean overall maladjustment scores.

A Rorschach sign of interpersonal difficulty that especially characterized the parents in the delinquent sample was their relative inability to see human movement of Card III. The shape of this blot makes it relatively easy to perceive human figures. In cross-cultural findings, this card most frequently elicits the human form. Seventeen out of nineteen of the mothers in our nondelinquent control did see human movement in this card, as opposed to only 16 out of 31 mothers of delinquents. This was a highly significant difference. The difference also reached significance in their sons. Among the nondelinquent controls, 16 out of 19 gave a human movement response to Card III compared with only 17 out of 31 responses of delinquents. Failure to see the most commonly perceived human form indicates problems in experiencing positive social attitudes. The comparative lack of the human movement response by delinquent subjects and their mothers matched the clinical observation that they had difficulty in adopting ordinary social attitudes. (Our sample of fathers was not different from our other sample on this variable.)

An interesting differentiation that one can make among the human movement responses is to classify them into those responses that indicate an active "extratensive," or expansive quality as opposed to those that are passive or stationary in nature. The normative controls tended to give many more active or expanding movement responses than did the delinquent subjects. While the delinquents also gave fewer passive movement responses, it was the actual difference in the number of active movement responses that most strikingly differentiated the two samples. This finding suggested that the nondelinquent controls were more apt to take an active, constructive, and outgoing stance in interpersonal relations.

"Outer Control": Control of Affectivity and Responsiveness to Stimuli

We found a greater constriction among the delinquent samples in the use of color responses (beyond the 1% level of significance). This difference was most notable in the mothers and least notable in the sons, with the fathers falling in between (table 6.3).

Not only did we compare in the Rorschach the overall use of

TABLE 6.3

Significant Differences in Color and Shading Reactions

| | Nondelinquents | | | | Delinquents | | | |
	Fa	Mo	Sons	Total	Fa	Mo	Sons	Total
Good form, dominant color (FC +)	1.67*	1.94	1.78*	1.80‡	.93	1.20	1.03	1.06
Poor form, dominant color (FC -)	.17	.06	.44*	.22	.10	.13	.17	.13
Pure color (C)	.06	.11	.39†	.19*	.10	.13	.03	.09
Color symbolism	.17	.11*	.11*	.13	.13	.00	.00	.04
Total color responses	3.28*	3.67†	3.33	3.43‡	2.20	2.37	2.47	2.34
Total shading (Y)	3.17*	3.22	2.28	2.89*	1.96	2.30	2.37	2.21
Texture (FT)	1.44	1.56*	1.17	1.39†	.93	.80	1.07	.93

*(P<.10)
†(P<.05)
‡(P<.01)

color (ΣC) but we differentiated among color responses that appeared in percepts in which the form was dominant over the color (FC), in percepts where the color dominated form (CF), and in responses in which the color was perceived with little concern with form (pure C). Form-dominant color responses represent a well-modulated, mature control over one's emotions, and we found significantly higher FC in the fathers of nondelinquents than in those of delinquents. Interestingly enough, some of the nondelinquent sons produced occasional poor-quality form-dominant responses (FC−). One can say, therefore, that some of their affect may have involved a forced quality. In other words, their expression of affect may have been somewhat artificially controlled.

Perception of shading and texture is related to passive sensitivity. A significant number of shading responses can indicate anxiety (FY, YF, Y), while textural responses may suggest a kind of passive, tactual sensitivity to the outside world (FT, TF, T). Consonant with the overall greater openness in the nondelinquent group as contrasted with the constriction of the delinquent group, the total score for texture (ΣT) was higher for the nondelinquent sample. The greatest difference between the two groups was found in the mothers. The overall difference in the shading

(FT, TF + FY, YF) or "vista" responses (FV) showed trends but did not reach significance; the sample as a whole in respect to such variables conformed well to the previous normative Japanese samples obtained in 1954 and reported by Murakami (1959, 1960).

Differences in Content Symbolism

Turning to content symbolism, the major overall differences between the groups were not to be found in the negative content (hostility, anxiety, and body preoccupation), but in the positive and dependent content (table 6.4). The nondelinquent subjects had significantly higher scores in some of the dependent and positive subcategories. What was especially suggestive was the overall high dependent content of the nondelinquent sons in contrast with their delinquent counterparts. The nondelinquent mothers, in particular, had the highest score for dependent and positive content, and the lowest of all scores on the total of unpleasant content.

There are some previous writings about Rorschach differences between delinquents and nondelinquents which emphasize the appearance of particular hostile symbolism; this was not a finding with our groups. We found no significant differences in hostile content in any of the subgroups, with one minor exception: The nondelinquent sons showed more freely perceived hostile responses. There was also a tendency for the mothers of delinquents to give more indirect hostility symbolism.

Minor differences in the anxiety responses were consistent with some of our clinical impressions from the interview material. For example, the fathers of nondelinquents did show a trend toward giving more dysphoric (Agl) responses, suggesting depressive moods. This finding fit in with our impression that some of these men were sometimes a bit self-reproachful concerning their occupational failure and lowered social status. The fathers of the nondelinquent group, in contrast to both mother groups and the fathers of delinquents, tended to give, to a minor degree, less of the diffuse anxiety signs (like the use of clouds). Such responses suggest diffusely experienced anxieties, rather than those of a more precise nature. The delinquent sample, generally, had a

TABLE 6.4

Mean Differences in Affective Symbolism in Respect to Total Summary Categories
and to Specific Subcategory Responses

	Nondelinquents				Delinquents			
	Fa	Mo	Sons	Tot	Fa	Mo	Sons	Tot
Total % of Hostile Responses	13.33	8.89	15.33	12.52	9.83	10.87	10.10	10.27
Hor (oral hostile)	.56*	.39	.50	.48	.17	.20	.30	.22
Hcmpt (competitive)	.11	.17†	.39*	.22†	.13	.00	.10	.08
Hh (indirect hostile)	.39	.72	.89*	.67*	.17	.67	.30	.38
Hsm (sadomasochism)	1.00*	.56	.83	.80*	.43	.60	.38	.47
Total % of Anxious Responses	16.89	17.50	22.06	18.81	21.90	21.90	24.60	22.80*
Athr (threatening percepts)	1.06	1.78†	2.50	1.78*	.67	.87	2.13	1.22
Aev (evasive percepts)	.28	.11	.11	.17	.57	.43*	.30	.45
Abal (loss of balance)	.06	.06	.39*	.17	.13	.10	.03	.09
Acnph (counterphobic)	.17	.44*	.06	.22	.20	.13	.23	.19
Agl (dysphoric-depressive percepts)	.56†	.33	.28	.39	.17	.47	.43	.3
Total % of Body Preoccupation	2.78	3.11	.50	2.12	5.43	2.00	3.60*	3.68
Bb (bone anatomy)	.06	.11	.00	.06	.37*	.23	.53†	.38*
Bd (disease or decay)	.00	.00	.00	.00	.17	.13	.07	.1
Bs (sexual anatomy)	.00	.12*	.00	.04*	.00	.00	.00	.00
Total % of Dependency Percepts	7.83*	10.00†	8.83‡	8.89‡	4.73	5.57	3.37	4.5
Dcl (clinging or hanging percepts)	.33	.44	.39*	.39*	.20	.23	.13	.15
Dch (childishly toned percepts)	.61†	1.22†	.94†	.93‡	.23	.53	.33	.37
Drel (religious precepts)	.11	.39	.06†	.20	.20	.33	.00	.18*
Daut (authority precepts)	.56†	.56	.56‡	.56‡	.10	.37	.10	.19
Dsub (submission precepts)	.28	.33	.17*	.26	.20	.20	.00	.10
Total % of Positive Affect	23.67†	25.44‡	20.61†	23.24‡	14.83	15.50	12.77	14.37
Ps (sensual-body percepts)	.56	.56	.67	.59†	.37	.33	.37	.36
Pch (child play)	.44	1.17†	.17	.50†	.30	.30	.20	.27
Prec (recreation-activity)	1.17	.94	1.67†	1.26†	.67	.67	.70	.68
Porn (ornamental percepts)	1.61†	1.33	.56†	1.17‡	.40	.73	.20	.44
Pstr (striving percepts)	.39	.89*	.83‡	.70‡	.30	.33	.20	.28
Pnar (body narcissism)	.11	.28	.22	.20*	.10	.10	.07	.09
Pcpt (competence)	.22	.22	.22	.22†	.13	.07	.03	.08
Total % of Neutral Percepts	29.94	32.22	30.22	30.80	37.13*	39.07	41.13†	39.11*
Total Unpleasant Affect	33.00	29.33	37.33	33.22	37.20	34.73	38.60	36.84

*(p<.10)
†(p<.05)
‡(p<.01)

trend toward evasive (Aev) responses, such as maps and diagrams that had no definite shape or outline. They also showed anxiety very indirectly in their perception of human pelvises. One could say that these bone anatomy (Bb) responses related to the generally nonideational nature of the delinquent records. Such responses are generally given by individuals who have very little direct insight into anxious or phobic states.

Finally, disease responses (Bdi) were given by 8 of the 93 members of the delinquent group, while no person in the nondelinquent group gave such a response. However, the trend was statistically insignificant because of the small sample. Therefore, in a minority of these records, one must consider some signs here and there of psychopathology.

The most notable differences were not found in the negative results, then, but rather in the use by the nondelinquents of dependent or positive symbolism. The delinquents had a much higher neutral content. Over 39% of their material was scored neutral, compared with a little over 30% of the material in the nondelinquent control sample. The dependent categories differed in that the nondelinquents produced almost 9% dependency responses, which was higher than scores previously obtained in American samples (see chaps. 3 and 4), and twice as high as the Japanese delinquent group. Looking specifically at the nature of the dependent content, the most striking difference was the tendency for the fathers, mothers, and sons in the nondelinquents to give childish, dependent (Dch) responses, in contrast to their delinquent counterparts. Nondelinquent fathers and sons also characteristically gave a significant number of authority symbols (Daut), such as helmets, badges, and emblems. This finding was very striking considering the nature of underlying social attitudes prevalent among delinquents. In our interview material with family members in the delinquent sample we found covert or overt attitudes antagonistic to formal authority, both in parents and children. The fact that positive symbols of authority were seen by the nondelinquents indicated their more conformist attitudes in contrast to their delinquent counterparts.

Whereas the sons and fathers gave these authority symbols, the mothers of nondelinquents, in contrast to the mothers of delinquents, gave various symbols of security, such as caves, indicative of a "female" sanctuary. In some nondelinquents we found that use of the dependent category suggested a strong capacity for a positive childish dependent identification. This finding is consistent with other evidence reported in the literature on Japanese personality (Caudill and Weinstein 1969; De Vos 1973; Doi 1971); it suggests that Japanese culture allows, and expects the expression as well, of positively toned dependency. Japanese cultivate an inner experience of considerably more dependency than one characteristically finds tolerated in American culture.

The contrasting absence of such responses in the delinquent records suggested possible alienation from meaningful dependent relationships in the families of delinquents. One can infer the likelihood of a greater cynicism about childish experience, parental nurturance, and interpersonal relationships in general among individuals of such families. Japanese are more at home than Americans in a subordinate position within an age-graded hierarchical structure, so that authority symbolism has a positive social meaning.

In essence, it was the absence of positive affect scores (Pos%) in the delinquent families that separated them most from the nondelinquent. The subcategories in which this difference was most notable were those suggesting positive sensual feelings (Ps), and positive responses suggesting active striving (Pstr). The positive sensual category provided only a trend to differentiate the two groups. These responses suggested a sensual pleasure related to tactual stimulation of various sorts, such as furry rugs and kissing. Forty-three percent of the nondelinquent controls gave such responses in contrast to 29% of the delinquent subjects. While only a trend, the relative absence of such responses in a delinquent group is consistent with the evidence elsewhere in the tests that difficulties in interpersonal closeness and dependency were more prevalent among members of these families than in those of nondelinquents.

The childhood activities subcategory (Pch) also showed only a trend, but one in the expected direction. It was principally in the mothers of the nondelinquents that one found such responses. Ten out of 19 mothers gave at least one such response, in contrast to only 6 out of 31 of the delinquent mothers. The type of content of these responses included characters from a child's storybook, clapping hands, and women playing patty-cake. The presence of Pch responses in a majority of records in the control sample of Japanese mothers is not surprising. It is congruent with other studies on Japanese culture which suggest that the average Japanese mother is most intent on an enduring emotional investment in her children. These mothers identified strongly with the maternal role, and also perceived the world, as much as possible, through the eyes of childhood. These responses have a very positive meaning to mothers. Contrastively, the relative absence of such responses in the mothers of delinquents suggested a lowered emotional investment in the activities of children and inferentially a lower cathexis of the mothering role. Considering the special role of mothers in the training of children, it is also noteworthy that 9 out of 19 mothers of nondelinquents gave positive "striving" responses indicative of achievement orientation, such as animals climbing uphill toward some goal. These responses were found in only 6 out of 31, a much smaller proportion of the mothers of delinquent subjects. Pstr responses therefore symbolically suggest a much stronger achievement drive in the nondelinquent mothers. We would infer that such drives are conveyed to their children, as we have described in our other publications (e.g., De Vos 1973).

It is interesting that the most positive emphasis found in the control fathers was on ornamental responses (Porn). Eleven out of 19 fathers gave responses like fancy vases and chandeliers— aesthetic objects of various kinds. Such responses were relatively absent in the fathers of delinquents. Whatever the lowered status of the men in the nondelinquent sample, they were still capable of significant "positive cathexis" or emotional investment in beauty.

The sons differed in respect to their positive recreational scores (Prec), which included various forms of play. The nondelinquent sons particularly gave various active human movement responses or saw individuals in playful activities. Such responses were relatively few in the delinquent subjects, and when they did appear, they lacked the intensity or verve found in the nondelinquent percepts. It was noteworthy that 8 out of 19 of the nondelinquent sons gave two or more recreational responses, indicating the live-ly positive attitude represented in their symbolic content. The corresponding absence of positive play responses in the delinquent subjects suggested a lack of fantasy outlets.

What was most evident overall was that both generations of the nondelinquent group gave significantly more positive responses on the Rorschach, 23% compared with 14%. These results were similar to what was noted in my original normative study (chap. 4). Many Issei and Nisei Japanese Americans, despite obvious personality difficulties of one kind or another, nevertheless, as an indication of their balanced, positive attitude toward life, would reveal a very positive social interest through positively toned symbolic material. In effect, whatever the psychological or social difficulties encountered, many Japanese evidence an optimistic view of their environment or are ready to project into their environment positive attributes. Thus, a basic difference was found between the attitudes of the families of delinquents and nondelinquents in that the latter took a more positive attitudinal stance toward life. Since both groups came from the same socioeconomic circumstances, we must look elsewhere for an explanation of the relative pessimism of the families of delinquents. These Rorschach results are consonant with the results obtained by examining family cohesion by other means, as we discuss in our volume on Arakawa ward (Wagatsuma and De Vos 1984).

Finally, we find that the Rorschach evidence is a striking confirmation of the incremental influence of personality variables in explaining why individuals are socially conforming or socially deviant.

References

Caudill, William, and Helen Weinstein
    1969   Maternal Care and Infant Behavior in Japan and America. *Journal for the Study of Interpersonal Processes* 32(1):12–43.
De Vos, George A.
    1952   A Quantitative Approach to Affective Symbolism in Rorschach Responses. *Journal of Projective Techniques* 16(2):133–150.
    1954   A Comparison of the Personality Differences in Two Generations of Japanese Americans by Means of the Rorschach Test. *Nagoya Journal of Medical Science* 17(3):153–265 (reprinted: no. 34, 1966).

1955   A Quantitative Rorschach Assessment of Maladjustment and Rigidity in Acculturating Japanese Americans. *Genetic Psychology Monographs* 52:51–87.

1961   Symbolic Analysis in the Cross-Cultural Study of Personality. Bert Kaplan, ed. *Studying Personality Cross-Culturally*, pp. 599–634. Evanston, Ill.: Row-Peterson.

1973   *Socialization for Achievement: Essays on the Cultural Psychology of the Japanese.* Berkeley, Los Angeles, London: University of California Press.

De Vos, George A., and Orin Borders

1979   A Rorschach Comparison of Delinquent and Non-Delinquent Japanese Family Members. *Journal of Psychological Anthropology* 2:425–441.

De Vos, George A., and Horace Miner

1959   Oasis and Casbah: A Study of Acculturative Stress. Marvin K. Opler, ed. *Cultural and Mental Health*, pp. 333–359. Evanston, Ill.: Macmillan.

De Vos, George A., and Hiroshi Wagatsuma

1972   Family Life and Delinquency: Some Perspectives from Japanese Research. William P. Lebra, ed. *Transcultural Research in Mental Health*, pp. 59–87. Honolulu: University of Hawaii Press.

Doi, L. Takeo

1971   *Amae no Kozo (The Anatomy of Dependency).* Tokyo: Kobunsho.

Fisher, Seymour

1950   Patterns of Personality Rigidity and Some of Their Determinants. *Psychological Monographs* 64(1):1–64.

Murakami, Eiji

1959   A Normative Study of Japanese Rorschach Responses. *Rorschach Kenkyu: Rorschachiana Japonica* 2:39–85.

1960   Rorschach Test Results from Special Sample of Japanese. Tsuneo Mutamatsu et al. eds. *The Japanese: Culture and Personality Empirical Research.* Nagoya: Mei Shobo.

Stevenson, Harold, Hiroshi Azuma, and Kenji Hakuta, eds.

1986   Child Development and Education in Japan, New York: Freeman.

Wagatsuma, Hiroshi, and George A. De Vos

1984   *Heritage of Endurance: Family and Delinquency in Urban Japan.* Berkeley, Los Angeles, London: University of California Press.

Chapter Seven

Clinical Inferences in Japanese Research

George A. De Vos

In this chapter[1] I illustrate how, Rorschach evidence in particular non-anticipated instances in normative group research, not only enhances or deepens our perceptions but may provide new evidence that can cause us to reorder our impressions gained from behavior or interview data.

The usefulness of the Rorschach as a clinical diagnostic instrument as well as a survey instrument was evident was applied to particular cases in our large-scale survey of personality and social attitudes in Japan, 1953–1955. In this chapter, therefore, I illustrate a fact known to psychologists working in Japan, but perhaps doubted by those who are convinced a priori that psychological testing cannot be used diagnostically outside Western culture. Indeed, there are at present a number of comparative studies being done collaboratively by Japanese and American psychologists that belie the idea that projective testing is culture bound (De Vos and Suarez-Orozco 1986).

There are at present more trained psychologists, including clinical psychologists, working in Japan than in any other country with the exception of the United States. The same theoretical and political issues that excite Western social scientists are discussed and argued among their Japanese counterparts generally, and among psychologists specifically. The varying adequacy of contemporary research on personality is reflected in the Japanese publications. If I were to generalize about Japanese psychological publications, I would comment that there is more description of results and a greater reluctance to theorize than is true for Western research efforts.

Specifically, the Rorschach test is used in a number of Japanese psychiatric facilities as part of diagnostic procedures. The use of the test to distinguish between disturbances of a neurotic or of a psychotic nature is an established part of modern psychiatry in Japan.

Although I have observed work in clinical settings I have not been personally involved in the direct analysis of particular cases. I have therefore selected for this volume two illustrative cases out of the research material of 1954 and 1960–1965 with which I have had personal familiarity. These cases were analyzed for both their symbolic connotations and their thought processes with my systems of scoring. I am illustrating here not only the system for affective symbolism featured in this book but also the system that I have developed for scoring thought disturbances and primary process thinking which we hope to present more fully in a succeeding volume.

The first individual discussed here, a junior high school student accused of rape, was not sent to a psychiatric facility but to a juvenile detention center. He came to our attention when we were gathering family samples working in the junior high schools of Arakawa ward, Tokyo, as already illustrated in chapter 6. His family history is fully discussed in a chapter of our volume on family and delinquency in Japan (Wagatsuma and De Vos 1984). In this case it became obvious from the test protocols that the boy's resorting to rape was but one manifestation of a deeper psychiatric problem as well as an unwholesome family situation.

Takeshi Ikawa, a Fifteen-Year-Old Rapist

By age fifteen, Takeshi Ikawa had raped several girls and had participated in a number of thefts. He was apprehended by the police and was subsequently sent to a juvenile detention home.

Takeshi was the only child of his father's second marriage, the youngest in a family of four boys. The first wife could not get along with a very difficult mother-in-law. As a result the man was induced by his mother to seek a divorce. As was usual in a previous era, the children remained with the man's family. A new wife was sought who would be more compliant. The Ikawa family lived in the back of a small candy and tobacco shop in Arakawa ward, Tokyo. The father, Hideo, age 49, was employed as a bookkeeper in a clothing store. The second wife, Takeko, age 44, managed the tobacco shop while the father was at work elsewhere. Takeshi lived with his parents, three half-brothers, and paternal grandmother in two tiny rooms.

Takeshi's Developmental History

The youngest son, Takeshi, the second Mrs. Ikawa's only child, was born not long after the remarriage. Mrs. Ikawa said, "I wanted to have my own children and was very happy when my son was born." She quickly adds, "Although when he does wrong I wish he had not been born."

As a young child he seemed to give them no special problems. While still quite small, he went to bed alone without any fuss. Mr. Ikawa remembers discussing with his wife that their boy was "easy to raise." However, as was the case in many of the delinquents studied, Takeshi wet his bed, even until he was in the fifth grade. Generally, Takeshi seemed to his parents no different from the older children except that "he eats meals somewhat more slowly than others, and he dislikes meat."

The first indication of the boy's delinquency was thieving, which his father first noticed when Takeshi was in the fourth grade. At that time he took 3,000 yen out of the drawer in his parents' store and treated a friend with the money. The parents knew nothing of the theft until the friend's mother came to them with a box of strawberries as a gift to express her gratitude for their son's having been so nice to her boy. They then pressed their son, and he confessed what he had done. They told him next time to ask for money instead of taking it from the drawer. Mr. Ikawa said, "I had heard of this sort of thing happening not infrequently in a store-owning family, and since it's not so unusual for children to take money from the parents without meaning to steal, I did not think it was too serious." As far as the parents knew, the boy did not steal from them again. The father's bland remarks about stealing did not conform to the facts known by the school; other acts of stealing by the boy had been reported. The boy himself in his own interviews admitted to more stealing than was mentioned by his father.

Takeshi's delinquency was not limited to repeated theft. At the age of fourteen he had his first experience of what was described as rape; the degree of compliance by the girl is not clear. He witnessed a friend of his raping a girl, after which he himself also forcefully attacked her.

First I felt disgusted, but then I somehow wanted to do it very much myself. Then I wanted to repeat it. This first experience left a strong impression on me, and it still remains in my mind as if it's printed there. I also thought I would not be caught, as my friend had gotten away. When I did it later myself, I would tell myself that I would not be found out. But afterward, each time I was constantly afraid of being caught. When my teacher would call me to his office, I always felt a kind of shock, thinking that they had found me out at last.

Takeshi had been apprehended by the police shortly before our contacts with him, and was subsequently to be sent to a detention home. In the boy's interview materials at this time, there was very little expression of what might be considered guilt about his delinquent acts. He seems to have been most concerned with having been caught. When he was asked how he felt when he was caught he answered tangentially, saying, "I wondered why they had found out and how come I had been caught—I still cant't answer that. The harder I think and the more I wonder, the more I feel confused. I still don't know why I was found out."

He said about his stealing that it was not because he liked the associated excitement but because he "needed more money." He liked spending money on children at the playground, going to movies, and treating his acquaintances to snacks. One gains the impression that this boy was desperately trying to buy contact with others and that his stealing was a means of having enough money so that other boys would show an interest in him. He said, "Recently I have felt more satisfied and do not want more money."

We were unable to obtain any detailed and relevant information about the patterns of family interaction and of child rearing, and therefore we could not reconstruct the process of the boy's personality formation. The following excerpts from remarks made by the boy may suggest the feelings he had toward his family members when contacted by us.

Concerning his paternal grandmother, who used to discipline him, he said:

> When I was a small child I felt annoyed at my grandmother for telling me uncomfortable things. Recently stronger thoughts come to my mind. When my grandmother bothers me too much, I frankly feel I wish to kill her, or something like that.

About his parents' discipline he said:

> When my mother tells me to be careful about my words, to talk more politely, or something like that, I feel rebellious. It is OK if she is not too persistent, but when she talks too much I feel I should talk back. I don't like to let her talk. . . .
>
> My father's not so nagging. When he is angry he is angry. But when he is friendly he is friendly. But I don't think I can say that I like my father. I think I like my mother better, even when I quarrel with her. . . . I feel somehow as if my father were a stranger. . . . Especially recently I feel a chill in my back when I see my father's face. I feel as if I were with a policeman. . . . My father does not tell me to study hard as my mother does. In this regard I think I like my father better than my mother.
>
> When I quarrel with my mother I tell her I want to become a real delinquent. She says, "Go ahead and try," and then I can no longer be angry with her. My mother has known my character since my childhood. Because she knows my character well, she knows that I am too cowardly to be a delinquent even if I tell her I will be.

He said that he got along with his second and third brothers but not with his oldest. He found that he could talk much more easily with his mother than with his father. He frankly said that he did not like his grandmother very much.

> I know my grandmother means well and wants to make me grow up well, but she keeps bringing up what happened in the past [meaning his delinquent behavior], and I get angry. Grandmother and Mother quarrel frequently—whenever they have time for it. My grandmother blames my mother, saying that as my mother did not raise me right I have become a bad boy. I get angry at at my grandmother, and I have quarreled with her. My father tells me to stop, and I stop.

Of the possible sources of this boy's sexual delinquency, the father says, "In short, he [the boy] slept with my wife until he was in the fifth or sixth grade. I wonder if this had any effect on him?" (It must be noted that this is most unusual even in Japan, where a child, especially the youngest, is allowed to remain close to its mother for a much longer time than is true in the United States.) From the interviews one can readily assume that the boy was sexually stimulated by sleeping in his mother's bed until he was twelve years old. He was known by the police to have stolen women's underwear on one occasion. The deviant mother-child contacts (sleeping next to the mother until age 12) we obtained from interview data go far beyond the normative cultural expectations of children sleeping next to parents.

The father seemed to be quite aware of the unusual sexualizing of the child by his mother. When asked why his son slept so long with his mother, the father replied, "Well, it was from force of habit. When he was a small child he slept with my wife, and it continued without our thinking about it very seriously." When asked if he felt that sleeping with the mother was a cause of his son's delinquency, the father replied, "Well, he slept with my wife, and if he was a precocious child, touching his mother's body and things of that kind caused him to be interested in a woman's body. . . . I think that way."

One wonders, since the father seemed, *ex post facto*, so aware of psychological motivation, why no precautions were taken earlier. Since this particular father admitted to a strong and continuing attraction to his widowed mother in the interviews about himself, one can speculate about his unconscious induction of a similar relationship between his wife and his youngest child, aided and abetted, perhaps, by the likelihood that the parental sexual relationship was, at best, muted and infrequent. Mr. Ikawa's mother had remained his primary attachment throughout his two marriages. We should consider the intrafamilial induction pattern (Wagatsuma and De Vos 1985 96–97; Johnson 1949) that led to the incestuous sexual stimulation of the boy: the father, with his strong unconscious attachment to his own mother, identified himself with his son, and his wife with his mother, thus recreating the image of his desired closeness between his mother and himself. By implicitly encouraging the closing tie between his wife and son, the father experienced vicarious sexual satisfaction of his own incestuous wish for his own mother.

There are numerous cases found in Japanese clinical settings of impotence, partial impotence, or sexual inhibition between husband and wife in family situations where the mother fastens tenaciously onto one son, usually the eldest. This mother-son relationship is, in effect, socially sanctioned by the concern for lineage in the traditional Japanese family system. The eldest son is encouraged to take permanent care of his mother and to put the interests of the mother over those of his wife when quarrels arise. The mother-son relationship is usually relatively conflict free, and only rarely, as in this case, does the pattern result in the sexual pathology of a child. Here there may have been seductive interplay between mother and child, in effect condoned and abetted by the father.

The boy said that he "daydreams a lot."

I thought of becoming a wealthy person and spending all my life just playing. . . . I would live alone so that nobody bothers me telling me what to do. . . . I don't like to be told what to do. I would go many places by car—I would be really wealthy. . . . I also daydream about a monster attacking my neighborhood. Houses and everything get smashed under the monstrous huge feet. Everybody is crushed and only I escape. The earth comes to its end and only I am left alone. . . . Things like that.

If we think of such a reverie in the context of his relationship with his seductive mother and his passive, condoning father, we can imagine Takeshi's daydream to express at least the wish that his father had protected him from his mother's tempting behavior. Another meaning of the daydream might be that he wished that only he remained in his father's favor. This would bring on the dangers of passive homosexual desires. In any event, the boy's wish that his mother would be destroyed by the monstrous feet makes us wonder whether his rape activity was in part an expression of his repressed rage at his mother.

Whether or not these conjectures are accurate, it is clear that his daydreams constituted evidence of his severe internal psychic turmoil, well illustrated in his projective test material. When most people daydream, their ego functioning is sufficiently strong that they can produce pleasant reveries. Not he, clearly, Takeshi's internal conflicts were overwhelming.

Takeshi's Rorschach Test

Takeshi Ikawa's record was the most severely disturbed of those obtained from our fifty families in Arakawa ward; it is highly suggestive of incipient schizophrenic thought disturbance. He showed an incapacity to delineate concepts clearly. His percepts encroached on one another; and he was incapable of keeping them separate. He used certain "queer" verbalizations that deepened the impression of "dynamic" feelings of inchoate motion throughout, accompanied either by a diffuse fear or a sense of "floating."

Card I. (7″) [the time taken to give the first response to the blot]
1. *I get the feeling that this is a fearful impression. It looks as if it is coming at me this way.* [free associations are in italics—answers to inquiry are in ordinary script] Because there is something like a wing. Looks like a butterfly as well. The impression that some things are combined. The top gives this feeling. Because it has protrusions. I feel that it is open and coming this way. [W FM+ A P (Confab)(Athr, Afant, Aobs)] (see app. A for definitions of the various subcategories.)
2. *Weird or . . . The impression that various animals are "combined."* The wings and other look like a butterflies, but the top looks like a snail. [W F— A)(Fab Comb)(Afant, Adef)] (A "fabulized combination" is an absurd combination of constituent parts that is highly suggestive of primitive thought processes. See Rapaport et al. 1946).

Card II (13″)
3. *I feel that this is also like a combination of animals.* Something like a snail. As a whole, it is weird, I feel. Seen individually, it forms something. Bears [pointing to hands and legs] and snails. . . Looks like a snail because of the slender shape. [W F— A)(Fab Comb)(Confab)(Afant Adef)]
4. *I get the feeling that it is a fur.* I get the feeling that something was stretched and pinned down (*hatte aru*). I feel so because of the shape of the bear. [W FT Fm— A (Dsub, Aobs)]
5. *I feel two of something doing something together.* Something like a snail or . . . not a person, not a human being. Two things

are talking about something to each other, I feel. Because it looks as if the hands and legs are being moved by them [W M−(H)(Fab Comb)(Confab)(Afant)] (The language is peculiar in structure. It is impossible to indicate this in translation.)

Card III. (15″)
6. *Lonesome feelings.* I get the feeling that it is a spirit fire. I have a weird and lonesome feeling because of it. Something slender is floating in the air. [D CF mF+ Rel (Athr, Dlo)]
   7. *Also a combination of human beings or animals.* "*Something is being done.*" The faces and other things give the impression of an animal. The figure is like that of a man. I feel that they are disputing over something. Doing something, looking at— facing each other. [D M+ (H) P (HH)]

Card IV. (11″)
8. *Fearful feeling. It looks as if it were ready to charge me.* This looks like a leg. It gives the feeling of bigness. Because the leg is like it is moving. Neither man nor animal but something. [D M−(H)(Athr, Afant)]
   9. *Like a fur.* I feel that something is put on and is spread. This may be because it is black. As the fur is spread and put on. [W FT+ Aobs P(Misc)]
   10. *Looks like a snail.* Protruding tentacle and other parts a little bit. Because it is of slender shape. [D F+ A (Adis, Adef, Aobs)]
   11. *Looks like a combination of something.* Like snail, like a monster, like a combination of furs. [W F+ A/H Fab Comb) (Athr, Afant, Aobs)]

Card V. (12″)
12. *I feel it is a butterfly. The feeling that something is flying—a weird feeling.* The impression of wings and others. From the leg part. Spreading the wings and looking this way, so it looks like. . . . No, it's facing that way because it has wings. But the wings are not regular but protruding. It would be good if there were no protrusions. [W F+ A P (Weird verbalization)(Aobs)]

Card VI. (9″)
13. *Looks like a tiger's fur.* Because the protruding parts are like legs and the top is like a face. The feeling that something is sticking to it. Because it spreads out and I see two. The legs and others. Only one should be seen if it's not a fur. I feel some pity. As it is being spread and stuck [pinned], it gives me the feeling that it is dead. [W FT Fm+ Aobj P (Hsm, Agl)]

Card VII. (13″)
14. *I get the feeling that it is combination of a cow, a horse, and a man or something like that.* The face and the mouth are like those of an animal, but the leg and the body look like a human. Like dancing, because it is spreading its arms. A little bit weird. Weird when seen as a whole. [W M− (H) P (Fab Comb)(Afant, Aobs, Prec)]

Card VIII. (16″)
15. *I get the feeling that it is a mixture*
  16. *of animals and*
  17. *plants.* The sides look like tigers as there are four legs, and this as a whole is like a flower. As it is spreading and the shape is like a wing. [W mF− Aobj (Fab Comb)(Afant)] [D FC+ Bot (Pnat)] [D FM+ A P (Neut)]
  18. *I get the feeling that it is bones.* As it is not neatly organized and has notches. Slender bones and thick bones are mixed together. Looks like bones, as there is a center and they spread as a whole. Beautiful. Because pink and orange colors are used (color naming). All are sticking to one another and doing something, as if animals, plants, and bones are stuck together. [D mF− Anat (Bb)]

Card IX. (10″)
19. *This represents the feeling of this being a human bone.* There is a center and it looks like a bone. [D F− Anat (Bb, Aobs)]
  20. *It represents something like a map.* A foreign map or . . . Protruding and like a map. As the vacant part is like a lake. The colors are like those of a map. The colors are beautiful. Many colors such as pink are used. [WS C/F− Map (Aev, Pnat)]

Card X. (10″)
21. *There are things like seaweed*
   22. *and things like birds.* A thing like seaweed looks like a tangle. It's slender. A thing like a bird is like a hen, as it is small. It gives a weird feeling as there is no bird in the sea. [DW F− Bot (Dsub)(Fab Comb)(Arb Comb)] [D F+ B A (Neut)]
   23. *It gives me the feeling that something is floating in the sky.* Have the impression that each one is floating. Like a will-o'-the-wisp. Red and yellow and others are beautiful if seen individually. [WS m, CF Sky (Contam)(Pnat, Misc)]

Card-by-Card Sequential Analysis and Comments

When presented the first card Takeshi stated immediately that it gave him a fearful feeling that something was coming his way. "It" was not clearly defined in the beginning; it turned out to be a butterfly. He was obsessively concerned in this card, as in some of the others, with the irregular protrusions at the sides of the card. He saw here and subsequently some weird combinations of animals and human forms. The little protrusions reminded him somewhat of a snail. There is what is called a confabulatory trend—he takes small protrusions on the blot and "confabulates" snails. He is to see several snails in the subsequent cards. The snail, symbolically, usually is a rather disgusting type of small animal, but one that is weak and boneless, protected by its own circular house into which it can withdraw. This characteristic of snails is salient in considering Takeshi's record.

   In his response to Card II the boy again showed some loss of a sense of reality, an incapacity to keep objects separate. We infer that he also had some difficulty in differentiating between what was inside himself and what was outside in the external environment, a basic deficiency in schizophrenic thinking. He again saw a "weird" combination of animals, bears, and snail, and produced a rather incoherent response. He had an autistic feeling of "movement" going on. He could not define the humans, even though he finally saw them, and he puts it in rather confused Japanese: "It looks as if the hands and legs are being moved by them."

On Card III he stated explicitly the feeling of lonesomeness that permeated his TAT responses. He saw a floating "spirit fire," which gave him "a weird and lonesome feeling." Then he saw a human form, but it occurred in a "fabulized combination" (in Rorschach terminology) of human and animal. His verbalization was in an extremely unsteady, queer Japanese. In response to Card IV, he had fearful feelings of something neither animal nor human. He saw the popular "fur" percept, then produced another snail response. He saw a "protruding tentacle" and other parts, which he did not define. Finally, he ended with a confused combination of something, "like a snail, like a monster, like a combination of furs."

He perceived Card V as the popular butterfly, but again with a peculiar verbalization. He said, "I feel it is a butterfly. The feeling that something is flying—a weird feeling." Although he tended to perceive the ordinary, usually perceived areas on this card, as well as on some of the others, it was with a peculiarly intrusive, unreal feeling of being moved that could not be integrated with his percepts, giving his responses a schizophrenic tone.

In Card VI he saw a tiger's fur where fur is often perceived, but again expressed a subjective emotional uneasiness. He felt a sense of "pity" at its being spread and stuck by pins, giving him the impression that it was dead. He showed himself here to be a very sensitive boy, quite unlike what we might think a callous rapist would be, nor did he offer any direct sexual content on his Rorschach. Instead, we received the impression of an overwhelmed ego that could no longer function adequately.

On Card VII he saw a peculiar combination of horse, cow, and man. He perceived dancing by something that was made up of the body parts of various animal forms. Overall, as in the records of both his parents (see Wagatsuma and De Vos 1984: chap. 15), we get a picture of a high degree of introversion, but his ego functioning is too disorganized for him to give valid, perceptually acceptable percepts.

In Card VIII he again picked out what are the usually perceived areas of the card. He actually saw a Japanese "popular" response, a flower, and the popular animals as tigers. His least appropriate response to this card was "the feeling that it is bones," which he could not integrate, saying that slender bones and thick bones were mixed together. He ended by expressing a confused feeling that all these percepts were somehow sticking together and doing something—animals, plants, and bones—in a confused configuration whose elements he could not keep separate.

Again on Card IX the feeling of bones came out. Then Takeshi responded to the blank central space area as depicting a lake on a map. He responded positively to the surrounding color, saying that the colors were beautiful, but he could not integrate them into any percept, and produced only a vaguely perceived "map."

In responding to Card X he struggled with the fact that he saw a marine view with seaweed, but there were birds present, and he argued with himself, saying that it was a weird feeling because there are no birds in the sea. Again, as on Card III, he saw some spirit fire or "will-o'-the-wisp" floating in the sky.

The prognosis for Takeshi had to be considered poor. What was regarded as poor schoolwork or laziness by his parents and teachers was, according to Rorschach evidence, probably symptomatic of an internal autistic withdrawal, which left no psychic energy for such constructive tasks as a systematic application to school assignments. When we look at the amount of raw affect poured into his TAT stories, in combination with this psychotic Rorschach, we feel safe in making a diagnostic evaluation of this boy as schizophrenic.

The TAT: A Brief Glance

Takeshi's TAT stories were a continual series of almost abstract statements about inner feelings of loneliness and depression. The faces of all the figures on the cards either expressed to him inner states of loneliness or had some strange or "eerie" quality. Schizoid withdrawal was apparent throughout. The time taken before commencing his stories was somewhat protracted. It took him over a minute before he responded to the first picture, nearly a minute for the second, almost two minutes for the third. He gradually warmed up to the task, however, and by the end was responding rapidly to each of the cards. Some excerpts:

J1 [a boy looking at a violin]. This child has a face suggesting he doesn't like to play the violin. His face seems to be somehow unhappy. He gives the feeling of being lonely. That's all.

In this card, as in many of the following, Takeshi paid attention first to the facial expression, which he sought to read. The boy's expression suggested to him a lack of interest in playing and unhappiness. Nothing more was given in the story except an inner feeling of loneliness. Throughout the following stories Takeshi either noted the facial expression or referred to the feeling given him by the card—almost invariably that of loneliness and isolation. There was considerable hesitancy and blocking.

J2 [a farm scene: a young woman in the foreground carrying books; a man plowing; woman in working clothes leaning against a tree]. Gives the impression that each is doing own thing for some reason. Mother is thinking about something and the woman seems to be looking at some book. The man is doing something to the horse. Gives the impression of poverty. That's all.

In Card 2 the boy saw that each person was doing something. There was no interaction, but each person was active. Takesi stated in the test of limits afterward that he liked the card because everyone was "doing something." One had the impression that he perceived the world as full of self-preoccupied people, none of them attached to him in any way. He felt a sense of poverty and deprivation within himself, which was projected continually into the environment.

J3 [figure slumped against bench]. Seems to be crying. Seems that there is some trouble with the leg. That's all. (?) Crying, clinging to the chair, and pressing the face against the board. The impression is that the leg is injured.

This picture evoked a story about an injury. A person, whose sex was not defined, is seen as crying over an injured leg, clinging to a chair, and pressing his face against a board—a desolate picture of abject helplessness, loneliness.

J6 [an older woman facing away from a young man standing with hat in hand]. Gives the impression that this man is unable to say what he wished to say. This woman expresses an unwillingness to listen. I get a feeling of loneliness. Both have faces that look tender. That's all.

In responding to the card usually evoking a mother-son situation, all Takeshi could specify was that the man was unable to communicate and that the woman's expression indicated an unwillingness to listen. Therefore he had a feeling of loneliness. However, he felt, looking at the faces, that they had "tender" expressions. Throughout this record there was no expression of any active aggressive attitude on the part of a protagonist, although various stories included either injury or killing being done by someone. Takeshi's identification always seems to be with the passive victim of aggression.

J8 [a dreamlike scene with a shotgun in the foreground; a young man looking away from a background scene of an operation or an attack with a knife on a prone figure]. Two persons are trying to kill someone at the place of one of them. Fearful atmosphere. The other one is going to the police station to tell, so it seems. . . . That's all.

On Card 8 Takeshi saw the two people as killing another person. He commented on the fearful atmosphere. The remaining person in the foreground is going to the police station to report what is going on. There is an appeal here to outside authority, the police, in a situation of violence.

J9 [a Japanese family scene: a young man in the foreground sitting distraught; two young women in Western clothes looking toward him; an older woman in kimono in the background]. Four persons seem to be in conflict. The woman and the child seem to be leaving home. The man keeps silent. Seems to be leaving and taking the clothes, and therefore the child seems to be lonely. Also the old woman seems to be lonely too. That's all.

Card 9, a Japanese card created at Nagoya, different from any of the cards adapted from the Murray set, elicited from Takeshi a theme of family conflict. Usually when this card is so used it is the male figure who is seen as leaving, but in this instance a young woman seems to be leaving the home. Takeshi identified mostly with a figure, inappropriately identified as a "child," who felt lonely in this situation, but he also saw the old woman as responding with a feeling of loneliness to the impending separation.

J11 [a Japanese card depicting a young boy possibly peeking into a room where a woman is standing in an inner kimono; there is a hat and briefcase on the floor seen from outside]. The child seems to be watching what his mother is doing. The child seems to be surprised. He keeps looking at what his mother is doing. The mother looks somehow lonely and is thinking about something. That's all.

This card often stimulates some impression of sexual curiosity, but Takeshi was so vague about what was going on that we do not know what sort of perception he had. He only expressed the child's feeling of surprise, watching what the mother was doing. We had the impression that for him his pervasive feeling of aloneness blocked out and took over, so that any other possibilities became secondary or muted.

J13 [a prone woman seminude in background on a futon; man in foreground, head down against forearm]. Seems that the woman had been killed. The man seems to be crying after seeing that the woman has been killed. As it is dark, it gives the impression of loneliness and fearfulness. That's all.

On Card 13 Takeshi saw a woman who had been killed by some unspecified person; and a man who was crying. There was no elaboration on what the relationships were in the story, but the fearful affect of loneliness and fright were again conveyed.

J18 [an older woman either holding or choking a figure in the foreground, who may have fallen]. This old woman is somehow going to kill this other woman. This old woman gives me an eerie feeling. It is dark, and the woman who is attacked seems to be trying to avert it.

In Takeshi's story to Card 18, the figure of an old woman, who was seen as "eerie," inflicted violence on a younger one, who attempted to protect herself. Again the identification was with the passive victim. After the test was over, Takeshi said that he disliked this picture the most.

J22 [a Japanese card: a street scene; a man walking away in one direction, a woman facing away in another direction; between them a young boy, his hands to his eyes]. The child seems to be crying. Well, well—he seems to be lost. The passersby are passing without paying any attention to the child. Usually someone would take him to the police station, but they seem to be passing him by.

On Card 22 Takeshi saw no one paying attention to a crying child. Not only had he been abandoned but also the passersby paid him no heed, so there was no one even to take him to the police station. He was completely alone, helpless and rejected.

J27 [two teenage students, boy and girl, in front of a coffee shop; another girl in the background]. These two seem to be in dispute. The woman who is watching gives me a strange feeling. That's all.

The last card was again seen by Takeshi as a dispute. There was no card that he saw as depicting a happy relationship. He saw the two people standing in front of the coffee shop as arguing, and he said that the woman who was watching gave him "a strange feeling." There was a sense of unreality running through Takeshi's whole TAT which deepened our impression of schizophrenic withdrawal. This record must be seen in relation to the situational crisis confronting Takeshi. Shortly after he was given this test he was sent to a detention home. His feelings of loneliness and rejection must certainly have been aroused to their fullest degree by his impending institutionalization.

Concluding Remarks

After examining both interview and projective test materials obtained from the Ikawa family, we found that Takeshi was a severely disturbed boy showing schizophrenic features, who seemed to have been driven to his rape activities by a strong, perhaps semiconscious, incestuous attachment to his own mother. Self-consciously, he was a compliant, passive figure in his own eyes; he said, "When I quarrel with my mother, . . . she says, 'Go ahead and try to become a delinquent.' Because she knows my character well, she knows that I am too cowardly to be a delinquent. . . ."

It was difficult to determine the degree of sexualization of Takeshi's relationship with his mother without much fuller revelation from the parents. From the mother's own story told for TAT Card 13, though it is the only clue available, one might speculate that there was some active but indirect unconscious seduction of Takeshi by his mother during the time he was sleeping with her, which ended when he was twelve years old. We have also seen some indications of unconscious induction on the part of the father, who might have obtained some vicarious satisfaction of his own incestuous attachment to his mother by observing his wife and son sharing a bed.

Seen superficially, Mr. Ikawa, the father, with high average intelligence and basically introversive orientation, had lived much in accordance with the traditional Japanese values in regard to his role as a son to his mother; he had maintained feelings for his mother that were stronger than those for his wives. When his first wife was rejected and sent home by his mother, he remained passive, siding with his mother. His basic attitude had continued to be the same in his second marriage. In most cases in Japan, however, the attachment between mother and son is well sublimated, so that the undercurrent of sexuality remains well hidden and does not disrupt the ego functioning of the family members. In the Ikawa family it did not remain thus hidden. Only in this regard did the family differ from many Japanese families, in which the husband often keeps a stronger tie to his mother than to his wife.

We could speak in a similar fashion of Mrs. Ikawa; it is culturally sanctioned, especially according to the traditional values of Japan, that a mother, rather than being the sexual mate of her husband, assumes a role of desexualized, dedicated caretaker of her parents-in-law, her husband, and particularly her son. Having a husband who is more strongly attached to his mother than to her, the wife, in turn, develops a stronger tie to her son than to her husband. In most instances, however, such an attachment is well sublimated, so that the undercurrent of sexuality remains hidden. In the Ikawa family, as we have said, it was not sufficiently sublimated, and Mrs. Ikawa's relationship with Takeshi was sexualized, contributing to serious disturbance of his ego development.

Mrs. Ikawa in her own projective material suggested an introversive person capable of responding to threat by affective withdrawal as an ego defense. Withdrawal behavior in the mother occurred within a generally intact ego; but the experience of such withdrawal tendencies by her infant could have had severely damaging effects on him. We may speculate that although the mother herself showed no signs of schizophrenia or thought impairment, the son's ego development may have been deeply affected by an experience of insufficient *emotional* closeness to his mother during infancy and early childhood. Takeshi's apparent withdrawal in the direction of schizophrenia might be explainable

in these terms, hastened by the threatened pubescent breakthrough of direct sexual feelings about his mother. The boy's active stealing from his parents no doubt reflected his feelings of
deprivation and his desire for warmth, which he sought by taking
money and buying friendship with his peers.

The nature of Takeshi's difficulties was at best highly specula-
tive on the basis of the incomplete knowledge provided by our
interview data and projective test protocols. More extensive contact over an extended period would have been necessary for us to
gain a more complete understanding.

In our research we had obtained the records of ten delinquent
boys whom we had classified as "isolates" based on their behavior
in school and on how they committed their acts of delinquency. It
should be noted that there were definite introversive trends in
both the Rorschachs and the TATs of the mothers of other isolates in our family samples. In effect, an introversive trend was
the major difference distinguishing the mothers of isolate children, delinquent or nondelinquent, from the mothers of the more
"social" delinquents.

What we are demonstrating in this case is the ability to use the
Rorschach cross-culturally in clinical situations to help understand behavioral deviancy, which in this case was related to possible mental illness. Takeshi's symbolic material is understandable;
so-called "queer" verbalizations in Japanese are quickly noted,
just as nonstandard usages are in English. Confabulatory trends,
inability to deal with the overly "real" impressions of blot material, incapacities to separate out distinct responses, and other
aberrant thought processes signify psychopathology in Japan as
they do elsewhere.

Takao, a Japanese Villager with an Ulcer

The ready cross-cultural applicability of Rorschach interpretation
of symbolic content to clinical cases was well demonstrated for
me in my observations of the use of the Rorschach with neurotic
patients in the Department of Psychiatry at Nagoya National University. Rather than discussing a case taken secondarily from
clinic files, it may be more dramatic to show the clinical relevancy
of the test cross-culturally by examining the record of a villager

who while being interviewed and tested by normative research complained to the interviewer about his illness. In what follows I compare the symbolic material of his Rorschach with clinical findings on ulcer-prone Americans.

In 1954, at age 46, Takao was a leading figure in his village's political activities. He was considered responsible for the introduction of dairying as a side occupation in his particular village. He had recently served for some time as village head. According to our interviews with him, he saw himself consciously as a leader. Looking at the opinion scales, interviews, the TAT, a Problem Situation Test, and figure drawings elicited from him, one gained the impression that he was a man who was strongly concerned with traditional Japanese values of family, household lineage, and community responsibility. The terminology used in some of his answers was suggestive of identification with samurai traditions. We found in studying village attitudes generally that members of his village did indeed trace their origins to samurai families.

Takao's appearance suggested a certain boyishness. He had regular, almost delicate features, although he comported himself in a somewhat assertive, direct fashion. There was a slight aura of physical weakness about him, but no obvious signs of physical defect. An interview by one of the Japanese psychiatrists during intensive interviews in this village brought out the fact that a few years before he had developed an ulcer of the stomach and had not felt well since. At the time of his interviews he was bothered with hepatitis and complained of attacks of fever, headaches, and "stiff shoulders"—a widespread Japanese complaint. He was spending considerable time in bed.

Takao had completed a course of education in an agricultural middle school. As the oldest child in the main lineage of his family, he assumed the succession of the household after his father's death. His aged mother continued to live with him in the family home. He was married at the age of 24 by means of a professional go-between. The marriage was a successful one by Japanese standards, although only one of Takao's seven children was a boy. Though exhibiting the tactfulness of the dutiful wife, Sachiko took considerable initiative, not only in the family but in the farming activities as well. She organized the daily chores and maintained the farm in spite of Takao's sporadic resort to bed rest. His 12-year-old son was Takao's favorite. A somewhat unusual closeness to an adolescent daughter was noted by the visiting members of the research team, who reported that they saw him lying under the same *futon* (bedding) with her, a fairly uncommon occurrence in a Japanese household.

Takao's Rorschach Test

Card I:
1. *Well, does this not seem to be a bat?* A bat sticks fast to something such as a wall and spreads out his wings. [W FM+ A P (Dcl)]
  2. *It looks like a moth.* Because this is the same with a bat. And this here indicates he is spreading out wings. [W FM+ A (alternate)]

Card II:
3. *These look like two puppies side by side.* These look like head and they are facing each other. They lift up their forefeet like this. [D FM+ A P (Dch)]
  4. *Although I turned the card to this direction [upside down] these still look like two puppies.* These are the same. These two quarrel and bleed. [D FM+ A (HH, Dch)]

Card III:
5. *What is this? Skeletons scattered about.* Skeletons are lying here scattered about. This is a head, shoulder, feet. Skeletons, and stones too, are scattered about the earth. [D F− Anat (Bb, Adeh)]
  6. [upside down]. *These look like somebody dancing in the dark at night.* On the upside down they raise their hands like this and dance. These two persons are back to back. [D M+ H (Prec, Agl)]

Card IV:
7. *This looks like an animal. Here is his eye. This looks like a small seafish in the sea.* For a small seafish, this is too short. These are its eyes. Say a lobster or something like that. This is some-

thing that cannot be determined clearly. The animal is swimming forcibly in the water, raising his head. [W FM+ A (Pstr, Aob)]

Card V:
8. *This looks like butterfly.* The butterfly raises his wings and is rubbing them together forcibly. [W FM+ A (Neut)]

Card VI:
9. *This looks like an emblem. Like the Order of the Golden Kite.* A kite stands up here; this looks like the Order of the Golden Kite. [W F+ obj (Daut)]

Card VII:
10. *This looks like a horse or animal that bends backward.* This raises forefeet and bends backward. [D F+ A (Neut)]

Card VIII:
11. *The young ones of an animal face each other and climb up.* They stick fast to something and climb up. [D FM+ A P (Dch Dcl Pstr)]

Card IX:
12. *I don't understand. These look like animals. These are eyes. They are back to back.* These look like eyes, two animals. Here are heads, and a back is inner side and a stomach is outer, I think so. [D F+ A (Aob)]

Card X:
13. *It seems to me that this looks like small animals in a sewer ditch swarming about.* I don't know, like bugs in a ditch. They are not clear; they are small. [W FM+ A (Adis)]

Summary Impressions

The most outstanding content feature of Takao's Rorschach record was its dependency symbolism, especially apparent in small animals. Although the record was rather sparse, the content was nevertheless highly consonant with the type of material obtained from American ulcer patients.

TABLE 7.1

Takao: Summary of Affective Scoring

(Total Responses: 13)

Hostility Hh, .5	4%	Dependency Dcl, 1, .3; Dch, 1, .5, .4; Daut, 1	32%
Anxiety Agl, .4; Adeh, .3 Adis, 1	14%	Positive feeling Preq, 1; Pst, .3	10%
Body preoccupation Bb, .3	2%	Neut, 5	38%
Total unpleasant	20%	Grand total	80%

Takao's record resembled those of individuals with a high pepsinogen level in the blood, a condition demonstrated to be closely indicative of a predisposition to ulcers (Weiner, Thaler, and Reiser 1957). Margaret Thaler [Singer], the psychologist in an interdisciplinary study using several physiological and psychological tests, scored the Rorschach records we obtained for their affective connotations, using my system (ibid.: 605–606). It was possible to differentiate on a statistical basis high secretors of pepsinogen from low secretors on specific Rorschach affective content criteria. In a second study similar statistical differentiation was possible between actual ulcer cases and control groups with other psychosomatic bodily disturbances (Thaler, Weiner, and Reiser 1957).

There seems to be some relationship between physiological propensity, unresolved psychological conflict, and social pressures which contribute to the formation of an ulcer. In Takao's case the nature of the symbolism was in line with the formulation of Alexander (1934) and others (Kapp, Rosenbaum, and Romano 1947; Minsky and Desai 1955; Streitfeld 1954), who saw as a common feature of ulcer patients a conflict related to the persistence of a strong infantile wish to be loved and cared for on the one hand and, on the other hand, the repudiation of these wishes by the adult ego concerned with social or professional ambition.

Table 7.2 demonstrates how Takao's Rorschach and Figure Drawing material (not shown here) coincides with ulcer-prone

TABLE 7.2

Rorschach (and Figure Drawing) Criteria Distinguishing
Subjects with High Pepsinogen Secretion (Ulcer-Prone
Subjects) from Those with Low Concentration in Comparison
with Takao's Rorschach Record*

(De Vos Scoring)	Responses: Cutoff Score	High Secretors (N=63)	Low Secretors (N=57)	Takao
Rorschach Content Criteria				
1. Percentage of hostile responses	25%+	13	27	(4%)†
2. Openly symbolized anxiety (Athr, Adif, Adef)	3+	27	14	(2)
3. Sadomasochistic (Hsm)	Present	11	20	Not
4. Anxious face details (Aobs)	Present	1	8	Not
5. Fantastic forms (Afant)	Present	1	10	Not
6. Overall percentage unpleasant	40%+	30	39	(19.5%)†
7. Dependent responses (Daut+Dch)	Present	37	21	(4)†
8. Oral symbolism (Hor, Dor, Por, Mor)	31%+	35	19	No
9. Neutral content	35%+	33	18	(38%)†
Other Rorschach Criteria				
10. Color-form responses (CF)	Present	31	17	(1)†
11. Texture (FT, TF, T)	Present	33	18	No
12. Small details (Dd)	8%+	35	20	No
13. F+%	Below 80%	32	43	(82%)†
14. Feminine figure on Card III	Present	11	20	Not
Figure Drawing Criterion				
15. Boyish rather than adult male figure	2	21	8	Spontaneous drawing of boy

Adapted from Weiner, Thaler, Reiser, and Mirsky 1957:60.

* Difference between high and low secretions at 5% or above level of significance.
† Indicates agreement between Takao and ulcer-prone subjects.

individuals on 11 of 15 criteria. As has been said, the outstanding
feature of Takao's record was its dependency symbolism (see
criteria 7). Takao gave three responses which showed a childish
immaturity in underlying self-perception. Responses in which the
young of animals are specifically seen where most individuals do
not so specify are scored as childish dependent (Dch). Card II,
right side up, was seen by him as "two puppies." Upside down it
was still two puppies; however, this time they were seen as quarreling and bleeding. Card VIII evoked the "young ones of an
animal [who] face each other." In the inquiry they "stick fast to

something and climb up." "Sticking fast" also appeared on the bat percept on Card I. Although the bat would usually be considered a normal response, the elaboration "sticking fast" is unusual and can be scored in a dependency subcategory. Clinging, hanging, or leaning responses are suggestive of a dependent attitude (Dcl).

Another form of dependent symbolism in Takao's record was found on Card VI, on which he perceived "the Order of the Golden Kite." This is a military order given by the emperor for distinguished service. By my criteria any percepts of seals, emblems, crests, or even bearded patriarchs are related to an implied authoritarian personality structure with a need for a dependent relationship with higher authority (Daut). An individual giving such responses may or may not in turn be assertive toward those he perceives as subordinate. However, identification with the authoritarian role is incomplete, and a dependent quality remains. This sort of response is usually found in an individual who has an essentially masculine identification rather than a feminine one (see criteria 15, table 7.2.). Takao did not give any feminine figures in his protocol.

The overall percentage of 31% dependency content in Takao's record was extremely high in comparison with usual norms for dependency needs, and became a salient feature of an otherwise sparse record. While dependency responses are common in Japanese records, as indicated in the previous chapter, dependency symbolism to the degree found Takao's record is unusual. It was a source of underlying conflict in Takao, as it is in hard-driving Americans with ulcers. In ulcer patients in the American study, the dependency score often tended to be high in a like manner.

Unlike some individuals in the ulcer-prone group, Takao did not produce much in the way of anxious symbolism (see criteria 2, table 7.2). The Japanese village group as a whole was extremely low in the production of indicators of anxiety in their content. It was noteworthy, however, that the single specific category that best differentiates individuals with ulcers, namely, depressive anxiety, Agl (Thaler, Weiner, and Reiser 1957), was represented in Takao's response to Card III. He saw there "skeletons . . . scattered about" rather than the humans popularly perceived on Card III. This proneness toward depressive moods in ulcer patients is related to frustration of their receptive needs.

The scattered skeletons further imply that Takao was concerned with body integrity. On the TAT test given him this concern was symbolized by his seeing the violin on Card 1 as "broken"—the only incidence of such a response in his village. In ulcer-prone individuals the overall percentage of hostile symbolism tends to be lower than for other groups (see criteria 1). In Takao's record there was only one hostile response, that of the quarreling dogs (Card 2). Direct hostile responses (HH) were found in only two of the 36 men tested in his village, so that seeing quarreling dogs suggests that Takao was perhaps somewhat more prone to interpret situations as being hostile or to react aggressively than were the village men generally. Yet, his percentile level for hostile affect was relatively low by overall normative considerations. Behavioral evidence supported this picture. An assertive, even testy, stance is not necessarily lacking in certain ulcer-prone individuals.

Labile activity is characteristic of ulcer-prone cases. Takao's one color response was a CF response in reaction to "blood" on Rorschach Card II. Even though limited to one-color response, his Rorschach record was consonant with the ulcer-prone group's general tendency toward less controlled color responses (see criteria 10). Lack of body preoccupation material was also consonant with the general finding that ulcer patients, although suffering from physical disability, are not particularly prone to give body content in their responses. Nor did Takao produce content which could be scored as oral in nature, contrary to some expectations that one would invariably find specific oral content in ulcer records. Statistically, one cannot separate an ulcer group from others by direct oral symbolism (Thaler, Weiner, and Reiser 1957).

In summary, the record on the only known individual with an ulcer in a projective test survey of Japanese villagers conformed remarkably to findings of research with content symbolism in American clinical groups. In this respect the record offered cogent support for the view that the Rorschach test functions effectively in cross-cultural diagnosis of unresolved personality problems defined in general psychoanalytic terms.

However, the nature of Takao's record was such that one would not automatically assume the likelihood of an ulcer. This would be asking for too great incisiveness on the part of the Rorschach in survey work. Nevertheless, it is interesting to note that the material was directly consonant with the expectations in American ulcer patients, once the fact of the ulcer was known. The point to be made is that the underlying use of symbolism in the Rorschach of this Japanese man appeared similar to that of Americans in spite of significant cultural differences.

Another note may be added without going into test detail. The Rorschach record of Takao's wife was that of a highly intelligent, creative personality, the most interesting record obtained in the village. The researchers in comparing notes came to the conclusion that much of the innovativeness of Takao was probably privately instigated by his wife and carried out publicly by him. Without the Rorschach and other projective test materials, we would not have guessed this state of affairs, considering how quietly his wife played the traditional woman's role in her overt, observable behavior.

Notes

1. This chapter contains excerpts from two previous publications: "Symbolic Analysis in the Cross-Cultural Study of Personality," in Kaplan (1961:391–405); and "Takeshi Ikawa," in Wagatsuma and De Vos (1984:394–430).

References

Alexander, R.
   1934   The Influence of Psychologic Factors Upon Gastrointestinal Disturbances: General Principles, Objectives, and Preliminary Results. *Psychoanalytic Quarterly* 2(4):501–539.
De Vos, George A.
   1976   The Interrelationship of Social and Psychological Structures in Transcultural Psychiatry. William P. Lebra, ed. *Culture-Bound Syndromes, Ethnopsychiatry, and Alternate Therapies.* Honolulu: University of Hawaii Press.
   1980   Book Review of "Schizophrenia: An International Follow-up Study." *Social Science and Medicine* 32:462–463.

De Vos, George A., and Marcelo Suarez-Orozco
  1986 Child Development in Japan and the United States: Prospec-
    tives of Cross-Cultural Comparisons. Harold Stevenson, Hiroshi
    Azuma, and Kenji Hakuta, eds. *Child Development and Education
    in Japan*, pp. 289–298. New York: Freeman.
Fisher, S.
  1950 Patterns of Personality Rigidity and Some of Their Determi-
    nants. *Psychological Monographs* 64(1):1–64.
Kaplan, Bert, ed.
  1961 *Studying Personality Cross-Culturally*. Evanston, Ill.: Row,
    Peterson.
Kapp, F., M. Rosenbaum, and J. Romano
  1947 Psychological Factors in Men with Peptic Ulcers. *American
    Journal of Psychiatry* 103:700–704.
Minsky, L.
  1955 Aspects of Personality in Peptic Ulcer Patients. *British Journal
    of Medical Psychiatry* 28·113–134.
Rapaport, David
  1945 *Diagnostic Psychological Testing*. Chicago: Yearbook Pub-
    lishers.
Schafer, Roy
  1954 *Psychoanalytic Interpretation in Rorschach Testing*. New
    York: Grune and Stratton.
Singer, Margaret Thaler
  1962 Personality Measurement in the Aging. James Birran, ed. *Hu-
    man Aging: Biological, Social, and Psychological*. Washington,
    D.C.: Government Printing Office.
Speisman, Joseph, and Margaret Thaler Singer
  1961 Rorschach Content: Correlates in Five Groups with Organic
    Pathology. *Journal of Projective Techniques* 25:356–359.
Streitfeld, H.
  1954 Specificity of Peptic Ulcer of Intense Oral Conflict. *Psycho-
    somatic Medicine* 16:315–326.
Thaler, Margaret, Herbert Weiner, and Morton Reiser
  1957 Exploration of the Doctor-Patient Relationship Through Pro-
    jective Techniques. *Psychosomatic Medicine* 19:228–239.
Wagatsuma, Hiroshi, and George A. De Vos
  1984 *Heritage of Endurance: Family Patterns and Delinquency
    Formation in Urban Japan*. Berkeley, Los Angeles, London: Uni-
    versity of California Press.
Weiner, Herbert, Margaret Thaler, and Morton Reiser
  1957 Etiology of the Peptic Ulcer. Part I. Relation of Specific

Psychological Characteristics to Gastric Secretion (Serum Pepsi-nogen). *Psychosomatic Medicine*, vol. 19 (special edition).
Weiner, Herbert, Margaret Thaler, Morton Reiser, and R. Mirsky
1957   Etiology   of   Duodenal   Ulcer.   *Psychosomatic   Medicine*
19(1):1–10.
Wynne, Lyman, and Margaret Thaler Singer
1966   Principles of Scoring Communication Defects and Deviances
in Parents of Schizophrenics. *Psychiatry* 29:260–298.

Part III

Algerian Arabs

George A. De Vos

In 1956 in Ann Arbor, I worked in collaboration with Horace Miner, an anthropologist at the University of Michigan, and with four research assistants, Hiroshi Wagatsuma, Akira Hoshino, Takao Sofue, and Mayumi Taniguchi. We did systematic blind analyses of the sixty-seven Algerian Arab Rorschachs obtained by Miner during his nine-month period of fieldwork in Algiers in 1950. Sixty-four of these records were obtained from men, and only three from women. Miner's plan to obtain comparable samples from both sexes proved to be impossible because of general problems in obtaining a female interpreter and interviewing women.

In the following two chapters I shall illustrate both psychological universals and culturally specific nuances in these Rorschach responses. These materials were published previously in our monograph, *Oasis and Casbah: Algerian Culture and Personality in Change* (Miner and De Vos 1960). The team of Japanese psychologists and I first completed the blind scoring of the records, both with a modified Beck system of scoring standard areas and determinants, F+%, and content frequency. Then we used my symbolic content system. Finally we did systematic case analysis of each record prior to staffing each case with Horace Miner and comparing the Rorschach results with the interview materials and background data obtained from the same individuals.

The only previously reported Rorschach work on North Africans was the early monograph published in 1935 by M. and R. Bleuler (1935). This previous monograph gave me an opportunity to compare my scoring of thought processes in the Algerian records with those published on Morocco.

Our own study gave me an opportunity to compare the Algerian Arabs with the 140 Japanese Rorschach materials previously obtained in the United States and the 724 protocols obtained in Japan.

In the context of the present volume I shall report some of the systematic differences between the Arabs who lived in an oasis, "Sidi Khaled," and those who had moved to the Casbah of Algiers at an early age, where they were influenced by their new status in an urbanizing, colonized Algeria. Subsequent to Miner's contact in 1950, the Algerian war broke out. To his knowledge several of the informants were killed in the subsequent successful struggle for independence against the French. In chapter 8, I shall present some systematic quantitative comparisons, and in chapter 9, some representative cases analyzed qualitatively, but in the context of our quantitative findings for the entire group. In each instance, I shall emphasize the symbolic thematic material and pay less heed to the formal analysis of determinants and other features of the records, which can be read more fully in our monograph. I shall refer to some results with Fisher's Rigidity and Maladjustment Scales, which had been used also with the American normal and maladjusted samples and with the Japanese. I shall give some systematic comparisons of the subscales of the symbolic content with some actual Arab beliefs and individual behavior. The overall material has been systematically compared both with my Japanese-American results and with the records of the control sample of normal neurotic and schizophrenic Americans loaned by Dr. Samuel J. Beck from his files at Michael Reese Hospital at Chicago. I shall excerpt only enough of the ethnographic material from the monograph to give the reader some background for the sample. Those interested in further details can refer to our volume, *Oasis and Casbah*.

References

Bleuler, M., and R. Bleuler
    1935   Rorschach's Ink-Blot Test and Racial Psychology: Mental Peculiarities of Moroccans. *Character and Personality* 4:97–114.

Miner, Horace M., and George A. De Vos
  1960 *Oasis and Casbah: Algerian Culture and Personality in Change*. Ann Arbor: University of Michigan Press.

Chapter Eight

Oasis and Casbah: Acculturative Stress

George A. De Vos and Horace Miner

The Colonization and Decolonization of Algeria

The Algerian revolt, which erupted in 1954, reflected the final unsuccessful attempt of the French to colonize and totally absorb the Algerian section of North Africa, directly across the Mediterranean.[1] Colonization had started a century earlier. After initial conquest, the city of Algiers came more and more to represent symbolically the difficulties of acculturation and assimilation of an Arab Muslim people into the French body politic. The city of Algiers stands as a symbol of a sequence of attempts at modernization and acculturation which directly or indirectly touched most Algerians. As a modern metropolis emerged from the ancient city of Al Dzeir, the old city declined to a native slum called the Casbah, named after the fortress that dominated this section of the old Barbary Coast. After first contact, the native population was continually decimated by cholera, typhus, and smallpox as well as periodic famine. The French brought in colonists, many from Spain and Italy, to settle the rich, more fertile, inland areas. These *colons* caused the native populations to put increased pressure on the remaining land resources. Intensified cultivation of the oases of the northern Sahara dangerously reduced their underground water sources. The children of the Arab cultivators, after efficient health practices were established, swelled the rural population beyond endurance and forced many to seek employment in the cities, where they became a depressed underclass of slum dwellers.

These oppressive colonialist conditions provided the setting for a militant nationalism that exploded in the post-World War II period and brought independence to Algeria in 1962. It was from among these dwellers of the Casbah that our urban sample was selected. Miner chose only those who came from a specific oasis, "Sidi Khaled," which he studied in detail. The sample therefore compares individuals who arrived, usually in early youth, in the Casbah from Sidi Khaled with people who remained on the oasis. Miner had in mind to explore how attitudes changed with direct acculturative contact within the French-dominated urban scene and whether or not the Rorschach records would reflect some systematic difference between the urban dwellers and those who remained within the oasis setting, where only indirectly exposed to French influence. The amount of contact varied somewhat among those sampled. Only two were born in Algiers itself of oasis parents; and Miner tested another two who had spent a considerable time in the city, but had returned to the oasis and were therefore included in the city sample. The age distribution ranged from 17 to 73 years of age, but only one subject was under 20, while four were over 60.

Miner went to considerable pains to select as random a sample as possible of the oasis men. Some Rorschach studies are done without the testers' having sought to obtain the trust of the group. Knowing of the Algerians' peopling of their world with *jinni* (genii), *jnun*, and other supernaturals and their suspicion that strange pictures and mechanical devices new to them might be inhabited with such dangerous spirits, Miner sought to achieve personal trust as best he could. In some instances, individuals who had been approached early refused to cooperate but later changed their minds when they saw that those who had cooperated had no ill effects. Some individuals, after as long as seven months agreed to take the Rorschach and answer the series of questions that Miner used. Miner ended with a sample of thirty-one men interviewed in the oasis and thirty-three Arabs selected for the city sample. Only six of the thirty-one men interviewed in the oasis were bilingual, speaking French besides their native form of Arabic. In contrast, twelve of the thirty-three Arabs selected in the city sample were bilingual, having excellent knowledge of French.

Miner, in quantitatively contrasting urban and rural samples, used only the extremes in terms of residence. He eliminated eleven of the oasis group who had more urban contact, leaving twenty (20) as his true oasis group. He eliminated five of the urban group who had less urban residence than one-quarter of their lifespan in the urban environment, leaving a sample a twenty-eight. For other purposes, when comparing the Arabs with Japanese or Americans, we used the total Arab male sample of sixty-four.

Miner in all cases used Arabic French interpreters so as to equalize the testing situation. It was through Miner's contacts in the oasis which had been well established that he obtained his city sample through either friends or relatives of individuals residing in the oasis. They informed their kinsmen in the Casbah that "the American" was coming. Miner was not identified with the French and did not suffer from the general hostility directed toward French colons or administrators. In the course of his contact, Miner was highly selective, using individuals as interpreters who not only had excellent knowledge of Arabic and French but also had a basic sympathy with and understanding of both the oasis people and those in the city. Miner also had the advantage of using an early wire-recording device which allowed playback of the subjects' responses so that the interpreting could be reviewed for possible flaws.

Miner took up to four hours with some of his subjects using a leisurely approach without pressing the individual to perform quickly. He spent as much or more time with the other forms of inquiry used during the interview sessions. The active presence of the interpreters, with whom all in the sample were closely acquainted, proved to put the informants at ease. For most it was the first contact with any recording device, and Miner initially used it to play music for them. The French had sometimes brought moving pictures to Sidi Khaled, so recorded sound was familiar from viewing movies. A telephone had been installed recently in the oasis, and some people were also familiar with radios.

The Setting

The date-growing oasis of Sidi Khaled in 1950 had a resident population of 5,300. The population had doubled in the previous century, but further expansion of the agricultural economy was stifled by lack of water. As a result, two-thirds of the men between the ages of 20 and 50 had to seek unskilled work in the cities of France and North Africa. A few of those who went to the cities returned after failing to find work or after accumulating a little capital. These returnees exerted some acculturative influence in the oasis, and a French school sporadically exposed a small group of boys to the three "R's." Despite these influences, life for most of the oasis dwellers continued in terms of traditional Arab culture.

Those who moved to Algiers, miles away, found themselves in a new physical world, peopled with what appeared to the newcomers as domineering French and with Arabs who had already altered many of their beliefs as a result of long interaction with the French. The secluded courtyard of the oasis gave way to the crowded apartment. Opportunities to work were controlled by the French or by relatively acculturated Arabs, and there were both economic and status advantages to adopting Franco-Arab city ways. To find a role in the life of the city, the migrant was inescapably forced, or lured, into adopting its patterns of life.

Within this oasis-urban comparative framework, we shall consider the cultural and Rorschach data collected in 1950 from sixty-four Arab men, largely between the ages of 20 and 50. Twenty of these men, to whom we shall refer as the "oasis group," either had never been outside the oasis setting or had had less than four months' residence in the city. The "urban group" consisted of twenty-eight men who had lived more than a quarter of their lives in the city. All had resided there longer than five years and most for more than twenty. Sixteen Arabs (referred to as group B) who had amounts of contact intermediate between these oasis and urban groups were excluded from the comparisons made of these two groups, but they figured in the overall analysis of Arab personality.

An attempt to work with subjects selected on a totally random basis proved utterly impractical. The oasis and urban groups, therefore, could not be said to be representative. Both groups of subjects were, however, chosen so as to provide a wide range of age, occupation, and prestige. Despite the informal method of selection, the oasis and urban samples were similar in terms of their basic demographic characteristics. Each of the subjects was interviewed concerning the same areas of culture and took a Rorschach test.

Some Psychological Variables Related to Cultural Change

For the purposes of this presentation we shall deal mostly with those Rorschach variables that showed significant relations to specific cultural beliefs and opinions. The measures that showed the closest relationship to cultural traits were not the Rorschach variables usually scored in quantitative analysis but (a) overall indices of rigidity and maladjustment, using methods of assessment developed by Fisher (1950) and (b) the De Vos system for scoring the affective implications of the content of Rorschach (app. A). Fisher's system had been used previously with Japanese-American data (see chaps. 3 and 4, above). There were certain model psychological patterns found in the Algerian protocols that did not differentiate between the urban and rural groups but were highly characteristic for the groups as a whole.

There were, for example, characteristic thought patterns in evidence that conformed remarkably to a pioneering Rorschach study by Bleuler and Bleuler (1935) done with Moroccans twenty years previously. Many individuals tended to create percepts full of arbitrary juxtapositions on the one hand or arbitrary discriminations on the other. The records were replete with modes of thought suggestive of what would be diagnosed in Western records as obsessive-compulsive character defenses. In the more extreme cases the type of illogical juxtapositions brought forward in the organization of the responses, as well as the modes of rationa lizing the responses given, were strikingly similar to those found in paranoid records in Western groups. An examination of certain individuals when there was sufficient background evidence available demonstrated that the patterns of thought indicated in the Rorschach were indeed related to behavioral evidence. In a number of instances the test seemed to differentiate as well between Arabs as it does between Americans, assuming sufficient knowledge of the cultural background. In the main, the determinants of Rorschach responses and the locations used in the percepts were similar for both the rural and urban groups. However, certain differences in the use of color, shading, and inanimate movement distinguished the urban-dwelling Casbah group from those of the oasis. The picture is a consistent one in which the urban group inferentially demonstrated more tendencies toward diffuse anxiety, less conscious control over affective reactions, and more tension over the control of impulses.

Rigidity and Maladjustment

On overall assessment of rigidity, using the Fisher rigidity scale, the Arabs scored extremely high. The group as a whole obtained a mean score over one standard deviation above the mean of a sample of American normals obtained by Beck et al. (1950). This score was considerably higher than the rigidity of maladjusted American groups (see table 8.1). On the maladjustment scale applied to the records, the mean score for the Arab group as a whole was directly comparable to that of an American neurotic sample and over two standard deviations above the mean of the American normal group.

While it does not follow that the Algerians should therefore be

TABLE 8.1

Rorschach Indices of Rigidity and Maladjustment in Arab and American Samples

		Arab			American		
	N	Oasis 20	Urban 28	Total Sample 64	Normal 60	Neurotic 30	Schizo-phrenic 30
Rigidity	Mean	51.0*	46.3*	50.1*	27.7	30.8	32.2†
	S.D.	10.3‡	20.2‡	14.0	15.3	15.3	16.8
Maladjustment	Mean	63.3*	61.8*	62.2*	34.0	65.8**	80.6**
	S.D.	19.8	26.1	20.2	16.2	31.7	23.8

Key to levels of significance:
  * Significance of difference from American normal .001.
  † Schizophrenic-normal American difference significant at .05.
  ‡ Oasis-urban Arab difference significant at .01.
  ** Neurotic-schizophrenic American difference significant at .01.

considered neurotic as a group, behavioral evidence was sufficient in a number of cases to indicate intrapsychic disturbance in certain capacities to adjust. In other cases, however, no overt maladjustment was perceivable.

The maladjustment and rigidity measures were not independent as to the variables scored. There was some tendency for individuals with excessively high rigidity of necessity to show these rigidity variables in the maladjustment scale as well. However, this sort of relationship was not always in evidence. These scales tended to co-vary only in the urban group. In some of the Casbah records the maladjustment scores were related to the presence of inflexible ego defenses, not readily adaptive to changes in the environment.

One might raise the question, at least in regard to these overall results with Algerians on a maladjustment score, of whether the type of personality integrations found modal for Arabs were sufficiently different from those of Americans or French to involve special problems in adaptation to Western life.

No significant difference was found between the oasis and urban groups in either mean rigidity or mean maladjustment. In the city, however, the mean rigidity score was somewhat lower and showed significantly greater variability because of the appearance in a minority of individuals, including those more successful in acculturation, of lower rigidity scores; their records were comparable to American norms. The number of these records was not sufficient, however, to lower the mean significantly below that of the oasis group, since the city group also had a number of individuals with high rigidity which co-varied with high maladjustment. The oasis group's rigidity and maladjustment scores did not co-vary. The most rigid records were in no case among the highest in maladjustment.

In the symbolic content of the Rorschach protocols, the proportion of unpleasant content was found to be significantly higher among the city Arabs, particularly in the content categories indicative of body preoccupation and hostility. These results, as was indirectly indicated by the results with color and shading and inanimate movement determinants, suggested that urban residence produced increased psychic stress for the Arabs. Two patterns of adjustment which appeared with some frequency in the city were only rarely found in the oasis. One centered around greater rigidity and internalization of aggression as suggested by anatomical preoccupations. Such records contributed heavily to the high mean maladjustment score found in the urban group. Another pattern suggested the development of a more complex, flexible ego, but one that had to cope with heightened internalized tendencies toward the overt expression of aggressive hostility. These individuals tended to see the environment as peopled with hostile and dangerous human forces. It is reasonable to believe from the Rorschach evidence that the degree of threat which the French represented to these Algerians was a reflection of intrapsychic stress as well as the continuing effect of objective political and economic issues.

Mental Approach: Perceptual Elaboration and Organization

Contrasting Rorschach responses indicated considerable difference between Algerians and Americans in their mental approach to the world about them (see De Vos and Miner 1960: 125 ff.). The utility of the test rested, of course, on the tendency for an individual's orientation to life situations to be reflected in the way he perceived the ten inkblot cards. For example, a reaction to the total blot area, in a "whole" or W response, suggested a more global or abstract orientation, whereas attention to large detail was more indicative of a pragmatic or concrete orientation. On the average, whole responses constituted 42% of all the responses given by an Arab, while members of the normal American group had a mean of about 19%. The total number of responses given by Algerians (mean 19), however, was much less than for Americans (mean 31). Nevertheless, the average number of the Algerians' whole responses was slightly higher than that of the American group. These results contrasted with the Bleulers' report of a mean of 2.7 whole responses for the Moroccans. A qualitative examination of the whole responses given by the Arabs revealed differences from those found in the American records. The Algerian W's were usually vaguely perceived things of indefinite shape, such as mountains or trees, or various sorts of "additive" or arbitrarily constructed combinations of items. The tendency of the Moroccans toward illogical, rather than systematic, thought, as noted by the Bleulers, was also readily apparent in these Algerian responses. Arbitrary juxtaposition of elements, rather than logical, carefully checked objectivity, seemed to guide the selection and combination of the percepts in many instances.

The low proportion of small or unusual details (Dd) was quite similar in the Algerian and the normal American groups, contrary to the Bleulers' findings of a high proportion of Dd responses in the Moroccans. Large detail responses are notably infrequent among the Algerians, implying a less matter-of-fact approach to problems.

The low response total did not indicate lack of mental activity on the part of the Algerian Arabs in meeting the Rorschach task. The responses were elaborated, albeit with arbitrary and illogical modes of thought that will be discussed later. The Algerians actually showed a great deal of intellectual push, in terms of a drive to organize their percepts into complex configurations. They obtained a mean Z score (a measure of organizational drive, developed by Beck [1944]) quite similar to that of the American sample, with its much higher response total.

Fluidity, Blocking, or Constriction in Associative Processes

The Algerian Arabs showed considerably more associative blocking than did the Americans. In addition to the rather low mean response total, they also evidenced blocking in their long delays before giving an initial response (46″ and compared to 32″ for normal Americans on Card I). In respect to a third measure of associative blocking—that of "rejection" or refusal to respond appropriately to an individual card—the Algerians were not significantly different from the American sample. These measures of associative blocking contributed considerably, however, to the group's high rigidity and high maladjustment scores reported above.

Other measures of psychic constriction were also significantly higher among the Algerians. They tended to withdraw responses or to deny previous responses during the subsequent inquiry. One noted an extreme tendency to constrict percepts, especially among the rural group, in the appearance of so-called oligophrenic responses, in which only one part of a percept usually seen as a totality was given as an answer. This sort of response occurred most frequently on Card III, where a number of individuals saw only human heads rather than total human figures.

A large proportion of the responses relating only to the form of the blots (F%) strongly indicated psychic constriction, as there was a relative lack of the use of color, movement, and other determinants. The Arabs generally showed no measurable difference from the normal American group in F%, except for the urban group, which was significantly lower. In both American and Arab groups, a large proportion of individuals received high scores on the rigidity scale for constriction of this measure.

The prevalence of a great number of rigid and constricted records would presuppose stereotypic thinking in a fairly large number of cases. This presupposition was borne out. Unlike Western records, it was not solely a high percentage of animal responses that indicated stereotypy in this group. Rather, it was through the additional pervasive use of botany and landscape content that some individuals revealed the narrowness of their range of interests and their lack of free use of imagination. As in the normal American sample, one must consider variations in intelligence in accounting for some of the more stereotyped records. Nevertheless, on the average, the Algerians did show a greater tendency toward stereotypy than the American sample.

Communality of Thought

The popular or P responses are those given most frequently to the various specific blot areas on the cards. The number of popular responses which an individual gives is a measure of his or her participation in the common thought of the group. In previous reports by Hallowell (1956) on certain acculturating American Indian groups, and in previous work of De Vos with the Japanese (chaps. 3–7), much similarity was found between the popular responses of these groups and those of Americans. To assess the relative use of populars in Algeria, the twenty-one American populars reported by Beck were slightly modified to produce a list of Western P's. Then a list was made of the twenty most popular Arab responses. The two lists overlapped in only eight of the

TABLE 8.2

The Twenty Most Popular Rorschach Responses
of Americans and Arabs

American Populars (Revised Beck)

Card	Location	Responses	Rank	Percentage of Respondents
I	W	* Bat, butterfly	3	75.7
	D4, D3	Human figure	8	31.7
II	D1, D6	* Animal	4	64.3
	W, D	Human figure	18	15.9
III	W, D1, D9	Human figure	5	59.2
	D3	Tie or ribbon	14	19.7
IV	W	Animal skin or furred animal	11	23.0
V	W	* Bat, butterfly, or bird	1	89.2
	d1	Leg	15	19.1
VI	W, D1	* Animal skin	6	43.2
VII	W, D9, D2, D1	Human head	16	17.2
VIII	D1	* Animal	2	88.4
	D3	Bones, ribs	18	15.9
	D4, D8	* Tree	12	22.3
IX	D3	Human figure	9.5	26.7
	D4	* Human head	9.5	26.7
X	D1	* Crab, lobster, or spider	7	40.7
	D2	Dog	13	21.7
	d5	Rabbit face	18	15.9
	D4	Vermiform animal	20	--

Arab Populars

Card	Location	Responses	Rank	Percentage of Respondents
I	W	* Bat, butterfly	11.5	12.5
	W, D2, D7, d8, D5	Mountain	7	20.4
II	D1, D6	* Animal	14.5	10.9
	Ws, Ds6, Ds5	Landscape	7	20.4
	d4	Architecture	9.5	14.0
	D2	Bird	11.5	12.5
III	W, D1, D9, D11, d6	Human figure, human head	5	21.0
	D1	Tree	18.5	9.4
	D5	Fish	4	21.9
IV	W	Sea animal	9.5	14.0
V	W	* Bat, butterfly, or bird	2	70.0
VI	W, D	* Animal skin	14.5	10.9
	W	Architecture	7	20.4
	D3	Winged animal	18.5	9.4
VII	W	Mountain	14.5	10.9
VIII	D1	* Animal	1	75.0
	D4, D8	* Tree	3	31.3
IX	D4	* Human head	18.5	9.4
	W, D9	Tree	14.5	10.9
X	D1	* Crab, lobster, or spider	18.5	9.4

* Common to both groups.

responses (table 8.2). The Algerians produced P's of a sort not previously reported as popular for any group. "Mountains in the distance," architectural features (mostly mosques) seen at a distance, and a number of "tree" responses were commonly seen. Such responses, particularly those involving distance, suggest that the desert environment affects perceptual habits. Human and animal life were also sometimes seen as being far off. Actually, the only mountains visible from Sidi Khaled are the Atlas, thirty miles to the north. Some of the human figure percepts reported for the Moroccans (Bleuler and Bleuler 1935) were also perceived as being distant or possibly hiding behind trees.

It seemed probable that the use of popular responses would be influenced by acculturative processes. To test this hypothesis, the occurrence of the twelve uniquely American popular responses was compared with the occurrence of the twelve uniquely Arab responses. Analyses were made of the effect of urban residence and of Koranic and French education on the type of popular responses given. There seemed no reason to doubt the assumption that French P's would be more like those of Americans than like those of the Arabs. In the urban Arab group, eighteen of twenty-eight individuals saw one of more uniquely American P's. Only two of the twenty oasis Arabs saw any of these P's. This difference was significant beyond the .001 level. As to the number who saw one or more uniquely Arab P's, there were twenty of twenty-eight in the urban group and nineteen of twenty in the oasis. This difference did not reach statistical significance but was in the hypothesized direction.

Continued French schooling was influential in the production of popular responses, as witnessed by the following results: Of thirteen individuals with more than one year of French education, seven used American P's, compared with fifteen of the remaining fifty-one Arabs ($P = .10$). The analysis also indicated that those without either French or Koranic education–factors that co-varied–tended more toward the production of uniquely Arab populars, but these trends did not reach significance.

In summary, the evidence indicated quite clearly that one result of moving from the oasis to the city was some development of Western ways of looking at things. The loss of distinctively Arab types of percepts was less marked and, presumably, more gradual. The impact of formal French education in the oasis showed similar effects. The fact that those who had some French education usually had also gone to Koranic school might have been related to the relatively slight loss of uniquely Arab perceptual norms among the educated men. These findings with regard to popular responses and education were the only instances in which French schooling was found to be related to a Rorschach variable.

The Arabs, as a whole, produced a very low average number of popular responses, even in terms of "Arab" populars (3.9 as compared with 6.8 for normal Americans). This relative lack of communality in P responses suggested a tendency for Algerian Arabs to be idiosyncratic in their perceptions, to think egocentrically, to be relatively insensitive to group pressures, and to be low in the need to conform. The inner-directed nature of the Moroccan psyche, as described by the Bleulers, and the individualism often mentioned as a component in Arab personality were both supported by this Algerian Rorschach evidence.

Subjective, Illogical, or Arbitrary Thought Patterns

In addition to the above modes of constriction, the Algerian records deviated from the normal American sample in terms of various ideal standards of logical, accurate, and objective thinking. In some ways the Arabs showed similarities to the thought patterns of our sample of neurotic Americans (see above). It is to be noted that the Rorschach signs of thought disorder are not, in themselves, diagnostic of specific pathology. As a matter of fact, the neurotic and schizophrenic American samples used in this report could not be clearly distinguished from one another by the frequencies of these disorders. In only a few cases could they be differentiated from the normal group. For adequate diagnosis, an intensive clinical analysis of an entire record is necessary. Most clinicians using the test have abandoned a "sign" approach to diagnosis in Rorschach work. We revert to tabulating signs only to demonstrate cultural differences in frequencies.

The accuracy with which the Arabs used the form of the test blots in arriving at their percepts, as measured by Beck's F+%,

was significantly lower than for the normal American group and
even somewhat below that of the neurotic Americans. Diffuse,
unclear, and confused responses lowered the scores on form
accuracy. Poorly perceived trees or animals were not infrequent.
Such responses alternated in some records, with quibbling over
details or arbitrarily distinguishing differences between the two
sides of the symmetrical blots. Among the urban Arabs, especially, poorly perceived anatomy contributed to very low F+%.

The oasis group was somewhat more prone to give direct
affective impressions of the blot, such as "It's frightening," "It's
very pretty," or "This one is much worse." In this group especially, there was much illogical elaboration of responses from a
personal association or experience called to mind by a portion of
the area included in the response.

A forced quality of thinking was revealed in the Arabs' tendency to give "whole" responses, no matter how distorted, to every
card or, compulsively, to include every area of the blots by giving
detailed responses. Often these details were then arbitrarily united. Vague, ill-defined responses were sometimes followed by
others which contained meticulous attention to detail, parts of the
blot being ignored to improve the accuracy of the percept. Occasionally, alternate percepts were given in an attempt to make the
answer more precise, but the individual felt compelled to decide
between the alternatives, even though he could not do so.

The Arab records may be best characterized as different from
the normal American sample in their pronounced tendency
to display modes of thought usually indicating obsessive-
compulsive and "projective" ego defenses. The types of thought
disorders listed under "Obsessive and Arbitrary Thinking" (see
Miner and De Vos 1960) were strikingly prevalent in both the
oasis and urban Arab records. Almost half the records manifested at least one occurrence of these indices. Such thought processes were somewhat more common in the neurotic American
group than among the schizophrenics. Notably present in the
Arab records were evidences of arbitrary, projective thinking of a
type found in paranoid clinical cases in which the ego structure is
still fairly intact. The Arabs were also more like the more abnormal American samples in indications of "impaired logic."

The Rorschach Content: Some Detailed Comparisons

The great psychic stress experienced by the Arabs in Algiers appeared in the significant differences in the affective tone of the urban group when compared with the oasis group, as well as when compared with samples of normal and maladjusted Americans (tables 8.3, 8.4). Comparison of the total Arab group with the normal Americans brought out a significant tendency on the part of the Arabs to produce in a higher proportion of "anxious" content. The average amount of anxious content, however, did not reach that obtaining for the neurotic Americans. The oasis and urban groups showed no difference from one another in this regard but were markedly different with respect to other types of "unpleasant" content.

The oasis group gave somewhat less hostile content and much less body preoccupation material (tables 8.3, 8.4). The proportion of all content scored as unpleasant among oasis Arabs was

TABLE 8.3

Comparison of Indices of Affective Symbolism

| | | Arab | | | | | | American | | | | | |
| | N | Oasis 20 | | Urban 28 | | Total Sample 64 | | Normal 60 | | Neurotic 30 | | Schizophrenic 30 | |
		Mean	S.D.	Mean	S.D.	Mean	S.D.	Mean	S.D.	Mean	S.D.	Mean	S.D.
Hostility		6.8%	8.6%	10.0%	7.9%	8.5%	7.4%	9.4%	7.1%	11.6%	6.9%	8.3%	7.7%
Anxiety		19.1	14.2	18.7	14.9	18.3	14.1†	13.8	7.6	22.6*	11.8	23.7*14.1	
Body preoccupation		2.0[b]	3.6	10.1[b]	19.0	5.7	12.4	4.1	4.9	9.3[ac]	12.8	19.3*[c]23.2	
Total unpleasant		27.9[b]	17.5	38.8[b]	23.8	32.5	22.8	27.3	12.0	43.5[ac]	13.2	51.3*[c]20.0	
Dependent		7.1	7.1	6.1	8.0	7.0	8.3	4.6	4.6	7.0	7.4	6.0	6.8
Positive		13.2	10.7	9.4	9.2	10.4‡	9.4	17.2	10.9	11.9[ac]	9.8	6.9*[c]	5.8
Neutral		49.3	19.6	43.0	37.5	45.3	29.0	49.3	15.6	35.3[a]	19.2	34.6*19.1	

Key to levels of significance:
 * = .001.
 ‡ = .01.
 † = .05.

[a] Comparison with American normal.
[b] Comparison between oasis and urban Arabs.
[c] Comparison between American neurotics and schizophrenics.

Categories do not total 100% because of omission of "Miscellaneous."

TABLE 8.4

Presence of Significantly High Scores in Hostility or Body Preoccupation

	N	Hostility*	Body Preoccupation*	Either or Both
Oasis	20	3	1	3
Casbah	28	7	6	12
Total Arab	64	10	7	15

(Oasis/Casbah) } P=.05

Presence of Mutilated or Distorted Humans, or Tension Responses
(Such as Explosions)

Scored under Hostile Symbolism	N	Humans Mutilated or Distorted (Hsm and Hhad)†	Tension Response (Hhat)†	Either or Both
Oasis	20	6	1	7
Casbah	28	13	8	17
Total Arab	64	28	10	34

(Oasis/Casbah) } P=.05

* 1 S.D. above mean of normal Americans:
   Hostile, 16%+
   Body preoccupation, 10%+

† See De Vos 1952 for a full description of criteria for scoring content.

almost identical with that of the normal Americans. It was significantly lower than that of the urban Arabs, who closely approached the control group of American neurotics. The similarity of the total Arab group to the normal Americans, on these measures, masks the wide oasis-urban differences.

The data on "positive" (pleasant and constructive) content showed the Arabs, generally, to be significantly lower in this dimension than the normal American sample and even slightly below the neurotics. As might be expected from the more open data on unpleasant content, the oasis Arabs gave more positive content than the city group, but the difference did not reach the level of statistical significance.

There was a larger amount of dependent affect in the total Arab sample than in the normal American. As was true for the comparable rise in dependency responses in the neurotic Americans, the difference was too slight, with such small samples, to be certain of its significance. In short, the evidence on the affective tone of responses was consistent with that from the rigidity and maladjustment scales and indicated some definite differences in intrapsychic stress between the oasis and urban groups.

Attitudes Toward People Expressed in Rorschach Content

The specific nature of human and animal content in the protocols can be used as a key to respondents' underlying attitudes toward people. Aggressive, deprecatory, submissive, anxious, and other attitudes are revealed through the types of animals or humans seen and the action or inaction attributed to them.

In their animal responses the Arabs showed no indication of overall active or passive trends through a preference for small, weak animals or large, fierce ones. There were distinct differences among individuals in this regard, however, as will be brought out in the individual sketches presented in the following chapter. The records did manifest some very distinctive characteristics in the way the Arabs handled human percepts. Rarely did they see human figures involved in some form of movement or engaging in positive activities. When very active movement was perceived, it was frequently attributed to a foreign or supernatural figure. A high proportion of responses involving humans presented them as incomplete or mutilated. The incidence of such responses was higher in the city, and usually involved bodies without heads or legs or, conversely, heads without bodies in blot areas where Americans perceived whole figures. In a large number of mutilated figures, specific reference was made to the genital area. Such attention to mutilation and to genital organs is also characteristic of the frequent internal anatomy responses found only in the records of those Arabs who had lived in the city.

The Arab men were not prone to see women among their human percepts. Only 12 of 82 such responses were of women. In three of the six female percepts given by the oasis Arabs and those in the intermediate group B, attention was drawn to sexual parts. In only one response was a woman perceived as associated with children. In a single instance, a percept of an Egyptian woman washing clothes, was there active movement. The general impression one gains is that the men did not tend to relate to women as social beings but rather as sexual objects. There were no responses that might possibly be interpreted as symbolic of a hated-but-feared woman even indirectly representative of feminine authority.

In the oasis there was a tendency to see strange humans or humanoid figures as supernatural in nature, particularly as devils and genii. In the urban group there was only one such reference, to "a savage or devil." When fantastic figures were seen by this group, the percepts were described as "monsters," "invisible men," or "Negro king who is half-animal." Quasi-political figures made their appearance: "capitalist," "communist leaders," "enemies," and "Russian dancers." These trends were minor indices of acculturative change.

In all, there are eight references to "Negroes." These percepts generally suggested a deprecatory attitude, though two responses were fairly positive ones of Negro dancers in the role of comic entertainers. The Algerian population, for Muslims, was rather unusual in its disdainful attitude toward Muslim blacks. There were a few other non-Arab human percepts, but only one was designated as a Frenchman, and he was described by an oasis Arab as hiding in a tree. A number of the responses given by the urban group were of humans perceived in extremely small segments of the blots. These responses seemed to be related to the use of other indications of projective defenses in the same records.

Another peculiarity noted in a few of these percepts was the occurrence of figures attached to each other in some way. They included enemies entwined, two genii bound together, Siamese twins, and women tied to posts. One could speculate that such figures somehow symbolized a helpless dependency on a hated object, from which one could not break away. In general, the humanlike percepts were described as being relatively passive or immobile, whereas those of animals showed a greater range of activity. It is clear that living things which the Arabs perceived as different or distant from themselves were more readily imbued with activity. The impression one gains from such results is that the Arabs may be affectively reactive, but they do not readily express their inner states nor are they capable of easily entering into rapport with one another. Instead, they are prone to project hostile and threatening attitudes onto others and onto the supernatural and therefore tend to be defensively hostile, rather than spontaneous, in their basic attitudes. The numerous responses depicting bodies with missing parts may be interpreted as reflecting a fear of emasculation not too deeply buried from consciousness.

Certain Inferences Concerning Cathexis

As previously mentioned in the comparison of rigidity and maladjustment, the most striking relevant difference between the urban and oasis Arabs was the correlation of these measures in the urban group. Those who were high on both measures also tended to be those who showed the greater amount of bodily preoccupation content. In most of these cases anal and sexual content was included with other anatomical concerns. The overall impression given by these records was such that it seemed relatively safe to assume that such results had a similar meaning, whether derived from the protocol of an Arab or from that of a maladjusted American.

Records high in anatomical preoccupation are usually produced by individuals who have severe hypochondriacal concerns or, in some instances, by individuals with homosexual problems (Rapaport, Gill, and Schafer 1945–46). In the most severe cases, such responses are found in psychotic reactions of various sorts. Moreover, hypochondriasis, as such, is more readily found in borderline paranoid cases, where projective defenses are strongly indicated. Body parts become the focus of hostile, destructive projections. In individuals concerned over "perverse" sexual practices, such as homosexuality, anal percepts or percepts of diseased tissues are sometimes forthcoming. In this connection, the increased number of anal responses among the urban Arabs was especially significant.

In the urban group, an alternative pattern to the high anatomical preoccupation of those with high maladjustment and rigidity scores was the significantly high proportion of percepts with hostile implications found in the records of those with low scores on both the rigidity and maladjustment measures. A great number of these percepts were of a type which sees bodies with parts missing or otherwise distorted or mutilated. This sort of response is usually found in individuals with sadomasochistic concerns or those preoccupied with castration fears. Such responses were significantly more prevalent among Arabs than in the normal American sample. Responses indicative of tension over the expression of hostile impulses were significantly more common in the urban Arab group than in the oasis group, but such responses appeared in one out of six of the American records as well. Kane (1957), on the basis of a study of American prisoners, concluded that hostility is part of a defensive reaction to a more basic feeling of inadequacy. This sort of individual does not necessarily recognize his own behavior as hostile but tends to deny it and project such feeling onto others.

Many of the sadomasochistic responses fit the type which Fisher and Cleveland (1954, 1956) describe as "permeable." (Their work on the relation of "soft" and "hard" or "permeable" and "impermeable" Rorschach content to body image and psychosomatic involvement has been a most promising approach.) Such responses suggest some penetration into an object through an opening or by violence. Soft, amorphous substances, such as smoke or clouds, are also high in "penetrability." Such penetration responses, either in connection with anatomical content or in more indirect symbols, suggested that some of the Arabs had an unconscious fear of penetration, as occurs in passive homosexuality. Such fear was probably being warded off, as unacceptable to the adult ego, through hypochondriacal displacement and particularly through the projection of hostility onto others. Such hostility would have been most likely to be projected onto authority figures toward whose power the Arabs felt vulnerable, such as the French. We note that on Fisher's and Cleveland's "penetration score" the urban Arabs scored significantly higher (2.8) than the oasis group (2.1; P = .05). The former were also significantly higher in amount of hostile anxiety reflected in their Rorschachs.

Sadomasochistic preoccupations were in evidence in about half the urban Arabs. The degree to which such concerns were disruptive of general ego functioning would have to be determined from

TABLE 8.5

Levels of Significance of Relationships Between Rorschach
and Cultural Variables*

	High Rigidity in Males	High Maladjustment in Males	Medium or High in Positive Content	High in Hostility and Body Preoccupation
Supernatural beliefs:				
Used charms			.05	-.01
Believed in genii				-.15
Believed in power of sahhara				-.05
Protected against or had been affected by evil eye			.05	-.01
Interpreted his dreams				
Believed in power of guezzana				
Cleanliness:				
Meticulous or clean	-.10	-.10		
Seclusion of women:				
Required veiling of one or both eyes	.10	.01		-.10
Forbade wife to go out with her mother				
Wife's seclusion ended at 56 years or older	.001	.01		-.15
Punishment of children:				
Beats severely or prefers beating	.05			-.15
Used isolation				
Used food deprivation	-.05	-.10	.05	

* Total sample analyzed with two-tailed tests of significance. Minus signs indicate an inverse
relationship between the variables.

analysis of the whole record. In some cases to be presented in the
next chapter, there was some assessment of how such orientations
were integrated into the total personality.

   In comparing the relationship of hostile and bodily preoccupation responses with supernatural belief elicited by Miner in his
interviews (table 8.5), a very striking relationship appears. Use of
Koranic charms by an individual was found to be *inversely* related, in a very significant fashion, to unpleasant Rorschach content. For the entire group, there was but a single individual who
both gave such responses and used charms. This suggested that a

culturally approved concern with this magical practice was, in some measure, an alternative to more internalized, intrapsychic methods of handling aggression. The increased stress apparent in the Rorschachs of urbanized Arabs was concomitant with a drop in belief in protective talismans.

The study of combat fliers under stress reported by Alexander and Ax (1951) demonstrated a significant increase in what we have categorized as hostile symbolism concerned with mutilation and body anatomy in those individuals showing psychic break-down under the stress of continual air raids over Germany. Those in the Casbah who could maintain a belief in charms, albeit with a tendency to be fairly high in rigidity, did not show either of the alternative content indicators of increased intrapsychic stress.

The relation of hostile content to externalized projection was supported in part by comparing belief in genii with belief in charms. As indicated, only one Arab with a strong belief in charms gave Rorschach responses indicative of hostility, and none gave bodily preoccupation responses. But of the ten individuals who had a strong belief in genii and who did not believe strongly in charms, four had markedly high scores in hostile affect. In these instances, strong belief in genii may be inferred to be related to a readiness to project hostility into human or humanoid beings.

Content as Related to Psychosexual Stages of Development

In spite of a tendency to give fewer responses in most affective subcategories, the oasis Arabs gave significantly more oral responses than the urban group. This difference consisted in the relative presence of hostile oral responses, usually represented by biting, aggressive animals; in positive oral responses, such as food or food preparation seen in a positive affective light; and a miscellany of responses suggesting oral concerns in an indirect fashion, as, for example, unusual attention paid to the mouths of animals or humans, food utensils, and the like. Neither group produced dependent oral responses, such as sucking or licking animals (though one oral-dependent record did appear in the intermediate contact group, B).

The reason for the lower number of oral responses in the urban group was not clear. There was concern with food production in the oasis, since it was an agricultural community; but, at best, such an explanation could not account for the greater number of specifically hostile oral responses in the oasis. A highly conjectural possibility was that those who remained in the oasis may have had somewhat stronger primary ties to maternal figures. While the amount of oral content was high in the oasis, the total Algerian material was not so characterized. The Arabs showed about the same amount of most types of oral content as the normal American sample.

A few of the urban Arabs gave anal and sexual content in the test. Six city Arabs gave two or more such responses, while no oasis Arab did so. Especially when the thinking processes and other subsidiary data are also considered, some of these and other individuals showed evidence of a general regression to, or fixation at what is described in psychoanalytic terms as the "anal" stage (Freud 1905). Although it is doubtful that every case of severe castration threat is necessarily related to anal-sexual preoccupation, many of the records gave a strong indication of retreat from genital sexuality, with a great deal of castration threat in evidence. Moreover, it is interesting that the Arabs were significantly higher than the Americans in the type of response called "anxiety gloom (Agl)," a category for scoring a respondent's concern with dead or dying things and suggesting a depressive, dysphoric mood. In American records, such responses are found quite often among men concerned with their potency as well as with aging generally.

The interview data suggested that fear of impotence was not rare among the Arabs, in spite of their polygyny and cultural norms overtly expressive of high virility among men. It might be argued that if the sexual expectations from men were great, the fear of impotence would have been commensurately great. While this was probably true, the Arabs' mental preoccupation with sex, as well as with such hypersexual activity as did occur, has commonly been interpreted, psychoanalytically, as stemming from deep-seated fear of impotence. The fear of retreating into passive homosexuality is one of the dangers besetting an individual who retreats from genital masculinity in the face of subconscious castration threat (Freud 1911).

Ego Defenses Used in Controlling
Emotions

Other aspects of Rorschach responses that provide evidence about personality are the types of reaction to the color in some blots, the use of shading or tones of gray, and the perception of three-dimensional "vista" in the blots. These determinants are considered in conjunction with the role of form and movement in the responses. The Algerian Arabs' generally low response total and the high incidence of responses that were determined solely by form must be taken as the frame of reference within which the other determinants were analyzed. The overall rigidity, thus revealed, characterized many of the records and influenced the interpretation of the occurrence of other determinants.

We note first that the proportion of Arab responses involving human movement was significantly lower than that of the normal American group, but the percentage of color responses was about the same. The ratio of movement to color responses was thus heavily weighted in an extratensive direction by the relative lack of movement responses. The conclusion would be that the Arabs were prone to be reactive to outer stimuli rather than to avoid such influences. In addition, there was a significantly higher proportion of shading responses among the Arabs than in the American group, which supported the above conclusion. In some individual cases where shading predominated, however, it indicated a more passive attitude toward environmental stimuli than the active one implied by color. Vista responses in some records suggested a tendency toward personal isolation as a defense against reactivity to the environment, but to a degree no greater than that in the American records.

Differences between oasis and urban Arabs suggested some acculturative shifts in the nature of the controls exercised over emotional reactions. The sixteen Arabs who were intermediate between the oasis and urban groups in amount of acculturative contact (group B) were considered in the analysis of the Arabs as a whole, but were not analyzed separately. The marginality of this group was apparent in their Rorschach protocols (see Miner and De Vos 1960).

Nine of them had gone back to the oasis from the city, and it is probable that there was psychological selectivity in this return movement. They were markedly higher than either of the other groups in number of responses, F%, and Dd%, and were much lower in C than either. There was some tendency for the city group to show less overall constriction (lower F%) and a somewhat greater loosening of outer controls, as evidenced in an increase in the proportion of poorly controlled color responses. Similarly, there was a significant increase in shading responses, with a greater increase in poorly controlled shading than in the more controlled responses. This trend was consistent with that of the color responses, but it did not reach the level of statistical significance.

The urban Arabs scored higher than the oasis group in the proportion of uncontrolled color responses, but they did not differ much from the normal American group in this respect. They did show, however, markedly fewer well-modulated color responses (FC+). Both in the lack of movement as a balance against color, and in the lack of well-modulated color, one finds indications of less emotional control than among normal Americans.

In spite of the lower F% in the urban group, there was no striking difference from the oasis Arabs in the use of human movement, which was quite low in both. Animal movement, as scored by Klopfer's system (Klopfer et al. 1954), showed no difference between the groups. There was, however, an almost fivefold increase in the number of inanimate movement responses in the urban sample. In many respects these responses were indicative of internal tension (Hhat), especially when they occurred in such content as "explosions."

It seems safe to generalize that, compared to the oasis group, the urban Arabs showed definite tendencies toward more poorly controlled responsiveness to outer stimuli, combined with a greater conscious experience of inner feelings of anxiety and tension. Whereas such tendencies could easily be related to observable emotional outbursts which occurred in both groups, it is uncertain how such behavior was held in check in situations where it might have produced reprisal. In some cases high rigidity was perhaps a defense against the unsanctioned display of affectivity, perhaps leading to retribution. In other cases anxiety and feelings of potential threat from the environment might have helped individuals control their reactive behavior. This latter, more open, affective pattern seemed to occur more frequently in the urban group. Whatever the conscious controls, the potential for open emotional expression was there. When the individual felt safe from reprisal, his inner tensions could seek release. When openly emotional behavior did occur, it was usually a momentary display. There was insufficient control of the potentially reactive affectivity to utilize it in the accomplishment of long-range goals.

As for the sort of behavior one might expect with this labile emotionality, the content of the color responses was not characteristically violent or negative in tone. The many flowers and colorful trees did not suggest hostile reactivity. However color responses were also represented by distorted and dismembered human figures that indicated that in some cases external stimuli perceived as hostile would be reacted with violence when the testee felt safe in doing so. Arabs are also capable of strong emotional expressions of a positive sort when moved by friendly feelings. Distrust of others, however, is a frequent barrier to such responsiveness.

Impression Gained from the Records of Three Arab Women

Three Arab women were tested by Dr. Agnes Miner through an interpreter. These few records offered no real basis for generalization, but certain similar characteristics in them were interesting enough to bear some comment. Two of the three records showed very high rigidity scores, and the maladjustment scores are also high because of a variety of factors essentially like those of the men. Two of the three records had more than the male average for dependent and submissive content. Combining positive and dependent affect in each of the three cases, we found 72%, 44%, and 40% of their responses so characterized. There was not a single bodily preoccupation response nor any hostile response.

The symbolic material suggests that these women have resigned themselves well within the narrow scope of their world. There was emphasis in their records on architectural responses (arches and mosques), on flowers and trees and, for two of the women, on ornaments and pretty clothes. The other woman stereotypically saw practically nothing but fruit trees or flowers. All these responses symbolize femininity or the female body (Freud 1900). Human content was almost lacking in these records, with only one movement response given to a tiny detail area. The color areas, in contrast, were relatively freely and positively used, albeit with some insufficiency of control. One record, with thirty-one responses, showed very adequate use of intellectual functions.

These results, briefly considered, supported the Miners' impression of lack of dissatisfaction among the Arab women over their subordinate lot in life and of their rather easygoing adjustment, sometimes with overall stereotypic and rigid behavior, but essentially without much inner turmoil. There was, in these three cases at least, no suggestion of suppressed or diffuse hostile feelings. Field observations also characterized the women as expressing affect more freely than the men.

It might be speculated that the men, in not assuming much "conscience" on the part of women, take an additional burden on themselves. The expectations directed toward a woman were not so great; she was not forced into a role full of stress and tension. The man, on the other hand, was much more subject to internal tension. While growing up he must have had to overcome severe feelings of threat from an aggressively perceived father (see below).

Personality Variables Related to Specific Cultural Beliefs

The characteristics of the urban Arabs as compared to those living on an oasis were in some cases related to changes in culture in a direct manner. The ensuing discussion will, therefore, consider the interrelationships among three types of variables: (a) personality characteristics; (b) urban contact; and (c) cultural beliefs associated with the seclusion of women, the punishment of children, and those connected with certain supernatural beliefs.

Tests of significance of relationships were based on chi-square, using a correction for continuity, or, particularly when theoretical cell frequency was below 5, Fisher's (1950) Exact Test was employed and the resultant probability doubled to provide the closest approximation of a two-tailed test.

Seclusion of Women

From the time of puberty women were carefully isolated from sight of men other than their close kinsmen and husbands. A woman's life tended to be narrowly restricted to her home, and when she did leave its confines she had to be veiled and accompanied by another member of the family.

The relation of three seclusion customs to personality variables in males was explored (table 8.5 above). The degree of veiling a husband required of his wife and the terminal age for her seclusion both showed a statistically verifiable, consistent relationship to male rigidity and maladjustment. The more restrictive customs were preferred by Arabs who were very high in these qualities and, interestingly enough, somewhat low in symbolic indications of hostility and body preoccupation in the content of Rorschach responses. Concerning the acceptability of the wife's mother as her chaperone, however, there was a striking lack of relationship to the psychological variables, despite the seeming similarity of the personality implications of all three seclusion customs.

If we place the evidence in the general context of what was learned about Arab personality, we conclude that the rigidity of the relatively maladjusted Arab man, whose psychological problems were by inference markedly sexual in origin, imposed strict controls on his wife and daughters. In the tendency for an inverse relationship to exist between severity of restriction and hostility or body preoccupation symbolism, we see evidence that the rigid, maladjusted Arab who followed such restrictive practices did not tend to develop more internalized and intrapsychically disturbing conflicts over the handling of his aggressions. In a sense, they were "taken out on the women" in acceptable cultural ways which produced no overt or even covert hostile tensions.

The above cultural expression of personality characteristics was based on analysis of the total male Arab sample. Beyond demonstrating its existence, it should be revealing to see how these apparently functional links between culture and personality operated under acculturative influences by contrasting urban and rural groups.

Considering veiling norms first, we noted that the shift to the more liberal custom of allowing the exposure of both eyes was so general in the city that only four of the urban Arabs continued to insist on more complete covering. The demonstrated personality implications of differences in veiling practice were, therefore, essentially an expression of the oasis situation.

The relationship of male maladjustment and female veiling norms was significant in the oasis group taken alone, where it was still possible to measure differences in attitudes. It was revealing, however, to examine the urban "traditionalists," despite their small number. Of these four more restrictive Arabs, all were high in rigidity, three were high in maladjustment, and three were low in both hostility and body preoccupation, paralleling the oasis findings.

It is meaningful to ask if the change in cultural norms occurred despite the apparent psychic "utility" of the oasis norms in personality integration, or whether the changes in cultural attitudes were paralleled by personality shifts attendant upon urban residence. We have already seen that overall indices of rigidity and maladjustment did not change in the city, but that Rorschach content symbolizing hostility and body preoccupation increased. The total evidence indicates, therefore, that change in attitudes toward veiling went on, despite its significant relationship in the oasis to certain personality traits and basic attitudes toward women that did not change with movement to the city. The urban increase in hostility symbolism or anatomical responses was consistent with the decline in severity in attitudes toward veiling. As will be further discussed in relation to supernatural belief, it would not be unreasonable to assume that the external social pressures of the Casbah affected cultural beliefs. With urbanization, changes in psychological integration occurred. The individual found himself bereft of beliefs and practices that made possible certain adjustments around culturally condoned beliefs and behavior which circumvented intrapsychic conflict. The person who was stripped of some reassuring religious and social beliefs was also more exposed to the French world and to what was perceived as its threatening domination. He tended to project the inner causes of his anxiety more on the *colons* and less on the supernatural.

There was less change in male attitudes between oasis and Casbah as to the age at which a woman might come out of seclusion. The relationship with content symbolism rigidity and maladjustment scores, nevertheless, was similar to the results with veiling; namely, those who were most rigid and maladjusted were more severe in adherence to custom, whereas those who gave more hostile or body preoccupation content in the Rorschach were prone to be less severe. In the oasis, the age at which a woman was released from seclusion was significantly related to rigidity at the .02 level, and in the city at .08. In the oasis the relationship to maladjustment did not reach significance, but in the city it was significant at the .05 level.

Punishment of Children

The psychological implications of the methods employed in punishing children were markedly varied (table 8.5). The use of isolation as a punishment showed no relation to the personality measures employed. The use of severe *physical punishment* was characteristic of the most rigid Arabs and of those who did not tend to show marked hostility or body preoccupation. But unlike seclusion customs, such beating of children showed no relation to maladjustment. Beating did not become less severe in the city, nor did rigidity decrease, but the verbal expression of preference for such beating as the best form of punishment did decline. An Algerian Arab man seemed to beat his sons through rigid adherence to the pattern he himself had received in childhood. The father's domination of his children was not altered by contact with the French, but he was probably not so likely to express, at least to a non-Arab, what he knew would be taken as an unduly punitive position.

The most rigid Arabs, however, were significantly less likely to punish children by *depriving* them of a meal, limiting their food, or even delaying their meals. The explanation here seemed to be that beating was the usual form of punishment and only the less rigid Arabs were likely to depart from the pattern and employ other means. Interestingly, it was also those who tended to be better adjusted and who gave a more positively toned affectual material in the Rorschach who punished by food deprivation; however, they showed no less tendency to use physical punishment. It was as though those who use deprivation as a rationalization to punish their children did so with the feeling that "it is for their own good." Despite the association of stable personality factors with food deprivation, this kind of punishment increased in the city (P = .06).

Supernatural Beliefs

Rigidity and maladjustment, which showed such striking relationships to the preceding culture traits, were not related to any of the six "supernatural" beliefs analyzed (table 8.5). However, the relation of maladjustment to belief or disbelief in fortune-telling *guezzanas* was significantly different in the city and oasis (P = .02). In the desert, eleven of the twelve disbelievers were very high in maladjustment. It is possible that a religious interdiction of fortune-telling was responsible for the tensions associated with the custom, but the direction of the relationship would have been hard to predict.

The most marked finding concomitant with belief in the supernatural was the inverse relationship between intensity of four beliefs and indications of hostility or body preoccupation. As with seclusion customs, belief in supernatural forces seemed to function to obviate aggressiveness either turned outward toward others or directed inward against the self as suggested in Rorschach content symbolism. Customs concerning charms, the evil eye (Roheim 1952; Servadio 1936), and love magic of the *sahhara* showed this pattern at statistically significant levels, while belief in *genii* showed a similar but less pronounced trend.

We have seen that fortune-telling was significantly and differently related to maladjustment in the oasis and city. Similarly, the use of dream interpretations was directly related to low anxiety in the city sample (P = .05), which differed from the oasis in this regard (P = .11). The only other significant finding with respect to supernatural traits in the subsamples was the inverse relation between the use of charms and hostility and body preoccupation responses in the urban group. The only beliefs which diverged from this pattern were the two involving prognostication: fortune-telling and dream interpretation.

One may provisionally conclude on the basis of these results that the personality implications of a belief in supernatural hold without regard for acculturative changes. Customs concerning charms, *genii*, and *sahharas* waned significantly in the city, where there was a concomitant increase in evidence of hostility and body preoccupation symbolism. But concern over the evil eye, which had similar personality implications, was not altered by urban contact. In fact, all the evidence we have presented indicates that culture change goes on in response to social pressures, without much regard for the previous personality implications of the traits involved. It would certainly have been impossible to predict which culture traits would change on the basis of our knowledge of their psychological significance for the individual in the oasis and our knowledge of the personality shifts attendant upon urban contact. There is probably some sort of threshold beyond which given personality types cannot adjust to certain cultural behaviors. Our investigation, however, seems to indicate there is a marked tendency for personality predispositions and cultural configurations to develop new kinds of equilibria during acculturation.

It is important to point out also that half the urban group came to the city when they were fourteen years of age or older; three-quarters were over nine years old. The changes which they underwent, both culturally and psychologically, demonstrate that the effect of early training and experience is not conclusive in personality formation. It is the continuity of influences throughout life, and not just the impact of early influences alone, that makes men what they are.

In summary, then, the evidence from Rorschach protocols, when viewed in relation to seclusion practices, discipline of children, and religious beliefs, showed a consistent pattern, namely that attenuation of traditional beliefs in urbanized Arab men was related to increasing intrapsychic tensions which were expressed in symbolic form in Rorschach content in a number of individuals. The minority position of the more acculturated urbanized Algerian Arabs was reflected in internalized personality adaptations in which the social environment was more directly experienced as hostile and threatening. The individual had to cope intrapsychically with the implications of this psychological set, since direct expression of reactive hostility was not usually possible. Attention was more directly focused on feelings of being oppressed by the dominant French. Arabs who adhered more tenaciously to traditional beliefs may have demonstrated greater rigidity in certain instances and scored higher on maladjustment indices, but in adhering to these traditional social and religious beliefs they were not forced into patterns of adaptation that caused them to experience social relationships as involving a great degree of personal threat coming from their own projected hostility.

A Note on the Cultural Setting of Arab Personality Formation

The above discussion has been concerned with certain demonstrable differences between urban and rural oasis Algerians. Elsewhere (Miner and De Vos 1960) we have discussed how these differences between the oasis and Casbah groups were greatly overshadowed by similarities in personality that were part of a modal configuration. These modalities suggested the effects of certain culturally widespread experiences in psychosexual development.

The Rorschach records in our sample were most characterized by ego defense related to problems over the internalization of disciplinary controls and unresolved feelings of threat from an overwhelming authority figure. While there were numerous signs of regression to what, in Freudian terms, was described as "anal sadism" (Abraham 1921; Fenichel 1945; Jones 1913, 1918), the Algerians as a whole were less characteristically concerned with the earliest stage of ego development in which personal relationships are concerned with nurturance. Oral symbolic material was not lacking, but it was not more prevalent than that found in numerous other groups.

Looking from the Rorschach to the Algerian culture, one finds that the fear of attack found in the Rorschach is directly explainable in terms of the behavior of the culturally dominant father, who in exercising his prerogatives was often given to uncontrolled rage and physical abuse. The Arab male was free to display violent affectivity toward women and children with no real pressure of sanctions to modulate or suppress such behavior. Fear of retribution checked such displays outside the home, but within its confines a man was free to display genuine affection or anger. Since there was an expectation that a father would resort to physical abuse if sufficiently angered, a child learned to avoid provoking him by any direct challenge of authority.

There was little room for logical discussion in the home and objective fact was not often used as a way of settling issues. The relationship of a wife to a husband did not allow for the experience of temperance or regard for the opinions of women. Nevertheless, part of the cultural tradition of women was how to handle men by guile and deceit.

One seemingly modally adaptive method the male child learned in relating to others at certain periods of his development was passive submission. This submission had certain sexual components. Early experience associated mother and other female adults and siblings with sexual stimulation. Later, very strong internalized sanctions were imposed against continued orientation toward these earlier sex objects. These sanctions are hypothetically related to the type of classical attempt at resolving the Oedipal rivalry described by Freud (1905, 1913) in his theory of the formation of neurosis. The very severe threat represented by the father was resolved by giving up the world of women, and the culture supplied a pattern of behavior that ideally suited this form of partial resolution.

A young boy left the world of women and younger children to join in the almost exclusive world of men found outside the walls of the home. He had a strong need to belong to this world of men. There was a culturally prevalent pattern of inducing young preadolescent males to the homosexual practices of older males. Homosexual submission as a means of placating a more dominant figure could be considered a culturally modal defensive maneuver, but the temporary assumption of a submissive relationship in directly sexual terms aroused strong needs for a compensatory assertion of one's active masculine identity in a world where to be a woman was so heavily disparaged. The young preadolescent, therefore, with further development attempted to become in his own eyes and those of others a virile male.

This experience of many preadolescent Algerian males upon entering the man's world was not unlike that of newcomers entering the exclusively male world of a prison. The younger, weaker-looking inmates are first pressured for their commissary privileges. If they succumb, pressure to submit to homosexual advances follows. As in the prison, little opprobrium was attached to the dominant individual among Algerian men, who was seen as "masculine" in so using another individual, but there was nothing but contempt for the passive individual who could not psychologically or physically protect himself. If homosexuality of the passive sort continued into adulthood, the man was despised by others. The most severe epithet one could apply to an Arab was to name him a passive homosexual.

As in a prison, a great deal of time and energy went into demonstrations of virility and masculinity. However, it was apparent that this emphasis on manliness did not lead to very easy or satisfactory relationships with women. The converse of the emphasis on virility was the concern with impotency, widespread in Arab culture. Diffuse feelings of threat and feelings of inner inadequacy were disguised in the more consciously tolerable distrust and suspicion of women. Repressed homosexual proclivities received conscious representation in jealous fantasies concerning the potential behavior of one's own wife with other males. Shaky over his virility, a man blamed his wife for his sexual inadequacy, even accusing her of using *sahharas* to make him impotent. Potential rage toward possible initiators of adultery with his wife went hand in hand with underlying Oedipal fantasies of his own adultery with the wives of others.

It is not difficult to relate these patterns to unresolved childhood rages toward an aggressive, dominant, and fearsome father. What is not so clear is what the effect of polygyny within the home had on the nature of the image of the father and that of the mother. It may well be that it served further to heighten the impression of the father's authority and dominance and to suggest the alternative submissive role as a mode of relating (see Adorno et al. 1950; Meissner 1978).

Since an immature individual who perceives himself as weak usually retreats from actual conscious rivalry or rebellion, the conscious feelings expressed toward the father emphasized respect rather than hostility. And so it was with the Arabs. One noted in most instances an active respect in men for their fathers. The better-adjusted men resolved possible difficulties by making an active identification with their fathers. It was noteworthy, however, that in individual Arabs who behaviorally had achieved such an identification, the sense of threat from outside forces did not disappear from their Rorschach records. Even when identifying with the role of an active, dominant male, a man had to continue to defend himself against his former passive proclivities. Paranoidlike projection and obsessive-compulsive character defenses were in common use to prevent a return to passive submission. It would seem that relatively few attained the dominant role without a severe struggle of some sort.

Once attaining some modicum of personal economic independence, the Arabs tended toward asocial seclusiveness in family life, each male within his own domain. A man made of his own home a fortress against outside attack, and yet memories of his own deviousness plus the above personality considerations made him mistrust even those within. As a child he probably observed how family members could intrigue against each other for the father's favor, or how they could combine in deceiving him. He learned how not to trust most people. Relationships of trust did not extend to women or subordinates but were limited to certain kinship ties where stringent social sanctions defined the limits of behavior, or to close ties of friendship with other men which sometimes had an unconscious homosexual flavor.

Not all men achieved a dominant masculine role. The nature of the extended family was such that it readily permitted a man to enter into a passive economic relationship with a brother, brother-in-law, or other near kin. A household might include one or more such dependent families, and such a relationship could be satisfactory to both. The support of kin attested to one's attainments as a family head. For the dependent, on the other hand, it allowed for a cessation of struggle against passive proclivities into a sometimes devious submissiveness—or into an adulation of the dominant figure as a paternal surrogate.

As we have suggested indirectly from our analysis of the Rorschach in the process of personality formation, supernatural beliefs can be presumed to bolster inner defenses. There is definite evidence that those individuals who actively employ supernatural forces have less internal tension. Some of the supernatural beliefs and practices of the Arabs seemed to be directly relevant to prevailing fears and concerns. It is not difficult, for example, to equate concern with love magic and the relatively common fear of impotence. The nature of the description of how one is attacked and penetrated by genii is almost a direct reflection of various forms of Rorschach symbolism found in certain records attesting to a fear of penetration. It is interesting to note the consciously emphasized heterosexual nature of the genii's attack in that certain informants averred that men are only possessed by female genii and the converse is true for women.

The fear of the evil eye is not limited to Arab culture, but its prevalence among the Arabs attests also to a fear of attack from the outside. Belief in the evil eye, with its emphasis on the destructive power of the eye of an envious person when turned on a desired object possessed by another, whether there is conscious intent or not, again suggests fear of penetration.

In the more stable social order of the relatively isolated oasis we found firmer beliefs and tendencies toward more secure though highly constricted personality patterns. Conversely, those who moved to the Casbah tended to suggest lessening belief on the one hand and more symbols of intrapsychic stress on the other. Even those who achieved a more adequate adaptation to their new half-Western and half-Arab environment often showed serious lack of development of more objective emotional and intellectual controls and the prevalence of a readiness to project fears and hostilities, all of which suggested that relationships between individuals remained difficult and uneasy.

A Comparison of Acculturative Stress: Arab and Japanese

The oasis/Casbah differences discussed above took on cross-cultural significance when I compared my original sample of acculturating Issei and Nisei in Chicago (De Vos 1954) with the overall results obtained from the normative sample of 724 Japanese in Japan (see above).

Arabs compared with the Japanese on overall Rorschach configurations were very different in many respects. However, within

TABLE 8.6

Increase in Hostility and Body Preoccupation Content
in Acculturating Minority Groups
(Men Only)

	N	Hsm*	Hhad*	Hsm+ N	Hhad %	Mean H%	Mean B%	Mean Pos%	Hostility N	Hostility %	Body Pre. N	Body Pre. %	H or B.P. N	H or B.P. %
AMERICAN														
Normal	30	2	3	4	13	9.2	5.4	16.1	5	17	5	17	9	30
Neurotic	15	4	3	5	33	15.1	10.3	11.3	5	33	5	33	8	53
Schizophrenic	15	3	4	5	33	10.9	15.9	7.3	5	33	10	67	11	73
Blacks‡	24	21	--	--	88	--	10.2	--	--	--	--	--	--	--
JAPANESE IN AMERICA														
Issei	25	9	1	10	40	12.2	14.6	17.6	8	32	9	36	14	56
Kibei	15	5	2	7	47	13.1	10.5	17.3	9	58	8	53	12	80
Nisei	30	12	3	14	47	10.7	12.7	18.3	9	33	12	40	18	60
JAPANESE IN JAPAN														
Urban	61	28	6	29	49	10.0	4.0	15.2	17	29	12	20	24	40
Rural	31	7	4	8	23	9.0	4.7	13.3	7	23	6	19	11	32
ARABS IN ALGERIA														
Urban Casbah	28	7	9	13	46	10.6	10.7	9.4	7	25	6	21	12	42
Rural Oasis	20	4	4	6	30	6.8	2.6	13.1	3	15	1	5	3	15
Total	64	17	19	27	--	8.5	5.7	10	16	16	7	11	15	23

Columns under *Significantly High†*: Hostility, Body Pre., H or B.P.

* Hsm are sadomasochistic responses, usually involving tissue mutilation. Hhad includes responses in which body parts are missing or distorted (DeVos, 1952).
† Significantly high defined at 1 S.D. above total American normal. Sample (Mean hostility 9.4 + 7.1 S.D.; body preoccupation 4.1 + 4.9 S.D.).
‡ The Goldfarb sample reported in Kardiner and Ovesey, 1951, included both men and women.

groups of Japanese or Arabs living in an acculturative situation, similar trends were found in the increased production of certain responses suggestive of the internalization of stress. When we compared men living within their traditional cultural environment with individuals of similar background living as members of a minority group within a Western cultural setting, specific forms of body content material and specific forms of hostile symbolism showed significant increase. Table 8.6 demonstrates, for example, significantly more body preoccupation content in the immigrant Japanese-Americans and in the urbanized Casbah Arabs than in comparable rural samples. Those in the Casbah reached a body preoccupation level of approximately 11% of their total responses, in contrast less than 3% of similar content found in the oasis group. These responses were concerned with both bone and flesh anatomy, disease, and sexual or anal anatomical percepts or organs. The Issei immigrant generation had an even higher percentage of anatomical responses, close to 15%. American-born Japanese Nisei men also has a very high level of body preoccupation (nearly 13%). The samples of acculturating individuals of Japanese background in the United States were significantly higher in body preoccupation than either 400 urban (4.0%) or rural (4.7%) samples obtained in Japan. The Japanese records showed levels of body preoccupation below those found in the American normal control group (5.4%).

I repeat that these results suggest that there may have been a turning in of hostility or an emotional withdrawal from difficult object relationships into an unhealthy self-preoccupation. Similar Rorschach results emphasizing the prevalence of anatomical responses were reported by Abel and Hsu (1949) for acculturating Chinese males.

This sort of interpretation can be extended to other groups showing the psychological effects of social stress other than that specific to acculturation. American blacks as a group are prone to primary family and secondary social experiences related to minority status which can only be thought of indirectly as related to an acculturation concept. Yet Goldfarb (1951) reported on a sample of Rorschachs obtained from blacks in which he found very high amounts of anatomical material, approximately 10% of the total responses given. (Other unpublished materials I have seen informally suggests high levels of anatomical responses among samples of American blacks.)

Table 8.6 shows that in the Arab Casbah group there was a general increase in hostile content compared with the oasis group, although not to a degree sufficient for statistical significance. The Japanese American groups were only slightly higher in hostile content than those found in Japan. However, if one examines specifically the number of responses from the various groups in the hostility subcategories of sadomasochism and body distortion (suggestive of castration anxiety), one finds that the urban Arab and Japanese American groups were significantly higher. These findings are related to Goldfarb's report on records obtained from American blacks that 21 of the 24 individuals tested in his sample had some sort of content suggesting mutilation of the body.

Again, the differential appearance of this specific content in certain cultural groups may result from stress experienced continually by people who live in a specific situation, as well as from specific psychosexual developmental experiences. It is the more emotionally constrictive Arab and Japanese rural groups (whose rigidity scores are the highest) who show the lowest amount of hostile symbolism. Among the urban Arabs, half of those tested left the oasis after age 14. Therefore, differences in the content of responses for the city dwellers cannot be directly attributed to the early developmental years. These results suggest the necessity for further exploration of the concept of intrapsychic stress as related to adult life experiences. It is noteworthy in this context that the Japanese urban male sample, taken in Japan, gave a very heavy incidence of mutilation responses in the age groups between 35 and 50; 22 of 28 individuals of this age in the urban group made such responses in contrast to the younger and older groups. These ages included most of the individuals who had been exposed to severe war experiences.

A Rorschach study of stress in American air force men participating in bombing raids over Germany (Alexander and Ax 1950) might be cited in support of the concept that environmental tension experienced as an adult is related to the reflection of intrapsychic stress in the Rorschach. It reveals that those individuals who showed the greatest psychological disorganization in coping with the chronic stress of bombing raids were specifically those who produced a great deal of sadomasochistic concern with mutilation in the content of their Rorschach responses. These responses, however, tended to disappear after fliers had recuperated from the tensions of combat.

Comparing the specific sadomasochistic material in the Arabs and Japanese, certain notable differences were observed. Japanese-Americans, in a number of instances, talked of crushed lungs or operations. These responses could have been related to concern over health. For example, tuberculosis—which was then prevalent among Japanese—was a very grave concern both in Japan and among acculturating Japanese-Americans, but the specific concern over health was often structured in sadomasochistic terms. In the Arabs the mutilation responses were more apt to be concerned with the tearing or penetration of the body as the result of a violent, aggressive act. Very often the mutilation was directly perceived as related to the sexual organs of men or women. These responses in Arabs seemed to be a reflection of specific continuing difficulties resulting from culturally patterned relationships between the sexes in Arab culture.

The question arises at this point whether symbolic material of this nature or of any other sort can actually be interpreted as meaning the same thing for Arab or Japanese personality structure as it would for American. It might be argued that certain statistical differences in supposedly symbolic content material have much more to do with culturally conditioned differences in perception than with underlying affective states.

If we take the Arab materials in regard to human content as an example, such an argument would point out that human movement responses are relatively lacking in the Arab records generally. Would it not hold that cloaked human figures, for example, are not as easily discernible as are humans in Western garb, whose limbs are emphasized? Moreover, the human form receives little representation in Arab art generally. There are some who would hold that it is against the Koran to represent the human figure. Likewise, Arabs are prone to give a number of vista responses that cluster sufficiently on certain cards to reach the level of being popular for the group. Could such results not be related to the habit of scanning the almost-always present desert horizon? Seeing figures in hiding and an emphasis on trees, with specific attention paid to the relative denseness of the leaves, can be readily seen as related to conditions of desert life.

Granting some cultural influence in making certain percepts more prepotent than others, one can still point out the relative prevalence of these responses in *certain* individuals in comparison with others. Also, these responses, when given by an individual, form part of a consistent pattern with other elements which are not suggestive of cultural prepotency, as pointed out in some of the individual cases to be considered in chapter 9. Moreover, the fact that certain ways of handling the blot are fairly common to groups as a whole does not necessitate the conclusion that the traits suggested are any less important in considering individual cases. The Arabs, for example, give many animal responses, although animals are no more portrayed in their art than are humans. There is, likewise, no reason culturally why the human head should be any more apparent on Card III than the entire body. Yet a number of Arabs saw human details or individuals at a distance, neglecting the more commonly seen whole humans for what would be considered more pathological material if found in American clinical records. The tendency to see *genii* or mythological *afreet*, other demonic forms, or to see humans only in antagonistic situations when they are perceived, is not without psychological significance. The manner in which the human form or other content material is handled or avoided is consistently suggestive of difficulties in human rapport general to the Algerian Arab group as a whole. In our study described above, close work by the Rorschach analyst with the anthropologist who knew the individuals concerned allowed Rorschach inferences to be checked against actual impressions of personalities based on observation. This collaboration brought out the usefulness of the Rorschach in individual cases.

In reference to the striking difference between acculturated and nonacculturated groups in the prevalence of anatomical mutilation material, it becomes obvious that groups in the acculturation situation rather than groups in a traditional cultural setting stress the anatomical and mutilation content. One cannot argue that the meaning of these responses is necessarily more benign or more readily perceived due to a lack of cultural repressions or other hypothetical cultural influences. For it is precisely the individuals in the stressful situation who are prone to this sort of perception, rather than those living in traditional settings.

Note

1. Adapted from Horace M. Miner and George A. De Vos, *Oasis and Casbah: Algerian Culture and Personality in Change* (Ann Arbor: University of Michigan Press, 1960).

References

Abel, Theodora M., and Francis L. K. Hsu
    1949   Some Aspects of Chinese Personality as Revealed by the Rorschach Test. *Rorschach Research Exchange and Journal of Pro-*

jective Techniques 13:285–301.

Abraham, Karl
1921   Contributions to the Theory of the Anal Character. *Selected Papers on Psychoanalysis*, pp. 370–392. London: Hogarth Press [1948].

Adorno, Theodor W., Else Frenkel Brunswick, Daniel J. Levinson, R. N. Sanford, Betty Aron, M. H. Levin, and William R. Morrow
1950   *The Authoritarian Personality*. New York: Harper.

Alexander, Franz
1934   The Influence of Psychologic Factors upon Gastrointestinal Disturbances: General Principles, Objectives, and Preliminary Results. *Psychoanalytic Quarterly* 3:501–539.

Alexander, L., and A. F. Ax
1951   Rorschach Studies in Combat Flying Personnel. Paul Hoch and Joseph Zubin, eds. *Relation of Psychological Tests to Psychiatry*, pp. 219–244. New York: Grune and Stratton.

Beck, Samuel J.
1944   *Rorschach's Test*. Vol. 1, Basic Processes. New York: Grune and Stratton.

Beck, Samuel J., T. Rabin, W. Thetford, and Molish
1950   The Normal Personality as Projected in the Rorschach Test. *Journal of Psychology* 30:141–198.

Bleuler M., and R. Bleuler
1935   Rorschach's Inkblot Test and Racial Psychology: Mental Peculiarities of Moroccans. *Character and Personality* 4:97–114.

De Vos, George A.
1952   A Quantitative Approach to Affective Symbolism in Rorschach Responses. *Journal of Projective Techniques* 16:133–150.
1954   A Comparison of the Personality Differences in Two Generations of Japanese by Means of the Rorschach Test. *Nagoya Journal of Medical Science* 17:153–265.
1955   A Quantitative Rorschach Assessment of Maladjustment and Rigidity in Acculturating Japanese-Americans. *Genetic Psychological Monographs* 52:51–87.

Durkheim, Émile
1915   *The Elementary Forms of Religious Life: A Study in Religious Sociology*. London: Allen and Unwin.
1933   *The Rules of Sociological Method*. New York: Macmillan.

Fenichel, Otto
1945   Early Mental Development (Continued): Development of Instincts, Infantile Sexuality. *The Psychoanalysis of the Neuroses*, chap. 5. New York: Norton.

Fisher, Seymour
    1950   Patterns of Personality and Rigidity and Some of Their Deter-
    minants. *Psychological Monographs*, Vol. 64, No. 1.
Fisher, Seymour, and S. E. Cleveland
    1954   Behavior and Unconscious Fantasies of Patients with
    Rheumatoid Arthritis. *Psychosomatic Medicine* 16:327–333.
    1956   Body-Image Boundaries and Styles of Life. *Journal of Abnor-
    mal and Social Psychology* 52:373–379.
Frazer, James G.
    1894   *The Golden Bough*, Vols. 1 and 2. New York: Macmillan.
Freud, Sigmund
    1900   *The Interpretation of Dreams*. Standard Edition, 1957, Vols. 4
    and 5. London: Hogarth Press.
    1905   Three Essays on the Theory of Sexuality. *Standard Edition*,
    1953, 7:123–245. London: Hogarth Press.
    1911   Psychoanalytic Notes on an Autobiographical Account of a
    Case of Paranoia (Dementia Praecox). *Standard Edition*, 1958,
    12:1–182. London: Hogarth Press
    1913   Totem and Taboo. *Standard Edition*, 1955, 13:1–61. London:
    Hogarth Press.
Goldfarb, W.
    1951   The Rorschach Results. A. Kardiner and L. Ovesey, eds. *The
    Mark of Oppression*, chap. 10. New York: W. W. Norton.
Hallowell, A. Irving
    1956   The Rorschach Technique in Personality and Culture Studies.
    Bruno Klopfer, ed. *Developments in the Rorschach Technique*.
    Vol. 2, *Fields of Application*. New York: Harcourt, Brace and
    World.
Jones, Ernest
    1913   Hate and Anal Erotism in Obsessional Neurosis. *Papers on
    Psychoanalysis*, 3d edition. London: Hogarth Press, 1923.
    1918   Anal-Erotic Character Traits. *Papers on Psychoanalysis*, pp.
    413–437. 5th edition. Baltimore: Williams and Wilkins, 1949.
Kane, Paul
    1957   Availability of Hostile Fantasy Related to Overt Behavior.
    Illinois Medical Journal 3:131–133.
Kapp, Frederic T., Milton Rosenbaum, and John Romano
    1947   Psychological Factors in Men with Peptic Ulcers. *American
    Journal of Psychiatry* 103:700–704.
Kardiner, A., and L. Ovesey
    1951   *The Mark of Oppression*. New York: W. W. Norton.

Klopfer, Bruno, Mary D. Ainsworth, Walter G. Klopfer, and Robert R. Holt
  1954 *Developments in the Rorschach Technique*. Vol. 1, *Technique and Theory*. New York: Harcourt, Brace and World.
Meissner, William W.
  1978 *The Paranoid Process*. New York: Aronson.
Miner, Horace M., and George A. De Vos
  1960 *Oasis and Casbah: Algerian Culture and Personality in Change*. Ann Arbor: University of Michigan Press.
Minsky, L.
  1955 Aspects of Personality in Peptic Ulcer Patients. *British Journal of Medical Psychiatry* 28:113–134.
Piaget, Jean
  1930 *The Child's Concept of Causality*. London: Kegan Paul.
Radcliffe-Brown, A. R.
  1922 *The Andaman Islanders*. Cambridge: Cambridge University Press.
Rapaport, David
  1945 *Diagnostic Psychological Testing*, Vol. 2. Chicago: Year Book Publishers.
Rapaport, David, Merton M. Gill, and Roy Schafer
  1945–46 *Diagnostic Psychological Testing*. Revised edition by Robert R. Holt. New York: International Universities Press, 1968.
Róheim, Géza
  1952 The Evil Eye. *American Imago* 9:351–363.
Servadio, Emilio
  1936 Die Angst vor dem bosen Blick. *IMAGO* 22:396–408.
Streitfeld, H. S.
  1954 Specificity of Peptic Ulcer to Intense Oral Conflict. *Psychosomatic Medicine* 16:315–326.
Thaler, Margaret, Herbert Weiner, and Morton Reiser
  1957 Etiology of Duodenal Ulcer. *Psychosomatic Medicine* 19(1):1–10.
Wolf, I.
  1957 Hostile Acting Out and Rorschach Test Content. *Journal of Projective Techniques* 21:414–419.

Chapter Nine

Some Individual Sketches

Horace Miner and George A. De Vos

Having presented a frame of reference derived from a general consideration of Arab Rorschach materials, we turn to some specific cases illustrative of personality variation.[1] They fall into two categories. The first five individuals were selected by Miner, the anthropologist who did the fieldwork in Algeria, from among the people best known to him, as representing varieties of acculturation. They varied from a youth who sought to identify with the French to a member of the nationalist underground movement.

The second group of five cases was chosen either because they were deviants in the community or because their Rorschach protocols presented unusual characteristics, or both. They ranged from psychotics to one man whose spontaneous, happy character stood out from the others.

Methodologically, these case studies initiated our collaborative effort. Each case was prepared independently on the basis of field observation and the Rorschach protocol. Then the two appraisals were brought together. In some instances (nos. 1, 2, 9, 25), personality estimates had been written in the field before the Rorschach test was administered. The other cases were worked up by Miner from field notes and memory. As all that he knew about Rorschach interpretation was learned after his fieldwork and no reference was made to the protocols in preparing the field observational sketches, his appraisal may be considered to be independent of the test results.

At this stage De Vos, the psychological anthropologist, knew little or nothing about Arab culture or personality and had no knowledge of the individuals concerned. In the collaboration, the Rorschach sketch was presented first and then points of convergence or disagreement with the field observations were brought out. All the available material was then used, as in standard clinical use of the Rorschach, to bring understanding to the apparent discrepancies. Through this process we gained progressive understanding of Arab personality and its particular reflection in the protocols. Some limitations found in the blind, cross-cultural use of the test have been commented upon. The ensuing cases present integrated pictures of the individuals, with remarks as to the problems involved in their derivation.

Patterns of Acculturative Adaptation

Case No. 1: A Young Man Who Wanted to Be Like the French. Ali once spent four months in France as a personal servant to a French man. As a teenaged oasis youth who intensely desired to identify with the French way of life, he used a mixture of European and Arab dress and was vain about his wristwatch, a certain mark of French contact. He wore a fez like an Arab urbanite and swore that he would never wear the more rural turban. His command of French was fair and, in general, he showed a surprising degree of superficial assimilation for one who had spent so little time outside the oasis. Apart from his sojourn in France, he had lived only two months in Algiers with his uncles. Beneath the clothes and speech, however, we found a core of cultural belief which was characteristically like that of the unacculturated oasis Arabs.

Ali's father had worked for many years in Algiers before marrying there and returning to Sidi Khaled, where he operated a store. While in the city, he learned very little French, but he did learn to respect the position of the French. He saw to it that Ali secured all the education possible at the French school in the oasis. While the father was not generally punitive toward the boy, he did initially force Ali to attend school. These six years of training stood in contrast to Ali's two years of Koranic education.

Ali was the youngest of the three children borne by his mother, who died when he was small. His elder brother was living in France, and his sister was married. After his mother died, his father married two local women, by whom he had a son and two daughters. Ali's relations with his stepmothers were apparently good, but he tended to deprecate some of their practices, such as tattooing, which his mother had not followed.

Ali was a constant braggart. He expressed his supposed superiority both verbally and actively in his arrogant behavior toward others, even his seniors. Occasionally he did this even with his father but never with non-Arabs or Ahmed (Case No. 2), who was his hero. In other relationships, however, his arrogance was so marked that Miner could not employ him as an interpreter. He was sometimes unable to live up to his boasts of superior ability, as when he claimed he was a good cook and sought such employment. When given the opportunity to cook for the anthropologist, Ali had to bring the cooked food from his own home, where one of his stepmothers had actually prepared it!

This sort of deceit, with its concomitant suspicion of others, was not unusual among the Arabs, but Ali was particularly marked by it. He was the only person who saw the possibility of using the anthropologist's wire recorder as a device to discover what people said about him in his absence. In the same vein, he maintained that, were he married, he would test his wife's fidelity by pretending to leave the house and observing what happened when she thought him gone.

There were marked compulsive traits in his behavior, particularly with respect to keeping himself and his clothes clean. Unusually meticulous in his dress, he removed his outer robe whenever there was a possibility that it might become soiled. While he was a servant, Ali was trustworthy but lazy, avoiding exertion as being beneath him.

While generally voluble, Ali was somewhat restrained in talking about sexual matters. There were some strong indications that he may have been the active partner in sodomy with his half-brother, three years his junior. This brother was known to have been severely beaten by the father for having had such relations with other young men. The two brothers had separate sleeping rooms, in spite of crowded living conditions in the father's house.

Ali's Rorschach protocol was characterized most readily as an obsessive-compulsive one in an individual of not much more than average intelligence. (see Rapaport et al. 1945–1946; Salzman

1968). He demonstrated a strong push toward achievement without much indication of real ability, emphasizing his somewhat shallow nature. Of 45 responses, only one was a whole response. Responses to rare details constituted 22% of the total. Another 9% were given over to the smallest of the more common areas used on the cards. He was extremely constrictive, both in the use of his intellect in any but a stereotyped manner and in the repression of inner awareness, but he showed less constriction in an extraversive direction, producing three color-dominant responses. He attempted to approach tasks in a rote manner, not integrating but enumerating. He counted off his percepts with exaggerated exactness, carefully noting "two rats," "two silkworms," "two bats," "two cocks," and so on. Since the symmetrical nature of the blots allows for two of each percept, this type of response is found only in compulsively organized individuals. The content revealed very little symbolic material. There was no human or animal movement. The only two percepts that might have involved force in any way were "falling snow" and "two killed rabbits fastened to a tree trunk." The latter response suggests some passive fear of mutilation. Most of the animals Ali perceived were small rodents or burrowing creatures, suggesting a rather ineffectual self-image underlying his exterior braggadocio. A number of his responses, consisting of small faces and protrusions such as sticks, legs, and the like, were scored as indicative of obsessive anxiety. Nothing else in the record was noteworthy.

The ego controls were basically sound, and the thinking processes showed nothing exceptional aside from the compulsive structuring of thinking generally. Ali's rigidity and maladjustment scores were close to the means for the entire group. He gave a total of four popular Arab responses in addition to four populars found in both Western and Arab records. These indicated perceptions fundamentally in conformity with the Arab group.

The general impression one gained of Ali was that his pro-French attitude was derived initially from his father's positive orientation toward the French and the fact that his mother represented the French-Arab cultural mixture of Algiers, in contrast to the rural Arab attributes of his stepmothers. He had been able to meet his achievement needs, in the face of his somewhat

limited abilities, by mild deceit and compulsive striving to conform to the external symbols of French identity. By application to
his studies in the French school, by attention to French standards
of cleanliness and speech, by attaching himself to the highly
acculturated Ahmed, and by being briefly employed in France, he
had been able to outstrip even his father. There may have been
some basic hostility to his father, but Ali's extremely superior air
probably also reflected his adolescence.

Case No. 2: A Man Who Could Live in Two Worlds. Tall and
somewhat more heavy-set than the average Arab, Ahmed was a
handsome man in his late thirties. His white turban and *gandoura*
were scrupulously clean, his nails well-tended, and his face close-
shaven every Friday. He lived in a house adjacent to that of his
parents. His father had two wives in polygynous marriage.
Ahmed's mother was the second wife, and he was the youngest of
her children. Ahmed had had but one wife, and only six of their
children were still alive. His household, however, also included
two nephews and a male servant who slept in the courtyard.

One wife was all he desired, he said, for he got along well with
her and had no liking for the inevitable quarreling which polygyny produced. Primarily though, Ahmed did not want the
additional children another marriage would entail. He had no
daughters and conceded that a girl would be desirable. His attitude toward women generally was conservative. He contended
that he had confidence in their morality but he was very restrictive concerning the movements of his wife, not even permitting
her to visit his garden, some distance from the house.

Ahmed's father had worked a year in Algiers but devoted most
of his life to his gardens in Sidi Khaled and to the teahouse which
he had established in the village. For brief periods he also held a
minor official position to which he was appointed by the French.
His contact with the French led him to enter Ahmed in the local
French school. The boy was a bright scholar, completing six
years' education with distinction. In addition, Ahmed had a
year's Koranic training from which he derived maximal benefit.
Not only did he memorize a quarter of the Koran, but he became
remarkably literate in Arabic.

In his youth, Ahmed went to France, where he worked for two

years in a factory. While there he dressed like a Frenchman, but on returning to the oasis he assumed Arab clothes except for sweater, shirt, socks, and bedroom slippers, which were not uncommon "street wear." His wristwatch was the most obvious symbol of his French contact. The effects of his acculturation were, however, much more marked than this.

He was an outstanding innovator in the community, having benefited from his dual cultural role both economically and politically. In addition to managing his large garden, irrigated with water from a gasoline-driven pump, he ran the teahouse which his father had started, operated a trucking service, and had served as a member of the elected *djema'a*, or village council. He seemed quite conscious of his bicultural role and aware of its advantages and disadvantages in different situations.

Ahmed's attitude of poise and composure, toward both French and Arabs, was so controlled that he never appeared entirely relaxed. The only real indication of inner strain was his habit of cracking his knuckles. Apparently a very pliant individual, he accepted suggestion with no show of insecurity or threat. But even in a mutual exchange of confidences, he was careful never to express hostility. He was not prudish and would speak freely on any topic other than his wife and his own feelings.

In spite of his close association with Miner and his readiness to converse, Ahmed never invited him to his home, although other Arabs were not as reserved or defensive in this regard. Instead, the two men usually met at Ahmed's teahouse, where his generosity toward others was often apparent. In the affective area he was generally reserved, except with his youngest son, who was three but still had a wet nurse, well beyond the normal time for weaning. The boy was frequently brought to the teahouse, where Ahmed held him on his knee and plied him with sweets.

Ahmed showed himself to be quite reactive to sensory stimulation. He loved his gardens and would put rose petals in his nostrils to savor them long and fully. In this sensitivity he was not unique among the perfume-loving Arabs. But he was unusual in that, during the hot, thirsty days of Ramadan, he frequently bathed in his garden pool and gargled the fresh, cool water. In so doing, he remained within the letter of the religious proscriptions but maximized his comfort. His supernatural beliefs adhered to

Islamic dogma, but he did not hold the elaborate beliefs about dream interpretation, the evil eye (Róheim 1952; Vereecken 1928), and genii which characterized others in the oasis.

Ahmed's Rorschach Test

Card I:

1. *An animal carcass.* That's the tail; these marks which are generally found on the back of the animal. He's dead because he has no head. [D F− Ad (Hhad)]

2. *A bird.* [W F+ A (Neut)]

3. *Resembles a relief of a mountain.* (Upper half—blot seen in vista) [D FV+ Lds (Aev)]

4. *Resembles a person.* There's the neck without a head. There are the hands, the feet, which are pulled off. Similar to the bones of the foot. The bones—where the bones of the foot penetrate through the flesh. It should have a thickness. It would be rotten if it were a real body. [D F− Hd Anat (Hsm, Bb, Bdi)]

Card II:

5. *A butterfly ready to eat* [D FM+ A (Mor)]

6. *A thumb.* The front's here; the back's there. It's not attached to the butterfly. The butterfly is poised on it to eat something. It resembles a thumb. You can see well the emplacement of the nail. The butterfly is poised on it. It penetrates underneath. [D FM+ A Hd (Mor)]

Card III:

7. *A tie.* A cravat. It has a butterfly tie and it has a knot. [D FC+ Cg P)(Porn)]

8. *The skeleton of a man.* The head, the holes of the eyes, the nose, and the mouth. [D F+ Death (Adeh, Agl)]

9. *The remains of the butterfly.* It's torn up in several pieces; the wings are gone; the body remains; all the rest is gone. [W F− Ad (Hsm, Aobs)]

Card IV:

10. *A fish.* A sea fish that has a kind of horn. It's soft because those things are a little elevated. [W F− A (Neut)]

11. *The stomach of a butterfly.* It's a butterfly that has been burned by something—a candle or something—and all that remains there is the stomach. [D F− Aanat (Hsm, Aobs, Mor)]

12. *A plant.* It's planted there and it grows. The leaves and shoots. This part is the old leaves. [(D F+ Bot)(Neut)]

13. *An edifice.* Two people are arguing. A construction like a minaret and two people arguing in the tower on top—very small. (Dd in Dl upside down as tower) [Dd M+ H O (HH, Drel)]

14. *A kind of toad.* There are the feet, the tail, the head. [W F− A (Neut)]

Card V:

15. *A bat.* [(W F+ ∧ P)(Neut)]

16. *A bird.* There are really differences with the head of the bat, in that the bat has no beak. [W F+ A (Neut)]

17. *A butterfly.* [W F+ A (Neut)]

18. *A head of leaf lettuce* (with rough edges). [W F+ Bot (Por)]

Card VI:

19. *A flying insect.* Head and wings; the wings are open. [D FM+ ∧ (Neut)]

20. *A tortoise.* The feet come out this way, tail, that's the shell. [(D F+ A)(Adef)]

21. *The head of a butterfly* (moustache seen from behind and above. [D F+ A (Aobs)]

22. *The mouth of a grasshopper.* It has a long thing, a tail; the mouth seen from below. [D F+ A (Dor)]

23. *A sparkplug* (these are the points). [D F+ Obj (Neut)]

Card VII:

24. *A butterfly with big wings.* [D F− A (Aobs)]

25. *The feet of a frog or a toad.* [D F− Ad (Neut)]

26. *A person with feet and hands.* [D F+ H (Neut)]

27. *Smoke* (goes up into the sky like that by layers). It rises from there as it forms. [W YF+ Smoke (Adif)]

Card VIII:

28. *A real butterfly.* [D F+ A (Neut)]

29. *A tree or something on which two animals are climbing.* A lion on each side; the lion may be clinging to the side. [D FM+ A P (Pstr, Dcl)]

30. *A decorative lamp of a house* (the lamp that one has in rich houses decorated in these ways). You put electricity or even candles in it and you hang it up from there. [W FT+ Orn (Porn)]

31. *The body of a butterfly.* It's made as if those two butterflies are stuck to one another by their back ends, tails, to make little ones. [D FM+ A, Sex (Msex, Aobs)]

32. *A tree on which animals are clinging.* (Identical with response 29.) [D FM+ A P (Dcl)]

Card IX:

33. *The back end of a dung beetle.* It's colored. It comes out at night and goes on the walls; it's black. It can be red or yellow. It depends upon the plants where it's found. [D CF− A (Man)]

34. *The body of a person* (stomach, a belt here, shoulders, the sleeve). This resembles a dress, looks like a woman shown with a dress, a silk dress; you can see the breast on either side. [DS M FC+H O (Porn, Ps)]

35. *The back part of a butterfly* (all the green, the body sticking out here. [D CF− Ad (Man Aobs)]

36. *Two deer heads* (head, eyes, and horns). [D F+ Ad (Neut)]

37. *A flower* (color and the form of petals). [D CF+ Bot (Pnat)]

Card X:

38. *A painting, a design* (in colors). [D FC+ Art (Porn)]

39. *The scorpion-stingers* (has a spine which curves in that form in the back). [D F+ Ad (Hh)]

40. *The winglike bones of a person's skeleton* (pelvic bones). [D F+ Anat (Bb)]

41. *A bird* (has a bill). [D F+ A (Neut)]

42. *Tree trunks* (a false pistachio). The twisting; it's not straight). [D F+ Bot (Neut)]

43. *The back end of a butterfly* (has two horns on the back). [D F− A (Man Aob)]

44. *Snails shells* (tail is here). This is the opening of the body.

The rolls on the shell are indicated by these lines. [D F+ A (Adef)]

45. *A bouquet of flowers, a little pot of plants* (a pot of glass with a design here). [W FC+ Bot (Porn, Pnat)]

46. *The form of a butterfly* (the head and the form). [D F+ A (Aobs)]

Although the Rorschach picture of Ahmed was generally in accord with the behavioral impression, it also revealed some surprising internal stresses. He was a flexible, extratensively oriented person rigidity score 32; with eight color responses out of a total of 46, five of them form-dominated. He showed extremely good outer control and could be pleasantly compliant whenever necessary. His emphasis on shading reinforced this picture. Positive affect was expressed in nine of his responses with a quantitative percentage of 19, close to the mean for the American group. Symbolically, these responses showed an aesthetic approach, emphasizing clothing and ornamentation as well as the beauty of nature.

A strong achievement orientation was indicated by the high response total and the emphasis on whole responses, which was found throughout the record, including the more difficult color cards. As was true for the Arabs generally, he was not systematic or methodical but showed his intelligence best when stimulated affectively in a positive way. What seemed lacking, somehow, was a mature inner life. His inner satisfaction still seemed basically bound to childish or infantile motives, but these wishes seemed to be strongly held back and repressed. The Rorschach suggested, therefore, that Ahmed's capacity to relate well socially did not carry over into deeper, more meaningful responsiveness as far as inner attitudes were concerned. In his deeper relationships he may have had no inner peace. There were strong sadomasochist tendencies related to an unresolved authority threat. His attention to anality was suggestive of strong latent homosexual submissiveness. In no quantitative score, however, did he suggest strong maladjustment, remaining within the low range.

The nature of his human content and an obsessive preoccupation with butterflies suffering various forms of destruction gave the record an unhappy tone, full of concern with sadomasochistic mutilation, until his mood shifted to a pleasurable one on the last three cards. Card I started with depressive content, "An animal carcass." Also seen was a person without a head. There was some preoccupation with the bones of the legs protruding without any feet. He decided they must have been made of stone because, if they had been flesh, they would have bloated up and rotted. On Card III the usual humans were for him perceived as skeletons. On Card IV he produced his only human movement: on the tower of a mosque seen at a distance were two marabouts, described as arguing. Card VII was a poorly perceived body of a person. The center of Card IX was seen as a woman dressed in a long gown revealing the form of her breasts.

It is interesting to follow a theme of butterfly percepts, for Ahmed saw butterflies on almost every card. They were not seen perseveratively, but rather in a different context and expressing different underlying affect from card to card. He unconsciously used the butterfly percept to express symbolically various fears and pleasures. One has the impression that he believed himself to be like a butterfly, basically rather soft and defenseless. To defend himself he had developed firm outer controls. His harder, outer social roles were represented by such shelled animals as snails and tortoises. On Card II the butterfly made its first appearance, "ready to eat," lighting on a thumb. The remains of the butterfly were found torn in several pieces on Card III. On Card IV the stomach of a butterfly had been burned by a candle. On Card V a butterfly appeared without elaboration and carried no special meaning. Only the head of a butterfly appeared on Card VI, followed by the mouth of a grasshopper. The butterfly had big wings on Card VII. Under the stimulation of color on Card VIII two butterflies were seen stuck together by their "back ends," clinging to a tree and copulating "to make little ones." The butterfly again appeared on Card IX but in a neutral tone. On Card X there were two butterflies. One response was again the "back end" of a butterfly, and the other a butterfly in pretty colors.

This preoccupation with oral, anal, and genital sexuality centering around butterflies suggests a time of experience in childhood or youth when Ahmed felt weak and vulnerable but nevertheless sought gratification as a favored and beloved child. The anthropologist from his notes suggested that he was probably considered attractive and was indulged. Later in life, he developed more mature outer controls and no longer resorted to the earlier passive techniques of gaining attention and indulgence. But passive narcissistic feelings, as well as a feeling of vulnerability to attack because of his passivity, remained strong but hidden currents underneath the surface poise and maturity.

It is noteworthy how Ahmed's particular personality development suited him for a bicultural role. In addition to his obvious intelligence, his poise, flexibility, and underlying "permeability" to others in social situations made him easily acceptable. It is doubtful that many individuals were able to maintain such a delicate balance between the French and Arabs without arousing animosity in one or the other, or even both groups.

Case No. 35: A Successful Businessman.   Rachid exemplified an Arab who sought to achieve business and social success in terms of modern industrial society without giving up his strong identity as an Arab. He lived within Muslim family and its marital ethics but in a manner which, by Western standards, emphasized their virtues rather than their deficiencies.

He was a well-nourished, strong-looking, middle-aged man. Energetic, intelligent, and sociable, he strove to further his business success and to establish and maintain an extended family in Algiers. He lived in an apartment in a mixed Arab-French quarter of the city. His wife was his father's brother's daughter, the preferred Arab match. Two other families closely related to him by similar marriages lived in the same apartment house, and Rachid thought of the whole group as "his" household. Despite their separate apartments, their lives were closely interwined, particularly as the women could visit one another without leaving the building.

Rachid spoke very good French, dressed meticulously in Western clothes, owned a car, and referred to himself as an "industrialist." Actually, he ran a small leather-goods shop, associated with a leather-working establishment in which he employed three young men.

Like most Arabs, he was antagonistic to French domination,

but he did not engage actively in politics. Normally a calm person, only unusual emotional strain caused him to lose his equanimity. Such a situation occurred when all six children in the extended family had whooping cough and one died. Rachid, who buried the child, was much more upset over the death than the child's own father was. The following day he burst into a tirade against economic conditions in Algeria. While these conditions were not directly related to the child's death, they were rationally couched criticisms against the lack of public health care provided by the French. On other occasions, Rachid was less rational in attributing to French domination the continuation of Arab customs of which he disapproved, such as the seclusion of women.

His supernatural beliefs conformed to Koranic dogma, but he had little belief in, or concern about, most of the peripheral areas of magic and prognostication. He interpreted "seizures by genii" in Western terms. In marked contrast was his firm belief in the power of a sorceress to make a man impotent with all but one woman; he was full of detailed information about such practices.

Rachid's father, a slipper-maker in the oasis, had married three women. He divorced his first wife because all her children died in infancy. Then he married again, and Rachid was the first child. Later he took a younger wife in polygynous marriage. As Rachid's mother grew older, she lost her place in her husband's bed but remained in his household.

As a child, Rachid had six years' training in the local French school and five years' Koranic schooling. Then he went to Algiers to work for relatives and later went to France as a worker. Upon his return to Algiers, he worked as an unskilled laborer until he was able to start his own leather-goods business. Married in his late twenties, he had seven children, only three of whom survived. But these three sufficed. In his struggle for economic security, he was one of the few Arabs in Miner's sample who used contraceptives. His belief that money was the most important thing in life was unequivocal.

His father and mother journeyed annually to Algiers to stay with him and to escape the desert heat of summer. On their last trip to Algiers his mother remained behind when his father returned to the oasis. Toward his father Rachid was respectful and deferential. Since there was a tradition against smoking in the family, he would hide and snuff out a cigarette in his pocket rather than have his father find him smoking. The father was proud of his son's success, which certainly helped Rachid's mother's position in the family.

The psychological picture presented by Rachid was fully in keeping with the overt picture and substantiated his strong identification with a paternal family role and strong achievement orientation. It also suggested, however, a propensity to use projective defenses, to connect and integrate thoughts in an arbitrary manner, and to feel vulnerable and threatened by potential dangers from outside. He also showed a somewhat volatile, affective potential, possibly related to the type of emotional outburst described by the anthropologist. In general, however, his introversive propensities were much more in the foreground on the Rorschach. He also showed a greater degree of personal flexibility than most Arabs (rigidity score of 25) and a stronger achievement orientation, albeit in pragmatic terms (D% = 76) rather than global (W% = 18). This high D% contrasted with the Arab mean of 51.

There was no doubt, when we approached the material from the standpoint of intellectual functioning, that Rachid was of superior intellectual caliber. In his 26 Rorschach responses, though he did not emphasize inclusive whole responses, he attempted to organize and elaborate his highly imaginative responses to a great extent. Although well defined in accuracy, their arbitrary and fanciful nature was sometimes removed from reality, especially in respect to human percepts. He symbolized a great deal so that the pressure of various affective promptings were very much in evidence. Considerable potential inner difficulty, which had to be overcome in maintaining outer equilibrium, was also apparent in these responses.

The record was full of symbolic expressions of a highly fabulized nature. Included were eleven responses with human or humanoid content, five of them having movement as a determinant. This amount of human content with movement (M) was in sharp contrast to the Arab records as a whole, although fabulization of a similar nature in human-movement responses was found in other records. Many percepts were original, some even containing a certain bizarre quality. For example, on Card II he saw "two monsters arguing. They're connected by their hands. Their hands are tied together. The body is like a monster and the head isn't human. The body's belted. . . ." On Card III he saw two poor, emaciated figures arguing either about something they both wanted or about which direction they should take "because of the blood between and in back of them. The blood shows they're in danger in front and behind; perhaps robbers." On Card IV he saw the head of a bearded Negro king whose body was that of an animal with a tail; also on this card he saw "someone hiding in the shadow, with a big nose and beard." He saw on Card V "a person with his head in the ground." On Card VI there were "two veiled women. Their hands are tied to a lamppost. You could say they look like ghosts arguing." On Card VII he described "the body of a person with a belt. It's a body without head or legs." He sees on Card X "a person coming down . . . like a parachutist, with two arms and two wings, which don't look much like wings." He also saw on Card X "two Alpinists . . . touching hands."

These responses were overdetermined by affect in a number of ways. Argumentation appeared in three of them. Being tied together or touching appeared in another three. Parts of bodies or bodies in unusual positions were seen. He paid special attention, in these responses, to the "belted" nature of the bodies. The figures were covered with coats or hair, and a bearded face appeared out of the shadow. One animal percept, on Card VII, involved animals "rearing back their heads as though to protect themselves." The humans on Card III not only disputed about dividing some gain but were afraid, arguing about which way to go to avoid the danger symbolized by blood. This content suggests a basically suspicious, defensive attitude, with a readiness to project hostility and feel threatened from the outside. The symbolic blood on Card III was the only use of bright color in the record. As was general for the Arabs, Rachid produced vista responses as well as demonstrating interest in the shading aspects of the cards. His five FM and three Fm responses showed, as in the case of his five M, suggestions of fabulization, but to a lesser degree.

His attitude toward coverings and containers caused him to produce the highest score of the Arab group on Fisher's Barrier

Score (Fisher and Cleveland 1958), a scale that correlated highly with achievement drive in research with American subjects. In Rachid's case, it was coupled with a high "penetration" score, suggesting a vulnerability to authority and a capacity to assume compliant roles.

The fabulized nature of his responses suggested a tendency to paranoid defenses, despite his more rational capacities. His belief in the evil eye and in the ability of a sorceress to inflict impotence contrasted with his conscious rejection of allied Arab supernatural beliefs in favor of Western concepts. The retention of some of the traditional beliefs may have come from very personal feelings in these areas, so that these beliefs resisted change in the face of a generally fairly rational attitude. Also his blaming the French for the Arab practice of secluding women may have stemmed from some personal feelings of ambivalence about this custom.

His assumption of a paternal role and establishing himself as a family head, with other relatives dependent on him, provided him with an outward show of success as a man. The anthropologist noted that, at one time when Rachid was talking about his mother, he made a "Freudian" slip and called her his "wife." His Rorschach responses of the Negro king with the body and tail of an animal and his percept of the bearded man hiding in the shadow suggested a lack of complete security in this identity as a successful male. He idolized his father but had not resolved his susceptibility to attack from power and authority, first represented by his father. The figures tied together represented a fear of submission and restriction. He saw "two sheep, killed and hung up. . . on a tree" on Card X; "a hide cut in two" (Card V); "legs without feet" (Card V); and "a body without head or legs" (Card VII). Concern over potency was suggested by a lamp (Card II), the two women tied to a lamppost (Card VI), and a lighted candle whose light was dim in the daytime (Card IX).

In summary, although Rachid identified with a patriarchal figure, he still had not fully resolved his Oedipal conflict. His special attention to a belief that a female sorceress could make men impotent with all except one woman suggested that a basic tie to the mother might prevent him from making a polygynous marriage like that of his father. In spite of underlying fears of threat to his potency and manliness, he had developed self-assertive strivings toward social accomplishment consonant with his superior intellectual abilities.

Case No. 50: An Overtly Aggressive Young Man.   Mohammed was initially a difficult case for us to understand, for certain of his manifest behaviors were in apparent opposition to characteristics suggested by analysis of the Rorschach material. The two sets of data were reconciled by inferring that his overtly assertive and aggressive behavior was a reaction against an underlying passive-oral orientation.

In his youth Mohammed made several trips to Algiers, where he stayed with his older brother. At eighteen, when he left the oasis permanently, he was rather wild and undisciplined. He had received a little training in carpentry from his father but even less after he came to Algiers to work under his brother's tutelage. Neglectful of his duties, he quarreled with and insulted the other workers and continually expressed a desire to go to France. Thinking that the experience of making his own way might be good for Mohammed, his brother paid his passage to the continent.

In France, Mohammed worked in a number of menial capacities. Out of a job at the end of a year, he returned to Algiers but not to his brother. Again he found no work and was a bicycle racer for a time. Finally, his brother persuaded a friend to take the youth into his shop. This time he settled down, married his father's brother's daughter, and drew close to his brother, whom he now holds in respect.

His alertness suggested fairly high intelligence; despite his lack of schooling, he had learned to speak French rather well. He wore European clothes and, while still liking native food, his preference was for a generally Western diet. His supernatural beliefs, however, were still like those of the oasis population, and his recently reformed behavior included a return to active religious life.

Mohammed expressed negative attitudes toward the French and toward those Arabs whose submissiveness stamped them as "Beni Oui Oui's." In the oasis, he had identified with a group of "young Turks" who opposed the older leaders of the village council and the dominant families of the community.

He seemed to form a rather close friendship with Miner and was relatively free of reticence and suspicion toward him. One reason for the positive relationship may have been his actively expressed desire to emigrate to the United States.

Some indication of his underlying personality was available, both in regard to the expression of aggression and to the nature of his concern with sexuality. According to his own account, he manifested at certain times highly explosive aggressive behavior. He told how he once hit a younger brother in "punishment" so hard that his jaw was swollen for days. When he was fourteen he hit a man on the head with a rock, leaving him unconscious "in a pool of blood." To punish him, his father beat him with a stick. While Mohammed was in France he had a fight with a Corsican co-worker who was bothering him, and beat the Corsican over the head with an iron bar.

Mohammed discussed sexual matters rather freely with the anthropologist. In this regard, he gave inferential evidence of homosexual play during childhood and expressed his adult interest in forms of heterosexual satisfaction other than intercourse, activities Freud (1905) designated as "polymorphous perverse." We gave certain other impressions concerning his sexual behavior, the possible meaning of which is better considered after presentation of the Rorschach data.

Mohammed's Rorschach was very complex, with a great deal of affective material in his 57 responses. It was, first, a record full of attention to the small details of the cards, with a meticulousness of approach and at times an exactness about trifling matters. There was a total of eight space responses, five of them to relatively rare areas. This reversal of figure and ground corresponded with the oppositional traits noted in his behavior. A certain intellectual querulousness was evident in such an approach. Like many of the Arabs, he was not attentive to the popularly perceived blot areas but was idiosyncratic in his percepts.

This was the record of a highly extratensive person. He was stimulated from without (M:C = 0:4) with a total of ten shading responses (4YF, 4FT, 2FC'), but there was a lack of more mature fantasy (M:FM = 0:5). His thinking exemplified the obsessive and arbitrary patterns noted earlier as being general in the Arab records. He had six responses in which elements were arbitrarily united, even to the extent of being somewhat bizarre: a bat with a crocodile head; a rare mosquito with big ears; two pigs holding a scarf; a mosquito on a fig; a bird on the belly of a woman; and a toad with a tail like a goat. He gave responses that were highly overvalenced with affect: "A head—big head—empty eyes—closed mouth—empty cheeks—much hair on the sides—a bone in the middle of the forehead." "It is from olden times—dead, but not long dead. It still has some flesh on it."

There were a number of mosquitoes in the responses, but it was not clear whether they were perceived as small, jabbing insects or as sucking ones. A great deal of attention was paid to the mouths in his percepts, and he also saw a human throat and the "neck" of a guitar. Three responses were of the bellies of women. In two of these the anatomy was perceived as cut open. In other responses he was particularly sensitive to musculature, seeing the strong shoulders of American bison and the shoulder of a camel, "in good condition, because it is muscular and thick." Hair was described with great detail as in "a jackal's tail." In the inquiry: "It's full of hair, the hair like cotton . . . full of hairs like wool"; "An open sweater with a zipper"; "It's knitted wool. . . ."

Since all these responses had an original flavor and were not suggested to others by the blots, they had special significance for him. They can be reconstructed into a picture of a person who had strong underlying oral-dependent needs which could at times be sadistically perceived. The need for tactual contact was strong, and the attention to musculature and soft qualities suggested strong body narcissism. Yet there was something repellent involved, as in the percept of the head with a bone in front and empty eyes. To interpret how these needs might be expressed in relation to a wife, one must know that "fig" was the expression for "vulva" in the colloquial French in which the Rorschach responses were given. With this knowledge, the "mosquito on a fig" response suggested indulgence in oral sexual behavior on Mohammed's part or some feeling of inadequacy with regard to his penis. He contended that he was inconvenienced by the ritual necessity of bathing after intercourse, to purify himself for prayer. To this he attributed the diminution of the frequency with which he had intercourse with his wife. He stated that early in marriage he had daily sexual relations but by the time of the interviews it occurred only three times weekly. From his wife it was learned that during one month they had intercourse only once and then at her request.

The examples which he gave of "Satan's dreams" consisted of beating up his father and sleeping with his mother. Reports of such dreams were not uncommon, but he added an idiosyncratic one about walking naked through the streets. This dream, it must be noted, is related to the suggestions of body narcissism found in the Rorschach content. Mohammed enjoyed showing pictures, which he carried with him, of himself as a bicycle racer. He openly discussed "variety" in intercourse but added that sodomy was forbidden. Nevertheless, he said that homosexual sodomy was frequent among boys and acknowledged the existence of animal contacts.

Relating the observational data to that of the Rorschach, one reached the conclusion that much of his aggressive surface behavior, of which he proudly boasted, and his exhibition of his masculine prowess and physique were counterpoised to underlying infantile, pregenital needs in which orality, both in the form of feelings of deprivation and of aggressiveness, played a very strong part. His masculine identification was therefore not a secure one. His belligerency and negativism were more acceptable to him than open passivity and dependency. His aggressiveness could be coupled with anti-French feelings, and he could vent anger on others who seemed submissive, as in the case of the "Beni Oui Oui's." His change in conduct, after his trip to France, from a belligerent obstreperous attitude toward his successful older brother to one of seriousness and respect may be explained by his shift in hatred of authority to hatred of the French.

His close relationship to the anthropologist seemed to contain certain dependent attitudes. It is to be noted, however, that these attitudes were well controlled and not intrusive. The relatively high number of Rorschach responses with positive affect suggested that, in spite of internal strain and defensive feelings, his overall attitude toward life was not lacking in a certain basic optimism.

Case No. 32: A Young Nationalist.   When Benazouz consented
to work as an interpreter for the anthropologist, Miner was curious as to why such an obviously capable and employable young
man should be available for temporary hire. Inquiry revealed that
Benazouz had just been released from prison. He had been
rounded up in Algiers, along with members of the two major
underground nationalist movements, following a disturbance and
bloodshed in a distant hill town. Nor was this his first arrest. During World War II he had dreamed that he was being arrested, and
his dream was soon fulfilled, when he was picked up on suspicion
that he was involved in black-market activities. Despite the likely
psychological interpretation of his dream, he professed innocence
and did, in fact, escape sentence.

    Benazouz was not, however, the colorful figure these incidents
might lead one to expect. As seen in 1950, he was a young man in
his twenties who affected a Western appearance and expressed
progressive, modern ideas. His European clothes were very neat,
and his total appearance was more French than Arab. Although
he had had only four years of French schooling and considered
himself essentially uneducated, his French was exceedingly good.

    This young man was one of the two Arabs in the sample who
were not born in Sidi Khaled. Both his parents were born in the
oasis and were postadolescent when their families moved to
Algiers. Related through their fathers, the husband and wife had
a traditional, lasting, and monogamous union. Benazouz was the
second of their three children. The father worked as a laborer in
a French winery—acceptable employment, despite the Muslim
antipathy to alcohol. While Benazouz gave the appearance of a
clerical worker, he had, in fact, had a succession of unskilled
jobs.

    His life goals were clear in his mind. Although he believed that
ideally a man should be married at twenty-two, he had not yet
married because it was important for him to have a good job first.
"If you are married, you have children in spite of yourself," he
said. He wanted a secure position, a comfortable apartment, and
four children including two girls "for their mother." Benazouz
had beaten his younger brother for keeping bad company and
refusing to go to school.

    His cultural values were a mixture of Western skepticism and deprecation of the backwardness of many of his fellow Arabs on the one hand, and unquestioning adherence to Koranic teaching on the other. His attitudes toward the seclusion of women were liberal. Indicating that these customs were not required by the Koran, he asserted they would not be necessary at all if adequate education were "permitted" (by the French, he implied). Polygyny, he thought, was declining in direct proportion to the increasing respect for women, who formerly had no rights. Now their protests against this custom, which produced so many quarrels among co-wives, were being heeded. His response, however, to the question of what he would do if he ever found a strange man in his house was the usual Arab one: "I would kill him." He erroneously considered this response unique.

He held only those supernatural beliefs, such as in the evil eye and genii, which he could trace to the Prophet and the Koran. Since Benazouz had the Westerner's faith in doctors and their medicines, he called the talebs, who made charms, "not men of science but charlatans." Nor did he believe in fortune-tellers, "who talk about everything and hit some things right." He maintained, however, that he could foresee his own future in his dreams and cited the instance of his first arrest, which he had already dreamed about. His only other supernatural belief was in sahharas, who had the magic power of making a girl love a man. He denied, however, that they had any power to impair a man's virility.

Throughout his contact with Benazouz, the anthropologist found him a reliable, relatively flexible person with whom to work. He showed a minimum of personal defensiveness, not finding it necessary to enhance himself at others' expense. He never made any reference to his nationalist activities.

The psychological integration suggested throughout his Rorschach protocol was somewhat more mature, with much less pervasive internal pressure over sexual conflict than was evident in the case of Mohammed (case No. 50). He showed strong obsessive-compulsive propensities (Dd% = 17, 5-space responses), obsessive and arbitrary thinking in the form of several instances of precision alternatives, exactness limitations, and arbitrary responses.

Benazouz's record suggested a person with much potential

anxiety (anxiety affective index = 30; total shading: 12 with 3 YF, 1 Y); sensitivity (5 FT); and responsiveness to environmental stimuli (1 FC', 2 FC, 3 CF). His sensitivity and responsiveness were well controlled (F+% = 86) but pervasive. He maintained an attitude of guardedness, giving a number of evasive responses such as maps. Even though Benazouz had strong labile propensities (3 CF, including a volcano), he attempted to remain objective and realistic. In spite of repression of inner resources (1 M), he was a relatively flexible person (rigidity score = 33), scoring eighth lowest among the Arabs in this regard and well within the range of the normal American sample. Certain deep-set feelings of inferiority (7 FV) were resolved by compensatory emphasis on self-assertion and aggressiveness. Many of his animals were fierce, aggressive creatures such as lions, crocodiles, bison, and eagles. Although there was an obvious concern with achievement of an assertive self-identity, at the same time there were suggestions of unresolved relationships with a strong authority figure. Benazouz wanted to be a bigger and stronger person than he already was.

His assertiveness could be oppositional and negativistic in nature (5S). This oppositional feeling was likely to be turned outward, since his responsiveness to his environment was strong and there were repressive forces at work preventing introversion (M:C = 1:4). His problem of self-assertion was probably related to the social realm, as he was strongly status-conscious, looking down on groups he considered primitive or simple. In his human responses he saw a pair of men on Card III (nonelaborated), but he also saw Negro heads, which he described as "not as good-looking as whites." In identifying idols as belonging to primitive Negro tribes, he remarked that they were similar to those of the American Indians. Such responses indirectly expressed both his derogatory attitude toward anything primitive, and respect for the power and prestige of white Americans. That he looked both ways in his acculturation was suggested by his relatively large number of popular responses, both in terms of American norms (total Beck P = 6) and in terms of responses popular only in the Arab sample (Arab P = 7). These results signified a combined awareness of Western percepts and a manifest sharing of modes of perception basically Arab in nature.

Benazouz respected horizons other than his own. He saw an American bison, a map of France, Swiss mountains, the mountains of California. These percepts may have been partially due to his interest in American films. One would guess that his anti-French attitudes did not extend to a general anti-Western feeling. In spite of maintaining his identity as a progressive Arab, his psychological propensity toward feelings of inferiority probably made his social identity an ambivalent one. Most likely, doubts concerning his self-identity were repressed or denied by compensatory but realistic political and social activities which continually affirmed his allegiance to Arab culture, at the same time expressing a belligerent attitude toward the hated, alien French. Later, during the early years of the Algerian rebellion, Benazouz disappeared. He was probably killed or imprisoned by the French, or he may have gone into hiding.

Some Deviant Adjustive Patterns

Case No. 26: A Retired Soldier.   A noncommissioned officer during the latter part of his career, Abderrahman had many years' service with the French army's native troops in Algeria. When Miner knew him he was past middle age, employed in a responsible but unskilled position in Algiers. Clean, dressed in European clothes aside from his fez, Abderrahman spoke good French, which he said he learned to read and write on his own. His only formal schooling had consisted of three years of Koranic training.

His father, a farmer in Sidi Khaled, married Abderrahman's mother after the death of his first wife. Abderrahman was their only son. The mother died when he was a small child. After his father's death, when the boy was eleven, he lived for three years with an uncle. At fourteen he came to Algiers, where the number of jobs had increased during World War I. His army service fell between the two wars. Retiring from the Spahis with a modest pension, Abderrahman married and divorced one wife before seeking his present mate from a nomad group. Her two children by a previous marriage were being reared as his own, a very unusual situation in this strongly patrilineal society. Of the six children he had had by this wife, only two were still living.

Abderrahman had a wealth of opinion concerning supernatural beliefs. His respect for modern medical techniques explained his contempt for traditional Arab practices, such as the use of charms. Insisting that a person's welfare depended upon one's own character, he claimed that few talebs were possessed of real supernatural power (*baraka*) but that the evil eye was the natural result of this power and aggressiveness. As for *afreet* (evil spirits), "Solomon purified the world of them. Hitler and Stalin are human *afreet*, and Stalin is the biggest *afreet* alive."

When questioned about sahharas, Abderrahman admitted that they could make love potions, which he considered harmful; the materials they used had been introduced by the French in order to weaken the people, he said. These substances attacked the stomach and lungs, whereas the ingredients used in the old days were harmless. "A sahhara takes a person's nail clippings or hair and puts them in a potion which makes the victim sick.[2] Fingernails are dirty. Even if you touch your eyes with dirty hands, you get eye diseases." He knew from old Arab books that the Arab drugs reinforced sexual powers, whereas the present ones just weakened a man. The authorities, however, closed their eyes to this, as they did to the drug traffic. Jewish women acted as intermediaries in introducing the new drugs because they could speak Arabic. He reiterated that through these practices European control was continued. His first wife tried to use this kind of magic on him, debilitating him so that he was powerless to sleep with other women. It was then that he studied the subject. He learned of two old Arab practices: A woman will love a man a great deal if he massages his penis with honey before intercourse; if a man washed his hands well and then gave a drink to a woman, it would make her love him. When questioned whether he followed these customs, Abderrahman says, "No. If a woman doesn't like me, I don't bother with her." Finally he took his wife home to her parents, intending to teach her a lesson and then to take her back in three or four months. She took his marriage papers with her, as well as other papers bearing his name, so he divorced her.

His bitterness towards the French appeared frequently. He also blamed them for the decline of Arab astrology. They had limited the study of this science by Algerians although they used it themselves, as witnessed by the observatories they had built.

His hostility was again evident when he discussed tattooing. He was careful to hide a tattoo of Western design on his hand, saying that he detested tattooing, introduced by early Catholics in North Africa before the Arab invasion. As a matter of fact, many of the indigenous Berbers, who did tattoo, were Catholic, but the emphasis on the religion of the French was significant. Abderrahman said that the French were responsible for the present lack of respect for women. Since the French occupation, if women were molested in the streets, the authorities would do nothing. If a woman was picked up as a prostitute, the police just let her go. He maintained that the Arabs did not want to keep their women shut up in the house but were forced to do so in order to protect them. Actually, he permitted his daughters to attend school, accompanied to and from class by their mother. When an older daughter was returning from school one day with her mother, she was accosted by some men, one of whom threatened the women with a knife. Only the screaming of the women frightened the men away, as the police did not even appear.

Abderrahman was distrustful of the purpose of the Rorschach testing as described, seeing the anthropologist's work as some sort of political inquiry. He believed the inkblots were deliberately constructed drawings. While in itself this suspicion was not diagnostic of paranoid pathology, it fit in with the nature of the record. He indicated, at the end of the testing, that he had a definite approach in mind in giving his responses, namely, to present the "real spirit of Arab mentality." In one sense he did this by presenting, in extreme form, certain types of thought found scattered with less intensity throughout many of the records. The responses of this anti-French soldier, if given in a psychiatric setting, could only be described as diagnostic of paranoid ideation, with grandiose overtones, in an extremely intelligent individual.

Abderrahman's Rorschach Test
(Abbreviated Summary)

Card I:

1. *Two invisible men arguing.* They are invisible because they are covered by these things. [(W)(HH)]

Card II:

1. *Communists separate themselves from all danger.* They infiltrate throughout the world. [(W)(Athr)]

Card III:

1. *Two men holding the world.* They are all red, black fellows—evil people. They are both cut in half. [(W)(Abal, Hsm)]

Card IV:

1. *A person—savage.* It's a devil. The arms go out from the body but come back into it. The top is a covering of some kind. [(W)(Afant)]

Card V:

1. *Something unseen which destroys all the greed of the previous cards.* In the center is a bird which is going through the other parts and encompassing it. [(W)(HH)]

Card VI:

1. *Something opens a breach in all the rest.* It splits open all. [(W)(Hsm)]

Card VII:

1. *A geographic thing with a passage very narrow and guarded, like the Suez or Panama Canal.* [(WS)(Adef)]

Card VIII:

1. *Green flags.* [(D5)(Daut)]
2. *A headdress of green.* [(D4)(Daut)]
3. *The liver.* [(D2)(Bb)]
4. *Red animals; the paw is black.* (D1) (He then combined these responses, saying, "The flag, headdress, and liver are all symbols of one people.") [(Daut)]

Card IX:

1. *The continuation of the other.* (Referred to Card VIII, continued his symbolization)
2. *Geographic design.* [(W)(Aev)]

Card X:

1. *A design—a crown.* With it perhaps one gains control of the world. [(Daut)]

2. *A big pillar in the crown.* [(Daut, Msex)]

3. *The red succeeds in becoming the greatest.* (Confabulation of all parts to a concept of control) The red will be eaten by the green until empty. [(Hor)]

Here are briefly some of the types of illogical and projective-type thinking found in Abderrahman's record:

1. Throughout the cards there was the use of grandiose, fabulized symbolism of world forces in conflict or great evils threatening to over-power and destroy. The red and the black of the cards were used to present various abstractions of such things as "greed" and "evil."

2. The affect attributed to the cards was overvalenced and extreme in nature. Attention was focused on the "feeling" in the cards. Form was not used much as a determinant except to start a chain of fabulized associative elaborations.

3. The language was "queer" and body parts were "vitalized" in an unusual way. For example, on Card IV: "It's a person—completely savage—*all that comes out of him* is savage. It's a devil." "The arms *go out from the body but come back into it.* They are not free. The top part is a covering of some kind. Black legs come out below. The covering represents the normal, but the thing isn't normal. It is set on a pillar instead of on its legs—savage—bad."

4. Continual attention to coverings, invisibility, hiding, and guarded passages such as the fortified Suez Canal on Card VII is found mostly in individuals of an extremely suspicious, paranoid nature.

5. The fear of penetration, which appeared in milder form in many of the other Arab records, took on a more malignant tone here. The feeling was represented almost independently of concrete content. For example, on Card VI: "It is something which opens a breach in all the rest and remains superior to all the rest. . . . It splits open all that was in the previous cards. This black represents the arrow which made the breach and turned part of the black into white. The black is evil that has become somewhat white and conserved its strength. It is strong because it is on top and has more arrows." (Here one can note the indirect sexual symbolism.)

6. Card VIII brought out an extreme form of illogical juxtaposition of elements, technically described as a "fabulized combination" or as

"confabulation." The language too had a queer flavor. *"Now you show me* green flags (indicating the deliberate purpose of the examiner). Above them is a headdress of green. The red is the liver. The red animals put their feet on the headdress, the flag, and the liver. The liver is just for them to put their feet on. The paw on the headdress is black. *You aren't doing this for a book."* (This implication that the anthropologist's work was political was a clear projection from the subject's own percept to the intentions of the tester.) "The flag, headdress, and liver are all symbols of one people." On the actual percept the subject commented, "It looks like a lung," but he continued to use the word "liver," which is similar to our "heart" in symbolic content. By symbolizing his response, the subject rationalized and thereby showed a need to maintain a surface logic. Such capacity helped explain how Abderrahman could continue to function without some breakdown that would make the manifest nature of his paranoia more overtly nonadaptive.

The above is sufficient to indicate to the clinically experienced person the unequivocally paranoid ideation of this record. The question may occur, is it fair to consider this record paranoid in the context of Arab culture, especially since the behavioral material presented an individual who seemed to have made an acceptable adjustment to French military service and who later held a position which demanded at least moderate responsibility? It is our considered opinion that the ideation presented on this Rorschach means the same as it would if it had been obtained from an American. What is not so easily determined from such a record (as is equally true for American records) is the nature of the positive ego forces which maintained the social adaptation of this person in spite of paranoid structuring. It is difficult to define and diagnose paranoid pathology in psychiatric interviews. If the paranoid delusion coincides with sufficient outer reality to make it plausible to others, the person can maintain himself very well without drawing any undue attention to himself. It is only when the stresses of life exacerbate a situation that a latent paranoid structure reveals itself by the increasing implausibility of a persecutory system or a compensatory grandiosity (see Meissner 1978).

There was nothing to indicate that Abderrahman was under any undue external strain which would have caused him to manifest such implausible ideation. Yet if we examine the report of his divorce from his first wife for weakening his sexual power through magic, we find a story with definite paranoid elements. It is noteworthy that it was the weakening of his sexual ability that was ascribed to the influence of outside malevolent forces. His culture helped disguise the pathology of his story because the belief system of relatively uneducated Arabs supported such ideation. In his case he gave a somewhat naturalistic explanation in terms of "drugs." Likewise, his hatred of the French and Jews and his blaming them for many of the evils of his own society was not uncommon for Arabs. We must, however, point out that structurally Abderrahman's ego was nevertheless using mechanisms of projection whatever the license he received from his culture.

Case No. 36b: A Man Possessed by Genii.   Thin to the point of emaciation, filthy, and ragged, Khaled was thirty-two years old. Living in the oasis in very squalid circumstances with his mother and an abnormal brother, he had been periodically possessed by genii for eleven years and worried about the increasing frequency of such occurrences.[3] His manner was nervous and distrait, but he conversed coherently and could answer questions, even though he tended to equivocate in his responses.

Khaled's father was a *taleb* who at one time had had a small store in the oasis. He had had four wives and was living with the last one. His first wife was his father's brother's daughter. He soon took a second spouse and, by subsequent marriages after the death of his second and third wives, maintained a bigamous household of two wives until he divorced the first, eighteen years ago. This woman was Khaled's mother, who had borne half of the husband's twelve living offspring. Severe in his relation to the boy, Khaled's father beat him frequently, once slapping him so hard that he knocked him unconscious. The father would not let him play but kept him occupied either in the store, working in the gardens, or going to school. In addition to the Koranic training which Khaled received from his father, he studied five years with other Arab teachers and also attended the French school for four years.

Khaled was fourteen when his mother was divorced. He continued to work in the store until it failed and also worked as a gardener. Making use of his Koranic training as a taleb, he taught children for a while. If we can trust his chronology, his first seizures by genii occurred before his first marriage. He was twenty-four when he married his father's brother's daughter, but the marriage did not last. Then he married one of his mother's relatives, who bore him two children. One of these, a boy of four, was still alive. His wife's father had taken Khaled's wife and child back to his home, but he permitted the lad to eat his noon meal with Khaled. This arrangement was highly anomalous, although understandable, since Khaled had been so debilitated the previous four months by his nightly seizures that he had not been able to work, thus existing only on the charity of relatives. It was not clear whether the withdrawal of his wife followed or preceded the increase in his seizures. One of Khaled's dreams, before the beginning of his present crisis, reflected his fear of aggression from his mother's relatives when he was not under his father's protection.

Even more anomalous was the fact that he and his brother lived alone with their mother, although she had relatives in the oasis. Clearly this woman and her two abnormal sons had been rejected by their kin, at least so far as living arrangements and marriages were concerned.

Khaled's epileptoid seizures were like those characteristically attributed to attacks by genii. His mother followed local tradition in blaming the seizures on sexual congress with a genie, although Khaled alluded to them only as attacks by genii. His brother was not bothered by genii and people simply thought he was crazy (*mahboul*). He had always been abnormal. Half-naked and covered only by a torn, filthy robe, he squatted silently in the courtyard, moving only to get food or to run to the wall to relieve himself.

It was interesting that this same family had other members who illustrated the third culturally recognized form of deviation, saintliness. Some of Khaled's cousins were regarded as holy because of their peculiar behavior, which consisted of never washing and of sitting for hours in the marketplace, completely withdrawn and speaking to no one.

We get some picture of what it is like to be attacked by genii from Kahled's own account:

I see things like smoke. My head tightens and I can't move or talk. When I get better, I get normal again. Until four months ago, I could fight it off with words of God, but then they get into my head, and I can't get them out. I can hear them laugh. They are like the wind. They wrap around me and I begin to feel them going into my chest. I begin to have fear. When they leave, I can talk and move. They go out like a shadow from my chest.

Khaled has sought charms to exorcise his genii from all the talebs in the region. Recently he even consulted a guezzana in an attempt to foresee his fate. Both with regard to this religiously disapproved practice and his search for help in books on love magic, his interview responses were evasive and contradictory. He even used his contact with the anthropologist to seek some Western medicine which might cure his condition. The only real help he had ever had was after his initial seizure, when a "great" taleb, who later died, cured him for a year with a Koranic charm and potion.

He felt threatened by the evil eye and believed that it was the source of his genii attacks. Similar seizures, which he experienced a year ago, he believed were due to the envious remark of a man who, seeing him hard at work in a garden, commented, "You have a motor in your back."

Khaled's Rorschach, approached quantitatively, does not evidence any outstanding disturbance. While his record showed certain disorders in the area of thought, these were found sporadically throughout the other records. There was, however, a combination of qualitative indications of severe pathology which did not contribute to the score on the maladjustment scale but which, nevertheless, attested to a malfunctioning ego structure. Khaled was one of the few Arabs tested who "edged" the Rorschach cards. This turning of the surface of the card almost horizontal to the line of vision has been clinically reported as quite a rare occurrence, found almost solely among psychotics. One conjecture as to the basis of edging behavior is that the person perceives something on the card as overly real and turns the card horizontally to see if the object is actually three-dimensional. Some approximation of this visual phenomenon may be found in a perfectly normal reaction to viewing bright red colors on color film transparencies under certain conditions when the red-colored images sometimes appear to stand out from the film. With debilitation of the ego, a similar effect may occur when an individual looks at the Rorschach cards.

Khaled also showed "confusion" and "fluidity" in certain responses. One could not determine whether this confusion was due to a lack of desire to commit himself or whether he had forgotten, in the inquiry, what he had said earlier in very vital terms: "Trees throw all their force into the end." He also made such remarks as "This is a picture that drives me crazy." On the other hand, the content of his responses was not bizarre or weird, nor was the use of determinants or location areas in any way aberrant. It was almost as though there were a healthy part of himself which fought off some debilitation that he felt as alien and "outside" himself. He somehow objectified his illness as an extraneous force but not necessarily a supernatural one. In attempting to obtain from the anthropologist American medicine to control his illness, he may have indicated that he did not attribute his sickness to supernatural forces alone.

Case No. 9: A Taleb Who Hennaed His Beard.   His relatives and neighbors thoroughly disliked sixty-two-year-old Said. They accused him of having the evil eye and maliciously gossiped about him for staining his chin whiskers with henna so that he would not be a "graybeard." He indirectly supported this interpretation by contending that Mohammed recommended henna, but not black dye, for beards. Henna, for Arabs, is associated with holiness. Said's vanity did not stimulate him to care for his person or clothes, both of which were dirty and unkempt. He spit on the walls of his room or under the carpet and wiped his nose on the sleeves of his robe.

A Koranic teacher, he ranted at his half-dozen pupils, often beating them, and was generally violent in his emotional expression. All his shouting and aggressiveness could not cover his cowardice. Once he brutally struck a boy with a stick when he caught the lad pushing his six-year-old daughter about in the street. When the boy's angry father came to Said's house, the taleb fled.

He had no obvious political convictions, nor any other kind, for that matter. He sought to please rather than to inform. His manner toward the anthropologist was unctuous, and he tried in every way to ingratiate himself. There was nothing unusual in his religious beliefs. Although he occasionally wrote charms for nomads and claimed to know how to exorcise genii, he was defensive about the lack of demand for his services.

Said's mother was his father's third wife, taken in polygynous marriage. She was divorced while Said was a young boy, and for eight years he was sent to live in a *zaouia* in the neighboring oasis of Ouled Djellal. There he studied under the marabout and other teachers of the religious fraternity. At thirteen, his father gave him a bride of eighteen, his father's brother's daughter. The surviving children of this marriage were four daughters, a very inadequate progeny for masculine-oriented Arabs. When his wife reached the climacteric, he married the daughter of another of his father's brothers, a woman more than ten years his junior. The fact that the co-wives were first cousins did not stop them from quarreling or even actively fighting.

The younger wife bore one son and three daughters. The mothers' rivalry extended to bickering among their children, but then the elder wife died and her daughters married. When asked if he wanted another wife, Said answered that he had "a young wife who pleased him greatly." Even this indirect reference to the sexual adequacy of his wife was very anomalous for an Arab and may also have reflected his desire to appear young and virile.

How much his son meant to Said was obvious when the boy fell seriously ill. The anthropologist brought in a doctor who was able to save the boy. Said was pitifully grateful. His strong attachment to his son was even more apparent when he literally fought the lad's battles for him, beating other boys who hurt his son. As in the case of the aggression against his daughter, his punitive violence toward other men's children went beyond local norms for rough coercion. He was equally undisciplined in his relation to his spoiled youngest daughter, whom he indulged in every way, giving her privileges usually reserved only for sons.

Said's Rorschach was not very revealing. A generally constrictive, stereotyped protocol of fifteen responses, the record did not suggest more than average intellectual functioning. The rigidity score of 71 was extremely high. He hedged cautiously on many of his responses. In his reactions to the last three cards he found an easy solution to the necessity of producing responses by giving practically the same content of "an animal in a tree" to all three. Subsequently, in the inquiry, he tried to rationalize the response by giving some details to make it acceptable. His thinking, in general, tended to be more concerned with self-justification than with being logical or coherent in organization. Of his fifteen responses, ten were of animals and three were of trees. Nothing very personal was revealed. In spite of his hedging and a tendency to withdraw earlier responses during the inquiry, he did not reject any card. He voiced difficulty throughout the test, stating that he could not understand it, and, at one point, that he was perspiring because of the strain, which made him "suffer." There was no doubt that he found the test an ordeal.

Of note was his total of eight Arab populars, a very high total when compared with the mean number of three populars for the group as a whole. Such emphasis on P responses usually suggests a need to conform to commonly held thought patterns. The populars in Said's record raised the question of what this meant in terms of his aberrant, disturbed behavior. His level of form adequacy was within the normal range and, with all its constriction, the record suggested no pathology. Whatever his difficulties, they did not seem to be due to lack of reality orientation. Rather, one might infer that he was sensitive to general opinion and would have liked to be highly regarded. He probably knew himself to be something of a bluffer, attempting to hide from others any revelation of his basic inadequacies. He maintained a very superficial, stereotypic perception of human relationships and, coupled with a basically undisciplined, primitive emotional structure, he was almost pathetically transparent as a sycophant. His undisciplined, even unprincipled behavior led him to be despised by others, in spite of his constant attempts to cover up and be accepted in his role as taleb.

Blind Rorschach analysis did not, in itself, suggest this sort of integrated picture. Although many of the elements were separately predicted, there was no accurate prediction of this man's primitive affectivity. As in a number of other cases, Said's color responses, despite their extratensive balance, did not reflect his propensity for uncontrolled emotional behavior.

Case No. 8: A Hawker of Charms and Nostrums.   By dint of eight years' Koranic schooling, Hocine presented himself as a *taleb-toubib*, a "teacher-doctor," adept at using magic for diagnosis and making charms for curing various ills. He was a specialist, self-styled, in venereal disease. Having no office, he carried the instruments and materials of his practice in his pockets and in a sack, setting up shop in cafes or wherever his clients might be. Sophisticated urban Arabs were contemptuous of him and laughed when Hocine denounced his more successful rivals as charlatans. A marginal person in a highly competitive profession, his dirty, slovenly appearance lost him possible wealthier patients.

Middle-aged, he had been in Algiers intermittently for eighteen years. He was next to the youngest of nine children in his father's household of four polygynous wives. The father, a gardener, had died, as had his three elder wives. Hocine's mother, wife, and children live in the oasis while he comes alone to the Casbah for half of each year. His grandmother was a guezzana, who, with a mirror immersed in a platter of water, could see the past and future. She also dealt with genii. Others of his paternal family have baraka (power) and specialize in making cuts on the foreheads of sick children to let out fever.

Hocine had seen genii and, as a *tour de force*, could make children or adults who were in a state of purity also see them. He claimed belief in, and was well informed about, all Arab supernatural forces. Showing marked interest in any kind of magical power, he would have liked to have "Solomon's ring," for then he could have controlled genii and been all-powerful. Hocine was sure that Aladdin's lamp, guarded by all the afreet, was somewhere in Algeria. In common with many other Arabs, he had "Satan's dreams." He said that a man's dream of intercourse with mother or sister was significant of good luck and success in business. A dream of fighting with one's father in which the son won indicated that the son would be devoted to his father. If the father won, the son would be dissatisfied and eventually quarrel with the father.

Hocine's protocol presented a picture of severe internal disturbance (maladjustment score, 86, the seventh highest score in the group). His low rigidity score of 29 indicated a failure to use ego-constrictive defenses to bind up his internal difficulties. Sado-masochistic content and signs of disturbed sexual adjustment pervaded the record. Such responses were found on six of the nine cards; Card V was rejected. The partial record follows:

Card II: The lower part of a woman, opened up. It's divided along here. The sexual part is also cut in two. This side is the part in which the baby is formed. The other side is the anus and rectum. You can't see the external sex parts.

Card III: A person cut in half, with two lungs. It's all part of one person when folded together.

Card IV: This way—a person cut open. The thigh. There is the backbone, split open. Even the backbone is opened up.

Card VI: The body of a person opened up. Just a body cut open. Those are the sexual parts below. It looks like a man. They are interior parts on the front of a man.

Similar responses were given to Card VIII, identified as a female vagina, cut open, and to Card X, described as the throat, kidneys, and sexual parts of a human.

Hocine's protocol indicated a strong desire for contact with others. He was probably painfully aware of the feeling of others toward him. One surmises that he was superficially compliant and passive (4 texture responses, 3 of them TF; 3 passive movement responses) and that he could not readily show direct aggression or anger. Covertly he was hostile and aggressive (hostility content, 18% of all responses; bodily preoccupation content, 19%), but he could not assertively express these emotions. A counterpart to his inability to overcome his helpless submission and attachment to power, which he expressed symbolically in the content of certain Rorschach responses, was his conscious preoccupation with the magical means of obtaining power. For example, on Card I he gave a borderline movement response, "two genii attached together"; and similarly, on Card IX, "Siamese twins attached at the legs, hands resting on something." The figures were tied to each other, symbolizing some ambivalence about deep dependency. A praying figure on Card III again suggested a dependent relationship on outside power.

Although Miner could provide no supportive evidence, Hocine

apparently tried to accomplish through slyness, deceit, and submission what he could not achieve by direct assertion. He felt pathetically vulnerable to attack at all times. His pervasive preoccupation with men's and women's bodies, split open and exposing their internal sexual organs, was evidence of the severity of his sexual disturbance. Such a record suggested that this man would engage in homosexual activities which, for him, would be an unconsciously directed means of wresting masculine power from other men.

This protocol, interpreted according to certain psychoanalytic surmises concerning homosexuality, is typical of those formed among men not able to master the difficulties arising from a dominant, overpowering father image. Hocine's resort to magic and, inferentially, to chicanery were the means of finding a formula to supply himself with what he did not obtain in his own distorted maturation. Through his manipulation of charms and nostrums he could gain at least some sense of power in reference to the weakness of others.

Case No. 25: A Happy Man. In contrast to the foregoing personalities, Amar was an unusually cheerful, outgoing individual, so well liked that he was often chosen as a semiofficial greeter for the village council or the *caid* (village chief). Living in the oasis community, he was a well-to-do landowner, forty-eight years old. He had remained totally Arab in habits and dress, but he was not anti-French. He said that politically he stayed to the middle of the road; some of his compatriots accused him of being too subservient to the French. He freely admitted that he had consulted the French administrator before agreeing to work with the anthropologist and that he was impressed by the latter's rapport with the administration. He had long represented his sib (clan) on the *djem'a*.

His strong sense of responsibility explained Amar's kindness and helpfulness. He liked to joke and to tease, but never maliciously. In most situations he appeared self-assured but not aggressive. The only indication of inner tension was his habit, like Ahmed's, of cracking his knuckles.

We can infer a strong paternal identification, as Amar's relationship with his father had been very good. He described the old man as generous and kindly. The father had died at the age of one hundred and three, having had four wives and thirteen children. It was interesting to note, with regard to identification, that Amar's marriage pattern was identical with that of his father: two monogamous marriages, each followed by divorce; then a subsequent polygamous marriage to two women. Having become a patriarch in his own right, Amar had twenty-three individuals in his household, including two married brothers and their families.

Some people said that Amar occasionally flew into terrible rages at home, when he scolded and yelled at his sons. He created a similar scene in the marketplace, screaming at a craftsman who had tried to cheat him. Religious but skeptical about peripheral supernatural beliefs, he had no faith in genii and told a humorous anecdote about one of his sisters. She wanted a divorce from her husband, who refused to let her go. Then she said she was being attacked by a genie, to which the husband replied that he would chase out the genie, and he beat her with a stick. "The genie left and never returned!"

Amar's Rorschach record confirmed the behavioral pattern. He ranked next to the lowest of the total group on the rigidity scale and ninth lowest on the maladjustment scale, while demonstrating in his affective symbolism a generally positive affective cathexis. A relatively open record when compared with Arab averages for the production of movement, color, and texture, it demonstrated a generally happy emotional adjustment. The color-dominated color responses, as well as the movement responses, were mild and pleasurable. The nature of his movement responses suggested a basically positive attitudinal stance toward others, with mature attitudes and expectations definitely predominating. One-fourth (25%) of the responses (8) were positive in tone, the amount of unpleasantly toned material being relatively low, not more than 9% of the total. (A critical level is above 40%.) Some sexual preoccupation appeared in his response to Card I: "A woman with a vulva." Since such content, however, was not repeated and since the tone of the record became increasingly positive, this response did not weigh heavily in the balance.

In terms of cognitive processes, the protocol was strikingly Arab in character. Amar's responses contained many unrealistic relationships, with no attempt made to be methodical. Beginning with small details, he sometimes shifted to a whole response; or he might respond with a series of details on one card, giving a whole response on the next. His reasoning throughout might be characterized as naïve and egocentric. His Rorschach record included six of the twelve specific responses found most popular for the entire Arab group.

Amar's record was singularly devoid of any hostile content. Instead, various positive features of nature (garden vegetables, fruit trees) or recreation (costumed Negro dancers, a moving picture) were paramount in his associations. His thinking processes coincided with the Bleulers' (1935) characterization of the Moroccans as self-centered, undisciplined, and illogical. But, in general, Amar showed a fairly rare personality pattern for an Arab. The record was significant in that his good adjustment in Rorschach terms corresponded with his good social adaptation.

Notes

1. Adapted from Horace Miner and George A. De Vos, *Oasis and Casbah: Algerian Culture and Personality in Change* (Ann Arbor: University of Michigan Press, 1960), chap. 9.
2. This concept of the means of accomplishing witchcraft is found throughout the world (Best 1922; Boyer 1979; Murphy 1958; Parin-Matthèy 1971; Poole 1983; Shirokogoroff 1924).
3. See Crapanzano (1980) for a psychological study of a Moroccan who was similarly possessed.

References

Best, Elsdon
  1922 *Spiritual and Mental Concepts of the Maori.* Wellington, New Zealand: Government Printer.
Bleuler, M., and R. Bleuler
  1935 Rorschach's Inkblot Test and Racial Psychology: Mental Peculiarities of Moroccans. *Character and Personality* 4:97–114.
Boyer, L. Bryce
  1979 *Childhood and Folklore: A Psychoanalytic Study of Apache Personality.* New York: Library of Psychological Anthropology.

Crapanzano, Vincent
    1980   *Tuhami: Portrait of a Moroccan*. Chicago: University of Chicago Press.
Fisher, Seymour
    1950   Patterns of Personality and Rigidity and Some of Their Determinants. *Psychological Monographs* 64(1).
Fisher, Seymour, and Sidney Cleveland
    1958   *Body Image and Personality*. New York: Van Nostrand.
Freud, Sigmund
    1905   *Three Essays on the Theory of Sexuality*. Standard Edition, 1953, 7:123–245.
Meissner, William M.
    1978   *The Paranoid Process*. New York: Aronson.
Murphy, Robert F.
    1958   *Mundurucú Religion*. University of California Publications in American Archaeology and Ethnology 49(1):1–154. Berkeley and Los Angeles: University of California Press.
Parin-Matthèy, Goldy
    1971   Witches, Shamans, and Female Healers. Paul Parin, Fritz Morgenthaler, and Goldy Parin-Matthey, eds. *Fear Thy Neighbor as Thyself: Psychoanalysis and Society Among the Anyi of West Africa*, pp. 212–247. Chicago: University of Chicago Press [1980].
Poole, Fitz John Porter
    1983   Cannibals, Tricksters, and Witches: Anthropophagic Images among the Bimin-Kuskusmin. Paula Brown and Donald Tuzin, eds. *The Ethnography of Cannibalism*, pp. 6–32. Washington, D.C.: Washington Society for Psychological Anthropology.
Rapaport, David, Merton M. Gill, and Roy Schafer
    1945–46 *Diagnostic Psychological Testing*. Revised edition by Robert R. Holt. New York: International Universities Press, 1968.
Roheim, Geza
    1952   The Evil Eye. *American Imago* 9:351–363.
Salzman, Leon
    1968   *The Obsessive Personality: Origins, Dynamics, and Therapy*. 2d edition. New York: Aronson, 1975.
Shirokogoroff, S. M.
    1924   *Psychomental Complex of the Tungus*. London: Kegan Paul, Trench, Trubner.
Vereecken, J. L. T.
    1928   A Propos du mauvais oeil. *Hygiene Mentale* 57:25–38.

Part IV

Native Americans

L. Bryce Boyer

In 1957, David M. Schneider, then professor of anthropology at the University of California, Berkeley, invited Ruth M. Boyer to gather data for her doctoral dissertation under his guidance, continuing and expanding work he had begun among the Apache of the Mescalero Indian Reservation in New Mexico. He invited me to collaborate in the work. She was to expand his research on social structure, but her primary task was to be an extensive and intensive study of the childhood socialization processes of the resident Chiricahua and Mescalero Apache. My task was to investigate Apache personality by means of psychoanalytically oriented therapeutic interviews with Apache informants. My principal research strategy was to use, as nearly as possible, the techniques of my psychiatric practice which allowed me to understand the transference and resistance phenomena at work in the treatment process. The ultimate goal of our project was to delineate the mutual interactive influences of social structure, socialization processes, and personality formation. We three collaborated during the summers of 1957 and 1958, but then Schneider's efforts were replaced by those of Harry H. Basehart, then professor of anthropology at the University of New Mexico (now emeritus), who had for some years been engaged in a land claims study for the Chiricahua and Mescalero tribes. The formal research affiliation of Basehart and the Boyers went on for the next five years and has continued informally subsequently. The Boyers' involvement in this research has persisted for over thirty years and has entailed active fieldwork each year. Our longest continuous period of fieldwork (in 1959–60) was for more than fourteen months.[1]

Although the Boyers had wanted to include projective techniques as research tools in the study of Apache personality, their use was strongly discouraged by the National Institute of Mental Health reviewers of our research grant requests; thus we omitted them initially. However, a field situation made their use appear to be imperative, and I began to administer Rorschach tests after but a few months of fieldwork in 1959.

The Chiricahua and Mescalero Apache were historically very close in all ways, used contiguous areas for their seasonal following of wild harvests and hunting, and as home bases for their hunting and raiding activities. There was much intermarriage between the members of the two tribes, and it seemed reasonable to assume that, given all their commonalities, their aboriginal personality structures would be very similar. However, the two groups were subjected to quite different deculturative and enculturative pressures. A reservation was established in 1873 for the Mescaleros in the heartland of their aboriginal nomadic existence, and they were acculturated relatively slowly by representatives of the Bureau of Indian Affairs during the ensuing years. By contrast, the Chiricahuas were taken in 1886 as prisoners of war from their homeland in eastern and southern Arizona, first to Florida, then to Alabama and Oklahoma, and were finally freed from their prisoner status in 1913, after twenty-seven years of captivity during which the stresses they encountered were much more precipitous and severe than those to which the Mescaleros had been subjected.

Gathering research data in the late 1950s, Basehart and the Boyers were struck by a sharp difference in the response patterns between the older Chiricahuas and Mescaleros, both of whom were eager to cooperate with the investigators' pursuit of knowledge. The aged Chiricahuas could talk freely and were capable of seeing common denominators between events which had occurred at different times and in different places. Asked a question, an old Chiricahua would spontaneously elaborate and generalize. By contrast, the old Mescaleros were simply incapable of giving information freely. Literally sweating in their effort to cooperate, they could only answer questions in the affirmative or negative and they could not elaborate. For them, events which appeared to the researchers to have obvious common denominators were unlike, simply because they had occurred at different times or in different places. They could not generalize.

It was obvious that this contrast in cognitive patterning in the personalities of the old people could not be studied by the research methods available to me. Thus I set about to learn from Bruno Klopfer the technique of administering the Rorschach test, and subsequently administered the inkblot test to all the Mescaleros and Chiricahuas who had spent six years or more of their childhood either on the reservation or in prisoner-of-war camps. Then, giving no information about the source of the protocols to Klopfer, I asked him to attempt to place them into two categories. He was able to divide them readily into two groups, one containing the aged Chiricahuas and the other the old Mescaleros. Having thus been *absolutely* convinced of the cross-cultural utility of the Rorschach on the basis of personal experience, I decided to use it for many other purposes in our continuing research with Apaches.

The Boyers have been engaged in other field studies that have had similar ultimate goals, although their involvement has been much less intense. Thus Arthur E. Hippler asked us to check his field data in Alaska and we spent three short periods with him, among the Yukon delta Eskimos and with two Athabascan-speaking groups, no doubt closely related to the forebears of the Apaches, the Tanaina and Tanana Indians. Subsequently we also spent a few weeks in northern Finland, accompanying Vilja and Tor-Björn Hägglund in fieldwork among two groups of Laplanders. I administered Rorschach tests to representative samples of people from all these groups and found their analyses to be valuable when related to cultural variables. A number of our papers have appeared in addition to the three following chapters, which were done collaboratively with George De Vos and graduate students under his supervision, principally Orin Borders and Richard Day (see references).

Note

1. The research of Schneider and the Boyers was supported by NIMH Grant M-2013; Grant M-3088 supported the formal affiliation with Basehart. Subsequent research with De Vos has been partially supported by faculty grants from the University of California, Berkeley.

References

Boyer, L. Bryce
  1987 Effects of Acculturation on the Personality Traits of Aged Chiricahua and Mescalero Apaches: A Rorschach Study. *Rorschachiana* XVI, pp. 67–73. Beiheft zur Schweizerischen Zeitchrift für Psychologie und Ihre Anwendungen, Nr. 63. São Paulo: Casa do Psicologo.
Boyer, L. Bryce, and Ruth M. Boyer
  1972 El uso del test de Rorschach como un adjunto de investigación en el estudio de los Apaches en la Reservación India Mescalero. *Revista Argentina de Psicología* 3:69–102.
Boyer, L. Bryce, Ruth M. Boyer, Florence R. Brawer, Hayao Kawai, and Bruno Klopfer
  1964 Apache Age Groups. *Journal of Projective Techniques and Personality Assessment* 28:397–401.
Boyer, L. Bryce, Ruth M. Boyer, and George A. De Vos
  1982 An Apache Woman's Account of Her Recent Acquisition of the Shamanistic Status. *Journal of Psychoanalytic Anthropology* 5:299–331.
  1987 Der Erwerb der Schamanenwürde. Klinische Studie und Rorschach-Untersuchung eines besonderen Falles. In: *Die Wilde Seele. Zur Ethnopsychoanalyse von George Devereux*. Ed.: Hans Peter Duerr. Frankfurt am Main: Surkamp, pp. 220–273.
Boyer, L. Bryce, Ruth M. Boyer, Hayao Kawai, and Bruno Klopfer
  1967 Apache "Learners" and "Nonlearners." *Journal of Projective Techniques and Personality Assessment* 31:22–29.
Boyer, L. Bryce, Ruth M. Boyer, Bruno Klopfer, and Suzanne B. Scheiner
  1968 Apache "Learners" and "Nonlearners." II. Quantitative Signs of Influential Adults. *Journal of Projective Techniques and Personality Assessment* 32:146–159.
Boyer, L. Bryce, George A. De Vos, Orin Borders, and Alice Tani-Borders

1978   The Burnt Child Reaction Among the Yukon Eskimos. *Journal of Psychological Anthropology* 1:7–56.

Boyer, L. Bryce, Bruno Klopfer, Ruth M. Boyer, Florence B. Brawer, and Hayao Kawai
1965   El Rorschach en el estudio de los grupos Apaches. *Revista Mexicana de Psicología* 1:565–574.

Boyer, L. Bryce, Bruno Klopfer, Florence B. Brawer, and Hayao Kawai
1964   Comparisons of the Shamans and Pseudoshamans of the Apaches of the Mescalero Indian Reservation. *Journal of Projective Techniques and Personality Assessment* 28:173–180.

Boyer, L. Bryce, Christine M. Miller, and George A. De Vos
1984   A Comparison of Rorschach Protocols Obtained from Two Groups of Laplanders from Northern Finland. *Journal of Psychoanalytic Anthropology* 7:379–396.

Day, Richard, L. Bryce Boyer, and George A. De Vos
1975   Two Styles of Ego Development: A Cross-Cultural, Longitudinal Comparison of Apache and Anglo School Children. *Ethos* 3:345–379.

De Vos, George A., and Orin Borders
1979   A Rorschach Comparison of Delinquent and Nondelinquent Japanese Family Members. *Journal of Psychological Anthropology* 2(4):425–442.

Klopfer, Bruno, and L. Bryce Boyer
1961   Notes on the Personality Structure of a North American Indian Shaman: Rorschach Interpretation. *Journal of Protective Techniques* 25:170–178.

Chapter Ten

Progressive Constriction in Apache Youth

Richard Day, L. Bryce Boyer, and
George A. De Vos

This study is a highly abridged effort to summarize and distill from a large body of ethnographic and psychological material some general patterns of personality development among the Mescalero and Chiricahua children of the Mescalero Indian Reservation.[1] Although the nucleus of this study was a nine-year, longitudinal comparison of Apache children's Rorschach responses with those of an equivalent sample of middle-class white youth, the data can be understood fully only within the framework of the psychological background of aboriginal personality patterns and the vicissitudes of acculturation as it was experienced by these two Native American groups.[2]

Perhaps a millenium ago, groups of hunting, gathering, and raiding Indians who spoke the Southern Athabascan language stock migrated southward from northwest Canada. They reached the Southwest by the sixteenth century and divided. One group was influenced heavily by the resident Pueblos and became the Navajo, while the others continued their nomadic existence and became the Apache. Subsequently, the Apache divided into seven tribes, each one of which conducted its own subsistence patterns within its own area. The Mescaleros and Chiricahuas became or remained most alike. Historically, the social structure and socialization practices were almost identical in these two Apache tribes, and it has been assumed that the aboriginal type of personality organization was likewise similar (L. B. Boyer 1964).

L. Bryce Boyer and Ruth M. Boyer (1972) suggested that aboriginal socialization practices stimulated and enhanced in Apache children the development of a strong aggressive drive. The social organization provided external outlets which turned this aggressivity away from intragroup expression in such a way that hostility was not internally disruptive. The net effect was that, generally speaking, the group benefited. It has been hypothesized that Apache child-rearing techniques originally evolved as a complex cultural response to the Athabascans' harsh ecological situation, even before their migration toward the American Southwest. Apache primary institutions were adaptive, and produced a hardy but suspicious people with a shallow emotional life: a perduring type of "typical" personality uniquely suited to aboriginal conditions, facilitating survival in a threatening and miserly physical environment (Hippler, Boyer, and Boyer 1976).

During the Indian wars of the nineteenth century, the Mescalero and Chiricahua Apache were two of the last Indian groups to give up their guerrilla resistance. In 1873, a reservation was established for the Mescaleros in the heartland of their traditional territory. The Chiricahua suffered a different fate. They were taken as prisoners of war in 1886 emprisoned in Florida and then Alabama, and finally transported to Fort Sill, Oklahoma. In 1913, after twenty-seven years, the Chiricahuas were "freed," and a majority of the tribe chose to join the Mescaleros on their reservation in New Mexico.

The immediate experience of deculturation or acculturative contact was markedly different for the two groups, but the long-term effects were a common state of severe social disorganization for both. In addition to the breakdown of traditional social roles, the disruptive, not always well-meaning efforts of governmental authorities helped undermine the integrative values at the foundation of Apache society.

The strictures of reservation life caused a progressive disintegration of their institutionalized religious-projective systems— their "secondary institutions," in the terminology of Kardiner and Linton (1939). These institutionalized beliefs and practices had served previously to adapt Apache psychologically to the demands of the physical environment. Although early socialization practices remained intact and a strong aggressive drive continued to be stimulated, the social system no longer provided stable, institutionalized outlets used for the common good.

In effect, the process of partial deculturation experienced after conquest created a crucial discontinuity in the Apache life cycle at the very point (about five or six years of age) when a developing child must begin to integrate the content of his or her previous primary group's socialization into a meaningful and productive social role outside the immediate family. Erikson (1950) has described the so-called "latency" stage as a period of psychosocial development in which the child learns to insert the self into a rudimentary division of labor and discovers the capacity to subordinate and transform previous infantile concerns into a productive self image that reflects the goals of his or her own society. Among the Apache, however, the vicissitudes of deculturation broke the established continuity of the life cycle. Over time, the rigorous training for adulthood roles during the childhood period and the teaching of discipline that had played such an important part in traditional Apache society came to be viewed as the responsibility of external authorities, especially the public schools.

Thus, the historical disorganization of Apache society and the concomitant abrogation of responsibility for latency socialization had the effect of isolating the young person from a meaningful psychosocial relationship with his or her own cultural heritage. Adult roles no longer actualized the anticipations of earlier stages of psychosexual development.

Erikson (1950) has pointed out that such a situation makes it extremely difficult for the child to achieve an initial feeling of mastery over a productive social role and hinders a *positive* experience of solidarity with one's culture mates.

The Apache child's separation from a productive relationship with his or her own cultural heritage was further aggravated by experience in the American public schools. Primary schooling took place on the reservation; but during the period in which these research data were accumulated, many of the teachers were bigoted, fearful, and unsympathetic whites. The child then attended junior high and high school in towns neighboring the reservation, where the socially dominant white and Hispanic American students were largely hostile. Indian children were often thrust, unprepared, into an alien institution that was founded on a set of interpersonal values normally proscribed within Apache society (i.e., intragroup competition). The children's inability to cope with the novel and conflicting demands of the public schools not only estranged them further from their learning environment but provoked a contemptuous attitude on the part of their teachers and non-Apache peers.

The Boyers (1972) observed that even though most Apache children were initially eager to attend grammar school, by the third or fourth grade they had become discouraged and withdrawn. Moreover, the difficulties met by Apache children in the Anglo school system recall Brody's (1966) comments on the process of cultural exclusion and its effects on the socially mediated aspects of ego formation: first, the denial of self-determination and human equality retards the development of a positive self-image; second, the lack of individual gain in collective situations blocks the development of incentive and long-range goals; and third, the failure to internalize a meaningful, consistent system of values may reduce the richness, continuity, and integration of information coming from the external environment (De Vos 1978). The impact of this exclusionary process too often resulted in a constricted range of ego-adaptive techniques and the deployment of simple but dramatic modes of defense. Both responses, in turn, further isolated the Apache child from the dominant white milieu.

Recent research has suggested that the successful navigation of childhood and adolescence in large part rests upon the experience of social health and cultural solidarity; in Erikson's words (1959:412), it must be based on a personal "identity [that] can produce a workable psychosocial equilibrium." With Mescalero and Chiricahua Apache, however, the psychohistorical process of deculturation acted to isolate contemporary generations of young adults from a sense of continuity with a meaningful cultural "patrimony," while their experience of exclusion from white society prevented a potentially ameliorative identification with a new cultural environment. The psychological effects of this situation on a single group of Apache children in the 1960s constitutes the subject of this chapter.

Using a white sample as our comparative template, we deal in section 1 with the formative patterns of ego development during the Apache children's grammar school years. From these data emerge some specific observations about the direction of Apache ego development in the early stage of latency and the manner in which the Apache's cultural context served to stimulate a divergence from the middle-class Anglo pattern.

Section 2 describes a follow-up study, nine years later, of the same Apache children during the period of adolescence in the late 1960s. Again using a comparative sample of white youth, we trace the longitudinal evidence of Apache constrictiveness as earlier styles of ego development transmute into later phases of personality organization. Our evidence permits us to offer some final comments on the observed psychological effects of the Apache children's elementary and high school experiences.

1. Childhood

The vast majority of children living on the Mescalero Reservation begin their education in a state-supported grammar school located in the district known as Agency. From 1955 through 1960, white kindergarten teachers considered about half of their Apache students to have adjusted adequately enough to the usual aims of grammar school education to warrant promotion to the first grade. The teachers called these children "learners." The other half were thought to require another year of instruction and were placed in a second year of kindergarten called "prefirst"; these children became known as "nonlearners."

In 1959–60, L. B. Boyer collected Rorschach protocols from a sample of fifty-four Apache schoolchildren, thirty of whom had been labeled learners and twenty-four, nonlearners. Most of these youngsters were the kindergarteners of 1958 and, at the time of testing, had an average age of 7.5 years. In 1961, the Otis Quick Scoring Form Em was administered to both groups of children. Subsequent qualitative interpretation of the intellectual aspects of the children's Rorschach protocols by Bruno

Klopfer and their beta scores from the Otis test showed no significant difference between the learners' and nonlearners' tested levels of intelligence (Boyer et al. 1967:27).

In 1969, we examined the final grammar school records of twenty-four of these learners and twenty-two nonlearners to compare their levels of performance. Those records, combined with their teachers' estimates, revealed that the nonlearners showed a lower level of school performance to a degree that had a statistical reliability of $P < 0.01$ (see also Boyer et al. 1967:27).

Two conclusions were drawn from these data: first, the initial division of Apache kindergarteners into learners and nonlearners was a significant index of their later grammar school performance, and second, the criteria upon which this classification was based had little relationship to the children's potential level of intelligence. In light of these results, it was decided to compare the learners' and the nonlearners' Rorschach protocols with a normative sample of white seven-year-olds (Sevens) to discover whether the teachers' identification of the two Apache groups of schoolchildren correlated with any significant features of their general personality organization.

The Data

The normative sample of Sevens used in this section was taken from the Ames, Learned, Metraux, and Walker (1952) study of children's Rorschach responses.[3] Their sample contained a total of 650 children drawn primarily from professional or managerial families; they scored at an average level of intelligence (pp. 23–25). Summarizing their research, the Ames group concluded that seven seemed to be a relatively difficult age for the white child, an age typified by "an adequate equilibrium with the external world, but a frequent disequilibrium with himself" (p. 227).

In terms of *external adaptation* to the social milieu, the Ames group observed that the Sevens generally displayed a strong internalized drive to deal productively with situations or tasks in their behavioral environment, an increased interest in and attention to the attitudes and feelings of other people, and a continued growth of their cognitive/intellectual capacities. In relation to *internal adjustment*, however, a majority of white seven-year-olds in this sample showed a definite "inwardizing of experience" (p. 220), along with a marked diminution in their awareness of aggressive impulses and a conspicuous inability to exteriorize unpleasant feelings and experiences. In addition to this element of "inner tension" (p. 227), they also suggested that seven might be "an age of extremes" (p. 228) in which emotional expression was pervaded by a general egocentricity.

Using these conclusions as a normative basis for comparison, we can now proceed to a more detailed study of the patterns that emerged from the protocols of our white and Apache seven-year-olds.

External Adaptation

The Apache children's internalized drive to deal productively with tasks in their behavioral environment (see table 10.1, total responses, rejections) and their sensitivity to the attitudes and feelings of others (see human responses) among both the learners and nonlearners compared favorably with the standards obtained from the Sevens' protocols. Furthermore, the differences that did appear between white and Apache children indicated not a difference in adaptive potential, but what would seem to be two contrasting modes of approach to external reality.

The Ames group was particularly impressed by the Sevens' critical attention to the accuracy of their percepts (see table 10.1; good form) and their desire to generalize on these initial responses by integrating them into an organized whole using all or most of the blot stimuli (see DW, WS responses). In contrast, both the Apache learners and nonlearners were significantly less critical than the white children about the accuracy of their percepts and uniformly failed to show an equivalent tendency to generalize and organize their responses. Instead, a majority of our Apache seven-year-olds were prone to deal with the blot stimuli as an unconnected series of large or small realistic details.

These data seemed to indicate a culturally determined difference in the style of cognitive approach which characterized white as opposed to Apache children. George D. and Louise S. Spindler (1957:148) found this same pattern of response within other Native American groups and suggested that it reflected "a practi-

TABLE 10.1

External Adaptation: Childhood

		Raw Scores		*Anglos/ Learners*		*Anglos/ Nonlearners*		*Learners/ Nonlearners*	
Variable	*Anglos*	*Learners*	*Nonlearners*	X^2	$P=$	X^2	$P=$	X^2	$P=$
Total responses:									
21 +	25	14	9						
13-20	50	7	8	12.49	0.01	2.26	0.30	3.8	0.20
0-12	25	1	5						
Rejections:									
mean no.	.34	.09	.45						
% rejecting	18%	9%	18%	n/a	n/a	n/a	n/a	n/a	n/a
Human responses:									
21 + %	25	7	8						
5-20 %	50	14	11	3.58	0.20	2.60	0.30	2.45	0.30
0-4 %	25	1	3						
Good form (F +):									
92 + %	25	3	3						
78-91 %	50	3	2	17.92	0.01	21.40	0.01	0.22	0.99
0-77 %	25	16	17						
D→W responses:									
3 +	50	4	0						
0-2	50	18	22	6.90	<0.01	17.67	<0.01	4.4	0.05
WS responses:									
2 +	50	1	1						
0-1	50	21	21	13.26	<0.01	13.26	<0.01	0.00	1.00
Mode of approach:									
Whole %									
62 + %	25	2	3						
37-61 %	50	2	5	24.34	<0.01	12.00	<0.01	1.98	0.80
0-36	25	6	6						
Large details									
51 + %	25	11	11						
33-50 %	50	5	5	6.79	0.10	6.79	0.10	0.00	1.00
0-32 %	25	6	6						
Small details									
14 + %	25	16	9						
1-13 %	50	5	7	17.66	<0.01	3.01	0.30	6.28	0.05
0 %	25	1	5						

All significant totals in the table with marginal tabulations were corrected for continuity.

cal approach to problem solving, in contrast to [a drive toward] abstract integration in terms of long-range goals." The Ames group believed that for the white child "the desire to generalize" was an inherently satisfying mode of approach to the external world. They made this comment after noting the frequency of "dynamic perseverations" in the Sevens' records, which they stated to be "not the result of an inability to modulate their drives as much as from an [internalized] desire to continue and improve on satisfying behavior" (Ames et al. 1952:228). In the Rorschach protocols of Apache children this type of "dynamic perseveration" simply did not occur.

The previous data on productivity showed that these contrasting styles of cognitive approach in the two sets of records were not related to the Indian children's willingness or motivation to exert substantial effort in dealing with external reality. Rather, we seemed to be observing the cognitive manner in which the children's self-motivated drive toward productivity finally became manifest within the context of problem situations.

In summary, we compared seven-year-old white and Apache subjects in relation to the major areas of personality development that the Ames group found essential in defining the quality of the Sevens' adaptation to external reality. Unlike white children, seven-year-old Apache were less critical about the accuracy of their own perceptions and took a more practical, less abstract approach to problem solving. Whereas the Sevens were likely to make expansive "dynamic perseverations" to maintain a "satisfying" level of generalization, the Apache children tended to react to stimuli by enumerating large or small realistic details. These observations further substantiated Bruno Klopfer's conclusion that the identification of an Apache child as a learner or nonlearner had little to do with the quality of the youngster's attachment to external reality.[4]

Internal Adjustment

The Ames group found a fundamental theme in the Sevens' protocols to be a "definite inwardizing of experience" (Ames et al. 1952:220). An essential component of this pattern was the frequency of human movement responses, which occurred "here more than at any age [up to ten years]" (ibid.). They interpreted this increase in human movement as a continuing "enrichment" of the children's inner imaginary life (pp. 67, 225).

Compared to the Sevens, the Apache children showed an equivalent frequency of human movement responses among both the learners and nonlearners. It appeared, therefore, that there was little difference in the manifest quality of reflective, imaginary controls across our sample of seven-year-old white and Apache children. A concern of more immediate significance, however, was the manner in which the children's formative ego characteristically handled their infantile, less socialized attitudes and impulses. It was when we focused our attention on the recurring patterns of coping and defense appearing in the Rorschach protocols that suggestive differences began to emerge among our Apache learner, nonlearner, and white subjects.

Consider, for example, the data on emotional integration (see table 10.2), which suggest that the Apache seven-year-olds as a group were more impulsive (FM: >M) and more apt to seek immediate gratification than were their white counterparts, who felt such impulses more often as an ego-alien tension (m). The use of animal movement in the Rorschach test is interpreted as a potential pressing into behavior of less socialized impulses and attitudes about which the respondent has little insight. Our data showed that both groups of Apache children generally used a significantly greater number of animal movement responses than did the seven-year-old white youngsters. Animal movement occurred with such frequency that the individual could be considered to be "ruled" by immediate needs for gratification in more than 90% of the nonlearners, 70% of the learners, but not more than 50% of the Sevens (Klopfer et al. 1954:289).

Although we cannot infer from these data that the children with a predominance of animal movement responses always show an immature, behavioral impulsivity, we can derive a continuum of emotional integration in which the greatest proportion of subjects showing an overt preoccupation with infantile needs is found among the Apache nonlearners, followed by the learners, and finally by our sample of middle-class white children.

The symbolic analysis of inanimate movement (i.e., "a rock falling") and associated Rorschach indices provided further insight into the quality of the children's awareness of impulses. In contrast to the preceding variable, inanimate movement responses are interpreted as a warning signal for forces that threaten to disrupt the subject's ego integration and usually reflect an inner tension owing to the suppression or repression of unacceptable (i.e., ego-alien) impulses and attitudes. Numerically, the white Sevens used these responses with a greater fre-

TABLE 10.2

Internal Adjustment: Childhood

Variable	*Anglos*	*Raw Scores* *Learners*	*Nonlearners*	*Anglos/ Learners* χ^2	$P=$	*Anglos/ Nonlearners* χ^2	$P=$	*Learners/ Nonlearners* χ^2	$P=$
Human movement (M):									
3 +	25	5	4						
0-2	75	17	18	0.09	0.80	0.43	0.70	0.09	0.80
Animal movement (FM):									
4 +	25	15	17						
0-3	75	7	5	15.11	<0.01	21.78	<0.01	0.37	0.70
Emotional integration:									
FM<2M	50	5	2						
FM≥2M	50	17	20	5.13	0.05	11.68	<0.01	1.52	0.30
Inanimate movement (m):									
1 +	50	5	2						
0	50	17	20	5.13	0.05	11.68	<0.01	1.52	0.30
Shading responses (T,Y):									
1 +	50	7	2						
0	50	15	20	1.50	0.30	11.68	<0.01	3.58	0.10
Morbid themes:									
1 +		13	0						
0	n/a	9	22	n/a		n/a		15.7	0.01
Color responses: FC									
2 +	25	15	11						
0-1	75	7	11	15.11	0.01	5.3	0.05	1.55	0.30
CF									
3 +	25	3	3						
0-2	75	19	19	1.36	0.30	1.36	0.30	0.00	1.00
C									
2 +	25	11	1						
0-1	75	11	21	5.3	0.05	3.70	0.10	9.30	0.01
Emotional control:									
FC > CF + C		10	13						
FC = CF + C	n/a	2	4	n/a		n/a		2.75	0.30
FC < CF + C		10	5						
Emotional rigidity:									
CF + C≥2		14	6						
CF + C≤1	n/a	8	16	n/a		n/a		5.83	0.02

All significant totals in the table with marginal tabulations were corrected for continuity.

quency than either the Apache learners or nonlearners, who concentrated predominantly on animal movement responses.

Statistical analysis showed that the difference rose to a clearly significant level only in a comparison of the white with the Apache nonlearners ($P<.01$), whereas the difference between the learners and the whites was of lesser significance ($P<.05$). We would infer from these results that the modal nonlearner, at the age of seven, was more preoccupied with his own self-centered needs than was the average middle-class Seven, who was generally engaged in a more strenuous effort to exclude infantile impulses from awareness and, consequently, more likely to experience them as ego-alien forces "working on him like an object" (Klopfer and Kelley 1946:279). The Apache learners, however, seemed to show a pattern of response that indicated that members of their group lay somewhere between these two contrasting modes of experiencing impulse.

Enlarging on this aspect of "internal tension" found within the white records, the Ames group commented on the Sevens' tendency to react dysphorically to the black and grey as shading or texture on the cards (see table 10.2, TY responses) and on the number of morbid themes found in the content of their responses. They suggested that the Sevens' effort to exclude infantile sexual and aggressive urges from awareness made it difficult for them to "externalize unpleasant feelings and experiences" (Ames et al. 1952:221), and that internalized hostile impulses emerged as morbid content on the Rorschach protocol.

While statistical analysis revealed no significant difference in the incidence of dysphoric reactions to the black and gray colors on the part of the Sevens and the Apache learners, the nonlearners gave significantly fewer of these TY responses than did the whites, with a reliability of $P<.01$. The learners also gave a greater number of morbid responses than did the nonlearners, to a degree that also reached a reliability of $P<.01$. Thus, compared to the nonlearners, both the Apache learners and the whites tended to show a more anxious sensitivity to their own aggressive urges and to be less needful of immediate gratification of egocentric desires.

In summary, we gathered evidence for the hypothesis that one essential difference among our three groups was the characteristic relationship of the children's formative ego to the infantile derivatives of their inner impulse life. In the white children, we found an "inner tension" that was related to their efforts to repress aggressive impulses, and an anxious sensitivity to the elements of the blots that stimulated the egocentric aspects of their personality. In contrast, our Apache subjects as a group showed less evidence of an effort to diminish their awareness of unsocialized aggressive impulses and a greater emphasis on their own needs for immediate gratification. Within our Apache sample, however, we have also pointed out that the learners, when compared with the nonlearners, showed a relatively greater anxiety concerning their experience of unintegrated aggressive impulses. We shall further observe, in succeeding data, how these differences in the characteristic experience of impulse were related to the possibility of being expressed behaviorally in an interpersonal, emotional context.

In terms of emotional reactivity to interpersonal stimuli (see table 10.2, color responses), most investigators expect to find an emphasis on labile impulsiveness among preadolescent children. Piotrowski (1957:251) observed that the child needs an opportunity to develop his emotions, to feel them and act them out, and experiment with them. If self-control habits are imposed too soon or too strongly, the child may lose much of his or her capacity for a deep, spontaneous emotional reaction.

Comparing these "ideal" developmental norms with the data from the Sevens, we find that the Ames group sample closely approximated the expectations of most theorists. The relative predominance of color over form in the color responses in the white records suggested the potential for a deeply felt, emotionally labile reaction to external stimuli and led the Ames group to term seven years "an age of extremes" (Ames et al. 1952:223). In contrast, only 23% of the Apache learners and 18% of the nonlearners showed a numerical predominance of color over form determinants in their color responses. This finding indicated that we might expect a large majority of the Apache children to demonstrate a significantly greater emphasis on control and restriction of emotional responsiveness than would a comparable sample of middle-class white children.

Furthermore, in terms of an *adult* measure of emotional rigidity (Klopfer et al. 1954:296), the Apache data showed that the nonlearners, when compared to the learners, demonstrated a more severe pattern of emotional constriction to a degree that had a statistical reliability of $P = 0.02$. Thus, by *adult* standards, the learners could not be classified as emotionally constricted, but in relation to the "ideal" developmental norms of childhood, they did show a modal overemphasis on affective self-control during a period of their lives that should have been characterized by an experimentation with and freedom of emotional reactivity. This relative overemphasis on emotional control among the majority of Apache children also indicated that neither the learners nor the nonlearners would be expected to show a deeply felt, interpersonal spontaneity. Although we found evidence for the hypothesis that the Apache child, particularly the nonlearner, was more concerned with egocentric impulses and attitudes than his white counterparts, the concomitant Apache emphasis on labile control suggested that these attitudes only infrequently (or in socially sanctioned circumstances [see Boyer and Boyer 1972]) were manifested in the form of immature but cathartic interpersonal reactions.

In summary, we would expect that a majority of white seven-year-olds, when compared to the Apache children, were more prone to respond egocentrically to emotional stimulation from their external environment. The dangers of emotional lability helped to explain the Sevens' more strenuous effort to keep primitive, uncontrolled, aggressive inner aspects of their personality from behavioral expression.

The white Sevens seemed to be moderating the behavioral demands of their environment and their inner emotional lability, such that the style of kinesthetic awareness apparent in their records was the most effective manner by which they could maintain an expected level of social integration, since a monitoring capacity of awareness (M) was already dominant over more infantile impulsive tendencies (FM). It was the struggle of the children's formative ego to deny these impulses direct behavioral expression which emerged in the prevalence of inanimate movement (m), the use of morbid content, and their dysphoric sensitivity to the dark colors in the blots (i.e., TY responses). Both

Klopfer et al. (1954:579–580) and De Vos (see discussion of Hhat responses in the appendix) have suggested that this pattern of inner tension indicates that the individual is capable, or is in the process, of making a successful adjustment to the adaptive demands of his social milieu. The "warning factor" implicit in the inanimate movement response also suggests that the individual has sufficient ego strength to maintain behavioral control over his inner impulse life.

Conversely, a significant number of Apache children showed an early emphasis on rigid emotional control in dealing with stimuli from the interpersonal environment. However, rather than attempting to control the primitive impulses arising from within through a process of ego modulation, Apache children often blocked the emergence of such impulses into the behavioral environment by severely restricting reactivity to interpersonal stimuli. It was as if one attempted to deal with impulse life by effectively "insulating" the self against potentially provocative emotional stimuli. Among the nonlearners we found this style of coping in its most extreme form, "which is characteristic of the individual whose interpersonal relationships are tense and formal, and who, although not well integrated into society gives the impression of being over-compliant" (Phillips and Smith 1953:46). It might be suggested that the nonlearners' lack of emotional integration, their maintenance of an over-compliant front, and the superficiality of their socialized color responses too often led to the style of interpersonal behavior attributed to the "passive aggressive" individual (Schafer 1951:55). During their ethnographic research, the Boyers (1972) observed that Apache children often responded to the rigors of a school environment by deploying "unconscious provocative techniques" that made their mistreatment by others almost inevitable.

Again, the learners lay somewhere between the nonlearners and white children in handling their egocentric attitudes and impulses. Although both groups of Apache children failed to reach the level of emotional integration found in the Sevens' records, the nonlearners continued to show a higher degree of emotional rigidity than the learners. The learners, even though they showed a relative developmental overemphasis on emotional control, still retained the potential for a deep and genuine response to the environment. In comparison with the white child, the majority of learners also showed the same evidence for a degree of internal tension over the exteriorization of unpleasant feelings and experiences, but they failed to show the same strenuous efforts to exclude egocentric attitudes and impulses from ego awareness. The learners in a general way, therefore, tended to manifest elements of both the preceding coping strategies in the effort to maintain an equilibrium between the structure of their inner lives and the demands of their social milieu.

Comment: Childhood

Sarnoff (1976; cf. Erikson 1950, 1959) has observed that during early latency (6–8 years) children must accommodate to society through a reduction of infantile omnipotent striving for sexual and aggressive gratifications. Sarnoff's description of this period as one in which "the superego is strict, denying the child real objects as drive outlets" (Sarnoff 1971:409) highlighted the Ames group's evidence of "inner tension" among a majority of their white subjects. Following Sarnoff, these results would seem to indicate that the Sevens were experiencing a period of disequilibrium preceding the attainment of more effective levels of ego functioning.

In contrast, the Apache children as a group remained more subject to their own egocentric needs for immediate gratification and attempted to control these infantile derivatives through a constriction of emotional responsiveness. The Boyers (1972) have suggested that this style of coping has prior developmental roots in the "precocious stoicism" of the Apache child:

By the time the child is three, he will have learned a style of control that will win approval. Initially when confronted [with a new sibling], he reacted with temper tantrums. After a few months he tensed the muscles with which he would have expressed the rage and suddenly became limp. . . . Later, confronted with a frustrating rival, the child responded automatically with muscular limpness and a facial expression of withdrawal. This form of Apache stoicism was usually established during the fourth year. It is clear that it involved turning hostility inward and was thenceforth used in the service of passive aggression (pp. 71–72).

Summarizing their observations, the Boyers (1972:72) conclude that this "precocious Apache stoicism" constitutes a form of "inconsistent ego development" (Winnicott 1961) that oftentimes continues beyond the earliest period of sibling rivalry and becomes established as a generalized means of passive self-control over aggressive responses stimulated by the social environment.

It has been observed that almost every culture begins the formal education of its children at a time when the Oedipal stage of psychosexual maturation is fairly well transcended. Psychoanalysts generally believe that the child's attention can be effectively turned to formal learning only after the basic conflicts about the expression and control of sexual and aggressive impulses have been reasonably well resolved. Sarnoff (1976) points out that the continued stimulating environmental experiences of the child's sexual and destructive aggressive urges during the period of latency may lead to interference with formal learning and may result in a withdrawal either into intense fantasy formation or in other extreme modes of maladjustive/maladaptive behavior or behavioral acting out and delinquency.

As previously noted in the introduction, early child-rearing practices among the Apache have remained basically intact since traditional times, but the later socialization of latency and post-latency children has changed markedly. Beyond the simple abrogation of previous responsibilities for latency training, the Boyers (1972; L. B. Boyer 1964; R. M. Boyer 1962) have observed in adult behavior a continuing, gross stimulation of the children's sexual and aggressive concerns, particularly in the households of Apaches who drink heavily.

In this context, we would hypothesize that the Apache children's developmental overemphasis on a controlled emotional reactivity may be viewed as an extension and generalization of earlier dramatic modes of passive reactivity in their effort to handle environmental overstimulation during latency. Moreover, it is reasonable to assume that the children would deploy this established mode of defense as a primary means of coping with the frustrations and conflicts stimulated by their experiences in the public schools. By generalizing upon this early culturally organized style of "emotional insulation," the Apache child may come to feel increasingly incapable of more modulated emotional responsiveness restricting the continued development of "secondary autonomy" (Hartmann 1939, 1955) and "ego effectance" (White 1963) necessary for a feeling of competence in dealing with external reality. We are suggesting that the contemporary environment that conditions the early development of an Apache child tends to stimulate an emphasis on inconsistent types of ego development with a selective permeability (De Vos 1978) that defensively constricts awareness and necessitates a repressive "motoric" mode of defense rather than an intraceptive or obsessive-compulsive ideational one. Although these simple but dramatic modes of defense may have an immediate adaptive value in light of the severe conflicts with which Apache children must cope, we have also suggested that such constriction may have detrimental effects by blocking the process of continued development and ideational differentiation.

We may now return to our initial inquiry concerning the personality features of the Apache children by which their kindergarten teachers identified the "learner" and "nonlearner" subjects. Even though both groups of Apache children showed a developmental overemphasis on passive self-control, significantly fewer learners "insulated" themselves from environmental stimuli to the extreme degree found among the majority of nonlearners.

First, the learners' greater potential for deeper emotional responsiveness more closely approximated the pattern found among white children and was, therefore, more congruent with the culturally derived expectations of their white teachers. Second, the nonlearners' extreme pattern of emotional constriction and their greater tendency to manifest passive provocative attitudes as a means of defense would have tended to create a tense interpersonal atmosphere bound to stimulate anxiety and frustration on the part of white teachers. In contrast, the learners' more productive, labile style of emotional response would have provoked, for the teachers, a more familiar interpersonal situation, conducive of a more secure style of interaction with their pupils. In terms of personality organization, these data suggest that the categories of "learner" and "nonlearner" usually correlated with the children's predominant modes of handling their inner impulse life and their contrasting styles of coping with external stimuli. We would further hypothesize that the *critical variable* involved in the initial identification of the learners and the nonlearners was the children's relative effectiveness in provoking feelings of interpersonal anxiety and frustration on the part of their teachers. This potential style of interpersonal interaction helps to explain the Boyers' (1972:74) observation that "although some teachers are genuinely concerned and empathic, a majority are frightened and contemptuous of the Apaches."

Finally, the ethnographic, evidence suggests that the genesis of the learners' and nonlearners' differential modes of response may have been tied to the relative difficulties they had encountered in their primary family experiences. The encounter of the Apache child with the attitudes and demands of the dominant culture, as personified in his grammar school teachers, was *not* the *original* cause of the pattern of emotional constriction found in their Rorschach protocols. The important question remains, however, as to the degree to which the children's experience of educational "channeling" had any positive ameliorative or further negative effects on the constrictive modes of coping and defense which had been evoked within the process of primary group socialization for many Apache children.

2. Adolescence

Nine years later, in 1969, we conducted a follow-up study of twenty-two each of the learners and nonlearners who had comprised our original grammar school sample. A second set of Rorschach tests was collected by L. B. Boyer. At the time of retest, the average age of the subjects was 16.5 years. Most had continued to reside on the Mescalero Apache Reservation. The purpose of the follow-up study was twofold: first, to trace the effects of the style of inconsistent ego development found in many of the children's records as seven-year-olds, and second, to discover if we could still accurately differentiate between the original learner and nonlearner groups.

To facilitate a cross-cultural development perspective, we again compared the Apache subjects with a sample of white middle-class adolescents drawn from the work of Ames, Metraux, and Walker (1959). Although they were not the same children described in section 1, the white sixteen-year-olds came from an equivalent socioeconomic background to that of the white Sevens, and also demonstrated an above-average level of intelligence.

The Data

In the Ames group sample, the white sixteen-year-olds (Sixteens) were found to be emerging from a period of relative introversive constriction and moving toward a relatively balanced, expansive, and outgoing phase of development. "Sixteen gets along well with himself and the world. . . . [Any] need to rebel against the outside world or restrict his experience and shut himself off is now less intense" (ibid.: 241).

Among their subjects, sixteen marked a developmental watershed in which previous introversive conflicts gave way and new, potentially productive energies became available to the adolescent. Positive indications of these new inner resources were reflected in the evidence of an "increasing emotional vigor and productivity" (p. 244), a greater concern with "self-identity and interpersonal relations," and a "new intellectual expansiveness and ambition." In a negative direction, the Sixteens' incomplete subordination of these new inner resources might lead to a certain degree of "inner tension" and a "tendency to react explosively to frustration" (pp. 216–217). Yet the pleasant affect, abstract content, and cognitive control found in their records indicated the availability of more sophisticated defenses (i.e., intellectualization) to augment their former mechanisms for coping with anxiety. In summary, the Ames group concluded that the sixteen-year-olds sought to find satisfying new directions of interest and expression (p. 246; Pumpian-Mindlin 1965).

Internal Adjustment

The Rorschach index of conscious kinesthetic awareness (M), an essential component in a relatively high level of ego functioning, is observed normatively to increase with the subject's age and continued psychological maturation. Over the nine-year period of the study, the control subjects in the Ames group samples showed

TABLE 10.3

Internal Adjustment: Adolescence

Variable		Raw Scores		Anglos/ Learners		Anglos/ Nonlearners		Learners/ Nonlearners	
	Anglos	Learners	Nonlearners	χ^2	P=	χ^2	P=	χ^2	P=
Human movement									
4 +	25	1	1						
2-3	50	4	5	20.76	<0.01	17.66	<0.01	0.12	0.99
0-1	25	17	16						
Animal movement									
4 +	25	16	12						
2-3	50	3	9	17.92	<0.01	8.43	0.02	4.65	0.20
0-1	25	3	1						
Emotional integration:									
FM<M		1	0						
FM=M	n/a	0	2	n/a		n/a		3.02	0.50
FM>M		21	20						
2FM<M		3	4						
2FM≥M	n/a	19	18	n/a		n/a		0.22	0.98
Color responses:									
FC									
2 +	10	13	9						
0-1	90	9	13	25.91	<0.01	12.97	<0.01	1.44	0.30
CF									
2 +	50	5	4						
0-1	50	17	18	5.13	0.05	6.90	0.01	0.12	0.99
C									
			5						
0-1	90	17	17	2.67	0.20	2.67	0.20	0.00	1.00
Emotional control:									
FC > CF + C		14	9						
FC = CF + C		2	6						
FC < CF + C	n/a	5	3	n/a		n/a		n/a	
O = O		1	4						
Emotional rigidity									
CF + C ≤ 1		15	16						
CF + C ≥ 2M	n/a	7	6	n/a		n/a		0.08	0.80

significant normative progress in the use of human movement responses, whereas the protocols of most of the Apache subjects actually evinced a numerical decline in the frequency of M (cf. tables 10.2 and 10.3). Both the learners and nonlearners showed a lack of progression in the use of human movement responses, which resulted in averages significantly below those of the Ames' Sixteens.

In terms of emotional integration (i.e., neutralization, sublimation), the white subjects showed a mean ratio of animal to human movement responses (1:1) that failed to reach a Rorschach "adult ideal" but nevertheless suggested "a mature spontaneity [and] an easy acceptance of inner impulses" (Ames, Metraux, and Walker 1959:241; see also Klopfer et al. 1954:289). In contrast, more than 80% of the Apache learners' and nonlearners' protocols continued to show a predominance of animal over human movement to a degree that usually indicates a restriction of conscious imaginal controls and a lack of monitored, socialized, "sublimated" (Hartmann 1955) pathways for drive discharge. Three basic consequences might be expected to emerge from this weakness of kinesthetic intraceptive sensibility and modulation of inner impulses among Apache youth, and a consequent ego restriction: first, a loss of productivity through the inability to take advantage of the personality's inner resources; second, a continuing preoccupation with egocentric impulses seeking immediate gratification; and third, a potential acting-out of ego-dystonic aggressive impulses and attitudes (Klopfer et al. 1954: 288; Phillips and Smith 1953:86). These impulses could only be actualized by some while in an altered state of consciousness, as when under the influence of alcohol.

To specify further the character of the lack of effective ego integration of ego-dystonic impulses, we scored the symbolic content of the learners' and nonlearners' animal movement responses following our thematic affective scoring system. Of the cumulative animal movement responses in the Apache records, 28% of the learners' and 34% of the nonlearners' responses showed an overt pleasurable (i.e., "animals playing") or aggressive (i.e., "animals fighting") content. The analysis in table 10.4 shows that aggressive themes were clearly predominant in more than 70% of the learners' and nonlearners' protocols.

Turning to the experience of impulse, the Ames group (1959:246) suggested than the mean occurrence of 1.0 inanimate movement responses in the white Sixteens' records indicated an element of "inner tension" caused by the incomplete subordination of their impulse life. This frequency of inanimate movement, however, was within a range that reflected a relatively effective ego structure that may have been in the process of making a controlled adjustment between the personality's inner resources and the adaptive demands of the social milieu (Klopfer et al. 1954: 267). In comparison, inanimate movement responses occurred in less than 10% of the sixteen-year-old Apache records. This

TABLE 10.4

Symbolic Analysis of Animal Movement Responses

1. Aggressive and Pleasurable Themes as a Percentage of Total FM

		Pleasurable		*Aggressive*	
% of total animal movement (FM)		*Learners*	*Nonlearners*	*Learners*	*Nonlearners*
0%	(all content neutral)	21	16	4	6
1-30%		1	5	9	5
31%	+	_0_	_1_	_9_	_11_
		22	22	22	22

2. Aggressive to Pleasurable Themes in Individual Protocols

Relationship	*Learners*	*Nonlearners*
Aggressive < Pleasurable	1	1
Aggressive = Pleasurable	4	7
Aggressive > Pleasurable	_17_	_14_
	22	22

figure suggests that a vast majority of the adolescent Apache subjects lacked a felt inner tension (in the form of ego-alien impulses) between the relatively unsublimated aspects of their impulse life and the more mature elements of their ego structure. At this juncture it is useful to recall the observation that "the absence of inanimate movement [in conjunction with other indices of conflict] may imply a cessation of the struggle towards integration" (Klopfer et al. 1954:267).

In summary, these comparative data led to the hypothesis that most of our sample of Apache adolescents showed a relative inability to integrate their inner aggressive motivations with a simple acknowledgment of impulse (i.e., inhibition), a structure of conscious acceptable fantasy, or a socially organized framework of goals (i.e., sublimation; Holt 1967:347). Furthermore, the Apache adolescents' apparent lack of felt inner tension with regard to the experience of impulse suggested that their state of emotional integration was not part of a developmental disequilibrium but reflected a stable internal adjustment that might be expected to remain a component of their modal personality structure throughout their life span. These data raised the question of the conditions under which this weakness of emotional integration might make itself manifest behaviorally and how unmodified egocentric impulses were normally controlled in everyday social interaction.

The above questions can, in part, be answered through an analysis of the white middle-class and Apache adolescents' contrasting styles of emotional reactivity to external, interpersonal stimuli (see table 10.3, color responses). The balance of emotional responsiveness among a majority of Sixteens was markedly more controlled than nine years earlier, but still maintained an essentially labile, reactive character. The Ames group (1959:242) interpreted this somewhat egocentric spontaneity of affective response as reflecting a new quality of "emotional vigor and productivity."

The Apache records demonstrated a much more controlled style of emotional reactivity: only 22% of the learners and 17% of the nonlearners showed the same labile balance of responsiveness found among most of the white sixteen-year-olds. In addition, a comparison of the adolescent Apache subjects with an *adult* measure of emotional rigidity suggested that 68% of the learners and 74% of the nonlearners used a massive general constriction of affective response to interpersonal stimuli. Piotrowski (1957) has observed that this pattern of nonresponse to color indicates a premature, socially motivated subordination of a child's emotional potential (cf. Phillips and Smith 1953:231) which may finally result in the subject's relative "inability or unwillingness to allow himself a strong emotional reaction even when the situation demands a deep affective response" (Klopfer et al. 1954:296).

This style of emotional constriction also had important implications for the Apache teenagers' characteristic manner of impulse control. In a "normal" state of consciousness it might serve as a compensatory mechanism that inhibited the acting-out of egocentric inner impulses that had neither been integrated within a structure of socially accepted goals, controlled through conscious fantasy, nor had lost their ego-dystonic quality (Loewald 1973). Therefore, this style of emotional reactivity may have affectively "insulated" the adolescent Apache from provocative tensions and conflicts in his interpersonal environment. However, with loss of inhibition under the influence of alcohol, acting-out behavior might have released pent-up impulses and permitted labile reactivity.

Piotrowski (1957:170) made such an observation. A rigid mode of impulse is often circumvented during periods of "diminished consciousness," such as those produced by alcoholic intoxication. This hypothesized potential for impulsive forms of acting-out during states of diminished consciousness is substantiated by the Boyers' ethnographic observations concerning the effects of alcohol on Apache behavior:

When sober, Apaches are as a rule courteous, gentle, shy, modest people. Rules for behavior are well defined and generally obeyed. Remarks pertaining to sexual matters are usually omitted and intragroup violence is proscribed. When intoxicated their behavior is quite otherwise. Modesty disappears and speech becomes "dirty"; violence is to be expected. . . . Suppressions seem to evaporate and conscious aspects of the superego seem to dissolve. (Boyer 1964:217–218)

In conclusion, the longitudinal data from the white and Apache records showed two contrasting, long-term patterns of personality development. The primary theme of the white pattern was the continuing progress of emotional integration and the development of reflective imaginal controls that bound the expression of inner impulses within a coherent ego structure. Within this framework, the white adolescents maintained a relatively labile style of emotional responsiveness and developed an increasingly productive relationship to their interpersonal milieu. The Ames group felt that for most white adolescents this pattern of growth resulted in a relatively rich, sufficiently introversive personality, characterized by a well-developed imaginal function and a self-sufficient, secure attachment to the external world.

Few Apache subjects showed this pattern. In most of the Indian records, including those considered here, there was little emphasis on conscious imaginal controls as a balance in emotional integration. Instead, these adolescent Apaches continued to show an undue pressure from unconscious impulses and attitudes that remained essentially unmodified and unintegrated within a coherent ego structure. We have hypothesized that this relative lack of emotional integration was balanced by a constriction of emotional reactivity that allowed for reactive control at the expense of individual productivity and spontaneity. For most Apache subjects this pattern of development resulted in a super-

ficially extroverted style of personality that emphasized a passive-
reactive orientation toward forces felt to be located in external
reality.

Field Dependence and Nonlearning

In cognitive terms we can infer that Apache youth remained field-
dependent (Witkin 1967; Witkin and Berry 1975). Elsewhere, De
Vos (1978, 1980, 1982) has discussed a type of defensive, constrictive psychological structure related to field dependence and
"nonlearning" found in given ethnic minorities.

Research on "cognitive style" attempts to overcome the criticism of the earlier approach to cognition simply through IQ tests.
It combines cross-cultural research in perceptual, cognitive, and
social development. Witkin and his colleagues (Witkin and Berry
1975; Goodenough and Witkin 1977; Kagan and Buriel 1977) developed the concept of cognitive style and related it to what they
term "psychological differentiation." They see in children a progression and maturation of thinking from less differentiated to
more differentiated concepts. Conceptually greater differentiation allows for the parts of a context to be experienced discretely.
Witkin believes that greater differentiation shows up in the cognitive domain as well as in perceptual discrimination. What has
been most exciting in this research are experiments that suggest
there is an interrelationship between maturation of perceptual
processes, cognitive styles, and other dimensions of personality.
This is to say, a cognitive style is also indirectly involved in self-
concepts and in the management of social relationships. We
would contend that a continuance dependence on the opinions of
one's peers also reflects problems with the internalization process
and a form of psychosexual identification involving a sense of
inner assurance.

The more global, less differentiated perceptual approach that
Witkin has called "field dependent" appears to be consistent with
a social interaction style in which the individual appears to be
sensitive to both positive and negative social cues. In contrast,
a more differentiated "field-independent" conceptual mode is
found in individuals who are more independent in decision making and more competitive in social interaction. U.S. children, at

least those who have greater field independence, seem to have experienced a type of childhood socialization encouraging separation from parents and individualized internalization and regulation of impulses.

In reviewing this research literature as a whole, however, De Vos finds that it blurs possible adaptive differences in regard to the specific effects of experiencing a given minority status and social self-identity from childhood on, and traditional patterns of cognitive and emotional development general to individuals within given cultural or subcultural settings.

Cognitive development must be judged differently in respect to social adaptation in an intact culture as compared, for example, with a situation of rapid change involving migration of people into new environments in which they are likely to be judged rather negatively or perjoratively, as Boyer describes for the Apache during the historical period. The adaptive value of cognitive development that takes place in children in such a minority situation is not strictly comparable with that occurring in a native setting. Part of the new social self-identity developing in some minorities is the possible partial internalization of some of the negative social attributions coming from the majority culture. A minority identity may foster particular defensive coping mechanisms, resulting in selective permeability or "nonlearning" in an attempt to ward off these attributions. Moreover, negative attributions from the outside give rise to resentments and increasing manifestations of deviant behavior, with further negative social consequences.

This point can be illustrated by an examination of studies in the late 1960s and the 1970s involving interdisciplinary research by psychologists and anthropologists into problems of formal education experienced in two subcultural settings, that of Mexican Americans (Kagan 1974; Kagan and Madsen 1971, 1972*a*, 1972*b*; Madsen 1967; Madsen and Shapira 1973; Ramirez and Price-Williams 1974) and native Hawaiians (Howard 1971; Gallimore et al. 1974).

There had been numerous earlier studies that amply demonstrated that Mexican-American children, on the average, when tested with traditional IQ and achievement tests, did poorly in American schools. There were even some studies reporting that the average IQ went down year by year. While these results were in keeping with observed school performance, the early studies made no attempt to explicate these results within the cultural or social context of Mexican-American children. Madsen took a new approach that considered the interpersonal attitude of traditional Mexican culture as well as cognitive performance in assessing what was operating in these minority children. It became obvious that emphasis on individual competition, which was characteristic of the U.S. schools, created difficulty for many Mexican-American children, who manifested field dependence when tested by the procedures developed by Witkin (Kagan and Buriel 1977).

Individual teacher-pupil interaction is the implicit U.S. method of learning, each child being expected to internalize a desire to perform well and meet the expectations of the teacher. Kagan and Madsen (1972b) found that Mexican-American children were consistently less rivalrous and avoided conflict more than Anglo-American children. These differences tended to increase with age, in contrast to the special emphasis on rivalry, especially among Anglo-American boys. The psychological use of the peer group is evidently part of a pattern of field dependence found in Mexican children; moreover, there is an avoidance of confrontation among Mexican-American children as a consequence of the sanctioning against such behavior by Mexican parents.

In comparing the behavior of mothers in six different cultures, Minturn and Lambert (1964) reported that Mexican-American and Anglo-American mothers were at the opposite extremes in tolerating peer-group competition of an aggressive nature. Mexican mothers, like Apache mothers, severely discouraged aggressive behavior between peers.

It is crucial to learn more about how the group may be involved in either learning or nonlearning in ethnic groups characterized by field dependency. One finds this issue more directly addressed in the studies of classroom competition and cooperation made by Gallimore and Howard (Gallimore, Boggs, and Jordan 1974; Howard 1971, 1974), who examined the learning difficulties of "culturally Hawaiian" children in U.S. schools. Although the category "Hawaiian" included all individuals with some trace of native Hawaiian ancestry, those who were considered culturally Hawaiian were not actually racially different from those who had become more assimilated to the dominant American cultural traditions. It was the children who remained culturally Hawaiian who showed the greatest difficulty in formal school settings.

Howard found that in such children the Hawaiian language and other institutional aspects of the culture had disappeared, but the children had been socialized in ways that deemphasized individual competitive behavior and stressed the positive social virtues of peer-group affiliation. This affiliative pattern of inter-relationship among Hawaiians was pervasive. Howard discusses how early parental interaction, especially between mother and child, was relatively nonverbal compared with U.S. middle-class patterns. Both adults and children were peer-group oriented. Commitments to workmate or childhood peers often superseded commitments to one's spouse or one's children. Howard points out cogently how investment of material or emotional resources were directed toward a loose social network rather than toward members of one's primary family. In a sense, one accumulated the goodwill of one's peers rather than material objects. Relationships generally tended to be nonhierarchical. This finding about nonhierarchy in the Hawaiian and Samoan family and community conflicts with some other reported generalizations (Werner 1979).

In the case of the Japanese, De Vos (1982) argues that one sees social interdependency in individuals who nevertheless have become field independent cognitively. One must distinguish, therefore, between individuals who internalize and identify with given social roles which may demand behavioral conformity with the social group, and individuals who have difficulty with internalization and therefore remain dependent *cognitively* as well as socially on a social group.

Our own longitudinal data with Apache youth, while not related in any direct way to the considerable research on field dependency, do also indicate a constrictive convergence of both Apache learners and nonlearners around a developmental pattern that seems to be a direct extension of the inconsistent ego development found, to varying degrees, in their seven-year-old protocols. These data confirm our earlier surmise that this defensive course of personality development would inhibit more effective forms of ego functioning and restrict the feeling of inner competence cognitively necessary to field independence. It would also inhibit one's social relationship to the external world. To illustrate these conclusions further, we turn again to the Rorschach indices of external adaptation.

External Adaptation

The cognitive data from the white and Apache subjects also reflected two quite different modes of attachment to the external world. Whereas Ames et al. (1959) were particularly impressed by the white sixteen-year-olds' commitment to deal productively with tasks in the external world, our sample of Apache subjects showed a general decline in previous self-motivated drive toward problem solving (see table 10.5, total responses). They were significantly more prone to react to a sense of frustration by completely withdrawing their efforts from a difficult situation (see table 10.5, rejections).

Some among the Ames sample gave evidence of a "global, inclusive" manner of perception using complex whole responses (Ames et al. 1959:244). There was even a relative overemphasis on cognitive/intellectual controls (see table 10.5, pure form and good form) among the Sixteens. Ames and her colleagues believed that this emphasis represented the youngsters' efforts to modulate their new inner resources through a more careful yet ambitious style of perception. In conjunction with the appearance of a high frequency of abstract content in their responses, this pattern suggested a new reliance on more sophisticated intellectual modes of defense to cope with the pressures of inner impulses and the demands of their environment.

Except in a few specific cases, this pattern of Rorschach variables was completely foreign to the sixteen-year-old Apache protocols. Both the learners and the nonlearners generally showed a less expansive, less ambitious style of response and lacked the white middle-class adolescents' overemphasis on cognitive/ intellectual controls and abstract content. While the emergence of this pattern in the Sixteens' records signified a new reliance on more sophisticated modes of defense, the data suggested that the Apache teenagers continued to rely on their earlier, more rigid means of controlling anxiety.

TABLE 10.5

External Adaptation: Adolescence

Variable	Raw Scores			Anglos/ Learners		Anglos/ Nonlearners		Learners/ Nonlearners	
	Anglos	*Learners*	*Nonlearners*	X^2	*P=*	X^2	*P=*	X^2	*P=*
Total responses:									
27 +	25	2	0						
14-26	50	8	10	7.53	0.05-	9.91	<0.02	2.22	0.50
0-13	25	12	12		.02				
Rejections:									
1 +	16	13	12						
0	86	9	10	18.47	<0.01	15.14	<0.01	2.20	0.50
Shading:									
texture (Fc)	68%		87%						
diffusion (K)	13%		8%						
vista (FK)	13%		2%						
projection (k)	6%		3%						
mean responses per record	1.6		3.4						
Inner controls over affectional needs:									
F ≤ Fc + FK			50%						
F > Fc + FK	n/a		50%						
Mode of approach:									
Whole %									
68 + %	25	1	2						
29-67 %	50	11	15	6.15	0.05	3.19	0.20	2.55	0.30
0-28	25	10	5						
mean	50%	34%	40%						
Large details									
58 + %	25	7	8						
31-57 %	50	14	11	4.70	0.10	1.86	0.50	1.42	0.50
0-30 %	25	1	3						
mean	44%	51%	57%						
Small details									
5 + %	50	17	6						
0-4 %	50	5	16	5.41	0.02	3.74	0.10	11.02	0.01
mean	4%	14%	3%						
Pure form (F):									
71 + %	25	0	0						
40-70 %	50	3	4	28.0	0.01	24.5	0.01	0.16	0.99
0-39 %	25	19	18						
Good form (F+):									
89 + %	75	8	8						
0-88 %	25	14	14	12.37	0.01	12.37	0.01	0.00	1.00

All significant totals in the table with marginal tabulations were corrected for continuity.

In the quality of interpersonal relationships, concern with the textural qualities of the blot stimuli had been observed, on one level, to reflect a "sensitivity to the *surface* of social contact" (Phillips and Smith 1953:273). After taking into account the spontaneous, productive nature of these adolescents' emotional responsiveness and their favorable balance of impulse life to object relations, the Ames group (1959:245) suggested that the sixteen-year-olds' frequency of textural responses (see table 10.5) reflected, on the first level, a greater interpersonal perceptiveness of others' reactions, and on the second level, "a frank pleasure in their own [needs] and reactions."

Although the adolescent Apache showed a higher mean frequency of textural responses than their white counterparts, our interpretation must be adjusted to take into consideration the context in which these responses appeared. For example, the emotional constriction found to be characteristic of a majority of Apache sixteen-year-olds belied any expectation that either the learners or the nonlearners would respond to their environment with "spontaneous emotional warmth and feeling" (Klopfer and Davidson 1962:136). In more than 50% of the Apache protocols we discovered a relative frequency of textural response, which, in relation to associated variables, suggested a deep awareness of others' needs that was out of balance with the availability of internal controls (see table 10.5, F:FT + FY). From this datum, we would hypothesize that a large majority of the sixteen-year-old Apache had a perceptive, tactful sensitivity to others' reactions and, for approximately half the subjects, this concern with the surface of social contact may have been an overt manifestation of deeper, largely unexpressed dependent-affectional needs. This use of shading and texture was also possibly consonant with a field-dependent, other-directed, social compliant stance in individuals lacking inner self-confidence.

As already indicated, this inhibition of felt dependent needs might have gone along with Piotrowski's (1957:197) predictions, which we interpret as suggesting that Apache's control would be considerably weakened during periods of "diminished consciousness." The Boyers' ethnographic observation was that among the Apache, periods of alcoholic intoxication were "a means of expressing [both normally proscribed] *dependent needs* and hostility" (1972:66–67).

Finally, the Ames group (Ames, Metraux, and Walker 1959: 245) observed that certain aspects of the white sixteen-year-olds' protocols showed "a desire to gain perspective on self, and relations to others" (i.e., in vista and reflection responses). In brief, they suggested that the Sixteens were engaged in a continuing adaptive effort to gain awareness of their own identity and its relationship to the larger social milieu.

Among the sixteen-year-old Apache, however, the paucity of such responses in conjunction with the preceding data suggested that they failed to show the same type of self-conscious concern with the relationship between self and social role apparent in the middle-class youngsters. The ethnographic and Rorschach materials also indicated that the Apache adolescent was more likely to assume a passive orientation toward the possibility of effective personal choice and a negative attitude toward the possibility of meeting socially approved goals. These data were summarized in the Boyers' (1972:75–76) observation that the Apache adolescent was too often forced to relinquish the *active* struggle for a *positive* relationship with his social milieu and instead might assume what Erikson (1959) has described as a "negative identity" (Pumpian-Mindlin 1965).

The data on external adaptation made it apparent that, over the nine-year period of this study, the majority of Apache subjects had moved away from an active, optimistic, and satisfying style of dealing with their external environment. At sixteen they generally showed a passive-reactive sensitivity to external pressure and a pattern of pessimistic withdrawal from situations that required a sustained application of effort. This apparent relinquishment of a positive, active stance must be viewed interactively with their sociocultural environment. As a group they failed to fulfill any of the potential for a practical, self-motivated approach to external reality which had been characteristic of many of their seven-year protocols.

Conclusions: Constriction into Adolescence

The data from a majority of our white and Apache adolescents reflected an elaboration and accentuation of disparate developmental patterns found in their childhood records. Most of the white middle-class adolescents showed a longitudinal pattern of response to the Rorschach tests which was in accord with the general theoretical expectations of psychoanalysts and developmental psychologists concerning the "normal" course of ego development in Western culture (Ames, Metraux, and Walker 1959:288 ff.). Middle-class Sixteens seemed to have reached a developmental plateau that was still unstable but was marked by a new, more productive access to the personality's inner resources and an increasingly secure, controlled, and satisfying relationship to the social milieu. The secondary themes of internal tension and external disequilibrium forecasts a process of further change in succeeding years, as the young adult searched for a more stable and mature equilibrium between the internal structure of his personality and the external demands of the sociocultural milieu.

Conversely, a majority of our Apache records showed a long-term convergence of the learners and nonlearners around patterns of further constriction. In the Apache records this pattern of personality organization was characterized by a constriction of both inner awareness and emotional reactivity. In a longitudinal perspective, we can observe how this defensive developmental pattern might cause a rigid inhibition of external expression and spontaneousness, and result in a passive-reactive approach to the external world. There may have been relative inability to take productive advantage of the personality's inner resources. The adolescent Apache protocols also showed little evidence that this style of personality organization was a transitory developmental disequilibrium. Rather, in most cases, it seemed to reflect a fairly stable, long-term difficult adaptation of the personality to its sociocultural milieu.

The Boyers (1972:76) provided a succinct summary of these two contrasting styles of adolescent personality in their observation that

the feeling of omnipotence which occurs frequently among white teenagers in our dominant culture . . . consists of the feeling that they can do anything if given the chance. Apache youth customarily experience no such adolescent or postadolescent phase. They see themselves as the products of defeated parents in a deteriorating culture. They have little optimism and but vague life goals.

The pattern of inconsistent ego development emerging from the Apache protocols seemed to have its roots in the psychohistorical vicissitudes of deculturation and forced minority status. An external social dominance was superimposed on the aboriginal pattern of psychosocial development found prevalent among the Mescalero and Chiricahua from a previous time. The severe disorganization of Apache society that followed their conquest and confinement on a reservation not only disturbed the essential "fit" between personality and social institutions but in succeeding generations stimulated an overreliance on coping mechanisms that emphasized internal social inhibitions and ideationally constrictive forms of cognitive socialization.

Defensive constrictiveness did not lead to adaptive learning in a white-controlled formal educational system, nor to occupational adaptability in the surrounding white social environment. The Apache child was not taught reliance on verbal skills that would have been useful in tasks requiring abstract thought. Moreover, lacking inner self-confidence and without a growing ability to modulate behavior, the Apache child reduced his opportunities to ally himself with any viable cultural tradition capable of integrating his previous psychosexual development with an acceptable, productive social role in the large society. In effect, the Apache child was "cut adrift" at a time when his society should have intervened supportively to provide a meaningful foundation for his continued psychosocial development outside the immediate family.

Growing up in a verbally uncommunicative and often neglectful family environment where parental interaction was disrupted by patterns of drinking, the growing child turned to groups of equally bereft peers. The individual child remained adrift in an unsupportive social milieu that often acted to stimulate and rearouse the vestiges of infantile sexual and aggressive conflicts. It was hardly surprising that the school-age child retreated to the simple but rigid defenses characteristic of earlier developmental stages. In addition to the historical impact of deculturation and depreciated minority status, the child's experience of exclusion from the dominant social milieu in the Anglo schools may have served to aggravate the effects of initial psychosocial discontinuities.

In our study, the convergence of both "learners" and "non-learners" around a pattern of inconsistent ego development indicated, on the one hand, that the children's experience of

educational "channeling" had little ameliorative effect on personality development and, on the other, that the learners' significantly more successful grammar school performance was, in
part, the result of their teachers' self-fulfilling expectations. The
learners in most instances did not maintain the relative promise
of their original protocols. Moreover, the ethnographic and
psychological data also suggested that the public schools on the
whole presented such a negative learning environment that it
had, in the samples evaluated, an overwhelmingly detrimental
impact across both groups of Apache children.

Although the protocols of the seven-year-olds demonstrated a
level of intellectual optimism and potential that might have been
used to promote a successful adjustment within the schools, the
majority of adolescent records showed an almost uniform retreat
from an active, self-motivated effort to deal with external reality
and a more widespread use of self-defeating modes of defense.

The Boyers (Boyer and Boyer 1972; Boyer et al. 1964) have
pointed out that the Apache have been caught in a maelstrom of
contradictory values, goals, and ethnic identifications which, until
recently, have been intensified by their experiences in the public
schools. The chronic pessimism, hopelessness, and lack of self-
esteem from which many Apache adolescents suffer is a result of
this experience and highlights their exclusion from the essential,
culturally mediated sources of ego development (Brody 1966).
In brief, we can only conclude that the style of personality found
in the adolescent Apache protocols indicates the failure of the
sociocultural environment to fulfill the growing child's need for a
secure, productive, and meaningful role in adult society. The following chapter illustrates these contentions with three individual
case histories.[5]

Notes

1. This chapter was modified from Richard Day, L. B. Boyer, and
George A. De Vos, "Two Styles of Ego Development," *Ethos* (1975)
3:345–379, and has been reprinted with permission of the publishers.

2. Detailed information pertaining to Apache history, social structure, and socialization is to be found in Basehart (1959, 1960), L. B.
Boyer (1979), R. M. Boyer (1962, 1964), Haley (1981), Mails (1974),

Moorhead (1968), Opler (1933, 1941, 1969), Shephardson (1961), Terrell (1974), Thomas (1959*a*, 1959*b*), and Worcester (1979).

3. The primary difficulty in using Ames, Learned, Metraux, and Walker's 1952 study for comparative purposes is their style of data reporting. In their study of children's Rorschach responses they only provided the mean and percentile data for each major scoring component, without any further indication of standard deviations or absolute sample size for each variable. This style of reporting made the problem of significance testing most difficult. In response, we constructed a "dummy" sample of 100 white children and distributed them in terms of the Ames group's percentile data. This procedure provided enough data in a sufficiently undistorted form to perform a simple chi-square test of significance. To provide continuity of statistical reporting throughout the present study, we retained this same method of significance testing with the Ames, Metraux, and Walker (1959) data from sect. 2.

4. In an attempt to explain the origins of the observed differences between these two groups of Apache children we hypothesized that the nonlearners would be found to stem from families in which there was more drunkenness and that there would be a high incidence of arrests among adults who were important emotionally to the children. There was a slight tendency in that direction, but the hypothesis was not borne out statistically. There was a slightly higher tendency for the learners to stem from families in which English was commonly spoken at home, but again there was no statistically significant difference (Boyer et al. 1968).

5. Since this chapter was written (1975) there have been encouraging changes in the school situation. At least one teacher has been learning to speak Apache. As traditional school personnel have retired, younger, more plastic teachers with some anthropological training have replaced them. For the last several years, the local school board has hired Mrs. Virginia Klinkole, a past president of the Business Committee of the Mescalero Tribe, as a liaison between Apache students and the faculty of Tularosa High School, which most reservation students attend. Her patient, wise words have begun to have beneficial effects.

References

Ames, Louise Bates, Janet Learned, Ruth W. Metraux, and Richard W. Walker
   1952   *Childhood Rorschach Responses.* New York: Hoeber.
Ames, Louise Bates, Ruth W. Metraux, and Richard W. Walker
   1959   *Adolescent Rorschach Responses.* New York: Hoeber.

Basehart, Harry W.
  1959 *Chiricahua Apache Subsistence and Sociopolitical Organiza-*
        tion. Albuquerque: University of New Mexico Mescalero–
        Chiricahua Lands Claims Project. Mimeographed.
  1960 *Mescalero Apache Subsistence Patterns and Sociopolitical*
        Organization. Albuquerque: University of New Mexico
        Mescalero-Chiricahua Lands Claims Project. Mimeographed.
Boyer, L. Bryce
  1964 Psychological Problems of a Group of Apaches: Alcoholic
        Hallucinosis and Latent Homosexuality Among Typical Men.
        Warner Muensterberger and Sidney Axelrad, eds. *Psychoanalytic*
        Study of Society 3:203–277. New York: International Universities
        Press.
  1979 *Childhood and Folklore: A Psychoanalytic Study of Apache*
        Personality. New York: Library of Psychological Anthropology.
Boyer, L. Bryce, and Ruth M. Boyer
  1972 The Effects of Acculturation on the Vicissitudes of the
        Aggressive Drive Among the Apaches of the Mescalero Indian
        Reservation. Warner Muensterberger and Aaron Esman, eds.
        Psychoanalytic Study of Society 5:40–82.
Boyer, L. Bryce, Ruth M. Boyer, Florence R. Brawer, Hayao Kawai,
    and Bruno Klopfer
  1964 Apache Age Groups. *Journal of Projective Techniques and*
        Personality Assessment 28:397–401.
Boyer, L. Bryce, Ruth M. Boyer, Hayao Kawai, and Bruno Klopfer
  1967 Apache "Learners" and "Nonlearners." *Journal of Projective*
        Techniques and Personality Assessment 31:22–29.
Boyer, L. Bryce, Ruth M. Boyer, Bruno Klopfer, and Suzanne B.
    Scheiner
  1968 Apache "Learners" and "Nonlearners." II. Quantitative
        Signs of Influential Adults. *Journal of Projective Techniques and*
        Personality Assessment 32:146–159.
Boyer, Ruth M.
  1962 *Social Structure and Socialization Among the Apache of the*
        Mescalero Indian Reservation. Doctoral dissertation, University of
        California, Berkeley. Unpublished.
  1964 The Matrifocal Family Among the Mescalero Apache: Addi-
        tional Data. *American Anthropologist* 66:593–602.
Brody, Eugene B.
  1966 Cultural Exclusion, Character, and Mental Illness. *American*
        Journal of Psychiatry 112:852–858.
Day, Richard, L. Bryce Boyer, and George A. De Vos
  1975 Two Styles of Ego Development: A Cross-Cultural, Longi-

tudinal Comparison of Apache and Anglo School Children. *Ethos* 3:345–379.

De Vos, George A.
1978 Selective Permeability and Reference Group Sanctioning: Psychocultural Continuities in Role Degradation. M. Yinger and S. Cutler, eds. *Major Social Issues*, pp. 9–24. New York: Free Press.
1980 Ethnic Adaptation and Minority Status. Walter Lonner, ed. *Journal of Cross-Cultural Anthropology* 11(1):101–124.
1982 Adaptative Strategies In American Minorities. E. E. Jones and S. Korchin, eds. *Minority Mental Health*, pp. 74–117. New York: Praeger.

Erikson, Erik H.
1950 *Childhood and Society*. New York: Norton.
1959 Identity and the Life Cycle. *Psychoanalytic Issues*, no. 1. New York: International Universities Press.

Gallimore, R., J. Boggs, and C. Jordan
1974 *Culture, Behavior, and Education: A Study of Hawaiian-Americans*. Beverly Hills, Calif.: Sage Press.

Goodenough, D. R., and H. A. Witkin
1977 *Origins of the Field-Dependent and Field-Independent Cognitive Styles*. Princeton, N.J.: Educational Testing Service.

Haley, James L.
1981 *Apaches: A History and Culture Portrait*. Garden City, N.Y.: Doubleday.

Hartmann, Heinz
1939 *Ego Psychology and the Problem of Adaptation*. 2d edition. New York: International Universities Press, 1958.
1955 Notes on the Theory of Sublimation. *Psychoanalytic Study of the Child* 10:9–29. New York: International Universities Press.

Hippler, Arthur E., L. Bryce Boyer, and Ruth M. Boyer
1976 The Subarctic Athabaskans of Alaska: The Ecological Grounding of Certain Cultural Personality Characteristics. Warner Muensterberger, Aaron H. Esman, and L. Bryce Boyer, eds. *Psychoanalytic Study of Society* 7:293–330. New Haven: Yale University Press.

Holt, Robert R.
1956 Gauging Secondary and Primary Process in the Rorschach Test. *Journal of Projective Techniques* 20:14–25.
1967 The Development of Primary Process: A Structural View. *Psychological Issues* 18–19:344–385. New York: International Universities Press.

Howard, A.
  1971   Households, Families, and Friends in a Hawaiian-American
         Community. Working Paper 19, East-West Population Institute,
         Honolulu.
  1974   *Ain't No Big Thing*. Honolulu: University of Hawaii Press.
Kagan, S.
  1974   Field Independence and Conformity of Rural Mexican and
         Urban Anglo-American Children. *Child Development* 45:765–771.
Kagan, S., and R. Buriel
  1977   Field Dependence-Independence and Mexican-American
         Culture and Education. Joe Martinez, Jr., ed. *Chicano Psychology*. New York: Academic Press.
Kagan, S., and M. Madsen
  1971   Cooperation and Competition of Mexican, Mexican-American, Anglo-American Children of Two Ages Under Four Instructional Sets. *Developmental Psychology* 5:32–39.
  1972a Experimental Analyses of Cooperation and Competition of
         Anglo-American and Mexican American Children. *Developmental Psychology* 6:49–59.
  1972b Rivalry in Anglo-American and Mexican Children of Two
         Ages. *Journal of Personality and Social Psychology* 24:214–220.
Kardiner, A., and Ralph Linton
  1939   *The Individual and His Society: The Psychodynamics of Primitive Social Organization*. New York: Columbia University Press
         [1965].
Klopfer, Bruno, Mary D. Ainsworth, Walter G. Klopfer, and Robert
  R. Holt
  1954   *Developments in the Rorschach Technique*. Vol. 1, *Technique and Theory*. New York: Harcourt, Brace and World.
Klopfer, Bruno, and H. H. Davidson
  1962   *The Rorschach Technique: An Introductory Manual*. New
         York: Harcourt, Brace and World.
Klopfer, Bruno, and Douglas Kelley
  1946   *The Rorschach Technique*. New York: Harcourt, Brace and
         World
Loewald, Hans
  1973   On Internalization. *International Journal of Psycho-Analysis*
         54:9–18.
Madsen, Millard C.
  1967   Cooperative and Competitive Motivation of Children in Three
         Mexican Sub-Cultures. *Psychological Reports* 20:1307–20.

Madsen, M., and A. Shapira
1973 Cooperative and Competitive Behavior of Urban Afro-American, Anglo-American, and Mexican Village Children. *Developmental Psychology*, pp. 16–20.

Mails, Thomas E.
1974 *The People Called Apache*. Englewood Cliffs, N.J.: Prentice-Hall.

Minturn, Leigh, and William W. Lambert
1964 *Mothers of Six Cultures: Antecedents of Child Rearing*. New York: John Wiley and Sons.

Moorhead, Max L.
1968 *The Apache Frontier: Jacobo Ugarte and Spanish-Indian Relations in Northern New Spain*, 1769–91. Norman: University of Oklahoma Press.

Opler, Morris E.
1933 *An Analysis of Mescalero and Chiricahua Apache Social Organization in the Light of Their Systems of Relationship*. Doctoral dissertation, University of Chicago. Private edition distributed by University of Chicago Libraries [1936].
1941 *An Apache Life-Way: The Economic, Social, and Religious Institutions of the Chiricahua Indians*. 2d edition. New York: Cooper Square Publishers, 1965.
1969 *Apache Odyssey: A Journey Between Two Worlds*. New York: Holt, Rinehart and Winston.

Phillips, L., and J. Smith
1953 *Rorschach Interpretation: Advanced Technique*. New York: Grune and Stratton.

Piotrowsky, Zigmunt A.
1957 *Perceptanalysis*. New York: Macmillan.

Pumpian-Mindlin, Eugene
1965 Omnipotentiality, Youth, and Commitment. *Journal of The Academy of Child Psychiatry* 4:1–18.

Ramirez, M., Ill, and D. Price-Williams
1974 Cognitive Styles of Children of Three Ethnic Groups in the United States. *Journal of Cross-Cultural Psychology* 5(2).

Sarnoff, Charles
1971 Ego Structure in Latency. *Psychoanalytic Quarterly* 40:387–414.
1976 *Latency*. New York: Aronson.

Schafer, Roy
1951 *The Clinical Application of Psychological Tests*. New York: International Universities Press.

Shepardson, Mary T.
    1961 Developing Political Processes Among the Navajo Indians.
        Ph.D. dissertation, University of California, Berkeley.
Spindler, George D., and Louise S. Spindler
    1957 American Indian Personality Types and Their Sociocultural
        Roots. *Annals of Political and Social Science* 311:147–157.
Terrell, John Upton
    1974 *Apache Chronicle: The Story of the People.* New York: Tho-
        mas Y. Crowell.
Thomas, Alfred B.
    1959a The Mescalero Apache, 1653–1874. Albuquerque: Universi-
        ty of New Mexico Mescalero-Chiricahua Land Claims Project.
        Mimeographed.
    1959b *The Chiricahua Apache, 1695–1876.* Albuquerque: Universi-
        ty of New Mexico Mescalero-Chiricahua Land Claims Project.
        Mimeographed.
Werner, E. E.
    1979 *Cross-Cultural Child Development.* Monterey, Calif.: Brooks-
        Cole.
White, Robert Winthrop
    1963 Ego and Reality in Psychoanalytic Theory: A Proposal Re-
        garding Independent Ego Energies. *Psychological Issues*, Vol. 2,
        No. 3, Monograph 11. New York: International Universities Press.
Winnicott, D. W.
    1961 The Effect of Psychotic Parents on the Development of the
        Child. *British Journal of Social Work* 6:13–20.
Witkin, H. A.
    1967 Cognitive Styles Across Cultures. *International Journal of
        Psychology* 2:233–250.
    1969 Social Influences in the Development of Cognitive Style. D.
        A. Goslin, ed. *Handbook of Socialization Theory and Research*,
        pp. 102–140. Chicago: Rand McNally.
Witkin, H. A., and J. W. Berry
    1975 Psychological Differentiation in Cross-Cultural Perspective.
        Journal of Cross-Cultural Psychology 6:4–87.
Witkin, H. A., D. Price-Williams, D. Bertini, M. Christiansen, B. Olt-
        man, M. Ramirez, J. Van Meel
    1974 Social Conformity and Psychological Differentiation. *Interna-
        tional Journal of Psychology* 9:11–29.
Worcester, Donald E.
    1979 *The Apaches, Eagles of the Southwest.* Norman: University of
        Oklahoma Press.

Chapter Eleven

Three Apache Brothers: A Longitudinal Comparison

L. Bryce Boyer, George A. De Vos, and
Ruth M. Boyer

There are very few longitudinal cross-cultural psychological studies of individuals or groups.[1] The previous chapter is a rare example in which members of a non-Western group were studied over time through the use of the Rorschach test. Along with the fifty-four Apache children whose tests were first taken during their early school period were three brothers whose records and those of their parents were obtained as part of the histories of family units being studied by the Boyers.[2] Their domestic unit was one of those included in an intensive and prolonged socialization study done rigorously during 1959 and 1960 (R. M. Boyer 1962). Ten years later the brothers were retested again along with other members of the childhood sample. More recently, after another decade, we again tested the three brothers as part of a smaller follow-up sample.

Introduction

As reported in chapter 10, Apache children showed an emotional control in dealing with the interpersonal environment, and some displayed a tendency to "insulate" themselves against being stimulated emotionally. When they reached adolescence, the majority revealed a passive-receptive sensitivity to external pressure. The personality organization of the Apache adolescent was characterized by a weakness of emotional integration and a constriction of emotional reactivity.

The three Yellowhorse brothers (a pseudonym) reported on in this chapter are fairly representative. The shift in the Rorschachs of the brothers we call Albert and Calvin conformed to the general constrictive shift in Apache responses from latency to adolescence into adulthood. However, Bridger, the middle brother, escaped this general impoverishment, although not without some cost.

A Background of Emotional Deprivation

As was true of many Apache families, the childhood home life of the three brothers was predominantly one of emotional and physical deprivation, inconsistency, and indirectly taught hypocrisy and irresponsibility.[3] During the rare periods when their parents were sober, they were usually affectionate, gentle, fun-loving, and considerate of each other and their offspring, but both drank to the point of deep intoxication whenever money was available from the father's occasional work at unskilled jobs or welfare. Quite simply, they then ignored their seven living children, regardless of their ages or needs. Both parents left home from time to time without warning or any discussion of where they might be going. The youngsters were left to their own devices for obtaining food and other care. Mr. Yellowhorse was a womanizer, and his wife partied but more customarily drank herself into solitary stupors. When they were recovering from drunken episodes, the mother bitterly reproached the father for his philandering and nonsupport, seeking to make him feel guilty by moralizing, and he in turn pummeled and cursed her. Each piously accused the other of delicts commonly committed by both of them, claimed his or her innocence, or blamed his or her actions on the other. The parents' platitudes pertaining to morality and responsibility contrasted starkly with their actual behavior.

The father's childhood had been unstable and marked by emotional deprivation. While he was yet an infant, his father had committed suicide, probably while drunk. His depressed mother became physically ill and died when he was but two years old; until then his principal caretaker had been a sister who was only four years older than he. We know well the deleterious effects on the development of the child's personality when his infancy has been spent with a depressed mother. When the mother of Mr. Yellowhorse died, the children were separated from one another, thereby losing the emotional support they had shared: while his siblings were dispersed among various maternal relatives, he was sent to live with his aged paternal grandparents, who already had in their charge a number of other children who had lost their parents through death or desertion. The care given to these youngsters appears to have been somewhat haphazard. All the sibs, like Mr. Yellowhorse, eventually became violent drunkards. His grandfather died a few years after Mr. Yellowhorse arrived, and his physically disabled grandmother sent her wards elsewhere. This time the boy was "adopted" by a nephew of his grandmother, a kindly, passive, and relatively acculturated man whose wife was a sanctimonious, reformed loose woman who treated her new ward shabbily at best, obviously preferring her own children to him. Whereas Apaches customarily are very respectful of and helpful to their elderly parents, she charged her own disabled mother "taxi" fare to take her shopping. Mr. Yellowhorse never called anyone *shimah* (mother) or *shitah* (father), a most unusual phenomenon on the reservation. He called his "foster parents" by their first names, which might well indicate that he felt scant emotional closeness toward them and certainly none of the traditional respect.

Mrs. Yellowhorse's childhood was quite different. She was the youngest of a large number of children whose parents were respected, loving, gentle Indians who did not drink to excess during her lifetime. She knew that her father had been a gay blade as a young man and a philanderer during the first years of his marriage, but she had an apparently happy childhood and early adolescence.

Apaches for many years have either attended grammar school on the reservation, where they comprise the vast majority of the students, or have been sent out to distant boarding schools or to neighboring towns, where they were a small minority among "Anglo" and "Spanish American" students. Mrs. Yellowhorse was educated in a neighboring town. While in high school she somewhat favored the customs of the majority white children and was especially interested in being sartorially attractive. Like her brothers and sisters, she retreated from her initial timid competi-

tion with her non-Indian classmates and became progressively
more interested in pursuing narcissistic pleasures and achieving
instant gratification. We may infer defensive retreat into an
Apache identity. Like most of her siblings, she stopped high
school before graduation. To the dismay of her parents, she and
most of her brothers and sisters became "problem drinkers" in
late adolescence or their early twenties.

As part of their childhood experience, both Mr. and Mrs. Yellowhorse had been heavily steeped in folklore. Throughout their
early years they had observed native religio-medical practices
as part of their everyday life. The paternal grandparents of Mr.
Yellowhorse were shamans, the grandfather being especially renowned. The mother of Mrs. Yellowhorse was a shaman, and her
father was the singer for a team of sacred masked Mountain Spirit
dancers (Bourke 1892; L. B. Boyer 1964, 1979; Opler 1941, 1946,
1947; see also chap. 12, below).

One custom about which both Mr. and Mrs. Yellowhorse
heard repeatedly as children may have affected the special behavior to be described below, which was directed toward the twin
daughters who were born after the three sons with whom we are
concerned. Traditionally, twins were thought to be the product of
"too much sex," a woman's intercourse with more than one man,
or the practice of witchcraft. The second-born twin, considered to
be unclean, was to be slain and "forgotten." The unwanted newborn was usually killed in a manner otherwise used to torture only
tribal enemies: its eyes were to be smeared with honey and it was
to be placed atop an anthill in the blazing sunlight, to die in
agony. The stated rationale for disposing of a twin was that no
mother could produce enough milk for two. However, aboriginally, when Apache mothers of infants died or left the home group
for any reason, their babies were wet-nursed, usually by the
mothers' sisters. It is our assumption that the harsh treatment of
twins was not only one of the numerous manifestations of the
ambivalence of Apache parents toward their children but may
also have contributed to guilt feelings of the parents. Although
the death of the second twin was culturally demanded, there may
well have been shame or guilt for the presumed sin which led to
the birth of twins.

Neither Mr. nor Mrs. Yellowhorse chose to follow the native

religious paths that were open to them; had either been so in-clined and deemed sufficiently moral, he or she could probably have become a shaman. It is probable that the brothers' mother left high school when a junior or senior to carouse with their father, who had renounced his education during his middle teens. Before their marriage when she was eighteen and he was twenty, she had no tribal court record. He, however, had been charged twenty times, seven for disorderly conduct (implicitly associated with drunkenness), twice each for liquor violations, disobedience of court orders, and escape, and one each for injury to public property, malicious mischief, failure to pay for purchases, and assault. He had an unknown number of arrests for drunkenness and disorderly, assaultive conduct in neighboring towns as well. Intoxicated, he was violent and at times forced his way into peo-ple's houses, those of white and Indians alike and whether they were or were not at home, seeking to steal or wrest money from the inhabitants in order to obtain more alcohol.

During the four years before their marriage, Mr. Yellow-horse's sentences amounted to 458 days in jail, nine months of probation, and $210 in fines. During the nineteen years of their marriage, he was charged eighteen times with disorderly conduct, often with assault, five times with failure to support dependent persons, and twice with failure to send children to school. His wife made most of the disorderly conduct charges and all of the other charges. He in turn also charged her with failure to care for dependent children. Jailed prisoners on the reservation fre-quently work out of doors, usually on the tribal farm, whenever weather permits. The children of this marriage often saw their father working among the prisoners.

When the Yellowhorses were married, a four-room tribal house was provided for them. They disliked the location and, after the birth of their first living child, they moved into an area near a brother of the mother, whose wife was willing to look after that infant, and subsequently, their later children when she knew of parental absences.[4] Although most Apache families tend to move about a great deal, more or less continuing the seasonal peregrinations of their nomadic forebears (Basehart 1959, 1960, 1967, 1970), this family stayed in the same general area until the parents died. They lived in a series of 9 × 12-foot tents with frame bases or tiny one-room shacks, even when they had seven children. Ordinarily the furnishings of the dwellings consisted almost entirely of boxes plus a bed for the parents, a cot or two for the children, and some kind of stove or cooking burner. There was scarcely room to move between the beds. At times, all the youngsters slept in blankets on the floor.

On two occasions when both parents were away drinking and had neglected to inform anyone that they would be absent, their dwelling caught fire and burned, and the little ones were rescued only by chance. The first time, the oldest child in the shelter was four, and the second time, either six or seven. On each of these occasions, the house had been furnished with borrowed goods, once including an electric refrigerator, but no attempt was made to repay the owners for the losses.

During the years when the Boyers knew this family, from 1959 until the parents died of causes directly related to drunkenness, the mother nine and the father ten years later, their children (with an exception to be mentioned below) were chronically undernourished and dressed in hand-me-downs, and were ordinarily dirty. They frequently had running noses and sores on their faces where the pus and mucus had irritated their skin. They had no handkerchiefs. Often during the cold or wet months one or more of the younger children suffered from severe bronchitis or pneumonia. Although the hospital provided by the Bureau of Indian Affairs was only about a quarter of a mile away, the children were rarely taken there and then usually at the behest of the mother's brother's wife, when they were nearly moribund. There is no record that the mother ever sought the freely available prenatal care.

The first child of Mr. and Mrs. Yellowhorse was stillborn. This infant was never mentioned by either of them in any listing of their offspring, and the fact was gleaned only by a perusal of the tribal census. Following the births of the three brothers, a fourth boy was born and died within a very short time. "They just let him die. He was never fed," said neighbors. Their next child received scarcely better treatment and was always sick and puny. Then twins appeared, the only female children born to this couple. Although it is usual that Apache infants of both sexes are dressed rather elegantly and kept as clean as possible, only the girls received such care in this family. They were clad in frilly, immaculate, well-ironed dresses when the mother was sober. Was this special treatment related to the sex of the twins? Or was there shame or guilt involved because of the stigma attached to the birth of twins? In any event, both girls became seriously ill when less than eighteen months old. Although the firstborn was taken to the hospital and medicated successfully, the younger remained at home, apparently left to die. The attitude of the parents toward this event was probably reflected in that of the three brothers. They made no mention of their sister's death at school. On the day after her demise the boys seemed totally unconcerned, laughing and playing with their classmates. The tenth child born to this couple died within a month of his birth, allegedly from starvation.[5] All the children, in the narrow confines of the tent-shacks, were regularly exposed to all of their parents' sexuality, their father's brutality and their mother's ambivalent behavior toward him, and to both parents' occasional affectional actions toward, and their generally callous neglect of, their children.

Mrs. Yellowhorse may have been much "meaner" than most Apache mothers. She was the only one observed by the anthropologist-author to actually kick a toddler in the face when he or she whiningly sought care. On the rare occasions when she was observed while neither intoxicated nor recovering from a hangover, she was a quiet, wistful, shy woman who sought desperately to dress attractively and to be clean. Mrs. Yellowhorse seemed hungry for contact with other women. When she saw them assembled at a neighbor's dwelling she would quietly join them, sitting either outside the group or on its fringes. It was not uncommon for her to appear, sit for a time, and leave, without uttering a sound or at most, one or two almost whispered words in Apache. In a one-to-one situation with the anthropologist-author, she was quiet and shy but willing to confide and to seek approval, often smiling, particularly when neither drunk nor suffering from hangover. She was eager to show how she lovingly bathed her little girls.

Mr. Yellowhorse generally avoided the Boyers, an unusual phenomenon for Apache men. He once indirectly sought psychiatric assistance with the psychoanalyst-author but failed to follow through. In his single interview he seemed rather dull and flat, and the content of his speech was pathetic indeed.

The Boyers met the Yellowhorses when Albert, Bridger, and Calvin were nine, eight, and six years old, respectively. Even then, Bridger was physically larger and healthier than his brothers and was more imaginative and interesting, both at home and at school. The Boyers were unable to determine if his parents or aunt gave him preferential care. He was absent from school less often than Albert and Calvin. On one occasion before Calvin attended school, their father was charged with failure to send the children to school. Although Bridger had been in attendance, Albert had been absent for eleven consecutive school days without being ill. In the grammar school on the reservation, Bridger's scholastic performance, while only in the middle range of Apache students, was better than that of his brothers. It is probable that Albert and Calvin were graduated from grammar school on the basis of age rather than accomplishment.

Following the death of Mrs. Yellowhorse, the younger children were dispersed among relatives and the three brothers were sent to an Indian boarding high school, far from the reservation. There, Apache students were frequently harassed by Navaho and Pueblo students, who greatly outnumbered them. Albert and Calvin turned to Bridger as their defender. They were truant more often than he and were disciplined more frequently for drinking and running away. Their schoolwork was spotty at best.

The second set of Rorschach protocols was obtained while they were in boarding school. Only Bridger acknowledged remembering L.B.B. He was neat, pleasant, and straightforward in contrast with Albert and Calvin who were untidy, cringing, and cadging. The results of the psychological tests administered to them by school officials are no longer available. However, L.B.B. remembers that Bridger's intelligence quotient was high normal in contrast with the much lower quotients of his brothers.[6]

While attending boarding school Bridger was found to have artistic talent and eventually was transferred to a specialized Indian school for the development of his capacities. There he did well and achieved some small fame for his paintings and sculptures, which sold in several Western states.

The Boyers did not see the three brothers during the period between obtaining the second and third protocols. The young men were only on the reservation for brief periods. Bridger married and had children and was generally responsible for his family. When he and they were on the reservation, he usually began to drink and carouse and to be somewhat undependable in doing unskilled work provided for him by the tribe. When away from the reservation, he worked fairly consistently as an artist, but much less so at Mescalero. We were unable to view any example of his art work or to obtain sophisticated descriptions of it.

Information concerning Albert and Calvin was fragmentary. They were said to have rarely worked and to have had transient marriages with unsupported and abandoned children, and to have been generally irresponsible. The Apache community described them as chronic drunkards and later perhaps as drug users. Calvin was considered to be very dangerous when drinking.

At the time of the third administration of the Rorschach test, the three brothers, coincidentally, had been on the reservation for about six months. Albert and Calvin seldom worked and were frequently jailed for drunkenness, often combined with assaults.[7] During the first two or three months of his presence on the reservation with his wife and children, Bridger also drank heavily. Then, however, an appeal was made to him by a relative to give up his drinking in order to assume the role of dancer in the Mountain Spirit team, a role which was then in the possession of one of his maternal cousins. He consented to accept the role and stopped his consumption of alcohol. He had been an upright and impressive member of the team for some three or four months when the protocols were obtained. First we present the protocols of the parents.

The Rorschach Data and Their Interpretations

Responses are shown in *italic* type. Replies during the inquiry are shown in parentheses. Tester's remarks are in square brackets.

Test of the Mother, Mrs. Yellowhorse

Age 31

Card I. (25")
1. *Bat.* (Flying, shape)   W FM_a+ A P (Neut)

2. *Butterfly*. (Sitting down) [Points out holes as spots on wings] WS FM_p+ A (Neut)

Card II. (rotated for 375″)
3. *Something standing up.* (Bears, got their paws together) W FM FT+ A P (Neut)

Card III. (45″ pause; edged card)
4. *A neck and a necktie.* (White shirt with tie. Shape) WS F+ Cg (Pnat)
(Additional: *Two people pull at something, got boots on.*) [DM+ H Cg (Hcmpt)]

Card IV. (rotated and edged for 15″)
5. *A hide, maybe bear.* (Spread out, fur side) W FT+ Aob P (Neut)

Card V, (inverted; 20″ pause)
6. *Butterfly*. (Flying, shape) W FM_a+ A P (Neut)

Card VI. (10″ pause)
7. *A hide* (Cat fur) W FT+ Aob P (Neut)

Card VII. (rotated and edged for 80″, inverted)
8. *A dam with water coming in.* (Grass on the ground) WS Fm FV+ Lds (Pnat)

Card VIII. (rotated and edged for 40″)
9. *Animals climb.* (Bears climb big rocks. Shape) W FM_a+ A P (Pstr)

Card IX. (rejected after 285″)
(Additional: *A dress with a zipper down it.*) [WSF+ Cg (Porn)]

Card X. (95″ pause)
10. *Rabbit face.* (I can see the eye) D F+ Ad P (Neut)

Time elapsed: 20 minutes
R = 10; W% = 80, S = 3, F% = 310, F+% = 100; FV = 1; M =
1; FM = 5; Fm = 1; FT = 3; FV = 1; C = 0; Neutral 70%; Rej =
1; Positive narcissistic = 1; Positive nature = 1; Positive striving
= 1.

(Additional: Hostile competitive = 1; Positive body narcissistic =
1; Positive ornamental = 1).

Overall, the Rorschach of Mrs. Mary Yellowhorse is fairly normal. There are no unusual responses suggesting any form of psychopathology, but she produces only ten responses, initially rejecting Card IX. A negativistic trend is suggested by her proneness to react to white spaces in three of her initial ten responses and to the central spatial area of Card IX in one of her two additional responses given during the inquiry following her free associations. Her perception of the white areas does not consist of an exact reversal of figure and ground; rather, she pays unusual attention to white spots in giving a butterfly response to Card I, and on Card VII she views the central area as water in a dam.

In her free associations, 80% of her responses score as simple animals, showing a rather stereotypic, narrow social vision. On Card I, she starts with a bat, then sees a sitting butterfly, with the white triangles as holes. She then quickly reveals an oppositional tendency in the way that she attends to the white spaces. She begins her protocol with an animal movement response, but the potential of the initial response becomes transformed into something that is more oppositional in tone. There is a lack of sustained push toward actualization.

Her symbolic material is fairly innocuous. The only outstanding idiosyncratic material is her percept of a white shirt with a necktie on Card III and a dress with a zipper on Card IX. This type of clothing response is very unusual in the record of a Native American. In addition to being idiosyncratic, they reveal in their complexity a potentially high level of intelligence. The organizational ability disclosed in these responses is that found in superior records. Its presence in this otherwise sparse protocol suggests that Mrs. Yellowhorse is not accustomed to using her intelligence nor has she a strong desire to do so. Yet with some unusual stimulus, she is capable of a high-level type of intellectual functioning.

It is also noteworthy that human beings appear only in the responses to Cards III and IX. She is very aware of her social environment (7 of 10 responses are Populars!).

The most notable characteristic of the entire record revealed by the final scoring of her protocol is that her record has a very high neutral stereotypic content (70%) but that affective material, when it is shown, yields positive narcissistic responses. Her responses to Cards III and IX, the white shirt with a tie and the dress with a zipper, symbolize social status and "dressing up," a narcissistic enhancement. These responses are, in a sense, parts of a potential social self that has gained no realization. She is not usually driven to fantasize except when responding to provocative narcissistic stimuli. We recall that during her high school days she sought to identify with the outside white culture but that that interest was not pursued nor was it sustained in her subsequent life so far as we could ascertain. Yet she did dress up her twin girls during their infancy, and the anthropologist-observer's notes indicate that Mrs. Yellowhorse herself was clean and neat when she had been sober for a few days.

There are two vigorous responses, the flying bat on Card I and the climbing animals on Card VIII. The balance in the perceived animal movement is in an active direction. She is heavily turned toward a potential intraceptiveness, but on an immature level. (Of her ten responses, five are animal movements in one form or another.) There is no human movement except in her additional response to Card III. One has the feeling that she could reveal more if provoked but that there is a chronic lack of incentive to use the capacities she has. She lacks any internal motivation to actualize herself through cognitive activities.

Her response to Card VII, the "feminine" card, evoked speculation on the part of the authors. Here she sees a large dam into which flows a trickle of water. She reverses figure and ground, visualizing an energy source flowing into a dam. This response is idiosyncratic: when Card VII elicits a dam and water response, ordinarily the water is seen as flowing out of the dam. The Boyers note that she was pregnant at the time the protocol was taken and believe that her response to Card VII had to do specifically with her gestational state, holding that her additional grass response symbolized pubic hair. L.B.B. postulates that one reason she allowed herself to become pregnant so often was that she felt more fulfilled when bearing a child, but to be a mother of a separate, live child gave her no sense of fulfillment in everyday life. De Vos interprets her response to Card VII to suggest that she chronically felt herself to be as unfulfilled and unproductive as if water flowed in but nothing was forthcoming. To De Vos, the fact that she was pregnant at the time the test was administered is somewhat irrelevant, since in her responses generally she suggested that nothing was let out. Such an idiosyncratic response demands further subsequent evidence before its meaning can be determined.

Test of the Father, Mr. Yellowhorse

Age 32   May 27, 1960

Quiet, courteous, apparently unthreatened.

First Test

Card I. (15″ pause)

1. *Butterfly.* (Sitting, Shape)   W FM_a+ A P (Neut)
2. *Beetle.* (Dead, shape)   D F+ A (Agl)
3. *Backbone.* (One piece, shape)   W F+ Anat (Bb)

Card II. (20″ pause)

4. *Pelvis.* (The white spaces are part of the design.)   W F+ Anat (Bb)

Card III. (25″ pause)

5. *Backbone.* (One piece of backbone)   W F− Anat (Bb)
6. *Bow tie.* (On a neck. Black coat, white shirt, red tie)   Ws FC+ Cg P (Pnar)
7. *Clay pot.* (With a red handle)   D FC+ Orn (Porn)

Card IV. (30″ pause)

8. *Cow's backbone.* (Black)   D FC′− AAnat (Bb)
9. *Rock from the bottom of the ocean.* (Shape and shading)   D FY + Nat (Adif)

Card V. (25″ pause)
   10. *Butterfly.* (Flying)   W FM_a+ A P (Neut)

Card VI. (15″ pause)
   11. *Rock found in the ocean.*   W FY− Nat (Adif)
(Shape and shading)

Card VII. (25 ″ pause)
   12. *Part of a leaf.* (Rotting,   W FY− Bot (Agl, Bdis)
turning gray)

Card VIII. (15 ″ pause)
   13. *Colored rock.*   W FCv Nat (Pnat)

Card IX. (30 ″ pause)
   14. *Backbone.* (Of a horse,   D F− AAnat (Bb)
shape)

Card X. reject   (Arej)

Time elapsed: 9 minutes.

$R = 14$; $W\% = 65$; $F\% = 50$; $M = 0$; $FM = 2$; $FC = 3$; $FC' = 1$; $FY = 3$; $A\% = 29$; Hostile $\% = 0$; Anxiety $\% = 27$. Bodily preoccupation $\% = 33$; Total unpleasant $\% = 67$; Positive $\% = 20$; Neutral $\% = 13$; Anxiety rejection $= 1$; Anxiety gloom $= 2$; Anxiety diffuse $= 2$; Bone anatomy $= 5$; Bdis $= 1$; Positive narcissistic $= 1$; Positive ornamental $= 1$; Positive nature $= 1$.

Mr. Yellowhorse revealed a great deal of inner disturbance at the time he was tested. He produced a very high level of unpleasant symbolism, principally with responses indicating bodily preoccupation. Additionally, he saw rocks at the bottom of the ocean, a dead beetle, and a rotting leaf, clearly revealing an anxious, gloomy, depressive trend. On the other hand, these responses were somewhat countered by a concern with aesthetics: he saw a clay pot with a red handle and, like his wife, a bow tie on a white shirt. However, he could not respond positively to the affect-arousing color stimuli of the last three cards. While he saw a colored rock on Card VIII, Card IX was for him a backbone, and he rejected Card X. Thus we have here revealed an individual who is turned in on himself; like his wife, he has an immature but active intraceptiveness but with a more unhealthy bottling up of emotions and impulses, a festering depressive feeling centered on bodily preoccupation, allowing no satisfactory social expression. His "backbone" responses suggest weakness rather than strength. While his wife has a latent inner vitality that in her adult years receives no external expression, he has inner feelings of insufficiency and weakness. Both parents have feelings of unrealized social status. However, while Mr. Yellowhorse dwells on his inadequacies and has little that is positive to externalize, the protocol of Mrs. Yellowhorse suggests that she is potentially active and resourceful. As we shall see in the records of all but one family member, little energy is put into constructive ideation and none in attempting to accomplish or to actualize. Of all the records of the family, that of Mr. Yellowhorse has the largest proportion of poor form quality in his responses because of the degree of bodily preoccupation which allows for less adequate responses to the form of the cards. Thus even his three "rocks" have an amorphous quality that also contributes to an overall poor form level.

The bodily preoccupation score of 33% and the total unpleasant score of 67% are very high and are commonly found only in rather disturbed individuals. At the same time, his positive affective expression of 20% is a counterbalance and indicates that emotionally he still seeks to maintain contact with his social environment.

Three of Mr. Yellowhorse's fourteen responses are rocks, twice seen at the bottom of the ocean. Rocks often symbolize an incapacity for feeling or at least an absence of softness or warmth, and at some level of consciousness the ocean is universally used to represent the mother. These percepts surely portray accurately Mr. Yellowhorse's childhood experiences, which we infer from interviews and our knowledge of his life history to have been characterized by severe maternal deprivation. Responses to the Rorschach are, of course, projections of the testee's qualities; the rock percepts no doubt indicate his scant capacity to be loving and warm to others. He is the only one of his family to produce a disease response, the rotting leaf, which is a sense of his own potential decomposition.

As will become more evident later, the main characteristic of this family's records is chronic cognitive constriction. With one exception, its members do not feel in themselves sufficient intellectual energy to strive for some form of satisfactory accomplishment.

It is interesting that there is no evidence of hostility in the protocol of Mr. Yellowhorse, in view of his regular drunken violence. Later we shall note that in the case of Calvin, whose frequent violence was feared by many people, only two hostility responses appeared on his first protocol. Many psychologists have noted that the acting out of violent impulses cannot be predicted reliably by means of the Rorschach test.

Tests of Albert, the Eldest Son

First Test

Age 10 years, 1 month   April 28, 1960

Shy and friendly; stacked the cards very neatly.

Card I. (100″ pause)

Hole, hole, hole, hole. [Naming   Unscorable
white spaces]

Card II. (10″ pause)

Something goes through here,   Unscorable
little road goes straight down,
dot, little line straight down and
around the bottom, little dot, little
dot. [Selects miniscule areas.
Would have continued endlessly
if tester had not removed card.
This was true also of all subsequent cards.]

Card III. (10″ pause)

Hole, square hole, hole goes   Unscorable
down, holes goes down, red line,
square hole, hole, hole. [Selects
only tiny white spaces; does not
relocate red line.]

Card IV. (10″ pause)

A hole goes down, a hole, a hole,   Unscorable
little holes goes down, black line,

a hole goes across, a white spot.
Card V. (10″ pause)
A hole goes down, a hole, a hole, little hole goes down, black line, a hole goes across, a white spot.	Unscorable

Card VI. (15″ pause)
White spot, white spot, black spot, little hole, white point, white hole goes across.	Unscorable

Card VII. (10″ pause)
White hole, white line, little black spot, a hole goes up, a white point goes up, little white mark, hole goes down, little black spot.	Unscorable

Card VIII. (10″ pause)
Hole, red spot, purple thing goes up, line goes down, skinny hole goes down, white mark goes down, white round hole, white spot, white hole goes down, red line goes down, blue spot, big hole, red and white little spot, little hole.	Unscorable

Card IX. (10″ pause)
Green and white hole, white line goes down, little hole goes down, blue line, hole, green spot, yellow arrow goes up, little white spot, two holes, little hole goes across, green crooked arrow goes down, little tiny white hole, pink spot.	Unscorable

Card X. (10″ pause)
A hole goes down, yellow spot, little black spot, a round hole green spot, white hole goes down, black line goes down, crooked arrow goes up, orange spot, white goes around.	Unscorable

Time elapsed: 25 minutes. Unscorable record.

Second Test

Age 20 years   July 7, 1970

Card I. (10″ pause)
    1. *Moth.* (Dead)   W F+ A P (Agl)
    2. *Bird.* (Two of them, sitting,   D FM_p+ A (Neut)
just the shape)
    3. *Dog head.* (Shape only)   D F Ad (Neut)

Card II. (15″ pause)
    4. *Two bears stand together.*   W FC′ FM_p+ A P (Neut)
(The shape and then the black)
    5. *Butterfly.* (Dead)   W F+ A P (Agl)

Card III.
    6. *Two people stand together.*   D M_p+ H P (Neut)
(Around a pot)

Card IV. (13″ pause)
    7. *Moth.* (Dead)   W F+ A (Agl)
    8. *Boar's head.* (The shape   D F T+ Ad (Neut)
and then the shading)

Card V. (5″ pause)
    9. *Butterfly.* (Flying. The   W FM_a− FY+ A P (Neut)
shape and the darkness)
    10. *Bat.* (Flying same as but-   W FM_a− FY+ A P (Neut)
terfly)

Card VI. (10″ pause).
    11. *Skin.* (Hairy side of cow)   W FT+ Aob P (Neut)

Card VII. (25″ pause)
    12. *Canyon.* (Shape and shad-   W FY− FV+ Lds (Neut)
ing)

Card VIII. (8″ pause)
    13. *Two lizards.* (Climb a hill;   W F M_a+ CF A P (Pstr)
the colors are colored dirt.)

Card IX. (30" pause)

14. *Canyon.* (Colored, with dirt walls)   W FV$_2$ CF Lds (Pnat)

Card X. (17" pause)

15. *Skull.* (The colors for the inside are more important than the shape.)   W CF− Anat (Agl, Bb)

Time elapsed: 20 minutes.

R = 15; W% = 73; F% = 26; F+% = 73; FV = 2; M = 1; FM = 5; FC' = 1; CF = 3; FY = 3; FT = 2; A% = 73; P = 6.

Hostile % = 0; Anxiety % = 27; Bodily preoccupation % = 7; Total unpleasant % = 34; Positive % = 13; Neutral % = 60; Anxiety gloom % = 27; 1 response each for Bone anatomy, Positive striving, and Positive nature.

Third Test

Age 30 years   July 1, 1980

Subject was uncooperative during inquiry, usually solely designating the areas which had been used. He refused to elaborate in the inquiry.

Card I.

1. *Moth.*   W FY+ A P (Neut)
2. *Sea horse.*   D F+ A (Neut)

Card II.

3. *Sting ray.*   D F+ A (Hha)
4. *Two cubs.*   D F+ A (Neut)

Card III.

5. *Two people.* (Stand together)   D M$_p$+ H P (Neut)
6. *Butterfly.* [red area]   D FC+ A (Neut)
7. *Bug face.*   FY− Ad (Athr)

Card IV.
    8. *Two shoes.*   D F+ Cg (Neut)
    9. *Ant's face.*   D FY− Ad (Athr Aobs)

Card V.
    10. *Bat.*   W FC'+ A P (Neut)

Card VI. (25″ pause).
    11. *Dog hide.*   W FT+ Aobj (Neut)

Card VII.
    12. *Two people, face each other.*   D M_p+ H P (Neut)

    13. *Little elephant.*   D FT+ A (Dch)

Card VIII.
    14. *Nice color to this one. Two iguanas.*   D FC+ A P (Neut)

    15. *Ram skull.*   DS F+ Anat (Bb)

Card IX. (30″ pause)
    16. *Hip bone.*   D F+ Anat (Bb)

Card X. (23″ pause)
    17. *Wishbone.*   D F+ Anat (Prec)
    18. *Two crabs.*   D F+ A P (Neut)

Time elapsed: 9 minutes. Responses given very swiftly except where noted.

R = 18; W% = 17; F% = 33; F+% = 89; M = 2; FM = 1; FC = 2; FY = 3; FT = 2; A% = 72; P = 7; Hostility % = 5; Anxiety % = 11; Bodily preoccupation % = 11; Total unpleasant response % = 27; Dependency % = 11; Positive % = 5; Neutral % = 56. Hostile anxiety, indirect = 1; Anxiety threat = 2; Dependent childish = 2; Bodily preoccupation = 2; Pleasant recreational = 1.

Albert's first protocol, obtained when he was ten, is essentially unscorable. It is characterized predominantly by his oppositional-obsessional approach, in which he finds holes everywhere, mostly in white spaces. We can remark with certainty only that this is an obsessional type of record in which the subject finds a magical way of handling the situation and maintains it throughout the testing. We might speculate that Albert's responding so often to the spaces as holes refers both to his negativistic traits and to an inner feeling of emptiness and despair about his chances of being able to obtain or accept emotional sustenance from without.

The record obtained ten years later is very different. Although it begins and ends with gloomy, depressive responses (a dead moth on Card I and a skull on Card X), Albert is much more affectively responsive and socially cooperative than formerly. He shows a need to participate in the common perceptions and preoccupations of his group (5 of his 15 responses are popular ones) and manifests an adequate reality sense in relating to his social world (F+% — 73) but in rather immature, stereotypic terms (A% = 73). There is one human movement response but there are four animal movement responses, indicating a continuing immature balance in his inner life and a relative lack of awareness of his own motives. There is a responsiveness to the color and shading characteristics of the blots, with three color-dominated color responses as well as two response sensitive to texture and three shading responses. In all, such attention to the nuances of the material presents us with an affectively open record, showing none of the constriction and difficulty recorded in his earlier protocol. He reveals an average level of intelligence.

In the symbolic material there is no expression of hostility. Some anxiety is revealed through a depressive trend, but to compensate there are also a number of positive responses throughout the record, suggesting Albert's attentiveness to, and investment in, his social world. At age ten he seemed to be fearful and emotionally constricted; at twenty he responds with a more emotionally open, albeit immature record. Nevertheless, all is not well with him affectively. On the last colored card he sees only a skull, reaffirming his proneness to depressive moods as a final offering.

At age 30 he races through the cards, giving 18 terse responses in 9 minutes, so as to divest himself with minimal effort of the task imposed on him. Remarkably, his protocol remains very similar to the record produced when he was 20. There is some suggestion of maturation reflected in the production of two human movement responses and two animal movement responses in this record as opposed to only one human movement and four animal movement responses previously. There is also a shift in the direction of exercising more control over his affective responsiveness. Color-dominated responses are no longer to be found. The number of shading and texture responses remains the same. He quickly produces six popular responses. There is a shift toward a more mundane approach. He is content, by and large, to respond to the large details of the blots; whereas previously he was more prone to use the entire blot, he now shows less interest in organizing his responses. He has turned more into his own body: percepts of distant canyons have been replaced by anatomical preoccupation. There is less positive material and curiously a trend toward dependent responses in the form of infant animals. The last three cards are handled no better than in the previous protocol. He can use the color on the "iguanas," a more precise reference to lizards than at age 20, but he then produces three anatomical responses before ending with the popularly perceived crabs on Card X. Symbolically, he gives among his animal responses three sea-dwelling creatures, suggesting, as does the iguana, cold-bloodedness. Overall, there is a retreat inward with a suggestion of greater passivity and dependency than was true at age 20, as well as some hypochondriacal binding up of anxiety. While he can now produce two human movement responses, in each instance the persons have passive postures.

In all, he reveals he is not a gifted person. He is somewhat more affectively open than many of his group, but he has little drive to externalize his average capacities or to apply himself with diligence to any task at hand.

Tests of Bridger, the Artist

First Test

Age 8 years, 8 months   April 26, 1960

Card I. (6'15" pause)
1. *Face with ear.* (Shape)   Dd F+ Ad (Aobs)
[Pointed to top hand area.]

Card II. (4′40″ pause)
    2. *Face*. (Horse)   Dd F Ad (Aobs)
(5′ pause)
    3. *Mouth*. (Bear)   Dd F Ad (Aobs)
(Additional: *Fox face*)   Dd F Ad (Aobs)

Card III. (30″ pause).
    4. *Bird*. (Face, the shape)   Dd F+ A P (Aobs)
    5. *Butterfly*. (Flying)   D FM_a+ A P (Neut)
(2′ pause)
    6. *Mouth*. (Skunk; the shape) Dd F− Ad (Mor)
(3′ pause)
    7. *Hand*. (The space of the   Dd F− Ad (Aobs)
edge)
(Additional: *Little chick*. (Walking; the shape); *Mouth*.

Card IV. (40″ pause)
    8. *Face*. (Just the mouth)
    9. *Fly*. (Flying; shape and   Dd FM_a− A (Neut)
shading)
(1′40″ pause)
    10. *Hand*. (Arm and hand)   Dd F− Hd Olig (Neut)
    11. *Face*. (Just the nose)   Dd F Hd (Aobs)
    12. *Hat*. (Winter hat)   D F− Hd (Aobs)

Card V. (10″ pause)
    13. *Mouth*. (Bird mouth)   D F+ Ad (Mor)
    14. *Face*. (Indian with long
nose)
    15. *Teeth*.   D F Hd (Aobs)
    16. *Face*.   Dd F− Hd (Aobs)
    17. *Face*.
    18. *Mouth*.
    19. *Eyes*.

Card VI. (10″ pause)
    20. *Face*. (Mouse face)   (Aobs)
    21. *Mouth*. (Lion)   (Aobs)
    22. *Nose*. (Fox face)   (Aobs)

23. *Eyes.* (Fox face)   (Aobs)
24. *Head.* (Mouse)   (Aobs)
25. *Nose.* (Rabbit nose)   (Aobs)
26. *Mouth.* (The white on the   (Aobs)
edge of the rabbit nose)
27. *Hair.* (The shape and the   (Aobs)
shading)
28. *Hill.* (Tree on it)   (Aobs)

Card VII. (10″ pause)
29. *Face.* (Rabbit, laughing)   (Aobs)
30. *Ears.*   (Aobs)
31. *Butterfly.* (Flying)
32. *Head.* (Rabbit)
33. *Hair.*
34. *Ears.*
35. *Nose.*
36. *Eyes.*
37. *Mouth.*

Card VIII.
38. *Face.* (Brown fox)   Dd F+ Ad (Aobs)
39. *Legs.* (Lamb, walking   D FM_a+ A P (Neut)
across the hills)
40. *Head.*
41. *Butterfly.* (Flies around in
the spring)
42. *Hill.*
43. *Butterfly.* (Flies around in   (Pnat)
the spring)
44. *Hand.* (Bear)
45. *Wood.* (That you chop)
46. *Face.* (Eagle)
47. *Mouth.*
48. *Nose.*

Card IX. (10″ pause)
49. *Head.* (Baby chick)   (Aobs)
50. *Bones.* (Bear bones)

51. *Eyes.* (In a bear face)
52. *Face.*
53. *Cow face.*
54. *Mouth.*
55. *Hand.* (Kangaroo)
56. *Face.* (The white part, of a
lion)
57. *Hand.* (Space)
58. *Nose.* (Bear nose)
59. *Hand.*
60. *Hole.*
61. *Ears.* (Cow ear)
62. *Nose.* (Rabbit)
63. *Eyes.*

Card X.
64. *Bones.* (Bear)
65. *Face.* (Rabbit)   D F+ A P (Neut)
66. *Face.* (It's a whole lion,   D FM_a+ A (P)
jumping; shape more than
color.)
67. *Lamb.* (Going to sleep)   D FM_p+ A
68. *Meat.* (Color more than
shape)
69. *Face.* (Bear)
70. *Spider.* (Walks around)   D FM_a+ A P (Athr)
71. *Eyes.*
72. *Face.* (Horse)
73. *Ears.* (On the rabbit)
74. *Bird.* (Two, flying, blue)
75. *Spiders.* (Try to fix the
bone)
76. *Ears.*
77. *Face.*

Time elapsed: 39 minutes, 30 seconds.

R = 77, few scorable; F% high; F+% low; other determinants low. A few populars. Oligophrenic restriction. Anxiety total very high. Dependent and oral symbolism present.

Second Test

Age 17 years   May 22, 1969

Card I. (72″ pause)
  1. *Mask.*   DS F+ Mask (Athr)
  2. *Bat.* (It has no face.)   D F+ A (Athr)

Card II. (40″ pause)
  3. *Bug.* (Like a crab)   D FC+ A (Neut)
  4. *A hide.*   D FT Aobj (Neut)

Card III.
  5. *A Fly.*   D F+ A (Athr)
  6. *Spider.* (Crawl)   D FM$_a$+ A (Athr)

Card IV. (19″ pause; inverted)
  7. *Bat.* (Dead)   W F+ A (Athr, Agl)
(inverted)
  8. *Hide.*   W FT+ Aobj P (Neut)

Card V.
  9. *Butterfly.* (Flying)   W FM$_a$+ A P (Neut)
  10. *Pelt.*   D FT+ Aobj (Neut)
  11. *Leaf.*   D FT− Bot (Neut)

Card VI. (8″ pause)
  12. *Hide.*   W FT+ Aobj P (Neut)
(inverted)
  13. *Leaf.*   D FT+ Bot (Neut)

Card VII. (82″ pause)
  14. *Moustache.*   W FT+ Hd (Mor)
  15. *Group of islands.*   W FV Lds (Aev)
  16. *Faces.* (Girls)   D F+ Hd P (Neut)

Card VIII. (10″ pause)
  17. *Inside a cave.*   W CF+ Nat (Pnat)
  18. *Flower leaves.*   D CF+ Nat (Pnat)

Card IX. (36″ pause)

19. *Group of flowers.*	W CF+ Bot (Pnat)
20. *Face.* (Of a cow)	DS F+ Ad (Neut)

Card X. (10″ pause)

21. *Group of insects.*	W FC+ A (Neut)
22. *Decorations.*	W CF+ Orn (Porn)

Time elapsed: 40 minutes.

R = 22; W = 45%; F% = 27; F+% = 95; M = 0; FM = 2; FC = 2; CF = 4; FT = 7; FV = 1.

Anxiety threat = 5; Anxiety evasive = 1; Adysphoric (Agl) = 1; Positive nature = 3; Positive ornamental = 1; Miscellaneous oral = 1; Neutral = 50%.

Third Test

Age 38 years   June 27, 1980

Card I. (20″ pause)

1. *Canyon, hill on both sides, wash coming toward you.* (inverted)	W FY FV− Lds (Mi)
2. *Face, mask, four eyes.*	DS F+ Mask (Athr)

Card II. (rotated for 80″, inverted)

3. *Sun coming out, pond in middle, reflection off water.*	WS FV− FY− FC+ Lds (Pnat)

Card III. (rotated for 50″)

4. *Outline of pottery, bottom part of vase, light reflects off the middle.* (inverted)	WS FC+ Orn (Porn)
5. *Part of a fly. Big eyes, legs in front.*	W F+ Ad (Athr)

Card IV. (rotated for 40″)

6. *Cowhide.*	W FT+ Aobj P (Neut)

Card V.
   7. *Butterfly.*   W F+ A P (Neut)
(inverted)
   8. *Butterfly.*   W F+ A P (Neut)

Card VI. (rotated for 60″)
   9. *Lake with reflection of*   W FV− FT+ Lds (Pnat)
clouds, with willows and cattails.

Card VII. (60″ pause)
   10. *Clouds move before the*   W Fm_a− TF+ Nat (Adif)
storm.

Card VIII. (30″ pause; card on it side.)
   11. *Cat on rocks with shadow*   WS FM_p+ A− Lds (Pnat)
and reflection on other side.

Card IX. (rotated for 40″)
   12. *It's hard.*   Cddes
(rotated for 2′ more, turned card on side)
   Colorful   (Arej)

Card X. (rotated for 50″)
   13. *Thunderstorm, lightning*   WS $C·m_a$ Nat O (Pnat, Aa)
strikes hard, makes colors move
around.

Time elapsed: approximately 15 minutes.

R = 12; W = 91%; F% = 33; F+% = 91; M = 0; m = 2; FV = 3; FC = 1; C = 1; FT = 1; FY = 2; P = 3; O = 3; Card description = 1.

Anxiety % = 35; Hostility % = 0; Bodily preoccupation = 0; Total unpleasant % = 35; Positive % = 35; Neutral % = 23; Anxiety reject = 1; Anxiety threat = 2; Indirect anxiety = 1; Diffuse anxiety = 1; Positive nature = 4; Positive ornamental = 1; Mi = 1.

At age 8, Bridger gives what can be described as an obsessional record and is very fearful. The content of his responses is a repetitive preoccupation with faces, teeth, noses, hands, and so forth. Only very small areas of the blots are used, and the record is essentially unscorable. It is characterized by what is termed "oligophrenic constriction." Thus, on Card III, where a common response is an entire human image, he manages only to see the head part, and where others see a bird he sees only the part which is the face of a bird. We might postulate that at this age he desperately sought to keep the facts of his life psychologically separated to avoid awareness of their gruesome reality.

Despite the fact that while in boarding school he was already perceived socially as the stalwart leader of his brothers, his second protocol, taken at this time, is still marked by fearfulness in the form of faces and flat, uninteresting responses through the first seven cards. He first sees a head-on a mask on Card I and a frightening headless bat. On Card II he sees a bug and then a hide. On Card III appear a fly, head-on and a spider, fearful figures on this card; on Card IV, a dead bat and a hide. After he sees the popular butterfly on Card V he again turns to a pelt and then a leaf, essentially nothing. After another hide and leaf on Card VI he gives his first original response, a moustache on Card VII, followed by a group of islands and the usual faces of girls in profile. It may be significant that on this "feminine" card he first sees a moustache. Perhaps he looks more to a male than to a female figure for softness and caretaking. In fact in his real life at this time, his sources of support were male teachers who appreciated his talents and encouraged him.

He responds affectively to the last three colored cards. His responses to the pastel-colored cards are quite different from his previous responses and those produced by other members of his family. He is stimulated by the colors in a positive way; he sees the inside of a cave and then, flower petals on Card VIII. Then he sees a group of flowers on Card IX, and decorations on Card X.

After an apprehensive start of this record at age 17, he manifests his capacity to be stimulated. He is opened up affectively by his environment, especially by nature. To be sure, he manifests fearfulness in dealing with people, as symbolized by masks, which also appear as symbols of fear of authority among Japanese youth (see, for example, De Vos 1966; De Vos and Borders 1979). It may also be significant that among Apaches, masked ceremonial dancers represent fearful figures of authority, omnipotence, omniscience, and discipline.

In Bridger's last record, nature is symbolized positively throughout. He does not go into himself: he remains constrictive in respect to introspection. There are no human responses at all. It is interesting that he sees inanimate movement but neither human nor animal movement, a tension about realizing inner impulses. Again he distances himself from his own inner promptings and is able to do so through the use of complex ego functions suggested by the perception of inanimate movement. He has become completely extratensive, responding sensitively and emotionally only to the outer environment. He is a doer and a responder, not a thinker or an analyzer. The protection afforded him by his artistic utilization of his extratensive controls does not, however, completely shield him from experiencing some forms of anxiety. Thus, on Card I he sees a mask, suggestive of threat, immediately after his initial distant view of a canyon. On Card II he discovers the use of symmetry as suggesting mirrored reflection and gives a highly creative and aesthetic response: he sees the sun coming out, a pond in the middle with a reflection coming off the water. On Card III we observe the same trends revealed on Card I, the emergence of a fearful percept, a fly seen head-on, after he initially perceived the outline of pottery and used the white space creatively as reflected light.

We can but postulate on why he was apparently able to develop the capacity to sublimate to the degree that he was. It is obvious from the anthropological data that he developed more ego strength and more sense of responsibility than either of his brothers; this is clearly reflected in his last Rorschach protocol. There is no evidence that his emotional succor from his actual parents differed from that of his brothers. It may be that he was more appealing to his mother's brother's wife, a major influence in the early and latency periods of all three brothers, but the Boyers' memory is not certain on this point. He did play with his cousins a great deal and was in and out of their dwelling at all times of day and night. There is no doubt that Bridger was the preferred brother in the boarding school situation where he lived for some years with his brothers Albert and Calvin. Subsequently, he attended another Indian school without them and indeed with but one or two other Apache students; there he was treated very well and for the first time found male figures with whom he could identify on a professional level, having an opportunity to capitalize on a personal gift, his artistic talent.

Tests of Calvin, the Third Son

First Test

Age 6 years, 5 months   March 8, 1960

Card I. (10″ pause)
1. *Man.* (Doing nothing; has   D F+ H (Hhad)
no head)

Card II. (20″ pause)
2. *Face.* (Woman, doing noth-   D F− Hd (Athr)
ing)

Card III.
3. *A nose.* (Man's nose)   DW F− Hd(Athr) confab)
                                       (Possible disguised W of
                                       card as face)
4. *A bird.* (Standing)   D FM$_p$+ A(Adeh)

Card IV. (10″ pause)
5. *A bear.* (Sitting on the tree.   W FM$_p$+ A O (Neut)
His arm)

Card V. (5″ pause)
6. *A kangaroo.* (Standing)   D FM$_p$ + A O (Neut)

Card VI.
7. *A hand.* (Black hand)   D FC′ Hd (Neut)
(5″ pause)
8. *A crow.* (Doing nothing).   D F+ A (Neut)
A hand. (The crow's wing point-
ing out)

Card VII. (30″ pause)

9. *A water.* (Shape and shad-   D FV+ Lds (Neut)
ing)

10. *A bull.* (Horned and with   D F+ AD (Hh)
an eye)

Card VIII. (5″ pause)

11. *A tiger, a tree, a head.*   D FM$_a$− F/C+ A P (Pstr)
(Climbing the green tree, tiger
because it's pink)

Card IX. (10″ pause)

12. *A tree.* (A green tree) *A*   D F+ Nat (Neut)
bear. [Could not relocate]

Card X. (5″ pause)

13. *A Head.* (Spider head be-   D F− Ad (Athr)
cause it's got ears)

14. *A man.* (Doing nothing)   D F− H (Neut)

15. *An eyeglass.*   D F− Orn (Neut)

16. *A goat.* (Yellow goat,   D FM$_a$+ A (Pstr)
climbing)

Time elapsed: 10 minutes.

The logic in the inquiry indicates some shift from what might have
been good responses in the free association. Either Calvin could
not relocate his responses or he avoided giving answers to the
actual percepts seen in the free association.

R = 16; W% = 6; F% = 69; F+% = 56; A% = 50; H = 2; Hd =
4; FM = 5; FV = 1; F/C = 1; FC′ = 1; P = 1; O = 2.

Hostility % = 12; Anxiety % = 25; Total unpleasant % = 37;
Positive % = 12; Neutral % = 50; Indirect hostility = 1; Distorted hostility = 1; Dehumanized anxiety = 1; Anxiety threat =
3; Positive striving = 2.

Second Test

Age 15 years, 7 months   May 21, 1969

Card I.
Rejected after 45″.   (Arej)

Card II.
Rejected after 95″.   (Arej)

Card III. (12″ pause)
   1. *Man pull something black.*   D M + H P (Hcmpt)
   2. *Lungs.*   D CF+ Anat (Bf)
   3. *Fish.* (Swim)   D FM$_a$+ A (Neut)

Card IV.
Rejected after 50″.   (Arej)

Card V. (102″ pause; card inverted)
   4. *Butterfly.*   W F+ A P (Neut)
   5. *Bat.*   W F+ A (Neut)

Card VI.
Rejected after 40″.   (Arej)

Card VII. (15″ pause)
   6. *Things stacked on top of*   W F$_v$ Obj (Aev)
each other. (Just things. Just the
shape)
   7. *Animal's head.* (Shape and   D F+ Ad (Neut)
shading)

Card VIII. (10″ pause)
   8. *Animals.* (Walk)   D FM$_a$+ A P (Neut)
(inverted)
   9. *Butterfly.* (It's just there.)   D F+ A (Neut)

Card IX.
(Rejected after 25″)   (Arej)

Card X. (10″ pause)
  10. *Spider.* (Walk)   D FM_a+ A P (Neut)
  11. *Sea lion.* (Stand up)   D FM_p+ A (Neut)
  12. *Rabbit's head.*   D F+ Ad P (Neut)

Elapsed time: 10 minutes.

R = 12; F% = 42; F+% = 91; A% = 75; M = 1; FM = 5; CF+ 1; P = 5. 5 rejections.

Anxiety % = 35; Hostility % = 6; Bodily preoccupation % = 6; Total unpleasant % = 47; Positive % = 0; Neutral % = 53.

Anxiety rejections = 5; Anxiety evasive = 1; Hostile competitive = 1; Bodily preoccupation flesh = 1.

Third Test

Age 26 years   July 27, 1980

Card I.
  Line in the middle and a white   (Aev)
dot, white dot.
  1. *Things go out, two dots.*   Dd F + Ad (Neut)
                              Card description (Aev)
  Shades, one light, one dark.   C des   (Aev)

Card II.
  Two lines in the middle, almost   C des   (Aev)
connect two colors of shades, one
light, one dark red.
Card III. (20″ pause, inverted)
  2. *Butterfly.*   D F+ A P (Neut)
  3. *Diamond shape between the* DS F− Ad (Mi)
eyes, straight lines through.

Card IV.
  Shades, just shading.   (Shading description)
                              (Aev)

Card V.
  4. *Butterfly.*   W F+ A P (Neut)

Line in the middle where fold   C des   (Aev)
the paper.

Card VI.
The same, just shades, watery,   C des   (Aev)
other colors, floating.

Card VII.
Really watery, watery water,   C des   (Aev)
colors.

Card VIII.
Colors and where the paper is   C des   (Aev)
folded and connected.

Card IX. Rotated for 50″.
All kinds of colors.   (Aev)

Card X.
A lot of beautiful colors.   C des   (Aev)

R = 4. Not a scorable record. The subject avoids giving true responses by giving card descriptions instead.

As was found frequently in the ten-year follow-up study of the Apache reported for the group of children as a whole in the previous chapter, Calvin's first record is more open and shows greater potential than is realized in his later records. We found such progressive constriction to be a characteristic of many psychological tests given during childhood and adolescence to Native Americans.

In his first record Calvin gives a most unusual response for a six-year-old Apache: on Card V he sees a kangaroo head-on. His record manifests vigor, but he also shows a childish fearfulness symbolized in faces and heads, which anticipates his later constrictiveness and evasiveness. In this first record there is some shifting from what seems to be spontaneously good responses in the free association to less adequate handling of these responses when he is directly questioned in the inquiry. He seems to be unable to locate some percepts, and when he is questioned about

others he seems to shift his percepts; perhaps he has seen something else he prefers and does not hesitate to revise his initial
responses. The epitome of this tendency is seen in his responses
to Card X. There, in the free association, he gives a head, a man,
an eyeglass, and a goat. In the inquiry the head is seen as a spider
head because it has big ears, but the spider head is seen in an area
which is more appropriate to a goat's head, and goats, not spiders, have big ears. There is a commonly perceived spider on Card
X, but he doesn't choose the appropriate spider. It is unusual for
a six-year-old to see a man on Card X, just as it is uncommon for
a six-year-old to give noses or hands as human details. The man
seen on Card I was in an area commonly selected for a human
percept, but that on Card X was a kind of stick figure in the center
of the card, an unusual response. He manifests a kind of fal-
lacious logic. Thus, on Card VI he sees a "hand" which turns out
to be a crow's wing, a peculiar usage. The animals he selects are
vigorous: a kangaroo, a bull, a tiger. In the area on Card VIII
where animals are usually perceived, he sees a tiger where his
brother Albert at 20 sees two lizards.

Ten years later, as a 15-year-old, Calvin reveals a totally different approach to the task of the test. He rejects five cards, including the first two. On Card III he begins with a vigorous perception
of the popular human response but then retreats quickly into
seeing lungs and finally a cold-blooded animal, a fish. Rejecting
Card IV he gives the usual butterfly and bat, the popular responses to Card V, rejects Card VI, then gives a kind of nonresponse to Card VII, "things stacked on top of each other." At age
six he had seen a bull here. No longer does he see tigers on Card
VIII but instead only walking animals. After rejecting Card IX he
sees the usual spider on Card X, a sea lion standing up, and the
popularly perceived rabbit. His unpleasant response level on this
meager record is high, 42%, due to the evasiveness which is now
his main mode of expressing anxiety. There are no positive responses such as appeared in the past record. What he does admit
seeing on this record are popular responses, appropriate but unimaginative. Like his brother Albert, he rejects cards after long
pauses, that is, willfully. His record at 15 is a most constricted
one, in sharp contrast to that obtained when he was six. He evi-

dences a strong sense of reality, but not personal investment in an active immersion in his environment.

At age 26 he has totally pulled back from giving a scorable Rorschach. He gives continuous evasive color naming or card description responses, one popular, the most common popular of all, the butterfly on Card V—and three borderline responses, such as seeing "things going out." He appears to be totally empty of any active investment in meeting social tasks. He claimed to be an artist, like his older brother Bridger, but his claim could not be supported. To L.B.B. his protocol was reminiscent of those of the pseudoshamans done in an earlier Rorschach study of Apaches (Boyer, Klopfer, et al. 1964), who claimed to possess supernatural powers but were not believed by many of their social group.

On the whole, Calvin's first record was much better than the initial protocols produced by his older brothers. Whereas they both were manifestly fearful and inadequate, his first record revealed positively creative and constructive aggressive potential. At age six he was the youngest of the three brothers. Among the Apache, at such an age during childhood, the youngest child is ordinarily the undisputed favorite and receives tender, solicitous care to the degree that the parents' egocentric orientation makes this possible. In the Yellowhorse family, with the temporary exception of the twin girls, no children who were born after the three brothers were treated as though they were truly children at all. An example of this phenomenon occurred during Mrs. Yellowhorse's Rorschach administration. Her two sons, respectively two and three years of age, were both ill and fretful but they were utterly ignored despite the fact that one resorted to an overt temper tantrum.

Comments

In order to understand the personalities of the three Yellowhorse brothers, the authors have referred to a general knowledge of Apache culture and the psychological norms that prevail. Life histories of parents or parental surrogates, field observations of the young men in childhood situations, and an awareness of the family's reputation contributed to the background data. As indicated, the Rorschach tests were given over a twenty-year time span and the protocols were interpreted, using a standard system and symbolic affective scoring. The combination of field observations and technical psychological interpretations yielded a suggestive picture of each of the young men at specific stages in their lives, not just behavioral aspects, but unconscious as well as conscious emotions and the means by which they were handled. Obviously, anyone looking at the disorganized Yellowhorse household during their early childhood could have predicted that the boys would be unable to develop deep and enduring object relations, but it would have been difficult to foretell the degree or kind of anticipated emotional impoverishment. What could not have been predicted is the fact that there is no *thought* disturbance in any of the records. Actually, as has been noted, the three brothers relate to a pattern that is all too common among many of the Apache of the same generation.

Albert, the oldest of the brothers, was friendly and outwardly cooperative at age ten, but he had already experienced a fearful despair concerning interpersonal relationships. Elder children among the Apache frequently experience severe parental rejection with the birth of ensuing siblings, and this, combined with an indoctrination of an ominous physical environment in the form of ghosts, wild men, and other cultural bogies including witches with their evil powers, makes growing up difficult at best (L. B. Boyer 1979, chap. 4; R. M. Boyer 1962). However, by the age of twenty, Albert appears to have conquered at least some of his anxieties, even though he still views his social world in "immature stereotypic terms" and is still prone to depressive moods. There is little change in the next ten years: Albert remains emotionally constricted, introverted, passive, and dependent, and shows little or no incentive to use whatever intellectual capacity he possesses.

Bridger, the middle brother, has an obsessional and fearful record at the age of eight. Life in his eyes is oppressive and cruel, and the inner turmoil he senses at this early period persists in the protocol obtained when he was an adolescent. Fortunately for Bridger, in contrast to his brothers, he possesses an artistic talent that touches his teachers and leads them to respond to him in a manner that enables him to achieve a means of feeling some personal accomplishment. Nonetheless, although he is stimulated positively by the pastel colors in his second Rorschach test, he remains fearful of dealing with people. His final protocol reveals that he has developed a capacity to sublimate to some degree and to enjoy the surfaces of nature. Nevertheless, he remains constrictive in respect to introspection. He has become completely extratensive, responding sensitively and emotionally only to the external environment. Like his brothers and others of his generation he acts and responds but does not think or analyze. In common with them, he has further developed an insulation against emotional interactions with people, the insulation developed by Apache by the time they have reached their middle adolescent years to ward off the continuing emotional traumata afforded by their everyday lives. Bridger is the only brother to have developed the capacity to sublimate; he can at least enjoy the surfaces of nature. Although his ego development is more mature than that of his brothers, the pervasiveness of early fears and distrust of interpersonal relationships persists throughout his records.

Calvin, like Albert, shows a certain openness in his first test, which was administered when he was six years old, and there he shows an imaginative ability lacking in his brothers' initial protocols. Later, however, his frankness dissipates and we see instead fear, constriction, and evasiveness. By the time Calvin is an adolescent, although he is fully aware of reality, he has become anxious, unimaginative, and rejecting and manifests the emotional insulation commonly seen in Rorschach protocols taken from Apaches during their teens. Life has dealt hard with him. The lack of a mother, however inconsistently responsive she was, combined with the traumatizing effects of grammar school and other latency experiences, appear to have had a profoundly negative effect on his emotional and intellectual growth.

In summary, it is apparent that the protocols of the Yellowhorse brothers resemble that of their father far more closely than that of their mother. It seems evident that the emotional impoverishment common to the childhoods of the father and the three brothers has had a profound effect. Mrs. Yellowhorse, whose own childhood was more emotionally gratifying, developed the capacity for more lasting interpersonal relatedness, but was unfortunately insufficiently strong to withstand the personal sense of inferiority toward and distance from a white culture she tasted briefly in school before she made an unfortunate marriage and became a "drop out" from life and an alcoholic, like her husband. The traumas of Apache childhood lead to age constriction—not to schizophrenic thought disorders.

Notes

1. One rare example is Madsen's (1982) recapitulation, forty years later, of Dennis's (1943) initial application to Hopi children of Piaget's (1929) classification of animistic thinkings. A recent example is Rabkin's report on a kibbutznik (1986).

2. This chapter has been adapted from L. Bryce Boyer, George A. De Vos, and Ruth M. Boyer, A Longitudinal Study of Three Apache Brothers as Reflected in Their Rorschach Protocols, *Journal of Psychoanalytic Anthropology*, 1983, 6:125–161, and is reprinted with permission.

3. In the Boyers' socialization study various criteria were chosen to divide the families on the Mescalero reservation into seven approximately numerically equal groups, and one family from each group was studied intensively for not less than six months. The Yellowhorse family came from the group with the lowest income level and the worst reputation as adjudged by both Apache and Anglos.

4. Apache housing generally follows the matrilocal pattern (R. M. Boyer 1964). We note that the brothers' father was placed with paternal rather than maternal relatives.

5. During 1959–60, some 30% of Apache infants on this reservation were found to have subdural hematomata, ascribed to a combination of dietary neglect and trauma (Clements and Mohr 1961).

6. The reliability of the results of intelligence tests which are administered to populations such as these has been questioned frequently, especially when the tests are administered to groups. The Iowa Tests of Basic Skills were administered to these Indian students. Zintz (1957–60) has found them to give results consistent with the school performances of this population, as did we (Day, Boyer, and De Vos 1975).

7. During the Boyers' early years on the reservation, they had free access to tribal records. However, in recent years such data have been withheld from them and all investigators, white or Indian. In consequence, the specific court charges leveled against the brothers were unobtainable.

References

Basehart, Harry W.
  1959   *Chiricahua Apache Subsistence and Sociopolitical Organization.* Albuquerque: University of New Mexico Mescalero-Chiricahua Land Claims Project. Mimeographed.
  1960   *Mescalero Apache Subsistence Patterns and Sociopolitical Organization.* Albuquerque: University of New Mexico Mescalero-Chiricahua Land Claims Project, Mimeographed.
  1967   The Resource Holding Corporation Among the Mescalero Apache. *Southwestern Journal of Anthropology* 23:277–291.
  1970   Mescalero Apache Band Organization and Leadership. *Southwestern Journal of Anthropology* 28:87–106.
Beck, Samuel J., Roy R. Grinker, and William Stephenson
  1954   *The Six Schizophrenias: Reaction Patterns in Children and Adults.* New York: American Orthopsychiatric Association.
Bourke, John G.
  1892   *The Medicine Men of the Apache.* Ninth Annual Report, Bureau of American Ethnology. Reprinted by Rio Grande Press, Glorietta, N. Mex. [1970].
Boyer, L. Bryce
  1964   Folk Psychiatry of the Apaches of the Mescalero Indian Reservation. Ari Kiev, ed. *Magic, Faith, and Healing: Studies in Primitive Psychiatry Today*, pp. 384–419. Glencoe, Ill.: Free Press.
  1979   *Childhood and Folklore: A Psychoanalytic Study of Apache Personality.* New York: Library of Psychological Anthropology.
Boyer, L. Bryce, George A. De Vos, Orin Borders, and Alice Tani-Borders
  1978   The "Burnt Child Reaction" Among the Yukon Delta Eskimos. *Journal of Psychological Anthropology* 1:7–56.
Boyer, L. Bryce, George A. De Vos, and Ruth M. Boyer
  1983   A Longitudinal Study of Three Apache Brothers as Reflected in Their Rorschach Protocols. *Journal of Psychoanalytic Anthropology* 6:125–161.
Boyer, L. Bryce, Bruno Klopfer, Florence B. Brawer, and Hayao Kawai
  1964   Comparisons of the Shamans and Pseudoshamans of the Apaches of the Mescalero Indian Reservation. *Journal of Projective Techniques and Personality Assessment* 28:173–180.
Boyer, Ruth M.
  1962   *Social Structure and Socialization Among the Apache of the Mescalero Indian Reservation.* Ph.D. dissertation, University of California, Berkeley unpublished.

1964　The Matrifocal Family Among the Mescalero: Additional Information. *American Anthropologist* 66:593–602.

Clements, William W., and Duane V. Mohr
1961　Chronic Subdural Hematomas in Infants. Paper presented at the Annual United States Public Health Service National Clinical Meeting, Lexington, Ky., April.

Day, Richard, L. Bryce Boyer, and George A. De Vos
1975　Two Styles of Ego Development: A Cross-Cultural, Longitudinal Comparison of Apache and Anglo School Children. *Ethos* 3:345–379.

Dennis, Wayne
1943　Animism and Related Tendencies in Hopi Children. *Journal of Abnormal and Social Psychology* 38:21–35.

Devereux, George, and Weston LaBarre
1961　Art and Mythology. Bert Kaplan, ed. *Studying Personality Cross-Culturally*, pp. 361–403. Evanston, Ill.: Row-Peterson.

De Vos, George A.
1952　A Quantitative Approach to Affective Symbolism in Rorschach Responses. *Journal of Projective Techniques* 16:133–150.
1961　Symbolic Analysis in the Cross-Cultural Study of Personality. Bert Kaplan, ed. *Studying Personality Cross-Culturally*, pp. 599–636. Evanston, Ill.: Row-Peterson.
1966　*Comparisons of Personality Differences in Two Generations of Japanese Americans by Means of the Rorschach Test*. Honolulu: University of Hawaii Social Science Research Institute, Reprint 14.

De Vos, George A., and Orin Borders
1979　A Rorschach Comparison of Delinquent and Nondelinquent Japanese Family Members. *Journal of Psychological Anthropology* 2:425–442.

De Vos, George A., and Horace Miner
1959　Oasis and Casbah: A Study in Acculturative Stress. Marvin K. Opler, ed. *Culture and Mental Health*, pp. 333–350.

Helm, June, George A. De Vos, and Teresa Carterette
1960　Variations in Personality and Ego Identification Within a Slave Indian Kin-Community. National Museum of Canada Bulletin 190, *Contributions to Anthropology*, Part 2.

Klopfer, Bruno, Mary D. Ainsworth, Walter G. Klopfer, and Robert R. Holt
1954　*Developments in the Rorschach Technique*. Vol. 1, *Technique and Theory*. New York: Harcourt, Brace.

LaBarre, Weston
1970　*The Ghost Dance: The Origins of Religion*. New York: Dell.

Madsen, Millard C.
1982 Animism and Related Tendencies in Hopi Children: A Replication of Dennis. *Journal of Cross-Cultural Psychology* 13:117–124.
Opler, Morris E.
1941 *An Apache Life-Way.* Chicago: University of Chicago Press. Reprinted by Cooper Square Publishers, New York [1965].
1946 The Mountain Spirits of the Chiricahua Apache. *Master Key* 20:125–131.
1947 Notes on Chiricahua Apache Culture. I. Supernatural Power and the Shaman. *Primitive Man* 2:1–14.
Piaget, Jean
1929 *The Child's Conception of the World.* New York: Harcourt, Brace.
Rabkin, Leslie Y.
1986 Longitudinal Continuities in the Personality of a Kibbutznik. *Journal of Psychoanalytic Anthropology* 9:319–338.
Singer, Margaret Thaler
n.d. Personality Measurement in the Aging. James Birran, ed. *Human Aging: Biological, Social, and Psychosocial.* Washington, D.C.: Government Printing Office.
Singer, Margaret T., and Joseph E. Speisman
1961 Rorschach Content: Correlates in Five Groups with Organic Pathology. *Journal of Projective Techniques* 25:356–359.
Streitfelt, H. S.
1954 Specificity of Peptic Ulcer to Intense Oral Conflicts. *Psychosomatic Medicine* 16:315–326.
Weiner, Herbert, Margaret Thaler, and Morton Reiser
1957 Etiology of the Duodenal Ulcer. Part I. Relations of Specific Psychological Characteristics to Gastric Secretion (Serum Pepsinogen). *Psychosomatic Medicine*, Vol. 19, special article.
Wynne, Lyman, and Margaret Thaler Singer
1966 Principles of Scoring Communication Defects and Deviances in Parents of Schizophrenics. *Psychiatry* 29:260–288.
Zintz, Miles V.
1957–60 *The Indian Research Study*: Final Report. 2 vols. Albuquerque: University of New Mexico College of Education. Mimeographed.

Chapter Twelve

Crisis and Continuity in the Personality of a Shaman

L. Bryce Boyer, George A. De Vos, and Ruth M. Boyer

As another form of longitudinal study we present two Rorschach protocols of an Apache woman taken at moments of crisis in the establishment of her career as a shaman.[1] The critical experiences and intrapsychic conflicts of "Dawnlight," an Apache woman, at the time she assumed her shamanic status have been described elsewhere (Boyer, Boyer, and De Vos 1982).[2] Herein we again examine her life history at a later point, with its problems and successes, within the context of the socialization patterns and social structure of her group.[3] A Rorschach protocol was obtained from Dawnlight two days following her first public professional performance. Another test was administered after an additional two years, during a period of stress perhaps aroused predominantly by the additional expectations directed toward her after she assumed an idiosyncratic shamanic role, one heretofore held only by men.

Background on the Social Functioning and Personality of Shamans

Studies of shamanism essentially began in northeast Asia, where an ecstatic aspect is a prominent feature of shamanic performance (Diószegi 1962; Diószegi and Hoppál; Ducey 1976, 1979; Eliade 1951; Lommel 1967; Ohlmarks 1939; Paulson 1965). The Tungusic-Siberian shamans were found to have been recruited from the "excitable," the "half-crazy," and the "deviant," and to have been "cured" of schizophrenia (Bogoras 1907; Czaplicka 1914; Jochelson 1905–08, 1924; Kim 1972; Nordland 1967; Ohlmarks 1939; Paulson 1965; Shirokogoroff 1924).[4] Acker-knecht (1943), generalizing and presenting a simplistic cultural definition of normality, held the shaman to be psychologically intact. Howells (1956), summarizing the then popular view, found the shaman to belong to a "psychological type" combining features of the severe hysteric and the schizophrenic (see also Silverman 1967).

This ecstatic component emphasized in Asian shamanism is largely absent in the behavior of American Indians assuming a shamanic type of healing role (Hultkrantz 1965, 1978; Luckert 1979:12). However, in his classic article, Devereux (1956) held the shaman to be always psychologically disturbed. He asked whether a "shamanistic and/or ethnic psychosis" is possibly the opening of an idiosyncratic psychosis, or (2) masks, "at the later stage," an underlying idiosyncratic psychosis, or (3) represents the terminal, restitutive manifestations of an idiosyncratic psychosis. Few detailed depth investigations exist of individuals during their accession of shamanship. In one of them, Day and Davidson (1976; Davidson and Day 1974), studying a Pilipina becoming a shaman, prefer Devereux's third category as an explanation of their specific instance.

Kroeber (1940) found not only shamans but the whole lay public of "primitive societies" to be involved in "curing" psychopathology and noted (p. 318) that "the psychopathologies that get rewarded among primitives are only the mild or transient ones," particularly of "the hysteric type, involving suggestibility or half-conscious volition. . . . The rewards seem to be reserved for individuals who can claim abnormal powers and controls, not for those *who are controlled*" (emphasis added). Kroeber's inference was clear, that the shaman is personally better organized and socially more effective, even though he shares some form of indigenous psychopathology. L. B. Boyer (1961, 1962, 1964c) agreed with Kroeber primarily on the basis of fieldwork with Apaches, which indicated that their shamans rarely if ever reintegrate after a serious psychological illness. A Rorschach study (Boyer, Klopfer, et al. 1964) demonstrated Apache shamans to be psychologically healthier than their culture mates. Some manifested the ability to use regression or primitive mental processes in the service of the ego and their social role, as has been found to be true of some artists (Kris 1952). The integrative capacities that allow them to adapt to society are considered socially useful and are sought after by others. The protocols of the Apache shamans varied widely in manifestations of creativity, liveliness, and relative presence of hysterical traits. The record of the one other shaman who was experiencing a life and professional crisis, as was Dawnlight, revealed perseverative qualities reminiscent of schizophrenia, but other responsive manifestations pointed instead to hysterical characterological features with oral and phallic fixations (Klopfer and Boyer 1961). This shaman also gave evidence of sexual identity confusion in his record—another feature we shall point to in the following protocols given by Dawnlight. The considerable psychological variability but general symbolic richness found in the Rorschachs of Apache shamans were similar to those found in a series of Okinawan shamans, collected by the late William Lebra and studied by De Vos but not reported on here. These women were not classifiable in any one personality category, and only a few suggested primitive thought disturbances.

Our present case, Dawnlight, gives some clinical evidence of having functioned previously with a more stable, perhaps more constricted personality pattern which decompensated somewhat under the stress of social circumstances. Some underlying weaknesses were exacerbated, and their partial resolution led to greater internal complexity. She was able to "compensate" through calling on available inner resources which could be directed toward a form of social integration that was strengthened or bolstered externally by the positive social expectations of her group. When there was strong social need for someone to take on the role of healer, Dawnlight succumbed to external expectations as well as internal pressures and took on the shaman's role.

Like other Apaches of the Mescalero Indian Reservation, Dawnlight believed that the shaman may use supernatural power at will either for culture-supporting purposes or in the service of witchcraft. She was also convinced that she might unintentionally harm her patients or others through her acquired power. She conceptualized herself as a parent of the group, with the capacity to be alternatively totally good or totally evil.

Dawnlight's record, like those of some other Apache shamans, revealed emotionally expressive content that was graphically symbolic in nature. Typically, Apache records are relatively bland and commonplace and their "psychopathology," if that term may be used, is most often expressed nonideationally by heightened emotional constriction (see chaps. 10 and 11). Dawnlight's protocol revealed that in the depth of her regression there was a resemblance to psychosis in a fashion similar to the shaman whose Rorschach was mentioned earlier (see Klopfer and Boyer 1961).

The record revealed possible repressed homosexuality and reflected also a conscious anxiety lest her internal "badness" prevail and cause her to become unintentionally a witch.

Apache Shamanism

In discussing the Rorschach records and Dawnlight we must refer to Apache beliefs about shamans and religiomedical philosophies and practices in a general social context.[5]

Although Dawnlight's position as a shaman and her possession of supernatural power appear to be strongly credited by members of her and her husband's extended families, some other Apache are less supportive. She herself may now be less certain of her shamanic capacity. Considered longitudinally, her second Rorschach protocol is much more constricted than the first; her psychological integration is less complex, perhaps less sound. We assume the relative reduction of integrity to be the result of overdetermined environmental and intrapsychic factors.

Her self-chosen idiosyncratic shamanic role was one that involved the transgression of a strong taboo, involving her assumption of a function traditionally performed only by men, and thereby the risk of putative supernatural or public censure. This risk still remains, although it now appears that an ancient and currently little-known Apache custom did provide a place in religiomedical practices for the assumption by a woman of a traditionally masculine function. This niche seemingly existed despite the fact that Apache custom did not provide an approved position for berdaches as was common among Plains Indians (Driver 1961; Lowie 1935). Interestingly enough, the homosexual conflict so apparent in Dawnlight's first record was absent in the more constrained second record. Instead there was a preoccupation with fear of incapacity and failure.

The basic concept of Apache religion is that of a vague, diffuse, supernatural power that pervades the universe and may enliven inanimate objects. To become effective, it must "work through" humankind. Inhabiting some animal, plant, natural object, or phenomenon, it will approach a human being when he or she is in an altered ego state, usually during a period of involuntary ordeal. If the person who has been approached accepts the power with its prescribed prayers, songs, and rituals, he is entitled to practice shamanism. As a shaman, he may use his supernatural power to intervene with powers or spirits who have been affronted by the actions of humans, or to counteract the malevolent efforts of witches and ghosts.[6] However, to "own" supernatural power is an awesome responsibility. While power has no intrinsic quality of good or evil, its human possessor may voluntarily use it for good (shamanic, culture-supporting) or for evil, witchcraft purposes. If he chooses witchcraft, his life and the lives of his family members are endangered. Additionally, since people are inherently both moral and immoral and sometimes perform actions involuntarily as well as think unbidden thoughts, those who own power might unwittingly use it for sinful purposes, thus inadvertently harming others or reaping personal supernatural retribution. Finally, the practicing healer and his family are vulnerable as a result of his shamanic activities. A power that has been especially affronted will demand a death. If the person who insulted it is cured due to shamanic intervention, the power will find a way to kill the curer himself or, if he chooses to deflect the vengeance onto one of his loved ones, that person will die. Inferentially, then, every shaman is also a witch.

Although in some Indian groups shamans perform ceremonies cooperatively, among these Apache each shaman owns his powers individually and acts alone. He fears that his powers might be stolen from him and is careful to guard against such theft by uttering only part of his prescribed ceremonies aloud when performing his rites. He is also afraid nonqualified listeners will be harmed by what they have taken in through their ears. Although members of other tribes could join forces in the Peyote religion (Gusinde 1939; Hollander 1935; La Barre 1938; Slotkin 1956), violence and murder resulted when these Apache sought to practice shamanism as teams, and peyote use among them was proscribed (Boyer, Boyer, and Basehart 1973; Opler 1936a).

The Apache have another set of individuals who possess supernatural power that is used in a culture-supporting way, ordinarily to alleviate problems confronting either the tribe as a whole or of small groups. These men are known in Chiricahua as ga^nheh, in Mescalero as *jajadeh*, and in English as Crown Dancers, Mountain Spirits, Masked Dancers, Devil Dancers, Horn Dancers, or Mountain God Dancers (Bourke 1892; Boyer 1964a, 1979a, 1979b; Boyer and Boyer 1983; Goddard 1916; Harrington 1912; Hoijer 1938; Kane 1937; Mails 1974; Opler 1941, 1946a). While both males and females may become shamans, in recorded times only men have been *jajadeh*.

The sacred dancers constitute an addition to Southern Athabascan religion which has diffused from the Pueblo Indians (Luckert 1979). They are "made" ga^nheh, mortals who represent the "true" underground supernaturals of the same name. Each team consists of at least six men: the singer or leader, four masked dancers, and one or more clowns. Ideally, the singer is approached by a "true" *jajadeh* while in an altered ego state and accepts the songs, rituals, and designs for a team of "made" Crown Dancers. Generally, the singership and thereby the ownership of a team is handed to a younger relative when the singer retires or is deemed to have become incompetent or immoral. If a shaman's solitary actions have been ineffective, Crown Dancers are sometimes hired to assist him in the cure of an individual. In the absence of a shaman, dancers alone may be employed.

Dawnlight's Acquisition of Shamanistic Status

Dawnlight, now a middle-aged woman, underwent typical Apache child-rearing experiences, and her life has followed the average expectable pattern for mature residents of the Mescalero Indian Reservation.[7] Since her mother and several other members of her extended family were shamans and her father owned the songs, ceremonies, and paraphernalia of a Crown Dance team, she was heavily exposed to traditional folklore and religiomedical philosophies and practices. Following the pattern of the great majority of modern young Apache, she lost her early interest in such matters, despite her knowledge that were she to pursue them, she was highly eligible to become a shaman. As a singularly beautiful teenager, she became interested almost solely in self-indulgence. She "stole" a handsome, hardworking man some dozen years her senior from his wife and children. Within a few months after they married, she and "Wide Eyes" had become drunkards. They remained so, living from hand to mouth in filth, for some fifteen years. She states, "We were just disgusting." As is true also for other Apaches (Freeman 1968), these Indians typically have a prolonged period of functional adolescence: many do not become responsible adults until they are of grandparental age (Boyer and Boyer 1976). After their marriage, Dawnlight and Wide Eyes gave up attendance at their childhood Christian churches, but soon after their oldest daughter had a baby, they joined an evangelistic, fundamentalist sect which forbade alcohol consumption and strongly censured involvement in native religious practices. As abruptly as they had become drunkards, they renounced drinking and became model citizens and parents. Just before Dawnlight first performed publicly as a shaman, she and Wide Eyes proudly celebrated fifteen years of teetotalism.

Wide Eyes, too, had come from a family steeped in traditional ways. When he and Dawnlight changed into responsible people, they turned strongly to old-time activities. Dawnlight became a proficient beadworker, much sought after as a seamstress of ceremonial costumes, tipis, and the like. She also turned her attention to native herbs, learning more about others' uses of them in addition to recalling her mother's practices. At first she used herbs only for members of her own nuclear family, but later her services were sought by members of her extended family. Indian music, live or recorded, was to be heard in their house at all hours of the day and night. Dawnlight and Wide Eyes gave no evidence that they were troubled by being involved both in such traditional pursuits and a Christian sect which strongly censured native religious practices.

As mentioned earlier, Dawnlight's father, "Smiles," had been the singer for a team of Crown Dancers, owning its ceremonies, songs, designs, and sacred paraphernalia. The singership had been owned by his mother's family for generations. The aged Smiles had earlier transferred the role to "James," one of his sons, after James, a recent grandparent, renounced insobriety.

Within a year after James became the singer, both of his and Dawnlight's parents died, and he quickly reverted to drunkenness. His performances were undependable and "shameful," and he stopped caring for the sacred paraphernalia, which became shoddy and filthy. The extended family members were concerned, fearing both supernatural retribution and loss of face. Although an older sister was living, she too was a drunkard, and Dawnlight held herself responsible for the welfare of her extended family. Accordingly, after her counseling and exhortations failed to rehabilitate James, she made an unusually courageous decision. Aboriginally, it was believed that if a female were even to *watch* as the singer painted and costumed the team's dancers before their holy performance, the "real" *jajadeh* would harm her. If she were to *handle* the sacred paraphernalia, she could expect serious retribution. In an illustrative story, a girl watched the painting and costuming and touched the "sword" and headdress; the following day she was found burned to a crisp in the ashes of the ceremonial fire around which the *ga^nheh* always dance. Nevertheless, after much trepidation, Dawnlight decided to take the paraphernalia under her own care, to clean and repair them, and to return them to James only when he became morally responsible once again.

When James did not improve, Dawnlight and other family members prevailed upon him to transfer the singership to his son "John," although the latter was only a little more than thirty years old. About a year after he handed down the singership to John, James died in an accident associated with drinking, and soon thereafter the older sister was murdered in a drunken brawl.

As mentioned earlier, Dawnlight's use of native herbs had increased following her renunciation of alcohol. For some years she had remembered having watched in girlhood her Lipan Apache mother's use of Lightning Power in a ceremony to cure a "paralyzed" woman. However, it had not occurred to her that she would ever believe herself to possess any supernatural power except perhaps that inherent in the prayers to the spirits of the herbs.

Following an injury, Wide Eyes suffered debilitating osteo-arthritis of one knee. He underwent several fruitless curing ceremonies and received much Western medical care without effect. He had much pain, always used a cane or crutches, and was "paralyzed." About six weeks following the death of her older sister, Dawnlight, probably remembering that the handling of the Crown Dance paraphernalia had not resulted in "bad luck," used her mother's "Lightning and Turtle Medicine" ceremony in an attempt to cure Wide Eyes.[8] The effort was remarkably successful.

During the next year, many misfortunes befell members of Dawnlight's extended family. In the most disastrous event, "Navaho Man," her paternal cousin and a shaman, suffered spastic quadriplegia as a result of a broken neck and was confined to a wheelchair. After each unfortunate occurrence affecting some family member, Dawnlight suffered episodes of anxiety that included apprehension of attack by unknown people or agents. We may assume that on some level of consciousness she feared that the unfortunate events were the result of supernatural retribution because of her transgression of the taboo against handling the sacred regalia or her practice of shamanism without first having had a "power dream." Dawnlight received transitory relief from her anxiety attacks through ceremonies conducted by local shamans. However, her reaction to Navaho Man's calamity was deeper and prolonged. It was finally relieved through the ministrations of a famous shaman in a distant pueblo. After he obtained sufficient autobiographical data from Dawnlight, he effected a cure by explaining to her that her extended family was being hexed by a powerful but unidentified witch who had been hired by Apache envious of her and Wide Eyes because the couple had been able to renounce drunkenness and become highly successful in traditional ways.[9] The astute shaman had supported Dawnlight's own defensive posture.

With the death of her sister, Dawnlight became the oldest member of the extended family and as such was accorded much respect. After she handled the sacred paraphernalia without incurring supernatural retribution and also successfully treated Wide Eyes' "paralysis," she received increasing esteem and was in constant demand as a counselor.

Soon John and Dawnlight developed a relationship which has been unrecorded and not disclosed previously to the Boyers. John's dance team was respected and hired frequently for the purposes which are usual for the Crown Dancers. Additionally, the team came to be employed to assist shamans whose previous ministrations had not effected cures.[10] Before the team danced on such occasions, John regularly consulted Dawnlight. He sought and received advice from her regarding diagnoses and modifications of ceremonies. Inferentially, he thus added her power to that of the shaman in charge while he also effectively made her into a consultant singer, and had her assume a masculine ceremonial role. Tribal members began to say that Dawnlight was the "power behind" the team; some even postulated that she actually owned the team.

Then Dawnlight had an experience which she retrospectively interpreted to be a power dream. Sometime following Navaho Man's tragic accident, she began to think that she would soon need to use the Lightning Medicine ceremony once again. Accordingly she obtained coals from a tree which had been struck by lightning. Then she dreamed that John came to her, recounting a dream of his own and seeking its interpretation.[11] In the first part of the dream within her dream, which she ascribed to John, a Crown Dance team were the protagonists. The team consisted of four shamans, including her father, and a clown. They went in tandem to the sacred fire and blessed it, the clown going last, as usual. In the second part of the dream, the clown went first to the fire and blessed it, being followed by the other members of the team. Dawnlight "knew" she had had a power dream when soon thereafter in reality John came to her, first telling her that he and his dance team had been requested to perform a ceremony for Navaho Man and then recounting a dream of his own which was identical to the dream within her dream. Dawnlight interpreted his dream to be a supernatural message which prescribed the actions of the dance team during the forthcoming ceremony, directing John to conduct it in a manner which constituted an unrecorded departure from the usual pattern and one new to the Boyers, in which the *clown* was to lead the dancers and be the first individual to bless the fire and the sufferer, Navaho Man.

After John had consulted Dawnlight and she had interpreted his dream, her and Wide Eyes' extended families expected *her* to take charge of the planning and conduct of the curing ceremony, and she did so. During the rite, the clown did indeed lead the dancers and first bless the fire and Navaho Man. The ceremony was the most solemn, peaceful, and beautiful the Boyers have ever attended. As far as they could observe, no participant or audience member entered an altered ego state.[12]

In light of the Rorschach protocol to follow, Dawnlight's spontaneous associations two days after the ceremony are highly relevant. She was eager to talk about the ceremony and its implications for her and invited the Boyers to her house for that purpose.[13]

After the amenities, Dawnlight talked immediately of her fear of witchcraft and of the duplicity of witches who, motivated by jealousy, pretended to be friendly but secretly sought to do harm. Her illustrative story depicted the actions of a witch who was part of the audience at the puberty ceremony of one of Dawnlight's daughters and, although smiling and offering assistance, really wanted to harm that daughter.[14] Later, while talking of witchcraft Dawnlight spoke of a previously unrecorded and perhaps idiosyncratically derived means whereby one might become a witch: by smelling the corpse of a witch, inspiring and incorporating his or her evil. This apparently new idea is a logical extension of the Apache view that witchcraft is accomplished through the invisible shooting of arrows, which have been tipped with tiny pieces of human cadavers or other offal, into intended victims. The arrows may be sucked or grabbed out of a sufferer from witchcraft by a shaman.[15]

There are psychological resemblances between the puberty ceremony and Dawnlight's debut as a shaman. The basic function of the ceremony is to assist a nubile maiden to become a moral woman, who will take responsible care of her future family (Opler 1941:82–134); Dawnlight's first public shamanic performance constituted a statement that she deemed herself responsible for the welfare of her extended family. The maiden is assisted by supernatural power through the mediation of her singer and her sponsor; Dawnlight was helped by supernatural power that she had come to possess. It is likely that in her complex transference relationship with the Boyers, she viewed them as her singer and sponsor. She was very eager to impart to them all her recently acquired ideas, to describe her behavior, and gain their blessing and support.

After talking of witches and their dangers, Dawnlight turned to the subject of death. She recounted a previously unreported means of avoiding ghost sickness, that of throwing the soles of the deceased person's shoes into his grave. She said the action was intended to give the soul of the dead individual easier access into the promised land and thereby diminish its resentfulness or loneliness, so that it would not be so likely to seek vengeance on loved ones or be lonely for them, and therefore less likely to drive them mad and cause them to commit suicide or act foolishly and be killed. The Boyers have attended many funerals and have never observed this action; no other informant has mentioned it. This may be yet another idiosyncratic idea introduced by this highly imaginative woman which may later come to be an accepted part of Apache folklore as a result of her shamanic authority (Opler 1946b). The homophony of "sole" and "soul" can scarcely be ignored. The two words in Apache have no similar homophony, but Dawnlight thought equally well in either English or Mescalero.

In her spontaneous progression of associations, Dawnlight then spoke of her physical reactions following the curing ceremony for Navaho Man. Her arms had become so stiff she could scarcely move them, and only after a long period of massage and exercise could she use them easily once again. She said she had taken Navaho Man's stiffness into her and because of that, she was even more certain that his spastic paralysis would be cured. It will be recalled that in the cure of an individual who has been bewitched, the shaman may suck or grab out the witch's arrow which has caused the illness or misfortune.

Next, Dawnlight turned to the subject of parental transmission of their own good or evil aspects to their children. She and Wide Eyes had had four children while they were still "disgusting" drunkards and each child had turned out badly, having predominantly immoral, irresponsible, and "mean" aspects. On the contrary, the three children born after their parents' renunciation of alcohol were thoughtful, loving, gentle, and good. Although she used different words to express herself, Dawnlight's explanation for this phenomenon was that children incorporate the parental model offered to them. As we shall see from her first Rorschach protocol, obtained immediately after she had expressed these thoughts, Dawnlight is cognizant of a fear that she might as a shaman transmit evil as well as good to others, as she believed she had done as a parent. Her conceptualization of the shaman/witch duality was clearly that of the mother who would be viewed alternately by her baby and herself as totally good or totally bad.

The Symbolic Analysis of Dawnlight's Protocols

The following is in outstanding example of how symbolism on the Rorschach can be helpful in understanding underlying attitudes as well as reflecting the structural dynamics of an individual's personality. Dawnlight reveals an exceptional intelligence, a very strong motivation for personal achievement, a vital active personality; but more than anything else, through a rather open, direct symbolic expression with content directly derivative from her culture, she presents both the positive and negative aspects of being invested with the power of a shaman.

The affective scoring of Dawnlight's first record permits some generalizations as to how she functions as an individual in comparison with usual group norms. In Dawnlight's case, she uses relatively less hostile content than the general norm (Hostility = 4%), whereas her anxiety content (36%) and bodily preoccupation (14%) are higher than normative expectations. The total (54%) of unpleasant affect is significantly higher than that so far found generally in nonclinical groups (see chap. 3). At the same time that she gives such a high percentage of negatively weighted content, she produces affectively toned symbolic material suggesting a positive social adaptation. She has a total of 10% dependency responses and 14% positive content for a combined total of dependent and positive material of 24%, which is higher than the usual norms and a direct counterindication to possible social withdrawal or manifest maladjustive symptomatology. Her Rorschach protocol, in sum, is a very rich, affectively open record in which we find both more positive and more negative material than is the general expectancy. The fact that there is a balance in symbolic content is counterindicative to a direct pathological interpretation of her negative, regressively toned symbolic material. We have found in the past that it is most infrequent that any such large percentage of positive symbolic material is given by individuals classified as either schizophrenic or neurotic.

Cultural referents are taken into account in the scoring of the material in addition to more universal psychodynamic considerations. For example, an owl in the Apache Rorschach context suggests a special meaning of disaster, since we know that the owl is seen by the Apache as a threat of death.[16] A response of an owl given by another Native American may not have the same threatening implications.

The First Rorschach

Card I:
(90″ pause)

1. *A design of a dancer, a Crown Dancer.* (He's dancing; the darkness, the shading is important.)

D_2 FY+ M + H (Drel, Daut, Prec, Athr, Porn)

2. *Crown Dancer. His face, bending down.* (His face is covered with a mask.)

Dd FY− H (Drel, Daut, Athr, Porn)

3. *Crocodile.* (The shape of it and the shading)

D_1 FY+ A (Hor)

4. *Tailbone, with the anus.* (Of the crocodile. I can't see the parts between.)

Dd FY− Ad (Ban) (arbitrary)

(120″ pause)

5. *Bat Wings.* (Flying. Black and the shading)

D FM_a FY FC′ + Ad (Athr)

6. *Teddy bear, its face.* (Furry and the eyes)

Dd FT+ A (Acnph, Pch Aobs)

Commentary.   On Card I we find the major themes that are to characterize this record throughout—themes of a positive and negative nature related to power and witchcraft. The Crown Dancer is a symbol of social control with both positive and negative features. Seen religiously, the Crown Dancer represents communal authority, but it is also a threatening figure to participants in ceremonies. To children, it is especially awesome. Seen secularly, the response has both esthetic and recreational aspects. It is, therefore, from the standpoint of its symbolic implications, very complex. Dawnlight's second response is again a Crown Dancer but with emphasis on his mask. The mask on the Rorschach is very often seen in the context of some implied threat. Should the response show preoccupation with eyes as well as masks, we infer obsessional, even paranoid, features to be present in the respondent.

Dawnlight's third response is to an area very often seen as that of a naked human body, usually a woman. She sees a crocodile, an oral aggressive response. Note that this early theme—hostile, threatening orality—is not a usual feature of this record and that it drops out as an important concern in her protocol.

The next response, the anus and tailbone, is more characteristic of Dawnlight's later preoccupations. The small area on the top of the card evokes for her the shape of buttocks. This type of response will appear again on Card III, where she again gives anal and sexual material. Here on Card I, therefore, is the first indication of what appears later and more directly as concern with the disavowed, which has homosexual implications. As communicated in her associations to L. B. Boyer during the course of the Rorschach, Dawnlight directly in her conscious thoughts related anal concerns and homosexuality to individuals practicing witchcraft. It is interesting to observe that similarly disavowed anal and homosexual material in the Middle Ages in Europe was also directly related to beliefs about the practice of witchcraft. The association of witchcraft, homosexuality, and anal preoccupation is also common in other cultures (Bogoras 1907; Czaplicka 1914; Eliade 1951; Housse 1939; Maestas and Anaya 1982; Parin-Matthèy 1971; Poole 1981).

The fifth response, the bat wings, is not to the whole area of the blot, which is the usual response to this card. Dawnlight picks out instead only a specific part. Had she seen the more usual bat, one would tend to consider it a more neutral type of response prompted by the suggestive shape of the entire blot, but since she goes to some trouble to pick out an unusual area, we must code the response as suggestive of a more threatening meaning. In Apache folklore the bat serves a dual role, a projection of both good and bad maternal images (L. B. Boyer 1979a, chap. 6; R. M. Boyer and L. B. Boyer 1981). The final response to the card, a teddy bear, is an affective reversal in that it suggests childlike innocence—a stuffed animal that is harmless, even comforting. At the same time one must note that it is in a seldom-used area and that she emphasizes the eyes as a small, rare detail. This response and the previous mask are obsessional-type responses of which one finds other examples in the following cards. "Bear" is one of the most irascible of the "powers" of these Apache, a fact that makes us even more aware of the counterphobic nature of the teddy-bear response.

After looking at the entire record one may also comment upon Dawnlight's responses to this card. Her very first response is that of the Crown Dancer, a ritual figure with both positive and negative aspects. Her preoccupation with anal-sexual material is repeated later. Another repetitive theme is that of a response suggesting threat followed by some kind of counterphobic reassurance—benign percepts replacing the possibility of threat, as in the use of the teddy bear. This defensive maneuver is an ability that she uses with great success throughout her record. This first card, therefore, evokes the internal ambivalences associated with the assumption of power as a shaman as well as suggesting the socially adaptive, integrative capacity to remain in good contact with her social group. Compared with most Athabascan and other American Indian protocols, this record is exceedingly rich and highly symbolic.[17] More characteristic for Native Americans' records are rather matter-of-fact, concrete protocols that give evidence of a good sense of reality testing but provide very little symbolic elaboration.

Card II. (30″ pause)

1. *Faces on totem poles.* (Looking some way. The color is important.) D_2 FC+ Rel Art (Aobs, Porn, Drel)

(120″ pause)

2. *Bears dance. Like in a   D$_3$ FM+ A P (Drel)
story.* [She refers to a story she
and her husband had told L.B.B.
earlier, having to do with Bear
Power and its magical connotations.] (Just the shape)

(30″ pause)

3. *Deer face.* (The shape and   Dd FY− Ad (Aobs)
the shading)

(60″ pause)

4. *Somebody sad, crying. The   D$_1$ Fm− Hd (Aobs, Agl)
tears are running down. Just her
face.* (You can see the tears running down.)

[Holding card with arm fully
extended.]

5. *Flying butterfly or moth.* (It   D$_1$ FM FC+ A P (Acnph,
is colorful.)   Pnat)

6. *From close up. A sheep*   (Aobs)
face. [Could not relocate]

Commentary.   The first response to Card II is a fairly curious
one. Totem poles are as esoteric to Apache as to whites and have
no traditional religious meaning within Apache culture. However, today a totem pole may be a somewhat indirect indication
of a pan-Indian identity. Note, nevertheless, that it is the faces on
the totem poles that are important to her. Faces and eyes are a
continuing theme in her record.

The second response is a fairly popular response to this card,
but for Dawnlight it has specific associations: The Bear Dance is
related to Bear Power and its magical connotations.

The third and fourth responses repeat her obsessional concern
with faces. Note that the fourth response is that of a crying face,
indicating concern with sadness. Among these faces she inter-
sperses a butterfly, which is a positive response. A final obsessional sheep's face was not relocated later in the inquiry, so the
last acknowledged percept is a colorful butterfly.

Card III. (24″ pause)

1. *The figure of a lady, pregnant. Her stomach is up top.* [Indicates the white area above the figures.] *The pelvis and the baby, two babies.* (It's the inside of a woman's body, bearing twins.) [During the inquiry she changed the location of the stomach from the white area to the red of D_2. The red D_1 remained the pelvis, although she also used D_3 as a pelvis and used D_4 as the babies.]

WS FC− H Anat Sex (Arbitrary)(Bch)

Commentary. The first response to Card III shows a loss of reality testing. It is what might be considered a psychotic-type response. The form has some reality but the assembly of parts is unreal. She produces an incipient childbirth concept, seeing the entire card as the insides of a woman pregnant with two babies. There is an arbitrary nature to what is seen inside; the location of the percept of the pelvis is moved from the center red area to that of the outside black area during the course of the inquiry, when she seeks to describe how and to what she responded in the initial free association. The "stomach" also does not hold its initial position as she later attempts to justify her perception. Nonpsychotic people rarely respond to Card III as a representation of pregnancy and childbirth. Note that contrary to Dawnlight's responses to the previous card, she does not attempt to give a second response but remains fixed on the entire card as representing pregnancy. As will be seen, subsequent responses deal with childbirth directly. From Card III on, she shifts her style to one that focuses on the total blot area, whereas in the first two cards she picked up some rare details and gave responses to separate specific regions of the cards. From Card III on she takes a different approach, which emphasizes attempts at an integration of the entire card area, at least for the first response.

Card IV.

(Her arm is extended; 30″ pause)

1. *The backbone of some animal.* (Looking down on the furry animal's back from the top) W FT+ Ad P (Neut)

(60″ pause)

2. *A Crown Dancer.* (Dancing. In his mask) W FT M+ H Rel (Daut, Athr, Porn)

Commentary.   In Card IV she first sees the entire card as a furry animal's back from the top, being highly responsive to the texture of this card and suggesting a social sensitivity. The Crown Dancer on Card IV is well perceived, repeating the theme of Card I. This card, often symbolic of the oppressive dominance of masculine authority, is handled without stress and with a socially adaptive symbol.

Card V.

1. *Grasshopper, flying.* W FM+ A (Athr)

2. *Bat with webbed wings.* W FC′ M+ A P (Neut) (Black, flying, furry)

(60″ pause)

3. *Something else flies.* (A black owl) W FC′− FM A (Athr)

Commentary.   On Card V she picks up the most frequently perceived bat, but she also supplies two alternate responses. Her very first response is that of a flying grasshopper, and the third of a black owl. It must be noted that the Apache are worried about grasshoppers, since at times they have been literally plagued with them, and as a matter of fact, at the time of the test there was a grasshopper invasion of the area. Note also that the owl heralds death in Apache thinking. These are therefore symbols of threat and anxiety.

Card VI. (30″ pause)

1. *It was folded up, but I'm only seeing half.* It's some design. [Unable to amplify.] W Card description (Aev)

(180″ pause)

2. *Plumes with feathers*. [She means they are feathers such as are worn in Indian headdresses during ceremonial but not necessarily religious dances. They are unrelated to the Crown Dancers. At this time she told a story in which an Indian used a feather from a headdress to guide a tornado away from his property and over the hill to destroy a city.]

D_5 FT+ Aobj (Drel, Porn, Acnph)

(Rotated for 60″)

3. *Rawhide*. (The smooth side)

W FT+ Aobj P (Ps, Acnph, Aobs)

(30″ pause)

4. *Some crawling creature. Eyes at sides. It's turned away to see.*

D_3 FY+ A (Acnph)

Commentary.   Her first response to Card VI is intellectual and evasive. She says it is a design but cannot elaborate. Her second response, "plumes with feathers," she associates to the feathers worn in Indian headdresses during dances which may be ceremonial, and then tells L.B.B. a story in which an Indian uses a headdress feather to guide a tornado away. In scoring the feather for its symbolic content, we note religious and ornamental value but also that the story suggests a counterphobic theme in which the feather is used magically to deflect a threat. It must be remarked that Card VI is commonly considered to have phallic content and that while she uses the phallic area first as noted above, she then veers away from such implications, saying that it consists of a crawling creature with its eyes turned away to the side. Clearly, the phallic area disturbed her, and we may suspect that her own phallic strivings make her anxious.

It may be, too, that inasmuch as the destroyed city of the story was a white man's city, her feelings for L.B.B., the recently discharged family shaman, were ambivalent at the time. Part of her interpolated response may have been determined by suppressed or repressed hostility toward him.

Card VII. (60″ pause)

1. *It's two women, one with a*   W M+ H [Sex]
black mouth, talking dirty. She's   P (Arbitrary)(Asex, Athr,
a witch and the other woman is   Drel, Bso)
afraid of her. The witch's breast is
down there. [At this time she told
a story of a female witch who
made a witch of another woman
by dancing naked with her.] (The
women are turned away from
each other, although they are
looking at each other.)

Commentary. Card VII gives us unusually direct material. Although the overall perception of dancing women is common, Dawnlight responds atypically by locating a witch's breast on a part of the blot that is usually perceived as a buttock area.[18] In this card she is making direct reference to an activity which she describes in other associations as being of a homosexual nature and related to witchcraft: two women dancing together. Being a shaman allows for some sex-role reversal in many regions of the world. The Apache female shaman whom she pictures as involved in homosexual relations is seen as the dominant or "male" partner in such a relationship. Perhaps Dawnlight's Crown Dancer responses reflect both her unconscious wish for and fear of the assumption of masculine powers. We may presume that a major psychological problem with which she is dealing at this time is how to handle the hostile homosexual impulses related to her supernatural power.[19] She projects her homosexual and aggressive wishes and fears of victimization. At the time of the Rorschach administration she was convinced that she and her extended family were being victimized by witchcraft, and was also afraid that her supernatural power might not be adequate to protect her family and herself. At the same time, she counterphobically challenged an unknown witch who had caused another shaman, Dawnlight's cousin, to become quadriplegic in an accident, despite his shaman's power and the power ascribed to L.B.B. as the family shaman. We see also in some of the responses a paranoid quality which may indicate that Dawnlight's ideation is an alternative to the breakthrough into consciousness of a direct homosexual wish to be victimized and thereby to passively obtain the witch's means of dealing powerfully and relatively safely with internal, omnipotently destructive self-representation. One must see that the assumption of the shaman's role exacerbates and heightens underlying homosexual anxiety. Locating a breast in the region of the buttocks suggests ambivalence about whether women are generative and nurturant or, conversely, poisonous and destructive. Many authors have suggested that witches are societally sanctioned projections of the "bad mother" introject (Hippler, 1971; Parin, 1971). The supernatural power Dawnlight has gained is obviously perceived by her to be a two-edged sword which may threaten her with certain inner potentials that she has not had to face previously.

Card VIII.

1. *These colors mean the day.*   W C symb FM+ A Anat P
The gray is the dawn, then morn-   O+ (Pnat)
ing, then evening and dusk. Some
animal travels during the day.
What is it? The animal gets ahold
of the day in the morning—you
can see the hand—and lets it go
during the night. The foot is
down there.

Commentary. After the disturbing material of Card VII, Card VIII appears as a poetic, symbolic liberating response. It is a beautifully organized representation of the integrated use of nature. It is very idiosyncratic among American Indians to find this type of symbolic response given to the Rorschach. The colors are directly, consciously symbolic. She sees the day as being traversed by animals from grey dawn to red "dusk." The Boyers know of no folktales that would be the source of this poetic thought. The response seems to be totally original, a poetic creation of Dawnlight. Following the difficulties and anxious implications of the previous cards, color and its underlying affectivity come as a relief. It is indicative of her sense of reality and her social adaptation that she is able to integrate both the common

percepts of the animals which are popularly seen on the sides of
this card and the varying colors in a type of response which is only
possible for a person of high intelligence with a capacity for constructive creativity. We find a graphic example of the counter-
balancing which goes on in the entire record between the negative
and positive content. In her artistic use of primary process thinking, one finds, therefore, constructive positive features as well as
fears of the disavowed and the destructive.

Card IX.

1. *Three colors, green in the*   W C naming (Aev)
middle. (120″ pause) A difficult
one. The colors make the differ-
ence. Green, red, orange.

2. *It's a picture of childbirth.*   W FT Fm− Hd Anat Sex
The baby is borning. The   (Anat, Bch, Bs)
woman's behind, the I-don't-
know-what-you-call-it-in English.
And part of the blood. [Means
the vagina and womb combined.]

Commentary.   Dawnlight first reacts to Card IX with intellectual evasiveness, naming the colors rather than giving a true response. Then she repeats her affective reaction to Card III. The
symbolism of childbirth and generativity are given again, but in
this instance the content is not handled with the intellectual disruption of the previous response. There is no disorganized shifting of the contents of her percepts. We remember that in becoming a shaman, she saw herself as the "parent" of her people.

Card X.

1. *Oh, my lord, it's beautiful.*   W FC Fm− Anat
Blue, gray, colors all over and   (Bs, Hha, Bch)
all connected to the red part, ex-
cept the orange. What's the red
part? It's a woman's body. Emit-
ting her parts all over, giving

good things to others and afraid she's giving bad parts too. [By woman's body means vagina and uterus. She said she excluded the orange area because it reminded her of a scrotum, full of seeds. She then spoke of how one's children might turn out badly, becoming irresponsible, immoral, and, in at least one case, dangerous and possibly murderous. She then shifted to talking about shamanism and how a medicine woman feared that her medicines and ceremonies might cause not only good but evil for others and maybe herself.]

2. *Baby's face, with a big eye.*

3. *Rabbit.* (Its head)

4. *A woman's tailbone. It's connected with witchcraft.* [At this time she told the story describing how a person can become a witch through smelling the corpse of a witch, by "inspiration."]

D F− Hd (Df, Aobs)

D₇ F+ Ad P (Neut)

D₈ F− Anat Sex (Asex, Drel, Bdi)

Commentary. On Card X she responded with positive enthusiasm, expressed through thinking that was heavily influenced by the primary process. The woman's body is "emitting her parts all over, giving good things to others," but the woman is afraid she is giving bad things too. A baby's face is found, and then a rabbit, and then the last response, in which a woman's tailbone represents the final anxiety about the witchcraft temptations connected with the role of shaman. Dawnlight tells L.B.B. an accompanying story illustrating how a person can become a witch through smelling the corpse of a witch, "inspiring," literally, the evil aura. Again she refers to women who dance naked together as being witches. It is interesting that she leaves out an orange part, in the center, because it reminds her of something male—a scrotum full of seeds. There is a rejection of any male generativity in her concept of herself.

All of Card X becomes a mystical representation of the role of the female shaman with its positive and negative features. This style of primary process thinking does not give everyone direct cultural license, but given the context of Dawnlight's having assumed the shaman's role there is specific license for regression in the service of the ego. Dawnlight is attempting to master an internal crisis which involves direct regressive welling up of unconscious material. At the same time, this threatening material is socially contained and positively expressed through her ritual practice rather than representing a private retreat into some form of psychosis. Records with "generativity" responses such as rebirth, eggs, and an unfolding of inchoate forces are not infrequent among individuals classified as acute catatonic schizophrenics. In Dawnlight, however, there is no attendant manifest retreat from social adaptation nor any indication in her daily life that she has been overwhelmed by the content of her unconscious.

Dawnlight has summarized for us on her last cards a meaning of shamanism that has not, to our knowledge, been recorded previously. She specifically equates the power of female generativity and its possible evil consequences with her shamanic role.[20] She is obviously fearful of her own evil potential that unconsciously involves homosexuality. She is afraid that her power will come back to harm her as well as others if she does not keep careful control over it. It is noteworthy that symbolically she leaves the record almost where she started with some anal implications—and that in her subsequent free association she mentioned one specific way of becoming a witch: that of smelling a decaying corpse. One may, of course, inadvertently become a witch through no desire of one's own. But the dancing together of naked women is certainly an intentional act, one in which one woman may sexually seduce another into the practice of witchcraft.

If this protocol is summarized in accord with standard Rorschach scoring, Dawnlight reveals an intellectual approach that shifts after the first two cards. She starts out selecting details, even rarely used areas, manifesting an initial inhibition which is overcome by Card III. Most subsequent responses are to the entire blot area (W% = 45). This latter approach suggests that she is ambitious, committed to tasks even beyond her capacity. She can overcome an initial constrictive anxiety; she can expand her perceptions to holistic imaginative concepts. She is fanciful and original, even idiosyncratic. There are moments of failure. On first looking at Cards VI and IX she again becomes constrictive and cannot give more than a description of the blot, without true content. Her use of enriched determinants of shading (FY = 7, FC' = 1, FT = 4) and the ratio of color and movement responses suggest an unusual responsiveness to her social environment (M = 3, FC = 8). Her use of color and shading throughout the record suggests a quick emotional responsiveness, but the balance is passive in that continued attention to the shading (FY = 7, FC' = 1) and texture (FT = 4) suggest wariness and sensitivity and a continual tendency to anxiety. Her inner life shows tensions and immaturity (M = 3, FM = 4), but it is strongly directed toward role responsibilities as represented in the human content of the Rorschach. The overall form level of her responses (F+ = 66%) is low. Only three of her twenty responses utilize pure form, suggesting a person swept up by her inner processes to the extent of endangering her grasp of reality. She produces seven popular responses in the midst of others of poor form that suggest autistic proclivities. Thus one presumes that there is a continual awareness and a need to return from her own preoccupations to sharing the perceptions of her ordinary social world. Although potentially imaginative, she does not extend her interests out into a wider realm (A% = 51). There can be a banality in her thought as well as an intense preoccupation with inner tensions.

The Boyers' behavioral observation would indicate that whatever the internal crisis being expressed symbolically on the Rorschach, certain other reintegrative social processes are also at work. Homosexuality for the Apache specifically implies witchcraft, whereas some other cultures in which homosexual shamans are tolerated do not at the same time imply that the homosexual person is necessarily a witch. Being a shaman gives license for sex role reversal in many regions of the world (Eliade 1951). However, there is no indication that Dawnlight is consciously using the role for purposes of sexual inversion. Note well how responsible she feels for the paraphernalia of the Crown Dancer, a masculine role, but she tries to stay away from assuming too direct a participation with these materials. She, as best she can, tries to keep to her role as woman.

We observe that there are certain areas of paranoid ideation going on, but again these are socially and culurally condoned. Dawnlight is convinced that she and her extended family are being victimized by witchcraft, and at some level she is worried about this. What seems to be occurring here is a projection of homosexual wishes into a fear of victimization triggered at least in part by several tragic events. On a personal level, these can be seen as possible paranoid fantasies; on a social level they are so well accepted and well defined that they draw no attention to her.

She counterphobically undertakes to battle a witch who is so powerful that she or he caused another shaman, Dawnlight's relative, to get a broken neck and become a quadriplegic. The degree to which Dawnlight is threatened by her own homosexual strivings determines the degree to which she is paranoid, according to Freud's classical concept (Freud 1911). While she may assume the shamanistic role defensively, the assumption of the role itself heightens her homosexual anxiety. While the culture allows for certain paranoid beliefs to be institutionalized, the Rorschach protocol suggests that paranoid defensiveness may be exacerbated by the possibility of having supernatural power. We may well ask how a person can continue in the social role of shaman should her magical desire to cure not be realized in particular cases.

The system itself perhaps, with its emphasis on the duality of power, the duality of good and evil, helps explain failure as well as create illusions of success. Since the system of belief has within it methods of avoiding failure, shamans can continue to believe in themselves. There is one concern, however, within this particular person which one will have to watch over the long run. Dawnlight had been precipitated into becoming a shaman by an ardent desire to cure a quadriplegic family member whose obvious physical problems did not lend themselves to the possibility of psychological cure. Opler (1936b) and Boyer (1964a) have observed that most shamans are careful to direct their attention to the types of problems which may be defined physically but in actuality are usually of psychological origin. Dawnlight had taken on a problem which could not be resolved by shifts of a psychotherapeutic nature. Only the future will disclose how the situation will be resolved and explained in Apache as well as in personal terms.[21]

Two Years Later

In the two years that followed, Wide Eyes' recovery from his painful knee affliction, his "paralysis," was maintained. However, Navaho Man's quadriplegia remained unchanged. Nevertheless, the curing ceremony at which Dawnlight made her public debut was considered successful by all the members of Dawnlight's and Wide Eyes' extended families. Their wholehearted belief in her possession of supernatural power had led them subsequently to seek her shamanic assistance for various problems, and they were well satisfied with the results of her ministrations. Other Apache were skeptical, disbelieving that Navaho Man would eventually recover. Opler (1936b) noted that Apache custom provided many loopholes which could be used by shamans to explain their failures, and commented that wise shamans usually avoided assuming the responsibility of treating either the chronically insane or the physically incurable. Dawnlight was thought to have been foolish to have undertaken the cure of a quadriplegic, but she also had potential loopholes. (1) Navaho Man had previously undergone curing ceremonies by renowned shamans from other tribes. If their ministrations were ineffective, at worst she was no less powerful than they. (2) Navaho Man had been an immoral shaman, and his supernatural powers might have been so affronted that they would not be mollified by the intervention of another shaman. (3) A very powerful unidentified witch, probably a member of some other tribe, was believed to have been hired by jealous Apache who wanted to harm Dawnlight, now the oldest member of her extended family, by harming an important member of that family. Until that witch could be identified and his or her hex counteracted, no cure could be expected. (4) It might appear that Navaho Man's recovery was at best slow, but that did not obviate the certainty that cure was imminent.

Dawnlight had not become a shaman of the usual kind. On her own she never performed ceremonies for the treatment of individuals. Although she had been a relatively sophisticated Apache herbalist before she assumed the shamanic role, she had renounced the use of native medicines. She never used her supernatural power except in conjunction with John's Crown Dance team. She explained this specific choice of a shamanic role by expressing the fear that if she treated individuals unassisted, she might inadvertently do something wrong which would result in supernaturally determined harm to her family or herself.

Dawnlight limited her shamanic activities to being what she called John's "aide." John consulted her before leading his dance team for any function, whether directed to the welfare of the tribe as a whole or to that of families or individuals. She advised him as to the optimal conduct of a wide variety of ceremonies, including dedications of public buildings both on and off the reservation, dancing for maidens at their puberty ceremonies, seeking to reduce marital discord, and cures of afflicted individuals. He continued to request assistance as he had done before. After she had a dream within a dream, John brought a matching dream of his own which she interpreted in terms of its prescription for a proposed ceremony. Dawnlight was the periodic custodian of the dance team paraphernalia, keeping them clean and repaired. She attended and quietly supervised each dance team ceremony.

Apaches try to believe that they can fool the supernaturals. Thus, they assume that both mortals and supernaturals will be envious or jealous if they have a beautiful child, and proclaim a particularly healthy and handsome baby to be ugly, to avoid having the child harmed or stolen. They share widespread beliefs about the evil eye (Róheim 1952; Servadio 1936; Vereecken 1928). Dawnlight's fear of being a shaman is reflected in her claim to be but an "aide," to deny that she is practicing shamanism while she is obviously doing not only that but leading a Crown Dance team, that is, assuming masculine powers. She hides behind the presumed omnipotent protection of John, the father surrogate who quite literally took over her father's magical powers. One of the major psychological problems resultant from Apache socialization is that of sibling rivalry. Dawnlight has achieved a resolution of this problem that, though acceptable to other people, still leaves her feeling insecure.

Dawnlight appeared to be less certain than she had been two years previously of her possession of supernatural power and of her shamanic capacity. Her protestations that Navaho Man had improved were too vehement and defensive, and she was reticent to discuss her activities and share her ideas with the Boyers, in contrast with her previous spontaneous eagerness. She was clearly conflicted. At the same time, though she sought to project onto them her self-accusations of incompetency if not chicanery, her reality-testing capacity kept her aware that they remained her noncritical friends.

Until our field trip in 1983, we believed that Dawnlight had assumed a totally idiosyncratic shamanic role: to our knowledge it is unrecorded, and we had not heard of anything resembling it in twenty-five years of gathering data pertaining to Apache religiomedical practices and philosophies. It is a role which is also unusual in that it entails a woman's challenge of taboos pertaining to powerful roles traditionally restricted to men.

In 1981, every Apache with whom the Boyers spoke agreed that the shamanic role assumed by Dawnlight was idiosyncratic and that there had been no historical precedent for it. Fears were expressed by others as well as Dawnlight that her choice of that role might lead to harm to herself or her family. By 1983, her assumption of that role appeared to have been accepted, and such fears were no longer expressed by her culture mates. Now Dawnlight said that as John's "aide" she was performing a traditional role in which a female relative of a somewhat undependable singer assumed the advisory function of the clown to him and the dance team and the messenger role of the clown to the people. She said that as a child she remembered having many times seen her mother helping her father care for the dance team paraphernalia and helping with the painting of the dancers, "just like she was the clown." A tribal leader, Dawnlight's half-sister by a different mother, who had previously asserted that she believed Dawnlight's shamanic role to be idiosyncratic, now said that she had taken over the traditional functions of the team's clown and stated in a matter-of-fact manner that Dawnlight was the "power behind the team." All our other informants were in agreement with her. History was being rewritten.

Other data that had been obtained in 1981 were modified substantially in 1983. Previously, the Boyers understood that Dawn-

light's shamanic intervention in behalf of Navaho Man com-
menced with the ceremony described above. Now they were told
that immediately following his hospitalization, when the doctors
said he was incurable, she visited him nightly four times, each
time blessing him with her Lightning and Turtle Power. She saw
improvement after each evening, so before performing the public
ceremony she knew that it was destined to be successful. Earlier,
she had said that she became John's helper only because he had
come to her after she'd had her dream within a dream and that
she had known that it was a power dream only after John asked
her for an interpretation of his identical dream. Now she said she
had had to become his aide because he periodically lapsed into
drunkenness despite her efforts and those of others a manifest
misremembering.

In 1981, she and Wide Eyes still attended services at the fundamentalist, evangelistic church with whose help they had been
able to renounce being drunkards. Perhaps a year following her
involvement in the public ceremony for Navaho Man, she and
Wide Eyes renounced attendance at that church, giving as the
reason the church's hostility toward Indian religion. We might
suspect that inasmuch as no apparent harm had come to Dawnlight or her family as a result of her actions, they felt less need of
support. Now they attended certain ceremonies such as funerals
and marriages in every other Christian church on the reservation,
but disclaimed doing so in search of help for themselves.

Dawnlight gave further examples of her new capacity to foretell the future. As an example, a year previously she claimed to
have had a dream or a vision which informed her that John's team
would be asked to participate in an important Catholic dedication
ceremony at Mescalero. Soon thereafter a nun who was the
daughter of a tribal member and who lived in a distant city came
to see her, claiming that she had had a vision while in her city
home in which God enfolded Dawnlight in his arms. Then John
came to Dawnlight, telling her he had dreamed he would be
asked to do something for the Catholic church in Mescalero. She
advised him to accept the charge. No word came from the church
for several months, but then the nun, commissioned by the new
bishop for the diocese, which includes not only Mescalero but
most of southern New Mexico, approached Dawnlight as the

power behind the dance team to obtain John's agreement that he would help dedicate a new cathedral in a city a hundred miles away. The Boyers were present when Dawnlight told the nun that she accepted the commission on John's behalf and agreed that she would attend and supervise the ceremony, which was to take place on the first of four nights of ceremonies involving Hispanic, Anglo, and Pueblo participation as well as Apache.

Although the Boyers continued to be beloved extended family members, there was increasing evidence of ambivalence on the part of Dawnlight toward L.B.B. Before her assumption of the shamanic status, his religio-medical assistance had been sought, especially by her, both in person when he was on the reservation and by telephone when he was not. After she became a shaman, his shamanic assistance was no longer requested. The day before the Boyers arrived in 1983, Dawnlight learned that one of her daughters was probably suffering from an incurable blood disease and might die within a few months. The family, including Dawnlight, obviously hoped for miraculous intervention on the part of L.B.B. and when none was volunteered reacted with mixed emotions.

An older daughter, one of the children born to Dawnlight and Wide Eyes while they were drunkards and whom Dawnlight had previously stated to have inherited her badness, had been "getting into trouble." The next evening, Dawnlight was scheduled to perform a ceremony intended to exorcise her daughter's badness. The Boyers were not invited to attend the ceremony, ostensibly because some relative had wondered whether L.B.B.'s presence might be harmful in some way. It was his impression that the hostility ascribed to the relative was Dawnlight's own and that it had resulted in part from his not having given hope of miraculous cure for the daughter with the blood dyscrasia. However, there were other reasons for hostility toward him. He had failed her expectations on several occasions. He had not gone to the reservation one time when she was severely troubled and had expected him to know of her need omnisciently. He had not magically killed the witch who was purportedly hexing her extended family, although at that time L.B.B. was the family shaman. But it is probable that the most important reason she distrusted him to the degree that she did was because she had projected onto him her own self-criticism for having dared to take over a masculine shamanistic role, thus symbolically replacing her father in her extended family. These Apache sometimes equate knowledge with possession of the phallus. Thus a woman who doubted a man's protestation of ignorance said, "I thought you knew everything. Your third leg hangs to the ground."

Comparison of Dawnlight's Two Rorschach Protocols

In comparing Dawnlight's two records, we find in the second protocol considerable evidence of a constrictive process, scarcely present in the initial Rorschach taken during the liminal period when she had just entered the role of shaman. Before directly examining the second record, let us note that, while there is a continuation of symbolism related to supernatural power, certain representations that were the themes evoked in the first record have been much diminished or are totally absent.

One theme that has almost disappeared is that of the Crown Dancer. A second theme no longer present is the perception of pregnancy, generativity, and female functions related to childbirth. A third theme now missing is concern with being homosexual and thereby becoming a witch.

An obsessional preoccupation with faces remains evident in both records. In the second protocol, however, Dawnlight's anatomical concern with the spine is modified to become also a concern with the absence of spines or the spinal column. In the second record the previous direct concern with masculine authority has disappeared. As for religious themes, in the second record concern with exorcism becomes explicit, but the ritual of religious authority of the masculine type, represented in the first record, disappears.

In both records there is a responsiveness to color on the Rorschach blots which can become imaginative, even poetic. It is in her responses to the black and white cards that one especially notes the greater constriction in the second record.

Summarizing what is very apparent: the first record was a more open one, elicited at a time of crisis and change. The second record suggests she has assumed a more chronic defensive posture in which she is more constrictive in coping with everyday reality. In the second record, a dangerously overt and florid concern with homosexuality, as well as other potential evils of the shaman's role, disappears from view. Nevertheless, we should note that her very last response to Rorschach blot X raises the question of whether religious singing is good or bad. We assume that Dawnlight lacks masculine authoritativeness, a quality which she perceives to be required of her shamanic role, or that she has it but is ambivalent about it and is therefore afraid.

The Second Rorschach

Card I. (20″ pause).

1. *A spine.* (Of some animal)	Dd F− Anat (Aobs, Bb)
2. *Head of a lizard.* (Just there)	Dd F+ Ad (Aobs)
3. *Cute owl with two eyes, hang onto something.* (I saw the eyes first)	Dd F− A (Aobs)
4. *Head, with arms out.* (Maybe Crown Dancer)	Dd FY− Hd (Drel, Daut, Porn)

Looking at the areas selected in her several responses to Card I, we note an evident ego constriction. She refuses to cope with the totality of the blot but selects instead little used, small locations starting with an anatomical response. Although she may have been stimulated to see a figure of a woman in the central area which is apparent to many, she does not respond overtly with this answer but goes in deeper and picks out only a central line and makes a spine of it. (The spine is what is broken in the paraplegic she cannot cure.) Then she selects another small area to see the head of a lizard. From this affectively ambiguous response, she goes to a third area, giving a more reassuring, positively turned response of a "cute" owl. The owl response is determined by its two large eyes which she pulls out of the deeply shaded area. There is both a counterphobic denial of anxiety indicated by insisting that the potentially fearful Apache symbol, the owl, is "cute" and, at the same time, a concern with eyes and faces which is to characterize a number of subsequent responses.

She then selects the upper center of the blot, to represent a head with the arms out. If we compare this with the previous record, we see that the upper portion of the Crown Dancer perceived in record 1 was located here.

Her response to the second card is much diminished. She now utilizes only a small blot area. This response continues the massive constriction that characterizes her responses to the first card. Instead of going in the direction of potentially pathological symbolism, she utilizes denial and an intellectually contrictive process, severely limiting her imaginative potential.

Card II.

5. *Two bears, dancing.*   D FM_a A P (Prec)

6. *Sad face.* (I see tears dripping down.) D_1 Fm FY− Hd (Aobs, Agl)

7. *Two faces, with moustache, on top.* (Man's face, look at each other.) D_2 FC FY+ Hd (Aobs)

On the second card she is able to respond quickly with a conventional movement percept. We must note that this card has red color, and as in her previous Rorschach, she gives evidence of a labile but positive reactivity to the warm colors. One can interpret this as a readiness for a positive warm response in social relationships. She then returns to her obsessional concern with faces. She sees a sad face, very dramatically, with tears dripping down. Here again, as on the first card, there is attention to eyes. The face does not threaten but is sorrowful. We can assume that in her shamanic role she is more aware of others' helpless expectations from her than of their potential hostility toward her. The following response to Card III is also of faces.

Card III.

8. *Two people, beat on a drum.* (That's all.)   W M_a+ H P (Drel, Daut, Prec)

9. *It's got no spine or tailbone. It's in the middle. The stomach is up top and missing from below in there.* (The insides of a person or   DS F− Anat (Aobs, psychotic confabulation, arbitrary paranoid forcing)

animal. The tailbone [D$_1$] *should*
be there [pointing to the area in
the space just behind and below
the buttocks of one of the drum
beaters] and the stomach [D$_2$]
there in the space between the
lap of a drum beater and the
drum.)

On the third card Dawnlight quickly sees the ordinary human
figures. They are envisioned as beating drums, suggesting a ceremonial setting. As in her previous record, she indicates her active
stance toward life in her characteristically active kinesthetic
motion. Her response is integrative, positive in nature. By it she
gives evidence of her social adaptability. She shares awareness of
common reality with others.

However, a psychopathological process becomes evident in her
next response. There is an autistic preoccupation with something
missing which is evident in the distortion of blot locations that
now takes place. She complains that there is no spine or tailbone
in the middle. The percept symbolically represents her anxiety as
well as a logical deformation in her thinking. She utilizes the
shape of the lateral red areas of the blot to associate to a stomach.
However, she relocates the stomach near the center. We get here
a conceptual disorientation and an incapacity to deal with the blot
areas as they are on the card. Again she goes inside the body,
following her anatomical preoccupation. The whole of the card
becomes confused and is finally perceived as a tailbone. This
associative chain suggests what is technically termed in Rorschach
language a "contamination." We assume the alogical transposi-
tion of location to have been stimulated at least in part by an
affect-laden response to the red area. The internal logic of her
needs supersedes the limitations of reality.

We can note here a "confabulatory" movement from a partial
perception of a tailbone in the central area to a tailbone which
becomes the whole blot. In this process, the stomach is moved
into another position to be part of the internal anatomy. We can
find sufficient evidence of the forgoing of logic and association to
suggest the same type of process involved in paranoid thinking.

A second observation we can make about the content is that, compared with the childbirth response elicited by Card III on the previous protocol, her present responses are far removed from possible sexual implications. She continues to be concerned with the inside of the body, but she concentrates mainly on the spine. The spine, a hard object, indicates firmness, perhaps authority, and may well represent qualities she fears she cannot have as a female. One can surmise her concern with the lack of a spine to symbolize an abiding sense of inner incapacity. It may be that she retains suppressed or regressed knowledge that her cure of the paraplegic shaman was unsuccessful and thus symbolizes doubly her inner feeling of powerlessness. On this record she pays no attention to female generativity. The symbolism throughout is focused on incapacity.

Card IV. (180″ pause)

10. *Rawhide.* (The shading is important.) $\quad$ W FY+ Aob P (Neut)

11. *Bull head.* (Two eyes, looking at me) $\quad$ D_1 FY FM+ Ad (Aobs)

12 *Spine, in the middle.* (Back part of an animal hide) $\quad$ Dd FY− Anat (Aobs, Bb)

On the fourth card she again manifests associative blocking to a totally black and white card on which there is no reassuring color. Nevertheless after a silence of three minutes she is able to give a global concept of an animal hide, a very common response to this card. This is the third of the first four cards to which she is able to give a popular, conventional response. Again, despite her ideational problems of paranoid arbitrariness, she is very much aware of the ordinary perceptions of reality. Then, she goes to the center of the blot, to an area that is commonly perceived as a head. She perceives a bull head, an active, massive figure. She again attends to the eyes looking out at her. The repetitive face response indicates the continuity of her obsessive wariness. And again, obsessionally, she focuses on the spine in the middle of the card. Once more we observe evidence both of anxiety and constriction and the continual concern with incapacity as represented by the spine. We interpret her anixety to be related both to the impossible task of curing a paraplegic client and to the more general continual anxiety evoked by the necessity to perform well in her accepted role as shaman, to fulfill others' dependent demands on her.

Card V.
13. *Bat.* (Flying)   W FM$_a$+ A P (Neut)
14. *Grasshopper, no spine.*   W FM$_a$+ A (Aobs)
[Unable to clarify what she meant] (Flying)

When Dawnlight first took the Rorschach test, she reacted to Card V with three responses that we interpreted to indicate anxiety. First she saw a grasshopper, then a bat, and lastly the dangerous owl, a very unusual response to this card although one of adequate form. As noted, there was at that time a plague of grasshoppers, and she was acutely worried about her garden. On the second test she promptly gives the popular bat response but then sees a spineless grasshopper. Her continuing anxiety pertains now to a feeling of incapacity. She attempts to deal with it obsessively, by displacing it from its source. As we find elsewhere in the second protocol, her defensive postures against anxiety do not work very well.

Card VI. (22″ pause)
15. *A shield.* (Indian shield   D$_2$ F+ Obj (Porn)
with feathers on it)
16. *Two hands, put together.*   Dd M$_p$+ Hd (Drel)
(Praying)
(180″ pause)
17. *An arrow, shot into the   Dd Fm+ Weapon (Hsm,
head or neck of something.*   Hhat)
[Couldn't identify the object
being shot into]

On Card VI, she first gives a positive response, a decorated (Indian) shield, well perceived in its ornamentation. Then she gives a religious response, two hands held together in prayer. She uses Card VI constructively, either to indicate ethnic symbolism, a protective shield and a supplication for power from the outside, a type of response viewed as a "dependency" response in our system of scoring. What continues throughout her record is a sufficient number of positive responses, or responses indicative of the investment in positive features of living which are usually absent in clinical patients tested with the Rorschach. She gives a number of responses scored either as positive or as dependent. These categories usually appear in individuals who are not clinically disturbed. The next percept is of an arrow that is being shot into the neck or head of something which cannot be identified, so that we have here a direct hostility response, actually the only one thus far so categorized.

Card VII.

18. *A witch-lady with a black, dirty mouth, watching a person. Just their heads.* (One on either side; both have bad mouths.)

D_3 M FY+ Hd P (Aobs, Athr)

On Card VII, she comes closest to a theme found in the previous record. In this instance it is only the heads of two witches with dirty mouths that are perceived. In the previous testing, this particular response was more elaborated, both in the blot area covered and in the associated comments given to the tester. In that protocol, she utilized the entire blot, and opened a discussion about the possibility of homosexual induction into becoming a witch. Structurally, the constrictive tendency here narrows down the area of the blot used, indicated in the location as well as in the lack of further association. We also note that this particular use of the two heads gives her another popular response, so that she now has given popular responses on five of the seven cards.

Card VIII.

19. *All the colors.* [Names them]

W Cnaming (Aev)

20. *Two faces. Face up the middle.*

D_6 FC− Hd P (Aobs)

21. *Something goes up into the air. Animal at the side. Person being relieved of something. It's a good one.* (The animals are

(DW FM+ A p (Pstr, Drel)) (additional Response)

medicine men relieving the persons of evil. I see it moving up in the turquoise and gray. The animals are pushing it out of the people below in the pink. They are Bear Power. Smoke and fire in the background.) [Could not relocate the face in the middle. The something going up was D_5 and the cylinder in D_3.]

On Card VIII, she uses the two commonly perceived animals as part of a theme of exorcism. The animals represent shamanistic practice in that the central part of the blot is being relieved of some evil that possesses it. She further elaborates that the animals are representative of Bear Power. This is an associative elaboration; since the animals look like bears, they represent Bear Power. She again uses the popular blot area, but in this instance, gives some indication of the type of imaginative response she gave in the first Rorschach series. Note also that there are faces in the center, observing the exorcism that is being conducted. The cooler colors are used to represent evil and the warmer colors are good, so that the gray and pastel blue of Card VIII represent the evil that is being exorcised. There are smoke and fire in the background. All the Crown Dance ceremonies are conducted in the presence of fire and smoke, and in the past the same was true of almost all the other shamanistic rites.

Another interesting note in respect to this response is that Dawnlight does not herself possess Bear Power. We can assume, with her feelings of incapacity, that she aspires to obtain other powers in addition to the Lightning-Turtle Power she has borrowed from her mother.[22] In the De Vos scoring system, this response, motivated by her wish to obtain Bear Power, constitutes an active striving. Combined with the other movement responses in her record, it indicates an active, assertive attitude, characteristic of her stance toward life.

Card IX. (180″ pause)

22. *It don't make sense. The green man [D_1] looks down at the*　　(DW M_pFC− H O)(Drel, Pstr, Athr)

baby's head [D₄]. He's a mon-
ster. The top one [D₂]. I don't
know. (The green one, diyiⁿ, up
top, good because of the color, is
fighting the monster-witch, and
the bottom [D₄, D₅] is the fallen
person. Someone will pray for
my daughter tonight.) [This last
remark pertained to an actual
ceremony in which she planned
to exorcise evil from a daughter
who was born during the time
she was a drunkard.]

Card IX gives Dawnlight some difficulty, but she manages to
produce a total integrated response to it. She sees the heads of
children in the pink area of the bottom, evil monsters threatening
them in the green, and shamans in the orange who seek to protect
thg children from harm. Once again, the warm colors (red and
orange) are used affirmatively, and the cool (green), negatively.
So the colors symbolically represent interaction between good
and evil, more specifically, the shaman's protection of a child
from the influence of the monster-witch. One must note that the
form level is fairly poor but the colors are used to delineate areas
that have some form nevertheless. A baby is very often seen in
the red area below and some kind of person or magician in the
orange area. Dawnlight's capacity to see warm colors in a positive
light on a symbolic level suggests the drawing of sustenance from
her social reactivity which is used to combat the anxieties stimulated by the black colors on the achromatic cards and by the cooler colors on the tinted cards. One might say that she draws sustenance from the outside and that it can be turned defensively
against her proneness to anxiety. The bright colors predominate;
they are strong affect that can be used integratively to overcome
danger and anxiety. Although as a shaman she is constantly
preoccupied with the themes of good and evil potentially emanat-
ing from herself, as manifested so unmistakably on the first protocol, at this moment she is acutely occupied with that theme,
inasmuch as on the evening of the day when the test was administered for the second time, she was to take part in a ceremony

intended to exorcise evil from one of the daughters born before she renounced drunkenness. She had recently restated her belief that she had imparted evil to all the children she then had. Taking this belief into consideration, we may assume that the green monster and its destructive wish toward the child was a projection of an aspect of her self-representation, although she consciously feared that her daughter was being bewitched by another as the result of hostility toward her and, by extension, her family.

Card X.

23. *Baby's face in yellow one.* D_{10} F/C Hd (Aobs)

24. *A man up there.* D_{14} Mp– (Neut)

25. *Spiders up there.* D_1 F+ A P (Neut)

26. *Butterflies.* D_{15} FM FC A (Pnat)

27. *Rabbit face.*   D F Ad P (Neut)

28. *You got all your colors there.*   W Cnaming (Aev)

(120″ pause)

29. *Face with open mouth.* (From the singing of the person) *saying that blue thing* (D_1). [The face was at the top of D_9.]   Dd M– Hd (Aobs) arbitrary

30. *A music sign.* (The red one in the middle) D_{12} F+ obj (Prec)

31. *The person is singing and all the rest are rejoicing, dancing. The man up there* (D_9) *is moving between the animals; you can see his eyes and the stick* (D_{14}) *in his hand. The blue monster animal was an open mouth and is mean. The butterflies* (D_{15}) *are happy and yellow. The Rabbit is as calm as he should be. Is the singing good or bad (diyi^n or enti^n)?* [Apaches generally believe red, "the color of sunrise," and yellow "the color of pollen," to be good, meaning that they may bring "good luck."]   DW M_a– H P O (Drel, Athr, Porn, arbitrary)

The last card starts with individual responses that are eventually turned into a total integration. The theme of the child is picked up again by seeing a baby's face in one of the yellow areas. In the blue Dawnlight sees spiders, then goes to more innocuous butterflies and the face of a rabbit. The rabbit face is a very common response, as are the spiders, in the blue area. Then she responds rather peculiarly that another part of the blot is "saying" the blue part. She sees the blue area of the blot as words, just as one finds words encircled by a balloon in a cartoon. It is interesting that in the inquiry she does not find the baby's face again but goes on to alternative responses about dancing, singing, and rejoicing, explaining that the man in the center is moving between the animals on each side of the blot. The cool blue here becomes a monster with an open mouth, but the butterflies of the warm yellow color are happy. The center of the black area is a person singing; again this figure is related, as in her other responses, to some kind of ceremonial activity. She ends the handling of this card by asking herself the question, "Is the singing good or bad?" Previously, on Card X, we had a much more global concept of the card as the representation of generativity of women who give birth to both good and evil objects. The question of good or evil remains here, but the response is much toned down and the reference to generativity is not forthcoming.

If we summarize the second record, we see that the identification with religious practice now has for her an integrative quality and gives her a feeling of adaptive participation rather than isolation. The last three cards all imply in one way or another some positive shamanistic functioning, but on the last card doubt is revealed about whether singing is really good or possibly could be evil. There is no such doubt on Card VIII, where evil is being driven out, or on Card IX, where the shaman is counteracting the monster that is attacking a fallen person or a child. The shaman on Card IX is unambivalently a protector. The central figure of Card X carries a stick, a scepter, "sword" of the *ga^nheh*, a symbol of potency, but the question remains whether his singing is good or evil, that is, whether he is practicing shamanism or witchcraft.

Dawnlight uses colors symbolically as she did in the initial Rorschach, but this time the record is much more constricted.

Nevertheless, under the stimulus of color she recovers her ability to give imaginative, holistic conceptions of very difficult, complex blots. The generativity of the shaman who can give birth to evil as well as good is replaced by the figure of the shaman in Cards VIII and IX as protective, an exorcist and combatant of evil. The child we can readily identify as her daughter, born during Dawnlight's drunken period and thus "bad." Subsequently, when she was no longer a drunkard, Dawnlight believed she had then imparted good things to her younger children, resembling her conceptualization of the shaman versus the witch. One might suppose that on a deep level the monster on Card IX is her disavowed self which is being combated by her present, professional self as shaman. The openness and crisis of the first record two years previously has been replaced with constriction and anxiety. We find no overt or florid concern with homosexuality, but there remains concern with evil and its potential.

Role Succession in Apache Aging

Given the inconsistencies and other traumatizing elements of their earlier socialization experiences, it may be surprising that many Apache are able to meet cultural expectations and become responsible people when they reach grandparental age. Both James and Dawnlight were able to do so, renouncing their drunkenness. James assumed the singership handed down to him by Smiles and for a while was able to handle that role adequately, though he required Smile's continual support to do so. Dawnlight became more and more like her mother in that she turned to traditionalism, including progressive involvement with her mother's religio-medical practices. We probably have here identification with her mother as part of healthy mourning (Freud 1917), made easier by cultural expectations.

James apparently did not share his sister's level of psychological maturity. When Smiles died, James was unable to continue to function adequately as the singer. Although there was an older sister, she had been unable to renounce her drunkenness and could not serve as a counselor and model for the extended family, as the oldest member is expected to do. Dawnlight assumed the responsibility of being the elder leader of the extended family, and her functioning in that role was welcomed. In doing so, however, she undertook a responsibility which had been assumed in the past very rarely if ever by women, namely, the care of the *jajadeh* team paraphernalia, despite her anxieties that she would be criticized by other Apache or punished by the "real" *ga^nheh*. It seems likely that in assuming this unusual role, she could mourn her father by identifying with his religio-medical role.

When her anxieties proved to be unfounded, Dawnlight allowed herself to perform a curing ceremony for her husband's "paralysis," although she had never had a power dream. With trepidation once again concerning supernatural retribution—that is, projected guilt—she used her mother's Lightning ceremony. To her amazement, the ceremony was successful and she was not punished. Subsequently she became much more actively involved in assuming a masculine role, becoming John's adviser and the power behind the Crown Dancer singership, assuming very literally her father's role as James' "aide." However, the Rorschach data suggest that her bisexual identification had been established earlier and was the source of intrapsychic conflict.

The first protocol, obtained when she felt so anxious about having assumed the idiosyncratic shamanic role, revealed much anxiety and creativity, in addition to her capacity to regress to, and quickly recover from, a psychotic-like state. She had anxiety connected with a self-picture of being potentially either all good or all bad and specifically equated the power of female generativity and its possible evil consequences with the female shaman's role. She revealed a fear that her own evil potential resulted from her bisexual identification, her unconscious homosexuality. Ultimately, she thus revealed anxiety lest her aggression get out of control. Such a fear is reasonably realistic for these Apache. Sometimes the best controlled of them become almost unimaginably cruel and lewd when in states of regression, often caused by intoxication.

During the ensuing two years, Dawnlight was confronted with little if any societal disapprobation. Even though her paraplegic uncle, Navaho Man, failed to improve after the curing ceremony she directed, almost everyone used massive denial and believed Dawnlight's intervention to have been at least partially successful. People now claimed they knew that in the old days, women had been the power behind the Crown Dance team when the singer felt insecure. That is, her personally selected shamanic role now received historical validation. The services of John's dance team were sought both frequently and far and wide. Although ostensibly people were asking for assistance from John as the owner of the power associated with his singership, everyone believed Dawnlight to be the power behind the dance team, and to be actually in charge. They were seeking if not primarily the use of her supernatural power, at least their combined powers.

One would think that with such public support, Dawnlight's anxieties would have been relieved. To the contrary, she seemed to be more fearful of the Boyers' disapproval, and her second Rorschach revealed a typical Apache manner of handling anxiety, that is, by greater emotional and cognitive constriction. A specific fear was symbolically portrayed, that of spinelessness, of incapacity. We have interpreted this to mean that she unconsciously recognized very well that Navaho Man had failed to improve and regarded herself as being also spineless, that is, incapable as a shaman. We would assume that she on some level of consciousness saw this failure as retribution for her temerity in taking over a masculine shamanic role, but we do not have direct evidence to support this assumption.

Stating the case differently, we observe that Dawnlight is anxious because through a sense of responsibility and inner unconscious pressures, she has usurped the ritual role of a man by becoming the power behind the *jajadeh* team. This was probably the first time in Apache history that a woman presumed such power. To do so ran the risk of supernatural retribution and public censure. One would say that she had presumed a form of masculine authority while knowing unconsciously that she was not equipped for the masculine role. We observe that a combination of social pressure and intrapsychic conflict-laden homosexual desires are the stimuli for the active efflorescence of her paranoia.

To be promoted or to be put in a position by others to assume a role for which one does not internally feel capable can lead to a personal decomposition of the type that Freud (1911) described in the Schreber case. That case became the classic exposition of paranoia. When promoted to the role of judge, Schreber came face to face with a deep sense of inner insufficiency as well as the dangers of usurpation, and regressed to his paranoid psychosis. Dawnlight's incapacity is related to a concept of usurpation similar to that experienced by Schreber, whose promotion, symbolically usurped a father's position. In both cases, the defense structure of the individual has within it a defense against an acknowledgment of homosexual impulses. We would term this a success psychosis. One observes that a success neurosis or psychosis may derive from one's being incapable to perform or, in other instances, from the fear that one's success may result in castration or annihilation (Boyer 1985). Of course, an alternate fear is that one's being successful may result in one's becoming a murderer or, in Dawnlight's case, a witch.

Moreover, when one assumes the authority role, one becomes subject to the hostility and envy accorded this status position. It is the experience of the hostility of the subordinate or rival which is projected at the time the individual assumes an authority position. It must be stated here that Dawnlight is not manifesting a persecutory fearfulness but rather that she is afraid of her own incapacity. And unlike what is evident in most paranoid records, there is suggested in her Rorschach protocol a socially integrative capacity to respond positively to others. This responsiveness may be the reason there are no overt signs of delusions which separate her clinically from those around her. On the contrary, others believe in her and forgo any questioning that might bring her into social disrepute.

Usually, when a person is seen as being paranoid, he has no social support. When an individual who may be structurally paranoid has social support, he or she is protected from direct confrontation. As long as there is a social need to believe, the person maintains a social adaptability. In such circumstance, one need not have an immediate crisis in the testing of one's beliefs. To a certain degree, the individual remains socially adaptive. There is no social withdrawal or withdrawal from the beliefs being espoused. Therefore Dawnlight's behavior is not interpreted negatively nor is the crisis exacerbated, as it would be if she were socially alone and isolated. People can have a potentially unstable structure but if they continue to receive sustaining social support, they cannot be considered as psychopathological.

Let us return to the popular idea that the shaman is a very

disturbed individual or has been "cured" of psychosis by assuming the shamanic role. Actually, Rorschach protocols reveal that shamans who show psychotic propensities are in the distinct minority. Dawnlight clearly was not seriously psychologically disturbed before becoming a shaman. To the degree that her subsequent Rorschach protocols reveal psychotic propensities, her "psychosis" can be judged to be a "success psychosis."

Clearly, the findings in the case of Dawnlight are not easily generalizable, suggestive though they certainly are.

Notes

1. Adapted from L. Bryce Boyer, George A. De Vos, and Ruth M. Boyer, "Crisis and Continuity in the Personality of an Apache Shaman," *Psychoanalytic Study of Society* (1985), 11:63–114. eds. L. Bryce Boyer and Simon A. Grolnick, pp. 63–114, Hillsdale, N. J.: Analytic Press.

2. See also chap. 10, n. 3, above.

3. Detailed data pertaining to Apache socialization and social structure are to be found in Basehart (1959, 1960), L. B. Boyer (1964a, 1964b, 1979a), R. M. Boyer (1962, 1964), Kunstadter (1960), MacLachlan (1962), and Opler (1933, 1941, 1969).

4. This formulation predates Freud's (1911) idea that the hallucinatory and delusional symptoms of psychosis are attempts at reconstituting a shattered ego. He wrote (p. 475), "[that] which we take to be a pathological product, is in reality an attempt at recovery, a process of reconstructions." Loewald (1979) has illustrated some of the complexities involved in defining pathological normality.

5. Here we present but the barest essentials of Apache religio-medical philosophies and practices. For more information, the reader is referred to other studies (Bourke 1892; Boyer 1964a, 1979a; Opler 1941, 1947).

6. The notion that insanity is the result of the influence of ghosts is widespread (Barrett 1917; Best 1922; Boyer and Boyer 1983; Gifford 1927; Steward 1929).

7. See n. 3; for details concerning Dawnlight's early life, see Boyer, Boyer, and De Vos (1982).

8. In a Lipan version of "Coyote Steals Fire," after Coyote stole fire from the Firefly people, they tried in every way to get the fire back and force the Apache to continue to eat raw meat (Opler 1940:111–114). When the forest was ablaze, the Firefly people prayed for rain and all of the fire was put out except some embers which Turtle protected with his

shell. Lightning struck Turtle many times in unsuccessful attempts to make him drop the fire and have it extinguished by the rain. The marks on the shell of the turtle came from the striking of the lightning. The first step of the ceremony used by Dawnlight to treat Wide Eyes' pain and "paralysis" involved her putting "coal or ashes" left on a tree which had been struck by lightning into her turtle shell and then mixing them with pure water. Four round, flat stones emblemizing Turtle were heated while hot and cold water was dripped onto them. If one or more of them had chipped or broken, the ceremony would have been stopped. The breakage would probably have meant that either Turtle or Lightning Power was displeased and, if used, would have "turned back" on Dawnlight or one of her loved ones.

9. To be outstandingly successful incurs resentment on the part of others, as reflected in some folklore (R. M. Boyer 1972). In a representative example, a high school boy did very well scholastically, whereupon a gang of his Apache peers responded by beating him up and torturing and killing his dog in front of him while holding him helpless.

10. This may be recent religio-medical behavior and we do not know its frequency. We had heard of its occurrence in the remote past but did not learn of or observe it during the years 1957–1988.

11. Ordinarily, Chiricahua and Mescalero Apaches believe that individuals' manifest dream contents have culturally defined symbolic meanings, signifying good or bad luck, and that they can be used to prescribe behavior in general. An occasional shaman is thought to have the power to use his own or others' dreams as vision experiences. Such men are called dream shamans and are said to be able to dictate specific behavior from their understanding of manifest dreams. Dawnlight's experience may constitute the first evidence that Lipan Apache held a similar belief.

12. The Boyers have never observed any participant in a public or private religio-medical ceremony enter into an obvious altered ego state.

13. L.B.B. had for some years been viewed as the shaman for Dawnlight and Wide Eyes' nuclear family, and a year previously he had successfully treated Dawnlight's episode of ghost sickness solely by means of interpretations pertaining to her hostility and guilt. Her transference toward him was mixed, of course, with close realistic object relations, and included his serving for her as an omniscient, omnipotent, and predominantly loving father surrogate.

14. It may be that Dawnlight expressed in this way a fear, perhaps unconscious, that L.B.B. might seek to harm her although pretending to be friendly. The first time she met the Boyers that year, she hugged

L.B.B., tearfully saying, "I wouldn't be standing here if you hadn't saved my life." Soon thereafter, however, she tactfully told him his services as family shaman were no longer required. The year after Dawnlight's assumption of the shamanistic status, R.M.B. informed her that she would be coming to the reservation alone; Dawnlight agreed to meet with her on an appointed date. However, when R.M.B. arrived, Dawnlight and her family were in another state, having decided at the last moment to attend a powwow there. We may suppose that the sudden decision was related to L.B.B.'s absence. Some years previously, while serving as the family shaman, he had not gone to the reservation at a time when the family expected him, assuming that he knew without having been informed by human communication that Dawnlight was suffering from ghost sickness and expected his assistance. She was bitterly disappointed and unforgiving when it became necessary for her to resort to a long-distance telephone conversation, and to achieve help through his interpretation of guilt related to her feelings toward the person who had been killed.

15. This means of curing an individual who suffers from witchcraft is very widespread among American Indians (Ackerknecht 1949; Kroeber 1925; Murphy 1958).

16. When an owl flies nearby at night, the Apache hear him say, "I am going to drink your blood." When the Apache is angry, he often says *shi zhade shi nah-i-shish*, "You make the blood rise to my throat." The owl clearly serves as a culturally supported bogey onto which oral aggression, in all its omnipotent primitivity, can be projected.

17. Although we possess and have examined many hundreds of protocols each from Apaches, Navahos, and several groups of northern Athabascans as well as other American Indian groups, we have elected not to present statistical validation for this statement in the present communication, beyond that afforded by articles to which we have referred in the citations.

18. This unusual Rorschach response is common in the associations of regressed patients in the analytic situation and those of young children (Isaacs 1948; Klein 1932). To them, the buttock represents the anus, the agent of expression of primitive, omnipotent, and omnidestructive aggression which has resulted from the frustration of being orally deprived. Such ideas are thought to be present side by side with the idea that one is either totally bad or totally good, ideas clearly present in the thinking of those who perceive their healers to be alternatively all good (shamans) or all bad (witches), such as the Apache and others who project onto their curers totally good or totally bad self-representations. As an example, many Latin Americans alternatively

call their healers (curanderos) witches (brujos), as we and many others have observed (Gillin 1948; Hudson 1951; Kiev 1968).

19. Today, most psychoanalysts believe that paranoia serves fundamentally as a means of dealing with primitive aggression rather than homosexuality per se (Meissner 1978). This would be a logical extension of the early ideas of van Ophuijsen (1920) and Stärcke (1920) that the earliest roots of paranoia stem from the infantile notion that his expelled feces (skybalum) would attack him, and the Kleinians' view that feces become persecutory symbolic equations of the bad breast of the schizoid position.

20. Numerous authors, seemingly writing of male shamans, have noted in many parts of the world, the acquisition and practice of shamanism and witchcraft or sorcery are conceptualized in oral and anal sadomasochistic terms, including literal or symbolic cannibalism and defecation (Angas 1847; Grey 1841; Howitt 1886, 1904; Hubert and Mauss 1909; Koch-Gründberg 1910; Róheim 1923, 1925; Salvado 1851; Seligmann 1910; Spencer and Gillen 1899, 1904; Threlkeld 1892).

21. We are indebted to Milton Lozoff, M.D., for an interesting suggestion. Recalling Freud's (1917) "Mourning and Melancholia," he hypothesized that Dawnlight's assumption of the shamanistic role may have had as one of its roots an attempt to mourn the loss of L.B.B., both as a real and a transference object through identification with his shamanistic status.

22. Another shaman was observed to acquire a new supernatural power when she was desperate about her physical incapacity (Boyer and Boyer 1977).

References

Ackerknect, Edwin H.
    1943   Psychopathology, Primitive Medicine, and Primitive Culture. *Bulletin of the History of Medicine* 14:20–67.
    1949   Medical Practices. Julian H. Steward, ed. *Handbook of South American Indians*, Vol. 5, pp. 621–643. Bureau of American Ethnology Bulletin 143, Washington, D.C.: Government Printing Office.
Angas, George French
    1847   *Savage Life and Scenes in Australia and New Zealand: Getting an Artist's Impressions of Countries and People in the Antipodes.* 2d ed. London: Smith, Elder.

Barrett, Samuel Alfred
  1917   Ceremonies of the Pomo Indians. *University of California Publications in American Archaeology and Ethnology* 12:397–441.
Basehart, Harry W.
  1959   *Chiricahua Apache Subsistence and Sociopolitical Organization.* Albuquerque: University of New Mexico Mescalero-Chiricahua Lands Claims Project. Mimeographed.
  1960   *Mescalero Apache Subsistence Patterns and Sociopolitical Organization.* Albuquerque: University of New Mexico Mescalero-Chiricahua Lands Claims Project. Mimeographed.
Best, Elsdon
  1922   *Spiritual and Mental Concepts of the Maori.* Wellington, N.Z.: Government Printer.
Bogoras, Waldemar
  1907   The Chuckchee: Religion. *Memoirs of the American Museum of Natural History* 11:277–536.
Bourke, John G.
  1892   *The Medicine Men of the Apache.* Bureau of American Ethnology, Ninth Annual Report. Reprinted by Rio Grande Press, Glorietta, N. Mex. [1970].
Boyer, L. Bryce
  1961   Notes on the Personality Structure of a North American Indian Shaman. *Journal of the Hillside Hospital* 10:14–33
  1962   Remarks on the Personality of Shamans, with Special Reference to the Apache of the Mescalero Indian Reservation. Warner Muensterberger and Sidney Axelrad, eds. *Psychoanalytic Study of Society* 2:233–254. New York: International Universities Press.
  1964a   Folk Psychiatry of the Apaches of the Mescalero Indian Reservation. Ari Kiev, ed. *Magic, Faith, and Healing: Studies in Primitive Psychiatry Today*, pp. 384–419, Glencoe, Ill.: Free Press.
  1964b   Psychological Problems of a Group of Apaches: Alcoholic Hallucinosis and Latent Homosexuality Among Typical Men. Warner Muensterberger and Sidney Axelrad, eds. *Psychoanalytic Study of Society* 3:203–277. New York: International Universities Press.
  1964c   Further Remarks Concerning Shamans and Shamanism. *Israel Annals of Psychiatry and Related Disciplines* 2:235–257.
  1979a   *Childhood and Folklore: A Psychoanalytic Study of Apache Personality.* New York: Library of Psychological Anthropology.
  1979b   Stone as a Symbol in Apache Folklore. R. H. Hook, ed. *Fantasy and Symbol: Studies in Anthropological Interpretation*, pp. 207–232. London: Academic Press.

1985 Christmas "Neurosis" Reconsidered. Vamik D. Volkan, ed. *Mourning, Depression, and Depressive States* pp. 297–376. New York: Aronson.

Boyer, L. Bryce, and Ruth M. Boyer
1976 Prolonged Adolescence and Early Identification: A Cross-Cultural Study. Warner Muensterberger, Aaron H. Esman, and L. Bryce Boyer, eds. *Psychoanalytic Study of Society* 7:95–106. New Haven: Yale University Press.
1977 Understanding the Patient Through Folklore. *Contemporary Psychoanalysis* 13:30–51.
1983 The Sacred Clown of the Chiricahua and Mescalero Apaches: Additional Data. *Western Folklore* 42:46–54.

Boyer, L. Bryce, Ruth M. Boyer, and Harry W. Basehart
1973 Shamanism and Peyote Use Among the Apaches of the Mescalero Indian Reservation. Michael T. Harner, ed. *Hallucinogens and Shamanism*, pp. 53–66. New York: Oxford University Press.

Boyer, L. Bryce, Ruth M. Boyer, and George A. De Vos
1982 An Apache Woman's Account of Her Recent Acquisition of the Shamanistic Status. *Journal of Psychoanalytic Anthropology* 5:299–331.

Boyer, L. Bryce, George A. De Vos, Orin Borders, and Alice Tani-Borders
1978 The "Burnt Child Reaction" Among the Yukon Eskimos. *Journal of Psychoanalytic Anthropology* 1:7–56.

Boyer, L. Bryce, George A. De Vos, and Ruth M. Boyer
1985 Crisis and Continuity in the Personality of an Apache Shaman. L. Bryce Boyer and Simon A. Grolnick, eds. *Psychoanalytic Study of Society*, Vol. 11, 63–114. Hillsdale, N.J.: Analytic Press.

Boyer, L. Bryce, Bruno Klopfer, Florence B. Brawer, and Hayao Kawai
1964 Comparisons of the Shamans and Pseudoshamans of the Apaches of the Mescalero Indian Reservation. *Journal of Projective Techniques and Personality Assessment* 28:173–180.

Boyer, Ruth M.
1962 *Social Structure and Socialization Among the Apache of the Mescalero Indian Reservation.* Ph.D. dissertation, University of California, Berkeley.
1964 The Matrifocal Family Among the Mescalero Apache: Additional Data. *American Anthropologist* 66:593–602.

Boyer, Ruth M., and L. Bryce Boyer
1981 Apache Lore of the Bat. Werner Muensterberger, L. Bryce

Boyer, and Simon A. Grolnick, eds. *Psychoanalytic Study of Society* 9:263–299. New York: Psychohistory Press.

Czaplicka, Marie Antoinette
1914 *Aboriginal Siberia: A Study in Social Anthropology.* Oxford: Clarendon Press.

Davidson, Ronald H., and Richard Day
1974 *Symbol and Realization: A Contribution to the Study of Magic and Healing.* Berkeley: Center for South and Southeast Asia Studies, University of California.

Day, Richard, and Ronald H. Davidson
1976 Magic and Healing: An Ethnopsychoanalytic Study. Werner Muensterberger, Aaron H. Esman, and L. Bryce Boyer, eds. *Psychoanalytic Study of Society* 7:231–292. New Haven: Yale University Press.

Devereux, George
1956 Normal and Abnormal: The Key Problem of Psychiatric Anthropology. J. Casagrande and T. Galwin, eds. *Some Uses of Anthropology, Theoretical and Applied*, pp. 23–48. Washington, D.C.: Anthropological Society of Washington.

Devereux, George, and Weston LaBarre
1961 Art and Mythology. Bert Kaplan, ed. *Studying Personality Cross-Culturally*, pp. 361–403. Evanston, Ill.: Row, Peterson.

De Vos, George A.
1952 A Quantitative Approach to Affective Symbolism in Rorschach Responses. *Journal of Projective Techniques* 16:133–150.

Diószegi, Vilmos
1962 How to Become a Shaman Among the Sagai. *Acta Orientalia: Academiae Scientiarum Hungaricae* 15:87–96.

Diószegi, Vilmos and M. Hoppál, eds. *Shamanism in Siberia.* Budapest: Akadémiai Kiadó.

Driver, Harold E.
1961 *Indians of North America.* Chicago: University of Chicago Press.

Ducey, Charles
1976 The Life History and Creative Psychopathology of the Shaman: Ethnopsychoanalytic Perspectives. Werner Muensterberger, Aaron H. Esman, and L. Bryce Boyer, eds. *Psychoanalytic Study of Society* 7:173–230. New Haven: Yale University Press.
1979 The Shaman's Dream Journey: Psychoanalytic and Structural Complementarity in Myth Interpretation. Werner Muensterberger, and L. Bryce Boyer, eds.; Gilbert J. Rose, assoc. ed. *Psychoanalytic Study of Society* 8:71–118. New Haven: Yale University Press.

Eliade, Mircea
  1951   *Shamanism: Archaic Techniques of Ecstasy.* Willard R. Trask,
         trans. New York: Bollingen Foundation [1964].
Exner, John E., Jr.
  1974   *The Rorschach: A Comprehensive System*, Vol. 1. New York:
         John Wiley.
Freeman, Daniel M. A.
  1968   Adolescent Crises of the Kiowa-Apache Indian Male. Eugene
         B. Brody, ed. *Minority Group Adolescents in the United States*,
         pp. 157–204. Baltimore: Williams and Wilkins.
Freud, Sigmund
  1911   Psychoanalytic Notes on an Autobiographical Account of a
         Case of Paranoia (Dementia Paranoides). *Standard Edition*, 1957,
         14:1–82. London: Hogarth Press.
  1917   Mourning and Melancholia. *Standard Edition*, 1957, 14:237–
         258. London: Hogarth Press.
Gifford, Edward Winslow
  1927   Southern   Maidu   Ceremonies.   *American   Anthropologist*
         29:214–257.
Gillin, John P.
  1948   Magical Fright. *Psychiatry* 12:387–400.
Goddard, Pliny E.
  1916   The Masked Dancers of the Apache. *Holmes Anniversary
         Volume*, pp. 132–236. Washington, D.C.: James William Bryan
         Press.
Grey, George
  1841   *Journals of Two Expeditions of Discovery in Northwest and
         Western Australia During the Years 1837, 1838, 1839.* London:
         T. and W. Boone.
Gusinde, H.
  1939   *Der Peyote Kult: Mödling, Sankt Gabriel, Festschrift*, pp. 401–
         499. Vienna: Missions-Druckerei St. Gabriel.
Harrington, M. R.
  1912   The Devil Dance of the Apaches. *Museum Journal* (Phil-
         adelphia) 3:6–9.
Hippler, Arthur E.
  1971   Shamans, Curers, and Personality: Suggestions Toward a
         Theoretical Model. *Transcultural Psychiatric Research* 8:190–193
         (abstr.).
Hoijer, Harry J.
  1938   *Chiricahua and Mescalero Texts.* Chicago: University of
         Chicago Press.

Hollander, Arie Nicolaas Jan den
   1935   De Peyote Kultur der Nooramerikaansche Indianen. *Mensch En Maatschapij* 11:17–29, 123–131.
Housse, Emile
   1939   *Une Epopée Indienne: Les Araucans du Chili.* Paris: Plon.
Howells, William
   1956   *The Heathens.* New York: Doubleday.
Howitt, Alfred William
   1886   On Australian Medicine Men, or, Doctors and Wizards of Some Australian Tribes. *Journal of the Royal Anthropological Institute of Great Britain and Ireland* 16:23–59.
   1904   *The Native Tribes of Southeast Australia.* London: Macmillan.
Hubert, Henri, and Marcel Mauss
   1909   L'Origine des pouvoirs magiques dans les sociétés australiennes. *Mélanges d'Histoire des Religions.* Paris: Alcan.
Hudson, William M., ed.
   1951   *The Healer of Los Olmos and Other Mexican Lore.* Texas Folklore Society Publication 24. Dallas: Southern Methodist University Press.
Hultkrantz, Åke
   1965   The Study of North American Indian Religion: Retrospect, Present Trends, and Future Tasks. *Temenos* 1:87–121.
   1978   Ecological and Phenomenological Aspects of Shamanism. Louise Bäckman and Åke Hultkrantz, eds. *Studies in Lapp Shamanism.* Acta Universitatis Stockholmensis. Stockholm Studies in Comparative Religion, No. 16, pp. 9–35. Stockholm: Almquist and Wiksell International.
Issacs, Susan
   1948   The Nature and Function of Phantasy. *International Journal of Psycho-Analysis* 29:73–97.
Jochelson, Waldemar
   1905–08   *I. Memoirs of the American Museum of Natural History* Vol. 10.
   1924   The Yukaghir and Yukaghirized Tungus. *Memoirs of the American Museum of Natural History,* Vol. 22, Part 2.
Kane, Henry
   1937   The Apache Secret Devil Dance. *El Palacio* 42:93–94.
Kiev, Ari
   1968   *Curanderismo: Mexican-American Folk Psychiatry.* New York: Free Press.
Kim, K.
   1972   Psychoanalytic Considerations of Korean Shamanism. *Journal of the Korean Neuropsychiatric Association* 11:121–129.

Klein, Melanie
   1932   *The Psycho-Analysis of Children.* London: Hogarth Press.
Klopfer, Bruno, and L. Bryce Boyer
   1961   Notes on the Personality Structure of a North American Indian Shaman: Rorschach Interpretation. *Journal of Projective Techniques* 25:170–178.
Koch-Grünberg, Theodor
   1910   *Zwei Jahre unter Den Indianern: Reisen in Nordwest-Brasilien*, 1903–05. Berlin: E. Wasmuth.
Kris, Ernst
   1952   *Psychoanalytic Explorations in Art.* New York: International Universities Press.
Kroeber, Alfred L.
   1952   *Handbook of the Indians of California.* Bureau of American Ethnology Bulletin 78. Washington, D.C.: Government Printing Office.
   1940   Psychosis or Social Sanction. *The Nature of Culture*, pp. 310–319. Chicago: University of Chicago Press, 1952.
Kunstadter, Peter
   1960   Culture Change, Social Structure, and Health Service: A Quantitative Study of Clinic Use Among the Apache of the Mescalero Reservation. Ph.D. dissertation, University of Michigan.
LaBarre, Weston
   1938   *The Peyote Cult.* University Publications in Anthropology, No. 13. New Haven: Yale University Press.
Lebra, William, and George De Vos
   n.d.   A Rorschach Study of Okinawan Shamans. Unpublished manuscript.
Loewald, Hans
   1979   Reflections on the Psychoanalytic Process and its Therapeutic Potential. Albert J. Solnit, Ruth S. Eissler, Anna Freud, Marianne Kris, and Peter B. Beubauer, eds. *Psychoanalytic Study of the Child* 34:155–167. New Haven: Yale University Press.
Lommel, Andreas
   1967   *Shamanism: The Beginnings of Art.* Michael Bullock, trans. New York: McGraw-Hill.
Lowie, Robert H.
   1935   *The Crow Indians.* New York: Rinehart [1956].
Luckert, Karl W.
   1979   *Coyoteway: A Navajo Holyway Ceremonial.* Tucson: University of Arizona Press, and Flagstaff: Museum of Northern Arizona Press.

MacLachlan, Bruce B.
  1962 *The Mescalero Apache Tribal Court: A Study of the Manifesta-tion of the Adjudicative Function of a Concrete Judicial Institution.* Ph.D. dissertation, University of Chicago.
Maestes, José Griego, and Rudolfo A. Anaya
  1982 *Cuentos: Tales from the Hispanic Southwest*, pp. 142–151. 3d printing. Santa Fe: Museum of New Mexico Press.
Mails, Thomas E.
  1974 *The People Called Apache.* Englewood Cliffs, N.J.: Prentice-Hall.
Meissner, William W.
  1978 *The Paranoid Process.* New York: Aronson.
Murphy, Robert F.
  1958 *Mundurucú Religion.* University of California Publications in American Archeology and Ethnology 49(1):1–154. Berkeley and Los Angeles: University of California Press.
Nordland, Odd
  1967 Shamanism as an Experiencing of the "Unreal." Carl-Martin Edsman, ed. *Studies in Shamanism*, pp. 166–185. Stockholm: Almqvist and Wiksell International.
Ohlmarks, Åke
  1939 *Studien zum Problem des Schamanismus.* Lund: C. W. K. Heerub.
Opler, Morris E.
  1933 *An Analysis of Mescalero and Chiricahua Apache Social Orga-nization in the Light of Their Systems of Relationship.* Ph.D. dis-sertation, University of Chicago. Private edition distributed by University of Chicago Libraries [1936].
  1936a The Influence of Aboriginal Pattern and White Contact on a Recently Introduced Ceremony, the Mescalero Peyote Rite. *Jour-nal of American Folklore* 49:143–166.
  1936b Some Points of Comparison and Contrast Between the Treatment of Functional Disorders by Apache Shamans and Mod-ern Psychiatric Trends. *American Journal of Psychiatry* 92:1371–1387.
  1940 *Myths and Legends of the Lipan Apaches.* Memoirs of the American Folklore Society, Vol. 36. New York: J. J. Augustin.
  1941 *An Apache Lifeway: The Economic, Social, and Religious Institutions of the Chiricahua Indians.* New York: Cooper Square Publishers. 2d edition, 1965.
  1946a The Mountain Spirits of the Chiricahua Apache. *Masterkey* 20:125–131.

1946*b*   The Creative Role of Shamanism in Apache Mythology. *Journal of American Folklore* 59:269–281.

1969   *Apache Odyssey: A Journey Between Two Worlds.* New York: Holt, Rinehart and Winston.

Parin, Paul

1971   Fantasy and Communication. Paul Parin, Fritz Morgenthaler, and Goldy Parin-Matthèy, eds. Patricia Klamerth, trans. *Fear Thy Neighbor as Thyself: Psychoanalysis and Society Among the Anyi of West Africa*, pp. 248–313. Chicago: University of Chicago Press, 1980.

Parin-Matthèy, Goldy

1971   Witches, Female Shamans, and Healers. Paul Parin, Fritz Morgenthaler, and Goldy Parin-Matthèy, eds. Patricia Klamerth, trans. *Fear Thy Neighbor as Thyself: Psychoanalysis and Society Among the Anyi of West Africa*, pp. 212–247. Chicago: University of Chicago Press, 1980.

Paulson, Ivar

1965   Der Schamanismus in Nordeurasien (Siberien). *Paideuma* 11:91–104.

Poole, Fitz John Porter

1981   Tamam: Ideological and Sociological Configurations of "Witchcraft" among Bimin-Kukusmin. *Social Analysis*, no. 8, pp. 58–84. November.

Róheim, Géza

1923   Nach dem Tode des Urvaters. *Imago* 1:83–121.

1925   *Australian Totemism: A Psychoanalytical Study in Anthropology.* London: Allen and Unwin.

1952   The Evil Eye. *American Imago* 9:351–363.

Salvado, Rosende

1851   *Memoire Storiche Dell'Australia, Particolarmente della Missione Benedettina di Nuova Norcia e degli Usi e Costumi degli Australiani.* Rome: S. Congregazione de Propaganda Fide.

Seligmann, Charles Gabriel

1910   *The Melanesians of British New Guinea.* Cambridge: Cambridge University Press.

Servadio, Emilio

1936   Die Angst vor dem bösen Blick. *Imago* 22:396–408.

Shirokogoroff, S. M.

1924   *Psychomental Complex of the Tungus.* London: Kegan Paul, Trench, Trubner.

Silverman, Julian

1967   Shamans and Acute Schizophrenia. *American Anthropologist* 69:21–31.

Slotkin, J. S.
1956 *The Peyote Religion*. Glencoe, Ill.: Free Press.
Spencer, Baldwin, and Francis James Gillen
1899 *The Native Tribes of Central Australia*. London: Macmillan.
1904 *Northern Tribes of Central Australia*. London: Macmillan.
Stärcke, August
1920 The Reversal of the Libido-Sign in Delusions of Persecution. *International Journal of Psycho-Analysis* 1:231–234.
Steward, Julian H.
1929 *The Clown in Native North America*. Doctoral dissertation, University of California, Berkeley, unpublished.
Threlkeld, Lancelot Edward
1892 *An Australian Language as Spoken by Awabakal*. Sydney: C. Potter.
van Ophuijsen, J. H. W.
1920 On the Origin of the Feeling of Persecution. *International Journal of Psycho-Analysis* 1:235–239.
Vereecken, J. L. T.
1928 A propos du mauvais oeil. *Hygiene Mentale* 57.25–38.

Part V

Conclusions: Transcultural Assessment Using Psychological Tests

George A. De Vos

Transcultural research on personality cannot be accomplished without some form of controlled comparison of individuals and groups. For standardized assessments of mental functioning within Western culture the psychiatrist or psychologist has usually relied on a battery of several personality tests which are used to measure a number of dimensions of mental competence, intellectual capacities, and personality controls operative in one's cognitive functioning and emotional expression. The question arises. What can one do with these helpful, if not completely satisfactory, present analytic tools when one leaves the normative cultural base on which they were originally validated?

Unresolved in the minds of many is whether one can use with validity in any given culture projective psychological techniques eliciting responses to relatively unstructured materials. There is considerable controversy today, especially among those who have concerned themselves with the study of mental health transculturally, whether one can presume validity for results obtained by the administration of identical psychological tests in highly divergent cultural settings. The examples provided in this volume argue for the feasibility of such comparisons, given due consideration for differences both in the cultural content of particular stimuli and in the culturally prevalent styles of response.

Projective tests, such as the Rorschach or the Thematic

Apperception Test, although presenting stimuli of an ambiguous nature, can have different meaning if one is analyzing the content directly. We have argued, however, that if one looks at expressive patterns, or the processes of thought involved in responding to the stimuli, one can make meaningful comparisons that transcend the specificities of individual cultural settings.

The use of tests cross-culturally is severely circumscribed when comparisons are made across the barrier of literacy. The cultural experience necessary to respond perceptually to unfamiliar written patterns has, no doubt, profound influences on the general organization of perception which affects radically the validity of standardized tests with nonliterate groups.

In many instances, one finds that insurmountable difficulties are involved in attempts at directly translating some individual items of objective questionnaires or structured tests for comparative use between literate cultures. As a consequence, those who are working in the field of psychodiagnosis have learned to delimit very carefully the use of questionnaires or objective methods when their subjects come from divergent cultural backgrounds.

However, even so-called "objective tests" that require yes-no or agree-disagree responses, when carefully prepared, can be applied cross-culturally to literate societies in order to obtain both within-group and between-group valid comparisons. For example, I have worked with the CPI (the California Personality Inventory) in Japan and Taiwan, as well as in the United States. In these literate, modern, but culturally very different settings, the norms were different but the subscales differentiated as they do in the United States. When statistically compared on overall scales, disregarding the weakness of some individual items, the CPI distinguishes delinquent from nondelinquent youths in India, Italy, and Japan (Gough 1960; Gough and Sandhu 1964; Gough, De Vos, and Mizushima 1965). Delinquent Chinese youth and their parents could be differentiated from members of nondelinquent families in both San Francisco and Taiwan (Abbott 1976; Abbott et al., n.d.). Objective tests, used judiciously, can produce valid results, contrary to the a priori judgment against such cross-cultural use.

Can conclusions be drawn as to the comparative quality of

thinking or the nature of ego mechanisms involved in the control of impulse or affect of members of such divergent cultures as the U.S., Japan, Algeria, and Apache? This volume gives our empirical evidence why we believe such efforts are indeed possible using a perceptual test such as the Rorschach.

Mental Health Considered Cross-Culturally

A Nonrelativistic, Transcultural Definition of Mental Health

Any transcultural definition of mental health is based implicitly on some theory of ideal standards of psychological functioning potentially realizable in human maturation, given facilitative socialization experiences. All psychodynamic theories today are based on a similar assumption: that there are universals of psychosexual maturation inherent in individuals rather than in culture. This assumption of universals in the possible sequence of maturation usually considered as psychosocial "development" seems to be borne out by what little controlled evidence has become available from perceptual and cognitive studies so far attempted in diverse cultural settings. One must distinguish what is simple physiological "maturation" from what is environmentally influenced "development." These concepts are directed toward explaining the same behavior, but they are distinct. Maturation emphasizes biological potential. Development emphasizes cultural actualization of potential.

The delineation of the parameters of human potential comprising intellectual maturation has received grossly insufficient study outside Western culture. Additional work on the physiological maturation of cognition, for example, is essential. One would presume that one parameter of any universalistic definition of mental health would be some definition of optimal maturation of conceptual-cognitive abilities in the individual. Psychosocial development depending on underlying maturation tends toward optimal adaptation to the environment, natural and social, as well as a modification of the surroundings to the advantage of the individual and the group. There is positive evidence that comparative development of cognitive processes can be tested by techniques other than those used in clinical psychology that hold promise although little more than a beginning has been made.

Cognitive studies and studies of causal thought both suggest that the same stages of "maturation" can make their appearance in other cultural settings at about the same physiological age period at which they occur in Western civilization. Price-Williams (1961) used the Piaget method of testing concepts of conservation of quantity among children of the West African Tiv tribe. He found no essential differences in the maturation of the concept of continuous and discontinuous quantities when his results were compared with those obtained normatively by Piaget in Switzerland (Flavell 1963).

However, other evidence suggests that culture patterns "developmentally" can impede or retard the appearance of these seemingly physiologically determined maturational stages. In comparative studies of children by Laurendeau and Pinard (1962) in Canada, and by Dubreuil and Boisclair (1960), in Canada and Martinique, there was found a retardation of approximately four years in Martinique subjects compared with French Canadians in the appearance of similar maturational stages. The stages appeared sequentially in the same order, but from the evidence, culturally induced impediments or the lack of a facilitative cultural atmosphere seemed to prevent the appearance of expected behavior at the anticipated time. As mentioned in the introduction, more work of the above nature in the field of cognitive development is necessary.

The relevance of the more recent work of Witkin (Witkin 1967; Witkin and Berry 1975) related to field dependence/field independence has been discussed extensively elsewhere (De Vos 1978, 1982). The results obtained by Witkin and those using field dependence studies in different groups suggest impediments to cognitive development in some groups relative to others. Their evidence points toward a generalization that in any indigenous cultural group of sufficient size (although one must not rule out the possible dysgenic inbreeding of mental defects or deficiency in a relatively small isolated community), one would find the biological capacities for the appearance of maturational potentials in cognitive development to be the same throughout Homo sapiens.

Nevertheless, the evidence also suggests that specific cultures may inhibit or impede the appearance of these maturational stages in a significant number of individuals in given cultural settings.

Mental Health as an Ideal, not a Normative Concept

There are adherents of relativistic theories of human adaptaton who believe that mental health can be defined by recourse to normative standards of mental functioning general to a group. They fail to realize that implicit in, and necessary to, the psychiatric transcultural approach is some universalistic concept of optimal levels of psychological functioning constituting mental health that would hold constant regardless of cultural variation. It is necessary to stress this point since it is only on this basis that one can presume to assess mental health transculturally by any controlled means. Clinical inferences derived from psychodiagnostic tests are made with reference to a physiologically determined range of possible functioning varying from grossly deficient to optimal along several parameters of mental functioning. This point has already been made very cogently by Hallowell in his perceptive article on the use of Rorschach cross-culturally (1957:72):

... for our present-day knowledge, imperfect as it may be in some respects, makes it necessary to differentiate a positive, higher, or optimal level of psychological functioning or psycho-dynamic adjustment... from a lower or less positive one... mental health, or an equivalent concept, is not culture bound but has universal significance both as a concept and a value. If this be so, then it may be possible to emerge from the chrysalis of an elementary cultural relativism.

The pertinence of a relativistic position in regard to subjective values cannot be gainsaid, however. Rating one culture over another in many instances becomes a matter of personal preference. Cultures, in one sense, can be viewed as patterns which selectively impede or foster various forms of imperfectly realized maturation in their members.

From the standpoint of scientific description, one must not impose one's own moral judgment but simply record what one finds. Nevertheless, only through the assumption that mental health is based on some absolute standards of psychosexual maturation related to normative distributions of personality traits is it possible for us to measure human functioning relatively.

Testing Aspects of Mental Health Cross-Culturally

Using optimal standards of emotional and intellectual coping as criteria, it does become possible in limited instances to arrive at some objective consensus concerning the relative efficiency of some cultures in the molding of personalities more or less capable of functioning at various levels of mental health. In the various chapters of this volume we have applied this contention to psychosocial problems. In Arab culture we discussed a patterning of suspiciousness that impedes social interaction (chaps. 8 and 9). In the Apache (chap. 10) there is progressive cognitive constriction noticeable during the formative school period. The Japanese, as we have indicated in chapter 4, pay a psychological price for their emphasis on social conformity experienced from childhood on. Beck's American normative group (1964) as discussed in chapter 3, manifested patterns of emotional responsiveness far less than ideal by Rorschach test criteria.

Although all cultures in one sense or other are imperfect compromises, some are manifestly less facilitative of cognitive or affective development in their members than others. Just as it is possible to differentiate stable, mature individuals from those suffering severe problems of intrapsychic adjustment, so, too, it is possible in specific cultures to differentiate between situations relatively conducive to the realization of human potentials from those producing severe internal conflicts or maladjustments among many of their members.

Specifically, in attempting transcultural comparisons of mental health, we can distinguish variabilities among individuals in very unlike culture groups in respect to intrapsychic adjustment. Further, we can come to some considered overall judgment concerning the relative prevalence in particular populations of such variables related to mental health, as psychological flexibility or rigidity. There are measurable differences in maturity or primitiveness in cognitive structures. There are differences in the relative proneness to resort to particular defense mechanisms. Finally, psychological variables usually found in Western culture marking neurotic or psychotic states do have the same "diagnostic" significance from one culture to the next as far as the status of mental health in any group is concerned.

The material on the Algerian Arabs in particular has addressed itself to some of these questions. It is for the reader to determine the degree to which these contentions have been answered by evidence.

In our own judgment, we believe it feasible, first, by means of unstructured tests, to attempt valid assessments of traits presumed to be associated with the mental health of a particular population or culture. Secondly, we can discriminate among individuals in any particular population or culture, regardless of literacy or other such dimensions, in respect to qualitative differences in their comparative state of mental health. We believe the material presented above has answered some questions in this regard.

Individual Differences

In every group whose Rorschach test protocols I have examined, I have found within-group differentiation possible. The chapters on individual Japanese (chap. 7), Algerians (chap. 9), and Apaches (chaps. 11 and 12), we believe, demonstrate an ability to use the Rorschach test in sketching personality profiles. In a later publication we plan to further illustrate this potential in more cases drawn from Ifaluk Atoll, Alaska, Israel, West Africa, the "outback" of Australia, and the Lapland area of Finland. Some of these normative samples, such as that gathered by Melford Spiro from Ifaluk, appear exceedingly aberrant to us (Spiro 1952). Nevertheless, within the Ifaluk cultural context, some deviant inhabitants "distinguished" themselves by giving even more unusual Rorschach responses that separated them from the other members of their group. Thus De Vos could identify from their protocols alone the two Ifalukese who were considered by their culture mates to be "deviant," "separate," and "strange."

Questions of Mental Health Related to Social
Maladaptation and Maladjustment

In assessing cultural patterns from a mental health standpoint, one is not limited to a consideration of the relative maturation of intrapsychic processes, but one must also examine the continual interaction of individual and environment, inner experience and social behavior, throughout the life cycle. A clear-cut definition of mental health in terms of inner adjustive considerations alone is impossible. In addition, varying normatively experienced socialization patterns conduce to patterns of inner adjustment that are potentially more or less adequate in meeting the environmental stresses of adulthood. Cultures also differ in the manner in which they provide a relatively satisfactory environment for various sex, age, and occupational segments of the population.

As we discussed fully in chapter 1, a further necessary differentiation, therefore, is to be made in clarifying the role of psychological assessment cross-culturally. "Personality" as a construct toward which the results of various tests are directed can pertain both to intrapsychic patterns and to patterns of social adaptation. Behavior patterns or social attitudes in any culture are not simply related to psychological structures but are interactive.

Nevertheless, social psychiatry or clinical psychology must differentiate between maladaptation simply from the standpoint of social functioning within a culture, and "disturbed" behavior resulting from intrapsychic difficulties. Adjustive difficulties (the traditional province of psychiatry) may take the form of physiological defects, rigid, visibly maladjustive defensive structures, or some other less easily observable failures in the complete maturation of ego functions which makes ordinary social life difficult if not impossible. What has our Rorschach evidence from a test quite specifically directed toward structure in personality contributed to the distinction between maladjustment and maladaptation?

Psychodiagnosis, by both psychiatrists and psychologists in Western culture, tends to rely heavily on the fact that there seems to be a great deal of congruence between forms of obviously maladaptive behavior from the standpoint of society, and specific forms of maladjustment in the organization of thought or emotional expression definable from the standpoint of intrapsychic processes. There are some superficial definitions of mental health that are derivative from this apparent congruency. The usual clinical psychodiagnosis is basically a differential diagnosis in which certain responses are quantitatively considered as revealing a propensity in the individual to manifest in overt behavior some signs of inner maladjustment. However, as in our work with Algerians, when a particular psychological test is given cross-culturally or, for that matter, when it is used in normative studies within Western subcultures, as in our study of Japanese Americans, reported in chapter 4, one frequently notes that a number of individuals show signs of maladjustment on tests. However, their manifest behavior does not readily reveal them to be different from those who show more adequate forms of mental functioning in their test results. Moreover, there has been sufficient experience now on the part of those who work with deviant populations, such as delinquents, to require caution in any assumption that one can judge some forms of socially deviant behavior as necessarily reflecting critical maladjustment. Chapters 5 and 6 are illustrative of this point. In considering the Rorschach records of delinquent and nondelinquent youth, only by statistical means do we find significant differences between groups. Individuals cannot be individually diagnosed "delinquent" or "nondelinquent" on the basis of one test of personality structure.

To illustrate the complexities involved in normative studies of nonclinical populations using the Rorschach, it is possible to refer to an unpublished study reported to me by Dr. Jean MacFarlane (personal communication, 1965). As part of a large-scale longitudinal study at the Institute of Human Development conducted at the University of California, various tests, including the Rorschach, were given periodically. There were also interviews conducted at specified times over a period of years so that the results obtained in childhood and adolescence could be compared with the behavior and attitudes of the same individuals at various life periods. In the study specifically dealing with Rorschach results, quartile division was made of extreme cases, dividing those with inconsistent ratings from those rated similarly on test results and behavioral evidence. These were records of cases given a prognostic rating "excellent" in adolescence in regard to social adaptation on the basis of behavioral and interview criteria, but at the same time given a "poor" rating for adjustment on the basis of the Rorschach. In addition to those excellent or poor on both measures there was a group rated excellent on the Rorschach but receiving poor prognostic ratings on the basis of behavioral evidence. Longitudinally, it was found in examining their subsequent social and occupational patterns over a period of years that many of the individuals who had been given excellent ratings on the basis of the Rorschach but poor ratings on the basis of their behavior as adolescents in many instances made productive and creative adaptations, but in less conventional careers. They, in many instances, came from families in which affective displays of both a positive and negative nature were more dramatically a part of family interaction than was characteristic for the American middle class. Those with good interview ratings but relatively poor Rorschach findings, demonstrating various forms of constriction, immaturity and particularly morbid content, tended to come from families where interpersonal patterns were maintained on a pleasant but "proper" basis. These latter cases demonstrated in their career choice and career abilities less capacity for a creative open use of fantasy. Instead, their life patterns were hampered, but generally not totally compromised, by the considerable expenditure of energy necessary to repress or inhibit any overt expression of what would be considered disruptive behavior. It was among those cases given poor prognostic ratings on the basis of *both* the Rorschach and the behavioral-interview evidence where one now finds the most personal problems appearing overtly as part of subsequent occupational and marital career patterns.

The use of psychodiagnostic tests on normative populations anywhere amply demonstrates the relatively rare appearance of individuals who seem to show some optimal psychological balance characteristic of full mental health as defined by ideal standards. Most individual personality formations are more likely to be characterized by some form or other of incomplete maturation. It is a characteristic of the Rorschach to reveal the relative pressure on behavior of unresolved unconscious processes. The limited view of an individual seen through the perspective of the

Rorschach sometimes tells us more about a potential malfunctioning than about the effective social resources available within the person. It tells us nothing about his or her immediate social environment integrative beliefs, or patterns of successful dependency, that help individuals meet any situation of potential stress.

The usual, clinical use of the Rorschach test depends on certain critical definitions of imbalance which, if exceeded, suggest some serious form of intrapsychic malfunctioning. Individuals using the test only in a clinic setting where, by definition, the patient usually appears as a result of disturbed behavior, are sometimes unaware of the relative frequency of the appearance of signs of similar malfunctioning in records of individuals who do not find themselves constrained to appear for clinical assessment. This fact leads the present authors to caution the users of psychodiagnostic instruments that they must differentiate between weaknesses, defects, or distortions of personality structure and the actual appearance of overt, psychiatrically designated symptoms.

In a study of schizophrenics in remission, Samuel J. Beck (1954, 1964) revealed in a five-year follow-up that, for the most part, the Rorschach patterns did not differ significantly from those obtained on the same individuals when they were first brought to the hospital for observation and treatment. Yet many of these individuals, at the time they were retested, had made some form of social adaptation in a sufficiently benign, nonstressful social environment, that they were able to function without further psychiatric guidance. This study was done before drugs were used to facilitate such adaptation.

One must recognize that individuals with neurotic or psychotic propensities may manifest symptoms only under conditions which have become too stressful for the individual to cope with without drawing critical attention to oneself. If it were otherwise there could be no social psychiatry, for the social psychiatrist must take into account systematic social or cultural stresses that contribute to the selective appearance of manifest patterns of intrapsychic disturbance in particular groups or cultures.

Even within our own culture it may be very difficult to recognize potential sources of stress from the outside. Such difficulties in understanding situational provocations often lead to the assumption on the part of some psychiatrists that particular manifest symptoms occurring in the neurotic or psychotic can occur without any environmental provocation whatsoever. Yet many individuals who have manifested psychotic symptomatology at some time in their lives may never again do so. One must assume some relationship of clinical patterns to environmental conditions, not simply to organic or biological deficiencies interfering with integrative capacities.

This lack of congruence between the personality structure revealed by the Rorschach test and the actual presence of symptoms should not lead one to dismiss as invalid what the test reveals concerning patterns of intrapsychic malfunctioning. The test does not pretend to measure the relative stress in the social environment in which an individual is functioning or one's immediate reactions to it.

Problems of psychodiagnosis are further compounded when we attempt to assess mental health in a non-Western culture. The incongruities between a psychodiagnostic picture on the Rorschach and the social adaptation of the individual may become even greater. One finds numerous examples of cultural patterns which, in effect, provide for types of expressive behavior which if occurring within our culture would be defined as symptomatic of some form of intrapsychic maladjustment. As we have already discussed in our Introduction, for example, trance behavior, indicating "loss of ego control," can be socially expressed, while the individual remains essentially conforming and within the bounds of prescribed behavior defined by the culture. Culture patterns may disguise patterns of personality rigidification which become apparent only if the requirements or modes of social adaptation are suddenly disrupted by changes in the social environment. Some such form of social change is much more apt to occur with the greatly increased tempo of communication throughout the world. Cultures whose members in greater proportion are unduly rigidified both intrapsychically as well as in terms of culturally prescribed behavior are apt to manifest numerous signs of social maladaptation in times of change.

Many cultures flexibly provide for deviant patterns for those individuals within the culture who have particularly aberrant tendencies resulting from intrapsychic personality structures that make easy conformity impossible. Such individuals can often take on some form of traditional, unconventional role, which in effect is one form of tolerated or even highly evaluated adaptation within the society, without incurring total ostracism. For instance, assuming the role of a holy man within Arab culture, as discussed by Miner and myself (chap. 9), provided for the possibility of a type of withdrawal from society which received a positive sanction and support as long as the role was at least minimally played according to prescribed expectations. Chapter 12 described an Apache shaman with severe internal conflict who received the social support of her group as she fulfilled a needed role. The degree to which certain forms of idiosyncratic religion or minor deviant social units within American culture are peopled by individuals who are thereby attempting to socialize intrapsychic tensions is an issue worthy of further systematic exploration.

Cross-culturally there are extreme variations in the type of responses elicited which gainsay ordinary clinical interpretations based on the usual quantitative scoring methods. Nevertheless, the Rorschach responses, as Hallowell (1957) justly pointed out, elicit standardized samples of behavior that can be interpreted in the context of culture as well as in terms of an individual's own patterns of thought and perception. Once the subject's sincere cooperation in meeting the task has been gained, the forthcoming responses, whatever their limitations or peculiarities, are valid examples of perceptual operations indirectly communicated by verbal means. The manner in which responses are communicated, the particular locations selected follow lawful forms of mental association that signify the relative presence of definable, prelogical modalities in thought. One cannot assume thereby, however, that such prelogical patterns directly relate to identifiable types of breakdowns in socially expected behavior.

This subject was discussed in detail in the two chapters on the Algerian Arabs. One may infer, comparing the thought patterns prevalent in the Arab group with those of the Japanese, that one could differentiate the relative ease with which they could meet situations demanding new types of decision making. But as was obvious in the case of the Arabs tested—including some with what can be termed highly paranoid ideation—when an individual continued to reside within a culture pattern familiar from childhood, he could remain socially adaptive as long as unchallenged by a new situation that would unduly tax potentially defective integrative capacities.

Unfortunately, many of the studies done with the Rorschach cross-culturally are not satisfactory in regard to the level of competence manifested by the investigator in the use of quantitative methods. Often no attention is paid to qualitative features of the record that have not been scorable within the limits of present generally accepted methods. The symbolic material which we have made central to this volume is often totally ignored.

In understanding the limitations of the Rorschach test cross-culturally one cannot overlook the fact that in a number of instances the material elicited from a particular culture group is not very revealing. Some groups are characterized by the type of constrictive ego defenses which seriously limit the material available for interpretation, as is the case of the Apaches discussed in chapter 10. When one has to deal with a great deal of constriction present in the perceptual apparatus one must employ other means to gain access to what might be the dynamics behind such constriction. Such problems of interpretation not only occur in cross-cultural studies but are frequently found in psychiatric settings within our own culture, where one is periodically faced with a guarded, constricted Rorschach record difficult to define as to possible pathology.

In spite of such obvious limitations it is our considered judgment that the material elicited when an individual genuinely attempts to cope with the assigned task is a valid sample of behavior related to mental functioning regardless of culture. But to gain valid inferences from this elicited behavior demands more from the interpreter than mechanical application of a scoring system. One must not forget that any scoring system of itself is simply a mnemonic device used to summarize the complex variables found in given responses. One cannot simply reify scoring symbols and extract mechanical interpretations, since it is always necessary to pass a considered judgment as to what any particular response implies, given consideration of other qualitative features found in the protocols which are not subjected to quantified scoring. The process of interpretation demands considerable experience with both normative and clinical populations of individuals who have exhibited some demonstrable forms of mental illness.

The Distinction Between Diagnosis of Mental Health and Socially Acceptable Therapeutic Intervention

There is confusion in the minds of some that defining members of a minority group as manifesting mental ill health would have negative social consequences. The use of "cross-cultural" definitions of mental illness is not necessarily related to institutionalization of the individual or some form of psychiatric intervention that serves to denigrate the individual as "mentally ill." This type of confusion can best be illustrated by citing a paper first presented at the First International Congress of Social Psychiatry. Guttentag and Denmark (1964) carefully analyzed Rorschach tests given to thirty institutionalized adult female Southern blacks who were in-migrants to New York and a comparable control sample of thirty black women working as domestic employees in wealthy homes in Nassau County and Queens County, New York. The samples were matched for age and socioeconomic status. The investigators found no significant differences in the standard scoring between the experimental and the control groups of blacks on the Rorschach. Both groups scored considerably below what are considered minimal standards of Rorschach expectations. They both exhibited a very poor level of form quality in their responses. What was more important from a symbolic standpoint was that both groups produced a great deal of direct sadomasochistic material similar to that reported by Goldfarb in his earlier clinical study of American black males conducted in collaboration with Kardiner and Ovessey (1951). To illustrate briefly: among the content responses mentioned in their 1964 report were: "A butterfly, someone tore the wings and it is still alive"; "I see two bugs standing and looking at some kind of dead meat at their feet"; "A vagina all red, raw, acid eating it away like when you get cancer, it spreads all over." Citing such material, these researchers conclude:

Since the two groups are not significantly different from each other the institutionalized population may be assumed to be a "normal" segment of the Southern Negro in-migrant group. . . . The clinical interpretation of the Rorschach rests on normative assumptions. In view of the findings of the study the clinical interpretations and diagnostic labels typically made in clinical settings of groups which are not part of the standardization population such as the Southern Negro, are thrown into serious doubt. In the case of the particular sub-culture investigated in this study there are only two possible evaluations of the Rorschach results. It is necessary to assume either that the entire sub-culture is "abnormal" and therefore in need of institutionalization, or that the Rorschach performance of an individual who comes from a racial, ethnic or sub-cultural group for which there are no norms cannot now be evaluated nor can any normative diagnostic label be applied to their Rorschach performance. . . . The diagnostic label of "psychotic" naturally carries with it the connotative implications of "potentially dangerous," "unable to care for oneself," etc., and it implicitly sanctions the institutionalization of the Southern Negro.

Aside from the overgeneralization from cleaning women to in-migrating Southern blacks in New York (the selectivity of this particular type of occupational function was not considered by the authors), there are particular conclusions in this presented paper that illustrate three of the apparent confusions concerning psychodiagnosis and a transcultural concept of mental health.

There is, first, the misconception already elaborated upon in the above discussion, that the Rorschach or perhaps even concepts of mental health rest only on normative assumptions. As we have indicated, regardless of the prevalence of certain response within any cultural or subcultural group, if they are indicative of intrapsychic disturbance, they can be so interpreted. Their frequency makes them typical, and statistically "normal," rather than "normal" in a mental health sense. The predominance of these responses, therefore, is an index of the prevalence of defensive cognitive functioning characteristic of the sample in question. As in the evidence cited in chapter 8, personality responses to stress are manifest in some minorities. One can generalize that more members of certain minority groups are under continuous social stress. This social condition leads to the production of symbolic sadomasochistic response that may appear in both the institutionalized and uninstitutionalized members of the subculture. One certainly should avoid a semantic confusion in the use of the words "normal" and "normative."

Secondly, the conclusions arrived at by the authors of this study would seem to oppose any possible assessment that serious psychological consequences can indeed result from growing up in an unhealthy national social climate brought about by systematic social denigration over several generations. Denigrated populations do have debilitative socialization experiences (De Vos and Wagatsuma 1966; Lee and De Vos 1981). Opposition to such a conclusion stems partially from the authors' misconception that the only "treatment" envisioned by psychiatrists for people showing problems of this nature is some form of institutionalization, drug administration, or perhaps shock therapy.

The authors also show a relativistic bias even more prevalent in anthropology. There is an understandable humanitarian inclination to shun any supposition that a particular American minority group may manifest, in some of its members, psychological debilitation as a result of the discrimination experienced through several generations. To do them justice, Guttentag and Denmark suggested in their paper that:

Alternative solutions [to unthinking institutionalization] might include job training, non-psychiatric housing and outpatient social services. These could substitute for society's present solution of institutionalization, and at the same time result in more constructive changes in the life of the individual Southern Negro in-migrant. (P. 6)

One must note that this paper was presented at a time when indeed it was a policy to more quickly institutionalize individuals with signs of mental illness. In the climate of the late 1980s, the opposite is more likely. It is only with considerable reluctance that individuals are institutionalized, in spite of their manifest incapacity in some instances to maintain themselves outside an institutionalized setting. (We have reached a stage in the treatment of the mentally ill today of more general understanding that environmental manipulation could allow for adequate utilization of individual resources despite the chronic handicap of mental illness. However, the financing necessary for such programs has not been forthcoming.

In effect, these authors were arguing that the diagnosis of mental health problems could be socially damaging, and to protect the individual it was safer to argue for cultural relativity. This tendency of avoiding psychological testing because results can be conceived of as socially damaging has been a type of thought that has been severely inhibiting the use of psychodiagnostic testing. Even in psychology one finds today a reluctance to use various forms of assessment because the social consequences are considered to be negative rather than helpful to the individual. This confusion of scientific findings with social policy is one of the drawbacks of today's climate, in understanding not only the usefulness but also the validity of personality assessment.

The third confusion in the Guttentag and Denmark paper is less apparent but illustrates the overlap between social definitions of maladaptation and of severe maladjustment based solely on an assessment of structural characteristics of the individual's personality. As we have indicated, the limitations of tests of intrapsychic organization applied to predicting social behavior should be explicitly recognized. It is naive to assume that such tests are direct measures of the manifest social adaptation of given individuals in every given environment. Nevertheless, properly interpreted, data from Rorschach tests, such as those presented by Guttentag and Denmark, provide supportive evidence for why the institutionalized sample of blacks would manifest statistically a very high rate of psychiatric disturbance, given their experience as in-migrants from small rural settings trying to adapt to life in New York. The fact that not everyone in the particular sample gave similar overt concrete expression of manifest difficulty does not counterindicate the validity of the Rorschach results, which suggest some form of mental debilitation to be rather general for some segments of rural blacks migrating from minority status in the American South to minority status in the urban North. Research with the Rorschach test can indeed produce findings that discomfort us. The effects of enslavement and denigration over several generations can be severely psychologically debilitative to a considerable number of a population so affected (De Vos 1978). It should make mental health workers all the more aware that individual therapy, no matter how beneficial, cannot by itself resolve social problems which can be ameliorated only by social means doing away with status inequality and systematic economic deprivation.

Mobility, Minority Status, and Problems of Mental Health: Research Evaluations by Means of the Rorschach Test

It is precisely in such stressful situations as social mobility or social change that assessments of intrapsychic adjustment are helpful in assessing mental health problems. One may accept the proposition that members of a group showing serious potential problems on measures of adjustment may not reveal any overt maladaptation as long as the individual remains within his or her own traditionally stable social group. Problems in inner adjustments are obviously more likely to reveal themselves under conditions of unusual environmental stress.

The geographically or socially mobile individual who leaves one's own society to enter into another host culture may face the extreme difficulties attendant upon becoming a member of a disparaged minority. Here community patterns in the original society may be more or less helpful during a period of readaptation. In the case of the Japanese meeting racial prejudice in the United States, cohesive community processes and a tradition of close family relationships supported the individual migrant against external rejection by white Americans. Some of our specific discussions in chapter 8 comparing the Rorschach responses of Japanese Americans and Algerian Arabs indicate how the Rorschach may serve to throw some auxilary light on the complex issues involved as they may affect particular individuals with given personality propensities in differing situations of minority status.

In our study reported partially in chapter 4, the Issei or immigrant generation of Japanese Americans produced patterns which we later found to remain highly similar to those found in a normative sample of 724 Rorschach protocols obtained from three villages and two urban centers in Japan. Those American-born Japanese Nisei who had been totally reared in the United States and had gone through the American public school system did not show the variety of disturbances evident among those who became "Kibei" by having been sent back to Japan for some period of time during childhood. The Kibei manifested more signs of maladjustment than those who had not been put in such a precarious position of cultural marginality.

As we reported, there was one systematic difference in the Japanese American records generally when compared with both majority Americans and normative Japanese: Japanese American records had a sadomasochistic flavor. We found similar systematic differences in affective symbolic material in comparing Arabs living in a rather encapsulated environment on an oasis when compared with individuals from the same oasis who had relocated to the Casbah of Algiers. Of principal interest again was the fact that in the urbanized sample one found a type of sadomasochistic material that was relatively absent in the records taken from individuals in the oasis. In other structural aspects of personality the Arab records were highly dissimilar to those of the Japanese.

These two samples of records share at least one similarity with the sample of American blacks obtained by Goldfarb as part of the study by Kardiner and Ovesey (1951) and the Guttentag-Denmark material just cited. The chronic debilitating effects of minority status on personality structure are evident. These groups so different in other respects *all* became characterized by the presence of considerable sadomasochistic content. The obvious inference is that individuals finding themselves in minority status in what they may perceive as a hostile and depreciatory host culture may be subject to a type of chronic social stress that does show up symbolically in their responses given to the Rorschach.

It must be noted that by American standards there is a vast difference in the perceptual adequacy revealed in the Japanese Rorschach from those reported on American blacks. The family-based intense socialization experiences of the Japanese-Americans equip them to meet the challenges of American middle-class social expectations in a far more integrated way than is true for many of the single-parent, lower-class American blacks.

The elaborate studies of Malzberg and Lee (1956) on the relationship of mental illness and geographic mobility point up the complexities involved in tracing out the influence of the simple factor of migration as related to the statistics of first admission for psychosis. Their statistics separate the minority nonwhite from the white population of the state of New York. They reveal that minority status itself in the stable, non-migrating part of the population showed a rate of admissions for both men and women almost twice that of the white majority population. In those under 30 years of age and with less than five years residence the incidence of those diagnosed as schizophrenic was three times as great in the nonwhite population as in the white. The type of Rorschach records reported for black subjects is certainly in line with expectations of a much higher rate of obvious malfunctioning.

In some yet unfinished research dealing with total families of Northern Athabascan Indian Slavey and Dogrib communities in Canada done in collaboration with anthropologist June Helm, we have obtained radically different Rorschach materials from two small groups within the same basic culture (Helm, De Vos, and Carterette 1960). One may speculate as to why this is so. Is it due to specific familial hereditary factors, or simply to idiosyncratic modes of socialization of a nonintegrative sort as far as mental processes are concerned, taking place in families of one tiny isolated community but not in the other? Helm could observe no apparent differences in child-rearing practices. The issue obviously cannot be resolved by the present data available. What we do know is that the Rorschach tests obtained in the Slavey Indian kin community, whose members as a group have shown some unusual economic enterprise in a cooperative sawmill operation, demonstrate in the total group more adequate personality patterns that approach what would be considered normal expectations in non-clinical testing in the United States. In contrast, some of the records obtained from a particular Dogrib settlement manifest types of associative debilitation usually found only in records of individuals of subnormal mental capacity or organic brain damage. These records suggest a level of functioning that would be insufficient for independent maintenance in the modern American culture. One would, therefore, question the present capacity of many of this particular group to meet the challenge of a more complex form of social or economic life should it be forced upon them.

Hallowell (1957), in his research with Ojibway in various stages of acculturation, noted significant differences in the various norms of his group. In his particular samples the more acculturated Lac de Flambeau people gave evidence of poorer mental health by Rorschach criteria than did other, less acculturated groups. The question arises whether these differences were a function of the stresses inherent in their marginal cultural position or of special factors related to socialization within the specific families of this particular settlement. Our speculation would be in the direction of attributing these differences to stressful acculturative circumstances, but we cannot be certain. We simply reiterate that at the present state of our knowledge the evidence is fragmentary. Psychological tests such as the Rorschach cannot answer problems that involve complex social or cultural issues; they only provide an ancillary form of behavioral evidence that pertains to the assessments of personality functioning within given social settings.

Problems Inherent in Contemporary Work with the Rorschach Test

From the standpoint of scientific research, our field of inquiry has obvious defects. For those cognizant of the difficulties entailed in well-controlled research, the standards of work with projective instruments even within Western culture, let alone the application that has been made with them cross-culturally, have suffered by objective comparison with what has come to be expected in other fields of psychology (see chapter 2; Lindesmith and Strauss 1950; Lindzey 1961).

Unfortunately, training toward higher standards of research in this area is generally lacking. After an initial period of uncritical enthusiasm, actual work in "cultural and personality" has abated. This situation is at least partially due to the fact that research foundations by and large have advisers who look askance at projects in which testing with projective tests is integral to the research design. It has become almost fashionable in present-day psychologically oriented social anthropology, or in psychology, for that matter, to decry any interest in such research. Certainly a younger generation of graduate students has been deflected from such interests. Lacking technical competence, graduates few have chosen to enter this relatively denigrated field. In the universities, more intensive training than that which now exists would be necessary to reinstate these studies as acceptable for incoming graduates to take on cross-cultural personality assessment as a specialization. Unfortunately there are no indications that such an increase in training will come about in the near future. Nevertheless, we hope by this volume to create some discontent with the neglect to which projective testing has been almost systematically accorded within academic psychology departments.

In surveying the present status of training programs in either psychology or anthropology in the United States, a country that has been in the forefront of studies of personality in culture, we have found very little provided in the graduate schools to improve the standards of present endeavors which would lead future social scientists to more satisfactory transcultural studies by controlled psychological methods. There is obvious need not only for the refinement or modification of present test methods but also for the development of newer techniques to be administered collaboratively in large-scale testing programs. Fortunately, the considerable efforts to do comparative work in Japan and the U.S., mainly by developmental psychologists, will soon attract attention (Stevenson, Azuma, and Hakuta 1986).

One would hope that the present hunting and gathering stage of collecting relevant materials eventually will be supplanted by a more evolved planned economy of scientific effort. The evidence now relevant to a general cross-cultural definition of mental health derived from efforts at psychological test assessment is at best comparable to the poorly related fragments and clues available to the archaeologist by means of which he must reconstruct cultural sequences. The evidence remains for the most part suggestive rather than conclusive.

In this volume, attempts have been made to illustrate the potential validity of transcultural diagnosis in mental health almost solely in terms of the Rorschach test, not because it offers the best potential means one can envision for comparative work, but simply because in our own judgment it is the only method so far that has been applied to date in a sufficient number of cultural settings to permit some comparative assessment of a sufficiently complex number of variables. It is hoped that other means will be found to deal more intensively or more satisfactorily with particular variables that can be considered only incompletely by use of this method. The Rorschach, whatever its limitations, has proven useful, since it is one of the few tests which economically, in approximately an hour's time, permits inferences to be made concerning a complex interplay of intellectual and emotional factors considered central in personality functioning.

Symbolic Analysis Cross-Culturally

As a final word we reiterate that the problem of assessing symbolic material cross-culturally in its broadest compass involves assumptions as to the universal nature of human maturational potentials. Judgments concerning mental or emotional functioning uses ideal rather than normative standards of maturation and must distinguish among forms of manifest social adaptation, degrees of intensity of social stress in the environment related to age and status, and relative strengths and weaknesses of intrapsychic personality structure.

Psychological tests can be applied transculturally only with considerable difficulty. Of the methods of testing now in general practice, the Rorschach as a relatively unstructured and economically efficient technique has been put to widest use. This test is a valid though imperfect means of obtaining perceptual responses related to a number of intrapsychic structures, but when applied cross-culturally, it has not always been adequately interpreted or flexibly adapted to the task. There remains controversy and misunderstanding as to its merits and deficiencies. We have chosen a number of empirical experiments to emphasize what we see as its relative merits. As a means of eliciting standardized evidence of psychological defenses or controls, the test supplies valuable evidence, including symbolic content, which cannot be readily obtained by other methods. Such results must not be interpreted out of context, however, but must be used in conjunction with other data in respect to the social environment.

Of itself it cannot uniformly predict the overt appearance of what is socially perceived as disturbed behavior, nor is it limited to assessing only negative features of personality. In using the test cross-culturally we have been less concerned with the clinical assessment of population, rather, especially in the context of symbolic analysis, we have sought out also the positive, integrative features of personality. These positive features function equally in the operation of unconscious mechanisms found in the logic and fantasy of humans everywhere. Our quantification of Rorschach symbols considers both the positive concerns and the unresolved features of personality. This interplay of symbol expressions has been the central focus of this book. We believe this volume to be a contribution to knowledge about our common humanity—an affirmative but critical statement which considers both our pleasures and aspirations as well as the finite nature of any present individual personality, which is not simply a resultant continuity of the vicissitudes of the past, personal or cultural, but a partaker of human consciousness directed toward an undetermined future.

References

Abbott, Kenneth A.
  1976   Culture Change and the Persistence of the Chinese Personality. George A. De Vos, ed. *Responses to Change: Society, Culture, and Personality*, pp. 74–104. New York: D. Van Nostrand.
Abbott, Kenneth A. et al.
  n.d.   *Family Patterns of the Chinese of San Francisco*. Unpublished manuscript.
Beck, Samuel J.
  1954   *The Six Schizophrenias*. Research Monograph No. 6. New York: American Orthopsychiatric Association.
  1964   Symptom and Trait in Schizophrenia. *American Journal of Orthopsychiatry* 34:517.
De Vos, George A.
  1954   A Comparison of the Personality Differences in Two Generations of Japanese Americans by Means of the Rorschach Test. *Nagoya Journal of Medical Science* 17(3):153–265 (reprinted no. 34, 1966).
  1961   Symbolic Analysis in the Cross-Cultural Study of Personality. Bert Kaplan, ed. *Studying Personality Cross-Culturally*, pp. 391–405. Evanston, Ill.: Row, Peterson.

1978 Selective Permeability and Reference Group Sanctioning: Psychocultural Continuities in Role Degradation. Minton Yinger and Stephen Culter, eds. *Major Social Issues: A Multi-Community View*, pp. 9–24. Glencoe, Ill.: Free Press.
1982 Adaptive Strategies in American Minorities. E. E. Jones and S. Korchin, eds. *Minority Mental Health*, pp. 74–117. New York: Praeger.

De Vos, George A., and Horace Miner
1959 Oasis and Casbah: A Study in Acculturative Stress. Marvin K. Opler, ed. *Culture and Mental Health*, pp. 330–350. New York: Macmillan.

De Vos, George A., and Hiroshi Wagatsuma
1966 *Japan's Invisible Race: Caste in Culture and Personality*. Berkeley and Los Angeles: University of California Press.

Dubreuil, G., and C. Boisclair
1960 Le Réalisme chez enfant à la Martinique at au Canada français: étude génetique and expérimentale. *Thoughts from the Learned Societies of Canada*, pp. 83–95. Toronto: W. J. Gage.

Flavell, J. H.
1963 *The Developmental Psychology of Jean Piaget*. Princeton, N.J.: D. Van Nostrand.

Gough, Harrison G., and H. S. Sandhu
1964 Validation of the C.P.I. Socialization Scale in India. *Journal of Abnormal Social Psychology* 68:544–547.

Gough, Harrison G., George A. De Vos, and Keiichi Mizushima
1965 A Japanese Version of the C.P.I. Social Maturity Index. *Psychological Reports* 22:143–146.

Guttentag, M., and F. Denmark
1964 Racial and Cultural Differences in Rorschach Performance: In Southern Negro In-Migrants, Institutionalized and Noninstitutionalized. Paper presented at the First International Congress of Social Psychiatry, London. August.

Hallowell, A. I.
1957 *Culture and Experience*. Philadelphia: University of Pennsylvania Press.

Helm, June, George A. De Vos, and Teresa Carterette
1960 Variations in Personality and Ego Identification Within A Slave Indian Kin-Community. *National Museum of Canada Bulletin 190, Contributions to Anthropology*, Part 2.

Kardiner, A., and L. Ovesey
1951 *The Mark of Oppression*. Cleveland and New York: Meridian Books.

Laurendeau, M., and A. Pinard
1962 *Causal Thinking in the Child.* New York: International Universities Press.
Lee, Changsoo, and George A. De Vos
1981 *Koreans in Japan.* Berkeley, Los Angeles, London: University of California Press.
Lindesmith, A. R., and A. L. Strauss
1950 A Critique of Culture and Personality Writings. *American Social Review* 15:587.
Lindzey, Gardiner
1961 *Projective Techniques and Cross-Culture Research.* New York: Appleton-Century-Crofts.
Malzburg, B., and E. S. Lee
1956 *Migration and Mental Disease.* New York: Social Science Research Council.
Miner, H., and George A. De Vos
1960 Oasis and Casbah: Algerian Culture and Personality in Change. University of Michigan, Museum of Anthropology, *Anthropological Papers*, No. 15. Ann Arbor, Mich.: University of Michigan Press.
Mizushima, Keiichi, and George A. De Vos
1967 An Application of the California Psychological Inventory in a Study of Japanese Delinquency. *Journal of Social Psychology* 71:45–51.
Murakami, Eijii
1962 Special Characteristics of Japanese Personality Based on Rorschach Test Results. Tsuneo Muramatsu, Ed. *Nihonjin-Bunka to Pasonarite No Jisshoteki Kenkyu* [The Japanese: An Empirical Study in Culture and Personality], pp. 206–235. Tokyo and Nagoya: Reimei Shobo.
Price-Williams, Douglas R.
1961 A Study Concerning Concepts of Conservation of Quantity Among Primitive Children. *Acta Psychologia* 18:297–305.
Schafer, Roy
1954 *Psychoanalytic Interpretation in Rorschach Testing: Theory and Application.* New York: Grune and Stratton.
Spiro, Melford E.
1952 Ghosts, Ifaluk, and Teleological Functionalism. *American Anthropologist* 54:497–503.
Stevenson, Harold, Hiroshi Azuma, and Kenji Hakuta
1986 *Child Development and Education in Japan.* New York: Freeman.

Witkin, H. A.
　1967　Cognitive Styles Across Cultures. *International Journal of Psychology* 2:233–250.
Witkin, H. A., and J. W. Berry
　1975　Psychological Differentiation in Cross-Cultural Perspective. *Journal of Cross-Cultural Psychology* 6:4–87.

Appendixes

Appendix A

A Thematic Manual for Scoring Affective Inferences

George A. De Vos

The system herein outlined[1] proposes a supplementary way of scoring all responses on the Rorschach for symbolic affect, just as they are usually scored for location, form, and other determinants. All responses given in the free association to the blots are examined for their affective tone and for their symbolic representation of underlying feelings. Inferences can be made more precise by judicious, nonsuggestive questions during the inquiry period. Even though direct evidence of affective tone is lacking, certain responses highly suggestive of underlying affective pressures of various sorts can be scored according to certain psychoanalytic interpretations of the meaning of such symbolism. This system for scoring affect was developed to aid in the quantification of the Rorschach for research purposes, as well as to provide a useful tool for clinical Rorschach work.

None of the inferences below is to be considered final; each has to be seen in the light of the particular record. The definitions are hypotheses that must be examined in context. Nevertheless, they do offer a quantifiable, organized approach to content symbolism.

To aid in the precision of scoring and interpretation, the criterion statements have been made explicit and the rationale of the categories has been made more directly pertinent to the psychoanalytic theory of

---

[1] This manual, describing and illustrating the criteria for scoring affective inferences in the studies reported in this volume, is being further modified from the present version by L. Bryce Boyer, Charles W. Dithrich, Hillie Hamed, John Stone, and Andrea Walt. The latest version will be used in a subsequent work.

libidinal progression and object cathexis, as well as to the affective tone of the responses.

Although I have made some considerable modification of subcategories since the publication of my first manual (De Vos 1952), the major categories reported here remain the same. In creating more subcategories, I kept in mind the dangers of too free proliferation resulting from trying to handle individualistic responses. Since 1952, new subcategories were added only insofar as they seemed to supply some elemental affective constituent not already singled out for consideration in a previous subcategory. Discussion of content analysis in the publications of Phillips and Smith (1953) and Schafer (1954) were helpful in revising the criteria for scoring.

Relation of the Scoring System to Psychoanalytic Theory

This system of scoring the underlying affective symbolism is organized around three major affective categories common to most psychoanalytic understandings of the emotions, namely *positive* valences toward objects; *hostile*, destructive, or antagonistic feelings; and dread, fear, or *anxiety* of either a diffuse or focused nature. For separate consideration I have brought together as one category various expressions of helplessness and *dependent* need, subservience to authority, and symbols of security. The responses in this category reflect object cathexis or attachment, in which dependency is salient, in contrast to those under the positive category, in which pleasure is uppermost. Approximately half the responses of many records are best considered a reaction to the form of the blots presented rather than a reflection of inner states. Here the content is banal and basically *neutral* in tone. There are some additional responses not easily categorizable that I have relegated to a special *miscellaneous* category.

Five underlying factors are variously operative psychodynamically in the responses scored in accord with the criteria of the categories and subcategories of this system of quantifiable scoring:

a. The positive or negative affective tone of specific content.

b. The nature of the cathexis involved in affective drives: Is cathexis basically to objects or to the self? Does the content suggest positive or destructively toned narcissism? To what extent is the narcissism of the primitive or the secondary, socialized variety? Is object cathexis essentially constructive or destructive in nature?

c. The psychosexual level of development suggested by the responses: What does the content suggest in terms of various libidinal development stages? Is there fixation on or regression to earlier stages of psychosexual development? Content often suggests in some manner the amount of energy or interest directed toward pregenital oral, anal, or phallic developmental stages.

d. The degree and nature of the socialization of the ego as a mediator between outer pressures and inner needs: What is the nature of the socialization and sublimation of libidinal interests? Are libidinal concerns expressed in a more or less direct manner in the content? Are ego defenses used to handle impulses as well as affects: Is repression, denial, projection, or displacement used? Are the affects expressed diffuse in nature, or localized?

e. The attitudinal stance or "set" taken toward an outside object: Is the affective relationship to objects structured in active or passive terms? Are outside objects related to in terms of dependent needs or in terms of active interests?

These five analysis factors are used to classify responses within the scoring system. Part of the complexity involved derives from the many combinations of these factors possible in responses and from differences in their relative pertinence to the particular responses. Most responses showing any kind of affective determination are located between the polarities of content, one polarity suggesting (a) positive, (b) outer object-oriented, (c) mature, (d) sublimated, or (e) active characteristics, and the other suggesting (a') threatening or destructive, (b') narcissistic, (c') primitive or aggressive, (d') defensive or (e') passive, receptive characteristics.

In modifying the categories and in redefining the scoring criteria, we have made more explicit statements below concerning the relation of certain scoring categories to these factors as they are understood in psychoanalytic terms. The major categories themselves differ as to how they are organized in respect to the factors just discussed.

Responses in the Positive category reflect positively toned attachments to objects and persons in the social world (a). In the Positive category, activity or passivity are also reflected (e, e').

The Hostile and Anxious categories are primarily organized around negative affective tone (a'), activity or passivity (e or e'). Within these categories as well as the others, relative degrees of maturation or primitiveness are apparent (c, c'). In the Hostile and Anxious categories there is an active or passive stance (e, e') taken toward destructiveness or fear of destructiveness.

Body preoccupation responses reflect most directly the nature of body cathexis (b') and the relative failure of satisfactory externalization of both impulses and affective responsiveness (d'). Many of these responses are narcissistic in tone (b').

The Dependent category reflects an attitudinal stance toward outside objects of a passive or receptive nature, a seeking for strength and protection from outside (e'). No matter how primitive the level on which this seeking takes place, there is attachment to the social world.

Variations in level of psychosexual development are found throughout these major categories. By means of the various subcategories one can specifically note various nuances in the expression of oral, tactual, anal, and phallic as well as genital or sublimated vectors in libidinal expression. Orality, for example, can be expressed in terms of oral aggressive percepts, in anxious terms, in percepts focused on oral dependent relations, in terms of gratification or oral needs, or in indirect percepts not showing any specific affective tone.

The relative emphasis on any of the five analytic factors differs with the subcategory involved. Certain of the subcategories explicitly suggest the direction of libidinal flow and the nature of object cathexis and whether it is anabolic or catebolic in nature. Certain subcategories, for example, scored under body preoccupation, suggest a destructively tinged turning in of affect into the primary narcissism of schizophrenia. Other subcategories, in the positive category, suggest a secondary narcissism in terms of a protective, erotically tinged self-love. Other subcategories suggest positive libido directed toward outside objects in nature or in the world of art. Some of the libido may be developmentally regressive, albeit positively directed to childish interest or activities.

The most noticeable modifications in the nature of the subcategories used in the present system have been alterations that allow for greater attention to symbolism of hostility or anxiety only suggested through defensive manipulation of symbolic content. The nature of certain symbolic material is such that reversals of affect are suggested. One gains an impression, however, that such defenses function only imperfectly so that the affects defended against are also apparent. Since the defenses are not iron-clad, the affect itself must be periodically apparent. This specific rationale or use of counterhostile and counterphobic denial as scoring categories is discussed under the appropriate subcategories below.

These differences in the nature of object cathexis, psychosexual levels, and defensive ego maneuvers in handling affect, as well as the other factors involved, are discussed in detail in the scoring criteria for various categories and subcategories below.

In categorizing responses that did not seem to fit into existing subcategories, we made an attempt to double-score (divide the weight between two factors) rather than to create innumerable new subcategories. The need for handling complex responses in terms of multiple determinants became increasingly apparent. Without some means of dealing with the inherent complexity found in many responses, the system could have become highly arbitrary. It was found necessary to double- and triple-score certain responses. In fact, some responses can legitimately be categorized as showing characteristics belonging to as many as five categories. However, this much complexity cannot be handled without making the system unmanageable from a quantitative standpoint. The following limits of quantitative scoring are offered as the best compromise between a highly complex, impressionistic analysis of each response, and an overly general or overly arbitrary constriction of responses to limited meanings.

1. Responses in which the affect suggested is complex in nature should be scored as blends, the most pertinent to the response being those selected. Most blends are of two categories. More rarely are responses sufficiently complex to warrant three scorings. Overscoring is to be avoided.

2. The scoring should be from the surface down; that is, the affect most readily described in the manifest content should be considered paramount, with deeper meanings secondary. In this way, an overweighting of certain general meanings of symbolism can be avoided and the emphasis kept at the level of idiosyncratic implications closer to the surface and more characteristic of the affectivity of the particular person.

List of Affective Categories

I. Hostility
  1. Hor   Oral aggressive percepts
  2. Hdpr   Depreciatory percepts
  3. HH   Direct hostility percepts
  4. Hcmpt   Competitive percepts
  5. Hh   Indirect hostility percepts
  6. Hha   Hostile-anxious percepts
  7. Hhat   Hostile-anxious tension percepts
  8. Hhad   Distorted percepts
  9. Hsm   Sadomasochistic percepts
 10. Hden   Denial of hostility percepts

II. Anxiety
  1. Arej   Rejection of percepts
  2. Aev   Evasion percepts
  3. Adif   Diffuse anxiety percepts

4. Acnph   Counterphobic percepts
5. Aobs   Obsessive-projective percepts
6. Adef   Defensive percepts
7. Abal   Imbalance-unstable percepts
8. Agl   Dysphoric-depressive percepts
9. Adis   Disgusting percepts
10. Athr   Threatening percepts
11. Adeh   Dehumanized figures
12. Afant   Fantastic, strange or weird percepts
13. Asex   Sexual anxiety percepts

III. Bodily Preoccupation
1. Bb   Bone anatomy percepts
2. Bf   Flesh or visceral anatomy percepts
3. Bs   Sexual anatomy percepts
4. Bso   Sex organs or activity percepts
5. Ban   Anal organ or anatomy percepts
6. Bdi   Disease or decay percepts
7. Bch   Childbirth percepts

IV. Dependency
1. Df   Fetal, embryonic, or newborn percepts
2. Dor   Oral dependent percepts
3. Dcl   Clinging or hanging on percepts
4. Dsec   Security percepts
5. Dch   Childishly toned percepts
6. Dlo   Longing percepts
7. Drel   Religious percepts
8. Daut   Authority percepts
9. Dsub   Submissive-dependent percepts

V. Positive Feeling
1. Por   Positive oral
2. Ps   Sensual-body contact
3. Pnar   Body narcissism
4. Pch   Child play
5. Prec   Recreation-activity
6. Pnat   Positively toned nature
7. Porn   Ornamental and decorative
8. Pstr   Striving
9. Pcop   Cooperative

VI. Miscellaneous
1.   Mor   Miscellaneous oral
2.   Man   Miscellaneous anal
3.   Msex   Miscellaneous sexual
4.   Mpret   Intellectual or social pretentiousness
5.   Mgrand   Grandiose or cosmic
6.   Mi   Affectively laden percepts of an indefinite nature

VII. Neutral

Total Unpleasant Affect = Hostility + Anxiety + Body Preoccupation

Quantitative Tabulation of Affective Inferences

Each Rorschach response is scored as one unit. Card rejection is also considered one unit. The total number of units for a record is therefore the response total plus the number of rejections.

When there is a *single* affective category scored per response, the affective category is given a unit value of *1*.

When a blend of *two* subcategories is scored for a single response, each category is given a unit value of *0.5*.

When there is a blend of *three* affective subcategories for a single response, each subcategory is given a unit value of *0.33*.

More than three—put remainders in parentheses: don't score.

Tabulation of Overall Indices of Affect

The total for each of the major categories is divided by the total number of units for the entire record (R, or response total + Number of card rejections) to give an overall percentile. The three major indices of hostility, anxiety, and body preoccupation are added together to form an index of unpleasant affect.

Based on the Beck American normal sample (see chap. 3), the list below gives the means and standard deviations obtained for the various indices:

		Mean	Standard Deviation
A.	*Hostile* content	9.4	± 7.1
B.	*Anxious* content	13.8	± 8.0
C.	*Bodily* content	4.1	± 4.9
D.	*Total Unpleasant* content	27.9	± 12.0
E.	*Dependent* content	4.6	± 4.6

F.	*Positive* content	17.1 ± 10.9
G.	*Neutral* content	49.3 ± 15.6

I. Hostility

There are numerous responses in which hostility and anxiety are present in the same response. Tension in an individual over hostile impulses is often accompanied by a considerable amount of anxiety. Nevertheless, in many responses the hostile nature of the content is sufficiently strong to warrant scoring as prevailingly indicative of underlying hostility. A response is to be scored hostile if a hostile element is definable in terms of one of the following 10 hostile subcategories. Responses scored separately under anxiety are those in which the hostile elements are definitely secondary or minimal. Certain doubtful cases can be resolved by double-scoring them with regard to the particular nuances of hostility and anxiety which they express. Some difficulty lies in determining the major identification of the subject when one figure in a response is seen as attacking another. In such cases our experience has been that the anxiety component usually seems the stronger. Careful questioning may bring out a manifestation of anxious identification with the attacked figure.

Throughout the following statements of criteria of scoring for Hostility, as well as other categories, there are numerous cross-references to blends. One should refer to the description of the other scoring categories involved in order to fully comprehend the rationale for the particular scoring suggested.

1. Hor. Oral Aggressive Responses.

These are responses in which the teeth are seen in an act of biting. Fangs, tusks, and teeth seen separately are also included in this subcategory. Some anxiety may accompany these responses; if sufficiently strong, a secondary scoring of anxiety should be made. Frankly oral aggressive animals such as sharks or alligators can be scored Hha, Hor (see below) to indicate a castration type of anxiety over being attacked, as well as the projected oral aggressiveness. Hor responses generally are characteristic of one group particularly prone to show such responses. There are a number of examples below in which oral aggressive symbolism is scored secondarily to other determinants.

Examples:
Hor   Couple of caterpillars eating something.
                       Fish eating the head of a frog.

Hor Hha	An alligator's head.
Hor Hsm Agl	Dead tree; the roots have been eaten away by something. (See Agl below for dysphoric-depressive anxiety response and Hsm for sadomasochistic implications.)
HH Hcmpt Hor	Two dogs fighting over something. They have big mouths. (See HH and Hcmpt below.)
Hden Agl Hor	Toothless face. (Denial of oral aggressiveness, but also depressive response in terms of loss or aging.)
Afant Hor	A head with darts coming out of its mouth, got real big teeth. (See Afant below.)
Bdi Hor	A decomposing corpse. The remains have been partially eaten away by two hyenas. (See Bdi below.)

2. Hdpr. Depreciatory Responses. Depreciatory responses are those in which there is a depreciation or dehumanization of human figures that implies indirect hostility. This scoring is to be distinguished from "dehumanized" responses (Adeh), discussed below under anxiety responses, in which human content is somehow altered or avoided in areas where such content is readily seen by others looking at the cards; the failure to see humans in dehumanized responses is thought to be due more to underlying anxiety than to a hostile feeling toward people as in Hdpr. However, in certain cases double-scoring is indicated. There is also the category Afant (see below under fantastic and weird anxiety responses), in which there is sometimes a combination of human and animal or plant elements in a fantastic response that may, in some cases, have some hostile motivation; but the major emphasis there is on an estrangement from human content in which underlying anxiety plays the major role.

a. Hdpr responses often are qualified by such adjectives as "silly," "awkward," and "foolish." Percepts such as clowns (without a strongly positive circus or festive atmosphere), minority group members, cartoons, drunks, and caricatures usually have a depreciatory value. Often depreciatory responses are accompanied by a certain amount of social pretentiousness (Mpret). In American culture this response is found relatively more often in women's records than in men's. It often implies extreme underlying ambivalence over one's own sexual and social role as well as a criticism of the opposite sex or another class or group. (A combination of fatness and depreciation of others in overly fat humans, for example, suggests a projection of one's own oral interests onto other individuals in a depreciatory way, as an unworthy, "disgusting" need.)

Examples:

Hdpr	A crying, ridiculous old man. A prime moralist, commiserating for sins. Two Negroes discussing. Negroid features apparent.
Hdpr Hor	Two cannibals around a pot.
Hdpr Hcmpt	Alphonse and Gaston, deep bows, but no one goes first.
Hdpr Hcmpt Dsub (Man)	Two women giving the bumps; there seems to be something on the hind part of the skirt so they can't come apart. What they are saying, I'll go my way and you go my [*sic*] way, and I hope we'll never meet again. (Competitive, dependent, depreciative, and anal implications; see below.)
Hdpr Adis	A woman working at an object, looking at again. It doesn't look human, too ugly.
Hdpr Adeh	Birds dressed up in man's clothes; looks like a cartoon or caricature.
Hdpr Athr Dch	Two old women, could be witches. They are riding on brooms. (See below under anxiety responses. However, depreciatory implications were most evident here, as "old woman" was said in a sneering tone.)
Hdpr Dcl Mor	Drunks hanging with one arm to a lamp-post.
Hdpr Dcl Msex	Two old maids, clinging to a pillar. (Clinging responses with indefinite sexual implications.)
Hdpr Mor	A fat woman dowager. This is a man flat on his back, sleeping, snoring; his mouth is open.

Hdpr Mor Athr	Two pot-bellied gargoyles.
Hdpr Mpret	Lackeys.
Hdpr Mpret Dsub	Two butlers bowling.
Mor Hdpr	Relatives of Mickey Mouse, lifting their pot of stew.

b. One type of response classified under Hdpr is a fairly rare one in which an incipient or potentially positive response is quickly distorted or denied. Such a response is an indication that the individual cannot permit himself positive feelings as part of a long-term maintenance of conscious as well as unconscious hostile attitudes. There is a directly hostile attitude toward positive feelings either in himself or in others. Such an attitude is often found in complex individuals who use sexual and social deviancy as a defense against the intrusion of ego-disruptive positive emotions. They can be double-scored with a positive affect category.

Examples:

Prec Hdpr	Two women dancing, kind of over-dressed . . . almost could be witches.
Pnat Hdpr	This is not a pretty flower. It is ugly (on Card VIII).

3. HH. Directly Hostile Responses.   Directly hostile responses are those in which fighting, verbal or physical conflict of some sort, is perceived. They usually indicate a projection of hostility. Such responses are given by individuals who are readily perceived as aggressive or hostile by others; however, the individuals may or may not be aware of their own hostile feelings. In psychotics, these responses are most often found in labile paranoid or manic records, but they are not specific to any maladjusted group.

Examples:

HH	A regular street fight.
	Two prehistoric animals fighting.
	Two animals trying to kick a tree.
	Two women glancing at each other, having words over a fence.
	Two buffaloes charging into one another with their heads.
HH Hcmpt	A couple of fighting cocks.

HH Hcmpt Hor	Two dogs fighting over something. They have big mouths.
HH Hsm	Roosters with their combs pulled off; they pulled them off each other.
HH Hden Prec	These animals are fighting, blood, no, they could be playing cheerfully with each other.
Hcmpt HH	Two men struggling to pull something away from each other.
Dsub HH	Siamese cats, but they hate each other. (A contaminatory response to Card III. The cats are seen as physically joined together, word play on Siamese twins and Siamese cats.)
Dsub HH Pstr	Two animals tied together fighting. (Inquiry) The fight was so fierce in trying to get loose that they have injured their legs. (There is a shift from injury due to fighting to one due to trying to get free of each other.)

4. Hcmpt. Competitive Responses.   This category[2] includes symbolic or attitudinal expressions of competition. These responses are usually double-scored with other affective categories, since the nature of the setting in which competition is expressed varies greatly, from a direct expression of hostility to an emphasis on the achievement or goal implied in the responses or to the playful interaction of contestants. The object of the competition may also vary greatly.

Examples:

Hcmpt HH	Two men struggling to pull something away from each other.
Hcmpt Prec	A tug-of-war. (Recreation response, see below.)
Hcmpt Pstr	Two small animals trying to see who can get the top of a pole first. (Positive striving, see below.)

---

[2] This is a newer category not scored separately in earlier research.

Hcmpt Mor	Two lions trying to get some supper first. (Miscellaneous oral response, since the response is not weighted directly in a hostile, oral, dependent, or positive direction. The competitive quality is strongest.)
Hcmpt Mpret	Two men arguing about some philosophical doctrine. (A pretentious response, see below.)
Hdpr Hcmpt	Alphonse and Gaston, deep bows, but no one goes first.
Hdpr Hcmpt Dsub (Man)	Two women giving the bumps; there seems to be something on the hind part of the skirt so they can't come apart. What they are saying, I'll go my way and you go my (sic) way, and I hope we'll never meet again.
Abal Psti Hcmpt	Two insects don't know which will go up the pole first—they look bewildered.
Prec Hcmpt Dsub	A three-legged race; the inner legs are tied together.

5. Hh. Indirectly Hostile-Phallic Responses.   Responses in this category indirectly reflect underlying concern with aggression or destruction. There is often a phallic aggressiveness suggested by these responses. They are distinguished from the following indirectly hostile anxiety responses (Hha) by manifesting less defensive or anxious concern with castration threat. Weapons, fires, sharp piercing objects form the major part of the responses classified under Hh. In women these responses suggest at times a fear of the male phallus as a destructive, sadistic organ so that their meaning can imply more anxiety in women. However, if no passive object of attack is seen, it can also mean a phallic identification in the woman (see below).

Indirectly related to this category are certain mythological or legendary figures that are usually seen with some underlying phallic as well as threatening implications. They are scored under (Athr) threat responses discussed below, but if a phallic quality is ascribed to them they take a secondary Hh scoring. Witches or harpies are the most prevalent examples.

Examples:

Hh	Fire.
	Fork.
	Spear used by Indians.
	Arrowheads.
	A Stone Age knife.
	Ducks bumping their heads.
	A collision between two wild deer.
	A horn of a bull.
Hh Adef	A tank with thick armor and a large gun mount in front. (See discussion of defensive responses below.)
	An anti-aircraft battery. This is a gun fortification guarding the entrance to the harbor.
Hh Athr Dch	A witch with long nails.
	A witch with a long, crooked nose.

6. *Hha. Indirectly Hostile-Anxious Responses.*

These responses are generally of two varieties: first, weapons and cutting instruments that function to cut off rather than pierce in thrusting motion. Second, pincers, clamps, tweezers, and such squeezing instruments suggest more latent anxiety in the form of castration threat than the previous Hh, indirectly hostile category. Some of these responses of claws of crabs and alligators' heads and the like may suggest underlying oral, aggressive fears as well as indicating concern with castration fantasies. Blood, unrelated to other content, is also scored in this category. If a blood response is organized within another percept, it is scored according to the total percept (e.g., with anatomy, Bf; with fighting, HH; with dissection or mutilation, Hsm).

Examples:

Hha	Tweezers.
	Worms with pincers.
	The claws of a crab.
	Blood spilled here.
Hor Hha	An alligator's head.
Hhat Hha Asex	A long drill; the head looks too big for the opening. (A woman's response.)

7. Hhat. Hostile-Anxious Tension Responses. These tension responses represent ego-alien hostile, aggressive affect which is being kept down with difficulty by generally suppressive but also in some cases repressive ego controls. There is concomitant underlying anxiety over the possibility that these controls are not sufficient to the task. A feeling of inner chaos, internal strife, or incipient explosiveness is projected into external conditions. Sometimes when grandiose or cosmic images are perceived, the response should be double-scored. There is sometimes an "anal" quality to these responses in terms of violent expulsion of gases and the like. The aftermath of explosions should also be scored, since they too show a concern with explosion, even though the person defensively moves the event back in time. Tension responses when directly related to human or animal tissue are usually scored as sadomasochistic responses (Hsm, see below).

Examples:

Hhat	Eruption of a mountain, volcano eruption. The dead calm after an explosion. The deadly fallout of the H-bomb; the white represents the burst center. A spinning top.
Hhat Ha	A nozzle shooting flame.
Hhat Hha Asex	A long drill; the head looks too big for the opening. (A woman's response.)
Hhat Adif	An atomic bomb explosion, cloud. The black, the clouds remaining.
Hhat Man	A jet plane, exhaust expended. An eruption of volcanic gases.
Hhat Mgrand	The image filled with movement; the colors representing antagonistic forces, repelling and crushing toward one another. A representation of world conflict. Whirling figures, going faster and faster as if they will whirl off into space.
Afant Hhat Man	A jet-propelled duck in flight; red contents expelled—jet propulsion could be combustible gas.
Pnat Hhat Pstr	A Japanese tree (artificially stunted); the pot looks broken, free to grow.

8. Hhad. Responses of Distorted or Incomplete Figures with Parts Missing or Disunited. These responses most often represent another type of indirect symbolization for castration anxiety in men or dissatisfaction with a feminine body in women, where there is a feeling of incompleteness or lack of integration in or partial dissolution of the body image. A sadomasochistic orientation may also be implied. When this is more pronounced, the response is scored directly as a sadomasochistic response (see Hsm, below).

Examples:

Hhad	A butterfly, the wings too large and ungainly
	A distorted dog, body twisted.
	A big gorilla, sitting there, head missing.
	Torso without arms.
	A large animal with stunted arms, an anthropoid.
	Bird without wings.
Adeh Hhad	A skeleton, the parts lying tossed around haphazardly. (Dehumanized response, see below.)
	A picture puzzle; these parts are to be combined into a man.
Df Hhad	Figure of a deformed child, head, eyes, curled up. (A fetal type response; see Df, below.)

9. Hsm. Sadomasochistic Responses. These responses symbolize sadomasochistic tensions and anxieties. By and large, this category includes responses wherein there is some violation of living tissue. However, by analogy it also includes responses like ripping cloth. These responses are in certain sense more extreme forms of the Hhat and Hhad responses in that the castration anxiety is often combined with an active, hostile tension. Some responses are the reverse of the tension response in that figures are crushed by outside forces overwhelming the individual. As such, they are double-scored with dependent, submissive responses. Generally speaking, extratensive movement or direction implies a more sadistic orientation, whereas images in which external forces destroy or mutilate an organism imply a more masochistic orientation.

Difficulty in defining the relative degree to which Hsm responses represent ego-syntonic or ego-alien attitudes, defended against by more or less successfully operative reaction formations, makes it judicious to conceive of these responses as sadomasochistic in tone rather than to attempt to be more precise as to the relative strength of the sadistic or masochistic features. Freud and others see sadomasochism as one syndrome, masochism often being a defense against sadistic impulses.

Examples:

Hsm	A bat with a wing shot off or torn off.
	Part of a frog being dissected.
	Reminds me of a dissection.
	Head of a dead dragon cut in half and flattened out.
	A cut and opened bear rug. (The nature of the description here necessitates scoring response as Hsm.)
	Looks like a section of the heart cut open.
	A piece of blue cloth; looks like it has been ripped.
Hsm Bdi	Discoloration on skin—some injury was incurred, wasting flesh.
Hsm Dsub	A smashed insect.
	A wolf that looks flattened out, like by a car.
	Person on a rock. He's been smashed on one side.
Hor Hsm Df	A pig embryo with milk teeth . . . They have to cut off their teeth sometimes because they hurt their mother. (See Df embryo responses, below.)
HH Hsm	Roosters with their combs pulled off; they pulled them off each other.
Bb Hsm	Lower portion of the brain, a dissection, the edge cut rather roughly. (A bone anatomy percept, see below.)
Bso Hsm	This looks like penetration of a virgin. This penis is going in with such violence that blood is splashing out.

10. Hden. Denial of Hostility Responses.   Some individuals attempt to cover or deny negative, hostile content by giving a response that is overly sweet or somewhat forced in an opposite direction to previous or subsequently released hostile content. (See also the discussion of counterphobic responses (Acnph) appearing as part of a sequence.)

This scoring is not an independent one, for the response has to be double-scored in terms of the forced affect as well as for its denial.

Examples:

Hden Hor	False teeth.
Hden Agl Hor	Old toothless face. (Denial of oral aggressiveness; also depressive response in terms of loss or age.)
Mor Hden	Mouthless face. (Denial of orality, either passive or aggressive.)
HH Hden Mgrand (Prec)	These figures are rushing toward one another as if to fight. It may end up as a gigantic symbolic dance symbolizing the age of peace after war.
HH Hden Prec	These animals are fighting, blood—no, they could be playing cheerfully with each other. These figures are not quarreling, but amiably discussing.

II. Anxiety

Responses scored under anxiety represent either various symbolic contents suggesting anxiety, or defenses against the breakthrough of underlying diffuse anxiety into consciousness. As was true for many of the responses scored in the hostile categories, there is a tendency toward fabulization in many of these responses. Responses in some of the following subcategories express underlying anxiety only very indirectly. What is sometimes apparent is a great deal of energy defensively used to repress or bind up anxiety by rejecting the response: by giving evasive content or by using specific obsessive or counterphobic defenses symbolized in some indirect way.

1. Arej. Rejection of Percepts.   Strictly speaking, card rejection (Arej) is not a content response to a card. However, the author included it under the anxiety category, since in guarded or constricted records, it was, in certain cases, the only indirect manifestation of unpleasant affect. Card rejection often reflects a type of defense against anxiety by quick withdrawal from a situation. Sometimes one gains the distinct impression that certain content is perceived but quickly avoided. At other times, one gains, rather, the impression of perceptual constriction due to paralyzing, anxious blocking. The nature of card rejection is not always easy to determine. Provisionally, card rejection is included in the anxiety category and weighted quantitatively as another response. The number of rejections present is added to the response total in the denominator in arriving at the overall percentage of anxiety responses in a record.

Example:
Arej   I can't see anything in this blot.

2. Aev. Evasive Responses.   The subject can become seemingly disturbed by the blot and seeks to evade close involvement through becoming vague as to the nature of his or her responses. Most maps that are not specific as to content are included among these responses. Surrealistic or nonobjective art and diagrams also often have an evasive quality. (Where the quality of dysphoric shading is emphasized rather than vagueness of outline or content, Adif is scored. See below.)

Examples:
Aev   Just a map.
                                An island in the Pacific. Could be any shape.

Aev Hh   A map, like red ink spilled. It has no definite form.

Aev Porn   Some sort of emblem. It's not clearly drawn.
                                The whole thing again could be some design. (See pleasure ornamental category below.)

3. Adif. Anxiety Expressed Through Diffuseness and Vagueness of Content.   This category[3] is to be distinguished from Aev, above. The Adif category includes clouds, shadows, smoke, and vaguely per-

---

[3] Adif was previously scored under Aa, an "indirect anxiety" category.

ceived anatomy with an underlying anxious quality to it. The responses scored in it do not have the sense of threat as clearly focused as those scored in the Athr category, below.

The use of diffuse dysphoric percepts demonstrates an intangible anxiety, one that cannot be brought into focus specifically, as is done, for example, in a phobic focus on certain animals or situations. It suggests free anxiety, not tied to specific symptoms. The person, therefore, is generally ready to be made anxious by circumstances, since there is nothing specific to react to or to cling to as a guide. When the diffusion is in terms of smoke, at times a suggestion of fear of loss through destruction also seems implied. Diffuse clouds in one sense are related to the more precise vista responses in that they suggest an ego unable to come to grips in any forceful, active way with external reality. They imply a feeling of diffuse, passive, inferiority in relation to the outside. Usually the diffuse nature of clouds suggests also a passive, anxious helplessness. Storm clouds imply a vague threat. Shadows suggest formless fears. Diffuse anatomical responses suggest fear coming from within the body and having a hold over the ego, without precision as to what the nature of the disturbance might be. Percepts of x-rays are usually included in this category.

Where anatomical responses show diffuseness in terms of shading and the inner content of the blot rather than the outline, they are double-scored with Adif. This category suggests individuals who would like to maintain an assertive, competent facade either socially or intellectually, with an inner capacity that is actually hollow in nature.

Examples:

Adif	Clouds.
	This is swirling smoke.
	There are deep shadows in this card.
	Clouds shifting by.
Adif Agl	Like the fire of Hell, swirling clouds.
Adif Athr	This is full of shadows in here. I can't make out what it might be—something fearful.
Adif Dsec	Smoke rising up—might be a burning house.
	This is a cave; the entrance looks dark and forbidding.
	A bottomless hole, black and fathomless.
Dsec Adif	A little house. It looks on fire. The smoke is billowing up on both sides.

Bdi Adif	This light and dark effect seems like an X-ray of some sore; it is not clearly in focus.
Dlo Adif	The future, like through a mist, thickness. (See symbols of future under Dlo.)

4. Acnph. Counterphobic Responses. This category was not scored in research prior to 1960. These responses are difficult to score without considering them in the context of the entire record. They are basically responses demonstrating a counterphobic defense in operation against anxiety. The manner in which it is put to use usually gives a clue either to the presence of a readiness to diffuse anxiety or to specific phobic material. Counterphobic responses are more readily perceived on the black and white cards than on the colored cards, since they are more difficult to catch on cards where the tone is more conducive to positive responses. These responses are also more readily apparent on the records in which the total content suggests underlying anxiety in other symbolic expressions. Counterphobic responses may be double-scored, since they very often have positive content and do manifest constructive ego controls.

There are two types of counterphobic responses: first, those given initially without any anxious content preceding; and second, those in a direct sequential relationship to some anxious response. Usually this type of response is given immediately following a response with dysphoric implications.

a. The first type of response is recognized for its forced quality, such as in responses to the black and white cards which are totally inappropriate to usual stimulus values.

Examples:

Acnph Pch	A toy gorilla. Comic book monster.
Acnph Pnat	A colorful, beautiful flower (Card IV). (Content itself is modified to make the card lose its threatening aspects.)
Athr Acnph Prec	Witches dancing happily.

b. Some responses suggesting feelings of kinesthetic insufficiency, of the counterphobic responses given. Men concerned defensively with their masculinity are more prone to give some responses to the cards manifesting virility or strength. They are sometimes given to responses that must be double-scored with Daut, or responses suggesting dependence on authority (see below). "Vocational" responses are common.

In boys, "masculine" activity of one sort or another is often perceived. Hysteroid women are more apt to give "beautiful" responses in inappropriate places or by attempting to efface a disturbing response by following it with the forced use of pleasant affect.

Examples from single records:

Acnph Daut	(Card I:) The shield of the United States. (This response was given by a policeman working in a large industrial plant who was supposed to keep order during a strike. He followed this response on subsequent cards showing diffuse anxiety and evasiveness. His response to Card I showed an attempt to use an official emblem or badge behind which he seeks to hide and to keep away his fears. But his later responses, symbolizing the pressure of diffuse, free-floating anxiety, reveal the unsuccessful nature of his counterphobic defenses.)
Athr	(Card IV:) A huge hulking form (2 sec. Then a pause of 5 sec.)
Acnph Pnat	A beautiful flower. (A woman gives a beautiful response after seeing a somewhat threatening figure, revealing a trend to cover over or retreat to a more pleasant topic. Such cover responses are very often found after unpleasant anatomical responses.)
Adis Bf	(On Card VIII:) A disgusting sight! Could be an operation. (Quickly followed by:)
Pnat Acnph	A distant hill clad in winter snow. (In this sequence of responses the subject first shows a concern with body integrity and then defensively retreats from it into nature at a distance.)[4]

---

[4] This sequence is taken from Theodora M. Abel and F. L. Hsu, "Some Aspects of Personality of Chinese as Revealed by the Rorschach Test," *Rorschach Research Exchange* and *Journal of Projective Techniques*, 1949, 13:285–301. In Abel and Hsu's sample, Chinese American men remained concerned with the body, whereas the women tended to give nature responses, perhaps defensively as a means of retreat from unpleasant dwelling on the body.

It is advisable to score counterphobic responses only in cases where there is evidence of phobic quality somewhere in the record. It is difficult to draw the line in some cases between a genuine positive affective reaction and one given with a defensive quality to it. This scoring should not be too readily used, since many positive responses also have a certain defensive quality. Scoring this type of response depends upon a great deal of experienced judgement. If there is some doubt, it is best not to score.

5. Aobs. Obsessive-Projective Responses.

a. This category[5] includes responses suggesting underlying anxiety defended against by either projective or obsessive-type defenses. Such responses can take the form of repetitive concern with protruding areas of the blots by producing a series of rare detail responses to such areas. Where the symbolic content itself suggests hostile or anxious preoccupation, such responses are double-scored under Hh or Hha (see above).

Examples from a 32-Response Record:

Hh Aobs	Here is a knife (Dd, Card II).
	Here is another knife (Dd, Card II).
Aobs	Here is a stick (Card V).

b. Another type of response included in this category is excessive concern with faces, profiles, and masks (see also Adef, below). Individuals giving such responses tend to have strong ambivalent concerns toward authority figures, feeling dependent and desiring nurturance but also tending to feel threatened by authority. There is frequently a projection of superego demands onto these figures when a fabulized threat is projected into these faces. They can be double-scored with Athr (see below). A feeling of having one's behavior scrutinized is often guilt-projected into external authorities. Such use of profiles and faces can symbolize what is usually termed a castration threat from parental or authority figures. (Large D's included as part of such a series are also scored Aobs.)

Examples from a 42-Response Record:

Athr Aobs	The face of a fox, rather frightening in appearance.

---

[5] Aobs includes responses scored in earlier research under Afc (faces and profiles) and certain other responses previously scored Aa.

Aobs	This is the profile of an Indian (Card II, upside down, D).
Aobs	Here is the outline of another face (Card II, Dd).
Aobs Porn	Like the face on a cameo . . . the shading looks like an old-fashioned cameo (Card IV, inner rare Dd).

A single nonrepeated face seen full face in large detail or even in an unusual detail in a record is usually better scored under another category, e.g., leering face (Athr); a clown's lugubrious face (Hdpr). However, two such responses in the same sequence of ten cards would deserve a double-scoring with Aobs.

Example in a 21-Response Record:

Aobs	A face with eyes (Card II).
	The center looks like a pair of eyes (Card IX). (This is most usual of the eye responses, even so, it deserves an Aobs scoring.)

c. The trend toward projection suggested in face responses is even more pronounced in responses in which only eyes or hands, pointing fingers, etc., are perceived in isolation. Such responses are in most cases even stronger indications of the projection of guilt over unacceptable impulses. Such responses are scored Aobs, even if only one such eye response is present in the record.

Example in a 23-Response Record:

Aobs	These small extensions look like roots coming from a stem (Card IV, Dd).
	These are like twigs (Card V, small usual d).
	These are like pointing fingers (Card VII, Dd).
	Eyes here in the center (Card IX, Dd).

Various types of Aobs responses are often found in the same record. Since the relative emphasis on obsessive or projective defenses varies from record to record, the two are included in the same category.

6. Adef. Defensive Responses.[6]   In addition to defensive responses this category includes those in which the content suggests pro-
tecting the individual from threat or danger or retreating from these.
Cloaks and covers are symbolically related to this type or response.
Masks at times may convey either a threatening or defensive quality;
however, they are usually scored under Aobs (see above). The Adef
category is related dynamically to Aobs. It is also suggestive of projective defenses.

Examples:

Adef	A warrior's helmet (inquiry) made of a thick metal to stand off blows.
	A suit of armor, the breastplate.
	A turtle's shell; he can pull in his neck very fast if need be.
	(Where threat is more directly implied, double-score under Athr, as below.)
Adef Athr	A figure wearing a cloak, somewhat hidden in it.
	A lion looking over his shoulder and running away.
	An animal running away from something.
	A fish with dorsal fin out as if in flight.
Ha Adef	A tank with thick armor and a large gun mount in front.
	An anti-aircraft battery.
	This is a gun fortification guarding the entrance to the harbor.

7. Abal. Responses Suggesting Anxiety Over Imbalance.
Responses suggesting feelings of kinesthetic instability or insecurity
are scored in this category. In these responses, instability or insufficiency is related to a feeling of anxiety over external support as being
untrustworthy, or a feeling of precariousness in one's own balance.
There is some anxiety about falling in one form or another. In some
responses there is an anxious "holding on." These last responses need a
double-scoring with dependent clinging responses (Dcl) as described
below.

---

[6] Adef was previously scored under Aa.

a. Feelings of falling or other insecurities about equilibrium in a percept can sometimes be related to guilt over masturbatory activities. Excitement due to autoerotic activities often brings with it concomitant anxieties. (In flying dreams symbolizing intercourse, one often finds a sudden anxiety about falling.) Falling seems to suggest both anxiety and anticipation of punishment. The feeling of falling also represents either loss of erection, or more generally anxious, helpless passivity as preferable to loss of control over an impulse.

Examples:

Abal	This looks like two animals balanced precariously on a rock. Rocks balanced on one another. A falling animal of some sort. Instability spreading out all over the place. A mouse treading precariously.
Abal Dcl	Mice barely hanging onto something.
Pcop Pstr Abal (Dcl)	Mountain climbers, uncertain; one is helping the other across an abyss.

b. An internal confusion or indecision when verbalized symbolically as part of a response is also scored in this category.

Examples:

Abal	A group of insects milling about not knowing what to do. The whole represents confusion to me.
Abal Pstr Hcmpt	Two insects don't know which will go up the pole first—they look bewildered.

8. *Agl. Depressive, Dysphoric, Gloomy Responses.*   Responses in this category suggest feeling of personal deterioration or the lack of inner warmth or vitality. These feelings may be attributed to concern with age, guilt, impotence, or in some cases actual physical deterioration or organic pathology.

Feelings of inner kinesthetic insufficiency, flabbiness, and inferiority which suggest depressive anxiety over a loss of vital life force are double-scored with the submissive-dependent category (Dsub). Many of these responses suggest severe guilt over the destructive implications of sexual impulses. For example, impotent feelings can be a defense against sadistic phallic impulses.

These responses are distinguished from the responses scored under the hostile distorted responses (Hhad) by the greater emphasis on depressive affect rather than on underlying castration anxiety. The loss, in a sense, has already occurred. The person has retreated to an impotent, submissive, or resigned defense against destructive feelings.

Examples:

Agl	This looks dull or lifeless, like dead leaf. Eroded soil, barren and sterile. A bat, looks frayed and worn, a dead specimen that is falling apart. An icy feeling like an iceberg.
Agl Hh	Fire and brimstone. (Punishment by fire.)
Agl Dsub	Jellyfish. (Inquiry) A rather soft, drifting animal without purpose.
Adis Athr	However, note: A jellyfish. (Inquiry) One must be careful when swimming. They are slimy to touch and some are poisonous. (Some jellyfish when seen as if slimy and poisonous are scored under Adis Athr, see below.)
Agl Dsub Asex	Body without backbone. Drooping arms.
Agl Mor	An emaciated figure. (Oral deprivation.)
Athr Agl	Devil, with a fire burning.
Athr Agl Dsub	Ghost without muscle.
Adeh Bb Agl	A skeleton, bones scattered about.
Pstr Agl	A figure struggling hard to free himself from a morass. There is a great struggle to pull himself out.
Pstr Dlo Agl	A lonely figure struggling up a steep hill.

9. Adis. Disgusting Responses. This category covers percepts of animals, objects, or material of a disgusting nature to the perceiver.

Types of disgust can vary widely in their implications depending on the sense organs involved as well as on the zones of the body. Thus, feelings of disgust can have oral, anal, olfactory, or tactual connotations. When an oral or anal quality is present it should be double-scored (see Mor, Man, below). Slimy objects involve tactual repulsion. They are the negative side of the positive sensual responses (Ps) discussed below. Poisonous animal responses usually combine a feeling of disgust with a feeling of threat.

Examples:

Adis	A furry spider. Looks like a slimy reptile. An earthworm.
Adis Bdi	A putrified corpse.
Adis Man	A dirty color. A splotch of mud—looks dirty. Poison gas. Some kind of smear, not pleasant to see.
Adis Mor	Decayed food.
Hdpr Adis	A woman working at an object. Looking at it again, it doesn't look human—too ugly.
Athr Adis	A sting ray. A beetle, might be of a poisonous variety. Jellyfish. (Inquiry.) . . . One must be careful when swimming. They are slimy to touch, and some are poisonous. (See Agl, above, for "jellyfish" with other implications.)

10.   Athr. Threatening Responses.   This category[7] includes threatening percepts or figures suggestive of threat or of being overpowering. The nature of the threat and the underlying dynamics implied differ with the nature of the fabulized material suggested. The category also includes fearful scenes of small objects being caught. Where a small animal is being overpowered, a double-scoring with dependent submissiveness is indicated (Dsub, below). Animals in flight from some implied threat are scored under Adef, above. The identification is with a weak figure that can be overpowered by a threatening force. There is a great deal of fabulization in many of these responses.

---

[7] Athr was formerly scored AA (direct anxiety).

Examples:

Athr	A dragon's head—massive, lots of hair.
	A wild boar; its face.
	A jack-o'-lantern.
	Baying wolves.
	A giant ray.
	A gorilla.
	Dracula, like in the movies.
	A Hallowe'en cat.
Athr Agl	Devil with a fire burning. (Threat of punishment; guilty feeling implied.)
Athr Acnph Prec	Witches dancing happily.
Athr Dsub	A spider about to catch a little leafhopper.
	A huge bird clutching toward this figure of a man here.
	Petals of a death flower opening to catch some insect.
Athr Dch	Witches, like a Hallowe'en nightmare.

11. Adeh. Dehumanization Responses. This scoring pertains to percepts that are substituted for more perceptually visible human responses in certain blot areas. Operationally this scoring has so far been virtually limited to certain types of "dehumanization" on Cards III and VII. This type of response suggests some incapacity to come to grips with human content directly. Where it results in a type of human devaluation, the response is scored under Hdpr as well. Where there is a merger of human and animal elements, where a certain weirdness or fantastic quality is more obvious, the response is scored under Afant (see below). The most common form of "dehumanization" is to see animals instead of humans. A second form of dehumanization is to make the figures into statues.

Examples:

Adeh	A duck; some kind of bird; a duck's head, that's all I see (Card III).
	Odd-looking animals with long necks.
	Could be giraffes.
	Something like a sheep.
	Stone statue of some human. Figures of two rabbits; they look almost human, facing away from each other (Card III).

Hdpr Adeh   Birds dressed in man's clothes; looks like a
                                   cartoon or caricature.

Afant Adeh   Like Martians, not human; some unearthly
                                   quality about them.

12. Afant. Fantastic, Strange, or Weird Responses.   This category includes responses of a grotesque, weird, or fantastic quality. Some
of these responses suggest feelings of strangeness of a vague, threatening kind. Others emphasize a grotesqueness of content with autistic
combinations of part animal–part human, or part mechanism-part animal, etc., when they are not commonly accepted mythological figures.
The emphasis in these responses is on the grotesqueness rather than on
their directly threatening nature. (Cf. Athr, above.) If both grotesque
and threatening, the response can be double-scored. These responses
suggest some disturbance in identification or body image, with some
sense of unreality about object relations. This disturbance can be related to an insecure sexual identification with fear of abnormality or to
some underlying anxiety about the reality-testing functions of the ego.

Examples:

Afant   Half-cobra, but from the legs down a
                                   woman in an evening dress.
                                   Weird sea monster like you'd see on the
                                   bottom of the ocean.
                                   Butterfly in flight; looks like an unknown
                                   from another world.

Afant Hor   A head with darts coming out of its mouth,
                                   got real big teeth.

Afant Hhat Man   A jet-propelled duck in flight; red contents
                                   expelled—jet propulsion could be com-
                                   bustible gas.

Afant Adeh   Like Martians, not human; some unearthly
                                   quality about them.

Afant Mor   Like the head of an animal, got lips like a
                                   man.

Aobs Afant   This looks like a mask—grotesque, face of
                                   a weird animal (in a sequence of faces).

*13. Asex. Indirect Expressions of Anxiety Concerning Sexual
Functions or Identity.*   This category includes a residual variety of

responses suggestive of veiled sexual fears, not scored under Hsm (hostile sadomasochism) or Hhad (distorted responses), or under any of the body preoccupation subcategories.

a. Fear of sexual organs, concern with penetration or seizure. Included here are phallic responses or thinly veiled fears concerning female orifices.

Examples from a record of a woman, age 25:

Asex	Large ears on a bunny rabbit; they are poking up (Card V).
	An elephant with a large trunk sticking up (Card VII).
	A drill and a shaft into the ground. The drill looks too big for the shaft (Card VI).
Asex Dsec	A cave, suggesting mystery and fear.
Athr Asex	Snakes. They are ready to strike.

b. Concern with potency.

Examples:

Asex	Limp arms.
Agl Asex	A dried-up stick.

c. This category does not include the giving of masculine-type responses by women or feminine responses by men, since one cannot infer any direct or indirect anxiety about sexual identification from such responses. It is concerned rather with responses that show more directly underlying anxiety about sexual identity. Such anxiety is implied where there is a mixture of sexes in one percept. Indirect reference to homosexual or other sexual perversions can be scored in this category as well. Responses making one mirror figure a man and one a woman are scored in this category.

Examples:

Asex	A man in a woman's dress.
	I can't make this out. Can be either men or women; two figures (?).
	I can't tell; high-heeled shoes, yet they have male dress.
Asex Bso	This looks like breasts, both breasts and a penis on this figure.
Asex Dch Pch	This is a man and a woman gnome playing patty-cake.

III. Body Preoccupation (Somatization Responses)

In general, responses of an anatomical nature are indications of affect narcissistically turned inward, or bound up in bodily processes. In psychoanalytic terms, the libido or life energy is not freely directed toward outside objects, but is turned inward so that an individual's body or its parts become the focus of erotic or destructive affects.

The type of self-cathexis known as secondary narcissism is not a primary determinant in the body preoccupation responses. In secondary narcissism, erotic components more than destructive affects are emphasized, and the result is a defensive form of self-love and love of objects only as they reflect or adhere to the self. Such structuring is often found in various types of character disorders. Certain symbolic manifestations of this tendency are scored under ornamental responses (Porn), narcissistic responses (Pnar), sensual responses (Ps), and pretentious responses (Mpret), below.

In the body preoccupation responses one finds, rather, a turning in of destructive rather than erotic affects. The self as a whole is not cathected with these affects, but instead specific organs become the focus of negatively toned feelings. Depending on the total personality organization and the methods of defense used by the individual, this binding up of affect in body organs (or withdrawal of affect from external objects) can appear in conversion phenomena, psychosomatic involvements, hypochondriasis, or the deeper withdrawal of schizophrenia. The nature of the anatomy responses given, and the total Rorschach picture, must both be examined to determine their implications.

In hysteria, other features of the records as discussed in Rorschach tests will bring out the presence of repression as a dominant defense. The anatomy material will generally be of a less malignant nature; the pelvis or specific organs with little elaboration are more usual.

Records with psychosomatic involvements vary greatly as to the content of the anatomy responses and the severity of ego disturbance. However, fantasy material is more apparent in responses other than the specifically anatomical, which remain fairly unelaborated in nature.[8]

Far more malignant elaborated anatomy appears in hypochondriasis in individuals guilty over homosexuality, and in schizophrenia. In in-

---

[8] The work of Fisher and Cleveland with "soft" and "hard," "permeable" and "impermeable" content as related to body image and psychosomatic involvements is an excellent approach to the reaction of body cathexis and content symbolism in the Rorschach. See, for example, "Behavior and Unconscious Fantasies of Patients with Rheumatoid Arthritis," *Psychosomatic Medicine*, 1954, 16:262–272.

dividuals guilty of perverse practices such as homosexuality, diseased tissue responses are often forthcoming, suggesting underlying guilt for destruction of the body by unnatural practices. Hypochondriasis is usually found in borderline paranoid cases, where projective defenses are strongly indicated. Body parts become the focus of hostile, destructive projections. It is often difficult to separate hypochondriacal anatomical responses per se from those of schizophrenia. In both cases there is usually more focus on visceral organs, and some of the responses are characterized by an autistic aura. The proportion of anatomical responses to response total increases with degree of malignancy.

Certain anatomical responses represent an intellectualizing defense emphasizing scientific interest in medicine, assertively covering anxiety feelings. Nevertheless, the basic meaning of anatomy responses, that is, some affective withdrawal from people as cathected objects, is implied. In intellectualizing responses, however, there is also compensatory emphasis on intellectual processes in a defensive way, suggesting a narcissistic ego orientation. Destructive affects are handled in a more sublimated manner by individuals giving such responses than is probably true for those giving anatomical responses who lack this intellectualizing facade. These responses usually are whole responses; they emphasize intellectual drive, but at the same time they have a certain vague quality resembling responses scored under the anxious evasive category (Aev, above).

The degree of malignancy of body preoccupation responses depends on the degree of fabulization and the nature of the thought disturbances manifested when the response is analyzed structurally. These ego control factors of anatomy responses are scored under thinking disturbance categories, which will be discussed in a separate manual. Therefore, the *affective* categories themselves only incompletely summarize quantitative severity. The quantitative use of anatomy, however, in itself is highly differentiating as to the degree of maladjustment indicated by anatomy responses. The quality and percentage of anatomy responses in records clearly differentiate between neurotic and schizophrenic disturbances over a large sample of individuals.

1. Bb. Bone Anatomy Response (Including Neural Anatomy). a. Bone anatomy is the least malignant anatomical response and is usually related to inhibiting, constrictive defenses. In the case of pelvis responses, constrictive attitudes toward sexuality are indicated. Bone anatomy is often a manifestation of underlying anxiety in an inhibited person. Spine responses are often symbolically overdetermined in terms of anxiety about one's strength of character (in women, a critical attitude toward men's strength; in men, related to inadequacy feelings).

Examples:

Bb	Rib cage.
	Spinal column.
	Cartilaginous masses behind the ear.
Bb Aev	This is vaguely suggestive of an X-ray or something like that—just an impression.
Bb Adif	This light and dark effect seems like an X-ray of some sort. It is not clearly in focus.
Bb Agl	Skull.
Bb Asex	Pelvis and backbone.
Bb Mor	Leg bone of a chicken (inquiry), like a fried chicken.

b. Some individuals concentrate on anatomical responses dealing with neural or brain tissue.[9] Very often these responses are intellectualized, as described above. They are often attempts to appear to be "expert." There is a narcissistic focus on intellectual processes, with certain individuals also displaying a constant fear of injury or dissolution. Intellect is in certain cases equated with potency.

Examples:

Bb	A cross-section of the spinal cord.
	An operation on the skull.
	Neuroanatomy chart.
	Neural tissue.
	Lower portion of the brain, a dissection, the edges cut rather roughly.
	Spine and nerve cord.
Bb Df	The neural groove of a chick embryo.

2. Bf. Flesh or Visceral Anatomy Responses.[10]   The flesh anatomy responses are usually of a more malignant nature than the bone anatomy responses. However, there are cases in which the experience of trauma or operations or a reality-oriented concern about a particular

---

[9]The former Bn (neural) category has now been combined with Bb.

[10]The particular examples listed here are not very autistic in nature. Rapaport, Gill, and Schafer (1946:331) and others give many autistic examples to which one can refer. There is usually a complex overlay of thought disturbance involved in autistic anatomical percepts.

organ or disease is the determinant of an anatomy response. This sort of fear is particularly apparent in lung responses, which often refer to fear of tuberculosis. Chest X-rays are similar in meaning.

Many of the flesh responses found in records are elaborated in a vague manner, with autistic overlays. A single word like "stomach" or "trachea" is not as pathognomonic as a more vague, diffuse elaboration of anatomy. Blood and other tissue fluids may or may not be seen as part of flesh anatomy responses. Elaborated dissection or violence to tissues should be double-scored for its sadomasochistic elements. Sexual anatomy and diseased anatomy are scored in separate categories (Bs and Bdi, below). Colons and other organ responses dealing with elimination are scored under Ban (anal organ percepts, below).

Responses with general references to internal anatomy are scored under Bf. They are double-scored with Bb if there is a specific reference to bone or neural parts.

Examples:

Bf	Lungs.
	All a liver.
	Hair pores in layers like in a book.
	Like an artery with red and blue blood; part of the human body from throat down to hips. These are the bones; this is the liver, heart, intestines.
	The color of flesh—meat (Cn, but scored affectively under Bf).
Bf Bb Mpret	A cross-section of the body, sliced through horizontally. One notes the various internal organs in their peripheral distribution round the central neural tracts. (Said in a rather pompous voice.)
Hsm Bf	Aftermath of an operation, a huge suture.

3. Bs. Sexual Anatomy Responses.   This category includes references to internal sexual organs not directly visible, except through surgically opening the body. These responses show body preoccupation focused on sexual functioning. They manifest a hypochondriacal concern with the organs as body parts when the responses relate to organs the same sex as the subject.

Examples:

Bs	Bleeding ovaries; it's that time of the month.
	Uterus.
	The Fallopian tubes of a frog.
	Ovaries of a mammal.
	A cross-section of a penis.
Bs Bdi	The sexual canal of a tapeworm.

4. Bso. Sex Organs or Activity Responses. This category includes percepts of external sexual organs and autistic references to the act of intercourse.[11] Perception of the external male or female sex organs is found in some normals but is more common in maladjusted individuals. These responses, since they are of external body parts, do not as readily suggest anatomical preoccupation as do the more strictly anatomical responses (Bs). They represent a more direct preoccupation with sexuality in terms of sexual identity and a feeling of frustration in heterosexual intercourse, sometimes with some underlying homosexual conflicts latent or manifest. So-called "liberated" individuals will give a few such responses to the more appropriate areas. Heterosexual relations in some individuals can have a counterphobic quality for them. Breasts are not scored in this category (see instead Dor, Msex, below).

Non-fabulized external sexual organ responses have, therefore, a minimum reference to body preoccupation. When some fabulization accompanies these responses, their meaning becomes more malignant. Perceptions of the act of intercourse are extreme examples of autistic sexual preoccupations.

Examples:

Bso	Penis.
	Vagina.
	Vulva.
	Looks like the testicles of a sheep.
Bso Hsm	This looks like penetration of a virgin. This penis is going in with such violence that blood is splashing out.
Bso Ban Ps	A woman's buttocks; the color, the shape somewhat reminiscent of the posteriors of

---

[11] See Phillips and Smith 1954, p. 150, for further examples.

Rouault's early paintings of prostitutes.
The flesh color and suggestion of the
texture of flesh.

Msex Dor   Looks like a brassiere; (in inquiry) you
                          almost can see the nipples. A woman's
                          breast.

5. *Ban. Anal Organ or Anatomy Responses.*   Percepts of both
internal and external anal body parts are covered in this category.
Attention to the anus itself may imply indirect interest in anal eroticism,
either latent or manifest, in the individual. The perception of internal
anal anatomy is of a more malignant nature, suggestive of underlying
paranoid or schizophrenic processes. Veiled anal interests are scored
under miscellaneous anal responses (Man, below), since there is less
direct anatomical preoccupation involved.

Examples:
Ban   Part of an intestinal tract—X-ray; dark
                          spots represent where waste materials are
                          gathered.
                          The alimentary canal—lower intestines.

Ban Bso   Anus and vagina.

Ban Mpret   A rectum, ready for a proctologist.
                          The ischial callosities of a Rhesus monkey.

Bso Ban Ps   A woman's buttocks; the color, the shape
                          somewhat reminiscent of the posteriors of
                          Rouault's early paintings of prostitutes.
                          The flesh color and suggestion of the
                          texture of flesh.

6. *Bdi. Disease or Decay Responses.*   Rotting or putrification of
flesh and decomposition or other malignant diseases of body tissues are
included in this category. These responses are most common in schizophrenics, but individuals very disturbed over "perverse" sexuality,
usually of a homosexual nature, can also evidence this type of anatomical preoccupation.

Examples:
Bdi   A wasting flesh.
                          Fungus growth on tissue.

	Diseased and healthy tissue—the colors suggest it.
Bdi Ban	A bloated body, probably drowned. The blue colors are caused by the gases formed during putrification.
Bdi Hor	A decomposing corpse. The remains have been partially eaten away by two hyenas.
Bs Bdi	The sexual canal of a tapeworm.
Hsm Bdi	Discoloration on skin—some injury was incurred.

7. Bch. Childbirth or Pregnancy Responses: Intrauterine Anatomy with Fetus. Autistic preoccupation with childbirth is suggested by these responses. In older women, they are somewhat less malignant than in men and can represent a severe hypochondriacal withdrawal and preoccupation with their loss of generative functions. In men, schizophrenic regression is more strongly implied. These Bch responses emphasize the woman's anatomy, whereas Df (fetal) responses, discussed below, are concerned primarily with the fetus and embryo.

Examples:

Bch	This looks like the opening babies come out [of], and here is the blood.
	A woman is pregnant; inside is the child.
	The water bag has just burst. The baby will be out soon.
	The woman is in stirrups, ready to give birth.

IV. Dependency

In responses included in this category, the emphasis is upon neither the positive nor the unpleasant aspects of the responses, but upon the extent to which the percept expresses an underlying dependent attitude in object relationships. Certain responses scored primarily under hostility, anxiety, or in the positive category may also strongly connote dependent attitudes which should be scored secondarily. Also to be noted in the responses subsumed under the dependent category is wish-fulfillment fantasy of a more or less regressive nature, the symbols obtained being symbols of childhood or infancy. Caves and hearths, babies and fetuses, oral dependent symbolism all suggest early regressive dependent need for the mother. Certain responses under the dependent category are expressed verbally in childish language, suggesting an ego identification at a childish level and the desire to maintain dependent relationships that would be disrupted by a more independent, sexually threatening adult identification. Submissive, clinging, religious, and longing responses suggest various forms of helpless dependency on outside forces or objects for nurturance. Authority responses suggest the need for strong figures as a means of partial identification in order to permit activity.

1. Df. Fetal, Embryonic, or Newborn Responses.   Fetal, embryonic, and small-infant responses are subsumed under this category. These responses suggest strong regressive tendencies or primitive fixations on the mother.

Examples:

Df	Embryos.
	Newly born babies.
	Newly born puppies.
	Profile of a baby.
	Fetuses in the upside-down position.
Df Hhad	Figure of a deformed child, head, eyes, curled up.
Df Bch	A pregnant woman with a child inside.
Df Dcl	Siamese twins, still connected to the mother by an umbilical cord. (Objects "tied" together often suggest a mutually dependent but hostilely toned relationship. See under Hhat or Dsub. The present response has no sense of tension related to the "tied" feeling and is more related to a feeling of "clinging" in a positive sense.)
Hor Hsm Df	A pig embryo with milk teeth. . . They have to cut off their teeth sometimes because they hurt their mother.

2. Dor. Oral Dependent Responses.   Oral dependent responses of a direct or indirect nature are included in this category. The emphasis is usually on the use of the mouth in a nonaggressive manner in obtaining oral supplies. Activities such as sucking, licking, and drooling are included in this scoring category. Breasts and udders also suggest dependent orality. (Breasts are double-scored with the miscellaneous sex category, Msex, below.) Concern with the mouth or lips or belly indirectly implied a similar passive-dependent oral-receptive orientation. These responses are to be distinguished from the oral-aggressive responses, which imply an aggressive taking of oral supplies. The positive oral (Por) category emphasizes object cathexis in terms of food or food-making materials. The positive sensual category (Ps) suggests the use of the lips in terms of their sensual qualities rather than in terms of their use in oral-receptive activity. The mouth used as a means of attachment is double-scored in the dependent clinging category as well (Dcl). Responses only indirectly suggesting food or oral content are scored in the miscellaneous oral category (Mor).

Examples:

Dor	Lips, lips here. (This response, depending on context, could also be Ps.) A bee sucking nectar through a long proboscis.
Dor Dsec	A mother bird bringing worms to her young in the nest.
Dor Prec	Two men drinking or smoking a water pipe, may have their mouths close to it.
Msex Dor	A woman's breasts, nipples here. Looks like a brassiere; (in inquiry) you can almost see the nipples.

3. Dcl. Clinging or Hanging-on Percepts. Clinging, hanging, or leaning responses suggest a dependence on outside objects for support. When anxiety is also indicated about the stability of support (see Abal, above), the response is double-scored with Abal. Certain types of clinging have hostile implications; holding on by the teeth suggests both dependency and oral aggressiveness.

Examples:

Dcl	A man holding onto a tree. An opossum hanging from a tree. Bears hanging onto something. A sleeping figure leaning against a pile of something.

Dcl Hor	A dog clinging to a rag with his mouth. (Not clear whether the hostile or dependent oral features are paramount, but the teeth are used to hold on.)
Dcl Hdpr Abal (Mor)	Drunk leaning against a building; if he moves the building will fall down.
Dcl Hdpr Mor	Drunks hanging on with one arm to a lamppost.
Dcl Dor Abal	Roots of a tree. It has a firm foundation, goes away down to receive nourishment. It's drawing water by tube. It also has roots wrapped around a large stone.
Hdpr Dcl Msex	Two old maids, clinging to a pillar.
Abal Dcl	Mice barely hanging on to something.
Df Dcl	Siamese twins, still connected to the mother by an umbilical cord. (Objects "tied" together often suggest a mutually dependent but hostilely toned relationship. See under Hhat or Dsub. The present response has no sense of tension related to the "tied" feeling and is more related to a feeling of "clinging" in a positive sense.)
Pcop Pst Abal (Dcl)	Mountain climbers, uncertain; one is helping the other across an abyss.

4. Dsec. Security Percepts. Responses indirectly suggesting wish fulfillment activities, usually in terms of the enveloping protection and nurturance of a mother, fantasies of return to the womb, are sometimes indirectly suggested. Vista often appears as a determinant in these responses. Sometimes a threat to security has to be double-scored. This category includes houses, caves, castles, hearths—symbols of being warm and enclosed. Sometimes the caves are fearful symbols or suggestive of vague foreboding.

Examples:

Dsec	This looks like a fireplace. Looks like a small house way in the distance.

This might be a castle on a hill.
A pair of bedroom slippers.
An old garden with a forest house on one
end.

Dsec Adif   A little house. It looks on fire; the smoke is
                       blowing up both sides.

Dsec Pch   A cave like in *Tom Sawyer.*

Agl Dsec   A bottomless hole, black and fathomless.
                       This is a cave; the entrace looks dark and
                       forbidding.

Drel Dsec   The spires of a church far off.

5. *Dch. Childishly Toned Percepts.*   Childish percepts, or objects
childishly perceived suggest indirectly a childish dependent orientation
when they are found in adults. Seeing the young of animals (or human
children) or using diminutives and a childish vocabulary in speech suggests a childish dependent identification. Fairy story creatures, grem-
lins, pixies, and the like, as well as more frightening figures such as ogres
and witches, are scored in this category. Frightening figures should be
double-scored with anxiety threat (Athr).

Examples:
Dch   These are bitty wee creatures.
                       These are puppies, or baby calves.
                       A hobgoblin.
                       Pixies looking at each other.
                       A gremlin peering out from behind a rock.
                       A little fairy creature.

Dch Hha Prec   Two witches dancing.

Dch Athr   An ogre seen from the bottom.

Dch Prec Acnph   Two angels dancing round a golden pot—
                       golden halos. (The response [to Card I]
                       was counterphobic when seen in
                       sequence.)

Hdpr Athr Dch   Two old women, could be witches. They
                       are riding on brooms.
                       A witch with a long, crooked nose.

Athr Dch   Witches, like a Hallowe'en nightmare.
                       A witch with long nails.

Asex Dch Pch	This is a man and woman gnome playing patty-cake.
Pch Dch	Santa Claus with his bag of toys. Two little baby rabbits, toys. Teddy bears. Bears playing patty-cake. A pretty jacket and pants for a little baby. Christmas stockings. A fairy godmother.
Pch Dch Ps	Fluffy lambs doing a dance.

6. Dlo. Longing Responses. Certain responses suggest a longing quality. Figures are seen reaching out, sometimes at a distance. A small figure far away is seen. There is some object at a distance or some distant goal. There is a wish fulfillment apparent, as in the security responses (Dsec, above). Dlo is an alternative scoring to Dsec, depending on the content. The future can be symbolic of longing.

Examples:

Dlo	The enchanted hills, a mist settling in. Looks like two figures in the distance reaching for something. A figure far off, like that of a man. (Response given by a 64-year-old widow.)
Dlo Sub	Arms outstretched, beseeching; (inquiry) a small figure at a distance. (Response by a 58-year-old man.)
Pstr Dlo Agl	A lonely figure struggling up a steep hill.
Dlo Adif	The future, like through a mist. The mist thickens.

7. Drel. Religious Responses. Responses with religious figures or religious concepts imply a feeling of dependence on external sources for succorance. Some figures of a patriarchal nature need to be double-scored with dependent authority responses or dependent submissive responses (Daut or Dsub, below).

Examples:

Drel	St. Peter's in Rome, like a religious symbol.

Drel Hsm	A crucifix.
Drel Dsec	The spires of a church far off.
Drel Dch	A statue of the Child of Prague. (Christ Child.)
Drel Daut	Moses.
Drel Dsub	Looks like a figure kneeling and praying, hands folded in prayer. Praying hands, held together in prayer.

8. Daut. Authority Responses.   Responses involving symbols or figures of authority imply an authoritarian personality structure with need for a dependent relationship on authority. The individual himself may in turn be assertive to those he perceives as subordinate, or he may be generally passive in human relationships. There is some indication, however, that the identification with an authoritarian role is incomplete and a dependent quality remains.

Bearded men, patriarchs, royal emblems, symbols such as the coat of arms of a state, scepters and the like are included in this category. Other categories suggesting authoritarian thinking are the depreciative (Hdpr), the dependent submissive (Dsub), and the pretentious (Mpret).

Examples:

Daut	The face of a stern old man.
	A patriarch, a long beard.
	A profile of a bearded man. (Given by a woman.)
Daut Acnph	The emblem of the U.S.
	An officer's insignia.
	A samurai helmet.
Drel Daut	Moses.
Porn Daut	The crown jewels on display.
	Coat of arms.
Porn Daut Mpret	A crown, like that found in Westminster Abbey. (Tone of teaching something, displaying knowledge.)

9. Dsub. Dependent-Submissive Responses. There are various types of responses suggestive of a submissive attitude to authority or to life tasks.

a. Some responses suggest a feeling of being manipulated from the outside by forces greater than oneself. Essentially the attitude to these outside forces is resigned, submissive, or helpless. Such individuals do not usually identify directly with butlers and servants. They risk revealing depreciatory or socially pretentious attitudes rather than simply giving expressions of submissiveness.

Examples:

Dsub	Two girls; their heads are bowed.
	An opossum, playing dead.
	A pawn, a chess pawn.
	A dog picked up by the fur of his neck.
	A heavily laden animal, probably a burro.
Dsub Adeh	A marionette.
Agl Dsub	Jellyfish. (Inquiry) A rather soft, drifting animal.
Agl Dsub Asex	Drooping arms.
	Body without backbone.
Dlo Dsub	Arms outstretched, beseeching. (From a 58-year-old man.)
Drel Dsub	Praying hands, held together in prayer.
	Looks like a figure kneeling and praying, hands folded in prayer.
Pst Dsub Mgrand	Atlas, holding up the world.

b. Some respnses suggesting feelings of kinesthetic insufficiency, impotence, or flabbiness are double-scored with depressive responses (Agl, above). Some have sadomasochistic features (Hsm, above).

Examples:

Hdpr Mpret Dsub	Two servants bowing.
Hsm Dsub	A squashed bug.
	A wolf flattened out by a car.
Prec Dsub Hdpr (Porn)	A puppet show; these are the decorations on the side. The puppets represent two butlers.

c. Helpless figures threatened by larger beings are double-scored with anxiety threat (see Athr, above).

Examples:

Athr Dsub	A spider about to catch a little leafhopper. A huge bird clutching toward this figure of a man here. Petals of a death flower opening to catch some insect.
Athr Agl Dsub	Ghost without muscle.

d. Figures joined together either in a Siamese-twin type of physical connection, or tied together, often suggest a tension over ambivalent dependent-hostile relationships (double-score with Hhat, above). Such figures inferentially suggest a feeling of being kept together with another hated figure by dependent ties that are conceived of in negative terms. The figure tied to often suggests a rival who is also tied to the same object of dependency; the two figures are therefore tied together by their mutual dependency on a third figure. In other figures, the bond in an ambivalent dependent feeling directed toward one another.

Examples:

Dsub HH	Siamese cats, but they hate each other. (A contaminatory response to Card III.)
Dsub HH Pstr	Two animals tied together fighting. (Inquiry) The fight was so fierce in trying to get loose that they have injured their legs. (There is a shift from injury due to fighting to one due to trying to get free of each other.)
Dsub Hhat	Two animals; their noses tied together.

V. *Positive Responses*

This general category includes various percepts suggesting positive object cathexis. Various levels of psychosexual maturity are represented. Fixation or displacement, as well as sublimation, may be inferentially represented when the emphasis in a response has oral, sensual narcissistic, or childish content. Nevertheless, the positive nature of the object cathexis implied in these responses indicates a capacity in the individual to relate to outside objects or to his or her own body with pleasure.

Responses in this category are usually counterindications for schizophrenic withdrawal. There is a seeming exception to this generalization, however, when positive responses are limited to the first two subcategories, Por and Ps. There are some patients in hospitals who are there not because they have withdrawn from reality but rather because they have been withdrawn from by their parents, in one way or another. Since the parents, their original object of cathexis, have died or are unwilling to continue to relate to a grown child in terms of primitive childish patterns of response, such individuals find themselves helpless in an adult world and welcome the security of institutionalization. Their prognosis is usually poor because the hospital itself and its personnel are objects of gratification to the patients. Such passivity in object cathexis is implied in their food and contact (oral and sensual) Rorschach responses. Nevertheless, the general affect in these responses must be seen as positive in tone.

Emphasis on recreational activity (Prec) or natural or ornamental objects of beauty (Pnat or Porn) demonstrates the capacity to become involved affectively with outside interests. A relatively large proportion of such responses is usually found only in the normal range of the population. Also included are responses of an upward striving nature (Pstr) showing purposeful intention of a positive nature and purposeful cooperative activities (Pcop) between two or more individuals. These two instrumental categories are found in achievement oriented individuals.

1. Por. Positive Oral Responses. Positive oral responses are scored only when the food mentioned is of a type to have common pleasant associations. Candy, ice cream, dumplings are usually positive in nature. Raw meat is not scored positively, since it implies a more aggressive orality than sweets or vegetables. Responses such as fried eggs may be considered positive in nature if given to the yellow area of Card X. These responses imply an oral vector in libidinal cathexis. What it means depends on the total configuration of the record. If food responses are the only expression of positive cathexis, we can think of serious libidinal regression as present. But if combined with other positive responses, they merely deepen the impression of positive cathexis.

Examples:
Por   Beer in ice.
                             Ice cream.
                             Strawberries.
                             Like cotton candy.

Dumpling fried in deep fat.
A drumstick. (The response does not
emphasize raw meat but is pleasant in its
associations.)
Cornucopia.

Por Pstr   Dogs trying to get at some jam, sportively.

Por Pstr Hcmpt   Two lions trying to get to some supper
first.

2. *Ps. Sensual-Body Contact Responses.*   Sensual pleasure may be
suggested in percepts relating to tactual stimulation of various sorts.
Furs, pelts, the texture of wood, the feel of cloth, often are perceived
pleasurably. Contacts such as kissing may have pleasurable connotations. The warming of hands over a fire also suggests a pleasurable
activity with sensual aspects. These responses suggest sensuous quality
in the personality perhaps suggestive of early libidinization of body-skin
contact. Sometimes these responses may be related to narcissistic propensities also in evidence in the ornamental (Porn) and narcissistic responses (Pnar) (see below). If these responses predominate in a record,
one can suppose that pleasure would tend to be rather egocentrically
conceived rather than in terms of heterosexual eroticism.

Examples:
Ps   A fur pelt.
                                  A fluffy dog.
                                  Velvety material.
                                  Sharkskin cloth.
                                  Lips. (So scored in a sensuous record or in
                                  one with sensuous associations in the in-
                                  quiry. Otherwise, it would be scored Dor.)

Ps Dch   Two men warming their hands over a fire.

Ps Dch Dor   Two puppies kissing.

Msex Ps   Panties. (Positive tone elicited in inquiry.)

3. *Pnar. Body Narcissistic Responses.*   Narcissistic responses
emphasizing personal adornment demonstrate object cathexis, albeit
directed egocentrically toward the self. These responses demonstrate an
incomplete development into external object relationships, but nevertheless they are positive in tone. (A number of responses to the mirroring of images in a positive context are included in this category.)

Examples:

Pnar

A girl doing setting-up exercise to keep trim.
A girl looking in the mirror, primping herself.
A well-developed male physique.
A necklace.
A peacock with his tail spread open.
An animal seeing his reflection in a pool of water; he is quite absorbed in what he sees.

4. Pch. Childish Pleasure Responses. Pleasure in childish games or other pleasurable childish content is scored in this category. Where the percepts are described with a childish tone, a double-scoring with Dch may be indicated. When these responses occur with frequency in a record, they suggest a nostalgic turning back to childhood in a flight from adult anxieties. One may assume the presence of difficulties in assuming an adult identification. Childhood is idealized as a period of happiness when one is not faced with the threatening nature of adult sexuality. A few such responses in adults who have children, however, imply a sharing of their children's happy activities, especially if other types of positive responses are equally forthcoming. Childhood figures, such as Santa Claus, are scored Pch Dch; such figures imply dependent succorant feelings. More indirect symbols of positive childhood experiences, such as Christmas trees, are scored Pch. Good-luck symbols, such as wishbones and horseshoes, are also scored in this category.

Examples:

Pch

Like a game where you clap hands.
Two kids, I guess—some sort of kids' game.
A Christmas tree.
Women playing patty-cake.
A horseshoe.
Clowns playing patty-cake, like at the circus.
Two characters like out of my child's fairy book.

Pch Hha Athr

An old woman playing patty-cake, maybe a witch.

Pch Dch	Santa Claus with his bag of toys.
	Two little baby rabbits, toys.
	Teddy bears.
	Bears playing patty-cake.
	A pretty jacket and pants for a little baby.
	Christmas stockings.
	A fairy godmother.
Pch Dch Ps	Fluffy lambs doing a dance.
Asex Dch Pch	This is a man and woman gnome playing patty-cake (Card II).
Porn Pch	A Chrismas tree ornament.

5. *Prec. Recreation Responses.*   Percepts of recreational and cultural activities, musical instruments and the like suggest positive object cathexis.

Dancing in certain cases can be a "masking activity"[12] for other activities which are disallowed and hence have a counterphobic quality. However, the ability to give such a positive response is in itself indicative of positive ego controls.

Examples:

Prec	A couple of figures dancing.
	A couple of jitterbugs.
	A sailboat.
	A violin.
	Ice skating.
	A ballet scene.
	The colors of a Mexican fiesta.
Prec Hdpr	Natives beating on drums for a dance.
Pst Prec Hcmpt	A sack race.
Prec Hcmpt Dsub	A three-legged race; the inner legs are tied together.
Prec Athr Dch	Dancing fairies with a lot of devils around.
Prec Dsub Hdpr (Porn)	A puppet show; these are the decorations on the side. The puppets represent two butlers.

---

[12] See Phillips and Smith 1953, 19:78.

Prec Pnar	A girl relaxing on a beach.
Prec Msex	A chorus girl with an elaborate costume. (Given by a man.) Girls doing a cancan.
Prec Mpret	The Ballet Russe premiere danseuse. A bust of Beethoven. The immortal Bard of Avon.
Hcmpt Prec	A tug-of-war.

6. Pnat. Pleasure in Nature Responses. Pleasure in the beauties of nature and living things expresses a type of positive object cathexis removed from the immediacy of personal or interpersonal concerns. Landscape, pretty butterflies, and graceful natural objects when not ornamental in nature are scored in this category.

Examples:

Pnat	A beautiful seashell. A Hawaiian butterfly pressed in a book. Leaves turning autumn colors. The Champs Elysees in spring. Woods and flowers. A snow scene, a medley of black and white. A tulip. An orchid. A flower. A scenic waterfall. A sunrise reflected in clouds.
Pnat Hhat Pstr	A Japanese tree (inquiry), artificially stunted. The pot looks like it is broken; now free to grow.

7. Porn. Responses Showing Pleasure in Art Objects and Ornaments. Responses that represent a positive feeling about beautiful objects, designs, and ornaments are indications of positive-object cathexis. Some of these responses represent a somewhat more sublimated form of those in the narcissistic category above, which refer more directly to personal body narcissism.

Examples:

Porn   A fancy ornamental bowl.
                                 A wallpaper design.
                                 A decorated totem pole.
                                 Winged Victory.
                                 A sculptured head.
                                 Beethoven as carved in marble.
                                 A vase for flowers.
                                 A pattern on a Japanese fan.

Porn Aev   A nonobjective painting, pleasing design.

Porn Daut   The crown jewels on display.

Porn Daut Mpret   A crown, like that found in Westminster
                                 Abbey. (In a tone of displaying knowl-
                                 edge.)

Porn Pch   A Christmas tree ornament.

8. *Pstr. Striving Responses.*   Responses emphasizing the active attainment of goals, when these goals are seen as positive, are another indication of the active cathexis of outside objects.

Examples:

Pstr   Two animals climbing a tree.
                                 Two parrots going to climb a pole.

Striving responses can at times suggest psychosexually regressive goals. If so, they can be double-scored (with Dch and Dor) as long as the goal is a nondestructive, positively toned one. The attainment of food by carnivorous animals, where there is no direct emphasis on either the animal as a carnivore or the destructive aspect of the striving, can be double-scored with a miscellaneous oral response (Mor). Certain of these responses, generally speaking, indicate active goal-directed attitudes with capacity to persevere toward the realization of life tasks.

Examples:

Pstr Dch Dor   Two puppies trying hard to get at their
                                 food.

Pstr Mor   Two animals climbing a hill, they may be
                                 seeking for food.

Sometimes, a feeling of constraint or burden is projected into striving responses. Percepts with burdens are scored as striving responses, even though the tone is essentially not a positive one. Nevertheless, there is the strong cathexis of a goal. In some "burden" responses there is an oppressive feeling of striving as a duty, rather than something spontaneously derived from one's own motivations. These responses are double-scored (with Dsub). In another type of striving response the motivation is positive but the striving is done in the face of counterforces. Some such responses can be double-scored for their depressive feelings (Agl) to indicate the dysphoric nature of the striving, as well as for passivity or submissiveness which is projected outwardly as not acceptable by the ego. Such responses are most probably linked to what is termed by Freud and others as moral masochism. Individuals evincing such responses emphasize perseverance in tasks toward long-range goals, sacrificing present pleasure for the future. Certain other responses of this type emphasize a competitive attitude (double-scored with Hcmpt).

Examples:

Pstr Dsub Mgrand	Atlas, holding up the world.
Pnat Dsub Pstr	A Japanese tree (inquiry), artificially stunted. The pot looks like it is broken; now free to grow.
Pstr Dlo Agl	A lonely figure struggling up a steep hill.
Pstr Agl	A figure struggling hard to free himself from a morass.
Pcop Pstr Abal Dcl	Mountain climbers, uncertain; one is helping the other across an abyss.
Pstr Prec Hcmpt	A sack race.
Hcmpt Pstr	Two small animals trying to see who can get to the top of a pole first.
Abal Pstr Hcmpt	Two insects don't know which will go up the pole first—they look bewildered.

9. Pcop. Cooperative Responses. Percepts of mutual or cooperative activities suggest concern with mutual assistance. Human or animal figures working cooperatively with each other are not infrequently perceived. Such percepts are very often complexly perceived and need double-scoring. For example, even though the figures are seen as fighting against a common enemy, they are scored in this category provided there is emphasis on some cooperative activity in their relationship.

Examples:

Pcop   Two women are carrying something
                                     together.

Pcop Por   A woman is cooking. The other is assisting
                                     her.

HH Pcop   Animals. They are struggling against their
                                     common enemy.

Pcop Pstr Abal (Dcl)   Mountain climbers, uncertain; one helping
                                     the other across an abyss.

VI. *Miscellaneous*

There are certain responses that cannot be categorized readily under
any of the above major categories. Some oral, anal, and sexual interests
are only indirectly suggested in a percept without any clearly defined
positive or negative valences.

Certain responses have an intellectually pretentious or grandiose
quality which is not scored under any of the major categories. These
responses suggest a compensatory reaction to underlying feelings of
inadequacy of varying degrees of severity, from snobbishness to the
grandiose compensatory self-evaluations found in paranoids or the cosmic inner struggles found in certain types of catatonic subjects.

Finally, there appears in certain records a type of fabulized response
that can be recognized as of personal significance to the individual, but
which a tester cannot categorize under any of the above categories.
These last are scored Mi, or indefinite.

1. Mor. Miscellaneous Oral Responses.   Certain responses indirectly concern eating or obtaining food without a hostile, dependent,
or positive quality that is directly ascertainable in the response. Often
they may have some other characteristic which can be double-scored.
Some responses suggesting oral deprivation can be double-scored in this
category with a secondary scoring for the depressive implications (Agl).

Examples:

Mor   Face of an old man, with vapor coming out
                                     of his mouth.
                                     Children trying to blow on something.

Mor Dch   Two children blowing a balloon.

Hdpr Mor	Relatives of Mickey Mouse, lifting their pot of stew.
Hdpr Mor	A fat woman dowager.
Hdpr Dcl Mor	Drunks hanging with one arm to a lamp-post.
Agl Mor	A very thin person. An emaciated figure.
Adis Mor	Decayed food.
Afant Mor	Like the head of an animal, got lips like a man.
Bf Mor	Tongue.
Prec Mor	Two men at a bar having a chat.
Pst Mor	An animal looking for food, climbing a tree. An animal trying to get some food with his paw.

2. Man. Miscellaneous Indirect Anal Responses. This category includes a variety of responses suggesting, in an indirect manner, interest in, or concern over, anal functions or the anal region of the body.

This response may indirectly suggest concern with feces in responses by perceiving dirt or mud, or concern with gases or eruption of lava. Interest in the buttocks, or the use of perspective emphasizing the posterior of a human or animal also suggests some sort of indirect anal reference. Jet planes lend themselves somewhat to this interpretation.

Examples:

Man	A person bending over, buttocks sticking out. A person looking through his own rear end, point this way. A stain; may be splattered mud.
Hhat Man	An eruption of volcanic gases.
Adis Man	A smear of some sort. A dirty color. A splotch of mud—looks dirty. Poison gas. Some kind of smear, not pleasant to see.

Afant Hhat Man   A jet-propelled duck in flight; red contents
                                   expelled—jet propulsion could be com-
                                   bustible gas.

Pch Man   Bumps a daisy.

3. Msex. Miscellaneous Sexual Responses.   Certain responses
suggest indirect sexual interest or concerns. Women's undergarments
suggest a certain curiosity or veiled interest with possible fetishistic implications when found in a man's record. Very often this category is used
to score secondarily some sexual overtones to a response scored under
another category.

   A sexual interest in the human form related to sexual characteristics
is also scored Msex.

Examples:

Msex   A corset cover like my mother used to
                                   wear.

Msex Dor   Looks like a brassiere; (in inquiry) you
                                   almost can see the nipples.

Msex Ps   Panties. (Positive tone elicited in the
                                   inquiry.)

Hdpr Dcl Msex   Two old maids, clinging to a pillar. (A
                                   veiled suggestion of equation of pillar with
                                   a sex organ.)

Prec Msex   A chorus girl with an elaborate costume.
                                   (Given by a man.)
                                   Girls doing a cancan.

Msex   Figure of a woman from waist down, trim
                                   hips.
                                   These are female figures, from the shape.
                                   This is the breast line.

Msex Hdpr   Two Africans—breast makes them
                                   female. They're black.

Msex Prec   Two female rabbits dancing coyly, and
                                   feminine attire makes them female.

4. Mpret. Socially and Intellectually Pretentious Responses.
The responses in this category show concern of an indirect nature with

social or intellectual status and the use of the intellect as a means of self-aggrandizement. These responses suggest a strong compensatory need. Like narcissistic responses, they also suggest pretentiousness as a form of defensive secondary narcissism in that in emphasizing one's own prowess there is a need to derogate the capacity of others so as to enhance one's own self. Some of these responses are related to the hostile depreciatory type of response (Hdpr). In scoring responses as Mpret, however, the emphasis is on self-enhancement rather than on the implied derogation of others. Some of these responses are related to the dependency authority (Daut) category insofar as there is a dependent identification with authority figures in the arts, politics, and so on. Pretension is often revealed through the nature of the language used in a response. When the language demonstrates a stilted or forced quality and is obviously used for show, a notation should be made about the expressive style.

Examples:

Mpret	A Lincolnesque face.
Hdpr Mpret	Lackeys.
Hcmpt Mpret	Two men arguing about some philosophical doctrine.
Bf Bb Mpret	A cross-section of the body, sliced through horizontally. One notes the various internal organs in their peripheral distribution round the central neural tract. (Said in a rather pompous voice.)
Prec Mpret	The Ballet Russe premiere danseuse. The immortal Bard of Avon.
Prec Porn Mpret	A bust of Beethoven. (Elaborated in pedantic style.)
Porn Daut Mpret	A crown, like that found in Westminster Abbey. (Tone of teaching something, displaying knowledge.)

5. Mgrand. Grandiose Responses. Responses in this category are expressions of internal states dramatized in cosmic or grandiose terms. Nations, for example, are symbolized as struggling with one another. Gigantic figures such as Atlas are seen holding up the world. Where the figures or symbols are seen in motion, there is usually outer representation of inner tension so that double-scoring with Hhat is often indicated. Such responses are related to primitive use of the introjective mechanism so that cosmic struggles are introjected and become symbols of internal concerns. They represent in extreme cases a pathological expansion of ego boundaries found in certain acute schizophrenics of the catatonic variety. They are also related to an outer projection of inner states of conflict onto world tensions. The individual becomes ego-involved with outer struggles as a means of avoiding a recognition of certain feelings as due to specific personal difficulties.

Examples:

Mgrand Athr Dsub	Represents the oppressive power of Russia, like a heavy oppression.
Hhat Mgrand	Whirling figures, going faster and faster as if they will whirl off into space.
Hhat Mgrand Dsub	The image filled with movement; the colors representing antagonistic forces, repelling and crushing toward one another.
HH Hden Mgrand (Prec)	All these figures are rushing toward one another as if to fight. It may end up as a gigantic symbolic dance symbolizing the age of peace after war.
Pstr Dsub Mgrand	Atlas, holding up the world.

6. Mi. Affectively Laden Responses of an Indefinite Nature. This scoring is used to score responses that cannot be readily assessed as belonging to any category, and yet the nature of the response makes it obvious that some sort of strong idiosyncratic affective push or personal symbolism is involved. Usually, case history material or other external clues are necessary to resolve the riddle. Case history material may help to locate certain responses more precisely than the series of generalizations presented above as a guide for meaning. In research work done on a quantitative basis, one has to sacrifice a certain amount of precision and define the meanings of responses according to what one discovers as their usual underlying affect.

VII. Neutral Responses

Responses determined principally by the formal qualities of the blot comprise 40 to 50 percent of ordinary normal records. Unspecified animals, humans, botany responses, and a miscellany of objects comprise the majority of neutral responses. Unspecified popular responses, such as bats or butterflies on Card I and II and crabs on Card X, are essentially neutral in tone unless there is some elaboration that suggests an affective valence. When certain responses, such as bats, are perseverated from one card to the next, they usually have no real affective tone. Excessive use of neutral responses is closely correlated in meaning to a high number of pure form responses without elaboration (F%) and a high percentage of banal animal responses (A%). Constrictive and stereotypic defenses are operative. A serious drop from the normal percentage of neutral responses, when not accompanied by an increase in positive responses, suggests severe maladjustment. Schizophrenic records generally are low in neutral responses. Severely guarded records, however, can mask underlying psychotic processes. There are differences in the underlying attitudinal identification related to various animal percepts. If no affective push beyond the mere expression of the response itself is available for assessment, no scoring is usually done unless there is a minimal amount of elaboration.

Examples:

Neut   Bats (Cards I and II).
                                        Two animals.
                                        Two bears.
                                        Two tigers.
                                        Rabbits.
                                        Horses' hoofs.
                                        Children.
                                        A flower. (No elaboration.)
                                        A man standing.
                                        Two people facing each other.
                                        A cow's head.

References

Abel, Theodora, and F. L. Hsu
    1949   Some Aspects of Personality of Chinese as Revealed by the Rorschach Test. *Rorschach Research Exchange and Journal of Projective Techniques* 13:285–301.
De Vos, George A.
    1952   A Quantitative Approach to Affective Symbolism in Rorschach Responses. *Journal of Projective Techniques* 16(2):133–150.
Fisher, Seymour, and Sidney Cleveland
    1954   Behavior and Unconscious Fantasies of Patients with Rheumatoid Arthritis. *Psychosomatic Medicine* 16:262–282.

1958   *Body Image and Personality.* New York: Van Nostrand.
Phillips, Leslie, and Joseph G. Smith
    1953   *Rorschach Interpretation: Advanced Technique.* New York:
    Grune and Stratton.
Rapaport, David, Merton Gill, and Roy Schafer
    1946   *Diagnostic Psychological Testing.* Chicago: Year Book Pub-
    lishers.
Schafer, Roy
    1954   *Psychoanalytic Interpretation in Rorschach Testing.* New
    York: Grune and Stratton.

Appendix B

Rorschach Location Areas

APPENDIX B : Location Areas according to Beck

Major Usual Details

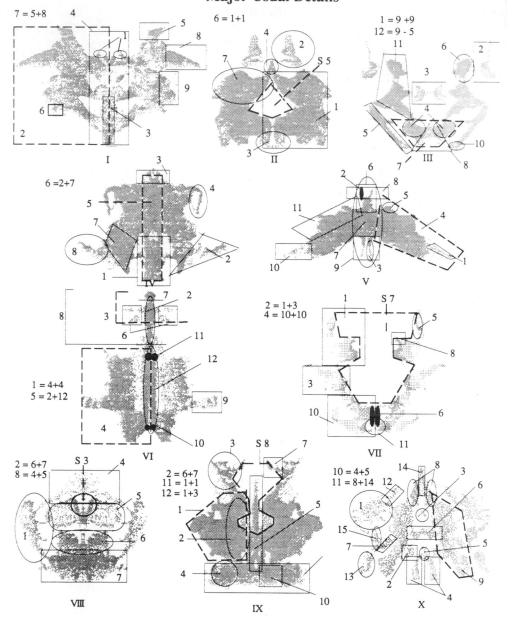

Unusual Details

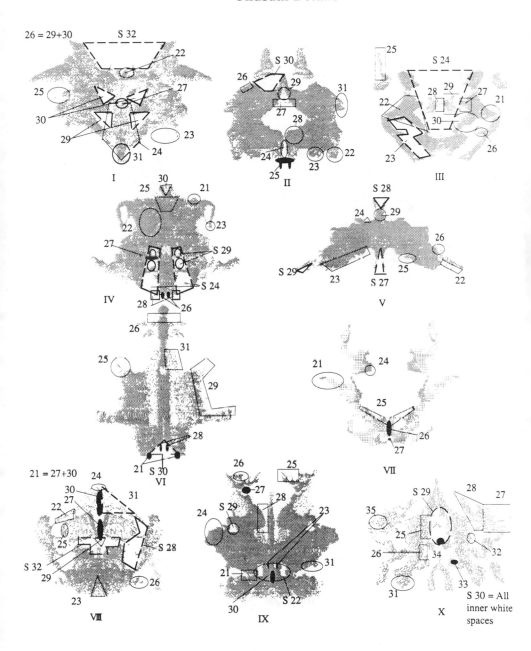

S 30 = All inner white spaces

Designer:	U.C. Press Staff
Compositor:	Asco Trade Typesetting Ltd.
Text:	11/13 Times
Display:	Times
Printer:	Bookcrafters, Inc.
Binder:	Bookcrafters, Inc.